# أهلاً وسهلاً

# أهلاً وسهلاً

## العربية الوظيفية للمبتدئين
## الطبعة الثانية


**مهدي العش**

منقحة مع آلن كلارك



دار جامعة ييل للنشر
نيو هيڤن ولندن

# Ahlan wa Sahlan

Functional Modern Standard Arabic for Beginners

Second Edition

With Online Media

Mahdi Alosh

Revised with Allen Clark

Yale University Press

New Haven and London

This book was originally accompanied by an audio CD and a DVD.
The audio and video files are now available at yalebooks.com/ahlan.
To access them, use the password aleppo.



| | |
|---|---|
| Publisher: | Mary Jane Peluso |
| Editorial Assistant: | Elise Panza |
| Project Editor: | Timothy Shea |
| Manuscript Editor: | Karen Hohner |
| Production Editor: | Ann-Marie Imbornoni |
| Production Controller: | Karen Stickler |
| Designer: | Mary Valencia |
| Typesetter: | J. P. Kang |

Printed in China

The Library of Congress has cataloged the DVD edition as follows:

Alosh, Mahdi.
Ahlan wa sahlan : functional modern standard arabic for beginners /
Mahdi Alosh ; revised with Allen Clark. — 2nd ed.
p. cm.
Includes index.
ISBN 978-0-300-12272-5 (cloth : alk. paper) 1. Arabic language—
Textbooks for foreign speakers—English. I. Clark, Allen, M.A. II. Title.

PJ6307.A395 2010
492.7'82421--dc22
2008049885

ISBN 978-0-300-21989-0 (pbk. with online media)

A catalogue record for this book is available from the British Library.

This paper meets the requirements of ANSI/NISO Z39.48-1992 (Permanence of Paper).

10 9 8 7 6 5 4 3 2 1

*To my wife*

Ibtissam

*and to the memory of my parents*

Falak and Abulfaraj

To access the audio, video, and Online Interactive Exercise Program, go to
**yalebooks.com/ahlan**
Password: **aleppo**

## CONTENTS


Introduction . . . . . . . . . . . . . . . . . . . . . . . . . . . . . . . . . . . . . . xix

Acknowledgments. . . . . . . . . . . . . . . . . . . . . . . . . . . . . . . . . . . . xxix

Lesson One الدَرْسُ الأوَّل . . . . . . . . . . . . . . . . . . . . . . . . . . . 2

Objectives. . . . . . . . . . . . . . . . . . . . . . . . . . . . . . . . . . . . . 3

1. School Surroundings . . . . . . . . . . . . . . . . . . . . . . . . . . . . 3

غُرْفَةُ الصَفِّ . . . . . . . . . . . . . . . . . . . . . . . . . . . . . . . . . . 4

2. Describing Location Using Prepositions. . . . . . . . . . . . . . . . . 4

3. Enumerating: The Coordinating Particle وَ. . . . . . . . . . . . . . . 6

4. Demonstratives: Gender Agreement . . . . . . . . . . . . . . . . . . . 7

5. Contrasting: The Particles لكِنْ and لكِنَّ . . . . . . . . . . . . . . . 8

A. The Strong Version (لكِنَّ) . . . . . . . . . . . . . . . . . . . . . . . 8

B. The Weak Version (لكِنْ). . . . . . . . . . . . . . . . . . . . . . . . . 9

6. Nominal Sentences. . . . . . . . . . . . . . . . . . . . . . . . . . . . . 10

7. Negating with لَيْسَ . . . . . . . . . . . . . . . . . . . . . . . . . . . . 11

8. Use of لكِنَّ and لكِنْ Combined with لَيْسَ. . . . . . . . . . . . . . 13

9. The Definite Article الـ: Assimilating and Non-Assimilating Sounds. . . . . . . . 14

10. Definite and Indefinite Nouns . . . . . . . . . . . . . . . . . . . . . . 17

Vocabulary المُفْرَدات . . . . . . . . . . . . . . . . . . . . . . . . . . . . 20

Lesson Two الدَرْسُ الثاني . . . . . . . . . . . . . . . . . . . . . . . . . .22

Objectives. . . . . . . . . . . . . . . . . . . . . . . . . . . . . . . . . . . . . 23

1. School Surroundings and Facilities . . . . . . . . . . . . . . . . . . . 23

جامِعَتي. . . . . . . . . . . . . . . . . . . . . . . . . . . . . . . . . . . . . 23

غُرفَةُ مَكتَبي. . . . . . . . . . . . . . . . . . . . . . . . . . . . . . . . . . 24

2. *Nisba* Revisited . . . . . . . . . . . . . . . . . . . . . . . . . . . . . . 27

Word Order and Gender Agreement. . . . . . . . . . . . . . . . . . . . 27

3. The *Iḍāfa* Structure (الإضافة) . . . . . . . . . . . . . . . . . . . . . 28

A. Cases of the Constituents of the *Iḍāfa* Structure. . . . . . . . . . . 29

B. Definiteness of an *Iḍāfa* Structure. . . . . . . . . . . . . . . . . . . 30

4. Identifying Objects: Demonstratives . . . 33
5. Colloquial Arabic . . . 35
Suppression of Short Vowels . . . 35
Quality of the Vowel Preceding ة . . . 36
Vocabulary المُفْرَدات . . . 38

Lesson Three الدَّرْسُ الثالِث . . . 40
Objectives . . . 41
1. Seeking and Providing Information . . . 42
أنا مِنْ جَبْلة . . . 42
2. Question Words . . . 43
A. Yes /No Questions . . . 43
B. Content Questions . . . 43
3. The Arabic Verb . . . 45
A. Verb Stem and Root . . . 45
B. Negating the Present-Tense Verb . . . 46
4. Cardinal Numbers 1–10 . . . 47
5. Learning How to Say "I Know" and "I Don't Know" . . . 50
6. Eliciting Information . . . 51
7. Expressing Admiration . . . 52
8. The Particle يا . . . 52
9. The Question Particle كَم . . . 52
المُفْرَدات . . . 58

Lesson Four الدَّرْسُ الرابع . . . 60
Objectives . . . 61
1. Describing Background . . . 61
طالِبَتانِ في جامِعَةِ حَلَب . . . 61
2. Forming Dual Nouns . . . 64
3. Number-Noun Agreement . . . 64
A. The Numbers *one* and *two* (1, 2) . . . 65
B. The Numbers *three* Through *ten* (3–10) . . . 65
4. Plurals of Non-Rational Nouns . . . 69

المُفْرَدات ........ 73

Lesson Five الدَرْسُ الخامِس ........ 74
Objectives ........ 75
1. Describing Family Members ........ 75
عائِلَةُ مازِن نَجّار ........ 75
2. Describing School Subjects ........ 76
طُلاّبٌ عَرَبٌ في أمريكا ........ 76
3. Arabic Last Names ........ 80
4. Objects of Verbs المَفْعولُ به ........ 81
5. Objects of Prepositions ........ 82
6. Ordinal Numbers الأعْدادُ التَرْتيبيَّة ........ 83
7. Pronouns of Separation ضَمائِر الفَصل ........ 86
المُفْرَدات ........ 92

Lesson Six الدَرْسُ السادِس ........ 94
Objectives ........ 95
1. Terms of Address ........ 95
يا آنِسَة! ........ 95
2. Expressing Regret or Apology ........ 99
3. Expressing Lack of Knowledge ........ 100
4. Expressing Degree ........ 101
5. The Present Tense: Negation and Conjugation ........ 103
A. Negation ........ 103
B. Conjugation ........ 103
6. Secrets of the Language: Prefixes and Suffixes ........ 104
A. Overall ........ 104
B. First Person ........ 105
C. Second Person ........ 105
D. Third Person ........ 105
7. Cardinal Numbers 11–999 الأعداد الأصْليّة ........ 107
A. Cardinal Numbers 11 and 12 ........ 107
B. Cardinal Numbers 13–19 ........ 107

C. Cardinal Numbers 20–90 .......... 108
D. Inside the Numbers .......... 110
E. The Number 100 (مِئة) .......... 110
المُفْرَدات .......... 114

Lesson Seven الدَرْسُ السابع .......... 116
Objectives .......... 117
جَرائِدُ ومَجَلاّتٌ عَرَبِيَّةٌ .......... 117
1. Inquiring about and Describing an Activity or Object .......... 119
2. Making Polite Requests and Offers Using the Imperative .......... 120
A. The Imperative .......... 121
B. Forming the Imperative .......... 121
C. Doubly Transitive Verbs .......... 123
D. Pronunciation of the Attached Pronoun هُ .......... 123
3. Cases of the Noun .......... 126
A. The Nominative Case الرَفْع .......... 126
B. The Genitive Case الجَـرُّ .......... 127
C. The Accusative Case النَصْب .......... 127
4. Expressing Possession with the Prepositions لِـ and مَعَ .......... 128
5. Attached Pronouns Suffixed to Verbs .......... 129
6. More on Arabic Names .......... 131
المُفْرَدات .......... 133

Lesson Eight الدَرْسُ الثامِن .......... 134
Objectives .......... 135
شاياً من فضلك! .......... 136
1. Requesting and Declining Things Politely .......... 136
2. Expressing Likes and Dislikes .......... 137
3. Adverbials of Time .......... 137
4. Food and Drink .......... 138
5. Describing Daily Activities .......... 139
6. The Imperative .......... 144
7. Prepositions and Attached Pronouns .......... 146

8. Plurals of Nouns . . . . . . . . . . . . . . . . . . . . . . . . . . . . . . . . . . . . . . . . . . . . . . . . . . . . . . . . 146
A. Sound Masculine Plurals جَمْع مُذَكَّر سالِـم . . . . . . . . . . . . . . . . . . . . . . . . . . . . . . . . 146
B. Sound Feminine Plurals جَمع مُؤَنَّث سالِـم . . . . . . . . . . . . . . . . . . . . . . . . . . . . . . . . . 147
C. Broken Plurals جَمْع تَكسير . . . . . . . . . . . . . . . . . . . . . . . . . . . . . . . . . . . . . . . . . . . . . 147
9. إضافة Structure Revisited . . . . . . . . . . . . . . . . . . . . . . . . . . . . . . . . . . . . . . . . . . . . . . 151
المُفْرَدات . . . . . . . . . . . . . . . . . . . . . . . . . . . . . . . . . . . . . . . . . . . . . . . . . . . . . . . . . . . . . . 153

Lesson Nine الدَرْسُ التاسِع . . . . . . . . . . . . . . . . . . . . . . . . . . . . . . . . . . . . . . . . . . . . . . . . . 156
Objectives . . . . . . . . . . . . . . . . . . . . . . . . . . . . . . . . . . . . . . . . . . . . . . . . . . . . . . . . . . . . . . 157
1. Telling Time . . . . . . . . . . . . . . . . . . . . . . . . . . . . . . . . . . . . . . . . . . . . . . . . . . . . . . . . . . 157
A. Morphological Structure . . . . . . . . . . . . . . . . . . . . . . . . . . . . . . . . . . . . . . . . . . . . . . . . 158
B. Grammatical Structure . . . . . . . . . . . . . . . . . . . . . . . . . . . . . . . . . . . . . . . . . . . . . . . . . . 158
C. Fractions of an Hour . . . . . . . . . . . . . . . . . . . . . . . . . . . . . . . . . . . . . . . . . . . . . . . . . . . 159
سَحَر في جامِعةِ حَلَب . . . . . . . . . . . . . . . . . . . . . . . . . . . . . . . . . . . . . . . . . . . . . . . . . . . 162
مايكِل براون في القاهِرَة . . . . . . . . . . . . . . . . . . . . . . . . . . . . . . . . . . . . . . . . . . . . . . . . . . 163
2. Telling Time Informally . . . . . . . . . . . . . . . . . . . . . . . . . . . . . . . . . . . . . . . . . . . . . . . . . . 169
3. Breaking Consonant Clusters . . . . . . . . . . . . . . . . . . . . . . . . . . . . . . . . . . . . . . . . . . . . . . 170
4. Suppressing the Initial Sound of the Article . . . . . . . . . . . . . . . . . . . . . . . . . . . . . . . . . . 170
5. Mass and Count Nouns . . . . . . . . . . . . . . . . . . . . . . . . . . . . . . . . . . . . . . . . . . . . . . . . . . 171
6. Numbers: Reading Hundreds and Thousands . . . . . . . . . . . . . . . . . . . . . . . . . . . . . . . . 171
المُفْرَدات . . . . . . . . . . . . . . . . . . . . . . . . . . . . . . . . . . . . . . . . . . . . . . . . . . . . . . . . . . . . . . 174

Lesson Ten الدَرْسُ العاشِر . . . . . . . . . . . . . . . . . . . . . . . . . . . . . . . . . . . . . . . . . . . . . . . . . . 176
Objectives . . . . . . . . . . . . . . . . . . . . . . . . . . . . . . . . . . . . . . . . . . . . . . . . . . . . . . . . . . . . . . 177
لُؤلُؤَة القَطامي فَتاةٌ عَرَبِيَّةٌ مِن قَطَر . . . . . . . . . . . . . . . . . . . . . . . . . . . . . . . . . . . . . . . . . . 178
1. Cultural Notes . . . . . . . . . . . . . . . . . . . . . . . . . . . . . . . . . . . . . . . . . . . . . . . . . . . . . . . . . 182
Family . . . . . . . . . . . . . . . . . . . . . . . . . . . . . . . . . . . . . . . . . . . . . . . . . . . . . . . . . . . . . . . . . 182
Women . . . . . . . . . . . . . . . . . . . . . . . . . . . . . . . . . . . . . . . . . . . . . . . . . . . . . . . . . . . . . . . . 182
The Gulf . . . . . . . . . . . . . . . . . . . . . . . . . . . . . . . . . . . . . . . . . . . . . . . . . . . . . . . . . . . . . . . 183
Names and Recent History . . . . . . . . . . . . . . . . . . . . . . . . . . . . . . . . . . . . . . . . . . . . . . . . . 184
Language in the Gulf . . . . . . . . . . . . . . . . . . . . . . . . . . . . . . . . . . . . . . . . . . . . . . . . . . . . . 184
Men's Head Gear . . . . . . . . . . . . . . . . . . . . . . . . . . . . . . . . . . . . . . . . . . . . . . . . . . . . . . . . 184

2. The Past Tense. . . . 185
A. Past-Tense Conjugation of the Verb دَرَسَ ‘he studied’ . . . . 185
B. Negating the Past Tense . . . . 187
3. Verbal Nouns المَصْدَر . . . . 188
4. Noun-Adjective Agreement Revisited . . . . 190
A. Number . . . . 190
B. Gender. . . . . 191
C. Case . . . . 192
D. Definiteness . . . . 193
المُفْرَدات. . . . . 198

Lesson Eleven الدَرْسُ الحادي عَشَر . . . . 200
Objectives. . . . . 201
يَوْميّاتُ طالِبٍ عَرَبيٍّ في أمريكا. . . . . 203
1. Describing Activities in the Past, Present, and Future . . . . 207
2. Expressing Sequence قَبْلَ، بَعْدَ . . . . 208
3. Expressing Certainty or Uncertainty. . . . . 209
A. The Particle أَنَّ . . . . 209
B. Verbs with Doubled Consonants . . . . 209
4. Reporting Other People’s Speech Using the Verb قالَ ‘say’ . . . . 211
The Particle إِنَّ. . . . . 211
5. Comparing and Contrasting Entities اِسْمُ التَفضيل . . . . 212
A. The Superlative. . . . . 213
B. The Comparative . . . . 213
6. The إضافة Structure: Dual and Plural. . . . . 214
7. The Verb كانَ . . . . 215
8. Calendars in the Arab World . . . . 217
A. The Islamic Calendar . . . . 218
B. The Western Calendar. . . . . 219
9. The Preposition بِـ. . . . . 220
10. Two of the Five Special Nouns (أب and أخ) . . . . 220
المُفْرَدات. . . . . 224

Lesson Twelve الدَرْسُ الثاني عَشَر . . . . . . . . . . . . . . . . . . . . . . . . . . . . . . . . . 228

Objectives . . . . . . . . . . . . . . . . . . . . . . . . . . . . . . . . . . . . . . . . 229

الفُصولُ الأَرْبَعَة والطَقْس . . . . . . . . . . . . . . . . . . . . . . . . . . . . . . . 231

1. Partitive Nouns . . . . . . . . . . . . . . . . . . . . . . . . . . . . . . . . . 236

2. Converting Temperature Scales . . . . . . . . . . . . . . . . . . . . . . 238

المُفْرَدات . . . . . . . . . . . . . . . . . . . . . . . . . . . . . . . . . . . . . . 240

Lesson Thirteen الدَرْسُ الثالِث عَشَر . . . . . . . . . . . . . . . . . . . . . . . . . . . . . . 242

Objectives . . . . . . . . . . . . . . . . . . . . . . . . . . . . . . . . . . . . . . . . 243

ماذا تَفعَلُ هالَة بُستاني كُلَّ يَوْم؟ . . . . . . . . . . . . . . . . . . . . . . . . . . . . 245

يَوْمِيّاتُ عَدنان مارتيني . . . . . . . . . . . . . . . . . . . . . . . . . . . . . . . . 246

1. Partitive Nouns and Phrases . . . . . . . . . . . . . . . . . . . . . . . . 252

2. Negating Imperative Verbs . . . . . . . . . . . . . . . . . . . . . . . . 252

3. Weak Verbs الفِعْلُ المُعْتَلّ . . . . . . . . . . . . . . . . . . . . . . . . . 253

4. Expressing Reason . . . . . . . . . . . . . . . . . . . . . . . . . . . . . . 255

5. Verb Position in Arabic Sentences . . . . . . . . . . . . . . . . . . . 255

6. Swearing or Giving an Oath Using the Preposition وَ . . . . . . . . 257

المُفْرَدات . . . . . . . . . . . . . . . . . . . . . . . . . . . . . . . . . . . . . . 259

Lesson Fourteen الدَرْسُ الرابع عَشَر . . . . . . . . . . . . . . . . . . . . . . . . . . . . . 262

Objectives . . . . . . . . . . . . . . . . . . . . . . . . . . . . . . . . . . . . . . . . 263

يَومِيّاتُ مايْكِل بْراوْن . . . . . . . . . . . . . . . . . . . . . . . . . . . . . . . . . 265

يَومِيّاتُ عَدنان مارتيني . . . . . . . . . . . . . . . . . . . . . . . . . . . . . . . . 266

1. Expressing Contrast with أمّا . . . فَـ . . . . . . . . . . . . . . . . . . . 268

2. Expressing Reason Using لِذلِكَ . . . . . . . . . . . . . . . . . . . . . . . 270

3. The Preposition لِـ Following the Verb قال . . . . . . . . . . . . . . . 271

4. The Position of Demonstratives in Relation to the Modified Noun . . . . . . . . 271

5. More on the Derivation of Relative Nouns (نِسْبَة) . . . . . . . . . . 272

المُفْرَدات . . . . . . . . . . . . . . . . . . . . . . . . . . . . . . . . . . . . . . 276

Lesson Fifteen الدَرْسُ الخامِس عَشَر . . . . . . . . . . . . . . . . . . . . . . . . . . . . . . 278

Objectives . . . . . . . . . . . . . . . . . . . . . . . . . . . . . . . . . . . . . . . . 279

أعيادٌ عَرَبِيَّةٌ وإسلامِيَّةٌ ومَسيحِيَّةٌ وأمريكِيَّةٌ . . . . . . . . . . . . . . . . . . . . . . . 281

عيدان إسلاميّان .................... 282
عيدان مَسيحِيّان .................... 282
أعْياد أمريكيّة .................... 283
سُعاد ريماوي..................... 284
1. The Five Nouns Revisited الأسْماءُ الخَمْسة .................... 287
2. Not Fully Inflected Nouns المَمْنوعُ مِن الصَرف (Diptotes).................... 289
3. The Passive Voice .................... 292
A. Past-Tense Passive .................... 292
B. Present-Tense Passive .................... 292
C. Agent فاعل and Deputy Agent نائب فاعل.................... 293
4. The Verb صارَ.................... 295
المُفْرَدات.................... 299

Lesson Sixteen الدَرْسُ السادِس عَشَر .................... 302
Objectives.................... 303
شَخْصِيّاتٌ أمريكيّةٌ وعَرَبيّةٌ .................... 306
1. Secrets of the Language: Forms of the Arabic Verb.................... 311
A. Patterns الأوزان and the Root System.................... 312
B. Verb Forms أوزان الفِعل .................... 317
C. Special Cases.................... 322
2. Ordinal Numbers Revisited .................... 324
المُفْرَدات.................... 329

Lesson Seventeen الدَرْسُ السابِع عَشَر .................... 332
Objectives.................... 333
عيدُ الفِطْرِ.................... 335
عامٌ دِراسيٌّ جَديدٌ .................... 337
1. Dual and Plural Nouns in إضافة Structures (مُثَنّى وجَمْع) المُضاف.................... 343
2. Expressing Frequency كُلّ، مَرّة.................... 343
3. Expressing Exception ما عَدا .................... 344
4. Explaining Reason Using لِـ and Its Case المضارع المنصوب (Subjunctive)... 344
5. Derived Forms: Active and Passive Participles اِسمُ الفاعِل واسمُ المَفعول .................... 346
6. Negating Past-Tense Verbs with لَمْ (المُضارِعُ المَجزوم) .................... 348

7. Weak Verbs الفعل المُعتَلّ ... 349
المُفْرَدات ... 357

Lesson Eighteen الدَرْسُ الثامِن عَشَر ... 360
Objectives ... 361
شَقَّةُ مايكِل الجَديدةُ ... 364
1. Expressing Intention: أرادَ أنْ + المضارع المنصوب ... 372
The Verb أعْجَبَ ... 374
2. The Noun of Instrument اسْمُ الآلة ... 375
3. Prepositions حُروف الجَرّ: Relational Concepts ... 376
A. Two Categories of Prepositions ... 376
B. Adverbs and Prepositions of Place ... 378
المُفْرَدات ... 385

Lesson Nineteen الدَرْسُ التاسِع عَشَر ... 388
Objectives ... 389
مايكِل براون في القاهِرَةِ والإسكَندَريَّة ... 392
عَدنان مارتيني في نيويورك وكَنَدا وفَلوريدا ... 395
1. Terms of Address in Written Communication ... 403
2. Adverbs of Time and Place ظَرف الزَمان والمَكان ... 404
3. Negating Future Time (لَنْ) ... 405
4. Relative Nouns (الَّذي، الَّتي) الأسْماءُ المَوصولة ... 406
A. Restrictive Relative Nouns الأسماء الموصولة الخاصة ... 407
B. Agreement with Non-Rational Plurals ... 408
C. Non-Restrictive Relative Nouns مَن and ما ... 409
D. Combining Relative Nouns with Prepositions ... 409
E. Indefinite Antecedents ... 410
F. The Referent as Object in the Relative Clause ... 411
5. Prepositions Revisited ... 413
6. Possessive إضافة ... 415
المُفْرَدات ... 418

Lesson Twenty الدَرْسُ العِشرونَ . . . . . . . . . . . . . . . . . . . . . . . . . . 422
Objectives . . . . . . . . . . . . . . . . . . . . . . . . . . . . . . . . . . . . . . . . . . . . . 423
رِياضاتٌ وأطعِمةٌ مُفَضَّلةٌ . . . . . . . . . . . . . . . . . . . . . . . . . . . . . . . . . . . 425
من يوميّاتِ مايكل براون . . . . . . . . . . . . . . . . . . . . . . . . . . . . . . . . . . . 427
1. Habitual and Progressive Past . . . . . . . . . . . . . . . . . . . . . . . . . . . . . 434
2. Colors . . . . . . . . . . . . . . . . . . . . . . . . . . . . . . . . . . . . . . . . . . . . . . 436
3. Comparative Nouns with Doubled Consonants . . . . . . . . . . . . . . . . . . 437
4. Weak Verbs Revisited (الفعل المعتلّ) . . . . . . . . . . . . . . . . . . . . . . . . . 438
المُفْرَدات . . . . . . . . . . . . . . . . . . . . . . . . . . . . . . . . . . . . . . . . . . . . 442

Lesson Twenty-One الدَرْسُ الحادي والعِشرون . . . . . . . . . . . . . . . . . . . . . 446
Objectives . . . . . . . . . . . . . . . . . . . . . . . . . . . . . . . . . . . . . . . . . . . . . 447
جُغرافِيَّةُ الوَطَنِ العَرَبيّ والوِلاياتِ المُتَّحِدةِ الأمريكيّة . . . . . . . . . . . . . . 451
الوِلاياتُ المُتَّحِدةُ الأمريكيّةُ . . . . . . . . . . . . . . . . . . . . . . . . . . . . . . . 454
سورِيَة . . . . . . . . . . . . . . . . . . . . . . . . . . . . . . . . . . . . . . . . . . . . . . . 455
وِلايةُ أوهايو . . . . . . . . . . . . . . . . . . . . . . . . . . . . . . . . . . . . . . . . . . 457
1. Geographical Directions . . . . . . . . . . . . . . . . . . . . . . . . . . . . . . . . . . 464
A. Adverbials . . . . . . . . . . . . . . . . . . . . . . . . . . . . . . . . . . . . . . . . . . 464
B. Prepositional Phrases . . . . . . . . . . . . . . . . . . . . . . . . . . . . . . . . . . . 464
2. The Noun كِلا / كِلتا (both of) . . . . . . . . . . . . . . . . . . . . . . . . . . . . . 465
3. Expressing Exception with إلاّ and غَيْر . . . . . . . . . . . . . . . . . . . . . . . 466
A. The Particle ما عَدا . . . . . . . . . . . . . . . . . . . . . . . . . . . . . . . . . . . . 466
B. The Particle إلاّ . . . . . . . . . . . . . . . . . . . . . . . . . . . . . . . . . . . . . . 466
C. The Noun غَيْر . . . . . . . . . . . . . . . . . . . . . . . . . . . . . . . . . . . . . . . 467
المُفْرَدات . . . . . . . . . . . . . . . . . . . . . . . . . . . . . . . . . . . . . . . . . . . . 470

Lesson Twenty-Two الدَرسُ الثاني والعشرون . . . . . . . . . . . . . . . . . . . . . . 474
Objectives . . . . . . . . . . . . . . . . . . . . . . . . . . . . . . . . . . . . . . . . . . . . . 475
الإذاعَةُ والتِلفاز . . . . . . . . . . . . . . . . . . . . . . . . . . . . . . . . . . . . . . . . 478
من يَومِيّات مايكل براون . . . . . . . . . . . . . . . . . . . . . . . . . . . . . . . . . . . 480
بَرامِجُ إذاعة وتلفزيون . . . . . . . . . . . . . . . . . . . . . . . . . . . . . . . . . . . . 482
1. Expressing Obligation with على . . . أن (have to) . . . . . . . . . . . . . . . . . 487
2. Expressing Possibility with the Verb أمكنَ . . . . . . . . . . . . . . . . . . . . . 489

3. The Structure لَمْ يَعُدْ ... 490
4. The Relative Noun ما ... 491
5. The Particle أنْ after Adverbs of Time ... 491
6. The Noun بِضْع ... 493
المُفْرَدات ... 496

Lesson Twenty-Three الدَرْسُ الثالِث والعِشرون ... 498
Objectives ... 499
عَدنان في مَدينةِ دِنْـفر ... 501
لالينيا تَزورُ المِنيا ... 504
1. The Use of the Particle فَـ ... 508
A. When Prefixed to Nouns ... 508
B. When Prefixed to Verbs ... 508
2. Functions of the Particle قَدْ ... 509
A. With Past-Tense Verbs (Perfect) ... 509
B. With Present-Tense Verbs ... 510
3. البَدَل (Substitution or the Permutative) ... 511
A Reminder about إضافة ... 512
4. The Particle إنْ ... 512
المُفْرَدات ... 515

Lesson Twenty-Four الدَرْسُ الرابِع والعِشرون ... 518
Objectives ... 519
أُسرَةُ عَدنان مارتيني ... 521
Terms of Address: أبو and أم ... 528
1. Comparative and Superlative Degrees Revisited ... 529
2. The Particles كَيْ and لِـ ... 530
3. Verbal Nouns Revisited المَصْدَر ... 531
4. Writing the *Hamza* ... 532
A. *Hamzatu-l-waṣl* همزة الوَصل (The Conjunctive *Hamza*) ... 532
B. *Hamzatu-l-qaṭ‘* همزة القطع (The Disjunctive *Hamza*) ... 534
In the initial position ... 534
In the medial position ... 534

In the final position . . . . . . . . . . . . . . . . . . . . . . . . . . . . . . . . . . . . . . . . . . . . . 537
Placement of double *fatḥa* (*tanwīn*) and other suffixes on a final *hamza* . . . 537
المُفْرَدات. . . . . . . . . . . . . . . . . . . . . . . . . . . . . . . . . . . . . . . . . . . . . . . . . . . . . 541

Appendix A: Arabic Alphabet and Diacritical Marks . . . . . . . . . . . . . . . . . . . . . . . . 545

Appendix B: A Key to the Arabic Sound System
and the Transliteration System Used in the Textbook . . . . . . . . . . . . . . . . . . . . . . . 548

Appendix C: Verb Conjugations . . . . . . . . . . . . . . . . . . . . . . . . . . . . . . . . . . . . . . . . 550

Appendix D: Answer Key. . . . . . . . . . . . . . . . . . . . . . . . . . . . . . . . . . . . . . . . . . . . . 564

Appendix E: Texts of Postcards and Letters from Lessons 19 and 24 . . . . . . . . . . . 611

Cumulative Vocabulary. . . . . . . . . . . . . . . . . . . . . . . . . . . . . . . . . . . . . . . . . . . . . . 615

English Index . . . . . . . . . . . . . . . . . . . . . . . . . . . . . . . . . . . . . . . . . . . . . . . . . . . . 655

Arabic Index . . . . . . . . . . . . . . . . . . . . . . . . . . . . . . . . . . . . . . . . . . . . . . . . . . . . . 662

Illustration Credits . . . . . . . . . . . . . . . . . . . . . . . . . . . . . . . . . . . . . . . . . . . . . . . . 667

# Introduction

This second edition of *Ahlan wa Sahlan* has undergone significant changes from the first edition. The new educational package presents the learner with multiple avenues to explore the Arabic language: a workbook, a textbook, dramatic and non-dramatic scenes on DVD, digitized MP3 files for the audio materials, digitized MP4 files for the video materials, an online interactive computer program, and a Web site. We provide the instructor with an Annotated Instructor's Edition of the textbook (explained in full later in this introduction) and online resources that include lesson plans, handouts, exercises, texts, and examinations to facilitate the use of the textbook and its supplementary materials.

Possibly the most noticeable change in the Second Edition is the separation of the *Letters and Sounds of the Arabic Language* workbook from the main textbook. Having two separate books allowed us to make numerous additions to the main textbook, including a great increase in the number of communicative exercises per lesson. On average, there are three communicative exercises per lesson, all of which are the result of over a decade of teaching with the functional approach to language learning. Only those communicative exercises that have been tested and revised, and have received a warm welcome in the classroom, have been blended into the textbook to reinforce lesson themes as well as vocabulary and grammatical items. The grammatical explanations throughout the Second Edition have been edited and rewritten, with additional examples and a generous number of tables that cleanly summarize many grammatical points in an easily digestible visual format, resulting in enhanced retention and recall. The grammatical summaries in the Second Edition have been expanded and include memory-enhancing tips and concise bulleted explanations. The vocabulary lists at the lesson level and the cumulative glossary at the end of the book have been greatly expanded to include more vocabulary from the main reading passages as well as those vocabulary items that are introduced in the DVD dialogues and scenes. The DVD dialogues set up the context for the language functions shown in the non-dramatic scenes, while the DVD scenes offer a glimpse into Syrian culture through natural interaction between and among Arabs and Westerners.

It was our intention that the overall feel of the Second Edition would be to convey the voice of a master teacher directly to the learner. A secondary goal in the development of these materials was to produce a textbook that not only engaged the student but was visually appealing as well. The concept of producing an attractive learning/teaching environment was the driving force behind publishing a full-color textbook, in order to stimulate the learner's desire to spend additional hours engrossed in the materials and pique the learner's curiosity about Arabic. But the use of colors also allowed us not only to highlight grammatical points but to open our lessons with full-color pictures representative of the Arab world, giving the learner a peek into its culture, heritage, and history.

***To the Student***

*What is the key to learning a foreign language well?* Before you embark on your journey in learning Arabic using *Ahlan wa Sahlan,* Second Edition, you may wish to take some time to reflect on this question. Over the past decade, students have offered nearly every conceivable answer after I pose it on the first day of my Arabic classes. The answer that I have become convinced is "correct" is: *to think in the language.* No matter what your original answer may have been, thinking in the language is central to learning a language well by practicing it on a minute-by-minute basis. This is possible even at the very beginning of your Arabic studies by containing your thoughts in Arabic, using an internal banter as practice, and gradually widening the scope of language use by introducing new words to your idiolect. Make this language your own by actively seeking out those vocabulary words that you use in your mother tongue. These are the words with which you will be expressing yourself and that, in turn, will create an Arabic persona. The more you practice, the more permanent your learning becomes and the stronger your individuality will become in Arabic. We encourage you to actively surround yourself with the language as much as possible, and we have made this quite easy for you in fact. Simply by visiting our Web site at **http://www.yalebooks.com/ahlan** you can download all of *Ahlan wa Sahlan*'s audio and video materials to your MP3 and MP4 players so that you may listen to or watch them wherever you are and whenever you wish.

Much has been said about the difficulty of learning Arabic. In fact, the United States government lists Arabic as a category four language—among the most difficult for an American to learn. You may view the notion of difficulty in one of two ways: as an obstacle or as a challenge. We tend to think that Arabic is not so much difficult for the Western learner as it is different. According to recent studies completed in 2006 in which Arabic grammar was compared to other world languages, it was found that verb conjugation in Arabic is logical (less complex than Spanish), its tense system is easier than English, and given that Arabic is a root-derivational language, it is quite mathematical and elegant in its dexterity—meaning that it is able to accommodate new concepts using its derivational qualities. What this means for you is that you can not only learn Arabic, but learn it well.

The instructional package before you includes:

- The textbook
- The *Letters and Sounds of the Arabic Language* workbook
- The DVD program (also available as downloadable MP4 files)
- The audio program on MP3 CD (also downloadable from the Web site)
- The online interactive program

All of these components are designed to work in concert, offering you a variety of sources that address and enhance the different skill sets of reading, writing, listening, speaking, and culture. We designed *Ahlan wa Sahlan* to guide you along on the most direct learning path to achieve functional language goals and proficiency. We also address known pitfalls and, in a section termed *Error prevention,* offer solutions before these problems become fossilized. It is our hope that this textbook will not only serve to anticipate pitfalls but will also allow you to experience the joy of learning one of the oldest living languages on the planet and the riches that it has to offer.

### *To the Instructor*

### Purpose and Approach

*Ahlan wa Sahlan,* Second Edition, provides learners with basic structural and lexical knowledge that will enable them to function completely in Arabic. The ability to perform language functions such as greeting others, thanking someone, introducing oneself, describing one's background, seeking and providing information, etc., in real life or lifelike situations is developed by engaging the learner in structured, practical activities and grammatical exercises. In every lesson, a variety of such activities is designed to build up overall language proficiency systematically. In this fashion, learners will be able take part in communicating with their classmates and their instructor by employing all five language skills in Arabic. The focus, therefore, is on performing language functions by using the language forms learned, not on analyzing them grammatically. This does not mean, however, that grammar is not important. On the contrary, grammar enables learners to use language forms appropriately and correctly—read "enables" here to mean "puts grammatical structures and explanations in the service of language use." For example, presenting, explaining, and practicing the subjunctive mood in Arabic should, in our view, always be related to a language function or functions through use in context. In this textbook, the subjunctive mood is dealt with in the contexts of expressing obligation, intention, and reason. As the learner tries to acquire the ability to express these functions, he or she will internalize accurate usage of the subjunctive, not for its own sake, but in order to express a given meaning.

In addition, presenting and practicing the Arabic language from functional as well as structural perspectives accommodate the needs and learning styles of most learners. Students learn differently; some benefit primarily from a functional presentation and practice, others find structural information useful. A functional presentation normally activates inductive cognitive processes, while structural presentations activate deductive processes. Research tells us that the human mind, regardless of how it acquires knowledge, assimilates, modifies, and reconstructs this knowledge and then uses it in appropriate, yet specific ways. The aim, in both modes of presentation, is developing overall proficiency and competency in using Arabic.

### Audience

This textbook is designed to take learners from the absolute beginner stage to the intermediate range. At the university level, this can be translated into a first-year program providing approximately 150 contact hours, the equivalent of three academic quarters or two semesters.

## The *Ahlan wa Sahlan* Instructional Package
### The Annotated Instructor's Edition

The Annotated Instructor's Edition provides a guided tour of how we have successfully taught from the first edition and earlier incarnations of this textbook for a combined total of more than twenty years at the university level. The comments and suggestions on how an instructor may wish to introduce certain complex ideas and concepts constitute a pedagogically sound and systematic process of teaching known as the instructional cycle: Review, Present, Practice, Apply, and Evaluate. Within the cycle, we leave the review and evaluation up to the discretion of the instructor and break exercises down into the present, practice, and application phases. Furthermore, the annotations offer additional communicative activities for nearly every lesson, answers to certain questions that students seem to pose almost every year, and some cultural notes. It is our intention to provide every available means to set you—the instructor—up for success in implementing the functional approach to language learning.

### The Student Textbook

*Lesson Format:* All of the twenty-four lessons have a similar format. They start with a list of learning objectives (both functional and structural) to introduce the user to the content, topics, and grammatical points that are covered. The objectives are followed by vocabulary presentations and reading passages accompanied by comprehension and communicative activities. The grammatical points presented in the lesson are tied to the functions used in the opening material, and cultural notes expand on key points of the readings. Each lesson concludes with a listening passage and a comprehension activity based on the DVD, followed by a list of the vocabulary presented in the lesson.

*Learning Objectives:* The objectives listed at the beginning of each lesson are of two types: (1) functional objectives that describe what learners will be able to do in Arabic at the end of the lesson, and (2) structural objectives that specify exactly which language forms need to be practiced and used in order to perform the functional objectives correctly.

*Activities:* Each lesson contains activities associated with each type of objective. There are two major types of activities: (1) classroom activities designed to develop interactive aural/oral communicative competence, and (2) out-of-class activities, which primarily focus on enhancing the listening/reading skill set through reading passages of varying lengths, recorded materials, and computer-assisted and written exercises. Written exercises follow the reading passages and are subdivided into five types: vocabulary, reading comprehension, writing, listening comprehension, and grammar exercises. There are also integrative exercises that combine two types, such as reading comprehension and writing. Each exercise is made up of one or more sections. For example, a vocabulary exercise may contain several sections, such as matching, categorization, odd word out, and multiple choice. Some vocabulary exercises precede the main reading passages, acting as advance organizers in establishing context and introducing key vocabulary words used in the passage. Reading comprehension and writing exercises immediately follow each reading passage to encourage immediate review and recall of the reading material. Grammar exercises have one or two sections each, since each grammar exercise deals with a specific point. They are structured and proceed from simple to complex.

Listening exercises (marked by the listening icon) provide practice in pronunciation, word recognition, and dictation, which, in turn, develops the ability to communicate orally by systematically guiding learners through communicative exchanges. Each dialogue or set of communicative phrases is presented at the beginning of each lesson, followed by oral practice of its component parts. Listening comprehension exercises usually comprise three types: content questions, multiple choice, and true-false. Content questions should be read before listening to the passage in order to guide learners to what they should listen for. Learners are expected to deal with true-false exercises at a level higher than mere recognition or simply labeling items true or false. They should elaborate on each item, amplify it, or correct it in order to reflect their understanding of the text.

It is recommended that the listening and reading exercises be done after the vocabulary has been covered, since the purpose of written vocabulary exercises is to reinforce the learning of the new words. The same thing applies to reading comprehension exercises, which must be done during or immediately after reading. Most of the written activities are expected to be done outside of the classroom. The instructor may provide feedback, though, in class or on paper.

*Reading Passages:* The reading material consists of simple communicative phrases, dialogues, expository prose, or personal journals written by the two main characters, Michael Brown and Adnān Martīnī. The reading passages are usually accompanied with illustrations, graphics, or maps. They are designed to provide the necessary contexts for the language functions listed in the objectives and constitute a source for the vocabulary and language forms needed to realize these functions. The reading passages also provide cultural glimpses of both the target and local culture. The content of these passages is expected to promote general cultural knowledge through the Arabic language. At an intermediate level, such as the one served by part of this textbook and by its sequel, *Ahlan wa Sahlan: Intermediate Arabic,* the amount of knowledge imparted to the learner through Arabic makes it partially content-based. In most foreign-language courses, content-based materials represent the first step toward discipline-based materials, where the learner is prepared to embark on dealing with original texts within a particular field of study.

Most of the passages here have been developed specifically for *Ahlan wa Sahlan.* Thus, the language is rather controlled, that is, it is not "authentic" in the traditional sense of the term, although it has been written by a native speaker. Authenticity is interpreted here, however, in a functional sense, where the language used by teacher and learner is considered authentic if it serves some genuine functional or communicative purpose, regardless of whether or not native speakers use the same forms orally to accomplish the same or similar linguistic goal (see the section below on the language situation in the Arab world). The written passages, on the other hand, can be considered both authentic in function and sociolinguistically appropriate, since the majority of them are expository passages, written communication (e.g., messages, postcards, letters), or personal diaries.

*Arab Culture:* The content of the reading passages offers cultural insights into the target and local (American) cultures. Since the two main characters are students at universities (Michael Brown is studying Arabic in Cairo, Egypt, while Adnān Martīnī studies computer science in Columbus, Ohio), heritage learners using this textbook might be able to identify with the activities and interests the characters describe. Students should take into account the fact that there is no single Arab culture, but rather a multiplicity of cultures. In fact, diversity rather than homogeneity characterizes the cultures of the Arab world. No one textbook can provide a comprehensive look at culture. Instead, the reading passages and the story line maintained through the lessons in *Ahlan wa Sahlan* attempt to show selected aspects of Arab culture. These include food and drink, clothing, customs, family, entertainment, sports, homes, schools, geography of the Arab world, significant Arab personalities, and festivities. The presentation of the cultural and language items proceeds from the immediate to the wider environment.

*Grammatical Explanations and Exercises:* The grammatical notes in this textbook are by no means comprehensive, nor do they constitute a reference grammar for the student. However, they are adequate for the tasks at hand, providing the necessary knowledge about structures that occur in the reading passages and the practice needed to internalize this knowledge. Grammar acquisition is not the goal of instruction, but rather a facilitating element to achieve the goal, which is developing the ability to use the Arabic language (Modern Standard Arabic) as native speakers would use it in formal and semi-formal situations. The ultimate test of its success is the students' ability to perform tasks specified in the functional exercises following the reading passages. Students are expected, for example, to provide a biographical sketch of themselves or of people they know, describe possessions and activities, express preferences and opinions, and be able to read and understand simple passages.

We suggest that the vast majority of grammatical explanations and exercises be read and done outside of the classroom, thus preserving valuable class time for conducting lifelike interactive activities with classmates and the instructor. Students can even read the grammar sections before working with the reading selection because this information is *about* the language and does not require special language skills. Grammatical explanations basically provide information or knowledge that can be learned without external help, whereas language abilities are skills that must be developed physically as well as cognitively with the assistance of an instructor and interaction with classmates. Instructors can, of course, provide brief feedback on their students' work on grammar exercises in class.

*Glossaries:* An Arabic-English vocabulary list containing the new words introduced in the lesson is found at the end of each lesson. At the end of the book, there is a cumulative glossary, or dictionary, containing all the words found in the individual vocabulary lists as well as key words from the listening and DVD passages. The vocabulary in the cumulative glossary is marked with the lesson number where each word first appears.

*Appendices:* Appendix A contains the Arabic alphabet with the different forms of the letters according to their positions in the word and the Roman symbol representing each letter. Appendix B contains a key to the sound system of Arabic and the transliteration system used in this textbook (that is, the Roman symbols used to represent Arabic letters). Appendix C has a representative sample of thirteen verb conjugation paradigms, showing tense, mood, imperative, verbal nouns, and active and passive participles. Appendix D contains an answer key to all of the discrete-answer exercises in the book, including listening and DVD exercises. Appendix E contains the texts of the handwritten postcards and letters that appear in Lessons 19 and 24.

**The Arabic Language**

*Modern Standard Arabic:* The Arabic variety used in this textbook is known in the West as Modern Standard Arabic (MSA) and as *al-fuṣḥā* (meaning "most elegant," "most eloquent," or "purest") in the Arab world. It is more or less invariable throughout the Arab world and is used for specialized functions, including classroom instruction, the electronic and print media, and formal situations. MSA is generally not used at home or on the street for interpersonal communication.

*Colloquial Arabic (The Dialects):* The previously described features of MSA differentiate it from the various spoken regional and local dialects, which vary considerably from place to place. Arabic dialects are oral for the most part, rarely being written. Variation among the dialects takes place at all linguistic levels: phonological, morphological, syntactic, and lexical. The dialects are numerous, but for convenience they may be grouped roughly into five categories: (1) Levantine (Syria, Lebanon, Palestine, and Jordan), (2) Iraqi, (3) Arabian (the Arabian Peninsula), (4) Egyptian (Egypt and Sudan), and (5) North African (Libya, Tunis, Algeria, and Morocco). Somalia and Djibouti are not normally included in these classifications because, although they are members of the Arab League, the Arabic in these regions is used mostly as a liturgical language and in some areas as a second language where it is learned formally. Therefore, this variety of Arabic is classifiable as MSA, or even classical Arabic, rather than as a dialect or colloquial variety.

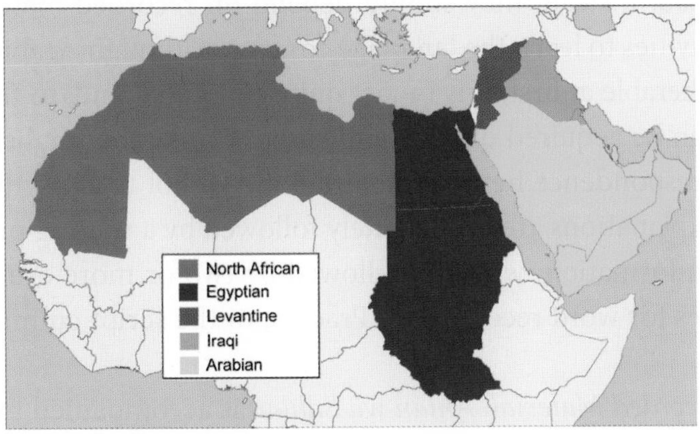


**Dialectal Regions of the Arab World**

The dialects are known collectively as colloquial Arabic (CA), which is distinct from MSA at all linguistic levels. Learning MSA before any colloquial variety provides learners with two advantages. First, a good foundation in MSA facilitates the acquisition of any dialect a learner might wish to learn later, for generally dialects are structurally less complex than MSA. Therefore, it may be easier for learners to acquire a colloquial variety after they have learned MSA because learning colloquial utterances involves applying deletion rather than augmentation rules. Secondly, and unlike local dialects, MSA is readily understood anywhere in the Arab world. In addition, by learning MSA, learners will be literate and have access to a vast heritage of ancient and modern literature, scholarly work, and the media.

Given this situation, some Arabists might object to using MSA as a vehicle for oral communication in situations normally reserved for colloquial Arabic. We recognize this sociolinguistic discrepancy and find that the response to that view may rest on educational and pedagogical grounds. First of all, for most Arabic programs reading is the primary goal, especially at institutions where there is a graduate program. Secondly, in order to avoid confusing learners with two varieties at the beginning stage, MSA may be used to fulfill both its own linguistic function (primarily reading and writing) as well as that of CA (speaking). In addition to the expected reading skills, learners will develop oral skills in MSA, which are, at any rate, required for proficiency in MSA; these skills can be transferred later to any dialect when the opportunity to learn it arises. Most of those involved in Arabic pedagogy agree that the ideal situation would be one that can replicate native-speaker performance in the classroom, but they also acknowledge the restricted nature of the classroom, which cannot accommodate this ambitious goal. Nevertheless, students should be made aware of this linguistic situation even if CA is not the target of instruction and should be presented, when appropriate, with CA equivalents of MSA communicative utterances in contexts in which they are used.

### The *Ahlan wa Sahlan* Learning Package

*Arabic Script:* The Arabic writing system is presented gradually over the six units of the *Letters and Sounds of the Arabic Language* workbook, along with communicative phrases and new vocabulary. During this initial phase (at least the first five units), learners are of course unable to read. Instead, they should depend on recorded material and classroom communicative activities to learn the language content. Although Arabic script might seem exotic and undecipherable at first, it is in fact quite consistent and, to the pleasant surprise of most learners, can be acquired quickly and easily. Unlike the English system, there is a high degree of correspondence between sound and symbol (each symbol represents one sound). Phonetic explanations are immediately followed by a writing practice exercise that is based on visual information, which is followed by two or more exercises that combine visual and aural cues for word recognition. Practice of the script culminates in a dictation exercise.

*Digitally-Recorded Material*: *Ahlan wa Sahlan* is accompanied by digital sound files that contain a rendition of dialogues or communicative phrases, new vocabulary, reading passages, listening passages, and oral drills recorded by native speakers at a near-normal speed. The audio material is signaled by a listening icon and includes sound-discrimination exercises as well as exercises for word recognition and listening comprehension. All the audio material for a given lesson is recorded in the sequence in which it appears in the textbook: new vocabulary, dialogues, and reading passages are followed by listening exercises and finally by a listening comprehension passage. In the first few lessons, learners are guided word-by-word and phrase-by-phrase on how to communicate orally and to recognize and produce the language forms correctly.

*DVD Dialogues and Scenes:* The DVD audio-visual materials that were developed for *Ahlan wa Sahlan* are intended to reinforce the main reading passages not only by establishing context, but also by bringing the subject matter to life. These DVD materials are divided into two separate learning tracks: non-dramatic language functions and dramatic scenes. The non-dramatic language functions establish context for the various language components covered in the lessons, expanding the learner's knowledge of the register and appropriateness of language use in different situations. The dramatic scenes reiterate and multiply the main reading passage themes, story line, and grammatical structures while offering a different source from which learners gather information. The dramatic story line takes Michael Brown, who studies at the American University in Cairo, to Damascus, Syria, where he visits his friend Steve who is studying at the University of Damascus. Because Michael Brown does not know the Syrian dialect on this short vacation, he poses questions to his Syrian interlocutors about the meanings of certain Syrian expressions. It is through these interactions that the learner is systematically exposed to new colloquial phrases that are translated for Michael from Syrian colloquial to Modern Standard Arabic (MSA). Additionally, the learner benefits from exposure to two different cultures, as the Egyptian culture is presented and described in the reading passages, while the Syrian culture is experienced through the DVD scenes. DVD comprehension questions get progressively more difficult with each lesson to continually present a challenge to the learners.

*Online Interactive Exercise Program:* Available with this textbook is an online computer-assisted language learning program. It provides drill and practice in the sound and writing systems of Arabic and contains a large number of vocabulary, grammar, and listening comprehension exercises. Much of the language material contained in the online exercise program mirrors the objectives found in the textbook.

The online exercise program contains drills and exercises designed to help in learning the sound and writing systems of Arabic quickly and easily. It combines the printed word, digitized voice, and pictures for an interactive and effective learning experience. The exercises include word construction, word recognition, matching, multiple choice, fill-in-the-blank, scrambled sentences and paragraphs, and much more. Each exercise format is intended to activate a different cognitive skill and sub-skill. Multiple-choice items make learners view a word in a linguistic context, matching lets them look at lexical items as pairs that share at least one semantic trait, and categorization makes them view words as collocations that have some common function in the language. Such cognitive exercises improve learning by re-organizing lexical items in the learners' cognitive structures.

> To access the Online Interactive Exercise Program, go to
> **http://yalebooks.com/awsexercises**
> Username: **aws2009**
> Password: **aleppo**

*Ahlan wa Sahlan,* Second Edition, along with the supplementary materials that accompany it, attempts to provide a learning environment conducive to effective acquisition of specific language abilities. These abilities, in their totality, create a measure of proficiency in Arabic. Upon completing this course, the average learner may achieve a proficiency level within the Intermediate Mid range established by the American Council on the Teaching of Foreign Languages (ACTFL). Naturally, results vary with respect to individual learner differences and may range between higher or lower proficiency levels.

Mahdi Alosh
Professor of Arabic and Applied Linguistics
Mahdi.Alosh@gmail.com

Allen Clark
Instructional Assistant Professor
The University of Mississippi
University, MS 38677

# Acknowledgments

I am indebted to so many individuals whose contributions improved the quality of this work, including students of Arabic at various institutions inside and outside the United States as well as colleagues who used the first edition and took time out of their busy schedules to provide me with feedback. I am especially indebted to my wife, Ibtissam, for putting up with the endless hours I spent on developing the material and for designing and programming the computer-assisted program that accompanied the first edition. I would like to acknowledge the extraordinary assistance and input by Allen Clark, who serves as a co-author of the second edition. He brings with him extensive experience in teaching the first edition as well as the perspective of the learner and the specialist. I also appreciate the expert assistance of Fayez Al-Ghalayini, whose meticulous editing of the Arabic portion of this textbook and assiduous input and profuse comments on the grammatical aspect improved the quality of this work and made it more accurate. I thank Lalainya Goldsberry, Hiba Abdallah, and Nevine Demian for providing factual and cultural information about Egypt. The peripheral materials associated with the textbook have received much assistance from several individuals. The online program has gone through several phases to which Abdulkafi Albirini, Allen Clark, Hanan Kashou, Rick Trinkle, Farah Combs, and J. C. Raymond contributed, each one in his or her area of expertise. I am also indebted to Khaled Huthaily, whose meticulous work on the program has made it more user friendly and effective. I thank Nonie Williams and Lana Khodary for the many hours they devoted to the recording of the audio material. I recognize the quality work by Dima Barakat and Maya Pastalides in designing, scripting, shooting, and producing the video program.

Finally, I thank the outside reviewers, whose comments on the manuscript and suggestions for improvements are gratefully appreciated:

Shukri Abed, Middle East Institute
Ghazi Abu-Hakema, Middlebury College
Abdulkafi Albirini, University of Illinois, Urbana-Champaign
Roger Allen, University of Pennsylvania
Muhammad Aziz, Yale University
Elizabeth Bergman, Georgetown University
Mirena Christoff, Brown University
Liljana Elverskog, University of North Texas
Fadia Hamid, Chagrin Falls Schools, Ohio
Eric Lewis
Summer Loomis, University of Washington, Seattle
Oraib Mango, Arizona State University
Ellen McLarney, Stanford University
David J. Mehall, University of Maryland
Harry Neale, University of California, Berkeley
Waheed Samy, University of Michigan

# أهلاً وسهلاً

# الدرسُ الأوّل

## Objectives

- Identifying objects in the school environment
- Describing location using prepositions
- Enumerating items using the coordinating particle وَ
- Introduction to demonstrative pronouns هذا هذِه هُنا هُناك
- Showing contrasts with لكِنْ and لكِنَّ
- Introduction to the nominal sentence and cases of its nouns
- Negating with لَيْسَ
- Introduction to the definite article ال: Assimilating and non-assimilating sounds
- Introduction to definite and indefinite nouns

### 1. School Surroundings

# غُرْفَةُ الصَفِّ

اِسْمي هالَة بُسْتاني. أنا طالِبَةٌ هُنا في جامِعَةِ حَلَب. لكِنّني مِن مَدينةِ دِمَشْق. هذِهِ غُرفةُ صَفّي. وَهذا أُسْتاذي. اِسْمُهُ الياس زِيادَة. هُوَ أَسْتاذُ رِياضيّات.

هالَة بُسْتاني

هُناكَ طاوِلَةٌ وَكُرْسيٌّ في غُرْفَةِ الصَفّ. عَلى الجِدارِ لَوْحٌ وَصورَةٌ وَساعَة. في الغُرفَةِ أَيْضاً بابٌ وَنافِذَة. هُناكَ صورةٌ عَلى الجِدارِ بِجانِبِ الباب.

## 2. Describing Location Using Prepositions

Prepositions usually acquire specific meanings from the context in which they are used. In the passage above, the preposition عَلى means "on" and في means "in." The prepositional phrase بِجانِب, which means "beside" or "next to," is made up of the preposition بِـ added to the noun جانِب 'side'. It is interesting to note that both the English and Arabic words use the sound *bi* before the word "side" in their respective languages.

عَلى

أمامَ

خَلْفَ

في

بِجانِب

تَحْتَ

فَوْقَ

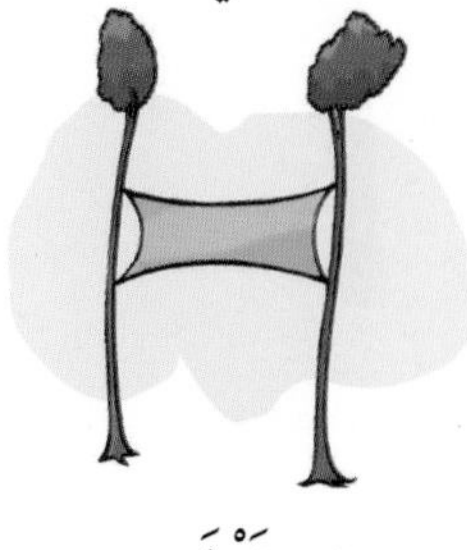

بَيْنَ

## تمرين ١

**Fill in the blanks:** Fill in the blanks in the following sentences with information from the reading passage.

١– هالَة مِنْ مَدينَةِ ________________.

٢– هِيَ طالِبَةٌ في ________________ حَلَب.

٣– في غُرْفَةِ الصَفِّ لَوْحٌ وَ ________________ وَ ________________ عَلى الجِدار.

٤– هُناكَ طاوِلَةٌ وَ ________________ عَلى الأَرْض.

٥– هُناكَ ________________ بِجانِبِ الباب.

٦– إلياس زِيادَة أُسْتاذُ ________________.

## تمرين ٢

**Matching:** Match words from the right-hand column with words in the left-hand column. Take the time to practice writing Arabic by writing both words in the middle column.

| | | | |
|---|---|---|---|
| ١ | لَوْح | | صورَة |
| ٢ | غُرفَة | | لكِنْ |
| ٣ | أُسْتاذ | | صَفّ |
| ٤ | جِدار | | في |
| ٥ | هُنا | | باب |
| ٦ | عَلى | | هُناكَ |
| | | | طالِب |

## 3. Enumerating: The Coordinating Particle وَ

Listing and enumerating things is a common language function used almost daily. It involves stringing a number of words together (e.g., "She speaks Italian, French, German, and Russian"). Unlike English, where the conjunction "and" is used only before the last enumerated item, Arabic requires the use of the conjunction وَ before every enumerated item, as in the example:

١ في غُرْفَتي طاوِلَةٌ وَكُرسِيٌّ وَحاسوبٌ وَمُسَجِّلَة.

- **Important:** The coordinating particle in Arabic is a prefix rather than an independent word. It should never be separated from the word it modifies (i.e., the word it precedes).

### تمرين ٣

**Conversation:** Ask your neighbors what they have in terms of those objects that we have studied thus far and then write a list using the conjunction وَ as in the examples below. Once you have gathered information on three of your classmates, report your findings to your teacher. As a follow-up exercise at home, try listing several objects that you own, that are in your room, or that are in your classroom.

١- عِندي سَيّارَة وَ__________ وَ__________.

٢- في غُرْفَتي طاوِلةٌ وَ__________ وَ__________.

## 4. Demonstratives: Gender Agreement

Demonstratives are used to identify objects by making reference to them—like "this" or "that" in English. Demonstratives are called determiners since they determine what you are talking about, as in the phrase "this room." In Arabic demonstratives are considered nouns. For example, the sentence **هذا أُسْتاذي** is made up of a subject (**هذا**) and a predicate (**أُسْتاذي**). This, as noted in section 6 of this lesson, is a nominal sentence because it starts with a noun.

In English, demonstratives agree with the nouns they modify in number but not in gender (e.g., this man/woman, those men/women), whereas in Arabic, they agree with the following noun in number as well as in gender. At this point, we shall consider the two forms used with singular masculine and feminine nouns. In the first example below, the word **كِتاب** 'book', which is masculine, is the noun modified by the demonstrative **هذا**. The second example contains the noun **صورة** 'picture', which is feminine and is therefore modified by the demonstrative **هذه**.

| | | |
|---|---|---|
| ٢ | هذا كِتاب. | *This is a book.* |
| ٣ | هذِه صورَة. | *This is a picture.* |

Two other demonstratives are used in the text above: **هُنا** 'here' and **هُناكَ** 'there'. The demonstrative **هُناكَ**, however, is also used in the sense of 'there is/are' to indicate the existence of an entity. It is used with singular (example 4), dual (5), and plural nouns (6).

| | | |
|---|---|---|
| ٤ | هُناكَ كِتابٌ عَلى الطاوِلة. | *There is a book on the table.* |
| ٥ | هُناكَ كِتابانِ عَلى الطاوِلة. | *There are two books on the table.* |
| ٦ | هُناكَ كُتُبٌ عَلى الطاوِلة. | *There are books on the table.* |

## تمرين ٤

Indicate the existence of five items, using **في** and **هُناكَ**, as in the following examples. Select five words that have been covered in this lesson and in the Workbook. Examples:

١– هَناكَ كِتابٌ عَلى الطاوِلَة.

٢– في الصَفِّ طالِبَة.

## تمرين ٥

**Identifying when to use هذا or هذه:** Indicate objects by using هذا or هذه, as in the examples. You will need to check the gender of each noun.

مِثال: ← 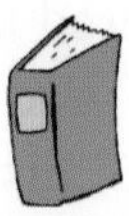 ← هذا ________ كِتاب ________.

مِثال: ←  ← هٰذِه ________ صورَة ________.

١- ←  ← ________ ________.

٢- ←  ← ________ ________.

٣- ←  ← ________ ________.

٤- ←  ← ________ ________.

٥- ← 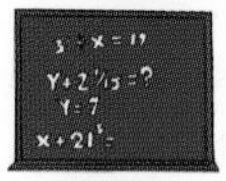 ← ________ ________.

٦- ←  ← ________ ________.

٧- ←  ← ________ ________.

## 5. Contrasting: The Particles لٰكِنْ and لٰكِنَّ

Showing contrasts between objects, people, states of affairs, and so forth can be done by using the word لٰكِنْ, which is used similarly to the English "but" or "however." There are two versions of this particle: (1) the weak version لٰكِنْ (pronounced *lākin*) and (2) the strong version لٰكِنَّ (pronounced *lākinna*).

### A. The Strong Version (لٰكِنَّ)

The strong version, as used in the main reading passage, must have either an attached pronoun suffixed to it or a noun that follows it. This noun or pronoun is considered the subject of لٰكِنَّ, which places it in the accusative case. Example 7 below is a sentence taken from our reading passage that contains the strong version لٰكِنَّ.

٧ أنا طالِبةٌ في جامِعَةِ حَلَب لكِنَّني مِن دِمَشق.

The word لكِنَّني is a combination of لكِنَّ and the suffix ني, which is the attached counterpart of the separate pronoun أنا, serving as the subject. لكِنَّ may be followed by a noun that is also the subject of the nominal sentence.

**B. The Weak Version (لكِنْ)**

You may also use the weak version لكِنْ in order to make contrasts, as in examples 8 and 9 below. The part contrasted after لكِنْ is a nominal sentence (e.g., عِندي دَرّاجة) whose preposed predicate is a phrase made up of the adverb عِندَ and the attached pronoun ي. A sentence beginning with such a phrase may be contrasted with a similar sentence using the weak version لكِنْ. Consider the following example:

٨ عِندي سيّارَةٌ لكِنْ لَيْسَ عِندي دَرّاجَةٌ.

However, a more acceptable and simpler style is to begin with the negative part:

٩ لَيْسَ عِندي دَرّاجَةٌ لكِنْ سيّارَة.

- **Note:** No changes occur in the forms of the constituents of the contrasted sentences as a consequence to the use of لكِنْ.

# 6. Nominal Sentences

Arabic sentences that do not start with a verb are called nominal sentences. The first noun is the "subject" or sometimes called the "topic," and the second is the "predicate" or the "comment." Both nouns are in the nominative case.

- Nouns in the nominative case are marked by a *ḍamma* on the end. If the noun is indefinite, the marker is double *ḍamma*, as in example 10 (عَرَبِيَّةٌ).

١٠    الطالِبَةُ عَرَبِيَّةٌ.

When the particle لكِنَّ is used with a nominal sentence, it causes the subject to change its grammatical case from nominative to accusative.

- Nouns in the accusative case are marked by a *fatḥa* for definite nouns and double *fatḥa* for indefinite nouns:

١١    الطالِبَةُ تونِسِيَّةٌ لكِنَّ الطالِبَ مَغرِبِيٌّ.

تمرين ٦

On a separate sheet of paper, combine each pair of sentences using لكِنَّ to contrast them. Remember that the noun that follows لكِنَّ must be in the accusative case and must be marked with a *fatḥa*. Consider the example:

مِثال:    سَيّارَتُكَ يابانِيَّةٌ. سَيّارَتُها أمريكِيَّةٌ.    سَيّارَتُكَ يابانِيَّةٌ لكِنَّ سَيّارَتَها أمريكِيَّةٌ.

١–    صورَةُ هالَة عَلى الجِدار. صورَتُكِ عَلى الباب.

٢–    دِمَشقُ في سورية. عَمّانُ في الأُردُن.

٣–    أنتِ مِصرِيَّةٌ. أنا سودانيٌّ.

٤–    حاسوبُ الأستاذِ أمريكيٌّ. حاسوبُ الطالِبِ يابانيٌّ.

٥–    جامِعتي في وِلايَةِ تكساس. جامِعتُكِ في وِلايةِ فلوريدا.

٦–    ساعَةُ الأستاذِ سُويسرِيَّةٌ. ساعَةُ الطالِبِ أمريكِيَّةٌ.

٧–    جَريدَةُ نيويورك تايمز أمريكِيَّةٌ. جَريدَةُ الأهرام مِصرِيَّةٌ.

٨–    مِفتاحي عَلى الكِتاب. مِفتاحُكَ بِجانِب التِلْفاز.

٩–    صورَةُ مونا ليزا إيطالِيَّةٌ. صورَةُ بابلو بيكاسو إسْبانِيَّةٌ.

١٠–    قَلَمُ الأستاذِ عَلى الطاوِلةِ. حَقيبَةُ الأستاذِ عَلى الأَرْضِ.

## 7. Negating with لَيْسَ

The statements in the example below are negated by لَيْسَ, which is used to negate nominal sentences. In a nominal sentence such as the one in the example, the predicate (which appears in blue) acquires the accusative case with the use of لَيْسَ (see also examples 12–14).

هذا لَيْسَ دَفْتَري.

هِيَ لَيْسَت أمريكيّةً. هِيَ كَنَديّةٌ.

- **Note:** When the man said the word دَفْتَري, it did not take an accusative marker (i.e., *fatḥa* or double *fatḥa*). This is because the pronominal suffix ي (= my) was attached in the place of the marker, preventing the *fatḥa* from appearing.

١٢ نادِيَةُ طالِبَةٌ. لَيْسَتْ نادِيَةُ طالِبَةً.

١٣ الأُسْتاذُ لُبْنانِيٌّ. لَيْسَ الأُسْتاذُ لُبْنانِيّاً.

- **Note:** لَيْسَ agrees with the noun it is negating in gender. Thus, if the noun at the beginning of the sentence is feminine, لَيْسَ must agree with it in gender and should have the form لَيْسَتْ.

**Note** also that the use of لَيْسَ makes the predicate accusative (لُبْنانِيّاً، طالِبَةً in examples 12 and 13). Accusative nouns are marked by *fatḥa* or double *fatḥa*. Regular rational (human) plurals that end with ونَ in the nominative case take the ending ينَ in the accusative case. When لَيْسَ follows the noun or pronoun, which is permitted, it should agree with it in number and in gender, as in the following example:

| *They are Canadians.* | هُمْ كَنَديّون. | ١٤ |
|---|---|---|
| *They aren't Canadians.* | هُمْ لَيْسوا كَنَدِيّين. | |

In example 14, لَيْسَ agrees with the pronoun هُم in gender and number (m., pl.). Note that the predicate in 14, a plural noun, takes the plural accusative marker ينَ instead of ونَ as a result of the use of لَيْسَ. If the predicate, however, is a prepositional phrase (مِن فِلَسطين in 15), no change takes place in the form of words. Contemplate the following:

١٥ مَحمود مِن فِلَسطين. مَحمود لَيْسَ مِن فِلَسطين.

| Conjugation | Pronoun | Number | Gender | Person |
|---|---|---|---|---|
| لَسْتُ | أنا | singular | ----- | 1st |
| لَسْنا | نَحْنُ | plural | ----- | |
| لَسْتَ | أنْتَ | singular | masculine | 2nd |
| لَسْتما | أنْتُما | dual | | |
| لَسْتُم | أنْتُم | plural | | |
| لَسْتِ | أنْتِ | singular | feminine | |
| لَسْتما | أنْتما | dual | | |
| لَسْتُنَّ | أنْتُنَ | plural | | |
| لَيْسَ | هُوَ | singular | masculine | 3rd |
| لَيْسا | هُما | dual | | |
| لَيْسوا | هُم | plural | | |
| لَيْسَت | هِيَ | singular | feminine | |
| لَيْستا | هُما | dual | | |
| لَسْنَ | هُنَّ | plural | | |

Table title: **Conjugations of لَيْسَ**

# تمرين ٧

**Using لَيْسَ**: Underline the predicate, which may be a word or a phrase, in each sentence. Then negate these sentences and phrases, using appropriate forms of لَيْسَ. Make changes to the predicate if necessary, according to the rules stated above. Consider the example:

مِثال: هذِه الطالِبَةُ مِن الأردُن. ← هذِه الطالِبَةُ مِن الأردُن. ← هذِه الطالِبة لَيْسَتْ مِن الأردُن.

١- أَسْتاذُنا مِصْريٌّ. ____________________.

٢- الحَقيبةُ عَلى الطاوِلةِ. ____________________.

٣- نَحْنُ سوريّون. ____________________.

٤- أنا أسْتاذٌ. ____________________.

٥- هذِه السَيّارَةُ أمريكيَّةٌ. ____________________.

٦- جامِعةُ هارفرد في وِلايةِ مِشيغان ____________________.

٧- أنا في الصَفِّ. ____________________.

٨- سوزانُ أوسْتَراليّةٌ ____________________.

٩- الدَفْتَرُ بِجانِبِ الهاتِفِ. ____________________.

## 8. Use of لٰكِنَّ and لٰكِنْ Combined with لَيْسَ

Contrasts are expressed in Arabic using لٰكِنْ and لٰكِنَّ. Remember that لٰكِنْ has no effect on the structure of the sentence, but with لٰكِنَّ the subject is in the accusative case:

١٦ لَيسَ عِنْدي حاسوبٌ لٰكِنْ حاسِبَة. *I don't have a computer, but I have a calculator.*

١٧ أُسْتاذُكَ مِنَ القاهِرةِ لٰكِنَّ أُسْتاذَها مِن تونِس. *Your teacher is from Cairo, but her teacher is from Tunis* (note the two endings on أستاذ).

# تمرين ٨

**Translation:** Use the following sentences as guides to form your Arabic sentences. Remember to provide the appropriate endings.

1. Your school is in Damascus, but his school is in Cairo.
2. She doesn't have a bicycle, but she has a car.
3. There's no newspaper in my bag, but there is a book on my table. (هُناكَ)
4. This is a tape recorder, but this is a television.
5. There's no calculator on the table, but there's an eraser and a ruler.
6. His car is American, but his computer is Japanese.

## 9. The Definite Article الـ: Assimilating and Non-Assimilating Sounds

The definite article in Arabic (the prefix equivalent to "the") is made up of the letters *alif* and *lām* (الـ) and is prefixed to nouns and adjectives. It is pronounced *al* when prefixed to words beginning with a sound that belongs to a group known as "moon" letters. They are thus called because long ago Arab grammarians used the word *qamar* قَمَر 'moon' to exemplify this group of sounds. If you prefix the definite article to this word, you have القَمَر, which is pronounced *al-qamar*.

- The sound represented by the letter ق and those in its class does not assimilate the ل of the definite article. In other words, the *lām* is pronounced as an *l* sound when prefixed to a word starting with one of these sounds. The sounds of this group are known as أحرُف قَمَرية 'moon or lunar letters'.

| Moon Letters (Non-Assimilating) |
|---|
| ء ب ج ح خ ع غ ف ق ك م هـ و ي |

In contrast, there are words which start with sounds that do assimilate the *lām* of the article; that is, a sound of this group causes the *lām* to be pronounced just like it. These are the "sun" letters, which were so named for the same reason cited above: Arab grammarians have used the word *šams* شَمس 'sun' to exemplify this class of sounds. If you prefix the article to this word, you have الشمس, which is pronounced *aš-šams* (*š* = *sh* as in shoe). As you can see, the *l* sound changes to *š*, thus resulting in two *š* sounds: one is the result of assimilating the *lām* of the article, and the other is the original initial sound of the word. The sounds of this group are known as أحْرُف شَمسِيّة 'sun or solar letters', and are listed on the following page.

### Sun Letters (Assimilating)

ت ث د ذ ر ز س ش ص ض ط ظ ل ن

You have been using the process of assimilation unconsciously. The morning greeting صَباحُ الخَيْر, for example, contains the article in the second word followed by a "moon" letter خ, which allows the *lām* of the article to be pronounced as *l*. Its response صَباحُ النور, on the other hand, contains the word النور, which starts with the "sun" letter ن that causes the *lām* of the article to assimilate to ن, thus resulting in *an-nūr*.

The article, whether or not it has an assimilated *l*, starts with an initial *a-* sound, which is basically a *hamza*. Thus, the word السودان 'the Sudan' is pronounced *as-sūdān* and البَيْت 'the house' is pronounced *al-bayt*. This particular pronunciation occurs only when these words are pronounced independently, that is, when they are not preceded by a word or a prefix. The definite article, however, loses the *hamza*, or the initial *a-* sound, if a word precedes it, such as the coordinating particle *wa* وَ 'and' or a preposition. This type of hamza is call *hamzatu-l-waṣl* هَمزَةُ الوَصْل. Consider the following examples:

| | | | |
|---|---|---|---|
| ١٨ | السودان | *as-sūdān* | (the Sudan) |
| | مِنَ السودان | *mina s-sūdān* | (from the Sudan) |
| ١٩ | البَيْب | *al-bayt* | (the house) |
| | وَالبَيْت | *wal-bayt* | (and the house) |

- **Important:** These processes affect only the pronunciation of the article, not its spelling.
- **Pronunciation tip:** One way of thinking about when to assimilate the *lām* and when not to is to compare the point of articulation of the sound that follows the *lām* with that of the *lām* itself. If the sound of the letter shares nearly the same point of articulation as the *lām*, then it is assimilated. In other words, "backed" consonants (those whose points of articulation are in the back of the mouth like the pharyngealized letters) are not assimilated, whereas the fronted letters, excluding the labials (those that occur on the lips like the *mīm* and the *bā'*), are assimilated.

## تمرين ٩

**Listen and recognize:** Listen to each word and mark the appropriate box. If the *l* of the article is pronounced *l*, then mark the box under the phrase حَرْفٌ قَمَريّ 'moon letter'. If the *l* is not pronounced as an *l* and you hear a doubled consonant, then mark the box under حَرْفٌ شَمْسِيّ 'sun letter'. If you are experiencing any difficulty in differentiating the sun and moon letters, it might be a good idea to write the word down on a piece of paper and then refer to the sun and moon letter tables on the previous two pages.

| حَرْفٌ شَمْسيّ | حَرْفٌ قَمَريّ | |
|---|---|---|
| ☐ | ☑ | مِثال: القَلْب |
| ☐ | ☐ | ١- |
| ☐ | ☐ | ٢- |
| ☐ | ☐ | ٣- |
| ☐ | ☐ | ٤- |
| ☐ | ☐ | ٥- |
| ☐ | ☐ | ٦- |
| ☐ | ☐ | ٧- |
| ☐ | ☐ | ٨- |

## تمرين ١٠

**Spelling Contest:** Add the letters together to make a word, and then in the left column write the meaning of the word.

| | | |
|---|---|---|
| ١- | جَ + ر + ي + دَ + ة + ي = | ______________ ______________ |
| ٢- | نَ + ظّ + ا + رَ + ةُ + ه = | ______________ ______________ |
| ٣- | ح + ا + س + و + بُ + كِ = | ______________ ______________ |
| ٤- | عِ + نْ + دَ + ه + ا = | ______________ ______________ |
| ٥- | ط + ا + و + ل + ة = | ______________ ______________ |
| ٦- | صَ + فَّ + كُ + م = | ______________ ______________ |
| ٧- | كُ + رْ + س + يّ = | ______________ ______________ |

## 10. Definite and Indefinite Nouns

Obviously, nouns marked with the definite article are definite and those which are not marked are indefinite. For example, the word كِتابٌ is indefinite and الكِتابُ is definite. There are other ways of making a noun definite, such as a suffixed possessive pronoun, e.g., كِتابي 'my book'.

- Unlike English, which has indefinite articles (*a* and *an*), there is no indefinite article in Arabic, though, as you have seen, the three *tanwīn* markers (double *fatḥa*, double *ḍamma*, and double *kasra*) on the end of a noun indicate an indefinite status.

## تمرين ١١

**Listen and recognize:** Listen as each word is pronounced and indicate whether it is a definite or indefinite noun by marking the appropriate box. A definite noun either contains the definite article ال (whether or not it is assimilated to the following sound) or has a possessive pronoun suffixed to it (e.g., كِتابي). An indefinite noun ends with a *tanwīn*.

| Definite | Indefinite | |
|---|---|---|
| ☐ | ☐ | ١- |
| ☐ | ☐ | ٢- |
| ☐ | ☐ | ٣- |
| ☐ | ☐ | ٤- |
| ☐ | ☐ | ٥- |
| ☐ | ☐ | ٦- |
| ☐ | ☐ | ٧- |
| ☐ | ☐ | ٨- |
| ☐ | ☐ | ٩- |
| ☐ | ☐ | ١٠- |

## تمرين ١٢

**Listen and respond:** Read the following dialogue and fill in the blanks with appropriate responses. After you have filled in the blanks, listen to the CD and respond during the pauses. Practice assimilating the *lām* at the correct times.

صَباحُ الخَيْر!

__________ __________!

كَيْفَ الحال؟

__________ __________. __________؟

الحَمْدُ لله بِخَيْر. عِندَك بَيْت؟

__________، __________ __________.

بَيْتُكَ في دِمشَق ؟

__________، __________.

تمام! أينَ هُوَ (= بَيْتُك) ؟

__________.

في بَيْتكَ حاسوب؟

__________، __________.

أين هُوَ؟

__________.

هَلْ أنْتَ أُسْتاذ في هذِه الجامِعة؟

__________، __________ __________ هُنا في __________ __________.

مَعَ السَّلامة!

____ __________!

## المُفْرَدات Vocabulary

Listen to the vocabulary items on the CD and practice their pronunciation.

professor, teacher . . . . . . . . . . . . . . . . (n., m.) أسْتاذ ج أساتِذَة

too, also . . . . . . . . . . . . . . . . . . . . . . . . (adv.) أيْضاً

on, in, by, with, for . . . . . . . . . . . . . . . . . . . (prep.) بِـ

to learn. . . . . . . . . . . . . . . . . . . . . . . . . (v.) تَعَلَّمَ

university . . . . . . . . . . . . . . . . . . . . . (n., f.) جامِعَة ج جامِعات

side. . . . . . . . . . . . . . . . . . . . . . . . . . (n., m.) جانِب

wall. . . . . . . . . . . . . . . . . . . . . . . (n., m.) جِدار ج جُدْران

Aleppo . . . . . . . . . . . . . . . . . . . . . . . . (n., f.) حَلَب

mathematics, calculus . . . . . . . . . . . . . . . (n., f.) رياضِيّات

of the sun, solar . . . . . . . . . . . . . . . . . . . . . (adj.) شَمْسِيّ

thing . . . . . . . . . . . . . . . . . . . . . . . (n., m.) شَيء ج أشْياء

class . . . . . . . . . . . . . . . . . . . . . . . (n., m.) صَفّ ج صُفوف

male student. . . . . . . . . . . . . . . . . . . . . (n., m.) طالِب ج طُلّاب

female student. . . . . . . . . . . . . . . . . . . . (n., f.) طالِبة ج طالِبات

on. . . . . . . . . . . . . . . . . . . . . . . . . . . (prep.) عَلى

room . . . . . . . . . . . . . . . . . . . . . . . . (n., f.) غُرْفَة ج غُرَف

you're welcome . . . . . . . . . . . . . . . . . . . . . . . عَفْواً

of the moon, lunar . . . . . . . . . . . . . . . . . . . . (adj.) قَمَرِيّ

but . . . . . . . . . . . . . . . . . . . . . (particle, weak version) لكِنْ

but . . . . . . . . . . . . . . . . . . . . (particle, strong version) لكِنَّ

if you would; please. . . . . . . . . . . . . . . . . . . . . لَو سَمَحْت

not . . . . . . . . . . . . . . . . . . . . . . . . . . (particle) لَيْسَ

place; store. . . . . . . . . . . . . . . . . . . . . . . . (n., m.) مَحَلّ

with . . . . . . . . . . . . . . . . . . . . . . . . . . . . (prep.) مَعَ

found. . . . . . . . . . . . . . . . . . . . . . . . . . (n., m.) مَوْجود

there, there is/are . . . . . . . . . . . . . . . . . (demonstrative) هُناكَ

and . . . . . . . . . . . . . . . . . . . . . . . . . . . . . . (conj.) وَ

# الدَرسُ الثاني

## Objectives

- Describing school surroundings and facilities
- Revisiting the *nisba*
- Introduction to an element of the *iḍāfa* structure
- Identifying objects by using demonstratives
- Introduction to an element of colloquial Arabic

### 1. School Surroundings and Facilities

## جامِعَتي

اِسْمي هَيْثم نَجّار. أنا طالِبٌ في كُلِّيَّةِ العُلومِ في جامِعَةِ دِمَشْق. في جامِعَتي عِدّةُ كُلِّيّات. هُناكَ كُلِّيَّةُ الهَنْدَسَةِ وَكُلِّيَّةُ الآدابِ وَكُلِّيَّةُ العُلومِ وَكُلِّيَّةُ الطِبِّ وَكُلِّيَّةُ التِجارَةِ وَكُلِّيَّةُ الحُقوق.

هُناكَ مَلْعَبٌ رِياضِيٌّ وَمَسْبَحٌ بِجانِبِ كُلِّيَّتي. في كُلِّيَّتي مُخْتَبَرٌ عِلْميٌّ وَهُناكَ مُخْتَبَرٌ لُغَوِيٌّ في كُلِّيَّةِ الآداب. المَكتَبَةُ بِجانِبِ كُلِّيَّةِ الحُقوق.

# غُرفَةُ مَكتَبي

اِسْمي راغِب طَبّاع. أنا أسْتاذُ رِياضِيّات في الجامِعَةِ الأُرْدُنِيَّة. في غُرفَةِ مَكْتَبي طاوِلةٌ وَكُرسيٌّ وَلَوْحٌ وَمَكْتَبَة. عِندي هاتِفٌ في مَكْتَبي. هاتِفي عَلى الطاوِلَةِ، لكِنْ لَيْسَ عِندي حاسوبٌ في المَكْتَب. هذِه حَقيبَتي عَلى الأرْضِ بِجانِبِ الطاوِلَة. مَكْتَبي في كُلِّيَّةِ العُلومِ في الجامِعَةِ الأُرْدُنيَّة.

$(س+ع)^٣$
هذِه حَقيبتي. هِيَ عَلى الأرْضِ بِجانِبِ الطاوِلة.


## تمرين ١

**Identity cards:** Fill out these identification cards for the persons described in the above passages. Indicate in the box (by writing down the appropriate word) whether this person is a student or a faculty member. Then complete the sentences with information from the texts.

الاسْم: ______________

الكُلِّيَّة: ______________

الجامِعَة: ______________

الإسْم: ______________
الكُلِّيَّة: ______________
الجامِعَة: ______________

١- هُناكَ ____________ كُلِّيّاتٍ في جامِعَةِ دِمَشْق.

٢- هُناكَ ____________ وَ ____________ بِجانِبِ كُلِّيَّةِ العُلوم.

٣- هُناكَ ____________ في كُلِّيَّةِ الآداب.

٤- راغِب طَبّاع ____________ في الجامِعَةِ الأُرْدُنِيَّة.

٥- هُوَ أُسْتاذ ____________.

٦- مَكْتَبُ الأُسْتاذِ راغِب في ____________.

٧- هُناكَ ____________ عَلى طاوِلَةِ الأُسْتاذِ راغِب.

٨- حَقيبَةُ الأُسْتاذِ راغِب عَلى ____________.

## تمرين ٢

**Read and emulate:**

**A.** Study the first passage in this lesson about **هَيْثَم نَجّار** and replicate it in writing, providing information about yourself and your school. You may provide actual names of buildings, colleges, and streets as applicable to your own situation.

**B.** Study the second passage in this lesson about **راغِب طَبّاع** and compose another passage similar to it, but in the third person, describing a professor you know. Make necessary changes in content and form to fit the new situation.

## تمرين ٣

**Conversation:** In groups of two, have one person describe his/her university or college to the other in Arabic. The other person should draw a picture of what he/she understands from the description on a separate sheet of paper. Once you are finished, the speaker compares how closely the drawing resembles reality. Now switch roles. Try to use as much of the language as possible, and if you cannot figure out how to say something directly, try to work around it.

## تمرين ٤

**Odd word out:** Underline the word that does not belong to each set and explain your choice if needed.

| | | | | |
|---|---|---|---|---|
| ١- | جانِب | جامِعَة | كُلِّيَّة | طِبّ |
| ٢- | مَلعَب | مَسْبَح | هَندَسَة | مُخْتَبَر |
| ٣- | مَكتَب | غُرْفَة | صَفّ | عِدَّة |
| ٤- | هذا | ذلِكَ | رِياضِيّ | تِلكَ |

## تمرين ٥

**Matching:** Match words from the right-hand column with words in the left-hand column. Take the time to practice writing Arabic by writing both words in the middle column.

| | | | |
|---|---|---|---|
| ١ | رِياضَة | | طِبّ |
| ٢ | مُخْتَبَر | | مَلعَب |
| ٣ | ذلِكَ | | سَكَن |
| ٤ | كُلِّيَّة | | لُغَوِيّ |
| ٥ | كِتاب | | تِلكَ |
| | | | مَكتَبَة |

## 2. *Nisba* Revisited

In Unit 5 of the Workbook, we derived relative nouns called *nisba* اِسْمُ نِسْبَة (which function like adjectives in English) from names of countries. The process involves adding a doubled يّ to a noun and can be applied to just about any Arabic noun. In the passage above, three *nisba* nouns are derived from the words رِياضَة 'sport', عِلْم 'science', and لُغَة 'language'.

| | | | | |
|---|---|---|---|---|
| ١ | رِياضَة *sport* | ← | رِياضيّ *athletic, sporty* |
| ٢ | عِلم *science* | ← | عِلميّ *scientific* |
| ٣ | لُغة *language* | ← | لُغَويّ *linguistic* |

If you recall, deriving a *nisba* from some nouns requires the addition of the letter و before suffixing يّ, as in example 3 لُغَويّ.

- In addition to the rules of derivation specified in Unit 5, note that if a noun is plural, it is generally changed to the singular before a *nisba* is derived. For example, the plural noun عُلوم 'sciences' must be changed to the singular عِلْم 'science' before deriving the word عِلميّ.

### Word Order and Gender Agreement

Adjectives in Arabic follow nouns and agree with them in gender, number, and case. For example, the noun مُخْتَبَرٌ may be modified by the adjective-like *nisba* عِلميّ (مُخْتَبَرٌ عِلميٌّ), which follows the noun and agrees with it in number (both being singular), gender (both being masculine), and case (both being nominative). If the noun is feminine (e.g., كُلِّيَّة), the adjective must also be feminine (e.g., كُلِّيَّةٌ عِلمِيَّةٌ), where the *tā' marbūṭa* on the end of عِلمِيَّة marks the *nisba* as feminine.

## تمرين ٦

**Construct the *nisba*:** Construct the *nisba* (adjective) from the pairs of words below. Derive a *nisba* from the second noun of each pair. The *nisba* must agree with the first noun in number and gender, as in the examples. You may wish to review the derivation rules explained in Unit Five.

| | | | |
|---|---|---|---|
| مُختَبَرٌ لُغَوِيٌّ | لُغَةٌ | مُختَبَرٌ | مِثال: |
| كُلِّيَّةٌ عِلْمِيَّةٌ | عِلْمٌ | كُلِّيَّةٌ | |
| | رِياضَةٌ | جَريدَةٌ | ١ |
| | طِبٌّ | كِتابٌ | ٢ |
| | مَدْرَسَةٌ | غُرْفَةٌ | ٣ |
| | صَباحٌ | صَفٌّ | ٤ |
| | جامِعَةٌ | طالِبَةٌ | ٥ |
| | اليابانُ | سَيّارَةٌ | ٦ |
| | الأُرْدُنّ | الجامِعَةُ | ٧ |
| | عَرَبٌ | اللُغَةُ | ٨ |
| | أمريكا | كُلِّيَّةٌ | ٩ |
| | عِلْمٌ | كِتابٌ | ١٠ |

### 3. The *Iḍāfa* Structure (الإضافة)

The phrases **مَدينَةُ دِمَشق** 'city of Damascus' and **جامِعَةُ حَلَب** 'University of Aleppo' may be familiar to you by now. They represent a structure in Arabic called *iḍāfa*. The term **إضافة** literally means "addition." It denotes "adding" one noun to another to form a relationship of possession or belonging. The *iḍāfa* structure binds the two (or more) nouns together, forming one entity. The main referent of this entity is represented by the first word of the structure.

**The *iḍāfa* structure is equivalent to three English structures:**

(1) The *of*-structure (e.g., City of New York, top of the hill, college of medicine)
(2) The apostrophe -*s* used on the end of nouns (e.g., Sandy's room, the instructor's car)
(3) Compound nouns (e.g., a car key, stock market, The Ohio State University)

| | | |
|---|---|---|
| *City of New York* | مَدينَةُ نيويورك | ٤ |
| *Sandy's room* (literally, *room of Sandy*) | غُرفَةُ ساندي | ٥ |
| *a car key* (literally, *a key of a car*) | مِفتاحُ سَيّارَةٍ | ٦ |

So far, you have used a number of *iḍāfa* phrases, including the following:

| | | |
|---|---|---|
| *the classroom* (literally, *the room of the class*) | غُرفَةُ الصَفِّ | ٧ |
| *University of Aleppo* | جامِعَةُ حَلَب | ٨ |
| *City of Damascus* | مَدينَةُ دِمَشق | ٩ |

- **Pronunciation tip:** As in examples 4, 5, 7, 8, and 9, when the first word(s) (= all but the last word) of the *iḍāfa* structure are feminine, the *tā' marbūṭa* must be pronounced like a *t* (= a regular ت). It parallels the phonetic rule in English of the possessive apostrophe -*s* in that when we say "Sandy's room," we must hear the *z* sound or we cannot tell that a possession is taking place. It is the same in Arabic; if we do not hear the ت sound at the end of feminine nouns in the structure, we cannot tell that a possession is taking place.

As you can see in the six examples above, the final noun of the *iḍāfa* structure does the possessing and the nouns that precede it are what is possessed. The first noun is the focus of the phrase. When reference is made to Sandy's room, for example, the reference is to the room (غُرفَة) rather than to Sandy. The second noun in an *iḍāfa* structure serves as added information to define the referent.

### A. Cases of the Constituents of the *Iḍāfa* Structure

An *iḍāfa* structure is made up of two or more nouns. The first noun in an *iḍāfa* structure can be in any grammatical case, depending on the position of the *iḍāfa* phrase in the sentence. The second noun of the *iḍāfa* structure (and others, if any), however, is always in the genitive case. The genitive case (known as حالَةُ الجَرِّ) is one of three grammatical cases of the Arabic noun which will be dealt with in various sections of this book. Nouns in the genitive are marked in a variety of ways. One of them is appending the short vowel *kasra* to the end of a definite noun. Examine the end of the second word in the examples below. You will notice that a *kasra* is written on the end of each one of them.

| | | |
|---|---|---|
| *the professor's car (the car of the professor)* | سَيّارَةُ الأستاذِ | ١٠ |
| *the classroom (the room of the class)* | غُرفَةُ الصَفِّ | ١١ |

**B. Definiteness of an *Iḍāfa* Structure**

The above phrases are definite by virtue of the definite article prefixed to the last noun.

**An *iḍāfa* structure is definite if:**

| | |
|---|---|
| (1) the definite article الـ is prefixed to the last noun of the structure | جَريدَةُ الطالِبِ |
| (2) an attached possessive pronoun is suffixed to it | جَريدَتُه |
| (3) it is a proper noun | جَريدَةُ مُحَمَّدٍ |

- **Note:** The first noun of an *iḍāfa* never takes a definite article or an attached pronoun. The first noun is, however, considered definite if the last noun of the structure is definite.

Now let's examine an indefinite *iḍāfa* phrase:

| | | |
|---|---|---|
| *a car key (a key of a car)* | مِفتاحُ سيّارَةٍ | ١٢ |

Notice that the last noun is marked with a double *kasra* (*tanwīn*). This marker denotes both a genitive case and an indefinite state (double *fatḥa* and double *ḍamma* also denote an indefinite state). Thus, if the last constituent of an *iḍāfa* structure is indefinite, the whole structure is indefinite. Likewise if the last noun is definite, the whole structure is definite.

Recognizing an *iḍāfa* phrase is relatively easy. First, it is made up of nouns that constitute the phrase. Second, the first noun is always indefinite and the second noun may be definite or indefinite.

## SUMMARY

- An *iḍāfa* structure is made up of two or more nouns that occur in succession.
- The first noun is the thing possessed and is the main noun of the phrase.
- The second noun is always in the genitive case (marked by a single or double *kasra*).
- The first noun is always indefinite; the second noun may be definite or indefinite.
- An *iḍāfa* phrase is definite if the last noun in the phrase has the definite article, if an attached pronoun is suffixed to it, or if it is a proper name.
- An *iḍāfa* phrase is indefinite if the last noun is indefinite.
- Indefinite nouns take *tanwīn* (ـــًــٌــٍ) on the final member of the construct.
- The *tā' marbūṭa* is pronounced like a regular ت in the *iḍāfa* structure for all words except the last one, where it is optional.

## تمرين ٧

***Iḍāfa* Identification:** Identify the *iḍāfa* phrases in the two passages at the beginning of this lesson and copy them down on a separate sheet of paper to turn in. There are 16 phrases altogether, including repeated phrases.

## تمرين ٨

**Form the *Iḍāfa*:** Form at least six *iḍāfa* structures from the following bank of nouns. After that, form three sentences using some of the *iḍāfa* structures that you have formed (you may use more than one *iḍāfa* per sentence). Pay close attention to the definiteness and the cases of these nouns to form the *iḍāfa* correctly.

| | | | | | | |
|---|---|---|---|---|---|---|
| صورَةُ | العُلوم | غُرْفَةٍ | الأَسْتاذِ | حَلَب | جامِعَةُ | الطِبِّ |
| مَكتَبُ | غُرفَةُ | كُلِّيَّةُ | الصَفِّ | المَدينَةِ | طاوِلَةُ | كِتابُ |

________________ ________________

________________ ________________

________________ ________________

١- ________________________________.

٢- ________________________________.

٣- ________________________________.

## تمرين ٩

***Iḍāfa* Construction:** Form *iḍāfa* phrases to express the following meanings, as in the example. Pay attention to the noun that is the focus of the phrase and the one that should receive the definite article.

Example: The door of the room بابُ الغُرفَةِ

1. The college of medicine ________________
2. The window of my room ________________
3. The car key ________________
4. Eyeglasses of a female student ________________
5. Sandy's female professor ________________
6. A bicycle of a male student ________________
7. A picture of Aleppo ________________
8. The classroom's door ________________
9. Ahmed's newspaper ________________
10. The Ohio State University ________________

## تمرين ١٠

**إضافة or نِسْبَة?** Write the word **نِسْبَة** next to the **نِسْبَة** constructions and the word **إضافَة** next to the **إضافة** structures.

١- سَيّارَةٌ يابانِيَّةٌ ____________

٢- أسْتاذُ رِياضِيّات ____________

٣- غُرفَةُ الصَفِّ ____________

٤- حَقيبَةُ طالِبَةٍ ____________

٥- الطُلاّبُ الكُويتيّون ____________

٦- صورَةُ مِصْرَ ____________

٧- صورَةٌ مِصْرِيَّةٌ ____________

٨- كُلِّيَّةُ العُلوم ____________

٩- كِتابُ الطِبِّ ____________

١٠- الكِتابُ الطِبِّيّ ____________

### 4. Identifying Objects: Demonstratives

The **demonstrative** "nouns" **هذا** (masculine) and **هذه** (feminine) refer to objects that are near. In order to refer to objects or people located far from the speaker, other forms are used. For the masculine singular, **ذلِكَ** is used, and for the feminine singular, **تِلكَ** is used.

The man in the drawing is identifying his car (سَيّارة), which is feminine, by using the demonstrative تِلكَ and his house (بَيت), which is masculine, by the demonstrative ذلِكَ. Both the سَيّارة and the بَيْت are far from him.

**Dual and Plural Demonstratives**

| | | | |
|---|---|---|---|
| هذانِ | (m., dual, nominative, close) | هذَين | (m., dual, genitive/accusative, close) |
| هاتان | (f., dual, nominative, close) | هاتَينِ | (f., genitive/accusative, close) |
| ذانِكَ | (m., dual, nominative, rare) | ذَيْنِكَ | (m., genitive/accusative, far; rare) |
| تانِكَ | (f., dual, nominative, rare) | تَيْنِكَ | (m., genitive/accusative, far; rare) |
| هؤلاءِ | (pl., m., f., close) | أولائِكَ | (pl., m., f., far) |

SUMMARY

- Demonstratives in Arabic are considered nouns.
- The Arabic demonstrative system distinguishes among referents in terms of gender, number, and proximity.
- The demonstratives هذا and هذه (masculine and feminine, respectively) are used to refer to something close.
- The demonstratives ذلِكَ and تِلكَ (masculine and feminine, respectively) are used to refer to something far away.

# تمرين ١١

**Using هذا or هذِه:** Identify the people and objects in the following pictures, using appropriate demonstratives (هذا, هذه, ذلك, تلك). Use هذا and هذه for objects close to the hand and ذلِكَ and تِلْكَ for objects far away from the hand. Be sure to pay close attention to the gender of the object. Consider the examples:

مِثال: هذا حاسوب. 

تِلكَ طالِبَة. 

١– ______________ 

٢– ______________ 

٣– ______________ 

٤– ______________ 

٥– ______________ 

٦– ______________ 

٧– ______________ 

٨– ______________ 

## 5. Colloquial Arabic

## تَذَوَّق الثَّقافة العَربيّة

**Suppression of Short Vowels:** A distinct aspect of phonological variation in colloquial Arabic is the suppression of one or more internal short vowels. For example, the word كِتاب is pronounced *kitāb* in Standard Arabic, but in urban areas in the Levant it is pronounced *ktāb*, where the *i* sound is dropped. The same process applies to جامِعَة (*jāmi'a*), which is pronounced *jām'a* in colloquial speech, where the short vowel *i* is deleted.

**Quality of the Vowel Preceding ة:** The word (مُسَجِّلَة) exemplifies another phonological process in Levantine colloquial Arabic: the change of the *a* sound preceding the *tā' marbūṭa* into an *e* sound (as in "net") after certain consonants in feminine nouns. For example, no change in the final vowel occurs in صورة, but the word طاولة (*ṭāwila*) is pronounced *ṭāwle* in Syrian colloquial speech, where the *a* sound changes into an *e* sound. Below is a classification of consonants in final word positions that are followed by the sound *a* in feminine nouns and adjectives in Syrian colloquial speech as well as those followed by the *e* sound. Please note that this is a general rule and that variations do exist.

Consonants preceding the ة followed by an *a* sound:

| |
|---|
| ح خ ع غ ق هـ و ر ص ض ط ظ ل |

Consonants preceding the ة followed by an *e* sound:

| |
|---|
| ب ج ف ك م ي ت ث د ذ س ش |

- **Pronunciation note:** The letter ق is usually pronounced as a glottal stop (i.e., *hamza*) in Arabic dialects in some urban centers, such as Damascus, Jerusalem, Beirut, Amman, and Cairo. In some other areas, it is pronounced [g] or [q].

## تمرين ١٢ AUDIO

**A. Listen and answer:** Select the alternative that best represents the information from the listening passage.

١- إسمُ الأسْتاذِ نَديم . . .

☐ ساحوري ☐ ساهوري ☐ سَمْهوري

٢- الأسْتاذُ نَديم مِن جامِعَةِ . . .

☐ القُدْس ☐ الآداب ☐ بير زَيْت

٣- مَكتَبُ الأسْتاذِ نَديم في كُلِّيَّةِ . . .

☐ الآداب ☐ العُلوم ☐ الطِبّ

٤- في مَكتَبِ الأسْتاذِ نَديم صورَةُ مَدينَةِ . . .

☐ بير زَيْت ☐ القُدس ☐ فِلَسطين

**B.** Mark the following statement صَواب (true) or خَطَأ (false) based on the information in the listening passage and correct any false statements.

٥- لَيْسَ عِندَ الأُسْتاذِ نَديم حاسوب. ______________________

٦- هُناكَ هاتِفٌ عَلى طاوِلَةِ الأُسْتاذِ نَديم. ______________________

٧- صورَةُ مَدينَةِ القُدسِ عَلى جِدارِ المَكتَب. ______________________

صَواب = 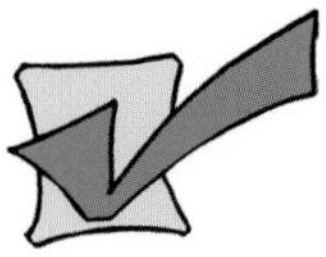

خَطَأ = 

## تمرين ١٣

**DVD: Watch Lesson 2.** When you are watching the dialogues, become an active participant by repeating what you hear, trying to imitate the sounds and inflections used in the scenes.

Answer the following questions:

١- في جامِعَةِ فادي عيسى عِدّةُ كُلِّيّاتٍ، ما هي؟

______________________ ______________________

______________________ ______________________

______________________ ______________________

٢- ماذا يُوجَدُ في مَكْتَبِ سامر نصر؟

______________________ ______________________

______________________ ______________________

______________________ ______________________

## المُفْرَدات Vocabulary

Listen to the vocabulary items on the CD and practice their pronunciation.

literature . . . . . . . . . . . . . . . . . . . . (n., m.) أَدَب ج آداب

ground . . . . . . . . . . . . . . . . . . . . (n., f.) أَرْض ج أراضٍ

those . . . . . . . . . . . . . . . . . . (pl., demonstrative) أولائِكَ

house, home . . . . . . . . . . . . . . . . . . . . (n., m.) بَيْت ج بُيوت

those . . . . . . . . . . . . . . . . . . . . (dual, nom.; *rare*) تانِكَ

trade, business, commerce . . . . . . . . . . . . . . . . (n., f.) تِجارة

that . . . . . . . . . . . . . . . . . . . . . . . . (n., f., sg.) تِلكَ

those . . . . . . . . . . . . . . . . . (dual, acc., gen.; *rare*) تَيْنِكَ

right, law . . . . . . . . . . . . . . . . . . . . (n., m.) حَقّ ج حُقوق

that . . . . . . . . . . . . . . . . . . . . . . . . (n., m., sg.) ذلِكَ

sport . . . . . . . . . . . . . . . . . . . . . (n., f.) رِياضَة ج رِياضات

of sports . . . . . . . . . . . . . . . . . . . . . . . . (adj.) رياضِيّ

medicine . . . . . . . . . . . . . . . . . . . . . . . . . . (m.) طِبّ

a number of, several . . . . . . . . . . . . . . . . . (n., f.) عِدَّةُ

science, discipline . . . . . . . . . . . . . . . . . (n., m.) عِلْم ج عُلوم

of science, scientific . . . . . . . . . . . . . . . . . . (adj.) عِلميّ

college . . . . . . . . . . . . . . . . . . . . . . (n., f.) كُلّيّة ج كُلّيات

language . . . . . . . . . . . . . . . . . . . . . . (n., f.) لُغَة ج لُغات

of language, linguistic . . . . . . . . . . . . . . . . . . (adj.) لُغَويّ

laboratory . . . . . . . . . . . . . . . . . . (n., m.) مُخْتَبَر ج مُخْتَبَرات

swimming pool . . . . . . . . . . . . . . . . . . (n., m.) مَسْبَح ج مَسابِح

office . . . . . . . . . . . . . . . . . . . (n., m.) مَكْتَب ج مَكاتِب

library; bookstore; bookcase. . . . . . . . . . (n., f.) مَكْتَبة ج مَكْتَبات

playground, sports field . . . . . . . . . . . (n., m.) مَلْعَب ج مَلاعِب

these . . . . . . . . . . . . . . . . . . . . (dual, f., nom.) هاتانِ

these . . . . . . . . . . . . . . . . . . (dual, f., acc., gen.) هاتَيْنِ

these . . . . . . . . . . . . . . . . . . . (dual, m., nom.) هذانِ

these . . . . . . . . . . . . . . . . . . (dual, m., acc., gen.) هذَيْنِ

engineering . . . . . . . . . . . . . . . . . . . . . (n., f.) هَنْدَسة

these . . . . . . . . . . . . . . . . . . . . . . . (pl., m.) هؤُلاءِ

# الدَرسُ الثالِث

## Objectives

- Seeking and providing information
- Asking yes/no and content questions
- Introduction to the Arabic verb
- Introduction to the cardinal numbers 1–10
- Learning how to say “I know” and “I don’t know”
- Eliciting information
- Expressing admiration
- Introduction to the particle يا
- Introduction to the question particle كَم

## تمرين ١

**Matching:** Match words from the right-hand column with words in the left-hand column. Take the time to practice writing Arabic by writing both words in the middle column.

| | | | |
|---|---|---|---|
| تِجارَة | | بَلْدَة | ١ |
| ثَلاثَة | | عُنوان | ٢ |
| عَفْواً | | العَرَبِيَّة | ٣ |
| مَدينَة | | رَقْم | ٤ |
| شارِع | | بِطاقَة | ٥ |
| لُغَة | | شُكْراً | ٦ |
| هُوِيَّة | | | |

1. Seeking and Providing Information

# أنا مِنْ جَبْلة

المَرأة: مَرحباً!

الرَجُل: أهلاً!

المَرأة: ما اسْمُكَ؟

الرَجُل: اِسْمي نِزار حَدّاد.

المَرأة: مِن أينَ أنْتَ؟

الرَجُل: أنا مِنْ جَبْلة.

المَرأة: أينَ جَبلة؟

عُنوان

الرَجُل: هذِه بَلْدَةٌ في سوريَة.

المَرأة: ما عُنوانُكَ؟

الرَجُل: ٥ شارِعُ ابنِ خَلدون.

المَرأة: أتَسْكُنُ في شَقّةٍ أم في بَيْت؟

الرَجُل: أسْكُنُ في شَقّة.

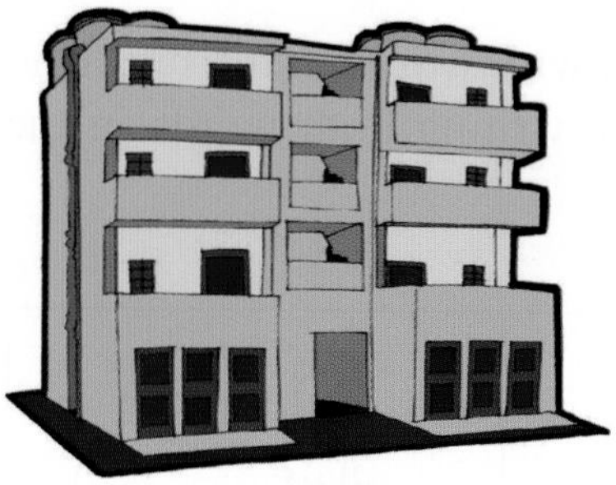

شَقّة

المَرأة: عِندكَ سَيّارة؟

الرَجُل: نَعَم، عِندي سَيّارَة.

المَرأة: هَل عِندكَ هاتِف في شَقّتِكَ؟

الرَجُل: نَعَم، عِندي هاتِف.

المَرأة: ما رَقْمُ هاتِفِكَ؟

الرَجُل: رَقْمُ هاتِفي سِتّة صِفْر واحِد خَمْسَة سَبْعَة تِسْعَة أرْبعَة.

شارِع

المَرأة: هَل عِندَكَ حاسوب؟

الرَجُل: لا. لَيْسَ عِندي حاسوب.

المَرأة: شُكْراً.

الرَجُل: عَفْواً.

**Reflecting on our reading:** In the above passage we were introduced to our first verb. From context, can you guess the meaning of أَسْكُنُ and تَسْكُنُ in the present tense of this verb?

أنا أَسْكُنُ في شَقَّةٍ وأَنْتَ تَسْكُنُ في بَيْتٍ.

## 2. Question Words

The main reading/listening passage included a variety of different ways to pose questions in Arabic. Let's take a look at some Arabic question particles and how they are used:

### A. Yes/No Questions

Yes/no questions may be posed either by rising intonation on the last word of the question, or by using the question particles هَلْ and أَ. As you can see from the exchanges between the woman and the man above, these question particles are inserted at the beginning of a sentence without causing any changes either in word order or in the forms of the words.

- **Note:** The particle أَمْ 'or' is used in questions (e.g., عِندَكَ سَيّارة أم دَرّاجة؟), its counterpart أَوْ 'or' is used in statements (e.g., اليوم أو غداً).

### B. Content Questions

Questions that seek information concerning time, place, manner, or reason use other question particles or words. In the above interview أينَ 'where' and ما 'what' are used. أين is used to inquire about the location of someone or something and ما inquires about the identity of something. The particle ما is followed by a noun or a pronoun (e.g., ما اسْمُك؟ 'What's your name?' ما هُو؟ 'What is it?'). On the other hand, أينَ 'where' and مَنْ 'who' may be followed by either a noun, a pronoun, or a verb:

١ أينَ جَبْلَة؟ مَنْ هُناكَ؟

٢ مَن هُوَ؟ أينَ هِيَ؟

٣ أينَ تَسْكُن؟

٤ مَنْ يَسْكُنُ في الشَقّة؟

The particle ماذا 'what' is usually used before verbs:

٥ ماذا يَدْرُسُ زياد؟

The question word كَيْفَ 'how' is used to inquire about a state of affairs, that is, the process or manner of doing something:

كَيفَ الحال؟ ٦

كَيفَ تَعْرِف عُنوانَه؟ ٧

- **Note:** These question words cause no change either in the form or order of the words in a sentence.

SUMMARY

- The particles هَلْ and أ are used for forming yes/no questions. They are placed at the beginning of a sentence, but they do not cause any structural changes.
- Question particles cause no change either in word form or order.

| | | | | | |
|---|---|---|---|---|---|
| **Yes/No Questions** | أَ | هَل | | | |
| **Content Questions** | أَيْنَ | ما | ماذا | مَنْ | كَيفَ |

## تمرين ٢

**Ask your neighbors:** Use the question particles above to pose these questions to your neighbors. Write your answers down on a separate sheet of paper and be prepared to report this information to your instructor. Find out . . .

1. the location of the library and whether it is a city or university library
2. whether or not he/she has a car and if so, where it is
3. if he/she has a morning class and if so, what it is
4. where the language laboratory is and what is in it
5. the identity of the professor of Arabic (who he/she is)

## تمرين ٣

**Conversation:** Interview a classmate or pretend to interview your favorite personality using the questions that we just learned to elicit information. Then write a short paragraph about that person in terms of name, address, origin, school, possessions, and place of residence. An example paragraph is presented below which gives information about **هالَة بُسْتاني**, the student who was described in Lesson 1.

هالَة بُسْتاني طالِبَةٌ مِن مَدينَةِ دِمَشق. عُنْوانُها ٨ شارِع الكَواكِبيّ في مَدينَةِ حَلَب. هِيَ طالِبَةٌ في جامِعَةِ حَلَب. لَيْسَ عِندَ هالَة دَرّاجَةٌ، لكِنْ حاسوب. تسْكُنُ هالَة في شَقَّة. هِيَ لا تَسْكُنُ في سَكَنِ الطالِبات.

## 3. The Arabic Verb

### A. Verb Stem and Root

The dialogue at the beginning of this lesson introduces the first verb in this textbook. There are two instances of the verb "to live": the first time it was used in second-person masculine singular (**تَسْكُنُ** 'you live') and the second time it was used in first-person singular (**أَسْكُنُ** 'I live'). In English, both instances have the same form: "live." In Arabic, however, verbs vary in form because, unlike English, person is indicated in verbs as a prefix, suffix, or both. In addition, the form of a verb is affected by tense, number, and gender. At this point, we will consider the present tense, or the imperfect, which indicates an uncompleted or unfinished action. The conjugation table below illustrates five forms which correspond to five personal pronouns. As we learned in Unit 4 of the Workbook, there are a total of 14 Arabic pronouns.

If you look closely, you will find that the initial letter of the verb forms changes because it is a prefix added to the stem of the verb (**سْكُن**). In the second-person feminine, the Arabic verb always takes a prefix as well as a suffix. As a rule, all present-tense conjugations must contain prefixes, but some have both prefixes and suffixes, and these attached suffixes indicate gender (**ين** 2nd f.sg. as in our example), or number (= **ان** for dual, **ون** for m.pl., **ـنَ** for f.pl.). We have highlighted in blue the prefix and suffix for second-person feminine singular to make the stem (**سْكُن**) apparent.

أنْتِ تَسْكُنينَ ← تَسْكُنينَ

Arabic verbs (and almost all derivatives) are generally organized in the dictionary according to their root, which is the minimal form of a word. Like most Arabic verbs, the root of the above verb is made up of the three letters (س ك ن). Unlike English, verbs are cited in the third-person masculine singular past tense (e.g., سَكَنَ 'he lived'). In other words, no true infinitive exists in Arabic (= to live; to reside); third-person past tense is used instead. Reflect on and memorize the following table:

| Present-Tense Conjugations of the Verb سَكَنَ | | |
|---|---|---|
| **English Verb Form** | **Arabic Verb Form** | **Separate Pronoun** |
| live | أَسْكُنُ | أنا |
| live | نَسْكُنُ | نَحْنُ |
| live | تَسْكُنُ | أَنْتَ |
| live | تَسْكُنين | أَنْتِ |
| lives | يَسْكُنُ | هُوَ |
| lives | تَسْكُنُ | هِيَ |

### B. Negating the Present-Tense Verb

Negating the present is done simply by using the negative particle **لا** (which as we have learned also means "no") before the verb. The use of **لا** does not affect the form of the verb in any way. Consider the following examples:

| | | |
|---|---|---|
| *I live in a house.* | أَسْكُنُ في بَيْت. | ٨ |
| *I don't live in an apartment.* | لا أَسْكُنُ في شَقَّة. | ٩ |

## تمرين ٤

**Asking/answering questions:** Now that we have learned how to form questions and the present-tense verb, let's put this knowledge to use. Answer the following questions about yourself on a separate sheet of paper.

١- ما اسْمُك؟

٢- ما عُنوانُك؟

٣- مِنْ أَيْنَ أَنْت؟

٤- ما اسْمُ جامِعَتِك؟

٥- هَل عِندَكَ / عِندَكِ دَرّاجةٌ أو سَيّارةٌ أو حاسوبٌ أو هاتِف؟

٦- هَل تَسْكُنُ / تَسْكُنينَ في شَقَّةٍ أَمْ في بَيْت؟

## 4. Cardinal Numbers 1–10

Cardinal numbers may be used for counting and labeling things. Let's consider counting first. The numbers in exercise 5 below represent the typed/printed form which is very similar to the handwritten form, except for number two which is written as follows: ٢. It starts from the top right-hand side, moves to the left and then down.

### تمرين ٥

AUDIO

**The Arabic numbers:** Listen and repeat after the recording. Read the numbers (and words) below from right to left. Copy them several times paying attention to the handwritten form of the number "two."

| 10 | 9 | 8 | 7 | 6 | 5 | 4 | 3 | 2 | 1 | 0 |
|---|---|---|---|---|---|---|---|---|---|---|
| عَشَرَة | تِسْعَة | ثَمانِيَة | سَبْعَة | سِتَّة | خَمْسَة | أَرْبَعَة | ثَلاثَة | اِثْنان | واحِد | صِفر |
| ١٠ | ٩ | ٨ | ٧ | ٦ | ٥ | ٤ | ٣ | ٢ | ١ | ٠ |

The numbers we are learning here are known as **cardinal numbers**, which are also used for labeling things (telephone numbers, car numbers, house numbers, etc.).

ما رَقْمُ هاتِفِكَ؟
رَقْمُ هاتِفي ٤٦٨٢٣٧٥.

At this point, you may say telephone numbers one digit at a time from left to right, as in English. Thus, the man on the telephone in the drawing might say his telephone number in the following manner:

أَرْبَعَة ـ سِتَّة ـ ثَمانِيَة ـ اِثْنان ـ ثَلاثَة ـ سَبْعَة ـ خَمْسَة

How do you think the man below might say his ID number?

## تمرين ٦

Do the following calculations:

| | | | |
|---|---|---|---|
| ١) | ٣ + ٥ = | ٥) | ٢ + ٨ = |
| ٢) | ١ + ٧ = | ٦) | ٦ + ٤ = |
| ٣) | ٩ − ٤ = | ٧) | ٨ − ١ = |
| ٤) | ١٠ − ٥ = | ٨) | ٧ − ٣ = |

- **Note:** The word for the plus sign is زائِد, for the minus sign is ناقِص, and for the word "equals" is يُساوي.

## تمرين ٧

**Translation:** You have just found the following identification card on the ground and wish to return it to its owner. Carefully translate this card into English on the lines below. Be sure to include the institution that issued the card, to whom it was issued, the address, telephone number, and card number.

جامِعَةُ حَلَب

**بِطاقَةُ هُوِيَّة**

الإسمُ: هالَة بُستاني

إِسمُ الأَبِ: وَحيد

العُنوانُ: ٥٢ شارِع المَنصور– دِمَشق

رَقْمُ الهاتِفِ: ٢٨٤٨٥٦٩

رَقْمُ الهُوِيَّةِ: ٩٧١٤٠٢

______________________________

______________________________

______________________________

______________________________

______________________________

## تمرين ٨

**A. Read and select:** Listen to and read the main text at the beginning of this lesson. Based on that information, select the best choice:

١- إِسْمُ الرَّجُلِ . . .

☐ نِزار　☐ جَبْلَة　☐ ابنُ خَلدون

٢- يَسْكُنُ الرَّجُلُ في . . .

☐ بَيْت　☐ شَقَّة　☐ الجامِعَة

٣- عِندَ الرَّجُلِ . . .

☐ سَيّارَة　☐ حاسوب　☐ دَرّاجَة

٤- رَقْمُ هاتِفِ الرَّجُلِ . . .

☐ ٦٠١٥٧٩٤　☐ ٤٩٧٥١٠٦　☐ ١٠٦٤٩٧٥

**B. Read and respond:** Respond in Arabic or English to these questions with reference to the dialogue:

5. What does the word جَبْلَة refer to? ______________________.
6. What is the woman's name? ______________________.
7. Copy the man's address. ______________________.

## 5. Learning How to Say "I Know" and "I Don't Know"

AUDIO

عادِل: كَمْ لُغَةً تَعرفينَ يا سَناء؟

سَناء: أعْرِفُ أربَعَ لُغات.

عادِل: ما هِيَ؟

سَناء: العَرَبِيَّة والإنكليزيَّة والفَرَنسيَّةُ واليابانيّة.

عادِل: ما شاءَ الله!! ما مَعْنى كَلِمَةِ "لُغَة" باليابانِيَّة؟

سَناء: آسِفَة. لا أعْرِف.

The verb عَرَفَ 'to know' in the dialogue above expresses knowledge about something. The phrase لا أعرف 'I don't know' expresses lack of knowledge of something. It is made up of the negative particle لا and the verb أعرف. Like English, this phrase is used very frequently and can come in handy in class, especially when you do not know the answer to a question.

## تمرين ٩

**Translation:** On a separate sheet of paper, translate the following sentences. Provide answers for those sentences which are questions. Remember that the Arabic question mark (= ؟) faces right, not left as in English (= ?).

1. Ask a woman where she lives.
2. Say that you do not live on Lincoln Street.
3. Ask a man whether he lives in an apartment or a house.
4. Say that your teacher (f.) lives in (name of a town).
5. Say that you do not know (a certain language).
6. Say that you do not know your instructor's (m.) address.
7. Ask a man what his telephone number is.
8. Ask a woman what her address is.

### 6. Eliciting Information

In order to inquire about the meaning of a word you do not know in Arabic, you may use the phrase **ما مَعْنى كَلِمَة . . .؟** 'What is the meaning of the word . . . ?' followed by the English word you wish to know. For example, to find out the word for "police," you may ask:

١٠ ما مَعْنى كَلِمَة "police" بِالعَرَبِيَّة؟

Note that the words **مَعْنى** and **كَلِمَة** are both nouns and together they form an **إضافة** structure. Notice also the preposition **بِـ** prefixed to the noun **العَرَبِيَّة** (**بِالعَرَبِيَّة**). It is one of a few prepositions that are directly prefixed to nouns. In this context, it means "in."

## تمرين ١٠

Ask your instructor about the meanings of at least six words in Arabic that you would like to know, using the phrase **ما مَعْنى كَلِمَة . . . ؟**. Give this exercise some thought in terms of asking about those words that you would like to add to your personal vocabulary but that have not been introduced thus far.

## 7. Expressing Admiration

One way of expressing admiration is by using the phrase **ما شاءَ اللّه** (literally "what God willed"). If someone informs you, for example, that he or she has nine children or has won a million dollars, this would be the appropriate response. It connotes joy for someone else's good fortunes devoid of any envy.

## 8. The Particle يا

This particle is called **vocative** because it is used to call the attention of someone (e.g., **يا سَناء! يا أُسْتاذ!**). It is used before names, terms of address, and titles, but never by itself. It has no equivalent in modern English usage, although the particles "Hey" and "Oh" are close in meaning. Consider this sentence:

| | | |
|---|---|---|
| *How are you, Ahmed?* | كَيْفَ الحالُ يا أَحْمَد؟ | ١١ |

## 9. The Question Particle كَم

In the dialogue in section 5, **عادِل** asks about the number of languages **سَناء** knows by using the question particle **كَم** 'how many'.

- **Note:** This particle should be followed by a *singular* indefinite noun. Contrast this with English in which the noun after "how many" is plural—"how many books do you have?"

١٢ كَمْ كِتاباً عِنْدَك؟

The word that follows **كَمْ** is in the accusative case **نَصْب**, meaning that the last consonant of the word takes a double *fatḥa*. Consider the following examples:

١٣ كَمْ سَيّارةً عِندَ توم كروز؟

١٤ كَمْ جامِعَةً في هذِه المَدينَة؟

١٥ كَمْ دَفْتَراً عَلى الطاوِلَة؟

- **Remember:** The *alif* above which the double *fatḥa* is written in examples 12 and 15 **كِتاباً / دَفْتَراً** serves only as a seat for this marker. It has no phonetic value.

- **Remember:** A silent *alif* must be provided except for words ending in ء preceded by a long vowel, ة, or ى.

> ### SUMMARY
>
> - The particle كَمْ is followed by a singular, indefinite noun in the accusative case.
> - The noun following كَمْ thus has a double *fatḥa* (ً) on its end كِتاباً.

## تمرين ١١

Complete the following questions with the appropriate form of the noun in parentheses as in the example. Remember that كَمْ must be followed by an accusative, singular, indefinite noun, and that the ة, ى, and ء do not require an *alif* to seat a double *fatḥa.*

مِثال: كَمْ (حاسوب) ____حاسوباً____ عِندَكِ؟

١- كَمْ (دَرّاجَة) ____________ عِندَكَ؟

٢- كَمْ (مِفْتاح) ____________ على الطاوِلة؟

٣- كَمْ (قَلَم) ____________ في حَقيبَتِكَ؟

٤- كَمْ (مُسَجِّلَة) ____________ عِندَكِ؟

٥- كَمْ (هاتِف) ____________ في بَيتِكَ؟

٦- كَمْ (جامِعَة) ____________ في هذِه المَدينَة؟

٧- كَمْ (كَلِمَة) ____________ في هذا التَمْرين؟

٨- كَمْ (أُسْتاذ) ____________ في هذِه الجامِعَة؟

## تمرين ١٢

**Ask your neighbor:** Find out from your neighbor how many . . . (Remember to use the singular accusative Arabic noun.) Write your answers down on a separate sheet of paper and be prepared to share your answers with your classmates.

1. languages he/she knows
2. televisions he/she has
3. computers he/she has
4. bikes he/she owns
5. cars he/she has
6. classes he/she has
7. instructors he/she has
8. keys he/she has

## تمرين ١٣

**Odd word out:** Underline the word that does not belong to each set and explain your choice if needed.

| | | | | |
|---|---|---|---|---|
| ١- | سَكَن | شَقّة | تِسْعة | بَيْت |
| ٢- | هَلْ | لَيْسَ | ماذا | كَمْ |
| ٣- | عِلْمِيّ | ياباني | عَرَبِيّ | إنْكليزيّ |
| ٤- | هاتِف | رَقْم | عُنْوان | طاوِلَة |

## تمرين ١٤

**Numbers:** Provide the numbers that have been requested in the following items. If the information is not available, indicate the reason in Arabic.

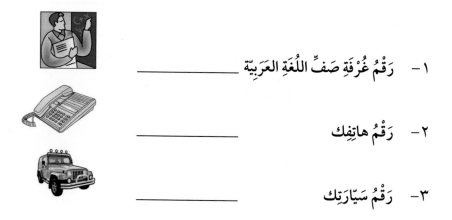

١- رَقْمُ غُرْفَةِ صَفِّ اللُّغَةِ العَرَبيّة ______________

٢- رَقْمُ هاتِفك ______________

٣- رَقْمُ سَيّارَتك ______________

٤- رَقْمُ شَقَّتِك ____________ 

٥- رَقْمُ هُويّتِك ____________ 

٦- رَقْمُ بَيْتِك ____________ 

## تمرين ١٥

**A. Listen and select:** Check the box that matches the information as expressed in the listening passages for this lesson.

١- وَفاءُ مِن . . .

☐ مَدينَةِ دِمَشق ☐ بَلْدَةِ الباب ☐ مَدينَةِ حَلَب

٢- عِندَ وَفاءَ صَفٌّ في . . .

☐ اللُّغَةِ العَرَبِيَّةِ ☐ اللُّغَةِ الإنكليزِيَّةِ ☐ التِجارَةِ

٣- عِندَ وَفاءَ . . .

☐ هاتِفٌ ☐ حاسوبٌ ☐ حاسِبَةٌ

**B. صواب أم خطأ:** Mark the following sentences **صواب** (true) or **خَطأ** (false) according to the information in the listening passage and correct any false statements in Arabic.

٤- تَسْكُنُ وَفاءُ في شَقَّة.

٥- وَفاءُ طالِبَةٌ في جامِعَةِ دِمَشق.

٦- تَعرِفُ وَفاءُ ثَلاثَ لُغات.

## تمرين ١٦

**Listen and respond:** Read the following dialogue and fill in the blanks with appropriate responses. After you have filled in the blanks, listen to the recording and respond during the pauses. Practice pronouncing *tā' marbūṭa* when it occurs in the *iḍāfa* structure.

السَلامُ عليكُم!

__________ __________!

كَيْفَ الحال؟

__________ __________. __________؟

الحَمْدُ للهِ بِخَيْر. أيْنَ سيّارةُ أسْتاذَتِك ؟

____________________ .

هَلْ عِنْدَها حَقيبة في سَيّارتِها؟

نَعَم، __________ __________ في __________.

ماذا هُناكَ في حَقيبَتِها ؟

في __________، هُناكَ __________ و__________ و__________ ؟

طَيِّب، ما اسْمُ أسْتاذَتِك ؟

__________ ريم.

هل هي أسْتاذةٌ في هذه الجامِعَة؟

نَعَم، __________ __________ في __________ __________.

مَعَ السَّلامة!

_____ __________!

## تمرين ١٧

VIDEO

**DVD: Watch Lesson 3.** When you are watching the dialogues, become an active participant by repeating what you hear, trying to imitate the sounds and inflections used in the scenes.

**Scene One:** Practice your numbers by counting with John. How high does John count? ___________

**Scene Two:** Answer the following questions:

١- ما جِنْسيَّةُ نبيل السَيِّد؟

أ - أمريكيَّة

ب- لُبنانيَّة

ج- سوريَّة

٢- هَل يَسْكُنُ نبيل السَيِّد في بَيْتٍ أم شَقَّة؟

______________________________

٣- ما رَقْمُ هاتِفِ نبيل السَيِّد؟

أ- ٦٦٢١٠٦

ب- ٦٦٢١٣٤

ج- ٦٦٢١٥

٤- ما رَقْمُ هاتِفِ بِلال السُلطان؟

أ- ٦٦٢٧٠٠٣

ب- ٦٦٢٧٠٥٦

ج- ٦٦٢١٥٣٠

# المُفْرَدات

Listen to the vocabulary items on the CD and practice their pronunciation.

a question particle to form yes/no questions . . . . . . . . . . . . أ

God. . . . . . . . . . . . . . . . . . . . . . . . . . . . . . (n., m.) الله

a 14th-century Arab historian. . . . . . . (proper noun) ابْنُ خَلْدون
and sociologist

two . . . . . . . . . . . . . . . . . . . . . . . . . . . . . (n., m.) اِثنان

four. . . . . . . . . . . . . . . . . . . . . . . . . . . . . (n., f.) أَرْبَعة

sorry . . . . . . . . . . . . . . . . . . . . (n., f.) آسِفة / (n., m.) آسِف

or (particle used in questions). . . . . . . . . . . . . . . . . (conj.) أَمْ

woman . . . . . . . . . . . . . . . . . . . . . . . . (n., f.) اِمرأة ج نِساء

now. . . . . . . . . . . . . . . . . . . . . . . . . . . . . . . . . (n.) الآنَ

English (language) . . . . . . . . . . . . . . . . . . . . (adj., f.) الإنكليزية

or (used with statements) . . . . . . . . . . . . . . . . . . . (conj.) أو

in, with, by. . . . . . . . . . . . . . . . . . . . . . . . . . . . . (prep.) بِـ

card. . . . . . . . . . . . . . . . . . . . . . . . . (n., f.) بِطاقة ج بِطاقات

small town. . . . . . . . . . . . . . . . . . . . . . . (n., f.) بَلْدة ج بَلْدات

nine . . . . . . . . . . . . . . . . . . . . . . . . . . . . . . (n., f.) تِسْعة

three . . . . . . . . . . . . . . . . . . . . . . . . . . . . . (n., f.) ثَلاثة

eight . . . . . . . . . . . . . . . . . . . . . . . . . . . . . (n., f.) ثَمانِية

name of a town in Syria . . . . . . . . . . . . . . . . . . . . (n., f.) جَبْلة

five . . . . . . . . . . . . . . . . . . . . . . . . . . . . . . . (n., f.) خَمْسة

man . . . . . . . . . . . . . . . . . . . . . . . . . . (n., m.) رَجُل ج رِجال

number . . . . . . . . . . . . . . . . . . . . . . . . . (n., m.) رَقْم ج أَرْقام

plus. . . . . . . . . . . . . . . . . . . . . . . . . . . . . . . (n., m.) زائِد

to equal . . . . . . . . . . . . . . . . . . . . . (v.) ساوى (يُساوي) مُساواة

seven . . . . . . . . . . . . . . . . . . . . . . . . . . . . . . (n., f.) سَبْعة

six . . . . . . . . . . . . . . . . . . . . . . . . . . . . . . . . (n., f.) سِتّة

to live, to reside . . . . . . . . . . . . . . . (v.) سَكَنَ (يَسْكُنُ) سَكَن

(student) living, residence, dormitory . . . . . . . . . . . (verbal noun, m.) سَكَنُ (الطُّلاّبِ)

street . . . . . . . . . . . . . . . . . . . . . . . (n., m.) شارِع ج شَوارِع

want, will . . . . . . . . . . . . . . . . . . . . . (v.) شاءَ (يَشاءُ) مَشيئة

apartment . . . . . . . . . . . . . . . . . . . . . (n., f.) شَقّة ج شُقَق

thank you . . . . . . . . . . . . . . . . . . . . . . . . . . . شُكْراً

zero. . . . . . . . . . . . . . . . . . . . . . . . . (n., m.) صِفْر ج أَصْفار

Arabic (language). . . . . . . . . . . . . . . . . . . (adj., f.) العَرَبيّة

to know . . . . . . . . . . . . . . . . . . . . . . (v.) عَرَفَ (يعرِفُ) مَعْرِفة

ten . . . . . . . . . . . . . . . . . . . . . . . . . . . . . (n., f.) عَشَرة

you're welcome (response to "thank you") . . . . . . . . . . . عَفْواً

address. . . . . . . . . . . . . . . . . . . . . . . (n., m.) عُنوان ج عَناوين

French (language) . . . . . . . . . . . . . . . . . . (adj., f.) الفَرَنْسِيَّة

word . . . . . . . . . . . . . . . . . . . . . . . . (n., f.) كَلِمَة ج كَلِمات

how many/much . . . . . . . . . . . . . . (interrogative particle) كَمْ

what (question particle used in front of nouns). . . . . . . . . . ما

what (used with verbs). . . . . . . . . . . . . . . . . . . . . . . ماذا

married . . . . . . . . . . . . . . . . . . . .(n., m.) مُتَزَوِّج ج مُتَزَوِّجون

meaning . . . . . . . . . . . . . . . . . (n., m.) مَعْنى ج مَعانٍ/ المعاني

minus . . . . . . . . . . . . . . . . . . . . . . . . . . . . (n., m.) ناقِص

question particle for yes/no questions . . . . . . . . . . . . . . هَلْ

identity. . . . . . . . . . . . . . . . . . . . . . . . (n., f.) هُوِيّة ج هُوِيّات

one . . . . . . . . . . . . . . . . . . . . . . . . . . . . . . (n., m.) واحِد

vocative particle used to call the attention of the addressee . . . يا

Japanese (language). . . . . . . . . . . . . . . . . . (adj., f.) اليابانِيَّة

# الدَرسُ الرابِع

## Objectives

- Describing background
- Learning how to form dual nouns
- Learning about number-noun agreement
- Introduction to the concept of non-rational noun plurals

### 1. Describing Background

# طالِبَتانِ في جامِعَةِ حَلَب

هالَة بُسْتاني وسَحَر حَلاّق طالِبَتانِ في جامِعَةِ حَلَب. هالَة مِن دِمَشق وسَحَر مِن دِمَشق أيْضاً. تَسكُنُ هالَة في شَقَّةٍ مَعَ سَحَر حَلاّق، والشَقَّةُ في البِنايَةِ رَقْمِ خَمسَة في شارِعِ الحَمَداني. رَقْمُ شَقَّتِهِما ٩. في شَقَّةِ هالَة وسَحَر غُرفَتانِ وسَريرانِ وطاوِلَتانِ وكُرسيّان. هالَة وسَحَر لا تَدرُسانِ في مَكتَبَةِ الجامِعَةِ بَلْ في شَقَّتِهِما.

تدرُس هالَة الطِبَّ وعِندَها الآن ثَلاثُ موادَّ وهِيَ الأحْياءُ والكيمْياءُ واللُغَةُ الإنكِليزيَّة. تَدرُس سَحَر التِجارَة وهِيَ تَعرِفُ ثَلاث لُغاتٍ هِيَ العَرَبيَّةُ والفَرَنسِيَّةُ والإنكِليزيَّة.

سَريرٌ    سَريرانِ    بِنايةٌ    بِنايتانِ

**Reflecting on our reading**: What rule can we make concerning the creation of the dual form in Arabic?

## تمرين ١

**Read and choose:** Select the best alternative according to the information in the passage above.

١- هالَة بُسْتاني طالِبَةٌ في . . .

☐ جامِعَةِ دِمَشق ☐ مَدينَةِ حَلَب ☐ كُلِّيَّةِ الطِبِّ

٢- تَسكُنُ هالَة في . . .

☐ بَيْتٍ ☐ شَقَّةٍ ☐ غُرفَةٍ

٣- تَسكُنُ سَحر حَلاّق . . . هالَة بُستاني

☐ مَعَ ☐ مِن ☐ عَلى

٤- هالَة وسَحَر . . . دِمَشق.

☐ مِن ☐ في ☐ مَعَ

٥- رَقْمُ شَقَّةِ هالَة وسَحَر . . .

☐ خَمسَة ☐ سَبعَة ☐ تِسعَة

٦- تَدرُس سَحَر . . .

☐ التِجارَة ☐ الأحْياءَ ☐ اللُغَة الفَرَنسِيَّة

# تمرين ٢

**صَواب أم خَطأ**: Mark the following statement **صَواب** (true) or **خَطَأ** (false) based on the information in the passage and correct any false statements in Arabic.

١- سَحَر أستاذةُ هالَة. ________________________.

٢- تَدرُسُ سَحَر حَلاّق ثَلاث موادّ. ________________________.

٣- تَسكُنُ هالَة مَعَ طالِبَةٍ مِن دِمَشق. ________________________.

٤- تَدرُسُ هالَةُ الطِبَّ في جامِعَةِ دِمَشق. ________________________.

٥- في غُرفَةِ هالَة سَريران. ________________________.

# تمرين ٣

**Matching:** Match words from the right-hand column with words in the left-hand column. Take the time to practice writing Arabic by writing both words in the middle column.

| | | | |
|---|---|---|---|
| ١ | مادَّة | | سَرير |
| ٢ | لُغَة | | أيْضاً |
| ٣ | كُرسيّ | | تَسكُنُ |
| ٤ | بِناية | | مَعَ |
| ٥ | تَعرِف | | الإنكليزيَّة |
| ٦ | في | | أحْياء |
| | | | شَقَّة |

# تمرين ٤

**Odd word out:** Underline the word that does not belong to each set and explain your choice if needed.

١- الرِياضِيّات الفَرَنْسيَّة الأحْياء الكيمياء

٢- شَقَّة بِنايّة بَيْت كُلِّيَّة

٣- دَرّاجَة طاوِلَة كُرْسيّ سَرير

## 2. Forming Dual Nouns

As you may have noticed, nouns (and adjectives) in Arabic are either singular, dual (two), or plural (more than two). Our main text for this lesson had numerous occurrences of the dual, which we will focus on in this section. The dual has two endings, depending on the case of the noun (or adjective):

**A.** If the noun is in the nominative case, the ending *–āni* انِ is suffixed to it:

| | | | |
|---|---|---|---|
| ١ | هذا كِتابٌ (singular) | ← | هذانِ كِتابانِ (dual) |

**Note** that the demonstrative هذا is a noun that serves as the subject in the above example. The word كتابٌ is a noun that functions as a predicate. In the dual, both acquire the suffix *-āni* انِ. This suffix is used for both definite and indefinite nouns. Normally the *kasra* on the end of the suffix is not pronounced in casual speech (e.g., the word كِتابانِ is pronounced *kitābān*).

**B.** If the noun is the direct object of a verb (e.g., أدرُسُ مادةً) or a preposition (e.g., في جامعةٍ), the suffix *-ayni* ـَيْنِ is attached to it. These are called the accusative نَصْب and the genitive جَرّ cases, respectively.

| | | | |
|---|---|---|---|
| ٢ | أدرُسُ مادّةً | أدرُسُ مادّتَيْنِ | (accusative case) |
| ٣ | في جامِعةٍ | في جامِعَتَيْنِ | (genitive case) |

- Notice the change of the ة to a regular *tā'* ت when the suffix ـَيْنِ is attached to it. Just like انِ, the suffix *-ayni* ـَيْنِ is used with definite and indefinite nouns.
- **Memory Device:** Examine the word "two" in Arabic: اِثنان (nominative) اِثنين (genitive; accusative). Notice that when we form the dual forms in nouns, all we are doing is taking the final two letters from the word "two" اِثنان and adding that ending to the noun. In fact, the use of اِثنان and اِثنين with dual nouns is redundant because duality is already expressed by *-ān* and *-ayni*. However, they are used for emphasis in this context.

## 3. Number-Noun Agreement

In order to express quantity, a number is combined with a noun. In the dialogue in Lesson 3, section 5, the woman specifies the number of languages she knows by saying: أعرِفُ أربَعَ لُغات. In Arabic, numbers are gendered—that is to say that they are either feminine (end with a ة) or masculine (do not end with a ة). You may be wondering why the number أربَع is masculine when the word for language لُغَة is feminine. Let's examine some rules that govern numbers in Arabic.

### A. The Numbers *one* and *two* (1, 2)

The numbers **1** and **2** follow their modified noun, because they act as adjectives and, like adjectives, agree with their modified nouns in gender, number, and case. They are usually used for emphasis, since the suffixes ان and ـَيْنِ denote dual number, as we discussed in section 2 in this lesson.

| | Dual | Singular |
|---|---|---|
| Masculine | كِتابانِ اِثنانِ | كِتابٌ واحِدٌ |
| Feminine | سَيّارتانِ اِثنَتانِ | سَيّارَةٌ واحِدَةٌ |

### B. The Numbers *three* Through *ten* (3–10)

1. The numbers **3–10** precede the noun they modify.

2. They have a reverse gender agreement with the singular counted noun; that is, if the counted noun is masculine, the number is feminine (by suffixing ـة to it) and vice versa. Consider the following example:

   ٤ أربَعُ سَيّاراتٍ أربَعَةُ كُتُبٍ

   The singular of سيارات is سَيّارَة, which is feminine; therefore the number modifying it أربَع is in the masculine form. Similarly, the singular of كُتُب 'books' is كِتاب, which is masculine; therefore, the number modifying it is in the feminine form in that it ends with a تاء مربوطة.

3. The specified noun being counted must be indefinite (no الـ), hence the تَنْوين on the end of the words.

4. The numbers **3–10** form an إضافة structure with the following noun, because these numbers are nouns. The plural counted nouns are thus marked with a double كَسرة, being *genitive* جَرّ and *indefinite.*

**Note** that the feminine form of the number **10** is pronounced عَشَرَة (e.g., عَشَرَةُ كُتُبٍ) and the masculine form is pronounced عَشْر (e.g., عَشْرُ سَيَّاراتٍ).

---

## SUMMARY

- ### The Numbers 1, 2

  Numbers **1** and **2** follow the noun they modify. These numbers function as adjectives and therefore agree with the preceding noun in gender, number, and case.

- ### The Numbers 3–10

  These numbers precede the noun they modify and have a reverse gender agreement with it. With the noun they form an إضافة structure. The noun following them is indefinite, genitive, and plural.

---

| Numbers 1–10 with Nouns | |
|---|---|
| Feminine مُؤَنَّث | Masculine مُذَكَّر |
| سَيَّارَةٌ واحِدَةٌ | كِتابٌ واحِدٌ |
| سَيَّارَتانِ اِثْنَتانِ | كِتابانِ اِثْنانِ |
| ثَلاثُ سَيَّاراتٍ | ثَلاثَةُ كُتُبٍ |
| أَرْبَعُ سَيَّاراتٍ | أَرْبَعَةُ كُتُبٍ |
| خَمْسُ سَيَّاراتٍ | خَمْسَةُ كُتُبٍ |
| سِتُّ سَيَّاراتٍ | سِتَّةُ كُتُبٍ |
| سَبْعُ سَيَّاراتٍ | سَبْعَةُ كُتُبٍ |
| ثَماني سَيَّاراتٍ | ثَمانيةُ كُتُبٍ |
| تِسْعُ سَيَّاراتٍ | تِسْعَةُ كُتُبٍ |
| عَشْرُ سَيَّاراتٍ | عَشَرَةُ كُتُبٍ |

# تمرين ٥

**A. Using numbers:** Hāla Bustānī is writing a journal entry about what she has in her apartment. Let's help her translate her list into English.

في بَيْتي ثَلاثُ طاوِلاتٍ وبِجانِبِ واحِدةٍ مِنها أربَعَةُ كَراسٍ ولَيْسَ هُناكَ حاسوبٌ واحِدٌ عَلى الطاوِلَةِ بَلْ ثَلاثةُ حَواسيب وأيضاً على الطاوِلَة تِلفازانِ اِثنانِ وفي غُرفتي ثَلاثةُ هواتِفَ وعَشَرَةُ كُتُبٍ وسَبعةُ دَفاتِرَ وسِتُّ نَظّارات.

______________________________________________

______________________________________________

______________________________________________

______________________________________________

______________________________________________

______________________________________________

**B.** Michael Brown, a student studying at the American University in Cairo thinks that he may have left his keys at home. Let's help him translate his thoughts into Arabic as he takes stock of what is in his book bag. Remember to use the appropriate form of the number and remember to pay attention to the word order. Refer to section 3 above as well as the word bank of plurals on the following page.

*I have a book bag, in which there are three pencils, four books, two telephones, three identity cards, a computer, and five keys.*

______________________________________________

______________________________________________

______________________________________________

______________________________________________

| | | | |
|---|---|---|---|
| بِطاقَة ج بِطاقات | حَقيبَة ج حَقائب | كِتاب ج كُتُب | نَظّارَة ج نَظّارات |
| تِلْفاز ج تِلْفازات | دَفْتَر ج دَفاتِر | كُرسيّ ج كَراسٍ | هاتِف ج هَواتِف |
| حاسوب ج حَواسيب | طاوِلَة ج طاوِلات | مِفْتاح ج مَفاتيح | |

## تمرين ٦

**Conversation: Number interrogation:** Ask your neighbor some questions about the number of objects that he/she owns. For the person answering, if you have that number, then simply answer "I have x objects." But if you do not have that number, then answer, "I do not have two cars; rather, I have three cars."

مِثال: هَلْ عِندَكَ سَيّارَتانِ؟

لا، لَيْسَ عِندي سَيّارتانِ ولكِنْ ثَلاثُ سَيّارات.

هَلْ عِندَكَ . . .

١- ساعةٌ واحِدَةٌ ________________.

٢- أربَعَةُ كُتُبٍ ________________.

٣- ثَلاثُ دَرّاجاتٍ ________________.

٤- حاسوبانِ ________________.

٥- نَظّارَتانِ ________________.

٦- خَمسَةُ دَفاتِر ________________.

٧- ثَلاثُ جَرائد ________________.

٨- أربَعُ حَقائب ________________.

# تمرين ٧

**Numbers in conversation:** Ask your neighbor the following questions and then record the answers on a separate sheet of paper. Be prepared to share this information with the rest of the class.

مِثال: كَمْ قَلَماً عِندَك؟

كَمْ مِفْتاحاً عِندَكَ وأينَ هي؟

Find out how many . . .

1. languages he/she knows and what they are
2. Arabic cities he/she can name and which ones
3. students he/she knows in this Arabic course and their names
4. classes he/she has and which ones
5. computers he/she owns and where they are
6. televisions he/she has and where they are

## 4. Plurals of Non-Rational Nouns

**Read this section closely and carefully:** In the dialogue in Lesson 3, section 5, the man refers to the four languages the woman knows, using the separate pronoun هِيَ 'she', which is feminine singular. He asks, ما هِيَ؟. The reason for using هِيَ is that all non-rational (or non-human) nouns are usually referred to in the feminine singular, regardless of gender.

That is to say that plural nouns, even those that are masculine when singular such as كِتاب ج كُتُب, are treated as feminine singular by using هي , هذه and تِلكَ. The same pronouns (هِيَ، هذِهِ، تِلكَ) are also used to refer to both feminine singular nouns such as ساعة as well as non-rational (non-human) plurals. Thus, the man's question ما هِيَ؟ may be translated in this context, "what are they?" rather than "what is it?" or "what is she?":

| | | | |
|---|---|---|---|
| ٥ | هذِهِ الكُتُبُ | *these books* | هذِهِ السَيّاراتُ | *these cars* |
| ٦ | تِلْكَ الكُتُبُ | *those books* | تِلْكَ السَيّاراتُ | *those cars* |

By contrast, rational plurals (those referring to people) are referred to by pronouns and demonstratives that agree with them in gender and number, for example:

٧ **هؤلاءِ الأساتِذة** *these instructors (m.pl .)*

٨ **هُم طُلاّب** *they are students (m. pl.)*

٩ **هؤلاءِ النِساء** *these women*

١٠ **هُنَّ طالِباتٌ** *they are students (f. pl.)*

## SUMMARY

- Non-rational plurals are referred to by feminine singular pronouns and demonstratives, regardless of the noun's gender in the singular.
- Non-rational plurals are treated as feminine singular. *Memorize this rule.*

| | **Singular** المُفْرَد | **Plural** الجمع | | | |
|---|---|---|---|---|---|
| مُذَكَّر (masculine) | كِتاب | كُتُبٌ | هِيَ كُتُبٌ | هذِه كُتُبٌ | تِلْكَ كُتُبٌ |
| مُؤَنَّث (feminine) | سَيّارَة | سَيّارات | هِيَ سَيّارات | هذِه سَيّارات | تِلْكَ سَيّارات |

# تمرين ٨

**Use of demonstrative pronouns:** Use the appropriate pronoun and demonstrative to refer to each of the following nouns. Note that the nouns listed may be singular, plural, masculine, or feminine. Also, use the proper demonstrative based on its proximity from the pointing hand.

| | | | | | | | | | |
|---|---|---|---|---|---|---|---|---|---|
| هذا | هذِه | هؤلاءِ | ذلِكَ | تِلْكَ | هُوَ | هِيَ | هُمْ | هُنَّ |

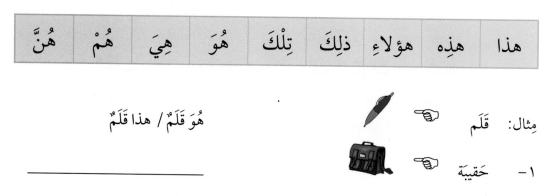

مِثال: قَلَم ☜  هُوَ قَلَمٌ / هذا قَلَمٌ

١- حَقيبَة ☜  ____________________

٢- كَراسٍ ☞  __________

٣- ساعَة ☞  __________

٤- بُيوت ☞  __________

٥- طُلاّب ☞  __________

٦- تِلفاز ☞  __________

٧- مَفاتيح ☞  __________

٨- طالِبَة ☞  __________

٩- نَظّارَة ☞  __________

١٠- سَيّارات ☞  __________

## تمرين ٩

**A. Listen and select:** Check the box that matches the information as expressed in the listening passage for this lesson.

١- اِسمُ الطالِبِ المَغرِبيِّ . . .

☐ عَبدُ الرَحمن ☐ عَبدُ الرَحيم ☐ عَبدُ الله

٢- يَدرُسُ الطالِبُ المَغرِبيّ . . .

☐ الأدبَ العَرَبيَّ ☐ اللُغَةَ الإنكليزية ☐ الطِبَّ

٣- الطالِبُ المَغرِبيُّ مِن مَدينَةِ . . .

☐ القاهِرة ☐ وُجدة ☐ عَيْن شَمْس

٤- في شَقَّةِ هذا الطالِبِ . . .

☐ حاسوبانِ ☐ تِلفازانِ ☐ سَريرانِ

**B.** **صواب أم خطأ**: Mark the following sentences **صواب** (true) or **خَطأ** (false) according to the information in the listening passage and correct any false statements.

٥- يَدرُسُ عَبدُ الرَحمنِ الأدَبَ العَرَبيّ.

٦- يَسكُنُ عَبدُ الرَحمنِ في شَقَّة.

٧- يَسكُنُ مَعَ عَبدِ الرَحمن طالِبٌ مَغرِبيّ.

٨- يَعرِفُ عَبدُ الرَحمن اللُغَةَ الفَرَنسيَّة.

## تمرين ١٠

VIDEO

**DVD: Watch Lesson 4.** When you are watching the dialogues, become an active participant by repeating what you hear, trying to imitate the sounds and inflections used in the scenes.

Answer the following questions:

١- ماذا يُوجَدُ في غُرْفةِ سارة؟

______________________ ______________________

______________________ ______________________

______________________

٢- كَم بِنْتاً وكَم وَلَداً في عائلة سارة؟ ______________________

______________________________________________

٣- أَيْنَ يَدْرُسُ الأولاد؟ ______________________

______________________________________________

______________________________________________

______________________________________________

## المُفْرَدات

Listen to the vocabulary items on the CD and practice their pronunciation.

biology . . . . . . . . . . . . . . . . . . . . . . . . . . . . . (f., pl.) أَحْياء

rather, but . . . . . . . . . . . . . . . . . . . . . . . . . (particle) بَلْ

building . . . . . . . . . . . . . . . . . . . . . . . . (n., f.) بِناية ج بِنايات

bag; briefcase . . . . . . . . . . . . . . . . . . . . . (n., f.) حَقيبة ج حقائب

closet, cupboard. . . . . . . . . . . . . (n., f.) خِزانة ج خَزائِن / خِزانات

study . . . . . . . . . . . . . . . . . . . . . . (v.) دَرَسَ (يَدرُسُ) دِراسة / دَرْس

bed . . . . . . . . . . . . . . . . . . . . . . . . (n., m.) سَرير ج أَسِرّة

small; young. . . . . . . . . . . . . . . . . . . . . . . . . (adj., f.) صَغيرة

school subject, course . . . . . . . . . . . . . . . . (n., f.) مادّة ج مَوادّ

with (someone; not thing). . . . . . . . . . . . . . . . . . . (prep.) مَعَ

middle . . . . . . . . . . . . . . . . . . . . . . . . . . . (adj., f.) وُسْطى

# الدرسُ الخامِس

## Objectives

- Describing family members
- Describing school subjects
- Learning about Arabic last names
- Introduction to objects of verbs
- Introduction to objects of prepositions
- Introduction to ordinal numbers
- Introduction to pronouns of separation

## ١. Describing Family Members

### عائِلَةُ مازِن نَجّار

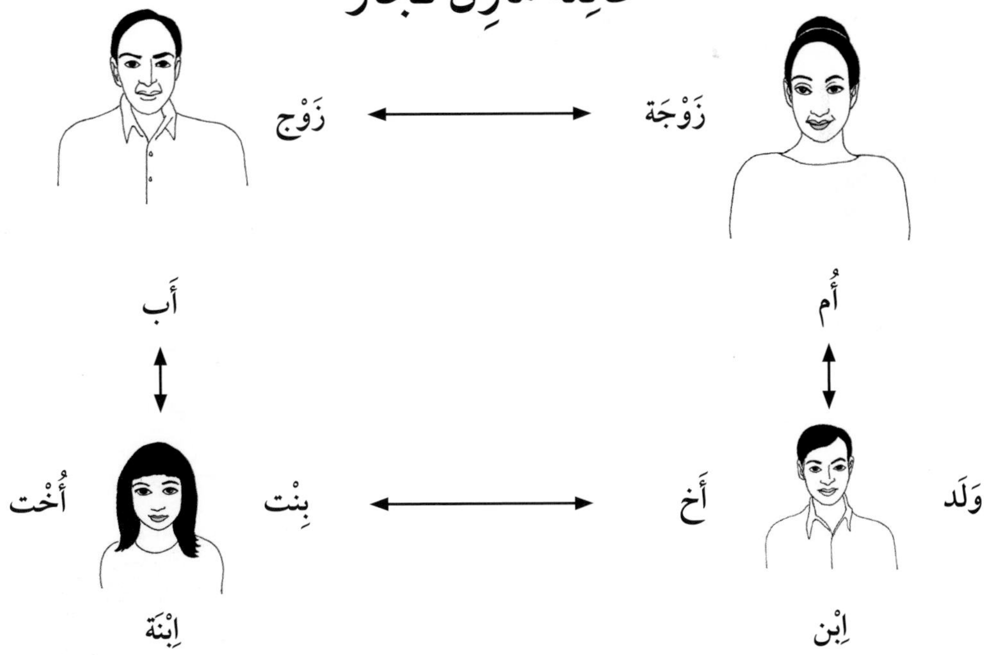

هٰذِه عائِلَةُ مازِن نَجّار. اِسمُ زَوْجَتِهِ ناديا الخولي. عِندَهُ ابنٌ واحِدٌ اسمُهُ أحمَد وَابنَتانِ: واحِدَةٌ اسمُها رانِيَة وواحِدَةٌ اسمُها رِحاب.

أحمَد في المَدرَسَةِ في الصَفِّ الثالِثِ الابتِدائِيِّ وأختُهُ رانِيَة في الصَفِّ الرابعِ وَرِحابُ في الصَفِّ السادِس. أحمَدُ الوَلَدُ الوَحيدُ في عائِلَةِ مازِن وَناديا.

## تَذَوَّق الثَقافة العَرَبِيّة

Women in most Arab countries (e.g., Syria, Egypt) retain their maiden names after marriage.

### 2. Describing School Subjects

## طُلاّبٌ عَرَبٌ في أمريكا

هذا عَدْنانُ مارتيني. يَدرُسُ عَدنانُ عِلمَ الحاسوبِ في جامِعَةِ وِلايَةِ أوهايو. هُوَ طالِبٌ عَرَبِيٌّ مِن سوريَّة. يَدرُسُ عَدنانُ الآنَ مادَّةَ الرِياضِيّاتِ ومادَّةَ اللُغَةِ الإنكليزيَّة.

أبو عَدنانَ وأمُّ عَدنانَ يَسكُنانِ في مَدينَةِ حَلَبَ في سوريَّة ويَسكُنُ مَعَهُما في البَيتِ إخوَةُ عَدنانَ الثَلاثَةُ وأختاهُ. لكِنَّ عَدنانَ يَسكُنُ في شَقَّةٍ في مَدينَةِ كَلَمبُس مَعَ طالِبَيْنِ عَرَبِيَّيْنِ، واحِدٌ مِن فِلَسطينَ اِسمُهُ زِياد نابُلسي وَواحِدٌ مِن لُبنانَ اِسمُهُ وَليد صايغ. يَدرُسُ زِيادُ مادَّةَ الهَندَسةِ ويَدرُسُ وَليدُ مادَّةَ الكيمْياء.

الكيمْياء

الهَنْدَسة

الأحْياء

في هذا الفَصْلِ الدِراسيّ يَدرُس زِياد هذِهِ المَوادَّ: اللُغَةُ الإنكليزيَّةُ والفيزياءُ والتَفاضُل. ويَدرُس وَليدُ في هذا الفَصْلِ مادَّتَيْنِ فَقَط هُما اللُغَةُ الإنكليزيَّةُ والأحْياء.

**Reflecting on our reading:** Can you deduce the meaning of **مادّة ج مَوادّ** from context? Do you see a pattern? Does it occur before or after certain nouns?

## تمرين ١

A. **Listen and select:** Check the box that matches the information as expressed in the passages in sections 1 and 2.

١- عائِلَةُ النَجّارِ فيها . . .

☐ اِبنٌ واحِد ☐ اِبنانِ ☐ ثَلاثَةُ أبْناء

٢- رانية في الصَفِّ . . . الابتِدائيّ.

☐ الثالِث ☐ الرابع ☐ السادِس

٣- وَليد صايغ طالِبٌ . . .

☐ سوريّ ☐ لُبنانيّ ☐ فِلَسطينيّ

٤- يَدرُس عَدنان مارتيني . . .

☐ مادّةً واحِدَةً ☐ مادَّتَيْنِ ☐ ثَلاثَ مَوادّ

٥- يَدرُس عَدنان مارتيني . . .

☐ عِلمَ الحاسوب ☐ الهَندَسة ☐ الكيمْياء

٦- يَسكُنُ عَدنان مارتيني في . . .

☐ سَكَنِ الطُلّابِ ☐ بَيتٍ ☐ شَقَّةٍ

٧- يَسكُنُ عَدنان مارتيني في . . .

☐ كاليفورنيا ☐ أوهايو ☐ تكساس

**B.** Answer these questions with reference to the passages.

٨- ما اسمُ أبي رانيةِ؟ ______________________.

٩- مَنْ يَدرُسُ مادَّةَ التَفاضُل؟ ______________________.

١٠- مَعَ مَنْ يَسكُنُ عَدنان مارتيني؟ ______________________.

١١- كَمْ مادَّةً يَدرُسُ عَدنان في هذا الفَصْل؟ ______________________.

١٢- ماذا يَدرُسُ زياد نابُلسي في جامِعَةِ أوهايو؟ ______________________.

## تمرين ٢

**صواب أم خطأ**: Mark the following statement **صَواب** (true) or **خَطَأ** (false) based on the information in the passage and <u>correct</u> any false statements.

١- رانِيَة أختُ رِحاب. ______________________.

٢- مازِن ابنُ ناديا. ______________________.

٣- أحمَد أخو رانية. ______________________.

٤- رِحابُ ابنَةُ أحمَد. ______________________.

٥- ناديا زَوْجَةُ مازِن. ______________________.

٦- أحمَد أبو مازِن. ______________________.

٧- أحمَد زَوْجُ ناديا. ______________________.

## تمرين ٣

**Family roles:** Check the appropriate box to indicate the family role of the people specified below. Each one may have more than one role.

| | أب | أم | زَوْج | زَوجَة | اِبن | اِبنَة | أخ | أُخْت |
|---|---|---|---|---|---|---|---|---|
| ١- أنا | ☐ | ☐ | ☐ | ☐ | ☐ | ☐ | ☐ | ☐ |
| ٢- أبي | ☐ | ☐ | ☐ | ☐ | ☐ | ☐ | ☐ | ☐ |
| ٣- أُمي | ☐ | ☐ | ☐ | ☐ | ☐ | ☐ | ☐ | ☐ |
| ٤- أخي | ☐ | ☐ | ☐ | ☐ | ☐ | ☐ | ☐ | ☐ |
| ٥- أُختي | ☐ | ☐ | ☐ | ☐ | ☐ | ☐ | ☐ | ☐ |

## تمرين ٤

**Odd word out:** Underline the word that does not belong to each set and explain your choice if needed.

| | | | | |
|---|---|---|---|---|
| ١- | تَفاضُل | أحْياء | أُخْت | كيمْياء |
| ٢- | وَحيد | فَصْل | مادَّة | فيزْياء |
| ٣- | زَوْج | اِبْن | وَلَد | أوَّل |
| ٤- | اِبنَة | عَلى | مَنْ | في |

## تمرين ٥

**Ask your neighbors:** On a separate sheet of paper, write down your neighbors' responses. Find out . . .

1. how many of your classmates study biology or engineering this term
2. who has a brother or sister and how many
3. who has a brother or sister in elementary school and if so, what grade
4. where your neighbor's family is from
5. where your neighbor's family lives now

Be prepared to report your findings to your class.

## تمرين ٦

**Writing a personal sketch:** On a separate sheet of paper, compose a paragraph about yourself modeled after our reading passage. Describe who you are, where you are from, what courses you are currently taking (studying), where you live, where your parents live, and whether you live with others. Use as much of the vocabulary as you can that we have learned so far—past-tense verbs as well as the possessive "have" and the particle "but." Be as creative as possible with your paragraph, displaying what you have learned so far. Use this writing exercise to focus on the words that you want to establish in your own vocabulary.

As a follow-up exercise, give a brief biographical sketch of at least one of your family members.

## 3. Arabic Last Names

### تَذَوَّق الثَقافة العَرَبيّة

Arabic last names generally refer either to place of origin, profession, an attribute acquired by one of the forebears of the family, or the person's father's and/or grandfather's names. For example, the surname مارتيني in the main reading passage is derived from the name of a small town in northern Syria near the city of إدْلِب called مارتين. As you can see, the name is a نِسبَة, or adjective, derived from the name of the town itself مارتين.

Similarly, the surname نابُلسي refers to نابُلُس, a town on the West Bank of the Jordan River. The surname صايغ is the word for a profession (goldsmith). Some names are composed of two or more proper names. The second name is usually the father's first name and the third one is the grandfather's first name (e.g., the man's name نِزار أحْمَد صالِح pictured below). In regions like the Arabian Peninsula and North Africa, some names may have the word بِن for ابْن 'son of' inserted after the first name, which explicitly shows the relationship (e.g., عَبّاس بِن مَسعود 'Abbas bin mas'ūd).

صالِح

أحمَد

نِزار

### تمرين ٧

**A.** The following is an advertisement for a book. On a separate sheet of paper, give the author's last or family name, and then explain the author's name in terms of the description above.

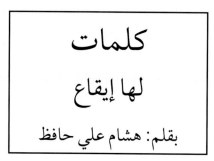

كلمات

لها إيقاع

بقلم: هشام علي حافظ

**B.** This is a heading from an Arabic magazine. Identify the two last names of the persons mentioned.

أحمد الشيباني كاتب العام
وفهمي هويدي يفوز بجائزة الأقليات الإسلامية

## 4. Objects of Verbs المَفْعولُ بِهِ

An object of a verb is a noun or a pronoun that is modified by the verb. In English, nouns that are *direct objects* are not marked for case (i.e., whether they are the subject or object), though pronouns are. Notice that the word "apples" remains unchanged in both positions in examples 1 and 2 in the table below. However, if a pronoun is used instead of "apples" in sentence 1, the pronoun "them" would be used (not "they").

| | Subject | Verb | Direct Object |
|---|---|---|---|
| 1 | I | like | apples (them). |
| 2 | Apples (They) | are | good food. |

In Arabic, nouns that are direct objects are in the *accusative case*. Western grammars use the term "accusative case," while grammars written in Arabic use the term نَصْب. There are different markers or endings that indicate this case:

**A.** A *fatḥa* فتحة appears at the end of the direct object if it is definite:

٣ يَدرُسُ وَليدُ الأحْياءَ

verb — subject — direct object

In this instance, يَدْرُسُ is the verb, وَليدُ the subject who performs the action, and الأحْياءَ is a definite direct object.

**B.** تَنوين فَتحة appears at the end of a direct object if it is indefinite:

٤ يَدرُسُ وَليدُ مادَّةً واحِدَةً.

In example 4, مادّةً is the direct object, which is indefinite; hence the use of تَنوين.

**C.** The suffix *-ayni* ـَيْنِ is attached to dual nouns in the accusative case (as in example 5) and the suffix *-īna* ِينَ to some sound masculine plural nouns (as in example 6). Both of these suffixes are used with definite and indefinite nouns.

(dual) يَدرُسُ وَليدُ مادّتَيْنِ. ٥

(plural) أعرِفُ ثَلاثَةَ أمريكيينَ. ٦

## 5. Objects of Prepositions

A noun preceded by a preposition is in a case called جَرّ in Arabic grammars and *genitive case* in Western grammars. An Arabic noun is marked in the genitive in four ways, three of which will be discussed at this point:

**A.** A *kasra* كَسْرة appears at the end of an object of a preposition if it is definite:

٧ يَدرُسُ عَدنانُ في الجامِعَةِ.

**B.** A double *kasra* تَنوين appears at the end of an indefinite noun:

٨ يَدرُسُ عَدنانُ في جامِعَةٍ أمريكيَّةٍ.

**C.** The suffix *-ayni* ـَيْنِ is attached to dual nouns and the suffix *-īna* ِين to some plural nouns:

٩ في جامِعَتَيْنِ (dual) أعْرِفُ المِصْريِّيْنِ (plural)

- **Note:** These suffixes are used with both definite and indefinite nouns (e.g., مِصريين، الجامعتين). Remember that adjectives agree with their modified nouns in number, gender, and case.

### SUMMARY

- The direct object of a verb is marked by a single فَتحة if it is definite, a double فَتحة if it is indefinite, and by suffixing ـَيْنِ to both definite and indefinite dual nouns and ِينَ to some sound masculine plurals.
- The object of a preposition is marked by a *kasra* if it is a definite noun, a double *kasra* if it is indefinite, and by suffixing ـَيْنِ to both definite and indefinite dual nouns and ِينَ to sound masculine plurals.

## تمرين ٨

**Recognizing grammar:** Underline the direct objects of verbs and draw a rectangle around the objects of prepositions. Provide the case markers where necessary. Be aware that some sentences contain both the object of a verb and the object of a preposition.

١- تَعرِفُ سَناء أربَعَ لُغاتٍ.

٢- أدرُس مادَّتَيْنِ في هذا الفَصْل.

٣- لا تَعرِفُ سامية عُنوانَ هالَة.

٤- تَدرُس هالَة مادَّةَ الأَحْياءِ في جامِعَةِ القاهِرة.

## تمرين ٩

**Conversation: Police investigation:** A theft has occurred in our classroom. The thief has stolen a **حَقيبة**. We need some background information that will help catch this criminal. Find out who . . .

1. is taking (studying) Arabic this term
2. has a book bag with two books in it and one notebook
3. lives in the dormitory
4. lives with two students
5. studies computer science
6. knows three French students

Have we caught our thief?

## 6. Ordinal Numbers الأعْدادُ التَرْتيبيَّة

Ordinal numbers are used to *order* items, hence their name (e.g., first, second, etc.). Arabic ordinal numbers are derived from cardinal numbers (e.g., one, two, etc.). While cardinal numbers 3–10 precede the noun they modify and form an **إضافة** structure with it, an ordinal number *follows* the noun and functions as an *adjective*. Examine the examples below:

| | | | |
|---|---|---|---|
| **Cardinal number** | *five lessons* | خَمْسَةُ دُروسٍ | ١٠ |
| **Ordinal number** | *the fifth lesson* | الدَرْسُ الخامِسُ | ١١ |

| Cardinal and Ordinal Numbers | | | | |
|---|---|---|---|---|
| Root | Ordinal (f.) | Ordinal (m.) | Cardinal | Digit |
| وَحَد | أُولى | أوَّل | واحِد | ١ |
| ثَني | ثانية | ثاني | اِثْنان | ٢ |
| ثَلَث | ثالِثة | ثالِث | ثَلاثة | ٣ |
| رَبَع | رابِعة | رابِع | أربَعة | ٤ |
| خَمَس | خامِسة | خامِس | خَمسة | ٥ |
| سَدَس | سادِسة | سادِس | سِتّة | ٦ |
| سَبَع | سابِعة | سابِع | سَبعة | ٧ |
| ثَمَن | ثامِنة | ثامِن | ثمانِية | ٨ |
| تَسَع | تاسِعة | تاسِع | تِسعة | ٩ |
| عَشَر | عاشِرة | عاشِر | عَشرة | ١٠ |
| | حادِيَةَ عَشْرَة | حادِي عَشَرَ | أحَدَ عَشَرَ | ١١ |
| | ثانِيَةَ عَشْرَة | ثانِي عَشَرَ | اثنا عَشَرَ | ١٢ |

**Note** that the cardinal number **واحِد** and its ordinal counterpart **أوّل** have different forms. Ordinal numbers 11 and 12 are indeclinable (i.e., they do not vary in case and only a **فتحة** can occur after the final letter).

Ordinal numbers may be feminine or masculine. As adjectives they agree with a preceding noun in gender, number, case, and definiteness.

١٢ هذا هُوَ الدَّرْسُ الحادي عَشَر *this is the eleventh lesson*

١٣ كِتابٌ ثالِثٌ *a third book*

١٤ في الدَّرْسَيْنِ الأوَّلَيْنِ. *In the first two lessons*

**Note** that the ordinal forms for numbers 2–10 follow the **فاعِل** pattern. This means that if you know the root letters of the number, you can just substitute them for the **ف ع ل** and add a **تاء مربوطة** when necessary. Be aware that when an ordinal number is definite, it will take the definite article **الـ** as a prefix, as can be seen in examples 12 and 14.

١٥ (ordinal pattern) **فاعِل(ة)**

## تمرين ١٠

**Matching:** Match words from the right-hand column with words in the left-hand column. Take the time to practice writing Arabic by writing both words in the middle column.

| | | | |
|---|---|---|---|
| ١ | فِلَسطين | | وَلَد |
| ٢ | فَصْل | | ثامِن |
| ٣ | بِنْت | | خَمسة |
| ٤ | سِتَّة | | دِرّاسيّ |
| ٥ | اِبن | | سادِس |
| ٦ | ثَماني | | اِبنَة |
| ٧ | خامِس | | عائِلَة |
| | | | لُبنان |
| | | | المَكتَبَة |

## تمرين ١١

**Fill in the blank:** Select words from the word bank that best complete the following sentences.

| | | | | |
|---|---|---|---|---|
| الثاني | زَوْجَة | مادَّةً | الابتِدائيّ | تَدرُس |

١- ________ هالَة مادَّةَ الرِياضِيّاتِ في هذا الفَصْل.

٢- كَمْ ________ عِندَكَ يا سالِم؟

٣- هَلْ أنتَ الابنُ ________ في عائِلَتِك؟

٤- أخي في الصَفِّ الرابع ________.

## 7. Pronouns of Separation ضَمائِر الفَصل

The independent personal pronouns (e.g., هُوَ، هِيَ) may be used to separate subjects from their predicates and also to distinguish sentences from phrases. When used as pronouns of separation, personal pronouns are comparable to the verb "to be" in English, as you can see in these examples from the passage:

| | | |
|---|---|---|
| *This is Mazen's family.* | هذِهِ هِيَ عائِلَةُ مازِن. | ١٦ |
| *Ahmed is the only child.* | أحمَدُ هُوَ الوَلَدُ الوَحيد. | ١٧ |

The subjects in examples 16 and 17 above are هذِهِ and أحمَد, respectively. The predicates represent the information about the subjects. The first predicate happens to be an إضافة structure عائِلَةُ مازِن (literally, family of Mazen) and the second predicate is a noun phrase الوَلَدُ الوَحيد (the only child) made up of a noun and an adjective. Note that both predicates are definite. Note also that these pronouns agree with the subjects in gender and number. Pronouns of separation are not used with indefinite predicates.

- The use of pronouns of separation is especially called for when the predicate is a single noun defined by the article, as in:

| | | |
|---|---|---|
| *This book . . .* | هذا الكِتابُ . . . | ١٨ |

The use of هُوَ in this context spells the difference between a noun phrase (18) and a sentence (19).

| | | |
|---|---|---|
| *This is the book.* | هذا هُوَ الكِتابُ. | ١٩ |

### SUMMARY

- Pronouns of separation are independent personal pronouns.
- They are used to separate subjects and predicates
- They distinguish a noun phrase from a sentence.
- The predicate must be definite.
- Pronouns of separation agree in number and gender with subjects.

## تمرين ١٢

**Pronouns of separation in use:** Change the following phrases into sentences by using the appropriate pronoun in the proper place.

١- هذه المِبراة. ______________________.

٢- الأستاذُ راغِب طَبّاع. ______________________.

٣- أخي نِزار. ______________________.

٤- هذا دَفتَرُ العائلَة. ______________________.

٥- هذانِ الطالِبانِ. ______________________.

٦- هؤلاءِ إخوَتي. ______________________.

## تمرين ١٣

**Filling out the دَفْتَرُ العائِلة:** In some Arab countries there is what is called a "family identification card," known in Arabic as **دَفْتَرُ العائِلة**. Fill out the first page of this document according to the information about the Najjār family in the main reading passage.

**دَفْتَرُ العائِلَة**

اِسمُ الأب: ______________________

اِسمُ الأم: ______________________

الوَلَدُ الأوَّل: ______________________

الوَلَدُ الثاني: ______________________

البِنْتُ الأُولى: ______________________

البِنْتُ الثانِية: ______________________

## تمرين ١٤

**Conversation:** Ask your neighbors questions concerning their family.

Find out from your neighbor . . .

1. if he/she has a brother or sister and if so, what his/her name is
2. where he/she lives (country, state, city, street) and whether he/she lives in a house or an apartment
3. what is in the house or apartment
4. what he/she studies, and where
5. if he/she is the only child

## تمرين ١٥

AUDIO

**A. Listen and select:** Check the box that matches the information as expressed in the listening passages for this lesson.

١- نَدى أستاذَةُ اللُغَةِ . . .

☐ الإنكليزيَّةِ ☐ الفَرَنسيَّةِ ☐ العَرَبيَّةِ

٢- نَدى لَها . . .

☐ ابنٌ واحِدٌ ☐ ابنانِ ☐ ثَلاثَةُ أبناء

٣- اِسمُ زَوْجِ نَدى . . .

☐ سامِر ☐ رامِز ☐ سَميح

٤- ابنُها في الصَفِّ . . .

☐ الثالِث ☐ الخامِس ☐ السابِع

**B. صواب أم خطأ:** Mark the following sentences **صواب** (true) or **خَطأ** (false) according to the information in the listening passage and correct any false statements.

٥- تَسكُنُ أُمُّ سَميح في دارِها. ______________________.

٦- سَميح بارودي هُوَ زَوْجُ نَدى حَفّار. ______________________.

٧- يَسكُنُ سَميحُ وعائلَتُه في مَدرَسةِ بَنات. ______________________.

٨- لِهذِه العائلَةِ ابنانِ وابنَة. ______________________.

# تمرين ١٦

**A. Verb conjugations:** Let's take a moment to review some verb conjugations. Give the independent pronoun with respect to the conjugated verb.

مِثال: أحمد يَدْرُسُ في المَدرسَةِ الابتِدائيَّة. ___هو___

١- هالة تَدْرُسُ في سوريَّة. ______

٢- هَلْ تَدْرُسينَ في كَندا؟ ______

٣- أَدْرُسُ في جامِعةِ بَيْروت. ______

٤- رانية تَدْرُسُ في المَكْتَبة. ______

٥- نَدْرُسُ في غُرفَةِ الصَفِّ. ______

**B.** Conjugate the verb with respect to the given pronoun. All verb conjugations are in the present tense.

مثال: هُم (دَرَسَ) ___يَدْرُسونَ___ عِلمَ الحاسوب.

أنا (دَرَسَ) ______ اللُغَةَ العَرَبِيَّةَ في جامِعَةِ وِلايةِ أوهايو. وأنتَ، هَل (دَرَسَ) ______ في هذِه الجامِعَةِ؟ ونَحْنُ (عَرَفَ) ______ أنَّ مايكل براون (دَرَسَ) ______ في الجامِعَةِ الأمريكيَّةِ في القاهِرة وهالَة بُستاني وسَحَر حلاّق (دَرَسَ) ______ في جامِعَةِ حَلَب. ولكِنْ أينَ (سَكَنَ) ______ هالَة وسَحَر؟ هَلْ (سَكَنَ) ______ في شَقَّة أم في بَيت؟

# تمرين ١٧

**Listen and respond:** Read the following dialogue and fill in the blanks with appropriate responses. After you have filled in the blanks, listen to the CD and respond during the pauses.

السلامُ علَيْكم!

__________ __________!

كَيْف الحال؟

____________________. ____________؟

الحَمْدُ لله بِخَيْر. هلْ لَك أَخ ؟

نعم، ______ __________.

ما اسْمُه؟

__________ __________.

هَلْ هوَ طالِبٌ في هذِه الجامِعة؟

نعم، هو _______ في _______ _______.

هَل عِنْدَه شَقّة ؟

نعم، ________ ________.

أيْنَ شَقَّتُه.

______________________________.

طَيِّب، شُكْراً ! مَعَ السَّلامة!

____ __________!

## تمرين ١٨ VIDEO

**تَمرينُ المُشاهَدة: شاهِدوا الدَرْسَ الخامِسَ على القُرْص الرَقْمي.**

١- مَع مَن يَسكُنُ هاني مُحَمَّد؟ ________________

________________

٢- ماذا يَدْرُس هاني؟ ________________

________________

٣- أَيْنَ يَسكُنُ أخو هاني؟ ________________

________________

٤- ماذا تَدرُس أُخْتُ هاني؟ ________________

________________

٥- مَع مَن يَسكُنُ عِماد حَسَن؟ ________________

________________

٦- في أَيَّةِ كُلّيّةٍ يَدرُسُ الطالِبانِ من مِصر؟ ________________

________________

## المُفْرَدات

Listen to the vocabulary items on the CD and practice their pronunciation.

father . . . . . . . . . . . . . . . . . . . . . . . . (n., m.) أب ج آباء
elementary. . . . . . . . . . . . . . . . . . . . . . . (adj.) اِبْتِدائيّ
son . . . . . . . . . . . . . . . . . . . . . . . . (n., m.) ابْنٌ ج أَبْناء
daughter . . . . . . . . . . . . . . . . . . . . . . . . (n., f.) ابْنَة ج بَنات
brother. . . . . . . . . . . . . . . . . . . . . . . . (n., m.) أَخ ج إخوة
sister . . . . . . . . . . . . . . . . . . . . . . . . (n., f.) أُخْت ج أَخَوات
mother. . . . . . . . . . . . . . . . . . . . . . . . (n., f.) أُمّ ج أُمَّهات
English. . . . . . . . . . . . . . . . . . . . . . . . (n., m.) إِنْكليزيّ
first . . . . . . . . . . . . . . . . . . . . . . . . (n., m.) أوَّل ج أوائِل
girl . . . . . . . . . . . . . . . . . . . . . . . . (n., f.) بِنْت ج بَنات
ninth . . . . . . . . . . . . . . . . . . . . . . . . (adj.) تاسِع
differential equations. . . . . . . . . . . . . . . . . . . . . . (n., m.) تَفاضُل
second . . . . . . . . . . . . . . . . . . . . . . . . (n., m.) ثانٍ (الثاني)
third . . . . . . . . . . . . . . . . . . . . . . . . (adj.) ثالِث
eighth . . . . . . . . . . . . . . . . . . . . . . . . (adj.) ثامِن
fifth. . . . . . . . . . . . . . . . . . . . . . . . (adj.) خامِس
of school, academic. . . . . . . . . . . . . . . . . . . . . . (adj.) دِراسِيّ
fourth . . . . . . . . . . . . . . . . . . . . . . . . (adj.) رابع
husband . . . . . . . . . . . . . . . . . . . . . . . . (n., m.) زَوْج ج أزْواج
wife. . . . . . . . . . . . . . . . . . . . . . . . (n., f.) زَوْجَة ج زَوْجات
seventh. . . . . . . . . . . . . . . . . . . . . . . . (adj.) سابع
sixth . . . . . . . . . . . . . . . . . . . . . . . . (adj.) سادِس
small; young. . . . . . . . . . . . . . . . . . . . . . . . (adj.) صَغير

child . . . . . . . . . . . . . . . . . . . . . . . . . . (n., m.) طِفْل ج أطْفال

tenth . . . . . . . . . . . . . . . . . . . . . . . . . . . . . . . . . . (adj.) عاشِر

nuclear family . . . . . . . . . . . . . . . . . . . . . . . (n., f.) عائِلَة ج عائِلات

(academic) term, season . . . . . . . . . . . . . (n., m.) فَصْل ج فُصول

only; no more than . . . . . . . . . . . . . . . . . . . . (particle) فَقَطْ

physics . . . . . . . . . . . . . . . . . . . . . . . . . . . . . . . . (n., f.) فيزياء

big . . . . . . . . . . . . . . . . . . . . . . . . . . . . . . . . . . . . (adj.) كَبير

chemistry . . . . . . . . . . . . . . . . . . . . . . . . . . . . . (n., f.) كيمياء

nice. . . . . . . . . . . . . . . . . . . . . . . . . . . . . . . . . . . . (adj.) لَطيف

who. . . . . . . . . . . . . (question particle and relative noun) مَنْ

sole, only. . . . . . . . . . . . . . . . . . . . . . . . (n., m.) وَحيد ج وَحيدون

middle . . . . . . . . . . . . . . . . . . . . . . . . . . . . . . . . (adj., f.) وُسْطى

boy . . . . . . . . . . . . . . . . . . . . . . . . . . . . . . (n., m.) وَلَد ج أَوْلاد

# الدرسُ السادِسُ

## Objectives

- Using terms of address
- Expressing regret or apology
- Expressing lack of knowledge
- Expressing degree
- Introduction to the negation and conjugation of the present-tense verb
- The secrets of the language: prefixes and suffixes
- Introduction to cardinal numbers 11–999

### 1. Terms of Address

## يا آنِسَة!

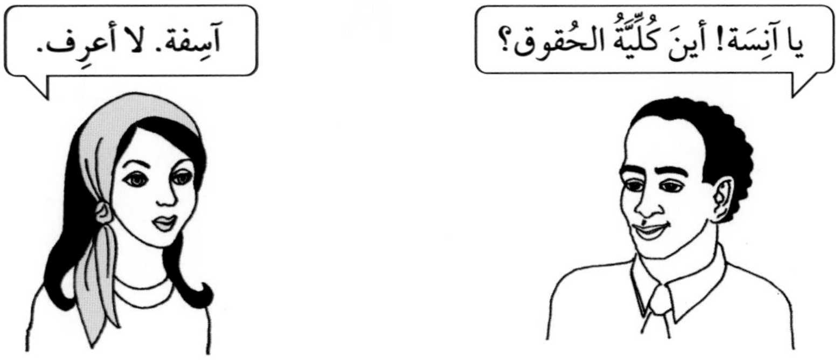

يا آنِسَة! أينَ كُلِّيَّةُ الحُقوق؟
آسِفة. لا أعرِف.

As in many languages, when people speak to each other, they use terms of address. Some Arabic terms of address also serve as titles. For example, the term آنِسة is equivalent to the English "Miss"; سَيِّدة is similar to "Mrs."; and the word سَيِّد is like "Mr." However, people may also use the words أخ 'brother' and أخت 'sister' to address strangers. The use of these terms is perceived to make the addressee feel safe, respected, and close—like a family member. In direct oral interaction, these terms may be preceded by the vocative **يا**, which is a particle used to call attention, as you may recall from Lesson 3. However, in indirect speech (e.g., when referring to someone) or in writing, the definite article **الـ** may be prefixed to the different terms of address (e.g., **الأستاذ أحمد**).

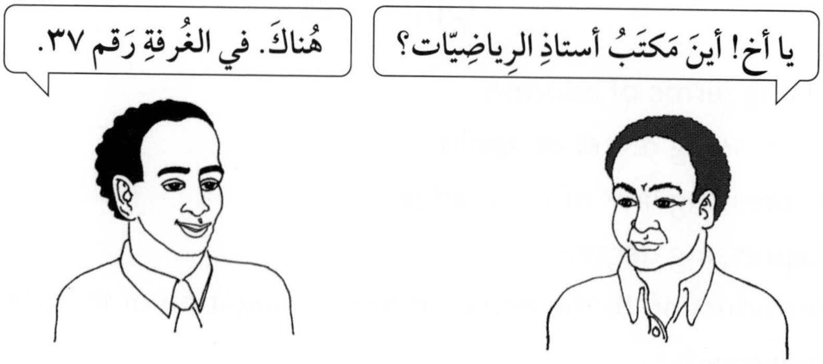


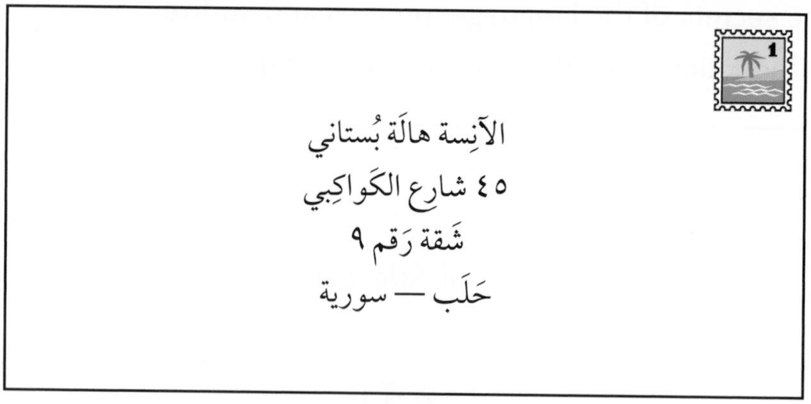
الآنِسة هالَة بُستاني
٤٥ شارِع الكَواكِبي
شَقة رَقم ٩
حَلَب — سورية

مَن أمينةُ المكتبَة ؟

اِسْمُها السَيِّدةُ نِداء خَيّاط.

شُكراً

عَفواً

**السَيِّدة نِداء خَيّاط**

- أينَ كِتابُكَ يا صَلاح؟
- آسِف يا أستاذ. كِتابي لَيسَ مَعي.

In speech you may use the article يا with either the first or the last names (e.g., an educated person named خَليل حدّاد may be addressed as يا أسْتاذ خَليل or يا أسْتاذ حَدّاد).

The plural forms of سَيِّد (سادة) and سَيِّدة (سَيِّدات) may be used to address groups of people, as in public gatherings. Consider the following example, where the MC is introducing a man named حُسَيْن زاهِر:

سَيِّداتي وَسادَتي . . .
الأستاذ حُسَيْن زاهِر!

| Use of Terms of Address | |
|---|---|
| **Oral (information)** | **Written (formal)** |
| يا سَيِّد أحمَد! | السَيِّد أحمَد ناجي |
| يا سَيِّدة رَنا! | السَيِّدة رَنا غلاييني |
| يا آنِسَة هَنادي! | الآنِسَة هَنادي زَيْتونة |
| يا أستاذ خَليل! | الأستاذ خَليل حَدّاد |
| يا أخ مُنذِر! | الأخ مُنذِر الدَجاني |
| يا أخت مُزْنة! | الأخْت مُزْنة القائِد |

## تمرين ١

**Read and select:** Review the dialogues in this lesson once more and check the box that corresponds with the information in these dialogues.

١- مَكْتَبُ أستاذِ الرِياضِيّات في . . .

☐ جامعةِ حَلَب ☐ مكانٍ لا نعرفه ☐ الغُرفةِ

٢- تَسكُنُ هالَة بُستاني في . . .

☐ شَقّةٍ ☐ غُرفةٍ ☐ شارعٍ

٣- اِسمُ أَمينَةِ المَكتَبة . . .

☐ هالَة بُستاني ☐ سامية ☐ نِداء خَيّاط

٤- صَلاح . . .

☐ لَيْسَ مَعَهُ كِتاب ☐ لَيْسَ مَعَهُ مِحفَظة ☐ لَيْسَ في الصَفِّ

٥- الآنِسةُ . . . أيْنَ كُلِّيَّةُ الحُقوق.

☐ تَعرِفُ ☐ لا تَعرِفُ ☐ لا تَتَكَلَّمُ

٦- صَلاح . . .

☐ طالِبٌ ☐ أستاذٌ ☐ أمينُ مَكتَبة

## تمرين ٢

**Terms of address in use:** On a separate sheet of paper, write how you would address these persons appropriately according to the contexts below. Imagine that you are . . .

1. writing an official business letter to **وَليد طَرَزي**, who has a university degree
2. addressing **محمود سالِم**, a lower-level employee in your office
3. addressing a young, single female secretary named **ريم مَعلوف** in person
4. writing to a lady whose name is **رَباب كَحّال**
5. writing to an older man who is not very educated, whose name is **عبد الرحيم حُسَين**
6. addressing your professor **فَريد قَدّورة** in person
7. writing to a female student whose name is **زَينَب حَمدي**

## 2. Expressing Regret or Apology

One way of expressing regret or apology is by using the word آسِف 'I'm sorry'. A man uses this form when talking about himself or another man in the third person. A woman would use آسِفة when talking about herself or another woman in the third person. As you can see, the words are the same except for the added تاء مربوطة that indicates femininity. Both آسِف and آسِفة are active participles, which are treated as nouns in Arabic. Thus, the rules that we learned about making the dual form can be applied here. آسِفان is said when two men are expressing regret or when talking about two men who are feeling apologetic about something. As you can see, آسِفان is formed by suffixing ان to the final radical, while the feminine form is آسِفتان. The masculine plural is made by suffixing ون to the form, resulting in آسِفون, while ات is suffixed to the feminine form, resulting in آسِفات.

Let's take a look at plural endings for nouns in the nominative case:

| The Sound Plural الجمع<br>*Suffix*: ون / ات | The Dual المُثَنّى<br>*Suffix*: ـانِ | The Singular<br>المُفْرَد | Gender الجِنْس |
|---|---|---|---|
| آسِفونَ | آسِفانِ | آسِفٌ | Masculine المُذَكَّر |
| آسِفات | آسِفتانِ | آسِفةٌ | Feminine المُؤَنَّث |

- **Note:** When the dual suffix ان is appended to the feminine form, the feminine suffix تاء مربوطة is retained, but it changes into a regular تاء. However, when the plural feminine ending ات is suffixed to the word آسِفة, the تاء مربوطة is dropped.

## تمرين ٣

**Conducting an official interview:** Seek out one of your classmates whose name you do not know. Apologize for not knowing his/her name and then conduct an interview with him/her using the correct term of address throughout. Find out and write down as much information as you can. Possible topics are place of origin, where he/she is living now, how many brothers and sisters he/she has, how many languages he/she knows, what he/she is studying this term, if he/she has/owns a car or bike. After you have exhausted your questions, switch roles. Be prepared to share your information with your classmates.

## تمرين ٤

Write down one word in each bubble to describe what the person or persons should say in order to express regret or apology. Proceed from right to left.

two men

one woman

one man

three men

three women

two women

### 3. Expressing Lack of Knowledge

You already know that the phrase لا أعْرِف 'I don't know' expresses lack of knowledge. It occurs as the first exchange in section 1 of this lesson. There are, however, other ways of expressing lack of knowledge. One of them involves the use of the phrase اللهُ أعلَم (pronounced *allāhu a'lam*), which literally means "God is the most knowledgeable." It is one of many phrases that involve the use of the word الله that we will cover over the course of this book. اللهُ أعلَم occurs in this exchange, signifying a lack of knowledge on the woman's part.

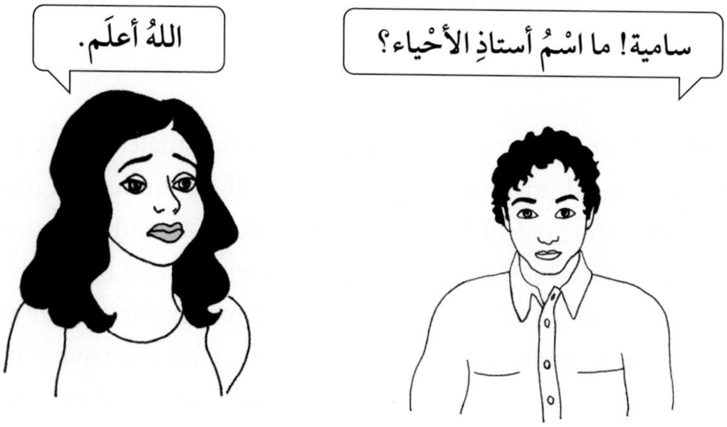
سامية! ما اسْمُ أستاذِ الأحْياء؟
اللهُ أعلَم.

## 4. Expressing Degree

Expressing degree refers to how well one does something. In the exchange below the woman tries to find out whether Marwān speaks تَكَلَّم English well. His response shows that he does not.

هَل تتكَلَّمُ الإنكليزيَّة جَيِّداً يا مَروان؟
لا، أتكَلَّمُها قَليلاً.

The adverbs جَيِّداً 'well' and قَليلاً 'a little' are derived from the adjectives جَيِّد 'good' and قَليل 'little', respectively, by suffixing a تَنوين, which is seated on a silent أَلِف.

- **Note:** These adverbs generally occupy the final position of a sentence.

### تمرين ٥

**Matching:** Match words from the right-hand column with words in the left-hand column. Take the time to practice writing Arabic by writing both words in the middle column.

| | | | |
|---|---|---|---|
| لُغَة | | جَيِّداً | ١ |
| أعْلَم | | آنِسة | ٢ |
| خَمسة | | يَتَكَلَّمُ | ٣ |
| قَليلاً | | أمينَةُ | ٤ |
| سَيِّدَة | | اللهُ | ٥ |
| مَكتَبة | | سَيِّداتي | ٦ |
| سادَتي | | | |
| لُبنان | | | |

# تمرين ٦

**Fill in the blanks:** Complete the following sentences with words from the word bank.

| اللهُ أعْلَم | الأخ | قليلاً | الآنِسة | سَيِّداتي | سادَتي | آسِفة |
|---|---|---|---|---|---|---|

١– ____________ هالَة لا تَسكُنُ هُنا بَلْ في سَكَنِ الطالِبات.

٢– أنا ____________ قَلَمي لَيسَ مَعي.

٣– أينَ مِفتاحُ السَيّارَة؟ ____________

٤– ____________ وَسادَتي، أهلاً بِكُم.

٥– أتَكَلَّمُ اللُغَةَ الإنكليزيَّةَ جَيِّداً والفَرَنسيَّةَ ____________.

# تمرين ٧

**Read and respond:** On a separate sheet of paper, respond to the following questions in Arabic with reference to the main reading passages on pp. 95–97 in this lesson. Improve your Arabic by writing your answers in complete sentences.

1. Does the woman know where the School of Law is?
2. What is Hala Boustani's address?
3. How would you introduce your favorite celebrity to an audience in Arabic?
4. How do you say that you speak a little Arabic?
5. What would you say if someone asks you about your professor's address, but you have no idea?
6. How would a woman express regret for not knowing how many students are in her son's class?
7. How would a man express regret for not knowing the name of his daughter's instructor?

# تمرين ٨

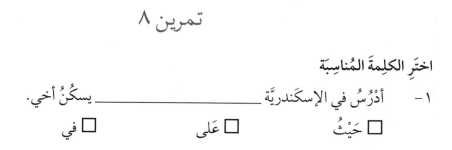

**اختَرِ الكلِمةَ المُناسِبَة**

١– أدْرُسُ في الإسكَندريَّة ____________ يسكُنُ أخي.

☐ حَيْثُ ☐ عَلى ☐ في

صَيْدلانيّة

٢- هذا كِتابٌ ________ .

☐ عَليم ☐ جَيِّدٌ ☐ أمين

٣- ريم عَلاّف ________ مَكتَبةٍ في جامِعَةِ تِشرين.

☐ صيدلانية ☐ قَليلاً ☐ أمينَةُ

٤- ________ لا أعرِفُ أينَ كُلِّيَّةُ الصَّيْدَلَة.

☐ شُكْراً ☐ آسِف ☐ مِن

٥- ________ هالَة الإنكليزيَّةَ جَيِّداً.

☐ تَتَكَلَّمُ ☐ أعْلَم ☐ تَسكُنُ

## 5. The Present Tense: Negation and Conjugation

### A. Negation

You have already used the present tense of the verb سَكَنَ ‘to live; reside’ in order to describe where one lives. For example, to indicate that you live in an apartment, you say: أَسْكُنُ في شَقة. However, if you do not live in an apartment, you can express that by inserting the negative particle لا in front of the verb:

١ لا أسكُنُ في شَقَّةٍ.

Negating present-tense verbs مُضارِع with the negative particle لا does not change either the structure of the verb or the word order of the sentence, as was described in Lesson 3.

### B. Conjugation

So far, only five conjugations have been used to refer to yourself, to an addressee (singular masculine and feminine), and to a third person (singular masculine and feminine). The following table lists all thirteen verb conjugations in the present tense according to person.

| Present Tense Conjugation of تَكَلَّمَ | | |
|---|---|---|
| Verb الفِعْل | Pronoun الضَمير | Person |
| أَتَكَلَّمُ | أنا | First المُتَكَلِّم |
| نَتَكَلَّمُ | نَحْنُ | |
| تَتَكَلَّمُ | أَنْتَ | Second المُخاطَب |
| تَتَكَلَّمينَ | أَنْتِ | |
| تَتَكَلَّمانِ | أَنْتُما | |
| تَتَكَلَّمونَ | أَنْتُم | |
| تَتَكَلَّمْنَ | أَنْتُنَّ | |
| يَتَكَلَّمُ | هُوَ | Third الغائِب |
| تَتَكَلَّمُ | هِيَ | |
| يَتَكَلَّمانِ | هُما (m. d.) | |
| تَتَكَلَّمانِ | هُما (f. d.) | |
| يَتَكَلَّمونَ | هُم | |
| يَتَكَلَّمْنَ | هُنَّ | |

## 6. Secrets of the Language: Prefixes and Suffixes

While memorizing the verb conjugations might seem to be a daunting task at first, here are some tips in terms of patterns that might simplify the matter. The generalizations that follow apply to every single Arabic verb in the indicative.

### A. Overall

As you can see, all present/imperfect-tense verbs take a prefix. The suffixes to present-tense verbs indicate either *gender* or *number*.

| Suffixes for Present-Tense Verbs | |
|---|---|
| ـانِ | for all duals, feminine and masculine |
| ـونَ | for masculine plurals |
| ـنْ | for feminine plurals |

What is the difference between the present-tense conjugation of أنْتَ and هِيَ? No differences exist. They are exactly the same and can only be distinguished through context.

**B. First Person**

The similarities between the conjugation of first-person singular and plural should be obvious. Examine the chart on the previous page to see what you can deduce. As you can see, the conjugation for the singular uses the هَمزة from أنا as the first letter of its verbs; similarly, the conjugation for the plural uses the نون from نَحْنُ as the first letter of its verbs.

٢ أنا ← أتَكَلّمُ

٣ نَحْنُ ← نَتَكَلَّمُ

**C. Second Person**

Take a close look at the second-person independent pronouns. Do you see any patterns? As you can tell, they all start with the same two letters أنـ. It is the third letter of these pronouns that indicates gender and number.

Now take a look at all of the second-person verbs. Do you see a pattern there? Each verb starts with a تـ, while their suffixes indicate *gender*, *dual*, or *plural* as can be seen in the Present-Tense Conjugation chart on the preceding page.

**D. Third Person**

All masculine verbs start with a يـ. You would think that all feminine verbs would start with a تـ to follow a pattern. Unfortunately we have an anomaly that has to be memorized. The feminine plural starts with a يـ. The suffixes follow the Present-Tense Conjugation chart on the preceding page.

تمرين ٩

**Fill in the blanks:** Conjugate the words in parentheses according to their modified nouns.

_____ (عَرَفَ) سَناء أَربَعَ لُغاتٍ ولكِنْ هَل

_____ (تَكَلَّمَ) ها جَيِّداً؟ كَمْ لُغَةً (تَكَلَّمَ)

مايكل براون؟ هُوَ _____ (عَرَفَ) اللُغة الإنكليزيَّة

جَيِّداً لكِنَّهُ _____ (تَكَلَّمَ) اللُغَةَ العَرَبِيَّةَ قَليلاً.

هُوَ _____ (سَكَنَ) في مَدينَةِ القاهِرَةِ حَيثُ

_____ (دَرَسَ) في الجامِعَةِ الأمريكيَّةِ. سَحَر

وهالة مِن دِمَشق لكِنَّهُما _____ (سَكَنَ) في حَلَب

حَيْث _____ (دَرَسَ) في جامِعتِهِما. وأَنْتُم، أَينَ

_____ (سَكَنَ) وماذا _____ (دَرَسَ) في هذا

الفَصْل؟

تمرين ١٠

**Conversation:** Find out how many people speak the following languages and how well they speak them. If your neighbors know other languages that are not included here, name them and indicate how well your neighbors speak them. Be prepared to report your findings to your instructor in Arabic.

١- الإنكليزيَّة _____.

٢- العَرَبِيَّة _____.

٣- الإسْبانِيَّة _____.

٤- الفَرَنسيَّة _____.

٥- اللاتينِيَّة _____.

## 7. Cardinal Numbers 11–999 الأعداد الأصْليّة

### A. Cardinal Numbers 11 and 12

These compound numbers *precede* the noun they modify and agree with the specified noun in gender.

| Feminine | Masculine | Case |
|---|---|---|
| إحْدى عَشْرَةَ سَيّارَةً | أَحَدَ عَشَرَ كِتاباً | Nominative, Accusative, and Genitive |
| اِثنتاعَشْرَةَ سَيّارَةً | اِثنا عَشَرَ كِتاباً | Nominative |
| اِثنَتي عَشْرَةَ سَيّارَةً | اِثني عَشَرَ كِتاباً | Accusative and Genitive |

**Note** that the number 11 is indeclinable; that is, it does not change with respect to case. However, the number 12 does change its form with respect to case. The forms اِثنا (m.) and اِثنتا (f.) are used in nominative case, while the forms اِثنَي (m.) and اثنَتَي (f.) are used when the noun is the object of a verb (accusative case) or a preposition (genitive case).

### B. Cardinal Numbers 13–19

Like the numbers 3–10, these numbers have reverse gender agreement with the singular of their modified noun. However, the reverse gender agreement is limited to the ones digits, not the tens, as you can see in the following example:

٤ ثَلاثَةَ عَشَرَ كِتاباً ثَلاثَ عَشْرَةَ سَيّارَةً

| Feminine المؤَنَّث | الأعداد | Masculine المُذَكَّر |
|---|---|---|
| ثَلاثَ عَشْرَةَ سَيّارَةً | ١٣ | ثَلاثَةَ عَشَرَ كِتاباً |
| أربَعَ عَشْرَةَ سَيّارَةً | ١٤ | أربَعَةَ عَشَرَ كِتاباً |
| خَمسَ عَشْرَةَ سَيّارَةً | ١٥ | خَمسَةَ عَشَرَ كِتاباً |
| سِتَّ عَشْرَةَ سَيّارَةً | ١٦ | سِتَّةَ عَشَرَ كِتاباً |
| سَبعَ عَشْرَةَ سَيّارَةً | ١٧ | سَبعَةَ عَشَرَ كِتاباً |
| ثَماني عَشْرَةَ سَيّارَةً | ١٨ | ثَمانِيَةَ عَشَرَ كِتاباً |
| تِسعَ عَشْرَةَ سَيّارَةً | ١٩ | تِسعَةَ عَشَرَ كِتاباً |

Reverse gender agreement exists between the first word of the number (the ones digit) and the noun. Notice that ثَلاثة and كتاباً exhibit a reverse gender agreement, while the tens digits agree in gender (e.g., عَشَرَ and كتاباً are both masculine).

- **Note:** All numbers 11 through 19 (except for the number 12, which shows a case marker) are invariable, with a فتحة on the end in all cases.
- **Remember:** The counted nouns are *singular indefinite accusative* (e.g., كِتاباً, سيّارَةً).

### C. Cardinal Numbers 20–90

These numbers (i.e., the tens) are nouns and therefore change in form according to case. The ending ونَ is used for the nominative case (subject) (e.g., عِشرون) and ينَ for the accusative and genitive cases (e.g., عِشرينَ). Like the numbers 11–19, the noun following them is singular, indefinite, and accusative in that تَنوين (ً) appears on the last radical. They are invariable with regard to gender; that is, they do not vary in form to match the gender of the counted noun. In the examples below the number 30 changes with respect to case, but not gender.

| Feminine المُؤَنَّث | Masculine المُذَكَّر | Case الحالَة |
|---|---|---|
| هُناكَ ثَلاثونَ جامِعَةً | عِندي ثَلاثونَ كِتاباً | **Nominative** |
| في ثَلاثينَ جامِعَةً | في ثَلاثينَ كِتاباً | **Genitive/Accusative** |

**Tens العُقود (20–90) with masculine and feminine nouns:**

| Feminine المؤنَّث | الأعداد | Masculine المُذكَّر |
|---|---|---|
| عِشرونَ سَيّارَةً | ٢٠ | عِشرونَ كِتاباً |
| ثَلاثونَ سَيّارَةً | ٣٠ | ثَلاثونَ كِتاباً |
| أربَعونَ سَيّارَةً | ٤٠ | أربَعونَ كِتاباً |
| خَمسونَ سَيّارَةً | ٥٠ | خَمسونَ كِتاباً |
| سِتّونَ سَيّارَةً | ٦٠ | سِتّونَ كِتاباً |
| سَبعونَ سَيّارَةً | ٧٠ | سَبعونَ كِتاباً |
| ثَمانونَ سَيّارَةً | ٨٠ | ثَمانونَ كِتاباً |
| تِسعونَ سَيّارَةً | ٩٠ | تِسعونَ كِتاباً |

## SUMMARY

- **The numbers 11 and 12 أحْكامُ العَدَد**

  Both words in the number agree in gender with the noun. The number 11 is indeclinable (i.e., it does not change with case), exhibiting a **فتحة** on the final radical of both words, whereas the words **اِثنا** and **اثنَتا** in the number 12 change to **اثنَي** and **اثنَتَي** in the accusative and genitive cases.

- **The numbers 13–19**

  The first word of the number (the ones digit) has a reverse gender agreement with the noun, while the second word (ten) agrees with the noun in gender. Neither the ones digits nor the tens digits change with case; they always have a **فتحة** on their final radical.

- **The numbers 20–90**

  These numbers have two forms: (1) nominative (e.g., **عِشْرون**) and (2) accusative and genitive (e.g., **عِشْرين**). The noun following these numbers is singular, indefinite, accusative (e.g., **سِتّون/ ستّين سيّارةً**).

### D. Inside the Numbers

As we have seen, the numbers **1** and **2** always agree in gender with the singular noun. This applies to 21, 22; 31, 32; 41, 42, etc.

| | | | |
|---|---|---|---|
| ٥ | **المُؤَنَّث** | واحِدةٌ وعِشرونَ سَيّارةً | اِثنَتان وعِشرونَ سَيّارةً |
| ٦ | **المُذَكَّر** | واحِدٌ وعِشرونَ كِتاباً | اِثنانِ وعِشرونَ كِتاباً |

As we have noted, the numbers 3–9 are always opposite the gender of the modified noun. This also applies to numbers 23–29; 33–39; 43–49, etc.

| | | |
|---|---|---|
| ٧ | **المُؤَنَّث** | ثلاثٌ وعِشرونَ سَيّارةً |
| ٨ | **المُذَكَّر** | أربعةٌ وعِشرونَ كِتاباً |

### E. The Number 100 (مِئة)

This is also a noun, which means that its case varies according to its position in the sentence. The counted noun following it is always singular indefinite. It forms an **إضافة** structure with the following noun, which is therefore genitive and indefinite, and takes a double **كسرة**:

٩ مِئَةُ كِتابٍ مِئَةُ سَيّارَةٍ

Since the word **مِئة** is a noun, it is subject to being made dual and plural. The dual is formed by suffixing **ان** for the nominative case or **ـَيْنَ** for both the genitive and accusative cases. The plural is formed by suffixing **ات** because it is a feminine noun, thus resulting in **مِئات** 'hundreds'. However, the plural form **مِئات** is never used with the numbers 100–999, but it is used in phrases such as:

١٠ مِئاتُ الكُتُبِ *hundreds of books*

- **Note:** In this usage, the counted noun (highlighted in blue) is plural, definite, and genitive.

Here is a list of multiples of 100 used with nouns:

| المُؤَنَّث Feminine | الأعداد | المُذَكَّر Masculine |
|---|---|---|
| مِئَتا (مِئَتَي) سَيَّارَةٍ | ٢٠٠ | مِئَتا (مِئَتَي) كِتابٍ |
| ثَلاثُمِئَةِ سَيَّارَةٍ | ٣٠٠ | ثَلاثُمِئَةِ كِتابٍ |
| أَربَعُمِئَةِ سَيَّارَةٍ | ٤٠٠ | أَربَعُمِئَةِ كِتابٍ |
| خَمسُمِئَةِ سَيَّارَةٍ | ٥٠٠ | خَمسُمِئَةِ كِتابٍ |
| سِتُّمِئَةِ سَيَّارَةٍ | ٦٠٠ | سِتُّمِئَةِ كِتابٍ |
| سَبعُمِئَةِ سَيَّارَةٍ | ٧٠٠ | سَبعُمِئَةِ كِتابٍ |
| ثَمانِمِئَةِ سَيَّارَةٍ | ٨٠٠ | ثَمانِمِئَةِ كِتابٍ |
| تِسعُمِئَةِ سَيَّارَةٍ | ٩٠٠ | تِسعُمِئَةِ كِتابٍ |

- **Note:** The number 200 loses its final نون because it is the first word of an أضافة structure, which is known in Arabic as المُضاف.

## تمرين ١١

**Conversation: Numbers in use:** Find out how many . . .

1. people in class know whose picture is on the 20-dollar دولار bill; the 50; the 100
2. TVs your neighbors have in their homes
3. students are taking biology this term
4. watches they have
5. phones they have
6. pens your neighbors each have in their book bags

And now write your answers down on a separate sheet of paper in complete sentences. Be prepared to share your answers with your classmates. A word bank of plurals follows.

| نَظَّارَة ج نَظَّارات | طالِب ج طُلّاب | دَفتَر ج دَفاتِر | تِلْفاز ج تِلْفازات |
|---|---|---|---|
| هاتِف ج هَواتِف | قَلَم ج أَقْلام | ساعَة ج ساعات | دَرّاجَة ج دَرّاجات |

## تمرين ١٢

AUDIO

**A. Listen and select:** Check the box that matches the information as expressed in the listening passage for this lesson.

١- يَسكُنُ عادِل مَحمود في . . .

☐ الإسكَندَريّة ☐ طَنطا ☐ القاهِرة

٢- عادِل مَحمود هُوَ . . . سامية.

☐ أخو ☐ أبو ☐ أخت

٣- تَدرُسُ سامية في جامِعَةِ . . .

☐ طَنطا ☐ القاهِرة ☐ الإسكَندَريَّة

٤- لِعَبدِ الحَليم . . .

☐ أختٌ واحِدَة ☐ أختانِ ☐ ثَلاثُ أخَوات

٥- تَسكُنُ سامية مَحمود الآنَ في . . .

☐ سَكَنِ الطالِبات ☐ بَيتِ أبيها ☐ كُلِّيَّةِ التِجارة

**B.** Answer these questions with reference to the listening passage.

٦- كَم أخاً لِسامية؟ ______________________.

٧- مَن زَينَب؟ ______________________.

٨- أهِيَ في المَدرَسةِ أم في الجامِعَة؟ ______________________.

٩- مَن تَهاني وماذا تَدرُس؟ ______________________.

**C.** Describe Samia's room in Arabic.

**D.** Compose a biographical sketch about yourself modeled after the listening passage.

- **Grammar note:** As can be seen in this lesson, the preposition لِـ 'to have' is very similar to عِندَ. Traditionally speaking, there has been a slight difference in usage in that لِـ was generally used for humans (= I have a son, daughter, friend, etc.), whereas عِندَ was used for everything else. In modern usage, عِندَ can be used in both cases.

## تمرين ١٣

**تَمرينُ المُشاهَدة: شاهِدوا الدَرْسَ السادِسَ على القُرص الرَقْمي.**

**المَشْهَدُ الأوَّل:**

١ – أَينَ مَكْتَبُ المُدير؟

**المَشْهَدُ الثاني:**

١ – اكْتُبْ ماذا تَعرِف/ تَعرِفين عن أستاذة الصف.

## المُفْرَدات

Listen to the vocabulary items on the CD and practice their pronunciation.

to be able. . . . . . . . . . . . . . . . . . (v.) اِسْتَطاعَ (يَسْتَطِيعُ) اِسْتِطاعة

sorry . . . . . . . . . . . . . . . . . (n., f.) آسِفة / (m.) آسِف

most knowledgeable . . . . . . . . . . . . . (n. superlative) أعلَم

God knows . . . . . . . . . . . . . . . . . . . . . الله أعْلَم

librarian. . . . . . . . . . . . . . . . . (n., m./f.) أمينُ/ أمينةُ مَكتَبةٍ

program. . . . . . . . . . . . . . . . (n., m.) بَرْنامِج ج بَرامِج

to speak . . . . . . . . . . . . . . . . . (v.) تَكَلَّمَ (يَتكَلَّمُ) تَكَلُّم

abundant . . . . . . . . . . . . . . . . . . . . . . . جَزيلاً.

good. . . . . . . . . . . . . . . . . . . . . . . . (adj.) جَيِّد

well . . . . . . . . . . . . . . . . . . . . . . . . (adv.) جَيِّداً

where, when . . . . . . . . . . . . . . . . . . . . (adv.) حَيْثُ

pharmacology . . . . . . . . . . . . . . . . . . (n., f.) صَيْدَلَة

knowledgeable . . . . . . . . . . . . . . . . . . . (adj.) عَليم

group of ten. . . . . . . . . . . . . . . . . . (n., m.) عَقْد ج عُقود

little . . . . . . . . . . . . . . . . . . . . . . . . (adj.) قَليل

a little . . . . . . . . . . . . . . . . . . . . . . . (adv.) قَليلاً

to, for, by . . . . . . . . . . . . . . . . . . . . . (prep.) لَـ

Don’t worry about it . . . . . . . . . . . . . . . . لا شُكْرَ على واجِب
(said when someone thanks you for something)

boss; director . . . . . . . . . . . . . . . . (n., m.) مُدير ج مُدَراء

help, assistance . . . . . . . . . . . . . . . (verbal noun) مُساعَدة

agreement. . . . . . . . . . . . . . . . . . . . (verbal noun) مُوافَقَة

worker, employee . . . . . . . . . . . . (n., m.) مُوَظَّف ج مُوَظَّفون

hundred . . . . . . . . . . . . . . . . . . . . . . . . (n., f.) مِئة ج مِئات

you (m.sg.) are able. . . . . . . . . . . . . . . . . . . . . . (v.) يُمْكِنُكَ

# الدَرسُ السابِع

## Objectives

- Learning about Arabic print media
- Inquiring about and describing activities or objects
- Making polite requests and offers using the imperative
  - The imperative
  - Doubly transitive verbs
  - The pronunciation of the pronoun ه
- Introduction to the cases of the noun
- Expressing possession with لِـ and مَعَ
- Introduction to attached pronouns suffixed to verbs
- Revisiting Arabic names

# جَرائِدُ ومَجلاّتٌ عَرَبِيَّةٌ

هُناكَ جَرائِدُ ومَجَلاّتٌ عَرَبيَّةٌ في مَكتَبَةِ الجامعَةِ.

جَريدةُ الأهْرامِ مِصْريّة.

جَريدةُ تِشْرينَ سوريَّة.

جَريدةُ الشَرْقِ الأوْسَطِ سُعوديّة.

جَريدةُ الرافِدَيْنِ عِراقيّة.

جَريدةُ الفِكْرِ تونسيّة.

مَجَلَّةُ الإكليلِ يَمَنيّة.

مَجَلَّةُ الفُنونِ مَغْرِبيّة.

مَجَلَّةُ العَرَبيِّ كُوَيتيّة.

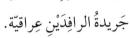

# الكَلِماتُ المُفيدَةُ في صُوَرٍ عَديدةٍ

قَرَأَ (يَقرَأُ) قِراءة



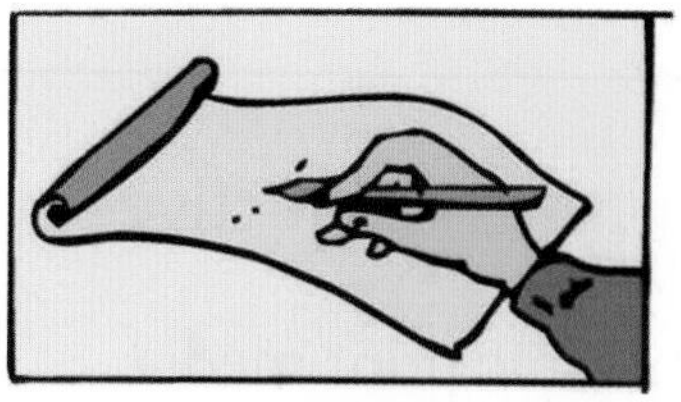

كَتَبَ (يَكتُبُ) كِتابة

مَجَلّة ج مَجَلّات

# مَن يَقرَأُ هذِهِ الجَرائِدَ والمَجَلّات؟

يَقرَأُ المَجَلّاتِ والجَرائِدَ العَرَبيّةَ طُلّابٌ عَرَبٌ في الجامِعةِ وطُلّابٌ أمريكيّونَ يَدرُسونَ اللُّغةَ العَرَبيّة.

# ماذا يَقرَأُون؟



يَقرَأُ الطُّلّابُ العَرَبُ في أمريكا الجَرائِدَ والمَجَلّاتِ العَرَبيّةَ في مَكتَبةِ الجامِعةِ عادَةً. يَقرَأُ عَدنان مارتيني جَريدةَ «تِشرينَ» ومَجَلّةَ «المَعرِفة» السوريّتَينِ عادَةً ويَقرَأُ أحياناً مَجَلّةَ «روز اليوسِف» المِصريّة.

عَدنان مارتيني

يَقرَأُ وَليد صايغ عادَةً جَريدةَ «النَهارِ» اللُّبنانيّة ومَجَلّةَ «المَجَلّةِ» السُعوديّة، ويَقرَأُ أحياناً جَريدةَ «الأهرامِ» المِصريّة.

وَليد صايغ

يَقرَأُ زِياد نابلسي عادَةً جَريدةَ «الرافدين» العِراقيّة، لكِنَّهُ يَقرَأُ جَريدةَ «الشَرقِ الأَوْسَط» السُعوديّة و«الأخبارَ» المِصريّة أيضاً. يَقرَأُ زِياد أحياناً مَجَلّةَ «الإكليل» اليَمَنيّة ومَجَلّةَ «المَوْقِف الأدَبيّ» السوريّة.

أيّةَ جَريدَةٍ تَقرَأُ يا عَبدَ اللطيف؟

أقرَأُ جَريدةَ النَهار.

- أيّةَ جَريدَةٍ تَقرَأُ يا عَبدَ اللطيف؟
- أقرَأُ جَريدةَ النَهارِ عادَةً.
  وأقرَأُ جَريدةَ المُجاهِد أحْياناً.
- هَل جَريدةُ النَهارِ سوريّة؟
- لا. هِيَ لُبنانيّة. المُجاهِد جَزائريّة.
- هَل تَكتُبُ في جَريدة؟
- لا. أنا لا أكتُبُ في أيّةِ جَريدة. أنا أقرَأُ الجَرائِد.

**Reflecting on our reading:** The word أيّ is used as a question particle. Can you deduce its meaning from context?

## 1. Inquiring about and Describing an Activity or Object

Inquiring about or describing an activity involves describing an action, which is expressed by a verb. However, in the exchange between ʿAbd al-Latīf and his friend the focus is on the object being read rather than on the action. In instances such as these, we use **أيّ** for both feminine and masculine objects to ask "which" (originally, no feminine form of it existed, but you may encounter **أيّةُ** in use, which is acceptable). As we have already seen, when we want to ask about an action we use **ماذا** followed by a verb. If the nature of the activity is known—reading, for example—then we would use that verb (e.g., "what are you reading?"). But if the activity is not known, then the generic verb **فَعَلَ** is used meaning "to do." Consider the following question and answer exchange.

The question word أيُّ is a noun; therefore, it forms an إضافة with a following noun and functions as subject or object in the sentence.

In summary, the interrogative (question) word used to inquire about objects is أيّ 'which', and the question word used to inquire about actions is ماذا 'what'.

If the request cannot be fulfilled, the words (m.) آسِف / (f.) آسِفة may be used, as in the exchange above.

## 2. Making Polite Requests and Offers Using the Imperative

As you can see in the exchange above, the phrase مِن فَضل is used along with the attached pronoun كَ. Any of the second-person attached pronouns (= كَ، كِ، كُما، كُم، كُنَّ) can be attached to this phrase to denote a polite request from someone or a group of people. A positive response to a request usually involves the use of a particular imperative verb تَفَضَّل/ تَفَضَّلي, which also signifies politeness. This verb carries many meanings that differ with respect to context.

For example, if someone has asked you if he/she can borrow your pen, it would be socially appropriate to use تَفَضَّل while handing the person your pen. In this instance,

تَفَضَّل could be roughly translated as "here you go." If you open the door for someone while saying تَفَضَّل, the meaning would be "come in"; if you seat someone while saying تَفَضَّل, it would mean "please (be seated)."



نعم. تَفَضّل. | مَعَكِ قَلَمٌ مِن فَضْلِكِ؟

## A. The Imperative

Requesting and offering something might involve the use of the imperative form of the verb you are using. Two imperative verbs أَعْطِ and تَفَضَّل are used in the dialogue found later in section C. The verb أَعْطِ 'give!' represents the second-person masculine singular conjugation, because it is *addressed to a man*.

- The imperative verb is not conjugated for the person speaking; it is conjugated for the person being addressed.

Likewise, the form تَفَضَّلي can be said by anyone, in fact, by any group of people, but it is addressed to an individual woman. There are basically five imperative forms of the Arabic verb corresponding to the five second-person pronouns. A table on the following page illustrates all of the possible forms of the imperative.

## B. Forming the Imperative

The imperative (command form) is formed from the present tense of any verb using the following steps:

1. Drop the prefix of the present-tense verb. If the letter following the prefix has a short vowel on it, do nothing (e.g., يَتَفَضَّلُ becomes تَفَضَّلْ; the تاء is followed by a فتحة).

Note that the final ضَمّة is also dropped:

Drop ضَمّة Retain فَتحة

١ يَتَفَضَّلُ ← تَفَضَّلْ

Drop ياء

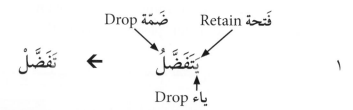

2. If the letter following the prefix is not followed by a vowel (that is, it has a سكون), replace the prefix with a همزة (*hamzat wasl*):

٢ يَكْتُبُ ← اُكْتُبْ

3. Place a فتحة on the initial همزة if the past-tense verb has four letters (e.g., أُعْطي → أَعْطِ), a ضَمّة if the middle short vowel of the present-tense verb has a ضَمّة (e.g., يَكْتُبُ → اُكْتُبْ); and a كسرة if the middle letter has a كسرة (e.g., يَجْلِسُ → اِجْلِسْ).

| Conjugation of أعطى (يُعْطي) | | | | |
|---|---|---|---|---|
| **Imperative** | **Present** | **Past** | **Pronoun** | **Person** |
| | أُعْطي | أَعْطَيْتُ | أنا | المُتَكَلِّم |
| | نُعْطي | أَعْطَيْنا | نَحنُ | |
| أَعْطِ | تُعْطي | أَعْطَيْتَ | أنتَ | المُخاطَب |
| أَعْطي | تُعْطِين | أَعْطَيْتِ | أنتِ | |
| أعطِيا | تُعطيانِ | أَعْطَيْتُما | أنتُما | |
| أَعْطوا | تُعْطون | أَعْطَيْتُم | أنتُم | |
| أَعْطين | تُعْطِين | أَعْطَيْتُنَّ | أنتُنَّ | |
| | يُعْطي | أَعْطى | هُوَ | الغائب |
| | تُعْطي | أَعْطَتْ | هِيَ | |
| | يُعطيانِ | أَعْطَيا | هُما | |
| | تُعطيانِ | أَعْطَتا | هُما | |
| | يُعْطون | أَعْطَوْا | هُم | |
| | يُعْطين | أَعْطَيْنَ | هُنَّ | |

| Imperative Forms of the Verb تَفَضَّل | | | | | |
|---|---|---|---|---|---|
| **Pronoun** | أنتَ | أنتِ | أنتما | أنتُم | أنتُنَّ |
| **Imperative** | تَفَضَّلْ | تَفَضَّلي | تَفَضَّلا | تَفَضَّلوا | تَفَضَّلْنَ |

### C. Doubly Transitive Verbs

Verbs that take an object are called transitive verbs. For example, in the sentence "I wrote a letter," the verb "wrote" is transitive because the word "letter" is the direct object of the verb "wrote." A limited number of verbs are transitive to two objects. One of them is the verb **أعْطى** 'to give'. In the sentence **أعْطِني جَريدةً** 'give me a newspaper' in the dialogue below, the two objects are the pronoun **ني** 'me' suffixed to the verb and the noun **جَريدةً** 'newspaper'.

- **Note:** The direct object of **أعْطى** will be in the accusative case; when indefinite, as in the example below, it will take a double **فتحة** on the final radical. When the direct object of a verb is definite, however, it will take a single **فتحة**.

أَعْطِني جَريدةً مِن فَضْلِكَ!

أيّةَ جَريدة؟

جَريدَةَ «الدُّسْتور» مِن فَضْلِك.

تَفَضَّل!

شُكراً!

عَفواً!

### D. Pronunciation of the Attached Pronoun هُ

AUDIO

As you know, this pronoun (pronounced *hu*) can only function as a suffix. However, if the preceding vowel is a **كسرة** (i.e., the short vowel *i*) or the long vowel **ي**, then it is pronounced *hi*. Listen to the recording and repeat during the pauses:

**فيهِ    إلَيْهِ    بِهِ    في بيتِهِ    أعْطِهِ**

## تمرين ١

**Conversation: Imperatives in use.** In groups of two, one person should pretend to be a newspaper vendor while the other is the buyer. The buyer will ask about various Arabic newspapers and magazines that were introduced in this lesson. Use the imperatives "give!" and "here you go" during this business transaction. **For a challenge** the vendor may wish to ask "which newspaper/magazine?" and ask for a lot of money, for example, "give me five American dollars!" Remember to be creative with the language and to use as much of your vocabulary as you can.

## تمرين ٢

**إِخْتَرِ الكَلِمَةَ المُناسِبَةَ حَسَبَ النَصّ:**

١- «الرافدين» ____________ عِراقيّة.

☐ مَكتبَةٌ ☐ مَجَلّةٌ ☐ جَريدَةٌ

٢- هُناكَ ____________ عَرَبيّةٌ في مَكتبَةِ الجامِعة.

☐ طالِباتٌ ☐ طُلاّبٌ وطالِباتٌ ☐ مَجَلاّتٌ وجَرائِدُ

٣- الفُنونُ ____________ مَغربيّة.

☐ جَريدةٌ ☐ مَجَلَّةٌ ☐ طالِبةٌ

٤- يَقرَأُ الجَرائِدَ العَرَبيَّةَ في المَكتَبَةِ طلاّبٌ ____________.

☐ أمريكيّونَ ☐ مِصْريّونَ ☐ يَعرِفونَ العَرَبيّة

٥- يَقرَأُ عَدنان مارتيني عادةً مَجَلَّةَ ____________.

☐ النَهار ☐ المَجَلّة ☐ المَعرِفة

٦- أَعْطى الرَجُلُ جَريدة ____________.

☐ الأهرام ☐ الدُسْتور ☐ تِشرين

٧- يَقرَأُ زِياد نابُلسي جَريدةَ ____________ عادةً.

☐ الأهرام ☐ الرافِدين ☐ تِشرينَ

٨- يَقرَأُ عَبدُ اللَطيف ____________.

☐ جَريدةً لُبنانيَّةً ☐ جَريدةً سوريّةً ☐ مَجَلّةً جزائريّةً

## تمرين ٣

**أكمِل الجُمَلَ التالية بكلماتٍ من المستطيل:**

| | | | | | | | | |
|---|---|---|---|---|---|---|---|---|
| تَفَضَّلي | آسِفَة | عادَةً | جَيِّداً | أيّة | مِن فَضْلِك | تَشَرَّفْنا | تَقرَأ | تكتُب |

١- ________ مَجَلّةٍ تَقرَأينَ يا هُدى؟

٢- أقرأُ مَجَلَّةَ العَرَبيّ ________.

٣- أينَ مَكتَبُ الأسْتاذِ طَبّاع ________.

٤- ________ لَيسَ مَعي قَلَم.

٥- يا طالِبَ اللُغةِ العَرَبيّةِ، هَل ________ جَريدةَ تشرين ؟

## تمرين ٤

**وافِقْ بَيْنَ الكَلِماتِ في العَمودَيْنِ** **Matching:**

| | | | |
|---|---|---|---|
| ١ | جَريدةٌ | | تَفَضَّلْ |
| ٢ | عادَةً | | مَعَهُ |
| ٣ | أعطِني | | مَجَلَّةٌ |
| ٤ | يَقرأ | | أحْياناً |
| ٥ | العَرَبي | | يَكْتُبُ |
| | | | الأهْرام |

## تمرين ٥

**Conversation: Scavenger hunt, using أعْطى، مِن فَضْلِك، تَفَضَّلْ**. In Arabic, politely ask for and return the following items to your neighbors. Be sure to write down the names of the people who gave you these items. Of course, the first one who completes the scavenger hunt wins.

1. a pair of sunglasses (solar glasses)
2. one biology or computer science book
3. three pencils
4. one identity card
5. two notebooks

Be prepared to report your "treasure" to your class.

## 3. Cases of the Noun

There are three cases of the noun in Arabic:

**A. The Nominative Case الرَّفع**

A noun is nominative مَرْفوع if:

1. it is the doer of the action, the agent, the *-er* form in English (like runner, writer, swimmer, etc.), or the subject of a verb in a verbal sentence. Like English, many Arabic words follow a form, that of **فاعِل**, which by no mere coincidence is the name for the active participle in Arabic **اِسمُ الفاعِل**. Consider the word **الطالِبُ** 'student' in the following example:

   *The student reads/is reading a newspaper* يَقرَأُ الطالِبُ جَريدَةً. ٣

2. it is the subject مُبْتَدَأ of a nominal sentence **الطالِبُ**, as in example 4

3. it is the predicate خَبَر of a nominal sentence **أمريكيٌّ**, as in example 4

٤ الطالِبُ أمريكيٌّ

**Note** that both nouns in example 4 are nominative, because they are the subject and predicate (topic and comment) of a nominal sentence, yet **الطالِبُ** is marked with a ضَمّة because it is definite, while **أمريكيٌّ** is marked with a double ضَمّة because it is indefinite.

- **Grammar note:** Singular Arabic nouns take two short vowels if indefinite and one if definite—exceptions are certain nouns called diptotes.

In the nominative case, the ending انِ is suffixed to dual nouns, and ونَ to sound masculine plurals.

٥ الطالِبانِ أمريكيّانِ. *The two students are American*

٦ الطُلّابُ أمريكيّونَ *The students are American.*

**B. The Genitive Case الجَـرُّ**

A noun is in the genitive case مَجْرور if:

1. it is the object of a preposition مَجْرورٌ بِحَرْفِ الجَرِّ

٧ في الصَفِّ *in the classroom*

2. it is the second part of an إضافة structure known as مُضاف إلَيْه

٨ مُخْتَبَرُ الكيمْياءِ. *the chemistry lab*

The genitive markers include the كسرة, the double كسرة, ـَيْنِ (*-ayni*) which appears on the final radical dual nouns, and ينَ (*-īna*) which appears on sound masculine plurals.

**C. The Accusative Case النَصْب**

This case is a bit more complex to define. But it can be readily said that if the noun is neither nominative nor genitive, then it is accusative مَنْصوب. We are already familiar with how to use النَصْب in two instances:

1. the direct object of a verb المَفْعول بِهِ:

٩ تَعرِفُ سَناء اللُغةَ الفَرَنسِيّةَ. *Sana knows the French language.*

2. the specification of quantity التَمْييز:

١٠ كَمْ كِتاباً عِندَكَ؟ *How many books do you have?*

١١ خَمْسونَ كِتاباً. *50 books*

- The accusative markers include the فتحة, double فتحة, ـَيْنِ (*-ayni*) for dual nouns, and ينَ (*-īna*) for sound masculine plurals.

## تمرين ٦

**Cases of the noun:** On a separate sheet of paper, rewrite each sentence giving the case of the underlined word(s) in each sentence. Provide the short vowels and then offer an explanation of why you chose that particular diacritic using Arabic terminology:

١- أستاذُ الصفّ مِن مَدينَةِ سوسة في تونِس.

٢- السَيّارة في الشارِع.

٣- كَمْ طالِب في الصَفّ؟

٤- يَعرِفُ أحمَد عُنوان هالَة.

٥- يَعرِفُ مايكل اللُغة العَرَبيّة قليلاً.

٦- تكتُبُ الطالِبة على وَرَقة في دَفْتَرِها.

٧- يَقرَأُ عَبدُ اللطيف كِتاب.

٨- مِفتاح سَيّارة الأستاذ في سَيّارتِه!

### 4. Expressing Possession with the Prepositions لِـ and مَعَ

Possession has been expressed so far with the adverb of place عِندَ followed by a noun or an attached pronoun. Consider the example:

١٢ عِندَ سامي سَيّارةٌ *Sami has a car.* عِندي سَيّارةٌ. *I have a car.*

Possession may also be expressed with the preposition لِـ by attaching either a pronoun or a noun to لِـ.

١٣ لي أُخْتانِ. *I have two sisters.* لِعادِلٍ أُخْتانِ. *Adil has two sisters.*

Like عِندي, the prepositional phrase لي may be translated as "I have"; although no verbs are involved in either case in Arabic.

**Note** that لِـ and عِندَ may not be used interchangeably. With reference to people, both the preposition لِـ and the adverb عِندَ may be used to express possession of something whether acquired or inherent (e.g., I have a car; I have two hands), but when it is used with reference to inanimate objects, only لِـ may be used:

١٤ لِغُرفَتي شُبّاكان *My room has two windows*

- **Note:** When the preposition لِـ (*li-*) is prefixed to a noun, it is pronounced *li*, but when prefixed to a pronoun, it is pronounced *la* (e.g., لَهُ، لَنا، لَكِ).

The use of the preposition مَعَ (Arab grammarians consider it an adverb) with a possessive pronoun (e.g., مَعي) denotes a form of possession. The phrase مَعي قَلَم, for example, means "I have a pen with me." In this context, this preposition means "along with," or "on my person," to be differentiated from عِندَ which alludes to a worldly possession.

## تمرين ٧

**Translation:** Express possession, using عِندَ, لِـ, and مَعَ:

1. Reema [feminine name] has two bicycles.

   ______________________________.

2. Our house has three doors.

   ______________________________.

3. Ahmed has got a car [with him] now.

   ______________________________.

4. I have a brother and a sister.

   ______________________________.

5. Do you have your eyeglasses on you?

   ______________________________.

6. Mrs. Boustani has a son and a daughter.

   ______________________________.

## 5. Attached Pronouns Suffixed to Verbs

So far, we have seen attached pronouns suffixed to nouns where they function as possessive pronouns (e.g., كِتابي 'my book', قَلَمُها 'her pen'). However, when these pronouns are suffixed to verbs and prepositions they serve as object pronouns, such as the English "him," "them," etc.

١٥ أعرِفُ ثَلاثَ لُغاتٍ وأتَكَلَّمُها جَيِّداً.

In example 15, the highlighted suffix ها (third-person feminine singular) in أَتكلّمُها means "them" (not "it" or "she") because this attached pronoun refers back to لُغات, which is a non-rational plural.

- **Remember:** Non-rational (i.e., inanimate) plurals are treated as feminine singular. This means that *any reference to such plurals is made in the third-person feminine singular, regardless of the gender of the singular noun.*

You will notice that pronouns attached to verbs are the very same pronouns that we attach to nouns and prepositions. There exists one exception, however; the first-person singular pronoun ي becomes ني when suffixed to verbs:

| | |
|---|---|
| *Nadia knows me from the university.* | ١٦ تَعرِفُني نادية مِنَ الجامِعة. |

## تمرين ٨

**Translation:** Translate the sentences below, providing the appropriate forms of the verbs with the correct attached pronouns. A reference table follows this exercise.

1. I know her.

   ________________________________.

2. He gave us a newspaper.

   ________________________________.

3. They (m.) know Arabic and speak it at home.

   ________________________________.

4. Give me (addressing a man) that magazine, please.

   ________________________________.

5. They (f.) know me.

   ________________________________.

6. Do you (f.) know them (m.)?

   ________________________________.

7. Give him (addressing a woman) your phone number.

   ________________________________.

| Attached Pronouns suffixed to Verbs | | | | | | | | | | | | | |
|---|---|---|---|---|---|---|---|---|---|---|---|---|---|
| الضمير المُنْفَصِل | أنا | نَحنُ | أنتَ | أنتِ | أنتُما | أنتُم | أنتُنَّ | هُوَ | هِيَ | هُما | هُما | هُم | هُنَّ |
| الضمير المتَصِل | ني | نا | كَ | كِ | كُما | كُم | كُنَّ | هُ | ها | هُما | هُما | هُم | هُنَّ |

## 6. More on Arabic Names

## تَذَوَّق الثَّقافة العَرَبيّة

Most Arabic first names have meanings. For example, the name **وَليد** (m.) means "boy" or "newborn," and the name **تَهاني** (f.) means "congratulations." There are also compound names (e.g., **عَبْدُ الله**). Such compound names containing **عَبْدُ** are only for males. The first word **عَبْدُ** means "servant, slave, creature." The second word is either **الله** 'God' or any one of the 99 other names of Allah, such as **عَبْدُ اللَطيف** and **عَبْدُ الهادي** (pronounced *abdu-l-laṭīf* and *abdu-l-hādī*). Thus, the popular belief that the word *Abdul* is an Arabic name is partially mistaken, since this word represents only the first part of the name **عَبْدُ** plus the definite article **الـ** of the second part.

## تمرين ٩

**Foreign names in news articles:** Examine these excerpts from an Arabic magazine and circle the foreign names that you can identify and then transcribe them in English. Five names appear in the first excerpt (on the right) and three in the second.

يقول جون كلارك غيبل "لقد قررت أن أجرب حظي في التمثيل عندما أحضر كلايد وير نص الفيلم (جيم السيئ) لأنني أحببته كثيراً. سأمثل هذا الفيلم مع ممثلين مجربين هما جيمس برولين وريتشارد راوندتري."

ساهم الكاتبان غراهم غرين وجون لو كاريه في ظهور نوع جديد من أدب الرواية الجاسوسية يتحدث عن جرائم فظيعة ترتكب على كلا الجانبين من جدار برلين أيام الحرب الباردة.

## تمرين ١٠

**Listen and select:**

**A.** Listen to the recorded passage and check the best alternative according to the passage.

١- أحمَد زَوج __________ .

☐ فاطِمة ☐ رانِية ☐ سَميرَة

٢- يَقرَأُ أحمَد جَريدَةَ __________ أحياناً.

☐ الدُستورِ ☐ الشَرقِ الأوسَطِ ☐ الأهرامِ

٣- فَريد __________ فاطِمة.

☐ اِبنُ ☐ زَوجُ ☐ أبو

**B.** Complete these sentences according to the information in the passage:

٤- فاطِمة لَها اِبنَتانِ هُما __________ و__________.

٥- تَقرَأُ فاطِمةُ جَريدةَ __________ .

٦- يَقرَأُ أحمَد عادةً جَريدةَ __________ .

**C.** **صواب أو خطأ** On the basis of the information in the recorded passage, mark these statements **خَطأ** or **صَواب** and correct the false ones.

٧- يَقرأُ أحمَدُ مَجَلّةَ الهِلال.

٨- سَميرة أُخْتُ بَشير.

٩- تَسكُنُ عائِلةُ أحمَد في عُمان.

## تمرين ١١

**تَمرينُ المُشاهَدة: شاهِدوا الدَرْسَ السابعَ على القُرْص الرَقْميّ.**

١- لماذا يُحِبُّ جون قِراءةَ الجَرائِدِ العَرَبيَّة؟ ______________________

______________________________________

٢- أَيّةَ جَريدةٍ يَقرَأ جون؟ ______________________

______________________________________

٣- أينَ المَحَلُّ الذي يَبيعُ الجَرائدَ العَرَبيَّةَ؟ ______________________

______________________________________

## المُفْرَدات

Listen to the vocabulary items on the CD and practice their pronunciation.

أَحَبَّ (يُحِبُّ) حُبّ، مَحَبّة (v.) . . . . . . . . . . . . . . . . . . . to like

أَحياناً (adv.) . . . . . . . . . . . . . . . . . . sometimes

أرادَ (يُريدَ) إرادة (v.) . . . . . . . . . . . . . . . . . . . to want

أعطى (يُعطي) أَعْطِ (imperative) (v.) . . . . . . . . . . . . . to give

إعْطاء (verbal noun) . . . . . . . . . . . . . . . . . . . giving

أيّ (n., m.) / أَيّةُ (n., f.) . . . . . . . . . . . . . . . . . which

باعَ (يَبيعُ) بَيْع (v.) . . . . . . . . . . . . . . . . . . . . to sell

تَفَضَّلْ/ تَفَضَّلي (imperative) (v.) . . . . . . . . . . . . . if you please

عادَةً (adv.) . . . . . . . . . . . . . . . . . . . . usually

فَعَلَ (يَفعَلُ) فِعْل (v.) . . . . . . . . . . . . . . . . . . . . to do

قَرَأَ (يَقرَأُ) قِراءة (v.) . . . . . . . . . . . . . . . . . . . . to read

قُرْب (adv.) . . . . . . . . . . . . . . . . . . . nearby, close

كَتَبَ (يَكْتُبُ) كِتابة (v.) . . . . . . . . . . . . . . . . . . . to write

مَجَلّة ج مَجَلاّت (n., f.) . . . . . . . . . . . . . . . . . . . magazine

مِنْ فَضْلِك (polite phrase) . . . . . . . . . . . . . . . . please

# الدَرسُ الثامِن

## Objectives

- Requesting and declining things politely
- Expressing likes and dislikes
- Introduction to adverbials of time صَباحاً، مَساءً
- Introduction to food and drink
- Describing daily activities
- Revisiting the imperative
- Revisiting prepositions and attached pronouns
- Introduction to plurals of nouns
- Revisiting the إضافة structure (multiple إضافة)

## الكَلِماتُ المُفيدةُ في صُوَرٍ عَديدة:

أَكَلَ (يَأْكُلُ) أَكْل

شَرِبَ (يَشْرَبُ) شُرْب

أَحَبَّ (يُحِبُّ) حُبّ

شايٌ

بَيْض

خُبْزٌ

جُبْنٌ

حَليبٌ

فنجان قَهْوةٍ

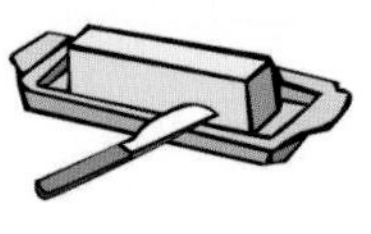

زُبْدةٌ

تُفّاحةٌ

بُرتُقالةٌ

# شاياً من فضلِك!

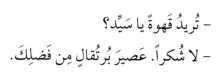

- تُريدينَ قَهْوَةً يا آنِسة؟
- لا. شُكراً. شاياً مِن فَضلِكَ.
- مَعَ السُكَّر؟
- نَعَم.
- حاضِر.

- تُريدُ قَهوَةً يا سَيِّد؟
- لا شُكراً. عَصيرَ بُرتُقالٍ مِن فَضلِكَ.

**Reflecting on our reading:** The waiters use the verb أرادَ in the preceding dialogues. Notice how in the cartoon bubbles the waiters express the same question without using the verb أرادَ. Based on this information, can you deduce the meaning of our mystery verb? The patrons do not use أرادَ, but they very well could have. Where would the verbs go in the preceding patrons' dialogues and what conjugations should the patrons use?

## 1. Requesting and Declining Things Politely

In the preceding dialogues, the woman and the man politely decline what the waiter is offering by using the expression لا شُكراً. They request their preferences politely by directly stating what they want followed by the phrase مِن فَضلِك 'if you please'.

- **Note** how the two waiters have used the appropriate terms to address their patrons (آنِسة and سَيِّد). Also, notice how the waiter responds to a request by using the word حاضِر 'ready, all set', meaning that the order will be placed right away.

## 2. Expressing Likes and Dislikes

The verb أَحَبَّ / يُحِبُّ 'to like' is used in roughly the same manner as its English counterpart. In order to express dislike, we precede the same verb with the negative particle لا.

| | | |
|---|---|---|
| *I like orange juice.* | أُحِبُّ عَصيرَ البُرتُقالِ. | ١ |
| *I don't like milk.* | لا أُحِبُّ الحَليبَ. | ٢ |

Remember that the noun (e.g., عَصيرَ البُرتُقالِ، الحليبَ) following أُحِبُّ 'I like' is the object of this verb and it must, therefore, be in the accusative case marked by a فتحة for singular definite nouns, or يْنِ for dual and ينَ for sound masculine plurals.

## 3. Adverbials of Time

An adverbial modifies a verb and indicates the time, place, or manner in which an action occurred. Usually, the adverbial is an indefinite noun to which a double فتحة is suffixed, indicating that it is in the accusative case نَصْب. The adverbial meaning may also be expressed with a prepositional phrase. For example, صَباحاً 'in the morning' may be expressed as a prepositional phrase: في الصَباحِ. Consider these two examples:

٣ صَباح ← صَباحاً مَساء ← مَساءً

Note that the noun in the prepositional phrase is always definite. The same preposition may be used to refer to the evening في المَساءِ. But with reference to noontime, another preposition is used: عِندَ الظُهْرِ. While the use of prepositions with respect to time may not seem intuitive at first, look again—for the Arabic pattern exactly mirrors the English "in the morning/evening" = في الصَباحِ/ المَساءِ and "at noon" = عِندَ الظُهْرِ. As you may have guessed, ظُهْراً is the adverbial of the prepositional phrase عِندَ الظُهْرِ.

Adverbials are extremely handy words that can describe frequency such as عادَةً 'usually; habitually' and أَحْياناً 'sometimes'. Another adverbial that can readily become part of your linguistic repertoire is كَثيراً 'a lot'. It is based on the adjective كَثير 'much'. This adverbial is used in the following passage to modify the verb أُحِبُّ, expressing degree, as in أُحِبُّ العَسَلَ كَثيراً 'I like honey very much.'

- **Error Prevention:** A common mistake among language learners is to confuse **كثيرة** (an adjective used to modify a single feminine noun or an inanimate plural) with **كثيراً** (an adverb that is used to modify verbs). Consider the examples:

٤ هُناكَ أوْراقٌ كثيرةٌ على مَكتَبي.

٥ أُحِبُّ البيتزا كثيراً وآكُلُها كثيراً.

## تمرين ١

**Adverbials in conversation:** With a partner, make a list of foods that you like and the degree you like them (a lot, a little). Mention the times of day (morning/afternoon/evening) that you (sometimes/usually) eat these foods. Be prepared to report both your and your partner's responses to the class.

## 4. Food and Drink

The types of foods and drinks consumed in different cultures and the manner in which people consume them vary tremendously. The following paragraphs illustrate the types of food and drink consumed at breakfast in the Arab and American cultures.

### ماذا يَشرَبونَ ويأكُلونَ صَباحاً؟

AUDIO

هذا مايكل براون. يَشرَبُ مايكل صَباحاً فِنجانَ قَهوَةٍ مَعَ الحَليبِ والسُكَّرِ. ويأكُلُ مايكل في الصَباحِ الحُبوبَ مَعَ الحَليبِ عادةً. لكِنَّ مايكل الآنَ في القاهِرةِ ويَأكُلُ هُناكَ صَباحاً الخُبْزَ والجُبْنَ والبَيْضَ ويَشرَبُ الشاي. يُحِبُّ مايكل القَهوةَ العَرَبيّةَ أيْضاً.

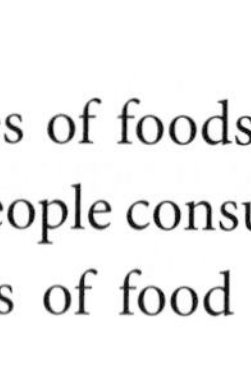

كأسُ ماءٍ

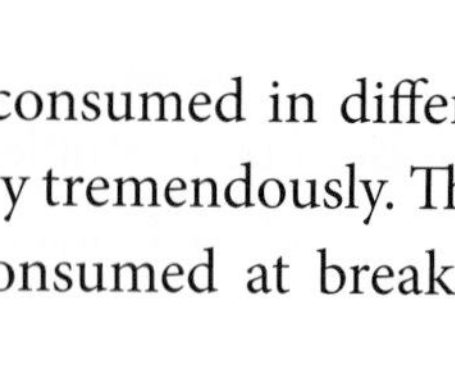

عَسَلٌ

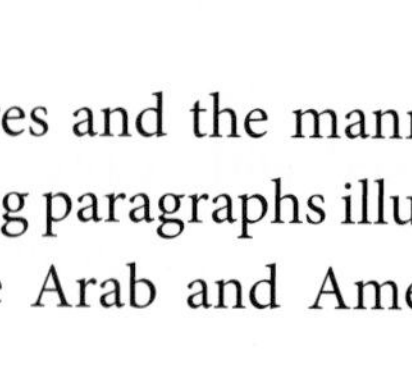

الحُبوبُ مَعَ الحَليبِ

هذِه هالة بُستاني. تَشرَبُ هالة كأسَ ماءٍ صَباحاً وتأكُلُ الخُبْزَ والجُبْنَ والزَيتونَ مَعَ فِنجانِ شاي. تَشرَبُ هالة الشايَ مَعَ السُكَّرِ عادةً في الصَباحِ لكِنَّها تَشرَبُ القَهوةَ دونَ سُكَّرٍ أحياناً.

هذِه كاثي وايت. هي تَدرُسُ اللُغةَ العَرَبيّةَ في جامِعَةِ آركانسو. تَشرَبُ كاثي فِنجانَ قهْوةٍ صَباحاً دونَ سُكَّرٍ أو تَشرَبُ كَأسَ عَصيرِ بُرتُقالٍ، لكِنّها لا تَشرَبُ الشاي. تَأْكُلُ قِطْعَةَ خُبْزٍ مَعَ الزُبدَةِ ومُرَبّى البُرتُقالِ أو العَسَلِ.

- يَأْكُلُ الأمريكيّونَ صَباحاً الحُبوبَ مَعَ الحَليبِ عادةً أو البَيْض ولَحْمَ الخِنْزيرِ ويَشرَبونَ عَصيرَ البُرتُقالِ أوِ القَهْوةَ أوِ الحَليب.
- يَأْكُلُ الفِرَنسِيّونَ عادةً الخُبْزَ والمُرَبّى في الصَباحِ ويَشرَبونَ القَهْوةَ.
- يَأْكُلُ العَرَبُ عادةً الخُبْزَ والجُبْنَ والزَيْتونَ صَباحاً ويَشرَبونَ الشاي.

وأنتَ يا طالِبَ اللُغَةِ العَرَبيَّةِ ماذا تَشرَبُ صَباحاً وماذا تأكُل؟

## 5. Describing Daily Activities

Describing activities involves the use of verbs. Some activities are performed habitually (e.g., eat), others are in progress (e.g., am eating). The former type of activity is described by the simple present in English and the latter by the present continuous, or progressive. In Arabic, the simple present is called the indicative, or **المُضارِع المَرفوع**, which is used for both the habitual and progressive aspects (e.g., **أقرأ** 'I read/am reading').

### ماذا يَفْعَلُ مايكل براون؟

أنا مايكل براون. أدْرُسُ اللُغَةَ العَرَبِيَّةَ في الجامِعَةِ الأمريكيَّةِ في القاهِرةِ في هذا الفَصْلِ الدِراسيّ. أسْكُنُ في شَقَّةٍ في شارِعِ المازنيّ. آكُلُ عادةً في شَقَّتي صَباحاً الخُبزَ والبَيْض وأشرَبُ الشاي. عِندَ الظُهرِ آكُلُ أحْياناً في مَطْعَمٍ اِسمُهُ «نِعْمة». آكُلُ هُناكَ الفولَ أو الطَعميَّةَ (الفلافِل). أُحِبُّ الفولَ والطَعْمِيَّةَ كثيراً، لكِنَّني لا أُحِبُّ اللَحْمَ. أحياناً آكُلُ سَلَطةً في مَقْصَفِ الجامِعَةِ. مَساءً آكُلُ في مَقْصَفِ الجامِعَةِ أو في مَطعَمٍ أو في شَقّتي.

# تمرين ٢

**Conversation: Eating in the Middle East.** In groups of two, pretend that you, like Michael, are eating breakfast, lunch, and dinner in an Arab city. Ask your partner how much, or how little, he or she would like the Middle Eastern plates that Michael mentioned. Record your answers on a separate sheet of paper and be prepared to report them to your class.

## زِياد يَقْرَأُ الجَريدة

AUDIO

أقرَأُ جَريدةَ النَهارِ وأشرَبُ قَهوةً.

- مَرْحَباً زِياد. ماذا تَفْعَلُ هُنا؟
- أقْرَأُ الجَريدةَ وأشرَبُ قَهوَةً. تَفَضَّلي اِجْلِسي، يا هادية.
- لا شُكراً. أيَّةَ جَريدَةٍ تَقْرَأ ؟
- جَريدَةَ النَهار. هُناكَ قَهوَةٌ في المَطْبَخ.
- لا أُريدُ قَهوَةً. شُكراً. أشرَبُ الشاي.

# تمرين ٣

**A. Listen and recognize:** Check the box that matches the information as expressed in the passages and dialogues for this lesson.

١- الآنِسةُ في ______________ .

☐ غُرفَةِ الصَفِّ ☐ المَطْعَمِ ☐ البَيْتِ

٢- يُريدُ الرَجُلُ ______________ .

☐ كأسَ ماءٍ ☐ فِنجانَ قَهوةٍ ☐ عَصيرَ بُرتُقالٍ

٣- مايكل براون في مِصرَ الآن. يأكُلُ صَباحاً ______________ .

☐ البَيْض ☐ الفولَ ☐ الحُبوبَ

٤- يُحِبُّ مايكل ______________ أيْضاً.

☐ القَهوةَ الأمريكيّةَ ☐ القَهوةَ العَربيّةَ ☐ الشايَ

٥- تَشرَبُ هالة بُستاني القَهوة ______________ .

☐ مَعَ سُكَّر ☐ دونَ سُكَّر ☐ مَعَ العَسَل

٦- تأكُلُ كاثي وايت صَباحاً الخُبزَ و ____________ .

☐ لَحْمَ الخِنزيرِ ☐ البَيْضَ ☐ العَسَلَ

٧- يأكُلُ مايكل الطَعْميّةَ في ____________ .

☐ مَقْصَفِ الجامِعَةِ ☐ مَطْعَمِ نِعمة ☐ شَقّتِه

٨- لا يُحِبُّ مايكل ____________ .

☐ السَلَطَةَ ☐ الفَلافِلَ ☐ اللَحْمَ

٩- يَقرَأُ زِياد ____________ .

☐ كِتاباً ☐ مَجَلَّةً ☐ جَريدةً

١٠- يَجلِسُ زِياد في ____________ .

☐ البَيْتِ ☐ الشارِعِ ☐ المَطْبَخِ

**B. صواب أو خطأ:** On a separate sheet of paper, mark these sentences either **خَطَأ** or **صَواب** according to the information in the reading passages and correct the false ones.

١١- يَشرَبُ مايكل القَهوةَ مَعَ الحَليبِ والسُكَّر.

١٢- تأكُلُ هالَة قِطعةَ خُبزٍ مَعَ الزُبدةِ والعَسَلِ صَباحاً.

١٣- تَشرَبُ كاثي كأسَ عَصيرِ بُرتُقالٍ صَباحاً.

١٤- تُريدُ هادية فِنجانَ قَهوة.

**C. Comprehension questions:** On a separate sheet of paper, answer the following questions on the basis of the information in the reading passages.

١٥- مَتى (when) يَشرَبُ مايكل الشاي في القاهِرة؟

١٦- مَتى تَشرَبُ هالَة الشاي؟

١٧- ماذا تأكُلُ كاثي صَباحاً؟

١٨- أينَ يأكُلُ مايكل ظُهراً؟

## تمرين ٤

**Odd word out:** Underline the word that does not belong to each set and explain your choice if needed.

| | | | | |
|---|---|---|---|---|
| ١- | فول | طَعْمِيّة | مُرَبّى | فَلافِل |
| ٢- | دونَ | ظُهْر | صَباح | مَساء |
| ٣- | عَصير | شاي | قهوة | بُرتُقال |
| ٤- | ماء | حَليب | خُبْز | شاي |

## تمرين ٥

**Matching:**

وافِق بَينَ الكَلِماتِ في العَمودَين:

| | | | |
|---|---|---|---|
| ١ | شاي | | مَساءً |
| ٢ | مُرَبّى | | حاضِر |
| ٣ | لَحْم | | قَهوَة |
| ٤ | صَباحاً | | بُرتُقال |
| ٥ | مَعَ | | عَسَل |
| ٦ | مَطْعَم | | كَأس |
| ٧ | يَشرَب | | خِنزير |
| ٨ | عَصير | | دونَ |
| | | | مَقصَف |
| | | | يأكُل |

## تمرين ٦

**اِخْتَرِ الكَلِمةَ المُناسِبة:**

١- أشرَبُ صَباحاً ________________ .

☐ قِطعَةَ خُبْزٍ ☐ عَصيرَ بُرتُقالٍ ☐ لَحْمَ خِنزيرٍ

٢- يأكُلُ سامي في ________________ عِندَ الظُهْر.

☐ مَطْعَمٍ ☐ مَكتَبٍ ☐ كُلِّيَّةٍ

٣- يأكُلُ أبي صَباحاً الزُبدةَ مَعَ ________________ .

☐ الزَيتونِ ☐ الجُبْنِ ☐ العَسَلِ

٤- تَشرَبُ أُخْتي صَباحاً ________________ فَقَط.

☐ الماءَ ☐ المَقصَفَ ☐ المُرَبّى

٥- يأكُلُ الأمريكيّونَ في الصَباحِ عادةً ________________ مَعَ الحَليب.

☐ القَهوةَ ☐ السُكَّرَ ☐ الحُبوبَ

## تمرين ٧

**Rearranging words:** Rearrange the words in each item to make meaningful sentences.

١- مِن، كأسَ، أريدُ، فَضلِكَ، ماءٍ

______________________________

٢- صَباحاً، سَمير، وَالجُبْنَ، الشايَ، ويَشرَبُ، الخُبْزَ، يأكُلُ

______________________________

٣- اللَحْمَ، الفَلافِلَ، يُحِبُّ، يُحِبُّ، لكِنَّهُ، مايكل، لا

______________________________

# تمرين ٨

**Likes and dislikes:** List three things you like and three things you do not like. For an extra challenge provide inflectional markers on the ends of words.

١- ________________________________________.

٢- ________________________________________.

٣- ________________________________________.

٤- ________________________________________.

٥- ________________________________________.

٦- ________________________________________.

## 6. The Imperative

The imperative form of the verb جَلَسَ 'to sit' is اِجلِسْ for the second-person masculine and اِجلِسي for the second-person feminine. The latter form is used in the dialogue on p. 140. It immediately follows another imperative verb تفضَّلي 'if you please', which is also imperative. The imperative is one of three forms of the Arabic verb: past, present, and imperative. It is normally used with the second person, as you can see in the table titled **Conjugation of** جَلَسَ on the following page.

**Notice** the changes which the verb undergoes in the imperative form. First remove the stem of the present tense (يجلِس → جلِس), then add a همزة with a كسرة prefixed اِجلِسْ. This is the form for the second-person masculine singular. The dual takes an ألف for a suffix (e.g., اِجلِسا), the masculine plural takes the long vowel و and a final *silent* ألف (اِجلِسوا), and the feminine plural takes نَ as a suffix. Contemplate and memorize the conjugations found in the following table.

| Conjugation of جَلَسَ (يَجْلِسُ) | | | |
|---|---|---|---|
| Imperative الأمْر | Present المُضارِع | Pronoun الضَمير | Person |
| | أَجْلِسُ | أنا | المُتَكَلِّم |
| | نَجْلِسُ | نَحْنُ | |
| اِجْلِسْ | تَجْلِسُ | أَنْتَ | المُخاطَب |
| اِجْلِسي | تَجْلِسينَ | أَنْتِ | |
| اِجْلِسا | تَجْلِسانِ | أَنْتُما | |
| اِجْلِسوا | تَجْلِسونَ | أَنْتُم | |
| اِجْلِسْنَ | تَجْلِسْنَ | أَنْتُنَّ | |
| | يَجْلِسُ | هُوَ | الغائب |
| | تَجْلِسُ | هِيَ | |
| | يَجْلِسانِ | (المُذَكَّر) هُما | |
| | تَجْلِسانِ | (المؤنَّث) هُما | |
| | يَجْلِسونَ | هُم | |
| | يَجْلِسْنَ | هُنَّ | |

## تمرين ٩

**The imperative:** Write down how you would politely ask the following people to sit down. Consider the example:

مِثال: اِجلِسا مِن فَضْلِكُما

1. A woman .________________________
2. A mixed group of five .________________________
3. A man .________________________
4. Four women .________________________
5. Three boys .________________________

## 7. Prepositions and Attached Pronouns

Attached pronouns may be suffixed to prepositions. In the exchange below, the first-person singular attached pronoun ي 'me' is suffixed to the preposition مِن 'from', resulting in مِنّي *minnī* 'from me'.

## 8. Plurals of Nouns

### A. Sound Masculine Plurals جَمْع مُذَكَّر سالِم

Some masculine nouns do not undergo any internal changes when put into the plural form. Such a noun usually refers to humans and is made plural by suffixing ونَ to it if it is the subject of a sentence (nominative رفع) and by ينَ if it is the object of a verb (accusative نصب) or a preposition (genitive جر). Such nouns are called **sound masculine plurals**:

| الجَرُّ والنَّصْب | الرَّفْع | المُفرَد |
|---|---|---|
| أمريكيّين | أمريكيّون | أمريكيّ |

Such nouns are called "sound" because no internal changes in the word occur and the same sequence of letters is retained intact in the plural form.

### B. Sound Feminine Plurals جَمع مُؤَنَّث سالِم

Some feminine plurals display the ending ات (e.g., ساعات / ساعة). These are called **sound feminine plurals**, since no internal changes ever take place. Note that the ة must be dropped before the suffix ات is attached. Case markers are indicated on the end of the plural suffix. Only two types exist and they are illustrated below:

1. A ضَمّة or double ضَمّة for the nominative رَفع:

ساعاتٌ ساعاتُ ٦

2. A كسرة or double كسرة for the accusative نَصب and the genitive جَرّ:

ساعاتٍ ساعاتِ ٧

### C. Broken Plurals جَمْع تَكسير

Other nouns, feminine and masculine, are made plural through internal changes whereby addition and/or deletion of long and short vowels occur. These are called **broken plurals**. A small sampling of those we have come into contact thus far follows:

| | | | |
|---|---|---|---|
| جَريدة ج جَرائد | بَيْت ج بُيوت | باب ج أبواب | أُسْتاذ ج أساتِذة |
| حَقيبة ج حَقائب | حَقّ ج حُقوق | حاسوب ج حواسيب | جِدار ج جُدران |
| صَفّ ج صُفوف | صُورة ج صُوَر | ساعة ج ساعات | دَفْتَر ج دَفاتِر |
| قَلَم ج أقْلام | غُرفة ج غُرَف | عِلم ج عُلوم | طالِب ج طُلاب |
| مِفتاح ج مَفاتيح | مَدينة ج مُدُن | كُرسي ج كراسٍ | كِتاب ج كُتُب |
| وَرَقة ج أوْراق | هاتِف ج هواتِف | نافِذة ج نوافِذ | مَكتَب ج مَكاتِب |

Note that the consonants remain unchanged in the plural form. Only short and long vowels are dropped, added, or their positions changed. Case markers appear on the end of the plural form just as they would on the end of a singular form:

| الجَرُّ | النَصْبُ | الرَفْعُ |
|---|---|---|
| كُتُبٍ | كُتُباً | كُتُبٌ |

You are strongly advised to memorize and practice the plural form of a noun along with the singular.

## SUMMARY

- Sound masculine plural nouns are formed by suffixing ون to subjects and ين to objects.
- Sound feminine plural nouns are formed by suffixing ات to the noun.
- Broken plurals are formed through internal changes in the word.

## تمرين ١٠

**Grammar identification:** Underline all sound masculine plural nouns and adjectives, place a dotted line under sound feminine plurals, and draw a box around broken plurals, as in the examples. There may be more than one plural form in each sentence.

مِثال: أساتِذةٌ أمريكيّونَ أمينات مَكتَبات طُلابٌ عَربٌ

١- السَيّاراتُ اليابانِيَّةُ سَيّاراتٌ جَيِّدةٌ.

٢- هؤلاءِ طُلاّبٌ ماليزيّونَ.

٣- هُناكَ بَناتٌ وأبناءٌ كثيرونَ في عائِلاتِ المِصريّينَ.

٤- في كُلِّيَّتي حواسيبُ كَثيرة.

٥- يأكُلُ السوريّونَ الجُبنَ والزَيتونَ صَباحاً.

٦- مَن مَعَهُ أقلامٌ في حَقيبتِه؟

## تمرين ١١

**Translation: Broken plurals.** Express these sentences in Arabic in which the broken plural has been used. Use the broken plural chart in part C of section 8.

1. We have three French (female) students in our class.

______________________________________________.

2. I have three pencils with me.

______________________________________________.

3. There are five telephones in this room.

______________________________________.

4. Do you know any Egyptian students?

______________________________________.

5. There are three tables and six chairs in the teachers' room.

______________________________________.

## تمرين ١٢

**A taste of the Middle East:** Take a close look at the menu on the following page. See if you can identify the eight foreign words. Once you are through, split up into groups of three. One person will play the waiter, and the other two people will play the part of the patrons. Emulate the dialogues that appeared at the beginning of this lesson by using the proper greetings, terms of address, and language used for taking and giving orders. Use the menu to make your orders. Be creative with the language, and use as much vocabulary from this lesson and the menu as possible.

# اللحومات

| | الوزن غ | السعر ل.س |
|---|---|---|
| سودة غنم مع بطاطا وخضرة وليمون | ٢٥٠ | ١٢٥ |
| بيض غنم مقلي مع بطاطا وخضرة وليمون | ١٥٠ | ١٤٠ |
| كلاوي غنم مع بطاطا وخضرة وليمون | ٢٥٠ | ١٢٥ |
| سودة دجاج مع بطاطا وخضرة وليمون | ٢٥٠ | ١٠٠ |
| نخاع بانيه + بطاطا وليمون | عدد١ | ٩٠ |
| نخاع مقلي + بطاطا وليمون | عدد١ | ٩٠ |
| نخاع مع البيض | عدد١ | ١٢٥ |
| نخاع سلطة مع خضرة وليمون | عدد١ | ٩٠ |
| سلطة لسانات | عدد١ | ١٠٠ |
| اسكالوب دجاج بانيه | ٢٠٠ | ١٤٥ |
| اسكالوب لحم بانيه | ٢٠٠ | ١٧٥ |
| شيش طاووق مع بطاطا وخضرة | ٢٠٠ | ١٢٥ |
| كوردون بلو لحم مع بطاطا وخضرة | ٢٥٠ | ٢٥٠ |
| اسكالوب دجاج بلو | ٢٥٠ | ٢٥٠ |
| شيش طاووق مع الفطر مع بطاطا | ٢٥٠ | ١٥٠ |
| شرحات مطفاية مع بطاطا وخضرة وليمون | ٢٥٠ | ١٢٥ |
| شرحات مع الفطر مع بطاطا وخضرة وليمون | ٢٥٠ | ١٥٠ |
| بيض مع لحمة | ١٥٠ | ١٢٥ |
| بيض مقلي عيون | عدد٣ | ٥٠ |
| مفركة فطر بلحمة وبصل | ١٠٠ | ١٠٠ |
| همبرغر مع البيض مع بطاطا | ٢٠٠ | ١١٠ |
| همبرغر مع جبنة مع بطاطا | ٢٠٠ | ١٣٠ |
| حمص باللحمة والصنوبر | ١٥٠ | ١٠٠ |
| سمك فيليه مع بطاطا وخضرة وليمون وطرطور | ٢٥٠ | ٢٥٠ |
| نقانق مع بطاطا وخضرة وليمون | ٢٥٠ | ١٢٥ |

# المقبلات

| | | صحن ١٥٠ غ |
|---|---|---|
| بابا غنوج | | ٣٠ |
| متبل | | ٣٠ |
| حمص ناعم | | ٣٠ |
| فتوش | | ٣٠ |
| تبولة | | ٣٠ |
| سلطة ناعمة | | ٣٠ |
| سلطة زيتون | | ٣٠ |
| سلطة شوندر | | ٣٠ |
| سلطة جرجير | | ٣٠ |
| حمص بيروتي | | ٣٠ |
| حمص بسمنة | | ٥٠ |
| حمص حب بلبن | | ٤٠ |
| حمص حب بزيت | | ٣٥ |
| فول بزيت | | ٣٥ |
| فول بلبن | ٢٥٠ غ | ٤٠ |
| بطاطا | | ٣٠ |
| سلطة فطر | | ٥٠ |
| سلطة ذرة | | ٥٠ |
| سلطة مايونيز ( روسية ) | | ٣٠ |
| يالنجي قطعة ٥ | | ٣٥ |
| لبن بخيار | | ٣٠ |
| لبنة مع زيت | ٧٥ غ | ٣٠ |
| جبنة | ١٥٠ غ | ٣٠ |
| جبنة قشقوان | ٧٥ غ | ٣٥ |
| جبنة مقلية | ١٠٠ غ | ٣٥ |

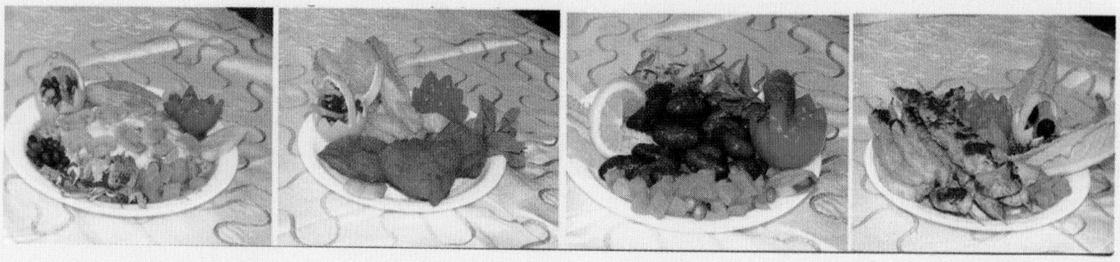

## 9. إضافة Structure Revisited

In this lesson, extensive use of the **إضافة** structure is made. There are 17 instances of it altogether throughout the passages and dialogues, including repeated ones. One example is **قِطعةُ** خُبز 'piece of bread'. This phrase is indefinite because the second (or last) part of the phrase is indefinite **خُبز**, whereas the phrase **عَصير** البُرتُقال is definite because of the definite article that is prefixed to the second part **البُرتُقال**.

One of the **إضافة** structures is **كَأس عَصيرِ بُرتُقالٍ**. Literally, it means "a glass of juice of orange." This phrase is a multiple **إضافة** because it contains more than two successive nouns. **كَأس عَصيرِ بُرتُقال** is an indefinite **إضافة** phrase.

## تمرين ١٣

**Grammar identification:** On a separate sheet of paper, write down at least six **إضافة** structures from the reading passages that appear at the beginning of this lesson, provide their meanings, and note whether or not they are definite.

## AUDIO تمرين ١٤

A. **Listen and select:** Check the box that matches the information as expressed in the listening passage for this lesson.

١- تَشرَبُ سُعادُ صَباحاً ________________ .

☐ قَهوةً ☐ ماءً ☐ سُكَّراً

٢- تَشرَبُ سُعادُ الشايَ صَباحاً مَعَ ________________ .

☐ السُكَّر والحَليبِ ☐ الخُبْزِ والجُبنِ ☐ الدَجاجِ واللَحْم

٣- تَأكُلُ سُعادُ ظُهراً ________________ .

☐ الدَجاجَ أو اللَحْمَ ☐ الجُبنَ أو الزَيْتونَ ☐ العَسَلَ أو المَرَبّى

**B. صواب أم خطأ:** Mark the following sentences صواب or خَطأ according to the information in the listening passage and correct any false statements.

٤- لا تُحِبُّ سُعادُ صيداوي أكلَ اللَحْمِ.

٥- تأكُلُ سُعادُ السَلَطَة مَساءً.

٦- تَشرَبُ سُعادُ القَهوةَ العَرَبيّة.

## تمرين ١٥

**تَمرينُ المُشاهَدة: شاهِدوا الدَرْسَ الثامِنَ على القُرص الرَقْمي.**

**المَشْهَدُ الأوَّل**

١- ماذا تُريدُ الآنِسة؟ ______________________________

______________________________

______________________________

٢- متى تُحِبُّ الآنِسة قِراءَةَ الجَرائد؟ ______________________________

______________________________

______________________________

**المَشْهَدُ الثاني**

١- ماذا تُريدُ أن تَشْرَب الآنِستان؟ ______________________________

______________________________

٢- ماذا سَتُحَضِّرُ الآنِستان على العَشاء؟ ______________________________

______________________________

3. From context, try to guess the meaning of the word حَسَناً: ______________

## المَشْهَدُ الثالِث

1. Circle the foods the woman with the glasses ate for breakfast (فَطور):

| | | | | | | | | |
|---|---|---|---|---|---|---|---|---|
| لَحْم | زَعْتَر | بَيْض | لَبَنة | أَرُزّ | مُرَبّى | خَضراوات | زُبْدة | زَيْتون |

٢- ماذا ستأكل الآنِستان على الغَداء؟ ______________________

______________________

## المُفْرَدات

Listen to the vocabulary items on the CD and practice their pronunciation.

to bring . . . . . . . . . . . . . . . . . . . . (v.) أحْضَرَ (يُحْضِرُ) إحْضار
rice . . . . . . . . . . . . . . . . . . . . . . . . (n., m.) أرُزّ
to eat . . . . . . . . . . . . . . . . . . . . . . (v.) أكَلَ (يأكُلُ) أكْل
orange. . . . . . . . . . . . . . . . . . . . . . . (n., m.) بُرتُقال
egg . . . . . . . . . . . . . . . . . . . . . . . . (n., m.) بَيْض
Come here! . . . . . . . . . . . (f., sg.)تَعالي (imperative, m., sg.) تَعالَ
apple . . . . . . . . . . . . . . . . . . . . . . . (n., m.) تُفّاح
to eat; to take; to reach for something . . . . (v.) تَناوَلَ (يَتَناوَلُ) تَناوُل
cheese . . . . . . . . . . . . . . . . . . . (n., m.) جُبْن ج أجْبان
to sit. . . . . . . . . (v.) (imperative) (اِجلِسْ) جَلَسَ (يَجلِسُ) جُلوس
ready, all set (polite expression) . . . . . . . . . (participle) حاضِر
grain, cereal. . . . . . . . . . . . . . . . . . (n., m.) حَبّ ج حُبوب
very well, okay (a response denoting agreement) . . . . (adv.) حَسَناً
to prepare . . . . . . . . . . . . . . . . (v.) حَضَّرَ (يُحَضِّرُ) تَحضير
milk . . . . . . . . . . . . . . . . . . . . . . . . (n., m.) حَليب
bread . . . . . . . . . . . . . . . . . . . . . . . (n., m.) خُبْز

vegetables, greens . . . . . . . . . . . . . . . . . . . خَضْراوات (n., f.)

light . . . . . . . . . . . . . . . . . . . . . . . . . . . خَفيف (adj.)

pig, swine . . . . . . . . . . . . . . . . . . خِنزير ج خَنازير (n., m.)

chicken . . . . . . . . . . . . . . . . . . . . . . . . . دَجاج (n., m.)

without . . . . . . . . . . . . . . . . . . . . . . . . . دونَ (prep.)

butter . . . . . . . . . . . . . . . . . . . . . . . . . . زُبْدة (n., f.)

wild thyme . . . . . . . . . . . . . . . . . . . . . . زَعتَر (n., m.)

olive . . . . . . . . . . . . . . . . . . . . . . . . . . . زَيْتون (n., m.)

sugar . . . . . . . . . . . . . . . . . . . . . . . . . . سُكَّر (n., m.)

salad . . . . . . . . . . . . . . . . . . . . . سَلَطة ج سَلَطات (n., f.)

tea . . . . . . . . . . . . . . . . . . . . . . . . . . . . شاي (n., m.)

to drink . . . . . . . . . . . . . . . . . . . . شَرِبَ (يَشْرَبُ) شُرْب (v.)

morning . . . . . . . . . . . . . . . . . . . . . . . . . صَباح (n., m.)

patty made from ground beans and spices fried in oil (Egypt) . . . . . . . . . . . . طَعْمِيّة (n., f.)

noon . . . . . . . . . . . . . . . . . . . . . . . . . . . ظُهْر (n., m.)

honey . . . . . . . . . . . . . . . . . . . . . . . . . . عَسَل (n., m.)

juice . . . . . . . . . . . . . . . . . . . . . . . . . . . عَصير (n., m.)

breakfast . . . . . . . . . . . . . . . . . . . . . . . . فَطور (n., m.)

patty made from ground beans and spices fried in oil (Syria) . . . . . . . فُلفُل ج فَلافِل (n., m.)

cup . . . . . . . . . . . . . . . . . . . . . . . فِنْجان ج فَناجين (n., m.)

fava beans . . . . . . . . . . . . . . . . . . . . . . . فول (n., m.)

piece . . . . . . . . . . . . . . . . . . . . . . . قِطْعة ج قِطَع (n., f.)

coffee . . . . . . . . . . . . . . . . . . . . . . . . . . قَهْوة (n., f.)

glass . . . . . . . . . . . . . . . . . . . . . . . كَأس ج كُؤوس (n., f.)

a great deal . . . . . . . . . . . . . . . . . . . . . كَثيراً (adverbial) meat . . . . . . . . . . . . . . . . . . . . . . (n., m.) لَحْم ج لُحوم

What's your opinion? . . . . . . . . . . . . . . . . . . ما رأيُك

water . . . . . . . . . . . . . . . . . . . . . . (n., m.) ماء ج مِياه

when . . . . . . . . . . . . . . . . . . . . (question particle) مَتى

jam, preserve . . . . . . . . . . . . . . . . . (n., m.) مُرَبّى ج مُرَبَّيات

boiled . . . . . . . . . . . . . . . . . . . . (passive particle) مَسْلوق

evening . . . . . . . . . . . . . . . . . . . . . . . . (n., m.) مَساء

kitchen . . . . . . . . . . . . . . . . . . . . (n., m.) مَطْبَخ ج مَطابِخ

restaurant . . . . . . . . . . . . . . . . . . . (n., m.) مَطْعَم ج مَطاعِم

cafeteria . . . . . . . . . . . . . . . . . . . (n., m.) مَقْصَف ج مَقاصِف

agree . . . . . . . . . . . . . . . . . . . . (active participle) مُوافِق

# الدَّرسُ التَّاسِع

## Objectives

- Telling time formally and informally
- Describing daily activities
- Giving background information
- Introduction to breaking consonant clusters
- Introduction to mass and count nouns
- Counting in the hundreds and thousands

### ١. Telling Time

## كَمِ الساعَة ؟

السّاعَةُ الواحِدةُ

Telling time formally in Arabic involves the use of ordinal numbers (= first, second, third, etc.; see Lesson 5). Telling time in a formal manner (using **فُصحى**) is a daily occurrence throughout the Arab world, particularly on radio and television programs. It is, therefore, the manner in which we will be learning to tell time in this lesson. You may have noticed from the caption below the clock face that **الواحدَةُ** is not an ordinal number, yet it is used to tell time. This is, in fact, the only exception. The feminine form of the cardinal number **واحِد** is used with the definite article, forming an adjective that agrees with the noun **الساعَة**.

**A. Morphological Structure**

There is no mystery in coming up with the correct form of the number. Simply take the root of the number (the middle column of the table below) and place it in the **الفاعِلة** form. 1:00 and 2:00 are given; the remaining times have blanks for you to fill in. 11:00 and 12:00 are exceptions and are dealt with later on in this section.

| العدد | الأصل | الساعة |
|---|---|---|
| واحِد | وحد | الواحِدة |
| اِثْنانِ | ثني | الثانية |
| ثَلاثة | ثلث | الـ_ا_ِ_ة |
| أَرْبَعة | ربع | الـ_ا_ِ_ة |
| خَمْسة | خمس | الـ_ا_ِ_ة |
| سِتّة | سدس | الـ_ا_ِ_ة |
| سَبْعة | سبع | الـ_ا_ِ_ة |
| ثَمانية | ثمن | الـ_ا_ِ_ة |
| تِسْعة | تسع | الـ_ا_ِ_ة |
| عَشَرة | عشر | الـ_ا_ِ_ة |

**B. Grammatical Structure**

The phrase used in telling time is a noun/adjective phrase:

١ السّاعَةُ الثانيةُ

As you can see in example 1, **السّاعَةُ** is a feminine noun, while **الثانيةُ** is its adjective. When we tell time in Arabic, the noun and adjective must agree in number, gender, case, and definiteness—in fact, telling time is always definite in **فُصحى**. Consider the example:

*What time is the Arabic class?* — مَتى دَرسُ العربيةِ؟

*At two o'clock.* — في السّاعَةِ الثانيةِ.

**Notice** that both the noun and the adjective take the genitive marker **كَسْرة** on their final radical, because they follow the preposition **في**. It follows that any time we are asked a question about time that requires **في** (= at) in the answer, the following noun and adjective will be in genitive case. This rule holds true when using times one o'clock through ten o'clock.

The compound numbers 11 and 12 are the exception to the rule because, as we mentioned in Lesson 6, they are indeclinable. That is to say, numbers 11 and 12 adhere to one set form regardless of case. Consider examples 2 and 3, paying close attention to how **السّاعةُ** (nominative) changes to **السّاعةِ** (genitive) following the preposition **في**, whereas the number does not change:

| | | |
|---|---|---|
| ٢ | الساعَةُ الحادِيَةَ عَشْرَةَ | في الساعَةِ الحادِيَةَ عَشْرَةَ |
| ٣ | الساعَةُ الثانِيَةَ عَشْرَةَ | في الساعَةِ الثانِيَةَ عَشْرَةَ |

**C. Fractions of an Hour**

Telling time with fractions of an hour differs a little from the way it is done in English. The fractions used are the words for *half*, *third*, *quarter* and *minute*. Examine the examples below:

**Note** that hours and fractions are connected with the conjunction وَ, and that all divisions of the hour are definite with the *exception* of minutes.

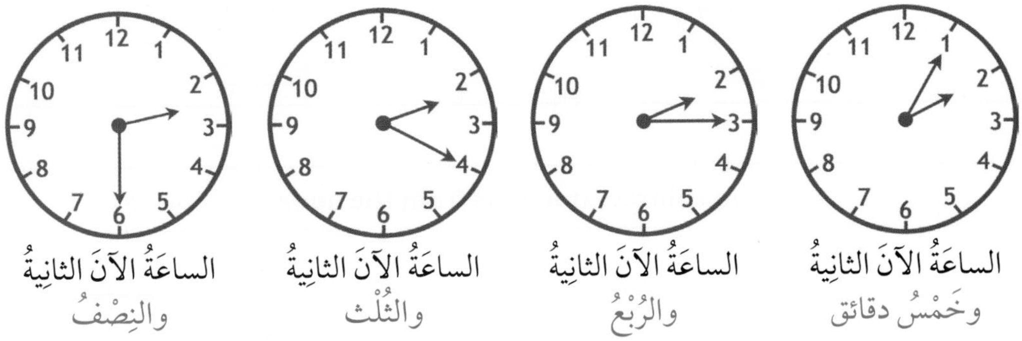


Notice that the minute hand of the four clocks that appear above is on the right-hand side of the clock dial, therefore the particle وَ 'and' is used. When the minute hand is on the left-hand side, إلاّ 'till' (as in, "a quarter till five," etc.) is used with hours and fractions. إلاّ is used for all times when the minute hand is on the left-hand side of the clock face except for the first nine minutes after the half hour mark (see clock face 2:35 below). The noun following إلاّ is accusative مَنصوب and indefinite, as in the highlighted examples:

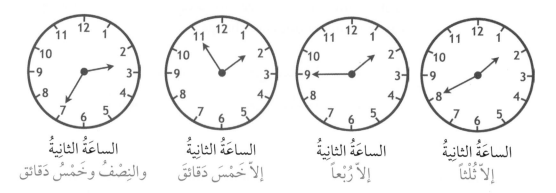

السَاعَةُ الثانِيةُ
والنِصْفُ وخَمْسُ دَقائق

السَاعَةُ الثانِيةُ
إلاّ خَمْسَ دَقائق

السَاعَةُ الثانِيةُ
إلاّ رُبْعاً

السَاعَةُ الثانِيةُ
إلاّ ثُلْثاً

A variation to saying 2:35 is: **السَاعَةُ الثانِيةُ وَخَمْسٌ وَثَلاثونَ دَقيقة**

The clock face below summarizes the information about the uses of و and إلاّ.

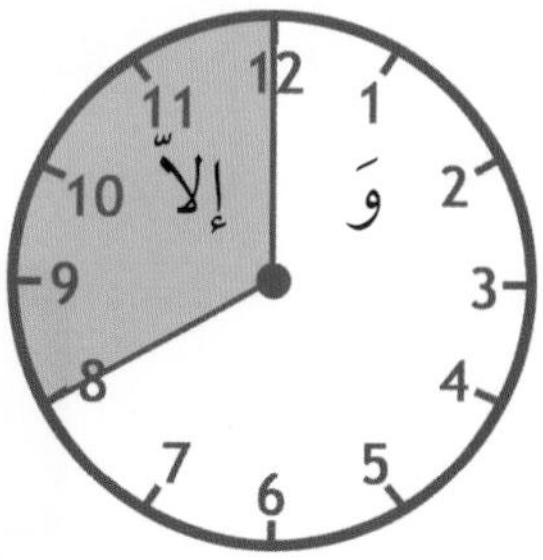


| To add fractions to the hour: | |
|---|---|
| *quarter after* | والرُبْع |
| *twenty after* | والثُلْث |
| *half-past* | والنِصْف |

| To subtract fractions from the hour: | |
|---|---|
| *quarter till* | إلاّ رُبْعاً |
| *twenty till* | إلاّ ثُلْثاً |

## SUMMARY

- The number indicating the time is an ordinal number: الساعةُ الثانيةُ وَالنِصْفُ.
- The numbers 11 and 12 are invariable: الساعةُ الثانيةَ عَشْرَةَ.
- The fractions of an hour used are: نِصْف، ثُلْث، رُبْع، دَقيقة.
- The particle وَ is inserted between the hour and fractions.
- The particle إلاّ is used to indicate times until the hour (40–59 minutes).

## تمرين ١

Under each clock face, indicate the time shown. Provide the short vowels on the ends of all words, assuming that الساعةُ is nominative مَرفوع.

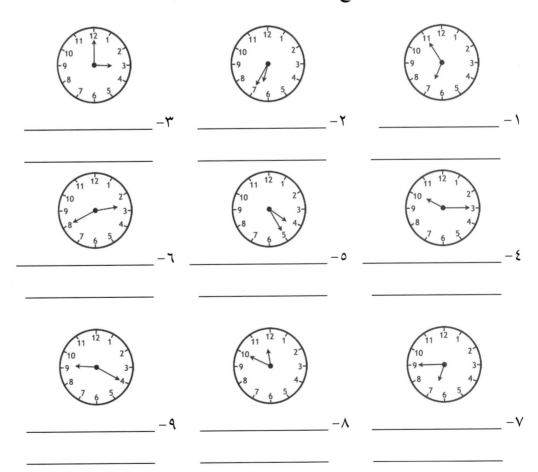

١- ______________________

______________________

٢- ______________________

______________________

٣- ______________________

______________________

٤- ______________________

______________________

٥- ______________________

______________________

٦- ______________________

______________________

٧- ______________________

______________________

٨- ______________________

______________________

٩- ______________________

______________________

## تمرين ٢

**Conversation: Making a مَوْعِد**. Make a **مَوْعِد** 'date' with someone in class to eat at a restaurant or to study at a friend's house or in the library. In order to mention as many times as possible, please do not settle on the first time mentioned; in fact, disagree as much as possible. Tell the person that you are in class, or that you are not at home, or that you have another appointment at that time; try to make up as many excuses as possible to elicit as many times as possible.

آسِفة، عِندي مَوْعِدٌ في
الساعَةِ السادِسةِ والنِصْف.

# سَحَر في جامِعةِ حَلَب

تَدرُس سَحَر حَلاّق التِجارةَ في جامِعةِ حَلَبَ في سورية. هِيَ مِن دِمَشق وتَسكُنُ مَعَ طالِبَةٍ مِن دِمَشق أيضاً اِسمُها هالَة بُستاني. عِندَ سَحَر أربَعُ مَوادَّ في هذا الفَصلِ هِيَ الرِياضِيّاتُ واللُغَةُ الإنكليزيَّةُ والمُحاسَبةُ والإحْصاء.

المُحاسَبةُ

الإحْصاء

مَوْعِدُ دَرْسِ الرِياضيّاتِ في الساعَةِ التاسِعَةِ صَباحاً، ومَوْعِدُ دَرْسِ اللُغَةِ الإنكليزيَّةِ في العاشِرَة. بَعْدَ دَرْسِ الإنكليزيَّةِ تَقرَأُ سَحَر مَجَلاّتٍ وجَرائِدَ إنكليزيَّةً في المَكتَبَةِ. عِندَ الظُهْرِ تَأكُلُ سَلَطَةً أو فَلافِلَ أو حِمَّصاً في مَقْصَفِ الجامِعَة. أحْياناً تَأكُلُ الكَبابَ الحَلَبِيّ. في الساعَةِ الواحِدَةِ مَوْعِدُ دَرْسِ المُحاسَبَةِ، وفي الساعَةِ الثالِثَةِ تَدرُسُ الإحْصاءَ. بَعْدَ ذلِكَ تَدرُسُ سَحَر في المَكتَبَةِ مِنَ الساعَةِ الرابِعَةِ إلى السادِسَةِ مَساءً مَعَ طُلاّبٍ وطالِباتٍ مِن صَفِّها.

# مايكِل براون في القاهِرَة

العَلاقات الدَوْليَّة

أنا الآنَ في الجامِعَةِ الأمريكيَّةِ بِالقاهِرَةِ أدرُسُ اللُغَةَ العَرَبيَّةَ وأدَبَها. مَوْعِدُ دَرْسِ اللُغَةِ العَرَبيَّةِ في الساعَةِ الثامِنَةِ صَباحاً وأستاذَةُ هذِهِ المادّةِ هِيَ زَيْنَب طَه. ومَوْعِدُ دَرْسِ الأدَبِ العَرَبيِّ في الساعَةِ الحادِيَةَ عَشْرَةَ واسمُ الأسْتاذِ عَبّاس التونِسي. أُحِبُّ دُروسَ العَرَبيَّةِ كَثيراً.

في مَقْصَفِ جامِعَةِ القاهِرةِ أتَكَلَّمُ عادةً بِالعَرَبيَّةِ مَعَ سَمير عَبدِ الفَتّاح وهُوَ طالِبٌ مِصْريٌّ مِن مَدينَةِ طَنْطا في مِصْر. هذا هُوَ أوَّلُ حَديثٍ بِاللُغَةِ العَرَبيَّةِ مَعَ سَمير.

سَمير: مَرحباً!

مايكِل: أهلاً!

سَمير: اِسمي سَمير عَبدُ الفَتّاح.

مايكِل: تَشَرَّفْنا. أنا مايكِل براون.

سَمير: تَشَرَّفْنا. مِن أينَ أنتَ؟

مايكِل: أنا مِن وِلايَةِ أوهايو في أمريكا.

سَمير: ماذا تَفعَلُ هُنا في القاهِرة؟

مايكِل: أدرُسُ اللُغَةَ العَرَبيَّةَ. وأنتَ؟

سَمير: أنا أدرُسُ الهَنْدَسَةَ. تَتَكَلَّمُ العَرَبيَّةَ جَيِّداً!

مايكِل: شُكراً. لَيْسَ جَيِّداً جِدّاً. وأنتَ، هَل تَتَكَلَّمُ الإنكليزيَّةَ؟

سَمير: نَعَم. قَليلاً. أينَ تَسكُنُ الآن؟

مايكِل: هُنا في القاهِرة.

سَمير: أعرِف . . . يَعني هَل تَسكُنُ في سَكَنِ الطُلاّب؟

مايكِل: لا، في شَقَّة.

سَمير: مَن يَسكُنُ مَعَكَ؟

مايكِل: لا يَسكُنُ مَعي أحَد. أسكُنُ وَحْدي.

سَمير: فُرصَة سَعيدة! مَعَ السَلامة.

مايكِل: مَعَ ألْفِ سَلامة.

## تمرين ٣

**A. Listen and select:** Check the box that matches the information as expressed in the passages for this lesson.

١- سَحَر حَلاّق مِن مَدينةِ ________________ .

☐ دِمَشق ☐ حَلَب ☐ القاهِرة

٢- تَسكُنُ سَحَر ________________ .

☐ وَحْدَها ☐ مَعَ طالِبة ☐ مَعَ ثَلاثِ طالِبات

٣- تَدرُسُ سَحَر في هذا الفَصْلِ ________________ .

☐ مَجَلاّتٍ وجَرائِدَ ☐ اللُّغَةَ الإنكليزيَّةَ ☐ اللُّغَةَ العَرَبيَّةَ

٤- تأكُلُ سَحَر عِندَ الظُهْرِ في ________________ الجامِعَة.

☐ مَكتَبَةِ ☐ مَقْصَفِ ☐ مَطْعَمِ

٥- مَوْعِدُ دَرْسِ المُحاسَبَةِ في الساعَةِ ________________ .

☐ العاشِرَةِ صَباحاً ☐ الواحِدَةِ بَعْدَ الظُهْرِ ☐ الثالِثَةِ بَعْدَ الظُهْرِ

٦- اِسمُ أُختِ مايكِل براون ________________ .

☐ مارثا ☐ لين ☐ كاثي

٧- يَدرُسُ مايكِل الآنَ في مَدينَةِ ________________ .

☐ سِنسِناتي ☐ كَلَمبَس ☐ القاهِرة

٨- يَتَكَلَّمُ مايكِل العَرَبيَّةَ في مَقْصَفِ الجامِعَةِ مَعَ ________________ .

☐ سَمير عَبدِ الفَتّاح ☐ زَينب طَه ☐ عَبّاس التونِسيّ

٩- يَدرُسُ سَمير عَبدُ الفَتّاح ________________ .

☐ العَلاقاتِ الدَوْليَّةَ ☐ الأدَبَ العَرَبيّ ☐ الهَنْدَسَةَ

**B. صواب أو خطأ:** Mark the following sentences **صواب** or **خطأ** according to the information in the main reading passage and <u>correct</u> any false statements.

١٠- عِندَ سَحَر حَلاّق ثَلاثُ مَوادَّ في هذا الفَصْل.

________________________________________

١١- تَقرَأُ سَحر الجَرائِدَ في المَكتَبَةِ بَعْدَ دَرْسِ المُحاسَبة.

______________________________

١٢- تَدرُسُ سَحر مَعَ طُلاّبٍ وطالِباتٍ مِن صَفِّها بَعْدَ دَرْسِ الإحْصاء.

______________________________

١٣- يَدرُسُ مايكِل الأدَبَ العَرَبيَّ مَعَ الأستاذِ عَبّاس التونسيّ.

______________________________

١٤- يَدرُسُ أخو مايكِل في جامِعَةِ وِلايَةِ أوهايو.

______________________________

## تمرين ٤

**A. Saḥar's daily schedule:** Fill in Saḥar's daily schedule according to the information in the main passage. List the types of activities she is involved in next to the appropriate times. Write your answers out in complete sentences, as in the example:

| الساعة | ماذا تَفعَلُ سَحَر؟ |
|---|---|
| ٨ | في الساعَةِ الثامِنَةِ تأكُلُ سَحَر الفَطور. |
| ٩ | |
| ١٠ | |
| ١١ | |
| ١٢ | |
| ١ | |
| ٢ | |
| ٣ | |
| ٤ | |
| ٥ | |
| ٦ | |

**B. Ask your neighbor:** Find out from your neighbor what he or she does on a daily basis and record your partner's information here.

| ماذا يَفعَلُ طالِبُ اللُّغَةِ العَرَبيَّةِ في صَفِّك؟ | الساعة |
|---|---|
| | |
| | |
| | |
| | |
| | |
| | |
| | |

**C. Provide your own schedule:** As in Saḥar's daily schedule, put the Arabic number in the right column and then describe your activities in a full and complete sentence with the time written out.

| ماذا أفعلُ كلَّ يوم | الساعة |
|---|---|
| | |
| | |
| | |
| | |
| | |
| | |
| | |

# تَذَوّق الثّقافة العَربيّة

**Women's Islamic Dress:** Islamic women's clothing includes wearing a headdress which covers the hair. Islamic attire has become popular among some women in the Arab world.

## تمرين ٥

**Family trees:** Below you will see two family trees: the Brown family tree in chart A and your own in chart B. Fill in the names in the Brown family tree based on the information provided in the main reading passage. In the space allotted for chart B, draw your own family tree or that of another family you know and label each person's relationship to you. In part C, write down details about the members of the family in chart B in a similar manner to Michael Brown's account of his family.

**A.** عائِلَةُ براون

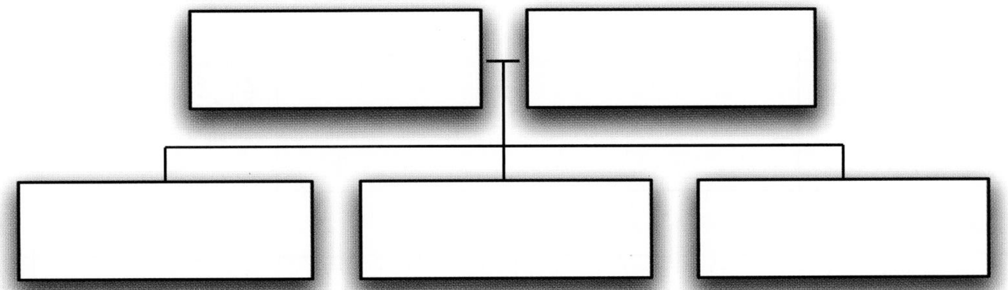

**B.** عائِلَةُ .........................

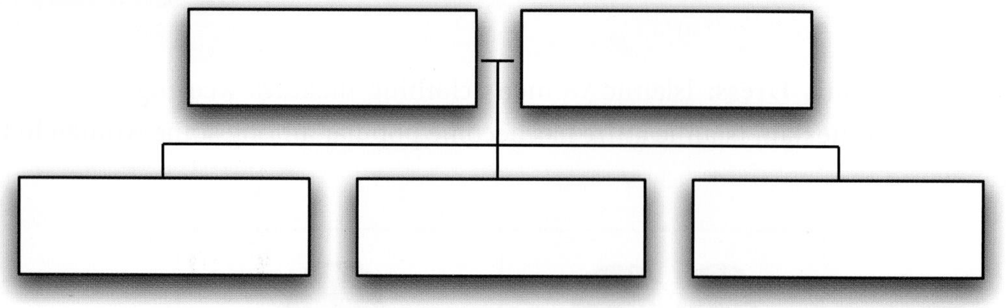

**C.** Summarize family tree B in writing.

______________________________________________

______________________________________________

______________________________________________

______________________________________________

______________________________________________

______________________________________________

______________________________________________

## تمرين ٦

**Matching:** **وافِقْ بَيْنَ الكَلِماتِ في العَمودَيْنِ**

| | | | |
|---|---|---|---|
| دَقيقَة | | أوَّل | ١ |
| العَلاقاتُ الدَوْلِيَّةُ | | الوِلاياتُ المُتَّحِدَةُ | ٢ |
| واحِد | | ساعَة | ٣ |
| صَفّ | | مادَّة | ٤ |
| أمريكا | | نِصْف | ٥ |
| ثُلْث | | | |

# تمرين ٧

**Odd word out:** Underline the word that does not belong to each set and explain your choice if needed.

| | | | | |
|---|---|---|---|---|
| ١- | رُبْع | نِصْف | ثُلْث | كَثير |
| ٢- | مَوْعِد | حِمَّص | كَباب | فلافِل |
| ٣- | إحْصاء | مُحاسَبَة | دَقيقَة | عِلْمُ الحاسوب |
| ٤- | ثالِث | تاسِع | واحِد | أوَّل |

## 2. Telling Time Informally

In many Arabic colloquial varieties, cardinal numbers are used instead of ordinal numbers to tell time informally. Also, the forms are not definite. Thus, to indicate 7:30 and 10:15, for example, in an informal way, you say:

٤ الساعة سَبعة ونِصف

٥ الساعة عَشَرة ورُبْع

This practice may still be acceptable in a formal setting when used orally, so long as the phonology and morphology (pronunciation and structure) of the words comply with the standard norms. Remember, however, that in writing it is recommended that you use the standard forms discussed above.

Also in informal speech, when indicating the minutes after or before the hour, you may drop the word for "minutes." Consider these examples:

٦ الساعة سَبعة وعَشَرة

٧ الساعة أربعة إلاّ خمسة

Bear in mind that the conjunction وَ (*wa*) is pronounced *w* without the *fatḥa* (e.g., *sab'a w 'ashara*).

## تمرين ٨

**Find out from your neighbors ماذا تُحِبُّ في التلفزيون**: Find out what television program your neighbors like and then write that information down in the table provided below. Be prepared to report this information to your classmates.

| كَم ساعةً؟ | مَتى (مِن أيّةِ ساعةٍ إلى أيّةِ ساعة) | ماذا يُحِبُّ في التَلفزيون | اِسمُ الطالِب |
|---|---|---|---|
| | | | |
| | | | |
| | | | |
| | | | |
| | | | |
| | | | |

### 3. Breaking Consonant Clusters

The question particles مَن and كَم end in a consonant and therefore acquire a suffixed كَسرة to prevent two consonants (a consonant cluster) from occurring (i.e., the final consonant of the question particle and the first consonant of the following word). Thus, to avoid a consonant cluster, which is not allowed in Arabic, a helping vowel كَسرة is inserted between the two consonants, but these particles are not to be considered genitive.

٨ كَمِ الساعة؟

٩ مَنِ الأستاذ؟

### 4. Suppressing the Initial Sound of the Article

The initial sound of the definite article (the glottal stop plus *-a*) is normally dropped when a prefix is attached to the word or preceded by another word. For example, the word العربية starts with the definite article *al-*, and is pronounced *al-ʿarabiyya* when the word stands independently. But with any prefix, take for instance the prefix بِـ, the *a-* part is dropped (*bil-ʿarabiyya*). The same process occurs when the conjunction **وَ** is prefixed (**وَالعربية** is pronounced *wa-l-ʿarabiyya*).

## 5. Mass and Count Nouns

A noun may refer to the general class of something, for example, cheese, water, air, etc. This type of noun is known as a mass noun. In Arabic, one way of creating a count noun from a mass noun is by simply adding a *tāʾ marbūṭa* to the noun:

١٠ تُفّاح *apples* تُفّاحة *an apple*

## تمرين ٩

**Forming count nouns:** Form count nouns from the following mass nouns that occurred in Lesson 8. Provide the meaning of each count noun you form.

١- بُرتُقال ______________ ٢- خُبز ______________

٣- زَيتون ______________ ٤- بَيْض ______________

٥- فول ______________ ٦- سُكَّر ______________

## 6. Numbers: Reading Hundreds and Thousands

The Arabic word for thousand is **ألف** (plural **آلاف**). **ألف** is a noun and, therefore, forms an **إضافة** structure with a counted noun. In a case such as this, the noun must be singular, genitive, and indefinite—hence it takes **تَنوين كَسرة**:

١١ ألفُ رَجُلٍ

Traditionally, Arabic numbers used to be read from right to left; that is, ones, tens, hundreds, and then thousands. When the number 1246 is read from right to left it appears in this manner:

١٢ سِتٌّ وأربَعونَ ومِئَتانِ وألف ٦ ٤ ٢ ١

Although this style is still practiced by a few radio and television announcers, another style of reading numbers is more prevalent today. When reading a number, you start with the highest category. Thus, in order to read 5246, read from left to right, as in English. Start with the thousands, then read the hundreds, skip the tens, read the ones, and then read the tens. Consider the example:

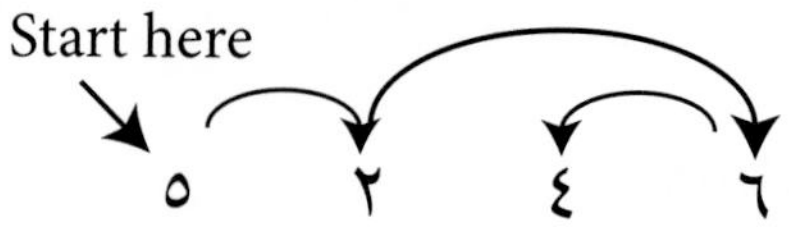


١٣ خَمسةُ آلافٍ ومِئتانِ وسِتٌّ وأربَعونَ

- **Note** that unlike English, the conjunction وَ is inserted before every category, as you can see in the examples above.

## تمرين ١٠

**Writing out numbers:** Spell out these numbers in words:

١- ٩٠٧ ____________________

٢- ٤٧٨٣ ____________________

٣- ١٣٦٨٥ ____________________

٤- ١٩٨٤ ____________________

٥- ٢٠١٠ ____________________

## تمرين ١١

**Forming questions:** Translate the following questions into Arabic and then answer them, as in the example:

Example: *What is Michael's sister's name?* (Use ما to form this question.)

ما اسْمُ أخْتِ مايكِل؟ اِسمُ أخْتِ مايكِل لين.

1. When does Saḥar eat in the cafeteria? (مَتى)

____________________

2. At what time does Saḥar have statistics? (في أيّةِ ساعَة)

____________________

3. What's the name of Michael Brown's Arabic language professor? (ما)

____________________

4. Where do Michael's parents live? (أينَ)

______________________________

## تمرين ١٢

**A. Listen and select:** Listen to the recorded passage and check the best alternative according to the passage.

١- اِسمُ هذا الطالِبِ ______________ .

☐ عَبدُ الله ☐ عادِل ☐ أشْرَف

٢- يَدرُسُ هذا الطالِبُ الأدَبَ ______________ .

☐ العَرَبيّ ☐ الإنكليزيّ ☐ الفَرَنسيّ

٣- أستاذُ مادّةِ اللُغَةِ الإنكليزيَّةِ هُوَ الدُكتور ______________

☐ جَزائِريّ ☐ ديـڤيس ☐ عَبدُ السلام

٤- أستاذُ مادّةِ الأدَبِ الإنكليزيِّ مِن ______________ .

☐ الأردُن ☐ مِصْر ☐ بريطانيا

**B. صواب أو خطأ:** Mark the following statements صَواب or خطأ based on the information in the recorded passage and correct the false ones.

٥- يَدرُسُ عادِل في جامِعَةٍ بريطانيَّةٍ.

______________________________

٦- أشرَفُ طالِبٌ في الجامِعَةِ الأردُنيَّة.

______________________________

٧- أستاذُ مادةِ اللُغَةِ الإنكليزيَّةِ بريطانيٌّ.

______________________________

٨- مَوْعِدُ مادَّةِ الأدَبِ في الساعةِ الواحِدَة.

______________________________

**C.** On a separate sheet of paper . . .

9. Write out the daily schedule of the person described in the listening passage.

10. Give the title used to refer to a university professor in the listening passage.

## تمرين ١٣

VIDEO

**تَمرينُ المُشاهَدة: شاهِدوا الدَرْسَ التاسِعَ على القُرص الرَقْمي.**

Practice telling time by writing the answers to the following questions in complete sentences:

١- في أيّةِ ساعةٍ يَسْتَيْقِظُ المُتَكَلِّم؟ ________________________________

________________________________________________

________________________________________________

٢- في أيّةِ ساعةٍ يَذْهَبُ إلى الجامِعة؟ ________________________________

________________________________________________

________________________________________________

٣- متى تَبدأ وتَنْتَهي دُروسُه ؟ ________________________________

________________________________________________

________________________________________________

٤- متى يَنام؟ ________________________________

________________________________________________

________________________________________________

## المُفْرَدات

AUDIO

Listen to the vocabulary items on the CD and practice their pronunciation.

one . . . . . . . . . . . . . . . . . . . . (n., m.) أَحَد ج آحاد

to wake up . . . . . . . . . . . . . . . . (v.) اِسْتَيْقَظَ (يَسْتَيْقِظُ) اِسْتيقاظ

statistics . . . . . . . . . . . . . . . . . . . . . . . (n., m.) إحْصاء

| | |
|---|---|
| to end | اِنْتَهى (يَنْتَهي) اِنْتِهاء (مِن) (v.) |
| except, minus | إلاّ (particle) |
| thousand | أَلْف ج آلاف (n., m.) |
| to begin | بَدَأَ (يَبْدَأُ) بِداية (v.) |
| after | بَعْدَ (prep.) |
| a third | ثُلْث ج أَثْلاث (n., m.) |
| conversation | حَديث ج أَحاديث (n., m.) |
| dip prepared from chick peas, sesame seed paste, lemon juice | حِمَّص (n., m.) |
| minute | دَقيقَة ج دَقائِق (n., f.) |
| international | دَوْلِيّ (n., m.) |
| quarter | رُبْع ج أَرْباع (n., m.) |
| o'clock, hour | ساعَة ج ساعات (n., f.) |
| relation | عَلاقة ج عَلاقات (n., f.) |
| to mean | عَنى (يَعْني) (v.) |
| literally "a happy opportunity" meaning "good to meet you" | فُرْصَة سَعيدة |
| kebāb, minced meat on a skewer with parsley and onion | كَباب (n., m.) |
| united | مُتَّحِد (adj., m.) |
| accounting | مُحاسَبة (n., f.) |
| time, appointment | مَوْعِد ج مَواعيد (n., m.) |
| to fall asleep, to sleep | نامَ (يَنامُ) نَوْم (v.) |
| half | نِصْف ج أَنْصاف (n., m.) |
| here | هُنا (demonstrative) |
| alone, by himself | وَحْدَهُ (adv.) |
| the United States of America | الوِلاياتُ المُتَّحِدةُ الأمريكيّة (n., f.) |

# الدَرسُ العاشِر

## Objectives

- Describing people, objects, possessions, and activities
- Learning about family, women, geography, history, and headgear in the Arabic-speaking world
- Introduction to the past tense: conjugation and negation الماضي
- Introduction to verbal nouns المَصْدَر
- Revisiting noun-adjective agreement (number, gender, case, definiteness)
- Learning about different names for family

## المُفرَداتُ الجَديدةُ في صُوَرٍ عديدة:

ذَهَبَ (يَذْهَبُ) ذَهابٌ إلى

عَمِلَ (يعمَلُ) عَمَلٌ

سائِقٌ ج سائِقونَ

فَتاةٌ جَميلةٌ

صَديقتانِ

طَويلٌ قَصيرٌ

قَويٌّ

# لُؤلُؤَة القَطامي فَتاةٌ عَرَبِيَّةٌ مِن قَطَر

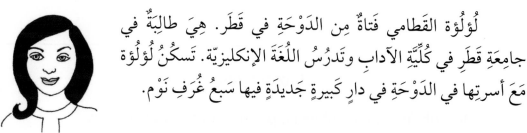

لُؤلُؤة القَطامي فَتاةٌ مِن الدَوْحَةِ في قَطَر. هِيَ طالِبَةٌ في جامِعَةِ قَطَرٍ في كُلِّيَّةِ الآدابِ وتَدرُسُ اللُغَةَ الإنكليزيّة. تَسكُنُ لُؤلُؤة مَعَ أسرتِها في الدَوْحَةِ في دارٍ كَبيرةٍ جَديدَةٍ فيها سَبعُ غُرَفِ نَوْم.

دار صَغيرة

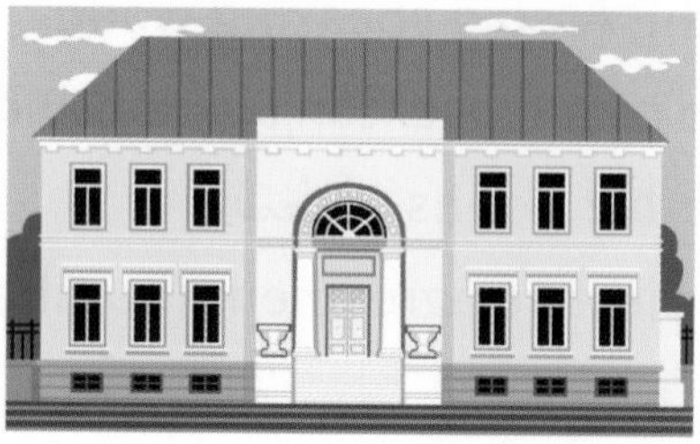

دار كَبيرة

غُرفةُ نَوْمٍ

تَذْهَبُ لُؤلُؤة إلى الجامِعَةِ بِالسَيّارَةِ مَعَ سائِقٍ هِنْديّ. هُناكَ سائِقٌ ثانٍ مِنَ الباكِسْتان تَذهَبُ مَعَهُ أمُّها إلى السوقِ وإلى بُيوتِ صَديقاتِها. لِعائِلَةِ القَطامي ثَلاثُ سَيّارات. الأولى سَيّارةٌ أمريكيّةٌ كَبيرةٌ (كاديلاك) وهِيَ لِلأُمّ. والسَيّارةُ الثانِيَةُ (مَرسيدس) ألمانِيَّةٌ وهِيَ لِلأب. والسَيّارةُ الثالِثةُ (تويوتا) يابانِيَّةٌ تَذهَبُ بِها لُؤلُؤة وإخوَتُها إلى الجامِعَةِ والمَدارِس.

لُؤلُؤة فَتاةٌ جَميلَةٌ. هِيَ لَيْسَتْ طَويلةً ولَيْسَتْ قَصيرةً لكِنَّ أُختَها الصَغيرةَ عائِشة طَويلَة. تُحِبُّ لُؤلُؤة دِراسَةَ اللُغَةِ الإنكليزِيَّة، وهِيَ تَذهَبُ إلى مَكتَبَةِ الجامِعَةِ بَعْدَ الظُهرِ وتَقرَأُ هُناكَ الجَرائِدَ والمَجَلاّتِ الإنكليزيّة.

لِلُؤلُؤة أُختانِ وأخَوان. أُخْتاها دانَة وعائِشة في المَدرسةِ الثانَوِيَّة. أخوها الصَغيرُ حَسَن في الصَفِّ العاشِرِ الثانَويّ. أخوها الكَبيرُ حُسَين في الكُوَيْتِ الآن. وهُوَ يَسكُنُ ويَعمَلُ هُناكَ. يَسكُنُ حُسَين في شَقَّةٍ في شارِع حَمَدِ المُبارَك. عِندَ حُسَين سَيّارةُ (پورش) ألمانِيَّةٌ وهِيَ سَيّارةٌ حَديثَةٌ وجَميلَةٌ لَها مُحَرِّكٌ قَويّ.

سَيّارةٌ قديمةٌ

سَيّارةٌ جَديدةٌ وحَديثةٌ

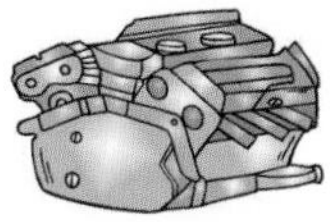

مُحَرِّكٌ

دَرَسَ حُسَيْن التِجارةَ في لَنْدَن وسَكَنَ فيها أربعَ سَنَوات. يُحِبُّ حُسَيْن العَمَلَ بِالحاسوبِ لكِنَّهُ ما دَرَسَ عِلمَ الحاسوب. حُسَيْن رَجُلٌ طَويلٌ ووَسيمٌ، لكِنْ لَيْسَ لَهُ زَوْجَةٌ الآنَ ولا يَسكُنُ أحدٌ مَعَهُ في شَقّتِه. يَلبَسُ حُسَيْن الكوفيّةَ والعِقال.

## تمرين ١

**Reflecting on our reading:** Explain the meanings of the following items in Arabic or English as they were used in the reading passage.

١– الدَوْحَة ____________________

٢– سَيّارةُ حُسَيْن ____________________

٣– شارِعُ حَمَدِ المُبارَك ____________________

## تمرين ٢

**A. Read and select:** Check the box that matches the information as expressed in the passages for this lesson.

١– لُؤلُؤة فَتاةٌ مِن ____________ .

☐ الكُوَيْتِ ☐ قَطَر ☐ الباكِسْتان

٢– تَدرُسُ لُؤلُؤة ____________ .

☐ اللُغَةَ الإنكليزيّةَ ☐ التِجارةَ ☐ العَلاقات الدَوْليّة

٣– تَقرأُ لُؤلُؤة المَجلاّتِ الإنكليزيّةَ في ____________ .

☐ البَيْتِ ☐ الصَفِّ ☐ المَكتَبَةِ

٤– تَسكُنُ لُؤلُؤة في ____________ .

☐ سَكَنِ الطالِباتِ ☐ شَقّةٍ ☐ دارِ أُسْرَتِها

٥- عِندَ عائِلةِ القَطامي ________________ .

☐ سَيّارتانِ ☐ ثلاثُ سَيّاراتٍ ☐ أربعُ سَيّاراتٍ

٦- دَرَسَ حُسَيْن التِجارةَ في ________________ .

☐ الدَوْحَةِ ☐ الكُوَيْتِ ☐ لَندَن

٧- يَعمَلُ حُسَيْن في ________________ .

☐ الكُوَيْتِ ☐ الدَوْحَةِ ☐ لَندَن

٨- لِحُسَيْن سَيّارةٌ ________________ .

☐ أمريكيّةٌ ☐ يابانيّةٌ ☐ ألمانيّةٌ

**B. صواب أو خطأ:** Mark the following sentences صواب or خَطأ according to the information in the main reading passage and <u>correct</u> any untrue sentences.

٩- في دارِ عائِلةِ القَطامي تِسعُ غُرَف.

________________________________________

١٠- تَذهَبُ أمُّ لُؤلُؤة مَعَ السائِقِ إلى السوق.

________________________________________

١١- تَقرَأُ لُؤلُؤة المَجلاّتِ الإنكليزيّةَ في كُلِّيَّةِ الآداب.

________________________________________

١٢- سَيّارةُ حُسَيْن لَها مُحَرِّكٌ قَويٌّ وجَميلٌ.

________________________________________

١٣- يَسكُنُ حُسَيْن مَعَ زَوْجَتِه في بَيْتٍ كَبير.

________________________________________

**C. Biographical sketch:** Sit down with one (or more) of your classmates and interview them in Arabic to find out as much personal information as you can about them and their family. Try to emulate one of the biographical descriptions in the main reading passage by asking about their house/apartment (big or small), their car (new or old, and the make), where they work, if they like their job, what they study, if they like their classes, how many classes they are taking, etc. Now, on a separate sheet of paper, describe the person you learned about. Be prepared to relate your sketch to your classmates orally.

## تمرين ٣

**Best choice:** Select the choice that correctly (or best) completes the sentence.

١- سَيّارَتي لَها ________ قَويّ.

☐ عِقالٌ ☐ شُبّاكٌ ☐ مُحَرِّكٌ

٢- في شَقّتي ________ نَوْمٍ واحِدَةٍ.

☐ غُرفةُ ☐ كوفِيّةُ ☐ مَجَلّةُ

٣- يَسكُنُ أبي في ________ كَبيرة.

☐ مَطْعَمٍ ☐ دارٍ ☐ وَسيمٍ

٤- لي ________ مِنَ اليابان.

☐ قَديمٌ ☐ قَصيرٌ ☐ صَديقٌ

٥- يَعمَلُ حامِد ________ في القاهِرة.

☐ سائِقاً ☐ طَويلاً ☐ جَميلاً

## تمرين ٤

**Odd word out:** Underline the word that does not belong in each set and explain your choice if needed.

١- قَصير مَكتَبَة مَجَلّات كُتُب جَرائِد

٢- سَيّارة مُحَرِّك صَديق سائِق كاديلاك

٣- اليابان ألمانيا الهِند دِراسة سورية

٤- أخ أخت أب لَبِسَ أم

٥- قَصير كَبير صَغير طَويل فتاة

# تمرين ٥

**Matching:** **وافِقْ بَيْنَ الكَلِماتِ في العَمودَينِ**

| | | | |
|---|---|---|---|
| ١ | سَيّارة | | جَميلة |
| ٢ | كَبير | | مَجَلات |
| ٣ | دار | | بِنْت |
| ٤ | طَويل | | حَديث |
| ٥ | وَسيم | | صَغير |
| ٦ | قَديم | | قَصير |
| ٧ | فَتاة | | سائِق |
| ٨ | مَكْتَبَة | | قَويّ |
| | | | بَيت |

## 1. Cultural Notes

## تَذَوّق الثَقافَة العَرَبيّة

**Family:** Arab families tend to be very protective of their children, even after they reach the age of eighteen. Children generally remain financially dependent on their parents and continue to live at home until they are married.

**Women:** Girls in particular are not allowed to be on their own, especially in the Arabian Peninsula region. Although young women are legally allowed to drive cars, they normally do not (Saudi Arabia is the only country in that region that prohibits women from driving, hence the need for chauffeurs **سائِقونَ**). Chauffeurs—mostly from India, Pakistan, and Bangladesh—drive the women of a household wherever they wish to go. Hiring foreign chauffeurs on a large scale has become an affordable practice thanks to oil revenues. Women have jobs **أعمال**, even in Saudi Arabia. Professional opportunities, though, are limited for women in the Arabian Peninsula. Most working women are teachers. From the author's observation, these restrictions seem to have had a positive effect on women's motivation and desire to excel and outperform men. Arab women have achieved excellence in various fields, in particular in education, literature, and the arts.

In the more secular Arab countries, such as Algeria, Egypt, Syria, Lebanon, Palestine, and Iraq, women have equal opportunities and find employment in almost all fields. Some women even hold cabinet positions in the government.

Men, on the other hand, have much more freedom of movement, and more professional opportunities are open to them. Young men are not expected to move out of the family house until they are married.

**The Gulf:** Arab states call it the Arabian Gulf **الخَليج العَرَبي** while Iran calls it the Persian Gulf **الخَليج الفارِسي**. As you can see on the map below, it is both Arab and Persian. Iran overlooks the eastern part of the Gulf, while the United Arab Emirates, Qatar, Saudi Arabia, and Kuwait are on the western part, and Iraq has a narrow outlet to the Gulf in the north. Bahrain is a small island in the western (Arab) side of the Gulf.

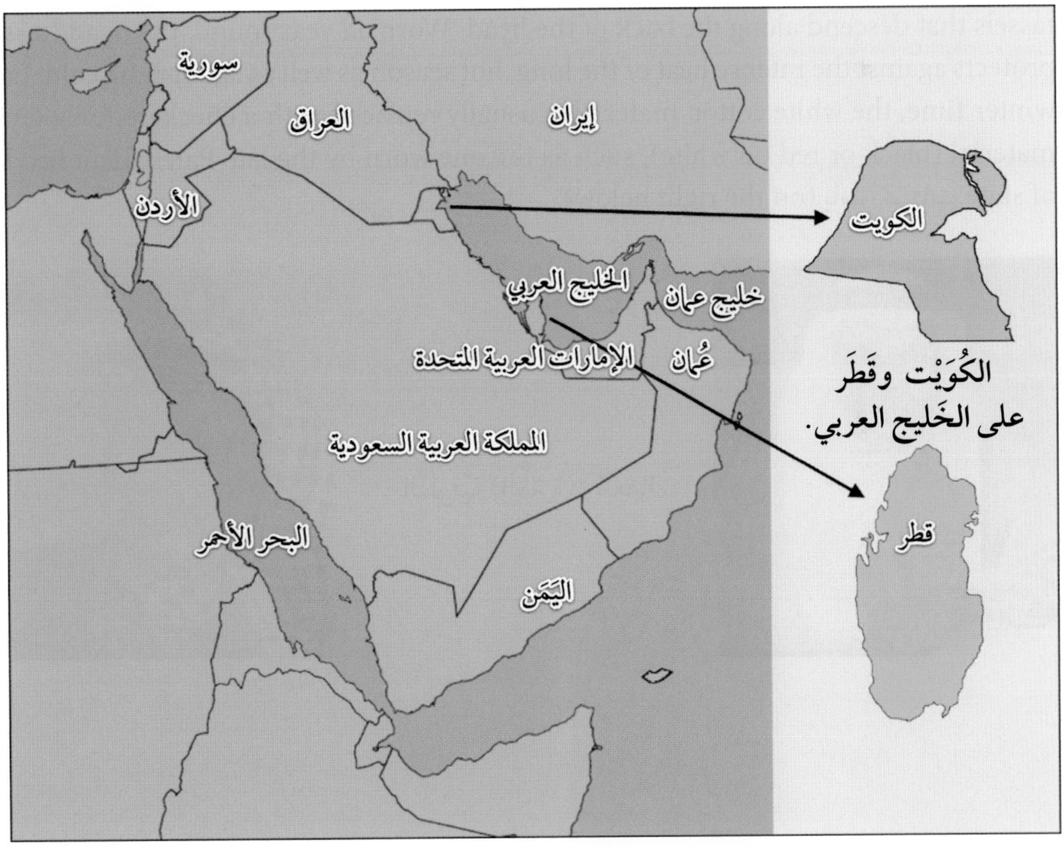


أينَ قَطَر والكُوَيْت؟

**Names and Recent History:** The personal name لُؤلُؤة 'pearl' is a common name for women in the Gulf region. It is reminiscent of the times that preceded the discovery of oil and the ensuing windfall of profits when the mainstay of the region was diving for pearls and fishing.

**Language in the Gulf:** As in most Arabic dialects, the Gulf dialect changes the هَمزة into either a واو or a ياء. Thus, لُؤلُؤة the main character of our reading passage, is pronounced *lulwa* in that part of the Arab world. Another popular name from our reading passage which refers to the ancient trade of pearl diving is دانة '*big pearl*'.

**Men's Head Gear:** The male head gear, is called غُتْرة in the Gulf area (also known as كوفيّة in the region of Greater Syria—بِلاد الشام—where it is still in use in rural areas). The more formal headdress (on the left below) is made of fine white cotton held in place with two thick bands made from a thick, black cord called عِقال which has tassels that descend along the back of the head. Worn all year round, the headdress protects against the intense heat of the long, hot season as well as against the cold. In winter time, the white cotton material is usually replaced with a checkered woolen material (black or red on white), such as the one worn by the late Palestinian head of state ياسِر عَرَفات (on the right below).

الكوفيّة (الغُترة) والعِقال

## 2. The Past Tense

Say that we were going to create our own language and one of the parameters that we had for making our language was to incorporate the pronoun into the verb. Let's, then, start with the past-tense verb. How would you incorporate the pronoun, as a suffix or a prefix? Since we are dealing with the past tense, we suggest a suffix, and that is exactly the way Arabic is patterned. Past-tense verbs take suffixes, and present-tense verbs take prefixes (as well as some suffixes that determine number and gender). In other words, all Arabic verbs have roots to which we add affixes (a prefix, infix, or suffix), as we have seen with present-tense verbs, and now we will learn about the past tense.

Verbs are conventionally cited in the simplest form, that of the past third-person masculine singular. All the verbs you have encountered are thus cited, although they have not been used in the past tense. In the main reading passage, there are two occurrences of the past: سَكَنَ 'he lived' and دَرَسَ 'he studied', both of which are third-person masculine singular. We will now take the verb دَرَسَ as an example of how suffixes are attached to verb stems so that we can apply this knowledge to stems that we have already covered.

### A. Past-Tense Conjugation of the Verb دَرَسَ 'he studied'

The root of the past-tense verb for all conjugations is دَرَسْ, to which the various suffixes are attached. For example, for the first-person plural (we), the suffix is نا. Here is how it is formed:

١ دَرَسْ + نا = دَرَسْنا

The same process is followed in forming the different conjugations for the other persons. Examine the different forms of the past for دَرَسَ in the table on the following page, paying attention to suffixes and how they correspond to pronouns.

| Suffix | Past-tense form | Pronoun | Person |
|---|---|---|---|
| ـتُ | دَرَسْتُ | أنا | المُتَكَلِّم |
| ـنا | دَرَسْنا | نَحْنُ | |
| ـتَ | دَرَسْتَ | أَنْتَ | المُخاطَب |
| ـتِ | دَرَسْتِ | أَنْتِ | |
| ـتُما | دَرَسْتُما | أَنْتُما | |
| ـتُم | دَرَسْتُم | أَنْتُم | |
| ـتُنَّ | دَرَسْتُنَّ | أَنْتُنَّ | |
| ـَ | دَرَسَ | هُوَ | الغائب |
| ـَتْ | دَرَسَتْ | هِيَ | |
| ـا | دَرَسا | (مُذَكَّر) هُما | |
| ـتا | دَرَسَتا | (مُؤَنَّث) هُما | |
| ـوا | دَرَسوا | هُم | |
| ـنَ | دَرَسْنَ | هُنَّ | |

After examining this table, do you notice any commonalities between the independent pronoun and the conjugated verb? As you can see, all second-person independent pronouns start with أنْـ followed by a suffix. It is the addition of this suffix to the root that creates the different conjugations. So, as long as you know the second-person independent pronoun, the conjugation is no more than placing the suffix on the verb stem.

- **Error Prevention:** The third-person singular past tense is so easy to make that many learners find themselves trying to find some suffix to add onto its stem. Remember that it only takes a فَتحة.

- **Note:** The third-person plural masculine form دَرَسوا has a <u>silent</u> أَلَف as its end. The verb is pronounced *darasū*. The أَلَف has no phonetic value at all.

**B. Negating the Past Tense**

One way of negating a past-tense verb is by using the particle **ما** before the verb. It does not cause any changes either in the verb itself or in the order of words within the sentence:

٢ دَرَسْتُ التِجارةَ. ما دَرَسْتُ التِجارةَ.

## تمرين ٦

**The use of ما:** Write down the names of everyone in class that did not . . .

1. drink coffee this morning
2. read the paper this morning
3. eat breakfast this morning
4. study this lesson
5. work this morning

Be prepared to report all of your findings to your classmates.

## تمرين ٧

**A.** Fill in the blanks with the appropriate past-tense conjugation of the verbs in the parentheses and then answer the comprehension questions that follow.

أنا وأخي __________ (ذَهَبَ) إلى دارِ أُمّي وأبي الكَبيرةِ في مَدينةِ مونْتَراي في وِلايةِ كاليفورنيا لِعيد الشُكْر. وهُناكَ أنا __________ (قَرَأ) الجَريدةَ الصَباحيّةَ و__________ (تَكَلَّمَ) مَعَ أسرَتي كثيراً. بَعْدَ الظُهْرِ، __________ (أكَلَ) لَحْماً وبَطاطا وأَرُزاً و__________ (شَرِبَ) شاياً وكوكا كولا وماءً. أُمّي __________ (أكَلَ) البَطاطا والأَرُزَ ولكِنَّها ما __________ (أكَلَ) اللَحْمَ وأبي __________ (أكَلَ) و__________ (شَرِبَ) كُلَّ شَيْء.

**B. Comprehension questions**: Answer in full and complete sentences *in Arabic*:

١- ما مَعنى "عيد الشكر"؟ (مِن كَلِمةِ شُكْراً)

______________________________

٢- ما مَعنى كَلِمَة بَطاطا؟

______________________________

٣- مَن ذَهَبَ إلى كاليفونيا؟

______________________________

٤- ماذا شَرِبْنا هُناكَ؟

______________________________

٥- ما مَعنى كَلِمَة "أرُز"؟

______________________________

## 3. Verbal Nouns المَصْدَر

A verbal noun is a noun derived from a verb. For instance, the noun دِراسَة 'study, studying', which is in our reading passage, is derived, as you may have guessed, from the verb دَرَسَ. It is treated exactly like a noun in the sense that it (1) can take the definite article; (2) can have possessive pronouns suffixed to it; and (3) changes according to number and case. The pattern of دِراسة (فِعالة) is only one of several verbal noun patterns which we will introduce in this book. By comparing the pattern of the verb دَرَسَ 'he studied' and the verbal noun دِراسة 'studying', you will notice that there are three differences (highlighted here in blue):

| | | | | | | | | |
|---|---|---|---|---|---|---|---|---|
| Verb | | سَ | | رَ | دَ | ← | دَرَسَ | ٣ |
| Verbal Noun | ـة | س | ا | ر | دِ | ← | دِراسة | ٤ |

In example 4 you will notice that:

1. The first consonant is followed by a كَسرة instead of فَتحة.
2. The second, or middle, consonant is followed by an added ألَف.
3. A تاء مَربوطة is suffixed to the resulting word.

The **فِعالة** verbal noun pattern is common, and the verb **قَرَأَ**, in fact, follows it:

٣ قَرَأَ ← قَـ رَ أَ Verb

٤ قِراءة ← قِـ ر ا ء ة Verbal Noun

**Notice** how the spelling of the **هَمزة** has changed from example 3 to example 4 because of the change in the preceding vowel (see Lesson 24 for detailed rules for writing the **هَمزة**).

Another verbal noun pattern that entails no changes in the basic form of the triliteral verb is **أَكَلَ** 'he ate'; only its short vowels are changed.

٧ أَكَلَ ← أَكْل

- **Note** that the short vowel on the last consonant of the verbal noun is not indicated. This is done because this word, being a noun, can have any one of the three short vowels that indicate case, depending on its position in the sentence.

Some verbs have two verbal noun patterns, such as **دَرَسَ**, which has **دِراسة** and **دَرْس**. Consider examples 8, 9, and 10:

٨ دَرْسُ العَرَبِيَّةِ جَيِّدٌ. *Studying Arabic is good.*

٩ أُحِبُّ دَرْسَ العَرَبِيَّةِ. *I like the Arabic class.*

١٠ في دَرْسِ العَرَبِيَّةِ. *In the Arabic class*

Other verbs that have a verbal noun pattern with no change in consonants include:

| المَعنى | المَصْدَر | المَعنى | الفِعْل |
|---|---|---|---|
| *drinking* | شُرْب | *to drink* | شَرِبَ |
| *wearing, attire* | لُبْس | *to wear* | لَبِسَ |
| *work* | عَمَل | *to work* | عَمِلَ |
| *living, residing, residence* | سَكَن | *to live, reside* | سَكَنَ |
| *doing, deed* | فِعْل | *to do* | فَعَلَ |
| *studying, lesson* | دِراسة | *to study* | دَرَسَ |

- **Remember:** A verbal noun has the same form whether you derive it from a past- or a present-tense verb.

## تمرين ٨

**Conversation using يُحِبُّ** and **يُريدُ**: Elicit the following information from your neighbor and then write it down on a separate sheet of paper. Your answers must include verbal nouns, which, in these examples, should be *definite*. If you have any trouble conjugating these two verbs, please refer to **Appendix C: Verb Conjugations** in the back of this book.

تُحِبُّ لُؤلُؤة دِراسَةَ اللُغَةِ الإنكليزيَّة.

Find out if your neighbor . . .

1. likes reading in the morning
2. wants to study (studying) mathematics
3. lives in the dorm (residence of students)
4. likes drinking coffee with his/her friends
5. has a family member who likes Arab food
6. knows anyone who wants to work (working) in Kuwait
7. wants to wear (wearing) the *kūfiyya*

## 4. Noun-Adjective Agreement Revisited

If you recall, adjectives follow nouns and they agree with them in *number*, *gender*, *case*, and *definiteness*. Let's review these points one by one.

### A. Number

Singular nouns are modified and followed by singular adjectives (example 11), dual (two) nouns are modified and followed by dual adjectives (example 12), and plural nouns are modified by (followed by) plural adjectives (example 13):

١١ وَلَدٌ طَويلٌ

١٢ وَلَدانِ طَويلانِ

١٣ أولادٌ طِوالٌ

- **Remember:** Plural non-rational nouns (those referring to inanimate objects) take feminine adjectives regardless of the gender of the singular noun

١٤ كُتُبٌ قَديمَةٌ

١٥ سَيّاراتٌ قَديمَةٌ

In example 14, كُتُبٌ is a plural of the masculine noun (كِتاب) while in example 15, سَيّارات is a plural of the feminine noun سَيّارة, and yet both are modified by the same adjectival form قَديمَة, which is feminine singular.

## تمرين ٩

**Adjective identification (number):**

1. Underline the adjectives in the following sentences.
2. Write صواب next to those which show correct noun–adjective agreement in number and خطأ next to those that do not.
3. Correct any and all mistakes.

١- عِندي هاتِفٌ يابانِيّة. ______________________

٢- تَأكُلُ سَلمى في مَطعَمٍ صَغير. ______________________

٣- عِندَ أخي كُتُبٌ قَديمات. ______________________

٤- إخْوَةُ مَحمود طِوال. ______________________

٥- هَل أولادُها الصَغيرُ مَعَها؟ ______________________

٦- في صَفِّنا كَراسٍ قَديم. ______________________

**B. Gender**

Singular masculine nouns must be followed by masculine adjectives (example 16) and feminine nouns by feminine adjectives (example 17).

١٦ مَطعَمٌ حَديثٌ

١٧ مَدرَسةٌ حَديثَةٌ

# تمرين ١٠

**Adjective identification (gender):**

1. Underline the adjectives in the following sentences.
2. Write صواب next to the sentences which show correct noun-adjective agreement in gender and خطأ next to those that do not.
3. Correct any and all mistakes.

١ - باريس مَدينةٌ فَرَنسيٌ. ______________________

٢ - عَدنان طالِبٌ سوريٌ. ______________________

٣ - مينيسوتا وِلايةٌ أمريكيَّةٌ. ______________________

٤ - جامِعَتُنا كَبيرٌ. ______________________

٥ - صَفُّنا صَغيرٌ. ______________________

٦ - حُسَيْن رَجُلٌ قَطَرِيَّةٌ. ______________________

**C. Case**

The adjective should have the same case as that of the noun it modifies. Examine these examples:

| | | |
|---|---|---|
| ١٨ | لُغَتي الأولى اللُغَةُ العَرَبِيَّةُ. | مَرفوع بالضَمّة |
| ١٩ | يَعرِفُ مايكِل اللُغَةَ العَرَبِيَّةَ. | مَنصوب بالفَتحة |
| ٢٠ | أتَكَلَّمُ مَعَ أستاذي بِاللُغَةِ العَرَبِيَّةِ. | مَجرور بالكَسرة |

In example 18, the adjective العَرَبِيَّةُ is nominative (مَرفوع) because the noun اللُغَةُ it modifies is the predicate of the sentence. As you can see, both display the same case marker: the ضَمّة.

In example 19, the adjective العَرَبِيَّةَ is in the accusative (مَنصوب) because the noun اللُغَةَ it modifies is the object of the verb يَعْرِف. The accusative case is marked by a فَتحة.

In example 20, the adjective العَرَبِيَّةِ is in the genitive case (مَجرور) because the noun اللُغَةِ is the object of the preposition بِـ. The genitive case is marked by a كَسرة.

- **Note:** There are case markers other than the three short vowels and تَنوين. These include ـانِ; ـيْنِ for dual nouns, and ون, ين for sound masculine plurals.

# تمرين ١١

**Adjective identification (case):**

1. Underline the adjectives in the following sentences.
2. Write صواب next to the sentences which show correct noun-adjective agreement in case and خطأ next to those that do not.
3. Correct any and all mistakes.

١- عِندي كِتابانِ جَديدَيْنِ. ________________

٢- يَدرُسُ سامي لُغَةً جَديدةٌ. ________________

٣- يَدرُسُ عَدنان في الجامِعَةِ الأمريكيَّةِ. ________________

٤- أعرِفُ رِجالاً وَسيمونَ. ________________

٥- هذِه شَقّةُ الطالِبَةِ السوريَّةُ. ________________

**D. Definiteness**

Both a noun and its modifying adjective are either definite or indefinite. A noun is definite if:

| Determining Definiteness of Nouns | |
|---|---|
| 1. | The definite particle الـ is prefixed to it (e.g., الكِتاب). |
| 2. | A possessive pronoun is suffixed to it (e.g., كتابي). |
| 3. | It is the first part of an إضافة structure, where the second or last part is definite (e.g., كِتابُ الأستاذ). |
| 4. | It is a proper noun; that is, a personal name (e.g., مايكل، عَدنان). |

Remember that a string of two words in which both the noun and the adjective are definite is considered a noun phrase—not a sentence (example 21). But if the noun is definite and the adjective is indefinite, this string is no longer a noun phrase; it is a sentence (example 22).

٢١ البابُ الكَبيرُ . . . — *The big house . . .*

٢٢ البابُ كَبيرٌ. — *The door is big.*

If the noun and the adjective are either both indefinite or definite, then they are a phrase (*a big house*; *the big house*). But if the first noun is definite and the adjective is not, then the string is a complete sentence (*The house is big*). The definiteness or indefiniteness of a phrase such as this depends entirely on context.

٢٣ بابٌ كَبيرٌ *a big house*

Thus, agreement in definiteness—when both the noun and the adjective are definite—signifies a noun phrase. Remember, however, that a string of two nouns where the first one is indefinite and the second definite is an **إضافة** structure (example 24).

٢٤ بابُ الصَفِّ

## تمرين ١٢

**Definitiveness: *phrase* or *sentence*?**

1. Label the following items "phrase," "sentence," or "both."
2. Write **صواب** if the phrase is grammatically correct and **خطأ** if it is incorrect.
3. Correct any and all mistakes. An example is provided.

مِثال: الدَرّاجةُ الإيطاليّةٌ ___phrase___ ___خطأ___ ___الدَرّاجةُ الإيطاليةُ___

١- أستاذ العَرَبيَّةِ. ______ ______ ______

٢- المَدينةُ القَديمَةُ. ______ ______ ______

٣- الكُرسيُّ صَغيرٌ. ______ ______ ______

٤- سَيّارةٌ حَديثَةٍ. ______ ______ ______

٥- صورةٌ الجَميلةٌ. ______ ______ ______

٦- الفَتاةُ قَطَرِيَّةٌ. ______ ______ ______

٧- هاتِفٌ جَديدٌ ______ ______ ______

٨- رَجُلُ الوَسيمُ. ______ ______ ______

٩- مُدُنُ الخَليجِ. ______ ______ ______

١٠- سَيّارتُكَ جَديدةَ. ______ ______ ______

١١- مَكتَبُها كَبيرٌ. ______ ______ ______

١٢- حاسوبٌ قَديمٌ. ______ ______ ______

## تَذَوَّق الثَّقافَة العَرَبيّة

**Family Affair:** As you may have noticed, two words for "family" are used, **عائلة** and **أسرة**. The former (**عائلة**) refers to the nuclear family or the unit that one supports (wife/husband, children). The latter (**أسرة**) is either the unit to which one belongs (mother, father, siblings) or the extended family (grandparents, uncles, aunts, cousins).

## تمرين ١٣

**Select the best choice:** Select the choice that correctly (or best) completes the sentence.

١- تِلكَ هِيَ كُلِّيَّةُ الآدابِ ________ .

☐ جَديدَةٌ ☐ جَديدٍ ☐ الجَديدةُ ☐ الجديدِ

٢- أينَ الكُتُبُ ________ ؟

☐ القَديمُ ☐ القَديمَةُ ☐ القُدَماءُ ☐ القَديماتُ

٣- تُحِبُّ هالَة مَدينَةَ دِمَشقَ ________ .

☐ قَديمٌ ☐ القَديمَ ☐ قَديمَةٌ ☐ القَديمَةَ

٤- عِندي دَرّاجَتانِ ________ .

☐ فَرَنسِيٌّ ☐ فَرَنسيّانِ ☐ فَرَنسِيَّتانِ ☐ فَرَنسِيّاتٍ

٥- اِسمُ الطالِبِ ________ سامي.

☐ الجَديدَ ☐ الجَديدُ ☐ الجَديدِ ☐ جَديدٌ

٦- تَسكُنُ الطالِباتُ ________ في سَكَنِ الطالِباتِ.

☐ الجَديدُ ☐ الجُدُدُ ☐ الجَديدةُ ☐ الجَديداتُ

## تمرين ١٤

**Sentence completion:** Complete these sentences with the correct form of the adjective صَغير, as in the two examples. Note that the masculine plural of صَغير is صِغار.

مِثال: عِندي بَيتٌ صَغيرٌ

أُختي صَغيرَةٌ

١- عِندَ سالِم سَيّارةٌ ________.

٢- أذهَبُ إلى الجامِعَةِ بِالسَّيّارةِ ________.

٣- يُحِبُّ أبي الأولادَ ________.

٤- ريما وغادَة بِنتانِ ________.

٥- ثَلاثَةُ مَفاتيحَ ________.

٦- هَل دِمَشقُ وبَغدادُ مَدينَتانِ ________.

٧- هَل أخوكِ ________ يا سَميرة؟

٨- يَجلِسُ عِماد في المَكتَبِ ________.

## تمرين ١٥

AUDIO

**A. Listen and select:** Choose the best alternative based on the information in the listening passage.

١- سَعيد طالِبٌ ________.

☐ سوريّ ☐ تونسيّ ☐ أمريكيّ

٢- يَدرُسُ سَعيدٌ ________.

☐ عِلمَ الحاسوبِ ☐ الكيمياءَ ☐ الطِبَّ

٣- يَسكُنُ سَعيد في ________.

☐ شَقَّةٍ ☐ بَيتٍ ☐ سَكَنِ الطُلّابِ

٤- لِسَعيد ________.

☐ أختانِ ☐ ثَلاثُ أخَواتٍ ☐ أربَعُ أخَواتٍ

**B.** **صواب أو خطأ**: Read these sentences, then mark each of them **صَواب** or **خَطأ** according to the information in the listening passage and correct the false information.

٥- يَدرُسُ سَعيد في جامِعَةِ ماساتشوسِتس. __________________

٦- يَدرُسُ برايَن الطِبَّ الآن. __________________

٧- فَرَح صَديقةُ سَعيد. __________________

٨- تَدرُسُ عَلياء في الجامِعَةِ. __________________

٩- عِندَ برايَن سَيّارةٌ. __________________

١٠- سَعيد لَيْسَ عِندَهُ دَرّاجةٌ. __________________

**C.** Write a brief summary of the passage in English.

## المُفْرَدات

Listen to the vocabulary items on the CD and practice their pronunciation.

immediate (parents, siblings) and extended family . . . . . . . . . . . (f., s.) أسْرة ج أسَر

Germany. . . . . . . . . . . . . . . . . . . . . . . . (n., f.) ألمانيا

German . . . . . . . . . . . . . . . . . . . . . . . . (adj.) ألمانيّ

Pakistan . . . . . . . . . . . . . . . . . . . . . . . (n., f.) الباكِسْتان

secondary . . . . . . . . . . . . . . . . . . . . . . (adj.) ثانَويّ

new. . . . . . . . . . . . . . . . . . . . . . . . (adj., m.) جَديد ج جُدُد

beautiful, good-looking . . . . . . . . . . . . . (adj.) جَميل ج (ون)

modern . . . . . . . . . . . . . . . . . . . . . . . (adj.) حَديث

house. . . . . . . . . . . . . . . . . . . . . . . . (n., f.) دار ج دور

chicken. . . . . . . . . . . . . . . . . . . . . . . . (n., m) دَجاج

study . . . . . . . . . . . . . . . . . . . . . . (n., f.) دِراسة ج دِراسات

to go . . . . . . . . . . . . . . . . . . . . . . (v.) ذَهَبَ (يَذْهَبُ) ذَهاب (إلى)

driver, chauffeur . . . . . . . . . . . . . . . . (n., m.) سائِق ج سائقون

market . . . . . . . . . . . . . . . . . . . . . . (n., f.) سوق ج أسْواق

friend. . . . . . . . . . . . . . . . . . . . . . (n., m.) صَديق ج أصْدِقاء

small child, young child . . . . . . . . . . . . (n., m.) صَغير ج صِغار

tall . . . . . . . . . . . . . . . . . . . . . . . (n., m.) طَويل ج طِوال

family that one supports . . . . . . . . (f., s.) عائلة ج عوائِل \ عائلات

cord used to hold a headdress in place . . . . . (n., m.) عِقال ج عُقُل

to work. . . . . . . . . . . . . . . . . . . . . . (v.) عَمِلَ (يَعْمَلُ) عَمَل

a man's headdress. . . . . . . . . . . . . . (n., f.) غُتْرة ج غُتَر/ غُترات

girl, young woman . . . . . . . . . . . . . . . . (n., f.) فَتاة ج فَتَيات

old, ancient . . . . . . . . . . . . . . . . . . . (adj.) قَديم ج قُدَماء

short . . . . . . . . . . . . . . . . . . . . . . . . . . (n., m.) قَصير ج قِصار

powerful, strong . . . . . . . . . . . . . . . . . . (adj.) قَويّ ج أقوِياء

big, large; old (in age) . . . . . . . . . . . . . . (n., m.) كَبير ج كِبار

headdress . . . . . . . . . . . . . . . . . . . . . . (n., f.) كوفِيّة ج كوفيّات

to wear . . . . . . . . . . . . . . . . . . . . . . . . . (v.) لَبِسَ (يَلبَسُ) لُبْس

particle used to negate past-tense verbs . . . . . . . . . (particle) ما

engine, motor . . . . . . . . . . . . . . . . . . (n., f.) مُحَرِّك ج مَحَرِّكات

handsome . . . . . . . . . . . . . . . . . . . . . . (adj., m.) وَسيم ج (ون)

India . . . . . . . . . . . . . . . . . . . . . . . . . . . . . . (n., f.) الهِنْد

Japan . . . . . . . . . . . . . . . . . . . . . . . . . . . . . (n., f.) اليابان

# الدرسُ الحادي عشر

التقويم الهاشمي
تصدره سنويا
محمد هاشم الكتبي بدمشق
١٤٣٠ هجري
الأربعاء
٢٠٠٨ غربي
المحرم
كانون الأول (ديسمبر)
٤
٣١
فجر شمس ظهر عصر مغرب عشاء
غ ١٢،٢٦ ١،٢ ٠،٧ ٩،٣٩ ١٢ ١،٢١
ز ٨،٥ ٤٢،٦ ٤٢،١١ ٢١،٢ ٤٢،٤ ٣،٦
كانون الأول
١٨ شرقي
Wednesday
31
December
٥٧٦٩ عبري
٤ طيبت
كل عام وأنتم بخير

## Objectives

- Describing activities in the past, present, and future
- Expressing sequence using قَبْلَ وبَعْدَ
- Expressing certainty or uncertainty using أظُنُّ أنَّ
- Reporting other people's speech using قال إن
- Introduction to the superlative and comparative degrees
- Introduction to the إضافة structure using the dual and plural
- Introduction to the verb كان
- Learning about Arab and Muslim calendars
- Introduction to the preposition بِـ
- Introduction to the five special nouns

## المُفردات الجَديدة في صُوَر عَديدة:

مَشى (يَمشي) مَشْيٌ

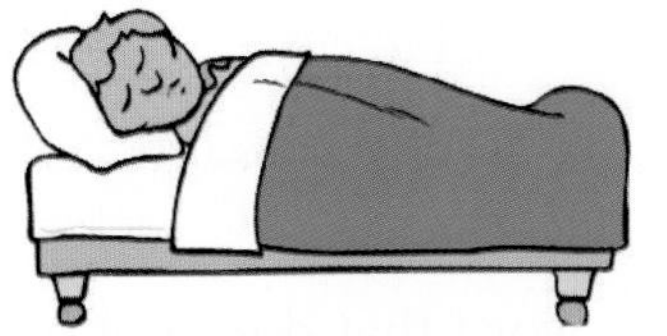

نامَ (يَنامُ) نَومٌ

فُندُقٌ

أمْس اليَوْم غداً

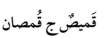

قَميصٌ ج قُمصان

## رُكْنُ المُفرداتِ الجَديدة:

| | |
|---|---|
| نَزَلَ (يَنْزِلُ) نُزول (في) | to stay at |
| وَصَلَ (يَصِلُ) وُصول (إلى) | to arrive |
| ظَنَّ (يَظُنُّ) ظَنّ (أنَّ) | to think (that) |
| قالَ (يَقولُ) قَوْل (إنَّ) | to say (that) |
| بَعيدٌ (عَن) | far (from) |
| قَريبٌ (مِن) | close (to) |
| قَبْلَ | before |
| بَعْدَ | after |

| Times | |
|---|---|
| *minute(s)* | دَقيقة ج دَقائق |
| *hour(s)* | ساعة ج ساعات |
| *day(s)* | يَوْم ج أيّام |
| *week(s)* | أُسْبوع ج أسابيع |
| *month(s)* | شَهْر ج شُهور/ أشْهُر |
| *season(s)* | فَصْل ج فُصول |
| *year(s)* | سَنة ج سِنون / سُنون |

The name of the chart below is **أيّامُ الأسبوع**. Take a look at the word **أسبوع**. Can you determine its three-letter root? If you can, its meaning will be a hard word to forget, because there are *seven* days in a week.

| أيّام الأسْبوع | | | | | | |
|---|---|---|---|---|---|---|
| يَوْم | | | | | | |
| السَبت | الجُمْعة | الخَميس | الأرْبِعاء | الثُلاثاء | الإثْنَين | الأحَد |
| *Saturday* | *Friday* | *Thursday* | *Wednesday* | *Tuesday* | *Monday* | *Sunday* |

- **Error Prevention:** To say "on" a day, we use **يوم الـ** or sometimes **في يوم الـ**, but we never use **على** in this case.

## تمرين ١

**Odd word out:** Underline the word that does not belong in each set and explain your choice if needed.

١- وَصَلَ شَهْر ذَهَبَ نامَ
٢- غُرفَة فُندُق مَطعَم مَقصَف
٣- الجُمْعَة يَوم الإثْنَيْن أيْلول
٤- كَبير بَعيد حينَ قَريب
٥- وِسادَة ساعَة بَطّانِيَّة شَرشَف

# تمرين ٢

وافِقْ بَيْنَ الكَلِماتِ في العَمودَيْنِ. **Matching:**

| | | | | |
|---|---|---|---|---|
| ١ | آب | | | أُسْبوع |
| ٢ | مَساءً | | | سَوفَ |
| ٣ | نَزَلَ | | | المِكسيك |
| ٤ | شُباط | | | السَبْت |
| ٥ | وِسادَة | | | فُندُق |
| ٦ | فاهيتا | | | سَرير |
| ٧ | شَهْر | | | ظُهْراً |
| ٨ | الأحَد | | | فِبرايِر |
| ٩ | كانون الثاني | | | طائِرة |
| ١٠ | مَطار | | | يَنايِر |
| | | | | أغُسطُس |

## يَوْميّاتُ طالِبٍ عَرَبيٍّ في أمريكا

هذا عَدنان مارتيني هو طالِبٌ عَرَبيٌّ مِن سورية يَدرُسُ عِلمَ الحاسوبِ في جامِعَةِ وِلايَةِ أوهايو. كَتَبَ عَدنان هذِه اليَوْميّاتِ حينَ أتى إلى أمريكا.

مَطارٌ

طائِرَةٌ

**الخَميس ١٤ أيْلول ٢٠٠٥**

وَصَلْتُ اليَوْمَ إلى مَطارِ كِنيدي في نيويورك في الساعَةِ السادِسةِ مَساءً. ذَهَبتُ إلى فُندُقِ شيراتُن في المطارِ وأَكَلتُ في مَطعَمِ الفُندُق. بَعْدَ ذلِكَ ذَهبتُ إلى غُرفَتي ونِمْتُ حَتّى الساعةِ السابِعةِ مِن صَباحِ يَوْمِ الجُمْعة. مَوعِدُ طائِرَتي في الساعةِ العاشِرةِ والنِصْفِ صَباحاً.

السَبْت الأحَد الإثنين الثُلاثاء الأرْبعاء الخَميس الجُمْعة
١
٧ ٨
١٤ ١٥
٢١ ٢٢
٢٨ ٢٩
أيلول
٢٠٠٥
تقويم


**مَواعِيد**
**عَدنان اليومية**

| الخَميس ١٤ أيلول ٢٠٠٥ | الساعة | الجُمْعة ١٥ أيلول ٢٠٠٥ |
|---|---|---|
| اللُغة الإنكليزيّة | ٩ | |
| | ١٠ | مَوْعِدُ الطائِرة العاشِرة والنِصف |
| | ١١ | |
| الرياضيّات | ١٢ | مَوْعِدُ الوُصولِ إلى مَطار كَلَمبَس |
| | ١ | |
| | ٢ | |
| الكيمياء | ٣ | |
| | ٤ | |
| | ٥ | |
| مَوْعِدُ الوُصولِ إلى مَطار كَنيدي | ٦ | |

**الجُمْعَة ١٥ أيْلول ٢٠٠٥**

وَصَلتُ إلى مَطارِ كَلَمبَس في الساعةِ الثانِيةَ عَشْرة ظُهْراً. حينَ وَصلتُ إلى المطارِ كانَ هِشام هُناكَ (هِشام هو صَديقُ أخي رامي). نَزَلتُ في شَقَّةِ هِشام. يُوجَدُ في شَقَّتِه غُرفَتا نَوْم وغُرفةُ جُلوسٍ واحِدة. غُرفةُ نَوْمِ هِشام أَكْبَرُ مِن الغُرفةِ الثانية. أظُنُّ أنّي سأسكُنُ مَعَهُ في هذا الشَهْر.

ذَهَبْنا أنا وهِشام أَمْسِ إلى السوقِ بِالسَيّارةِ وهي بَعيدةٌ عَنِ الشَقّة. اِشْتَرَيْتُ وِسادةً وشَرشَفينِ وبَطّانِيّتَينِ لِسَريري، واشْتَرى هِشام قَميصاً جَديداً بِخَمسةٍ وعِشرينَ دولاراً. بَعْدَ ذلِكَ أكَلنا في مَطعَمِ مِكسيكيٍّ قَريبٍ مِن شَقَّتِه. أَكَلَ هِشام فاهيتا بِاللَحْمِ وأنا أكَلتُ فاهيتا بِالدّجاج. يُحِبُّ هِشام الأَكْلَ المِكسيكيّ. سآكُلُ غَداً في مَطعَمٍ عَرَبِيٍّ إنْ شاءَ الله.

**الأَرْبعاء ٢٠ أيلول ٢٠٠٥**

كُنْتُ اليَوْمَ في الجامِعَة. ذَهَبْتُ إلى دُروسي ومَشَيْتُ في الجامِعةِ. أظُنُّ أنَّ جامِعَةَ ولايةِ أوهايو كَبيرةٌ جِدّاً. يَقولُ هِشام إنَّها أكْبَرُ جامِعةٍ في الوِلاياتِ المُتَّحِدَةِ الأمريكيّة. في الساعةِ الخامِسةِ مَساءً مَشَيْتُ إلى الشَقَّة. قَبْلَ ذلِكَ مَشَيْتُ إلى مَكتبَةِ «إس بي إكس» القَريبةِ مِن الجامِعةِ واشْتَرَيْتُ كُتُبي مِنها. اِشْتَرَيْتُ سَبعَةَ كُتُبٍ وثَلاثَةَ دَفاتِرَ بِمِئتَينِ وسِتَّةٍ وسَبعينَ دولاراً. سأقرَأُ قَليلاً قَبْلَ النَوْمِ وسَوْفَ أكتُبُ إلى أبي وأمّي.

## تمرين ٣

**Conversation:** You have just arrived at the Cairo airport and you need someone to meet you there to take you to your new apartment. Relate the following information to your friend, trying to incorporate the words from the word bank:

| | | | |
|---|---|---|---|
| *to arrive* | وَصَلَ (يَصِلُ) وُصول (إلى) | *to come* | أتى / يأتي / إتيان (إلى) |
| *to do* | فَعَلَ (يَفْعَلُ) فِعْل | *to buy* | اِشْتَرى / يَشْتَري / شِراء |

1. your plane's time of arrival
2. what street your new apartment is on
3. when your friend wants to eat lunch and who is buying (paying)
4. what you want to do in Cairo and on what day
5. when you want to go to the markets so you can buy some new ___________

## عُطلةُ نِهايةِ الأسبوعِ في البِلادِ العَرَبيَّةِ

يَذهَبُ الطُلّابُ إلى المَدارِسِ سِتَّةَ أيّام في الأُسْبوعِ في بعضِ البِلادِ العَرَبيَّةِ ويَعمَلُ الناسُ سِتّةَ أيّامٍ في الأُسْبوعِ أيْضاً. ويَوْمُ الجُمْعَةِ هو عُطلَةُ نِهايةِ الأُسْبوعِ. في سورية عطلةُ نهايةِ الأسبوعِ هي يوما الجمعةِ والسبتِ، لكِنَّ عَطْلَةَ نهايةِ الأسْبوعِ في لُبنانَ هي يَوْما الجُمْعَةِ والأَحَد.

## تمرين ٤

AUDIO

**A. Listen and select:** Check the box that matches the information as expressed in the passages for this lesson.

١- وَصَلَ عَدنان إلى مَطارِ كِنيدي ________________ .

☐ في الساعةِ العاشِرة ☐ في الساعةِ السادِسة ☐ بِالسَيّارة

٢- كانَ مَوْعِدُ طائِرةِ كَلَمبَس في الساعةِ ________________ .

☐ السادِسة ☐ العاشِرةِ والنِصْف ☐ الثانِيَةَ عَشْرة

٣- هِشام ________________ .

☐ صَديقُ عَدنان ☐ أخو رامي ☐ صَديقُ رامي

٤- حينَ وَصَلَ عَدنان إلى مَطارِ كَلَمبَس كانَ هِشام في ________________ .

☐ المَطار ☐ الجامِعة ☐ الشَقَّة

٥- يوجَدُ في شَقَّةِ هِشام ________________ .

☐ غُرفَةُ نَوْمٍ واحِدة ☐ غُرفَتا نَوْم ☐ ثَلاثُ غُرَفِ نَوْم

٦- في هذا الشَهرِ سَوفَ يَسكُنُ عَدنان في ________________ .

☐ شَقَّةِ هِشام ☐ فُندُق ☐ سَكَنِ الطُلاّب

٧- اِشْتَرى هِشام ________________ .

☐ كُتُباً ☐ قَميصاً ☐ وِسادةً

٨- اِشْتَرى عَدنان كُتُباً بِـ ________________ دولاراً.

☐ ٧٢٦ ☐ ٦٢٧ ☐ ٢٧٦

**B. صواب أم خطأ:** Mark the following sentences صواب or خطأ according to the information in the main reading passage and correct any untrue sentences.

٩- سَيَسكُنُ عَدنان في غُرفَةٍ كَبيرة.

________________________________________

١٠- وَصَلَ عَدنان إلى كَلَمبَس يَوْمَ الجُمْعَة.

________________________________________

١١- ذَهَبَ عَدنان إلى دُروسِه في الجامِعَةِ يَوْمَ الثُلاثاء.

---

١٢- يَظُنُّ عَدنان أنَّ جامِعَةَ وِلايَةِ أوهايو أكبَرُ مِن جامِعَةِ دِمَشق.

---

## 1. Describing Activities in the Past, Present, and Future

You are already familiar with the past and present forms of the Arabic verb. The past denotes an action that has been completed, and it is formed by adding suffixes. The present describes an action that is not complete yet, and it is formed by adding prefixes (with suffixes indicating gender and number). The future describes an action that has not occurred yet, but will take place at a later time. It is formed by prefixing the future marker سَـ (the first letter of the future particle سَوْفَ) to the present-tense form of the verb (indicative **المُضارِع المَرفوع**) or by inserting **سَوْفَ** right before the present-tense verb. There is no difference in meaning between using **سَوْفَ** or سَـ.

| | Present | | Future |
|---|---|---|---|
| ١ | يَدْرُسُ | ← | سَيَدْرُسُ / سَوْفَ يَدْرُسُ |

- **Note:** No change in the verb form is involved when using either **سَوْفَ** or سَـ.

### تمرين ٥

**Conversation: Using the future particles سَوْفَ و سَـ**. Find out from your neighbor what he/she is planning on doing at particular times on certain days of the week, or what he/she is planning to do this weekend **عُطلة نِهاية الأسبوع هذه**. The person responding might wish to answer using: "I think that I . . ."

**Example:** *What are you doing this Friday?*
*I think that I am going to read at the library Friday evening.*

**مِثال:** ماذا تَفعَلُ يَوْمَ الجُمْعة؟
أظُنُّ أنّني سأقْرَأُ في المَكتَبَةِ يَوْمَ الجُمْعة مَساءً.

Some topics that you might wish to ask about are: eating, sleeping, writing, reading, studying, buying, talking, going, and walking.

Write your answers down on a separate sheet of paper, and be prepared to report your answers to your classmates.

## 2. Expressing Sequence قَبْلَ، بَعْدَ

The word for **adverb** in Arabic is ظَرف, which means "vessel" or "container," referring to how an action or a state is situated, as in أشربُ الحليبَ صباحاً 'I drink milk in the morning', where the action (drinking) is specified to take place in the morning, which is the adverb. The words قَبلَ 'before' and بَعدَ 'after' are adverbs of time and place (e.g., قَبلَهُ 'before him/it'), but they are used as prepositions with other nouns (قَبلَ الفُندُق 'before the hotel'; بعدَ الظُهر 'afternoon'). In the preceding reading passages, they are used with reference to time.

These two adverbs behave just like prepositions in that the noun that follows them is مَجرور (genitive) marked by a كَسرة with definite nouns, ـيْنِ with dual nouns, or ينَ with sound masculine plurals.

## تمرين ٦

Describe the following events with respect to Adnān's schedule, using the adverbs قبل وبعد. If you wish to specify the number of hours before or after an event happens, use the preposition بـِ.

مِثال: دَرْسُ اللُغةِ الإنكليزيّة بَعْدَ الفَطور بساعةٍ وقَبْلَ دَرْسِ الرياضيّات بثَلاثِ ساعاتٍ.

| الخَميس ٧ أيلول ٢٠٠٥ | الساعة |
|---|---|
| الفَطور | ٨ |
| اللُغة الإنكليزية | ٩ |
| | ١٠ |
| | ١١ |
| الرياضيّات | ١٢ |
| | ١ |
| | ٢ |
| الكيمياء | ٣ |
| | ٤ |
| الذَهاب إلى السوق | ٥ |

١- دَرسُ الرياضيّات ________________________________

________________________________________________

٢- دَرسُ الكيمياء ________________________________

________________________________________________

## 3. Expressing Certainty or Uncertainty

When you are not absolutely certain of something, you may use the verb ظَنَّ 'think' to express the degree of certainty you have. This verb is immediately followed by the particle أنَّ 'that', which must be followed by either a pronoun or a noun (highlighted in blue in examples 2 and 3).

٢ أينَ هالَة؟ - أظُنُّ أنَّها في المَدرَسَةِ الآن.

٣ أينَ كِتابي؟ - أظُنُّ أنَّ الأستاذَ يَقرَأُه.

**A. The Particle أنَّ**

In example 2, the suffix ـها attached to أنَّ refers back to هالة. In example 3, أنَّ is followed by a noun الأستاذَ. Note that a فتحة appears on the last radical of الأستاذُ. This is because أنَّ makes the nouns and pronouns that follow it accusative (مَنصوب). Other markers of the accusative include a double فتحة (for indefinite nouns), ـَيْنِ (for dual nouns), or ـِينَ (for sound masculine plurals).

Remember that the subject and predicate in a nominal sentence are nominative (مَرفوع بِضَمّة) if they are not modified by أنَّ. The subject of أنَّ is in the accusative (مَنصوب) while its predicate remains in the مَرفوع/nominative (highlighted in blue in example 4).

٤ أظُنُّ أنَّ أختَكِ طَويلةٌ.

**B. Verbs with Doubled Consonants**

The verb ظَنَّ is made up of two consonants, the ظاء and the نون. The نون is a doubled consonant, as can be seen by the شَدّة. The conjugation of doubled verbs is slightly different from those with three different consonants.

- **Note:** The doubled consonant (e.g., the doubled نون in أظُنُّ, تَظُنُّ, and يَظُنُّ) occurs in all conjugations in the present and in the third person in the past (e.g., ظَنَّ), but not in the first and second persons in the past.
- As a rule, the second radical (consonant) of doubled verbs (such as the نون of ظنّ) appears twice in the first- and second-person past tense (refer to the table below entitled تَصريف الفِعْل ظَنَّ). Notice, though, that the شدة is absent from these conjugations.

| تَصريف الفِعْل ظَنَّ | | | |
|---|---|---|---|
| | الضمير المنفصل | الماضي | المُضارِع |
| المُتَكَلِّم | أنا | ظَنَنْتُ | أظُنُّ |
| | نَحْنُ | ظَنَنّا | نَظُنُّ |
| المُخاطَب | أنْتَ | ظَنَنْتَ | تَظُنُّ |
| | أنْتِ | ظَنَنْتِ | تَظُنِّين |
| | أنْتُما | ظَنَنْتُما | تَظُنّانِ |
| | أنْتُم | ظَنَنْتُم | تَظُنّونَ |
| | أنْتُنَّ | ظَنَنْتُنَّ | تَظْنُنَّ |
| الغائب | هُوَ | ظَنَّ | يَظُنُّ |
| | هِيَ | ظَنَّتْ | تَظُنُّ |
| | هُما (مُذَكَّر) | ظَنّا | يَظُنّانِ |
| | هُما (مُؤَنَّث) | ظَنَّتا | تَظُنّانِ |
| | هُم | ظَنّوا | يَظُنّونَ |
| | هُنَّ | ظَنَنَّ | يَظْنُنَّ |

## تمرين ٧

**Conversation using ظَنَّ أنَّ**: Find out what your neighbor thinks of your favorite movie/actor/car/athletic team/song, etc. If your neighbor does not like your favorite movie, see if you can relate why you like it so much.

As a follow-up exercise, try this exercise again after completing section 5 of this lesson concerning the use of superlatives; using them could go a long way in convincing your classmate why you think your favorite movie/actor/car, etc., is so good.

## 4. Reporting Other People's Speech Using the Verb قالَ 'say'

### The Particle إنَّ

The verb قال is followed by the particle إنَّ 'that', which is very similar to أنَّ (the difference, as you may have noticed, is the فَتحة or the كَسرة following the هَمزة). إنَّ must be followed by either a pronoun or a noun, which will be مَنصوب (accusative).

- **Remember:** If a noun is the subject of a nominal sentence (= a sentence starting with a noun) and is preceded by أنَّ or إنَّ, the predicate of the sentence remains مَرفوع (nominative) as is seen in example 5:

٥ يَقولُ عَبدُ الرحمنِ إنَّ مَكتبَهُ كَبيرٌ.

Example 5 illustrates how إنَّ affects its subject and predicate in that مَكتبَ is مَنصوب (accusative indicated by a فَتحة) and كَبيرٌ is مَرفوع (nominative indicated by a تَنوين ضَمّة).

- **Note:** The verb قال is followed by the particle إنَّ while أنَّ follows all other verbs that require it.

## تمرين ٨

**Use of أنَّ or إنَّ:** Use either أنَّ or إنَّ before the nouns in parentheses and provide the correct endings for the nouns that follow them.

١– يَظُنُّ سَميحٌ ________ (الجامِعَة) بَعيدةٌ.

٢– تَقولُ ريم ________ (سَيّارتها) قَديمةٌ.

٣– هَل تَظُنّينَ ________ (الكِتاب x ٢) بِعِشرينَ دولاراً؟

٤– أظُنُّ ________ (مَدينَة) سان فَرانسيسكو جَميلةٌ.

٥– يَقولُ صَديقي بَشّار ________ (الطُلاّب) لَيْسوا في الصَفِّ.

٦– تَقولُ سُعاد ________ (السَيّارة x ٢) (جَديدَة x ٢).

## تمرين ٩

**Conversation using قالَ إنَّ:** Talk with one of your classmates to find out whom he/she spoke to today either on the telephone or in person. Ask about who said what to whom. Report what your neighbor said during his/her conversation to the class.

مِثال: ماذا قالَتْ ليسا لآلَن؟ – قالَتْ إنّها سَتَشْتَري حاسوباً.

## 5. Comparing and Contrasting Entities اِسْمُ التَفضيل

When we compare or contrast things, we compare their attributes by using adjectives. In English, there are two degrees of comparison: the comparative and the superlative degrees. As you know, the comparative degree is formed by suffixing "-er" to adjectives or by using the word "more" before them (e.g., taller, bigger, more beautiful). The superlative degree is formed by suffixing "-est" to adjectives or by using the word "most" (e.g., tallest, biggest, most beautiful).

In Arabic, both degrees of comparison are formed by using the pattern أفْعَل. To form the comparative/superlative degree in Arabic, add a هَمزة to the beginning of the three-letter root of any word and, *voilà,* you have the superlative. To derive the verb from an adjective, we must first learn how to recognize an adjectival pattern. One adjectival pattern that we are familiar with at this point is the *letter, letter,* ي, *letter* pattern.

| The Adjectival Pattern | | | |
|---|---|---|---|
| ٣ | | ٢ | ١ |
| ـل | ـيـ | ـعـ | فـ |

- **Note:** When explaining grammatical patterns, grammarians use the following formula: the **فاء** represents the first letter of any word, the **عين** the second letter, and the **لام** the third letter. Any other letter that you see in this pattern is an added letter. From now on, we will be using these three letters to explain the various patterns of Arabic words.

The added letter in our example is the **ي** that follows the **عين**, giving us the adjectival form **فَعيل**. Consider the formation of the comparative degree from several adjectives that we already know:

٦ كَبير أكْبَر
٧ بَعيد أبْعَد
٨ قَريب أقْرَب
٩ جَميل أجْمَل

### A. The Superlative

As we have stated, to form the superlative, we use the **أفْعل** pattern. The superlative forms an **إضافة** structure with the following noun, which may be singular (example 10), dual (example 11), or plural (example 12). The plural form may be definite or indefinite.

١٠ هِشام أطْوَلُ طالِبٍ في الصَفِّ.
١١ هِشام وسامي أطْوَلُ طالِبيْنِ في الصَفِّ.
١٢ هِشام وسامي وعَبدُ الرَحيم أطْوَلُ طُلاّبٍ (أو :الطُلاّبِ) في الصَفِّ.

### B. The Comparative

To form the comparative degree, just add **مِن** (= than) after the **أفْعل** pattern.

١٣ هالَة أطْوَلُ مِن أُختِها. *Hāla is taller than her sister.*

- **Note:** If a pronoun is used in the comparison, it attaches to the preposition **مِن**.

١٤ هالَة أطوَلُ مِنها (مِن + هِيَ = مِنْها).

## تمرين ١٠

**Forming the comparative/superlative:** On a separate sheet of paper, translate the following sentences into Arabic and change the adjectives between parentheses to the **أفْعَل** pattern. Context will dictate whether you use the comparative or superlative degree.

١- سان فرانْسيسكو (جَميل) ديترويت.

٢- جامِعةُ ويسكونسن واحِدةٌ مِن (كَبير) الجامِعاتِ في أمريكا.

٣- سَناء (طَويل) طالِبةٍ في الصَفّ.

٤- أريحا (قَدَم) مَدينةٍ في العالَم.

٥- حاسوبُ هُدى (كَبير) حاسوبي.

٦- اِشْتَرى هاني (حَديث) سَيّارةٍ في السوق.

٧- باريس وروما (جَميل) مَدينَتَيْنِ في أوروبا.

٨- سَناء (طَويل) أنا.

## تمرين ١١

**Conversation using أفْعل**: Find out who in the classroom. . .

1. is the oldest
2. is the youngest
3. is the tallest
4. is the shortest
5. has a car newer than your instructor's car
6. lives closest to the university/college you attend
7. lives farther away from the university/college than your instructor

Remember to take notes in order to report your findings.

### 6. The إضافة Structure: Dual and Plural

If you recall, an **إضافة** structure is made up of at least two parts: the first member is a noun called **مُضاف** 'added' and the second member is a noun called **مُضاف إلَيْهِ** 'a noun to which another noun is added'. If the **مُضاف** is dual, we drop the final **نون**

(e.g., example 16). Similarly, we drop the final **نون** from sound masculine plurals (e.g., example 17).

١٦ غُرفَتانِ + نَوْم = غُرفَتا نَوْم.

١٧ سائِقونَ + السَيّارات = سائقو السَيّاراتِ.

The **نون** in **غُرفَتان** and **سائقون** is dropped because these nouns function as **مُضاف** (i.e., the first part of an **إضافة** structure), meaning literally 'two rooms of sleep' and 'drivers of cars'.

## تمرين ١٢

**Identify the إضافة:** Examine these two advertisements (the middle rectangles) and circle all instances of **إضافة** structures. There are nine **إضافة** structures.

| | |
|---|---|
| سيارة بسعرمغر. يرجى الاتصال على الهاتف ٦٦٧٤٦٣٢-إياد. | للمراجعة الرجاء الاتصال بالهاتف ٤٥٧٩٨٤٤. |
| مطلوب سائقي شاحنات للعمل في شركة المطاحن. يتراوح الراتب الشهري من مئتي دينار إلى ثلاثمئة دينار. | دار في شارع الجلاء مع هاتف وبرّاد وغسالة وتلفاز. ثلاث غرف نوم وغرفتا جلوس وغرفة طعام مع المفروشات. الإيجار السنوي ٦٠٠ ألف ليرة. |
| قطعة أرض في صحنايا صالحة | محل تجاري في وسط المدينة |

## 7. The Verb كانَ

The verb **كانَ** is the Arabic equivalent of the verb "to be" and it conjugates like any other hollow verb (i.e., the middle radical is a long vowel). While **كانَ** is rarely used in present-tense sentences, it is used frequently in past-tense sentences (example 18) and when you want to express future time (example 19). There are present-tense sentences, however, that require the use of this verb, as in example 20.

١٨ كُنتُ أمْسِ في مَكتَبي في الساعةِ الثامِنةِ.

١٩ سَأكونُ في مَكتَبي في الساعةِ الثامِنةِ غَداً.

٢٠ أكونُ في مَكتَبي في الساعةِ الثامِنةِ صباحاً.

The adverbs أَمسِ 'yesterday' in example 18 and غَداً 'tomorrow' in example 19 define the time of an action. The adverb أمسِ requires the use of the past tense, while غداً requires the use of the present tense with the future particle.

| تَصريف الفِعْل كان | | | |
|---|---|---|---|
| المُضارِع | الماضي | الضمير المنفصل | |
| أكونُ | كُنْتُ | أنا | المُتَكَلِّم |
| نكونُ | كُنّا | نَحْنُ | |
| تكونُ | كُنْتَ | أنْتَ | المُخاطَب |
| تَكونينَ | كُنْتِ | أنْتِ | |
| تَكونانِ | كُنْتُما | أنْتُما | |
| تَكونونَ | كُنْتُم | أنْتُم | |
| تَكُنَّ | كُنْتُنَّ | أنْتُنَّ | |
| يَكونُ | كانَ | هُوَ | الغائب |
| تكونُ | كانَتْ | هِيَ | |
| يَكونانِ | كانا | هُما (مُذَكَّر) | |
| تَكونانِ | كانَتا | هُما (مُؤَنَّث) | |
| يَكونونَ | كانوا (silent *alif*) | هُم | |
| يَكُنَّ | كُنَّ | هنَّ | |

The verb كانَ (and others in its class) differs from other regular verbs in that: (1) it provides a time frame for a nominal sentence; and (2) it causes the predicate of a nominal sentence to be مَنصوب. You are already familiar with another member of its group used for negation, لَيْسَ, which has the same effect on its predicate.

٢١ الفَتاةُ جَميلةٌ.

٢٢ كانَت الفَتاةُ جَميلةً.

The predicate جَميلة in example 21 is in the nominative case, but in example 22 when كانَ precedes جَميلة, it becomes accusative (مَنصوب) marked by a double فَتحة indicating indefiniteness.

## تمرين ١٣

**Fill in the blank:** Use the correct from of **كانَ** (past or present depending on context) to complete these sentences.

١- ____________ عليّ في الدارِ البَيضاء غَداً.   *Casablanca

٢- صَديقي أحمَد وزَوجَتُه ____________ في المَطعَمِ أمْس.

٣- مَن ____________ في المَطارِ حينَ وَصَلَتْ طائِرةُ دانة؟

٤- أنا وعائِلَتي ____________ عِندَكُم في الأسْبوعِ المُقْبِل.

٥- الأستاذُ والطُلّابُ ____________ أمامَ بابِ الجامِعَةِ بَعْدَ ظُهْرِ أمْس.

٦- هِيَ وأخوها ____________ في المَطعَمِ يَوْمَ الأحَدِ الماضي.

٧- أينَ ____________ أمْس يا هالَة؟

٨- مَتى ____________ في مَكتَبِكَ يا أستاذُ عادَةً؟

- **Note:** In addition to expressing possession, the adverbial phrase **عِندَ** + a noun or a pronoun signifies being at a particular location. For example, the phrase **عِندَ البابِ** means 'at the door'.

## تمرين ١٤

**Communicate, using كانَ:** You have just seen your favorite celebrity at the airport. Tell your classmate all about the encounter, who was with you, who was with the celebrity, what was said. and anything else that you would find interesting from your real or fictional encounter.

### 8. Calendars in the Arab World

Generally, two calendars are used in the Arab world: the Islamic lunar calendar and the Western solar calendar. The names of the months of the Western calendar vary from country to country. In the eastern part of the Middle East, the names of indigenous Babylonian-Semitic months are still in use, whereas in Egypt and North African countries two varieties of the Roman months are used.

In most Arab countries, the weekend عُطْلَةُ نِهايَةِ الأسبوع is one day: Friday. The week normally starts with Saturday, the first working day of the week in some countries, while it is Sunday in others. In Syria, for example, the weekend is Friday and Saturday. In Lebanon, however, where there is a substantial Christian community, Sunday is considered part of the weekend.

## A. The Islamic Calendar

The Islamic calendar is based on the lunar cycle, and its beginning is marked by the emigration هِجْرة of the Prophet *Muḥammad* from Mecca to Yathrib (*Medīna*) in AD 622, hence the designation هِجْريّة of the Islamic calendar (abbreviated as هـ). A lunar year is eleven days shorter than the solar year that is the basis for the Gregorian or Western calendar.

| شُهورُ السَنةِ الهِجريّة | | | |
|---|---|---|---|
| رَجَب | ٧ | مُحَرَّم | ١ |
| شَعبان | ٨ | صَفَر | ٢ |
| رَمَضان | ٩ | رَبيعُ الأوَّل | ٣ |
| شَوّال | ١٠ | رَبيعُ الآخِر | ٤ |
| ذو القِعْدة | ١١ | جُمادى الأولى | ٥ |
| ذو الحِجّة | ١٢ | جُمادى الآخِرة | ٦ |

| رَجَب ١٤٢٨ هـ | | | | | | |
|---|---|---|---|---|---|---|
| الجمعة | الخميس | الأربعاء | الثلاثاء | الإثنين | الأحد | السبت |
| ٦ | ٥ | ٤ | ٣ | ٢ | ١ | |
| ١٣ | ١٢ | ١١ | ١٠ | ٩ | ٨ | ٧ |
| ٢٠ | ١٩ | ١٨ | ١٧ | ١٦ | ١٥ | ١٤ |
| ٢٧ | ٢٦ | ٢٥ | ٢٤ | ٢٣ | ٢٢ | ٢١ |
| | | | | ٣٠ | ٢٩ | ٢٨ |

التقويم الهِجْريّ (الإسلاميّ)

## B. The Western Calendar

The Western calendar finds its roots in the Gregorian calendar and is called **التَقويم الغَربي** (the Western calendar) or **التقويم الميلادي** (**الميلادي** means "the birth" in reference to the birth of Christ). The abbreviation م is used to indicate the word **الميلادي**, a designation of Western calendars. The names of the months used in Egypt are listed in gray next to the indigenous names used in Greater Syria and Iraq.

| شُهورُ السنةِ الميلاديّة | | | | | |
|---|---|---|---|---|---|
| ١ | كانون الثاني | يَنايِر | ٧ | تَمّوز | يوليو / يولية |
| ٢ | شُباط | فِبرايِر | ٨ | آب | أغسطَس |
| ٣ | آذار | مارِس | ٩ | أيلول | سَبْتَمْبَر |
| ٤ | نيسان | أبريل | ١٠ | تِشرين الأوّل | أكْتوبَر |
| ٥ | أيّار / مايِس | مايو | ١١ | تِشرين الثاني | نوفَمْبَر |
| ٦ | حَزيران | يونيو / يونية | ١٢ | كانون الأوّل | ديسَمْبَر |

| تشرين الأول ٢٠٠٥ م | | | | | | |
|---|---|---|---|---|---|---|
| السبت | الأحد | الإثنين | الثلاثاء | الأربعاء | الخميس | الجمعة |
| | | | | | | ١ |
| ٢ | ٣ | ٤ | ٥ | ٦ | ٧ | ٨ |
| ٩ | ١٠ | ١١ | ١٢ | ١٣ | ١٤ | ١٥ |
| ١٦ | ١٧ | ١٨ | ١٩ | ٢٠ | ٢١ | ٢٢ |
| ٢٣ | ٢٤ | ٢٥ | ٢٦ | ٢٧ | ٢٨ | ٢٩ |
| ٣٠ | ٣١ | | | | | |

**التقويم الميلاديّ**

# تمرين ١٥

**Fill in the blank:** Complete the following sentences with appropriate months.

١- يأتي شَهْرُ تَمّوز بَعْدَ شَهْرِ ____________.

٢- يَأتي شَهْرُ آذارَ قَبْلَ شَهْرِ ____________.

٣- شَهْرُ ____________ هو الشَهْرُ السادِسُ في التَقويم الميلادي.

٤- الشَهْرُ الثاني عَشر هُوَ ____________.

٥- شَهْرُ ____________ هُوَ الشَهْرُ الثامِنُ في التَقويم الإسلامي.

٦- في الأُسْبوعِ ____________ الأيّام.

٧- يَأتي يَوْمُ الخَميسِ قَبْلَ يَوْمِ ____________.

٨- يَوْمُ الإثنَيْنِ بَعْدَ يَوْمِ ____________.

٩- يَوْمُ عُطْلَةِ نِهايَةِ الأُسبوعِ في البِلادِ العَرَبِيَّةِ هُوَ ____________.

١٠- عُطْلَةُ نِهايَةِ الأُسْبوعِ في أمريكا هِيَ يَوْما ____________.

## 9. The Preposition بِـ

As is the case with most prepositions, بِـ acquires its meaning from context. So far, three meanings have been used, as exemplified by these sentences:

٢٣ اِشْتَرَيْتُ كِتاباً بِعِشْرينَ دولاراً.

٢٤ أنا أكبَرُ مِن أختي بِسَنَتَيْنِ.

٢٥ ما مَعْنى "police" بِالعَرَبِيَّةِ؟

The preposition بِـ, as you can see, functions only as a prefix and causes the modified noun to be مَجْرور (genitive), as indicated by the ي in examples 23 and 24 and the كَسرة in example 25.

## 10. Two of the Five Special Nouns (أب and أخ)

There are five nouns in Arabic which behave in a different manner from other nouns. Regular nouns are marked for case by short vowels, whereas these five nouns are marked by long vowels. We already learned two of them: أب and أخ. Compare the three cases illustrated in example 26 with those in example 27, paying close attention to how أبو takes the long vowel equivalent of the short vowels of example 26.

| | ٢٦ | ٢٧ |
|---|---|---|
| مَرفوع | هذا كِتابُ حازِم. | هذا أبو حازِم. |
| مَنصوب | اِشتَرَيْتُ كِتابَ حازِم. | إنَّ أبا حازِم في الدارِ. |
| مَجرور | لِكِتابِ حازِم. | لِأبي حازِم |

The noun أبو (مَرفوع) in example 27 serves as the predicate of the sentence; أبا (مَنصوب) is modified by the particle إنَّ, which makes the subject of a nominal sentence accusative; and أبي (مَجرور) is the object of a preposition. All five special nouns take the long vowel equivalent of the short vowel specific to each case. For example, the nominative رَفْعٌ takes a و instead of the ضَمّة, the accusative نَصْبٌ takes an ألف (ا) instead of the فَتحة, and the genitive جَرٌّ takes a ي instead of the كَسرة.

## تمرين ١٦

**Two of the five nouns:** Provide the correct case markers for the nouns in parentheses, using short or long vowels as appropriate

١- هَل هذا الكِتابُ لـ (أخ + هيَ) ____________________

٢- أدرُسُ (اللُغَة) العربِيَّة. ____________________

٣- يَعمَلُ (أب) سامية في الدارِ البَيضاء. ____________________

٤- هذا (الكِتاب) لَيسَ لي. ____________________

٥- يَدرُسُ صَديقي في (جامِعَة) دِمَشق. ____________________

٦- إنَّ (أب) سَليم صَديقُ أبي. ____________________

## تمرين ١٧

**A. Listen and select:** Check the box that matches the information as expressed in the listening passage for this lesson.

١- ذَهَبَ حَسّان إلى ________________ .

☐ دِمَشق ☐ الرِياض ☐ القاهِرة

٢- حَسّان لَهُ ________________ .

☐ اِبنٌ واحِدٌ ☐ اِبنٌ وبِنتٌ ☐ ثَلاثَةُ أبناء

٣- نَزَلَ حَسّان في ________________ .

☐ فُنْدُق ☐ شَقَّةِ أخيهِ ☐ دارِ أبيه

٤- في بَيْتِ أبي حَسّان ________________ .

☐ غُرفتا نَومِ ☐ ثَلاثُ غُرَفِ نَوْم ☐ أربَعُ غُرَفِ نَوْم

**B. صواب أو خطأ:** Mark the following sentences صواب or خطأ according to the information in the listening passage and correct any untrue sentences.

٥- ذَهَبَ حَسّان إلى الرِياضِ بِالسَيّارةِ مَعَ زَوْجَتِهِ.

________________________________________

٦- كانَ أبو حَسّان في المَطارِ حينَ وَصَلَ حَسّان وعائِلَتُه.

________________________________________

٧- حَسّان طالِبٌ في مَدرَسَةٍ ثانَويةٍ في دِمَشق.

________________________________________

٨- رانِية أصغَرُ مِن رائِد بِسَنَتَيْن.

________________________________________

## تمرين ١٨

VIDEO

**تَمرينُ المُشاهَدة: شاهِدوا الدَرْسَ الحادي عَشَر على القُرص الرَقْمي.**

١- لماذا يَذْهَبُ سامِر وستيف إلى مَطار دِمَشْق الدُوَليّ؟ ______________________

______________________________________________

٢- مَتى وَصَلَ عَدنان إلى سوريَّة؟ ______________________

______________________________________________

٣- مَتى سَيَصِلُ مايكل إلى دِمَشْق؟ ______________________

______________________________________________

٤- كَيْفَ تَعَرَّفَ سامِر على مايكل؟ ______________________

______________________________________________

٥- مَن سَيُقابِلُ عَدنان وستيف غداً؟ ______________________

______________________________________________

6. Try to guess what the word **أكيد** means from context and write your answer here:

______________________________

## المُفْرَدات

Listen to the vocabulary items on the CD and practice their pronunciation.

August . . . . . . . . . . . . . . . . . . . . . . . . (n., m.) آب

to come . . . . . . . . . . . . . . . . . . . . (v.) أتى (يأتي) إتيان (إلى)

Monday . . . . . . . . . . . . . . . . . . . . . . . (n., m.) الإثْنَين

Sunday . . . . . . . . . . . . . . . . . . . . . . . (n., m.) الأَحَد

March . . . . . . . . . . . . . . . . . . . . . . . . (n., m.) آذار

Wednesday . . . . . . . . . . . . . . . . . . . . (n., m.) الأَرْبِعاء

week . . . . . . . . . . . . . . . . . . . . . (n., m.) أُسْبوع ج أَسابيع

to buy . . . . . . . . . . . . . . . . . . . . (v.) اِشتَرى (يَشتري) شِراء

certainly, surely . . . . . . . . . . . . . . . . . . . (exclamation) أكيد

yesterday . . . . . . . . . . . . . . . . . . . . . . . . . (adv.) أَمْسِ

that (after verbs similar to "think") . . . . . . . . . . . . (particle) أَنَّ

that (after the verb for "say") . . . . . . . . . . . . . . . (particle) إنَّ

hopefully (*lit.* "God willing") . . . . . . . . . . (set phrase) إنْ شاءَ الله

May. . . . . . . . . . . . . . . . . . . . . . . . . . . . (n., m.) أيّار

September . . . . . . . . . . . . . . . . . . . . . . . (n., m.) أَيْلول

some . . . . . . . . . . . . . . . . . . . . . . . . . . . . . . . بَعْض

October . . . . . . . . . . . . . . . . . . . . . (n., m.) تِشرين الأوَّل

November . . . . . . . . . . . . . . . . . . . . . (n., m.) تِشرين الثاني

to be acquainted with. . . . . . . . . . . (v.) تَعرَّفَ (يَتعَرَّفُ) تَعرُّف (على)

calendar . . . . . . . . . . . . . . . . . . . . . (n., m.) تَقويم ج تَقاويم

July . . . . . . . . . . . . . . . . . . . . . . . . . . (n., m.) تَمّوز

Tuesday . . . . . . . . . . . . . . . . . . . . . . . . (n., m.) الثُلاثاء

to come . . . . . . . . . . . . . . . . . . . . (v.) جاء (يَجيءُ) مَجيء

sitting . . . . . . . . . . . . . . . . . . . . . . . . (verbal noun) جُلوس

Islamic month (*Jumādī al-āḳira*) . . . . . . . . . (n., f.) جُمادى الآخِرة

Islamic month (*Jumādī al-'ūlā*). . . . . . . . . . (n., f.) جُمادى الأولى

Friday . . . . . . . . . . . . . . . . . . . . . . . . . (n., m.) الجُمعة

till, until . . . . . . . . . . . . . . . . . . . . . . . . (particle) حَتّى

June . . . . . . . . . . . . . . . . . . . . . . . . . . . (n., m.)حَزيران

when . . . . . . . . . . . . . . . . . . . . . . . . . . . . (adv.) حينَ

Thursday. . . . . . . . . . . . . . . . . . . . . . . . (n., m.) الخَميس

lesson. . . . . . . . . . . . . . . . . . . . . . . . . (n., m.) دَرْس ج دُروس

Islamic month (*ḏū al-ḥijja*) . . . . . . . . . . . (n., m.) ذو الحِجّة

Islamic month (*ḏū al-Qi'da*) . . . . . . . . . . . . (n., m.) ذو القِعدة

wonderful, awesome . . . . . . . . . . . . . . (active participle) رائع

Islamic month (*Rabī'al-āḳira*) . . . . . . . . . . . (n., m.)رَبيع الآخِر

Islamic month (*Rabī'al-'awwal*) . . . . . . . . . . (n., m.) رَبيع الأوَّل

Islamic month (*Rajab*). . . . . . . . . . . . . . . . . (n., m.) رَجَب

Islamic month (*Ramaḍān*). . . . . . . . . . . . . . . (n., m.) رَمَضان

to visit . . . . . . . . . . . . . . . . . . . . . . . (v.) زارَ (يَزورُ) زِيارة

shall, will. . . . . . . . . . . . . . . . . . . . . . . . (future particle) سَـ

Saturday. . . . . . . . . . . . . . . . . . . . . . . . . . (n.,m.) السَبْت

year. . . . . . . . . . . . . . . . . . . . . . . (n., f.) سَنة ج سَنَوات / سُنون

shall, will. . . . . . . . . . . . . . . . . . . . . . . (future particle) سَوْفَ

February . . . . . . . . . . . . . . . . . . . . . . . . . (n., m.) شُباط

bed sheet. . . . . . . . . . . . . . . . . . . . . .(n., m.) شَرْشَف ج شَراشِف

Islamic month (*ša'bān*) . . . . . . . . . . . . . . . . (n., m.) شَعبان

month . . . . . . . . . . . . . . . . . . . . . . (n., m.) شَهْر ج أشْهُر / شُهور

Islamic month (*šawwāl*) . . . . . . . . . . . . . . . . (n., m.) شَوّال

Islamic month (*ṣafar*) . . . . . . . . . . . . . . . (n., m.) صَفَر

guest . . . . . . . . . . . . . . . . . . . . . (n., m.) ضَيْف ج ضُيوف

airplane . . . . . . . . . . . . . . . . . . . (n., f.) طائِرة ج طائِرات

to think, to believe . . . . . . . . . . . . . . . . . . (v.) ظَنَّ (يَظُنُّ)

tomorrow . . . . . . . . . . . . . . . . . . . . . . . . (adv.) غَداً

hotel . . . . . . . . . . . . . . . . . . . . . . (n., m.) فُنْدُق ج فَنادِق

to meet. . . . . . . . . . . . . . . . . . . . (v.) قابَلَ (يُقابِلُ) مُقابَلة

to say . . . . . . . . . . . . . . . . . . . . . . (v.) قالَ (يَقولُ) قَوْل

before . . . . . . . . . . . . . . . . . . . . . . . . . . . (adv.) قَبْلَ

close, near . . . . . . . . . . . . . . . . . . . . . . . . (adv.) قَريب

shirt . . . . . . . . . . . . . . . . . . . . . . (n., m.) قَميص ج قُمْصان

to be (was, were) . . . . . . . . . . . . . . . . . (v.) كانَ (يَكونُ) كَوْن

December . . . . . . . . . . . . . . . . . . . . . (n., m.) كانون الأوَّل

January. . . . . . . . . . . . . . . . . . . . . . . (n., m.) كانون الثاني

objection. . . . . . . . . . . . . . . . . . . . . (active participle) مانِع

enthusiastic . . . . . . . . . . . . . . . . . . (active participle) مُتَحَمِّس

Islamic month (*muḥarram*) . . . . . . . . . . . . . . . . . (n., m.) مُحَرَّم

to walk . . . . . . . . . . . . . . . . . . . . . (v.) مَشى (يَمْشي) مَشي

airport . . . . . . . . . . . . . . . . . . . . . . (n., m.) مَطار ج مَطارات

to sleep. . . . . . . . . . . . . . . . . . . . . . . . (v.) نامَ (يَنامُ) نوم

to stay (in a place) . . . . . . . . . . . . . . . . . (v.) نَزَلَ (يَنْزِلُ) نُزول

sleeping . . . . . . . . . . . . . . . . . . . . . . . . . (verbal noun) نَوْم

April . . . . . . . . . . . . . . . . . . . . . . . . . . . (n., m.) نيسان

pillow . . . . . . . . . . . . . . . . . . . . . . . (n., f.) وِسادة ج وَسائِد

to arrive, to reach a destination . . . . . . . . . (v.) وَصَلَ (يَصِلُ) وُصول

day . . . . . . . . . . . . . . . . . . . . . . . . . . (n., m.) يَوْم ج أيّام

today . . . . . . . . . . . . . . . . . . . . . . . . . . . . (adv.) اليَوْم

diary, daily journal . . . . . . . . . . . . . . . . . . (n.) يَوْمِيّة ج يومِيّات

# الدَرْسُ الثاني عشَر

## Objectives

- Describing the four seasons
- Describing the weather
- Introduction to the partitive nouns بَعض – كُلّ – مُعْظَم
- Converting temperature scales

## المُفردات الجَديدة في صُوَر عَديدة:

زَهْرة ج أزْهار

غَيْمة ج غُيوم

شَجَرة ج أشْجار

سَبَحَ (يَسْبَحُ) سِباحةٌ

## الطَقْسُ

غائِم

ماطِر

صَحْو / سَماءٌ صافيةٌ

نَهار

٢٤ ساعة =

لَيْل

حارّ

دافِئ

مُعْتَدِل

بارِد

## تمرين ١

**Matching:**

وافِقْ بَيْنَ الكَلِماتِ في العَمودَين

| | | | |
|---|---|---|---|
| ١ | رَبيع | | مَطَر |
| ٢ | حارّ | | مِئَوِيَّة |
| ٣ | غائِم | | خَريف |
| ٤ | شاطِئ | | صَحوٌ |
| ٥ | لَيْل | | سَماء |
| ٦ | ثَلْج | | بَحْر |
| ٧ | دَرَجة | | نَهار |
| | | | بارِد |

## تمرين ٢

**Odd word out:** Underline the word that does not belong to each set and explain your choice if needed.

| | | | | |
|---|---|---|---|---|
| ١- | شَجَرة | زَهْرة | خَضراء | ثَلْج |
| ٢- | طَقْس | بُحَيْرة | مُعْتَدِل | دَرَجة حَرارة |
| ٣- | مَطَر | شاطِئ | بَحْر | بُحَيْرة |
| ٤- | دافِئ | بارِد | فَصْل | حارّ |
| ٥- | ريح | مَطَر | ثَلْج | أَسْبوع |

# الفُصولُ الأَرْبَعَة والطَقْس

يَسْقُطُ المَطَر

في السَنةِ أربعَةُ فُصولٍ هِيَ الرَبيعُ والصَيْفُ والخَريفُ والشِتاءُ. فَصْلُ الرَبيعِ جَميلٌ. الأَشْجارُ خَضْراءُ والأَزْهارَ مِن كُلِّ لَوْن. يَسْقُطُ المَطَرُ أَحْياناً، لكِنَّ الطَقْسَ مُعْتَدِلٌ دائِماً. الشَمسُ ساطِعَةٌ في مُعْظَمِ الأَيّام. أَشْهُرُ هذا الفَصْلِ هِيَ آذارُ ونيسانُ وأَيّار.

شاطِئ البَحْر

يَأتي فَصْلُ الصَيْفِ بَعْدَ فَصْلِ الرَبيع. الطَقْسُ حارٌّ في الصَيْفِ والسَماءُ صافِيَةٌ. يَذهَبُ الناسُ في الصَيْفِ عادةً إلى شاطِئِ البَحْرِ أو البُحَيْرةِ ويَسْبَحونَ هُناك. شُهورُ الصَيْفِ هِيَ حَزيران وتَمّوز وآب.

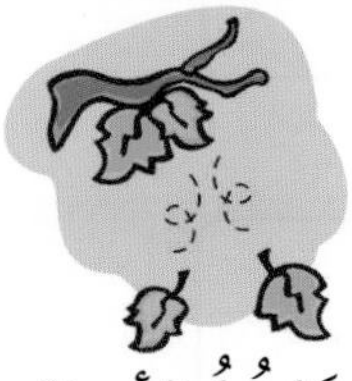

تَسْقُطُ الأوراق

أَشْهُرُ فَصْلِ الخَريفِ هِيَ أَيْلولُ وتِشرينُ الأَوَّلُ وتشرينُ الثاني ويَأتي هذا الفَصْلُ بَعْدَ فَصْلِ الصَيْف. هُناكَ غُيومٌ في السَماءِ في الخَريفِ وتَهُبُّ الرِياحُ وتَسقُطُ أوراقُ الأَشْجار. يَذهَبُ كُلُّ الطُلّابِ إلى المَدارِسِ والجامِعاتِ في هذا الفَصْل.

يَسْقُطُ الثَلْجُ

هُناكَ ثَلاثةُ أَشْهُرٍ في الشِتاءِ أَيْضاً وهِيَ كانونُ الأَوَّلُ وكانونُ الثاني وشُباط. في هذا الفَصْلِ يَسْقُطُ المَطَرُ أو الثَلْجُ ويَكونُ الطَقْسُ بارِداً عادَةً. يَذهَبُ بَعْضُ الناسِ في أمريكا في الشِتاءِ عادةً إلى وِلايَتَيْ أريزونا وفلوريدا لأَنَّهما دافِئَتانِ في هذا الفَصْلِ.

**Reflecting on our reading:** The verb **سَقَطَ** was used in different contexts in the main reading text. Can you use the different contexts to deduce its meaning?

الجُمْعة ١٦ آذار ٢٠٠٧
الطَقْسُ اليَوم
ماطِرٌ
مَطَر كُلَّ اليَوم. تَصِلُ
دَرَجةُ الحَراراةِ إلى ١٢
مِئويَّة نَهاراً و٦ دَرَجات
لَيْلاً. بِرياحٍ خَفيفة.

الثُلاثاء ١٧ تَمّوز ٢٠٠٧
الطَقْسُ اليَوم
حارٌّ وصَحو
تَصِلُ دَرَجةُ الحَرارةِ إلى
٣٦ مِئويَّة. رِياحٌ خَفيفة.
السَماءُ صافية.

الإثنين ١ تِشرينُ الأوَّل
٢٠٠٧
الطَقْسُ اليَوم
مُعْتَدِل وغائِم
تَصِلُ دَرَجةُ الحَرارةِ إلى
١٨ مِئويَّة نَهاراً و١٢
دَرَجة لَيلاً. رِياحٌ قَويّة.
غُيومٌ في النَهار.

الجُمْعة ٢٥ كانون الثاني
٢٠٠٨
الطَقْسُ اليَوم
بارِد
يَسْقُطُ الثَلْجُ مِن الصَباح
حتّى المَساءِ. تَصِلُ دَرَجةُ
الحَرارةِ إلى –٢ مِئويَّة.
لَيسَ هُناكَ رِياح.

- **Note:** The word **يَوْم** means 'day', whereas **اليَوْم**, with the definite article means 'today'.

# تمرين ٣

**A. Listen and select:** Check the box that matches the information as expressed in the passages for this lesson.

١- في السَنةِ أربعَةُ ____________ .

☐ شُهور ☐ فُصول ☐ أسابيع ☐ أيّام

٢- شَهْرُ تِشرينَ الأوّلِ مِن أشْهُرِ ____________ .

☐ الخَريف ☐ الشِتاء ☐ الرَبيع ☐ الصَيْف

٣- الطَقْسُ في الرَبيعِ ____________ .

☐ حارٌّ ☐ بارِدٌ ☐ مُعْتَدِلٌ ☐ كَبيرٌ

٤- يَذهَبُ بَعْضُ الناسِ في أيّامِ الصَيْفِ الحارّةِ إلى ____________ .

☐ البَحْرِ ☐ الغُيوم ☐ الرِياحِ ☐ الشَمْسِ

٥- يَذهَبُ بَعْضُ الأمريكيّينَ في الشِتاءِ إلى ____________ .

☐ المَدينةِ ☐ ألاسكا ☐ الغُيوم ☐ أريزونا

٦- تَهُبُّ الرِياحُ في فَصْلِ ____________ .

☐ الرَبيعِ ☐ الصَيْفِ ☐ الخَريفِ ☐ الشِتاءِ

**B. Short answer:** Answer these questions according to the information in the reading passages.

٧- في أيِّ فَصْلٍ تكونُ الأشْجارُ خَضراء؟ ____________

٨- مَتى تَكونُ الشَمسُ ساطِعةً في مُعْظَمِ الأيّام؟ ____________

٩- هَل توجَدُ بُحَيرةٌ قَريبةٌ مِن مَدينَتِك؟ ما اسْمُها؟ ____________

١٠- في أيِّ فَصْلٍ يَكونُ الطَقْسُ حارّاً؟ ____________

C. **صواب أو خطأ**: Mark the following sentences **صواب** or **خَطأ** according to the information in the main reading passage and correct any false statements.

١١- يَسقُطُ الثَلجُ في الخَريف.

_______________________________________________

١٢- تَصِلُ دَرَجةُ الحَرارةِ في الشِتاءِ إلى -٢ (ناقِص اِثنَين) مِئَويَّة.

_______________________________________________

١٣- الطَقْسُ غائِمٌ في الصَيْفِ في مُعْظَمِ الأيّام.

_______________________________________________

١٤- طَقْسُ اليَومِ ماطِرٌ.

_______________________________________________

## تمرين ٤

**Reporting the weather:** With a partner, write a description of today's weather, providing as much detail as you can. Write your weather report in the same fashion as your favorite local weather reporter. Be sure to mention both the local and national weather concerning:

1. what the weather will be like tomorrow in the morning, afternoon, and evening
2. what the weather will be like on certain days of the week (like a four-day forecast)
3. what the weather will be like on the weekend
4. how long the weather will be sunny, rainy, overcast, etc.

Once you are finished, report the weather in front of class as if it were being broadcast.

## تمرين ٥

**Using وَصَلَ إلى in sentences:** On a separate sheet of paper, translate the following sentences into Arabic. Each sentence will contain the verb وَصَلَ. Remember that you may need to use the preposition إلى when the destination is specified.

1. Hani's flight arrived at 9:30.
2. I arrived in this city in 2006.
3. The temperature in the summer reaches 40 degrees Celsius in my city.
4. We have reached lesson 12.
5. The temperature will reach negative five at night.

## تمرين ٦

**Rearranging words in sentences:** On a separate sheet of paper, rearrange the words in each item to make meaningful sentences.

١- تِلْكَ- ما - في - البُحَيْرة - سَبَحْتُ

٢- أختي- مِفتاحُ - هذا - شَقَّةِ - بابِ

٣- أيّار - حَزيران - شَهْرُ - شَهرِ - بَعْدَ - يَأتي

٤- غَدٍ - الطَقْسُ - بَعْدَ - سَيَكونُ - صَحْواً

٥- الصَيْفِ - شاطِئِ - في - إلى - الناسُ - البَحْرِ - يَذهَبُ

٦- لِصَديقاتِها - غَداً - قالَت - إلى - إنَّها- زَينَب - المَغرِبِ- سَتَذْهَبُ

٧- جَيِّدَةٌ - العَرَبِيَّةَ - إنَّ - لي - لُغَتي- أُستاذي - قالَ

٨- مِن - السَبتِ - إلى - في - بِالقِطارِ - حَلَبَ - دِمَشقَ - ذَهَبْتُ - يَوْمِ

## تمرين ٧

**Conversation about travel and weather:** You have just returned from a trip to Alexandria, Egypt. Your partner wants to know:

1. when you arrived (on what day and at what time)
2. what the weather was like in Alexandria
3. when you went to the beach and what you did at the beach
4. what hotel you stayed at
5. how many days you were there
6. with whom you went

7.   with whom you spoke and whether you spoke to them in Arabic
8.   what you talked about
9.   how long you were on the plane

Words to remember:

| نَزَلَ (في) | تَكَلَّمَ (مَعَ) | وَصَلَ (إلى) | قالَ (إنَّ) |
|---|---|---|---|
| شاطِئ | طائِرة | فُنْدُق | الطَقْس |

## 1. Partitive Nouns

Partitive nouns are words that denote *part* of a whole, hence their name. We have encountered three of them so far: مُعْظَمُ 'most', بَعْضُ 'some', and كُلُّ 'every, all, the whole'. These nouns form an إضافة structure with the nouns that follow them.

The meaning of each of these nouns varies depending on whether the modified noun is definite, indefinite, singular, or plural. Take time to read and reflect on the following table:

| | | |
|---|---|---|
| *most of the* | مُعْظَمُ اليَوْمِ | مُعْظَمُ |
| *most of the* | مُعْظَمُ الأَيّامِ | |
| *most of the* | مُعْظَمُ أَيّامِ الأسبوعِ | |
| *part/some of the* | بَعْضُ اليَوْمِ | بَعْضُ |
| *part of a* | بَعْضُ يَوْمٍ | |
| *a number of* | بَعْضُ أَيّامٍ | |
| *some of the* | بَعْضُ الأَيّامِ | |
| *some of the* | بَعْضُ أَيّامِ الأسبوعِ | |

| | | |
|---|---|---|
| *the whole* | كُلُّ اليَوْمِ | كُلّ |
| *every* | كُلُّ يَوْمٍ | |
| *all of the* | كُلُّ الأيّامِ | |
| *all of* | كُلُّ أيّامِ الأسبوعِ | |

The second part of an إضافة is مَجرور 'genitive', marked by a كَسرة or تَنوين كَسرة. Note that الأيّام and أيّام الأسبوع are both definite and therefore take a كَسرة, whereas يَوْم is indefinite and therefore marked by تَنوين كَسرة. These structures may be used as adverbs of time دَرَسْتُ مُعْظَمَ اليَوم or as adverbials qualifying time كُلُّ الأيّامِ بارِدَةٌ in nominal sentences.

- **Error Prevention:** The difference between كُلّ الـ and كُلّ is similar to English in that whenever you want to say "every day/week/month," the phrase you would use is indefinite كُل (يَوْم، أسبوع، شَهْر) in both languages, whereas when you are speaking about "*the* whole day/week/month" you would use the definite article كُلّ (اليَوْم، الـأسبوع، الشَهْر) in both languages.

## تمرين ٨

**Using مُعْظَمُ, بُعضُ, and كُلّ:** Translate the following paragraph into Arabic, paying close attention when to use مُعْظَمُ, بُعضُ, and كُلّ. Provide inflectional endings each time you use مُعْظَمُ, بُعضُ, or كُلّ.

*Every weekend during the summer, some of my friends and I go to the beach. Friday night I usually walk on the beach with my friend Leila and we talk about all of our classes. On Saturday, I usually read or swim most of the day. Some of my friends do not like reading and studying on the beach, but I like it. We are in our car most of the day Sunday on our way home. Summer is a beautiful season of the year.*

## 2. Converting Temperature Scales

You may convert a Fahrenheit scale to a Celsius scale by simply subtracting 32 from the temperature reading, multiplying the result by 5, and then dividing by 9. For example, to convert 78° F to the Celsius scale, here is what you do:

| | | | |
|---|---|---|---|
| ١ | ٧٨ – ٣٢ | = | ٤٦ |
| ٢ | ٤٦ × ٥ | = | ٢٣٠ |
| ٣ | ٢٣٠ ÷ ٩ | = | ٢٥,٥٥ |

In order to convert from Celsius to Fahrenheit, follow the reverse process: multiply by 9, divide by 5, and then add 32.

### تمرين ٩

**Temperature conversion:** What is the equivalent of each of these temperature readings?

١- ٣٨ مِئَوِيَّة ________________

٢- ٨٤ فَرنهايت ________________

٣- ٣٢ فَرنهايت ________________

٤- ٢٠ مِئَوِيَّة ________________

٥- ٩٢ فَرنهايت ________________

### تمرين ١٠

AUDIO

**A. Listen and select:** Listen to the recorded passage and select the best alternative.

١- في أوَّلِ يومٍ كانَ الطَقْسُ في النَهارِ ________________ .

☐ بارِداً ☐ مُعْتَدِلاً ☐ حارّاً

٢- ذَهَبَ الزَوْجُ والزَوْجَةُ إلى صافيتا في فَصْلِ ________________ .

☐ الشِتاءِ ☐ الرَبيعِ ☐ الصَيْفِ

٣- وَصَلَ الزَوْجُ وزَوْجَتُهُ إلى صافيتا يومَ ______________ .

☐ الخَميسِ ☐ الجُمْعةِ ☐ السَبْتِ

٤- يَعمَلُ الزَوْجُ في مَدينَةِ ______________ .

☐ صافيتا ☐ دِمَشق ☐ حَلَب

B. صواب أم خطأ: Mark the following sentences صواب or خَطأ according to the information in the listening passage and correct any untrue sentences.

٥- ذَهَبَ الزَوْجُ والزَوْجةُ إلى صافيتا بِالقِطار.

______________________________

٦- كانَتِ الأَشْجارُ خَضْراءَ في صافيتا.

______________________________

٧- تُريدُ الزَوْجَةُ السَكَنَ في حَلَب.

______________________________

٨- الطَقْسُ بارِدٌ في صافيتا.

______________________________

9. Write a summary of the listening passage in English. Try to avoid translating literally.

## تمرين ١١

VIDEO

**تَمرينُ المُشاهَدة: شاهِدوا الدَرْسَ الثاني عَشَر على القُرص الرَقْمي.**

١- لماذا يُحِبُّ فَصْلَ الصَيْف؟ ______________________________

______________________________

٢- لماذا يُحِبُّ فَصْلَ الرَبيع؟ ______________________________

______________________________

٣- لماذا يُحِبُّ فَصلَ الشِتاء؟ ______________________________

______________________________

٤- كَم شَهْراً في السَنة؟ ______________________________

______________________________

5. Recite the names of the months along with John. If you have problems remembering the names, refer to section 8.B of Lesson 11.

## المُفْرَدات

Listen to the vocabulary items on the CD and practice their pronunciation.

green . . . . . . . . . . . . . . . . . . . . . . (adj., m.) أخْضَر ج خُضْر

cold. . . . . . . . . . . . . . . . . . . . . . . . . (adj., m.) بارِد

sea . . . . . . . . . . . . . . . . . . . . . . (n, m.) بَحْر ج بِحار

lake. . . . . . . . . . . . . . . . . . . . . . (n., f.) بُحَيْرة ج بُحَيْرات

some . . . . . . . . . . . . . . . . . . . . . . . . . . (n.) بَعْض

snow . . . . . . . . . . . . . . . . . . . . . . (n., m.) ثَلْج ج ثُلوج

hot . . . . . . . . . . . . . . . . . . . . . . . . . (adj., m.) حارّ

heat. . . . . . . . . . . . . . . . . . . . . . . . . (n., f.) حَرارة

autumn. . . . . . . . . . . . . . . . . . . . . . . . (n., m.) خَريف

green . . . . . . . . . . . . . . . . . . . . . . (adj., f.) خَضْراء ج خُضْر

warm. . . . . . . . . . . . . . . . . . . . . . . . . (adj., m.) دافِئ

degree (temperature), step . . . (درجة حرارة) (n., f.) دَرَجة ج دَرَجات

spring . . . . . . . . . . . . . . . . . . . . . . . . (n., m.) رَبيع

wind . . . . . . . . . . . . . . . . . . . . . . (n., f.) ريح ج رِياح

flower . . . . . . . . . . . . . . . . . . (n., f.) زَهْرة ج زَهَرات / أزْهار

brilliant, shining . . . . . . . . . . . . . . . . . . (adj., m.) ساطِع

to swim . . . . . . . . . . . . . . . . . . . . (v.) سَبَحَ (يَسْبَحُ) سِباحة

to fall. . . . . . . . . . . . . . . . . . . . . . (v.) سَقَطَ (يَسْقُطُ) سُقوط

sky . . . . . . . . . . . . . . . . . . . . . . (n., f.) سَماء ج سَماوات

beach. . . . . . . . . . . . . . . . . . . . . . (n., m.) شاطِئ ج شَواطِئ

winter . . . . . . . . . . . . . . . . . . . . . . . . . (n., m.) شِتاء

tree . . . . . . . . . . . . . . . . . . . . . . . . (n., f.) شَجَرة ج شَجَرات

sun . . . . . . . . . . . . . . . . . . . . . . . . (n., f.) شَمْس ج شُموس

pure; clear, not cloudy . . . . . . . . . . . (f.) صافِية (adj., m.) صافٍ

clear, fine (of weather) . . . . . . . . . . . . . . . . . . (adj., m.) صَحْوٌ

way, road. . . . . . . . . . . . . . . . . . . . . . (n., f.) طَريق ج طُرُق، طُرُقات

weather . . . . . . . . . . . . . . . . . . . . . . . (n., m.) طَقْس ج طُقوس

worker, laborer (Labor Day) . . . (عيد العُمّال) (n., m.) عامِل ج عُمّال

cloudy, overcast . . . . . . . . . . . . . . . . . . . . . . (adj., m.) غائِم

rain cloud . . . . . . . . . . . . . . . . . . . . . . (n., f.) غَيْمة ج غُيوم

every, all, the whole. . . . . . . . . . . . . . . . . . . . . . . . . . . (n.) كُلّ

color . . . . . . . . . . . . . . . . . . . . . . . . (n., m.) لَوْن ج أَلْوان

night . . . . . . . . . . . . . . . . . . . . . . . . . . . . . . . (n., m.) لَيْل

rainy . . . . . . . . . . . . . . . . . . . . . . . . . . . . . (adj., m.) ماطِر

rain. . . . . . . . . . . . . . . . . . . . . . . . . . (n., m.) مَطَر ج أَمْطار

moderate. . . . . . . . . . . . . . . . . . . . . . . . . . . . . . (adj.) مُعْتَدِل

most . . . . . . . . . . . . . . . . . . . . . . . . . . . . . . . . . . (n.) مُعْظَم

minus . . . . . . . . . . . . . . . . . . . . . . . . . . . . . . (n., m.) ناقِص

daytime . . . . . . . . . . . . . . . . . . . . . . . . . . . . . (n., m.) نَهار

# الدَرسُ الثالِثَ عَشَر

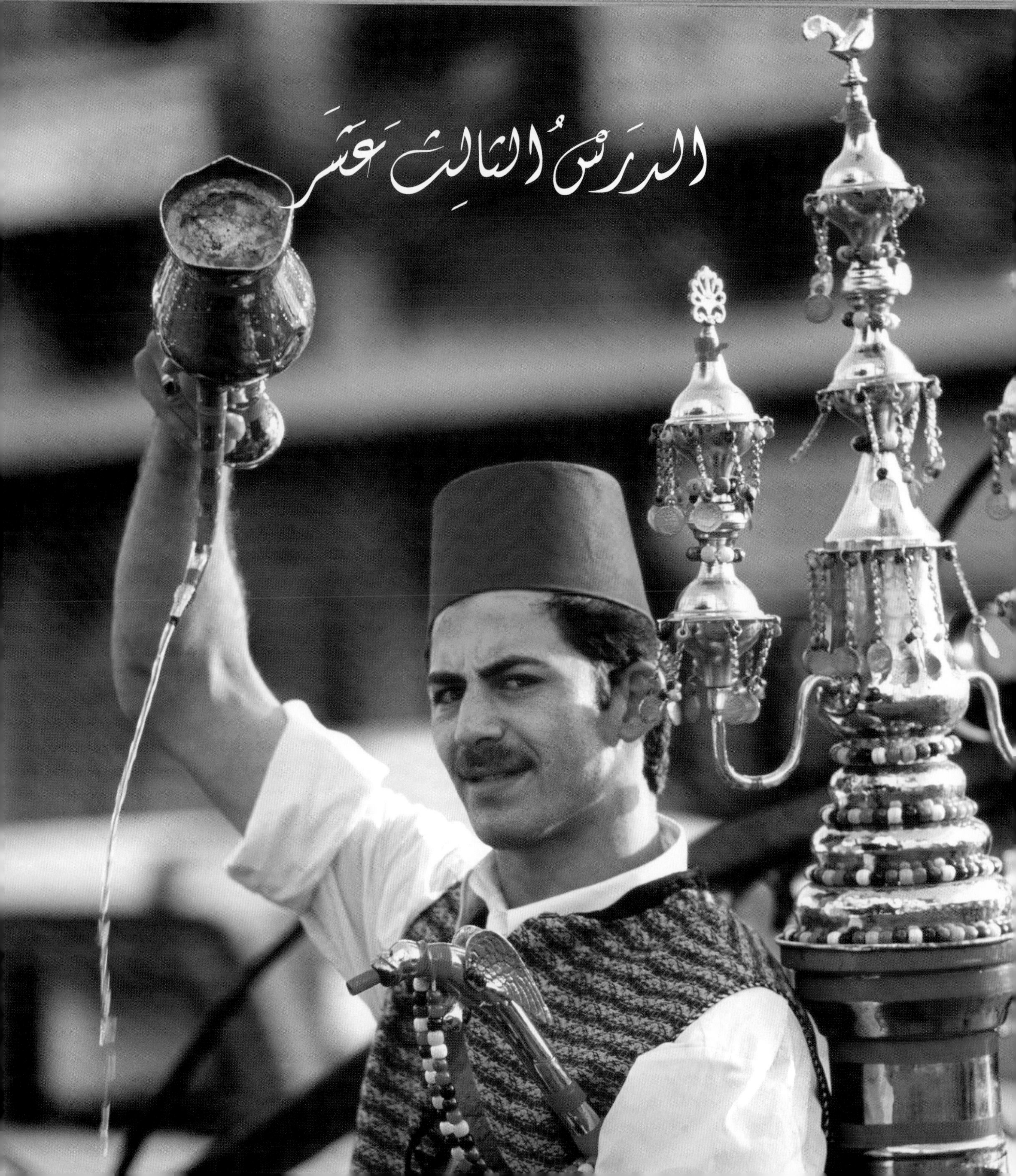

## Objectives

- Describing daily activities
- Revisiting partitive nouns كأسُ حليبٍ – فنجانُ شاي – قِطعةُ خُبزٍ
- Introduction to negating imperatives
- Introduction to weak verbs
- Expressing reason using the particle لأنَّ
- Introduction to the preferred position of the verb in the Arabic sentence
- Swearing or giving an oath using the preposition وَ

## المُفردات الجَديدة في صُوَر عَديدة:

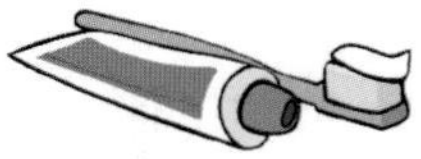

فُرشاةُ الأسنانِ ومَعجون

نَظَّفَ (يُنَظِّفُ) تَنْظيف

اِسْتَحَمَّ (يَسْتَحِمُّ) اِسْتِحمام

نَهَضَ (يَنْهَضُ) نُهوض

شاهَد (يُشاهِدُ) مُشاهَدة

# تمرين ١

**Matching:**

وافِقْ بَيْنَ الكَلِماتِ في العَمودَينِ

| | | | |
|---|---|---|---|
| ١ | اِسْتَحَمَّ | | مَعْجون أسْنان |
| ٢ | فُرشاة | | ذَقْن |
| ٣ | نَسِيَ | | حافِلَة |
| ٤ | سَرير | | غَسَلَ |
| ٥ | كَباب | | مَطعَم |
| ٦ | حَلَقَ | | فَلافِل |
| ٧ | مَقْصَف | | مَوْعِد |
| | | | نَوْم |

# تمرين ٢

**Odd word out:** Underline the word that does not belong to each set and explain your choice if needed.

| | | | | |
|---|---|---|---|---|
| ١ | فُرشاة | ماء | قَهوة | شاي |
| ٢ | فَطور | غَداء | طِبّ | عَشاء |
| ٣ | حافِلَة | سَيّارَة | دَرّاجة | حاسِبَة |
| ٤ | كَباب | صابون | فَلافِل | فول |
| ٥ | سِنّ | وَجْه | لَبَن | يَد |
| ٦ | مادَّة | مُسَلسَل | بَرنامَج | تِلفاز |
| ٧ | نَهَضَ | اِسْتَحَمَّ | غَسَلَ | مَرَّة |
| ٨ | وَرَقَة | مُشاهَدَة | كِتاب | رِسالة |

# ماذا تَفعَلُ هالَة بُستاني كُلَّ يَوْم؟

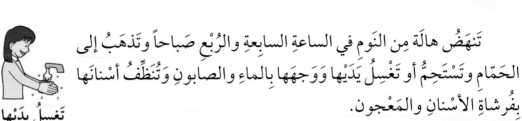

هالَة بُستاني طالِبةٌ تَدرُسُ الطِبَّ في جامِعَةِ حَلَب. تَسكُنُ في شَقَّةٍ مَعَ صَديقَتِها سَحَر حَلاّق.

تَغسِلُ يدَيْها

تَنهَضُ هالَة مِن النَومِ في الساعةِ السابِعةِ والرُبْعِ صَباحاً وتَذهَبُ إلى الحَمّامِ وتَسْتَحِمُّ أو تَغْسِلُ يَدَيْها وَوَجهَها بِالماءِ والصابونِ وَتُنَظِّفُ أَسْنانَها بِفُرشاةِ الأَسْنانِ والمَعْجون.

تُحَضِّر الفَطور

بَعدَ ذلِكَ تَذهَبُ إلى المَطْبَخِ وتُحَضِّرُ طَعامَ الفَطور. تَأكُلُ هالَة على الفَطورِ عادَةً بَيضَتَينِ أو قِطعَةَ خُبزٍ وقِطْعَةً مِنَ الجُبْنِ مَعَ كأسِ حَليب.

في يَومِ الجُمْعة تُحَضِّرُ هالَة وسَحَر البَيْضَ أو الفولَ المُدَمَّسَ على الفَطورِ وتَشربانِ الشايَ بَعدَ الطَعامِ.

حافِلة

في الساعةِ الثامِنَةِ تَذهَبُ هالَة إلى الجامِعَةِ بِالحافِلة. لا تَذهَبُ إلى الجامِعَةِ بِالسَيّارةِ لأَنَّها لَيسَ عِندَها سَيّارة.

في الساعةِ الثامِنةِ والنِصْفِ تَصِلُ إلى الجامِعَةِ وتَذهَبُ إلى المَكتبَةِ وتَدرُسُ هُناكَ حَتّى الساعةِ الحادِيةَ عَشْرة.

تأكُلانِ الغداء

في الساعةِ الحادِيَةَ عَشرةَ تَذهَبُ إلى دَرْسِ الكيمياءِ مَعَ صَديقَتِها غادة. وفي الساعةِ الثانِيةَ عَشْرةَ تَذهَبانِ مَعاً إلى مَقصَفِ الجامِعَةِ وتَأكُلانِ الغَداءَ هُناكَ. تَأكُلُ هالَة أحياناً الكَبابَ الحَلَبيَّ وأَحْياناً الفَلافِلَ، لكِنَّ غادة تَأكُلُ لَبَناً أو سَلَطَةً فَقَط، وأَحْياناً تَأكُلُ التَبّولَة.

بَعدَ ذلِكَ تَذهَبُ هالَة إلى المُخْتَبَرِ من الساعةِ الواحِدةِ إلى الساعةِ الثالِثة. بَعدَ المُخْتَبرِ تَذهَبُ إلى دَرْسِ الأَحْياء.

طعام العَشاء

في الساعةِ الخامِسَةِ تَرْجِعُ إلى البَيْتِ وتَكونُ في شَقَّتِها في الساعةِ الخامِسَةِ والرُبْع. في المَساءِ تُحَضِّرُ هالَة طَعامَ العَشاءِ، وتَأكُلُ عادةً الزَيْتونَ والجُبْنَ أو الخُضَرَ أو البَيْضَ المَقْليَّ وتَشرَبُ فِنجانَ شاي بَعدَ العَشاء.

الأخبار

تُشاهِدُ هالَة التِلفازَ قَليلاً كُلَّ لَيْلَةٍ. تُحِبُّ مُشاهَدةَ المُسَلْسَلاتِ العَرَبيّةِ والأمريكيّةِ وبَرامِجَ الأَخْبارِ مِنَ العالَم. تَذهَبُ هالَة عادةً إلى سَريرِها في الساعةِ العاشِرةِ والنِصْفِ عادةً أو في الساعةِ الحادِيَةَ عَشْرةَ على الأَكْثَر.

| رُكْنُ المُفْرَداتِ الجَديدةِ | | | |
|---|---|---|---|
| busy | مَشْغول ج مَشْغولونَ | to forget | نَسِيَ (يَنْسى) نِسيان |
| early | مُبَكِّر | late | مُتَأَخِّر |

# يَوْمِيّاتُ عَدنان مارتيني

**الثُلاثاء ٩ تِشرينَ الأوَّل ٢٠٠٧**

حَلَقْتُ ذَقْني

نَهَضْتُ اليَوْمَ مِنَ النَوم في الساعةِ السابِعةِ إلاّ ثُلْثاً. اِسْتَحْمَمْتُ وحَلَقْتُ ذَقْني بِرُبعِ ساعةٍ ثُمَّ أَكَلْتُ فَطوري (كأسَ حَليبٍ وقِطعَةَ خُبزٍ مَعَ الجُبْنِ) ومَشَيْتُ إلى الجامِعةِ.

وَصَلتُ إلى صَفّي في الساعةِ الثامِنةِ والنِصْفِ تَماماً. لا أُحِبُّ هذِهِ المادَّةَ (لُغاتِ الحاسوب) لأنَّها في وَقْتٍ مُبَكِّرٍ جِدّاً. وَصَلَ بَعْضُ الطُلاّبِ مُتَأَخِّرينَ إلى الصَفِّ اليَوْم. حينَ رَجَعْتُ إلى البَيْتِ مَساءً كانَ هُناكَ وَرَقةٌ مِن زِياد على بابِ غُرفَتي. كَتَبَ فيها: «لا تَنسَ العَشاءَ اليَوْمَ في مَطعَمِ علي بابا في الساعةِ السابِعةِ مَعَ تِم وليسا.» نَسيتُ مَوْعِدَ هذا العَشاءِ واللهِ.

**الأربعاء ١٠ تِشرينَ الأوّل ٢٠٠٧**

بَعدَ دَرسِ لُغاتِ الحاسوبِ ذَهَبْتُ إلى المَكتبَةِ وقَرأتُ ساعَتَينِ ثُمّ أكَلْتُ الغَداءَ في مَقصَفِ الجامِعةِ وذَهَبْتُ إلى عَمَلي في مُختَبَرِ الحاسوب. أعْمَلُ هُناكَ خَمسَ عَشْرةَ ساعةً في الأسبوع. بَعدَ الظُهرِ ذَهَبْتُ إلى دَرسَيْ الرِياضِيّاتِ واللُغةِ الإنكليزية. رَجَعْتُ إلى المَكتبَةِ مَرّةً ثانِيَةً وقَرأتُ دُروسي حَتّى الساعةِ الثامِنةِ مَساءً. بَعدَ ذلِكَ مَشَيْتُ إلى شَقّتي وأكَلتُ العَشاءَ مَعَ زِياد في الشَقّة.

ما أكَلْنا أمْسِ في مَطْعَمِ علي بابا. تَكَلّمَتْ ليسا أمسِ بِالهاتِفِ وقالَتْ إنّها مَشْغولةٌ جِدّاً. سَنَأكُلُ مَعاً (أنا وزِياد وليسا وتِم) مَساءَ يَوْمِ الجُمْعَةِ إن شاءَ الله. ذَهَبْتُ إلى النَوْمِ في الساعةِ الحادِيَةَ عَشْرَةَ بَعدَ مُشاهَدةِ بَرنامَج «سِتّونَ دَقيقة» على التِلفاز. أُحِبُّ مُشاهَدَةَ هذا البَرنامَج. لا أُحِبُّ كِتابَةَ الرَسائِلِ عادةً لكِنّني سَأكتُبُ رِسالَةً إلى أبي وأمّي غَداً إنْ شاءَ الله.

## تمرين ٣

**Ask your neighbors:** Find out what your neighbors do on an average day and then write that information down on a separate sheet of paper. Some subjects that you may wish to ask about are:

1. what time they wake up in the morning
2. when they shower/brush their teeth
3. when/where they eat breakfast/lunch/supper
4. what they usually eat for breakfast/lunch/supper
5. what time they go to school, and how they get to school
6. what subjects they study and on what days
7. what time they return home
8. what time they go to bed

Report your findings to your classmates, giving as much detail about each person as you can.

# تمرين ٤

**A. Listen and select:** Check the box that matches the information as expressed in the passages for this lesson.

١- تسكُنُ هالَة بُستاني الآنَ في ____________ .

☐ حَلَب ☐ القاهِرة ☐ دِمَشق

٢- تَنْهَضُ هالَة مِنَ النَوْمِ في الساعةِ ____________ .

☐ السادِسَةِ ☐ السابِعَةِ ☐ الثامِنَةِ

٣- تَذهَبُ هالَة إلى الجامِعَةِ ____________ .

☐ بِالحافِلَةِ ☐ بِالسَيّارةِ ☐ مَشْياً

٤- تَأكُلُ هالَة الغَداءَ مَعَ صَديقَتِها ____________ .

☐ سُعاد ☐ غادَة ☐ سَحَر

٥- مَوعِدُ دَرسِ الأَحْياءِ في الساعةِ ____________ .

☐ الواحِدَةِ ☐ الثانِيَةِ ☐ الثالِثَةِ

٦- يَأكُلُ عَدنان على الفَطورِ ____________ .

☐ الزَيْتونَ ☐ البَيْضَ ☐ الجُبْنَ

٧- وَصَلَ عَدنان إلى دَرسِ لُغاتِ الحاسوبِ ____________ .

☐ في مَوْعِدِهِ ☐ مُبَكِّراً ☐ مُتَأخِّراً

٨- ما أكَلَ عَدنان العَشاءَ مَعَ أَصْدِقائِهِ يَومَ الثُلاثاءِ لأَنَّ ليسا كانَت ____________ .

☐ مُبَكِّرَةً ☐ مَشْغولَةً ☐ مُتَأخِّرَةً

٩- يَعمَلُ عَدنان في مُخْتَبَرِ الحاسوبِ ____________ في الأسبوع.

☐ عَشْرَ ساعاتٍ ☐ خَمسَ عَشْرَةَ ساعةً ☐ عِشْرونَ ساعةً

١٠- يُحِبُّ عَدنان ____________ .

☐ مُشاهَدَةَ التِلفازِ ☐ كِتابَةَ الرَسائِلِ ☐ بَرنامَجَ سِتّونَ دقيقة

B. **Fill in the blank:** Complete these sentences with information from the reading passages.

١١- تَسْكُنُ هالَة بُستاني مَعَ ____________________.

١٢- تَرْجِعُ هالَة إلى شَقَّتِها في الساعةِ ____________________.

١٣- تذهَبُ هالَة إلى السَريرِ في الساعةِ ____________________.

١٤- لا يُحِبُّ عَدنان مادَّةَ لُغاتِ الحاسوبِ لأَنَّها ____________________.

١٥- نَسِيَ عَدنان مَوْعِدَ ____________________.

١٦- يَقرَأُ عَدنان دُروسَهُ عادَةً في ____________________.

C. **صواب أو خطأ:** On a separate sheet of paper, mark the following sentences **صواب** or **خَطأ** according to the information in the main reading passage and <u>correct</u> any untrue sentences.

١٧- تَأكُلُ هالَة بُستاني الفولَ على الفَطورِ كُلَّ يوم.

١٨- تذهَبُ هالَة إلى النَومِ في الساعةِ العاشِرةِ مَساءً.

١٩- تُنَظِّفُ هالة وَجهَها بِالفُرشاةِ والمَعْجون.

٢٠- لَيْسَ عِندَ هالَة سَيّارة.

٢١- تُحِبُّ هالَة مُشاهَدَةَ بَرنامَج سِتّونَ دَقيقة.

٢٢- يَحلِقُ عَدنان ذَقنَهُ قَبْلَ النَوم.

٢٣- نَسِيَ عَدنان دَرسَ لُغاتِ الحاسوب.

٢٤- تَكَلَّمَ عَدنان بِالهاتِفِ وقالَ إنَّهُ مَشْغول.

٢٥- سَيَأكُلُ الأَصْدِقاءُ الأَرْبَعَةُ العَشاءَ مَعاً يَومَ الجُمْعَة.

٢٦- سَيَكتُبُ عَدنان رِسالةً يَوم الأربِعاء.

## تمرين ٥

**Sentence construction:** On a separate sheet of paper, rearrange the words in each item to make meaningful sentences.

١- على - الفولَ - هالَة - الغَداءِ - تَأكُلُ - المُدَمَّسَ

٢- صَباحاً - مُشاهَدَة - الأخْبارِ - أُحِبُّ - بَرامِجِ

٣- السَبْتِ - السَيّارة - زَوْجي - يَوْمَ - يَغسِلُ

## تمرين ٦

**Paragraph construction:** On a separate sheet of paper, construct a meaningful paragraph by rearranging the following sentences. Do not change the position of the first sentence. Practice your script by writing the entire paragraph out.

١- اِسْمي رَوضَة قطّان.

أُحَضِّرُ عادَةً فَطوراً كَبيراً لي ولِزَوجي وأولادي.

نَرجِعُ إلى البَيْتِ في الساعةِ الثامِنَةِ مَساءً

في الساعةِ الرابِعَةِ بَعدَ الظُهْرِ أذهَبُ وأولادي إلى دارِ أبي وأمّي.

أعْمَلُ أمينَةَ مَكتَبَةٍ في الجامِعَةِ الأُردُنِيَّةِ في عَمّان.

لكِنَّني أنهَضُ مُتَأخِّرَةً في يَوْمِ الجُمْعة (في التاسِعَةِ أو العاشِرة).

وأحْياناً نَأكُلُ الحِمَّصَ إلى جانِبِ الزَيتونِ والجُبْن.

حَيْثُ أتَكَلَّمُ مَعَهُما ومَعَ أُختي وأَخي.

بَعدَ الفَطورِ أُنَظِّفُ الدارَ وأغسِلُ القُمْصان.

أُحَضِّرُ أحياناً الفولَ المُدَمَّسَ والبَيْض المَقْليّ.

أذهَبُ إلى عَمَلي في الساعةِ السابِعَةِ كُلَّ يَوْم.

## تمرين ٧

**Frequency of activities:** On a separate sheet of paper, construct three sentences. In the first sentence describe an activity which you do *every day* كُـلَّ يَوم; in the second describe an activity you *usually* عادَةً do; and in the third describe an activity you *sometimes* أحْياناً do, as in the example below.

مِثال: آكُلُ الكَبابَ الحَلَبيَّ على الغَداءِ عادةً.

## تمرين ٨

**Fill in the blanks:** Complete the following sentences with words from the list.

| | | | | | | | |
|---|---|---|---|---|---|---|---|
| الحَلوى | تَنهَضينَ | عيدٌ | المَعجونِ | الشايَ | تَبّولَةً | فَجْرٌ | الصابونِ |

١- تَشرَبُ هالَة __________ بَعدَ الفَطور.

٢- أغسِلُ يَدَيَّ بِالماءِ و__________ .

٣- هَلْ تأكُلُ __________ بَعدَ الطَعام؟

٤- مَتى __________ مِن النَومِ يا لَيْلى؟

٥- أُنَظِّفُ أسْناني بِالفُرشاةِ و __________ .

٦- آكُلُ __________ فَقَط على الغَداء.

## تمرين ٩

**A day in the life of . . . :** On a separate sheet of paper, write a paragraph in which you describe your daily activities either on a typical day of the week or on the weekend. Model your description after the main reading passages in this lesson.

# تمرين ١٠

**Find out from your classmates.** Ask your speaking partner about the following:

1. what time he/she goes to sleep
2. where he/she goes at night, and with whom
3. what time he/she gets back home
4. what he/she likes to do (watch movies or television, go out to eat, go to a friend's house)
5. when/what he/she eats/drinks
6. what he/she likes to watch on the weekends

## 1. Partitive Nouns and Phrases

Just like the noun بَعْض, which denotes part of a whole, there are nouns that, when used with other nouns as إضافة structures, effect a partitive meaning. In this lesson, three such phrases occurred: كَأسُ ماء 'glass of water', فِنجانُ شاي 'cup of tea', and قِطعَةُ خُبز 'piece of bread'. The first word of each phrase signifies a specific amount of the complete whole.

- **Note:** A partitive meaning can also be achieved through a prepositional phrase, as in قِطعةٌ مِنَ الخُبز, which literally means "piece of bread," the same meaning conveyed by an إضافة structure.

# تمرين ١١

**Partitives in context:** Translate the following short paragraph into Arabic. If you can, try to incorporate both إضافة and prepositional phrases to express the italicized words.

> I woke up this morning and then fixed breakfast. For breakfast I ate *some eggs*, a *slice of bread*, and *some pieces of cheese*, and I drank *two glasses of orange juice* and a *cup of coffee*.

## 2. Negating Imperative Verbs

An imperative verb is used for making requests or giving commands, such as أعطِ، اِجْلِسْ and تَفَضَّلْ (refer to Lesson 7, section 2). Negating an imperative verb is done with the negative particle لا. It is used before the verb and it *affects* its form. With لا, the verb changes its form from the imperative to a form of the present tense called المُضارِع المَجزوم (jussive).

١ أُكْتُبْ ← لا تَكْتُبْ

The jussive form of the present is similar to the regular (indicative) present المُضارِع المَرفوع, but with two differences: (1) the inflectional marker ضَمّة that appears on the final radical of the regular present is replaced with a سَكون (as in example 1); and (2) in all but one conjugation that ends with a نون, the نون is dropped (as in example 2). The exception is the conjugation for أنْتُنَّ, where the نون remains (as in example 3).

| | الضَمير | المُضارِع المُخاطَب | | المُضارِع المَجزوم |
|---|---|---|---|---|
| ٢ | أنْتُم | تَكتُبونَ | ← | تَكتُبوا |
| ٣ | أنْتُنَّ | تَكتُبنَ | ← | تَكتُبنَ |

- **Note:** The final أَلَف in the second-person masculine plural conjugation of المضارع المجزوم (jussive) (example 2 above) is silent. The أَلَف is, however, dropped when an attached (object) pronoun is suffixed to the verb (as in example 4):

٤ تَكتُبوا + ها = تَكتُبوها

## 3. Weak Verbs الفِعْلُ المُعْتَلّ

A weak verb is called مُعتَلّ in Arabic because it contains حَرف عِلّة, which is a long vowel in the first (فاء), second (عين), or third position (لام) of the verb (e.g., وَصَلَ، قالَ، نَسِيَ). A weak verb is known as an **assimilated verb** الفِعْلُ المِثالُ if the first radical is a long vowel (example 5), a **hollow verb** الفِعْلُ الأجْوَفُ if the second radical is a long vowel (example 6), and a **defective verb** الفِعْلُ الناقِصُ if the third radical is a long vowel (example 7).

Notice that in المُضارِع المَجزوم, the long vowel is replaced with its short vowel counterpart (e.g., أَلَف becomes فَتحة) in the second-person masculine singular (see also the imperative conjugation of these verbs in Appendix C).

| | الماضي | المُضارِع المُخاطَب | | المُضارِع المَجزوم |
|---|---|---|---|---|
| ٥ | وَصَلَ | تَصِلُ | ← | تَصِلْ |
| ٦ | قالَ | تَقولُ | ← | تَقُلْ |
| ٧ | نَسِيَ | تَنسى | ← | تَنسَ |

The process of deleting the long vowel in the imperative only occurs with the second-person masculine singular. Another difference between **المُضارِع المَرفوع** and **المُضارِع المَجزوم** is that the final **نون** is deleted (examples 8, 9, and 10) in all cases except for the imperative of أنتُنَّ (examples 11, 12, and 13).

| | الضَمير | المُضارِع المَرفوع | | المُضارِع المَجزوم |
|---|---|---|---|---|
| ٨ | أنْتِ | تَصِلينَ | ← | تَصِلي |
| ٩ | أنْتِ | تَقولينَ | ← | تَقولي |
| ١٠ | أنْتِ | تَنسَيْنَ | ← | تَنسَيْ |

**Note** that the feminine second-person plural form does not undergo any changes:

| | الضَمير | المُضارِع المَرفوع | | المُضارِع المَجزوم |
|---|---|---|---|---|
| ١١ | أنْتُنَّ | تَصِلْنَ | ← | تَصِلْنَ |
| ١٢ | أنْتُنَّ | تَقُلْنَ | ← | تَقُلْنَ |
| ١٣ | أنْتُنَّ | تَنسَيْنَ | ← | تَنسَيْنَ |

## تمرين ١٢

**Negating the imperative:** On a separate sheet of paper, express each of these situations in Arabic.

1. In order to decrease the amount of graffiti, you write a sign asking people not to write on the walls.
2. You remind a male friend not to forget the time of his flight.
3. Ask a woman not to give her phone number to someone (him).
4. Ask a man not to sit on a particular chair.
5. Inform two friends that there is no class today (ask them not to go to class).

## 4. Expressing Reason

Expressing reason is accomplished by using the particle لِأَنَّ 'because', which is a compound word made up of the preposition لـ 'for' and the particle أَنَّ 'that'. Just like إِنَّ and أَنَّ , لِأَنَّ must be followed by a noun or a pronoun. For example, the phrase "because I" is expressed as لِأَنِّي, and "because the teacher" is rendered as لِأَنَّ الأَستاذَ .

- **Remember:** The noun following لِأَنَّ must be مَنصوب, as indicated by the فَتحة on the final radical of الأَستاذ (refer to Lesson 11, section 3A for an explanation of أَنَّ and إِنَّ). Questions whose answer requires the use of لِأَنَّ start with لِـماذا 'why' (e.g., لِماذا تَسكُنُ هُنا؟).

# تمرين ١٣

**Conversation:** In pairs, one person should play the role of the "interrogator" who is going to be asking a lot of probing questions. The other person should come up with reasonable excuses. Choose your reason or reasons for (1) coming to class late; (2) returning home late last night; or (3) not showing up to your dinner date with your friends. Both partners should take a couple of minutes to prepare the questions they want to pose or the excuses they want to make. Switch roles after the role-play has reached its conclusion.

**Follow-up exercise:** Report everything that happened in your role-play to your classmates, using the verb "to say."

## 5. Verb Position in Arabic Sentences

Conventionally, the Arabic verb occupies an initial sentence position, as in example 14:

١٤   تَدرُسُ الطالِباتُ في المَكتبة.

In this example, the verb تَدرُسُ agrees with the subject الطالِباتُ in gender, but not in number. That is to say, تَدرُسُ is singular though the subject of the sentence is plural. Compare the sentence structure of example 14 with a sentence that starts with a subject الفاعل:

١٥   الطالِباتُ يَدرُسْنَ في المَكتبَة.

As you can see, the verb in example 15 agrees with the preceding subject not only in gender, but also in number.

- The rule that we can state here is: *If the verb <u>precedes</u> the subject, it agrees with it in gender, not in number.* Memorize and follow this rule.

If the subject is of a mixed gender (both men and women are mentioned), use the gender of the first noun:

١٦ يَسْكُنُ أخي وأختي في بَيْتي.

Consider the following sentence from our main reading passage:

١٧ تُحَضِّرُ هالَة وسَحَر البَيْضَ على الفَطورِ وتَشرَبانِ الشايَ.

In example 17, the first verb تُحَضِّرُ is singular because it *precedes* the subject (هالَة وسَحَر), even though subject is dual. The second verb تَشرَبانِ is dual because it *follows* the dual subject.

## SUMMARY

- If the verb precedes the subject, it agrees with it in *gender*, not in *number*. The verb, therefore, will always be in the singular if it precedes its subject.
- If the verb follows the subject, it agrees with it in gender *and* number.

## تمرين ١٤

**Verb conjugation:** Provide the correct form of the verb in parentheses with respect to tense, gender, and number. The verbs are listed in third-person past-tense masculine singular. Look for contextual clues to determine tense.

مِثال: أخَواتُ صَديقي (عَمِلَ) الآنَ في سوقٍ كَبيرة.

أخَواتُ صَديقي <u>يعْمَلنَ</u> الآنَ في سوقٍ كَبيرة.

١- كُلُّ الطُلاّبِ (دَرَس) ________ اللُغَةَ الإنكليزيَّةَ في المَدارِسِ الآنَ.
٢- (وَصَلَ) ________ صَديقاتي مِنَ الرِباطِ أَمْسِ.
٣- (عَمِلَ) ________ أبي وأُمّي في مَدينَةِ الرِياضِ حينَ كُنْتُ صَغيراً.
٤- أخي وزَوجَتُهُ (سَكَنَ) ________ في مَدينَةِ حَلَبَ في سوريَة حَتّى الآن.
٥- صَديقي وعائِلَتُهُ (اِنْتَقَلَ) ________ إلى دارٍ جَديدَةٍ في الشَهْرِ الماضي.
٦- (لَبِسَ) ________ سامي وأخوه الكوفِيَّةَ والعِقالَ عادَةً.
٧- (دَرَسَ) ________ مُعْظَمُ صَديقاتِ هالَة اللُغَةَ الإنكليزيَّةَ الآن.

## 6. Swearing or Giving an Oath Using the Preposition وَ

This preposition is used either to add emphasis to one's words or to swear solemnly **وَاللّهِ** 'by God'. The noun modified by it is **مَجرور** (genitive), marked either with a **كَسرة** appearing on the final radical of singular and broken plural nouns or **ي** instead of **أَلِف** and **واو** in dual and sound masculine plurals (see section 3, "Cases of the Noun," in Lesson 7).

## تمرين ١٥

**A. Listen and select:** Check the box that matches the information as expressed in the listening passage for this lesson.

١- سَيَغسِلُ هاني قُمصانَهُ يَوْمَ ________ .

☐ الجُمْعَةِ ☐ السَبْتِ ☐ الأَحَدِ

٢- سَيَذهَبُ هاني عِندَ الظُهرِ إلى ________ .

☐ مَكتَبَةِ الفارابي ☐ مَطعَمِ الصَحّة ☐ دارِ صَديقِهِ

٣- يَدرُسُ غَسّان في جامِعَةِ ________ .

☐ دِمَشق ☐ بِرمِنغهام ☐ حَلَبَ

٤- في السَنَةِ المُقْبِلَةِ سَيَكونُ غَسّانُ في ________ .

☐ سوريَة ☐ بريطانيا ☐ أمريكا

٥- سَيأكُلُ الأَصْدِقاءُ الثَلاثَةُ العَشاءَ في مَطعَمِ ________ .

☐ الفارابي ☐ الصَحّةِ ☐ الجامِعَةِ

**B.** صواب أو خطأ: Mark the following sentences صواب or خطأ according to the information in the recorded passage and <u>correct</u> any false statements.

٦ –	عِندَ هاني سَيّارة.

_____

٧ –	يَدرُسُ غَسّان الأَدَبَ الأَمريكيّ.

_____

٨ –	سَيَأْكُلُ الأَصْدِقاءُ الثَلاثَةُ العَشاءَ في الساعةِ السابِعة.

_____

٩ –	عامِر صَديقُ هاني وغَسّان.

_____

**C.** In Arabic, describe what the narrator will do on that weekend morning.

**D.** In Arabic, compose a biographical sketch of the narrator's friend.

## تمرين ١٦

تَمرينُ المُشاهَدة: شاهِدوا الدَرْسَ الثالِثَ عَشَر على القُرْص الرَقْميّ.

Place a number next to the following sequence of events in the order that is described in the scene. Her first daily activity is already given:

| | |
|---|---|
| ١ | تَسْتَيْقِظُ في الساعةِ السابعةِ والنِصْفِ. |
| | تَسْتَمِعُ إلى الموسيقا وهي تَشرَبُ القهوة مع زَوْجِها. |
| | في الساعة الثالثة تَعودُ إلى البيت وتُحَضِّرُ الغداء. |
| | في المساء تَذهَبُ وزَوجُها لِزيارة العائلة أو الأصدقاء. |
| | تُشاهِدُ التلفاز وتَنام في الساعةِ الثانيةَ عشرةَ ليلاً. |
| | تَغسِلُ وَجهَها وتُنَظِّفُ أسنانَها. |
| | تَغسِلُ الصُحونَ ثم تُغَيِّرُ ملابِسَها. |
| | تَعودُ إلى البيت لِتُحَضِّرَ العَشاء وتُرَتِّبَ البيت. |
| | تُحَضِّرُ الفَطور. |

## المُفْرَدات

Listen to the vocabulary items on the CD and practice their pronunciation.

to bathe, to take a bath or shower. . . . (v.) اسْتَحَمَّ (يَستَحِمُّ) استِحْمام

to move, to relocate. . . . . . . . . . . . . . . (v.) اِنتقَلَ (يَنتَقِلُ) اِنْتِقال

in need of . . . . . . . . . . . . . . . . . . . . . بِحاجَةٍ (إلى)

program . . . . . . . . . . . . . . . . . . . . (n., m.) بَرنامَج ج بَرامِج

salad made with finely chopped parsley, . . . . . . . . . . (n., f.) تَبّولة
cracked wheat, tomatoes, lemon juice, and olive oil

then, and again . . . . . . . . . . . . . . . . . (conjunction) ثُمَّ

to prepare . . . . . . . . . . . . . . . . . . . . . (v.) جَهَّزَ (يُجَهِّزُ) تَجْهيز

bus, tram. . . . . . . . . . . . . . . . . . . . . (n., f.) حافِلة ج حافِلات

to prepare, to make . . . . . . . . . . . . . (v.) حَضَّرَ (يُحَضِّرُ) تَحْضير

to shave . . . . . . . . . . . . . . . . . . . . . (v.) حَلَقَ (يَحْلِقُ) حَلْق

bathroom . . . . . . . . . . . . . . . . . . . . (n., f.) حَمّام ج حمّامات

news story . . . . . . . . . . . . . . . . . . . . (n., m.) خَبَر ج أخْبار

vegetables . . . . . . . . . . . . . . . . . . . (n., f.) خُضرة ج خُضَر

chin (when used with "to shave," . . . . . . . . . . (n., f.) ذَقْن ج ذُقون
it signifies shaving one's beard)

to organize. . . . . . . . . . . . . . . . . . . . (v.) رَتَّبَ (يُرَتِّبُ) تَرْتيب

to return, to go back . . . . . . . . . . . . . . (v.) رَجَعَ (يَرْجِعُ) رُجوع

letter, message. . . . . . . . . . . . . . . . . (n., f.) رِسالة ج رَسائِل

tooth . . . . . . . . . . . . . . . . . . . . . . . (n., f.) سِنٌّ ج أَسْنان

to watch . . . . . . . . . . . . . . . . . . . (v.) شاهَدَ (يُشاهِدُ) مُشاهَدة

soap . . . . . . . . . . . . . . . . . . . . . . . . . . . (n., m.) صابون

plate . . . . . . . . . . . . . . . . . . . . . . . . (n., m.) صَحْن ج صُحون

to return . . . . . . . . . . . . . . . . . . . . . . (v.) عادَ (يَعودُ) عَوْدة

world . . . . . . . . . . . . . . . . . . . . . (n., m.) عالَم ج عَوالِم

break; vacation . . . . . . . . . . . . . (n., f.) عُطْلة ج عُطْلات/ عُطَل

dinner . . . . . . . . . . . . . . . . . . . . . (n., m.) عَشاء ج أعْشِية

lunch . . . . . . . . . . . . . . . . . . . . . . (n., m.) غَداء ج أغْدِية

to wash . . . . . . . . . . . . . . . . . . . . . (v.) غَسَلَ (يَغْسِلُ) غَسْل

to change something . . . . . . . . . . . . (v.) غَيَّرَ (يُغَيِّرُ) تَغيير

brush . . . . . . . . . . . . . . . . . . . . . . (n., f.) فُرْشاة ج فَراشٍ

breakfast . . . . . . . . . . . . . . . . . . . . (n., m.) فَطور

to spend time . . . . . . . . . . . . . . . . . . (v.) قَضى (يَقضي) قَضاء

writing . . . . . . . . . . . . . . . . . . . . (verbal noun) كِتابة

much, a great deal . . . . . . . . . . . (n., m.) كَثير ج كَثيرون / كِثار

because. . . . . . . . . . . . . . . . . . . . . . (particle) لأَنَّ

yogurt . . . . . . . . . . . . . . . . . . . . . . (n., m.) لَبَن

why. . . . . . . . . . . . . . . . . . . . . . . . (particle) لِـماذا

one coming early . . . . . . . . . . . . (n., m.) مُبَكِّر ج مُبَكِّرون

one coming late . . . . . . . . . . . . . (n., m.) مُتَأخِّر ج مُتَأخِّرون

stewed . . . . . . . . . . . . . . . . . . . . . . (adj.) مُدَمَّس

once, one occurrence. . . . . . . . . . . . (n., f.) مَرّة ج مَرّات

show, (television) series . . . . . . . . (n., m.) مُسَلسَل ج مُسَلسَلات

watching . . . . . . . . . . . . . . . . . . . (verbal noun) مُشاهَدة

busy . . . . . . . . . . . . . . . . . . . . . . (n., m.) مَشْغول ج مَشْغولون

together . . . . . . . . . . . . . . . . . . . . . (adv.) مَعاً

paste . . . . . . . . . . . . . . . . . . . . . . (n., m.) مَعْجون ج مَعاجين

fried . . . . . . . . . . . . . . . . . . . . . . . (adj.) مَقليّ

to forget . . . . . . . . . . . . . . . . . . . . (v.) نَسِيَ (يَنسى) نِسْيان

نَظَّفَ (يُنَظِّفُ) تَنْظيف (v.) . . . . . . . . . . . . . . . . . . . . . . . . . to clean.

نَهَضَ (يَنهَضُ) نُهوض (v.) . . . . . . . . . . . . . . . . . . . . . . . . . to get up

وَاللّهِ . . . . . . . . . by God, I swear, really (used to add emphasis)

وَجْه ج وُجوه (n., m.) . . . . . . . . . . . . . . . . . . . . . . . . . face

يَد ج أيْدٍ (n., f.) . . . . . . . . . . . . . . . . . . . . . . . . . . . hand

# الدرس الرابع عشر

AL Fattat
الفتات
ل.س SP
Fatteh With Olive Oil 50 ٥٠ فتة بزيت
Fatteh with Gee 60 ٦٠ فتة سمنة مع الصنوبر
Fatteh With Meat & Pines 100 ١٠٠ فتة بلحمة
Fattah With Meat ( Muscles ) 150 ١٥٠ فتة بلحمة موزات مع الصنوبر
Fatteh Chicken 80 ٨٠ فتة دجاج ربع فروج مع الصنوبر
Fatteh With Tounges 125 ١٢٥ فتة لسانات مع الصنوبر
Fatteh With Brains 125 ١٢٥ فتة نخاعات عدد١ مع الصنوبر
Fatteh Makadem 75 ٧٥ فتة مقادم عدد٢ مع الصنوبر
Fatteh 250 ٢٥٠ فتة كوكتيل ( لسان + نخاع + مقادم ) مع الصنوبر
Hot Drinks
المشروبات الساخنة
Acup Of Tea 25 ٢٥ شاي
Coffee 25 ٢٥ قهوة
Express Coffee & Milk 45 ٤٥ نسكافة مع حليب
Tisane ( Flowers ) 25 ٢٥ زهورات
Milk 35 ٣٥ حليب
Cold Drinks
المشروبات الباردة
Orange Frish Juice 50 ٥٠
Juice ( Raoukh ) 25 ٢٥
Cola 25
ACup Of Liquid Yogurt
Mineral Water
بابا غنوج
متبل
حمص ناعم
فتوش
تبولة
سلطة ناعمة
سلطة زيتون
سلطة شوندر
سلطة جرجير
حمص بيروتي
حمص بسمنة
حمص حب بلبن
حمص حب بزيت
فول بزيت
فول بلبن
بطاطا
Pastry
Cheese pie 15
meat pie 20
pinach pie 15
asted kubbeh 25
low Cheese Pies 25
za Daimeter 15 CM 25
شوربة عدس
ليس لدينا أي فرع آخر
اللحومات
Price Wieght السعر الوزن
s.p grm ل.س غ
Meats
Lamb Liver 125 250 ١٢٥ ٢٥٠ سودة غنم مع بطاطا وخضرة وليمون
Lamb Testicles 140 150 ١٤٠ ١٥٠ بيض غنم مقلي مع بطاطا وخضرة وليمون
Lamb Kidney 125 250 ١٢٥ ٢٥٠ كلاوي غنم مع بطاطا وخضرة وليمون
Chicken Liver 100 250 ١٠٠ ٢٥٠ سودة دجاج مع بطاطا وخضرة وليمون
Brains bane 90 1 ٩٠ عدد١ نخاع بانيه + بطاطا وليمون
Fried Brains 90 1 ٩٠ عدد١ نخاع مقلي + بطاطا وليمون
Brain With Egg 125 1 ١٢٥ عدد١ نخاع مع البيض
Brains Salad 90 1 ٩٠ عدد١ نخاع سلطة مع خضرة وليمون
Toungues Salad 100 1 ١٠٠ عدد١ سلطة لسانات
Escallope Chicken Bane 145 200 ١٤٥ ٢٠٠ اسكالوب دجاج بانيه
Escallope Meat 175 200 ١٧٥ ٢٠٠ اسكالوب لحم بانيه
Shish Tawook 125 200 ١٢٥ ٢٠٠
Meat Cordon PLO 250 250 ٢٥٠ ٢٥٠
Escallope Chicken Plo 250 250 ٢٥٠ ٢٥٠
Shish Tawook With Mushroom 150 250 ١٥٠ ٢٥٠
Meat Steak 150 250 ١٥٠ ٢٥٠
With Meat 125 250 ١٢٥ ٢٥٠

## Objectives

- Describing activities in the past, present, and future
- Expressing contrast with the أمّا . . . فَـ structure
- Expressing reason using لِذلِكَ
- Introduction to the preposition لِـ following the verb قالَ
- Introduction to the position of demonstratives in relation to the modified noun
- Revisiting the derivation of relative nouns

## المُفردات الجَديدة في صُوَر عَديدة:

زار (يَزورُ) زيارةٌ

قِطارٌ

مَحَطّةٌ ج مَحَطّاتٌ

مَشْهورٌ ج مَشْهورونَ

مُهَنْدِسٌ ج مُهَنْدِسونَ

الصِحافةُ

## تمرين ١

**A. Select the best choice:** Select the choice that correctly (or best) completes the sentence.

١- جِمي كارتَر رَجُلٌ ______________ .

☐ مَشْهور ☐ مُتَوَسِّط ☐ مُهَنْدِس

٢- ذَهَبَ سالِم إلى تونِس في ______________ الصَيف.

☐ بَلْدةِ ☐ بِطاقةِ ☐ عُطْلةِ

٣- تَسكُنُ سَناء في ______________ «القَنَوات» في مَدينةِ دِمَشق.

☐ حَديث ☐ حَيّ ☐ حَبّ

٤- سَتَدرُسُ أختي في جامِعَةِ الجَزائِر في فَصلِ الخَريفِ ______________ .

☐ الحارّ ☐ الأوَّل ☐ المُقْبِل

**B. Odd word out:** <u>Underline</u> the word that does not belong to each set and explain your choice if needed.

| | | | | |
|---|---|---|---|---|
| ٥- | شَمْس | حارّ | بَصَل | صَيْف |
| ٦- | مَوْعِد | سَرير | قِطار | مَحَطَّة |
| ٧- | أَرُزّ | عَدَس | بَصَل | طَقْس |
| ٨- | عيد | شاطِئ | بَحْر | بُحَيْرة |

## تمرين ٢

**Sentence construction:** On a separate sheet of paper, rearrange the words in each item to make meaningful sentences.

١- فِلَسطينِيَّةٌ – «المُسَخَن» – مَشْهورَةٌ – أَكْلَةٌ

٢- الإسْكَندَرِيَّة – بْراون – زارَ – مايكل – مَدينَة

٣- شاطِئ – هُناكَ – على – البَحْرِ – ناسٌ – كانَ – كَثيرونَ

٤- مَساءً – القِطارِ – سامية – مَحَطَّةِ – وَصَلَتْ – إلى

# تمرين ٣

**Paragraph construction:** On a separate sheet of paper, construct a meaningful paragraph by rearranging the following sentences. Do not change the position of the first sentence. Practice your script by writing the entire paragraph.

١- أَحْمَد حِجازي رَجُلٌ مِن مَدينَةِ حَلَب.

بَعدَ أربَعِ ساعاتٍ ونِصْفٍ وَصَلوا إلى طَرْطوس.

لكِنَّ طَرطوسَ لَيْسَتْ قَريبَةً ولَيْسَ عِندَ أحْمَد سَيّارة.

بَعدَ خَمسةِ أيّامٍ رَجَعوا إلى حَلَبَ بِالقِطارِ أيْضاً.

أرادَ أحْمَدُ زِيارةَ مَدينَةِ طَرطوسَ مَعَ عائِلَتِه.

نَزَلوا في طَرطوسَ في فُنْدُقٍ قَريبٍ مِن شاطِئِ البَحْر.

وطَرطوسُ مَدينَةٌ صَغيرَةٌ على الشاطِئِ السورِيّ.

كانوا في مَحَطَّةِ القِطارِ في حَلَبَ في الساعةِ السابِعَةِ صَباحاً.

لِذلِكَ ذَهبوا إلى هُناكَ بِالقِطار

## يَومِيّاتُ مايْكِل بْراوْن

**الأربِعاء ٢٢ أغُسْطُس (آب) ٢٠٠٧**

بَعدَ دَرسِ العَرَبيَّةِ بَعدَ ظُهرِ اليَومِ ذَهَبتُ إلى مَطعَمٍ مَشْهورٍ في حَيِّ المُهَندِسينَ اِسْمُهُ "العُمْدَة" مَعَ أصدِقائي حُسَيْن أحْمَد وهِبَة عبد الله وجِنِفَر كولي. يَدرُسُ حُسَيْن التِجارةَ وتَدرُسُ هِبَة الصِحافَة. أمّا جِنِفَر فَهيَ طالِبَةٌ أمريكيَّةٌ مِن جامِعَةِ واشِنطَن في سانت لويس تَدرُسُ اللُغَةَ العَرَبيَّةَ في الجامِعَةِ الأمريكيَّةِ في القاهِرة. أكَلْنا هُناكَ "الكُشَري" وهِيَ أكْلَةٌ مِصْرِيَّةٌ مِن الأرُزِّ والعَدَسِ والمَعكَرونَةِ والبَصَل. أُحِبُّ الكُشَريَّ كَثيراً، لكِنَّني حينَ آكُلُ الكُشَريَّ أشرَبُ كَثيراً مِن الماءِ بَعدَ الطَعام. لِذلِكَ ما أكَلْتُ كَثيراً مِنَ الكُشَريّ. كانَ المَطعَمُ نَظيفاً وكانَ هُناكَ بَعضُ الناسِ البريطانِيّينَ والإيطالِيّين.

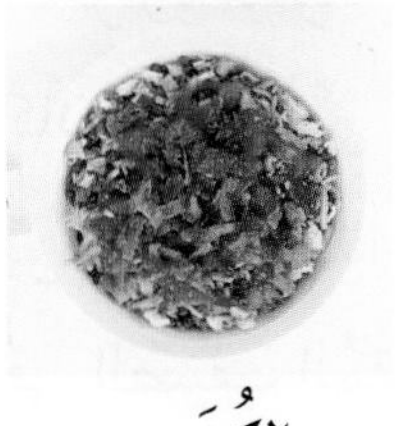

الكُشَري

**الخَميس ٢٣ أغُسطُس (آب) ٢٠٠٧**

يَقولُ حُسَيْن إنَّ الطَقسَ غَدّاً سَيَكونُ حارّاً. قُلْتُ لَهُ إنّي سَأذهَبُ في عُطلَةِ نِهايَةِ الأسبوعِ هذِهِ إلى مَدينَةِ المِنيا. قالَ لي إنَّ المِنيا حارّةٌ أيْضاً، وهِيَ أحَرُّ مِنَ القاهِرَة. سَأزورُ أُسْرَةَ صَديقي سَمير أحْمَد هُناكَ وسَأنزِلُ عِندَهُم. سَأذهَبُ بِالقِطارِ مِن مَحَطَّةِ الجيزة. ثَلاثُ ساعاتٍ ونِصْف مِن هذِهِ المَحَطَّةِ إلى المِنيا. مَوعِدُ القِطارِ في الساعةِ السابِعَةِ صَباحاً مِن كُلِّ يَوْم. سَيَكونُ أخو سَمير في مَحَطَّةِ القِطار حينَ أصِلُ إلى هُناك.

## يَومِيّاتُ عَدنان مارتيني

**الجُمْعَة ٣١ آب ٢٠٠٧**

بَعدَ دُروسي اليَومَ ذَهَبْتُ إلى المَكتَبَةِ وقَرَأتُ أكْثَرَ مِن ساعَتَيْن. كانَ هُناكَ صَديقي تِم نِكَلز وقالَ لي إنَّ الطَقسَ سَيَكونُ حارّاً غَداً وبَعدَ غَدٍ وإنّ عُطلةَ نِهايَةِ الأسبوعِ هذِهِ طَويلةٌ لأنَّ يَومَ الإثنَيْن ٣ أيلول هُوَ عيدُ العُمّال، لِذلِكَ سَيَذهَبُ يَومَ السَبتِ مَعَ صَديقَيْنِ إلى "سيدَر پوينت" وهي مَدينَةُ مَلاهٍ على شاطِئِ بُحَيْرَةِ إيري، والطَقسُ هَناكَ أبْرَدُ مِن طَقسِ كَلَمبَس. قالَ لي تِم "تَفَضَّلْ مَعَنا." سَأذْهَبُ مَعَهُم إنْ شاءَ الله لأنَّني ما زُرتُ "سيدَر پوينت" حَتّى الآن.

**الإثنَين ٣ أيلول ٢٠٠٧**

كانَ الطَقسُ جَميلاً جِدّاً في "سيدَر پوينت" وكانَت الشَمْسُ ساطِعةً ودَرَجَةُ الحَرارةِ مُعْتَدِلَة. بُحَيْرَةُ إيري كَبيرَةٌ، وهي أكبَرُ مِن كُلِّ البُحَيراتِ القَريبَةِ مِن كَلَمبَس. كانَ هُناكَ ناسٌ كَثيرونَ على شاطِئِ البُحَيْرَةِ وكانَ بَعْضُ الناسِ يَسبَحونَ في الماء. كانَ يَومُ السَبْتِ هذا مِن أجْمَلِ أيّامِ الصَيف. سَأزورُ "سيدَر پوينت" مرةً ثانية مَعَ أصدِقائي في الصَيْفِ المُقْبِلِ إن شاءَ الله.

## تمرين ٤

**A. Listen and select:** Check the box that matches the information as expressed in the passages for this lesson.

١- «العُمْدة» إسْمُ ______________ .

☐ صَديقِ مايكِل ☐ حَيٍّ في القاهِرةِ ☐ مَطعَمٍ

٢- الكُشَريُّ أكْلَةٌ ______________ .

☐ مِصْريَّةٌ ☐ بريطانيّةٌ ☐ إيطاليّةٌ

٣- كانَ «العُمْدة» ______________ .

☐ قَريباً ☐ نَظيفاً ☐ جَميلاً

٤- سَيَذهَبُ مايكِل إلى المِنيا مِن ______________ .

☐ مَطارِ القاهِرةِ ☐ مَحَطَّةِ الجيزَةِ ☐ حَيِّ المُهَندِسين

٥- ذَهَبَ عَدنان بَعدَ دُروسِهِ إلى ______________ .

☐ المَكتَبَةِ ☐ الصَفِّ ☐ الشارِعِ

٦- ذَهَبَ عَدنان في عُطلَةِ نِهايَةِ الأسبوعِ إلى مَدينَةِ ______________ .

☐ كَلَمبَس ☐ دِمَشق ☐ مَلاهٍ

٧- عيدُ العُمّالِ في يَومِ ______________ .

☐ السَبْتِ ☐ الأحَدِ ☐ الإثْنَيْنِ

٨- إسْمُ صَديقِ عَدنان ______________ .

☐ تِم ☐ مايكِل ☐ جِنِفَر

**B. صواب أو خطأ:** Mark the following sentences صواب or خَطأ according to the information in the main reading passage and correct any false statements.

٩- مِنَ القاهِرَةِ إلى المِنيا خَمسُ ساعاتٍ بِالقِطار.

١٠- مَوعِدُ قِطارِ المِنيا في الساعةِ التاسِعَة.

١١- كانَ الطَقسُ في «سيدَر پوينت» غائِماً.

١٢- سَيَذهَبُ عَدنان إلى «سيدَر پوينت» في الصَيفِ المُقبِل.

**C.** Form three questions about the reading passages.

# تمرين ٥

**Conversation:** Describe an interesting vacation that you took in your life. Explain why you did or did not enjoy your vacation, where you went, what happened, how you got there, in which season you traveled, with whom you traveled, how long you stayed, and when you returned.

How well did your partner listen? Once you have finished speaking about your vacation, the person who listened will now relate your interesting vacation story to you and see how it matches up with the original version. Once you are finished, switch roles.

## ١. Expressing Contrast with أمّا . . . فَـ

The أمّا . . . فَـ combination is used to contrast two things, similar to "however, as for, as to, but, yet" in English. The first word of this clause أمّا signals that the following noun or noun phrase (underlined in example 1) is being contrasted with something else (the word highlighted in blue in example 1). The conjunction فَـ introduces the contrasted item and is *prefixed* to it.

١ سَيّارَةُ يُوسُف قَديمةٌ أمّا سَيّارةُ أحْمَد فَجَديدَةٌ.

The particle فَـ is usually followed directly by a verb if the sentence contains one, as in example 2.

٢ أَتكَلَّمُ العَرَبيَّةَ أمّا مايكِل فَيَتكَلَّمُ الإنكليزيَّة.

- **Note:** The grammatical case of the item after أمّا should be the same case as the item being contrasted. In example 1, both سَيّارَةُ يوسُف and سَيّارةُ أحْمَد are nominative مَرفوع since they function as subjects. Consider example 3:

  ٣ أتكَلَّمُ العَرَبيَّةَ جيِّداً أمّا الفَرَنسيةَ فأتكَلَّمُها قليلاً.

  In example 3, the word العَرَبيَّةَ is the direct object of the verb أتكَـلَّمُ, therefore it is accusative مَنصوب, and so is its contrast الفَرَنسيةَ.

Now that we can identify the فَـ . . . أمّا combination, the issue that remains to be resolved is where to place the فَـ particle in our discourse. The particle فَـ should be placed exactly where a comma would be placed in English.

٤ أُحِبُّ الحِمَّص أمّا أمّي فَتُحِبُّ التبولة. *I like* ḥimmus. *As for my mother, she likes* tabūleh.

٥ مايكِل براون في القاهِرةِ أمّا عَدنان فهُوَ في كَلَمبَس. *Michael Brown is in Cairo. As for Adnan, he is in Columbus.*

## تمرين ٦

**Find out from your neighbor using فَـ . . . أمّا**: Find out who in your class . . .

1. likes German cars/Italian cars
2. has visited the city of Aleppo, Syria/the city of Paris, France
3. watches the news/reads the paper
4. bought a new telephone/bought a new computer
5. wants to visit *ḳān el-ḳalīlī* bazaar in Egypt/*el-ḥamidiyya* bazaar in Syria

Now on a separate sheet of paper, write your findings down in contrastive sentences in Arabic paying close attention to the correct placement of the particle فَـ. You may rely on your sense of comma placement in English to guide your فَـ placement in Arabic. Be prepared to report your findings to the class.

## تمرين ٧

**Sentence construction using فَـ . . . أمّا**: On a separate sheet of paper, translate the following items into English, using the structure فَـ . . . أمّا, as in the example:

**مِثال: مَدينةُ نيويورك كَبيرَةٌ / مَدينةُ توليدو صَغيرَة**

**مَدينةُ نيويورك كَبيرَةٌ أمّا مَدينةُ توليدو فَصَغيرَة.**

١- نَهْرُ النيلِ طَويلٌ / نَهْر بَرَدى قَصيرٌ

٢- يَسكُنُ نادِر في شَقّةٍ / تَسكُنُ ناديا في سَكَنِ الطالِبات

٣- أخي مُهَندِس / أختي أستاذة

٤- اِشتَرَيْتُ مِحفَظةً / اِشْتَرتْ زَوْجَتي نَظّارةً

٥- مَدينةُ طَرابُلُسَ الشامِ في لُبنانَ / مَدينةُ طَرابُلُسَ الغَرْبِ في ليبيا

٦- أُحِبُّ عَصيرَ البُرتُقالِ / أنْتِ تُحِبّينَ الحَليب

## 2. Expressing Reason Using لِذلِكَ

One way of expressing reason is by using the prepositional phrase لِذلِكَ (pronounced *lid̲ālika*). It is made up of the preposition لِـ 'for' and the demonstrative ذلِكَ 'that'. Together, they mean "for that reason." The use of لِذلِكَ adds an air of sophistication to your sentences, while not, in any way, affecting sentence structure.

٤ أُحِبُّ الفولَ المَدَمَّسَ لِذلِكَ آكُلُهُ كُلَّ يومٍ.

If you want to ask about reason, you may use the particle لِماذا 'why'.

لِماذا تَدرُسُ اللُّغَةَ العَرَبيَّةَ؟

### تمرين ٨

**A. Sentence composition using لِذلِكَ**: Combine the two ideas by using لِذلِكَ.

١- المَكتَبَةُ قَريبةٌ / مَشَيْتُ إلَيْها.

______________________________

٢- يُحِبُّ مَحمودٌ البيتزا كَثيراً / يأكُلُها كُلَّ يوم.

______________________________

٣- سَحَر مِن دِمَشق وتَدرُسُ في جامِعَةِ حَلَبَ / تَسكُنُ في شَقَّةٍ هُناك.

______________________________

**B. Translation using لِذلِكَ**: Express these meanings in Arabic using لِذلِكَ.

4. I don't have a car; therefore, I went by train.

______________________________

5. We sat in the classroom for a half hour, but the teacher did not show up. So, we went to the library.

______________________________________________

6. Souha likes swimming. For this reason, she lives on the shore of a lake.

______________________________________________

## 3. The Preposition لِـ Following the Verb قال

The verb قالَ is followed by the preposition لِـ when the addressee is specified (e.g., "I told Adnān": قُلْتُ لِعدنان).

- **Pronunciation note:** The preposition لـ is pronounced *li* when prefixed to nouns (e.g., قال لِعدنان) and لَـ *la* when prefixed to pronouns (قال لَهُ).

## تمرين ٩

**Using قالَ**: On a separate sheet of paper, express the following sentences in Arabic, using the verb قالَ.

1. My professor told me that he would be in his office at nine.
2. Maḥmūd told his wife that he stayed at the Sheraton Hotel in Damascus.
3. He told her also that he ate at al-Sharq Restaurant every day.
4. Marwān says that his brother will arrive at the train station at 4 p.m.

## 4. The Position of Demonstratives in Relation to the Modified Noun

In Arabic, demonstratives (e.g., هذا أو هذِه) are considered and treated as nouns. They may be objects of verbs (e.g., أَعْطِني هذا), or of prepositions (e.g., أَعْطِني مِن هذا), or they may be subjects of nominal sentences, as in examples 5 and 6.

| | | |
|---|---|---|
| ٥ | هذا هُوَ أُسْتاذُ العَرَبيَّةِ. | *This is the Arabic teacher.* |
| ٦ | هذا أُسْتاذٌ. | *This is a teacher.* |

A demonstrative may be one of the constituents of a noun phrase (not a sentence):

| | | |
|---|---|---|
| *this book* | هذا الكِتابُ | ٧ |

- **Note:** In a noun phrase, if the noun modified by a demonstrative has a possessive pronoun suffixed to it (e.g., كِتابي) or is part of an إضافة structure (e.g., عُطلةُ الأسْبوعِ), the demonstrative should follow this noun or noun phrase, as in examples 8 and 9:

| | | |
|---|---|---|
| *this book of mine . . .* | كِتابي هذا . . . | ٨ |
| *this weekend . . .* | عُطلَةُ الأسْبوعِ هذِهِ . . . | ٩ |

In example 8, هذا (m.) refers to كِتاب (m.), while in example 9 هذِهِ (f.) refers to عُطلَةُ (f.).

- If the demonstrative precedes a noun or noun phrase like those in examples 8 and 9, the result is a full and complete sentence:

| | | |
|---|---|---|
| *This is my book.* | هذا كِتابي. | ١٠ |
| *This is the weekend.* | هذِهِ عُطلَةُ الأسْبوعِ | ١١ |

## تمرين ١٠

**Using demonstratives:** Express these phrases and sentences in Arabic, using appropriate demonstratives in the right positions:

1. This is our professor. ____________________
2. this holiday of yours (f., sg.) ____________________
3. these friends of mine ____________________
4. This is my car. ____________________
5. these eyeglasses (sg.) of my mother's ____________________

## 5. More on the Derivation of Relative Nouns (نِسْبَة)

The relative noun (*nisba*) مِئَويّ is derived from مِئة by dropping the final تاء مَربوطة and suffixing a واو and then the relative suffix يّ. When deriving relative nouns, an additional **واو** is required before the relative suffix **يّ** in some nouns, such as **أسرة سَنة، مِئة، سَماء،** (see Unit 5, section 6 in the Workbook).

- **Note:** Relative adjectives are normally derived from singular nouns, but as you will see later, they may also be derived from plurals.

## تمرين ١١

Derive relative adjectives **نِسبَة** from these words:

١- أوروبا ______________

٢- سَنَة ______________

٣- سَماء ______________

٤- شِتاء ______________

٥- ميلاد ______________

٦- مِئَة ______________

٧- خَريف ______________

٨- أُسْرَة ______________

## تمرين ١٢

**Writing enhancement:** On a separate sheet of paper, describe a visit you made to a real or imaginary place. Mention your destination, the reason for going there, what you did there, when you went and how, where you stayed, and when you returned. Briefly describe the place in terms of size, people, and weather and any interesting conversations that you had with the people there.

## تمرين ١٣

A. **Listen and select:** Check the box that matches the information as expressed in the listening passage for this lesson.

١- رامِز الخولي مِن مَدينَةِ ______________ .

☐ طَرابُلُس ☐ حِمْصَ ☐ دِمَشق

٢- أكَلَ رامِز وزوجَتُهُ فَطوراً صَغيراً لأنَّهُما ______________ .

☐ لا يَأكُلانِ الفَطورَ ☐ في طَرابُلُسَ ☐ سَيَأكُلانِ غَداءً كَبيراً

٣- وَصَلَ رامِز وزَوجَتُهُ إلى طَرابُلْسَ في الساعةِ ____________ .

☐ التاسِعةِ ☐ الحادِيَةَ عَشْرَةَ ☐ الواحِدةِ

٤- أكَلَ رامِز وَزَوجَتُهُ على الغَداءِ ____________ .

☐ فولاً ☐ كَباباً ☐ أطعِمةً لُبنانِيَّةً

B. **Fill in the blank:** Complete these sentences with information from the listening passage.

٥- يَعمَلُ رامِز ____________ .

٦- يَسكُنُ رامِز وزَوجَتُهُ في مَدينَةِ ____________ .

٧- ذَهَبَ رامِز وزَوجَتُهُ إلى طَرابُلْسَ في فَصْلِ ____________ .

٨- أكَلَ رامِز وزَوجَتُهُ طَعامَ الغَداءِ في مَطعَمٍ اسْمُهُ ____________ .

C. **صواب أو خطأ:** Mark the following sentences **صواب** or **خَطأ** according to the information in the listening passage and correct any false statements.

٩- إسْمُ زَوجَةِ رامِز سِهام.

______________________________________________

١٠- مَشى رامِز وزَوجَتُهُ في السوقِ بَعدَ الغَداء.

______________________________________________

١١- كانَ الطَقسُ بارِداً وجلَسا في غُرفَةٍ دافِئة.

______________________________________________

١٢- ذَهَبَ رامِز وزَوجَتُهُ إلى طَرابُلْسَ بِالحافِلة.

______________________________________________

## تمرين ١٤

**تَمرينُ المُشاهَدة: شاهِدوا الدَرْسَ الرابع عَشَر على القُرْص الرَقْميّ.**

**المَشْهَدُ الأوّل**

١- لماذا جاءَ مايكل إلى دِمَشق؟ ________________________

________________________________________

٢- كَم يَوماً سَيَبقى مايكل في دِمَشق ولماذا عليه أنْ يَرجِع إلى القاهِرة؟ ____________

________________________________________

٣- كَيْفَ الحياة بالقاهِرة في رأي مايكل؟ ________________________

________________________________________

٤- مَن يَنْتَظِرُ مايكل عِند قَوس باب شَرقي؟ ________________________

________________________________________

**المَشْهَدُ الثاني**

١- ماذا يَدرُسُ سامِر وفي أيّةِ كُلّيّة؟ ________________________

________________________________________

٢- ماذا يُفَضِّلُ مايكل العامية أم الفُصحى؟ ________________________

________________________________________

٣- إلى أين سَيذهَبُ كُلٌّ مِن ستيف وسامِر ومايكل؟ ________________________

________________________________________

________________________________________

________________________________________

# المُفْرَدات

Listen to the vocabulary items on the CD and practice their pronunciation.

| | |
|---|---|
| rice | أرُزّ (n., m.) |
| extended family | أُسْرة ج أُسَر (n. f.) |
| to wait | اِنتَظَرَ (يَنْتَظِرُ) اِنتِظار (v.) |
| onion | بَصَل (n., m.) |
| neighborhood, borough | حَيّ ج أحْياء (n., m.) |
| to visit | زارَ (يَزورُ) زِيارة (v.) |
| to do (Syrian colloquial) | ساوى (يساوي) (v.) |
| what (Syrian colloquial) | شو (interrogative particle) |
| journalism | صِحافة (n., f.) |
| worker, laborer | عامِل ج عُمّال (n., m.) |
| colloquial | عامّيّة (active participle) |
| lentils | عَدَس (n., m.) |
| break, vacation | عُطلة ج عُطَل/ عُطلات (n., f.) |
| weekend | عُطْلَةُ نِهايَةِ الأُسْبوعِ (n., f.) |
| mayor | عُمْدَة ج عُمَد (n., m.) |
| celebration, festivity, feast day, day, holiday, eid | عيد ج أعْياد (n., m.) |
| Labor Day | عيدُ العُمّال |
| Classical Arabic (*lit.*, “most eloquent”) | فُصْحى (superlative) |
| to prefer | فَضَّلَ (يُفَضِّل) تَفْضيل (v.) |
| train | قِطار ج قِطارات (n., m.) |
| arch | قَوْس ج أقْواس (n., m.) |
| lightly salted, partially dehydrated yogurt with olive oil | لَبْنة (n., f.) |

for this reason, therefore . . . . . . . . . . . . (demonstrative) لِذلِكَ

station . . . . . . . . . . . . . . . . . . . . . . . . (n., f.) مَحَطّة ج مَحَطّات

crowded . . . . . . . . . . . . . . . . . . . . . . . . . . (adj.) مُزْدَحِم

famous, well-known . . . . . . . (participle) مَشْهور ج (ون)، مَشاهير

pasta, macaroni . . . . . . . . . . . . . . . . . . . . . . . (n., f.) مَعْكَرونة

place of entertainment . . . . . . . . . . . . . . (n., m.) مَلْهىً ج مَلاهٍ

engineer . . . . . . . . . . . . . . . . . . . . . (n., m.) مُهَنْدِس ج مُهَندِسون

clean . . . . . . . . . . . . . . . . . . . . . . . . . . . . (adj., m.) نَظيف

end . . . . . . . . . . . . . . . . . . . . . . . . . . (n., f.) نِهاية ج نِهايات

# الدَرسُ الخامِسَ عَشَر

## Objectives

- Describing events such as national and religious festivities
- Providing personal information
- Revisiting the five nouns and diptotes
- Introduction to the passive
- Introduction to the verb صارَ

## رُكنُ المُفْرَداتِ الجَديدة

| | |
|---|---|
| to celebrate | اِحْتَفَلَ (يَحْتَفِلُ) اِحْتِفال (بِـ) |
| to fast | صامَ (يَصومُ) صَوْمٌ / صِيام |
| feast / holiday | عيدٌ ج أعيادٌ |
| revolution | ثَوْرةٌ ج ثَوْرات |
| Messiah | مَسيحٌ |
| type / kind | نَوْعٌ ج أنْواعٌ |
| independence | اِسْتِقلالٌ |
| education | تَعليمٌ |

## تمرين ١

**Odd word out:** Underline the word that does not belong to each set and explain your choice if needed.

١- تَربية تَعليم فَجْر مَدرَسة

٢- الأضْحى الفِطر الفِصْح الجَزيرة

٣- إسلاميّ ابْتِدائيّ مُتَوَسِّط ثانَويّ
٤- فَجْر حَلوى ظُهر مَغرِب

## تمرين ٢

وافِقْ بَيْنَ الكَلِماتِ في العَمودَين.

**Matching:**

| | | | |
|---|---|---|---|
| ١ | إسلاميّ | | المَسيح |
| ٢ | عيدُ الشُكْر | | رَمَضان |
| ٣ | عيدُ الأَضْحى | | ثانَويّة |
| ٤ | عيدُ الميلاد | | ٤ تَمّوز |
| ٥ | عيدُ الفِطْر | | مَسيحيّ |
| ٦ | عيدُ اسْتِقلالِ أمريكا | | الحَجّ |
| | | | ديك حَبَش |

## تمرين ٣

**Fill in the blanks:** Choose the appropriate word to complete the sentences.

| | | | | | | | | |
|---|---|---|---|---|---|---|---|---|
| الاسْتِقلال | وُلِدَ | ذو الحِجّة | تَعليم | إسلاميّ | رَمَضان | طَعام | لأنَّ | نَوْع |

١- إيرانُ بَلَدٌ __________ لكِنَّهُ لَيسَ بَلَداً عَرَبيّاً.

٢- اِنتَقَلَتْ أُختي إلى قَطَر __________ عَمَلَ زَوجِها صارَ هُناكَ.

٣- __________ جورج واشنطُن في وِلايةِ فرجينيا في سَنةِ ١٧٣٢.

٤- تَحتَفِلُ سورية بِعيدِ __________ في ١٧ نيسان.

٥- ما __________ سَيّارتِكَ يا أستاذ؟

٦- يَصومُ المُسلِمونَ في شَهرِ __________.

# أعيادٌ عَرَبِيَّةٌ وإسلامِيَّةٌ ومَسيحِيَّةٌ وأمريكيَّةٌ

في البِلادِ العَرَبِيَّةِ هُناكَ أعيادٌ عَرَبِيَّةٌ وإسلامِيَّةٌ ومَسيحِيَّة. يَحْتَفِلُ كُلُّ بَلَدٍ عَرَبِيٍّ عادةً بِعيدِ اسْتِقلالِه أو بِعيدِ ثَوْرَتِه. هذِه أعيادُ الاسْتِقلالِ والثَورةِ في بَعضِ البِلادِ العَرَبِيَّة.

| البَلَد | عيدُ الاسْتِقلال | عيدُ الثَوْرة | العَلَم |
|---|---|---|---|
| تونِس | ٢٠ آذار | ----- |  |
| الجَزائِر | ---- | ١ تِشرين الثاني |  |
| سورية | ١٧ نيسان | ٨ آذار |  |
| العِراق | ---- | ١٧ تمّوز |  |
| عُمان | ١٨ تِشرين الثاني | ---- |  |
| لُبنان | ٢٢ تِشرين الثاني | ---- |  |
| مِصر | ---- | ٢٤ تمّوز |  |
| المَغرِب | ٣ آذار | ---- |  |
| اليَمَن | ٢٢ أيّار | ---- | 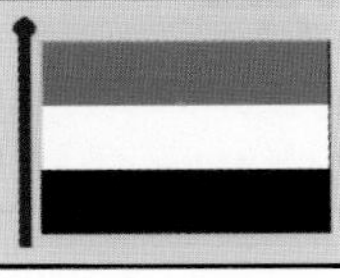 |

تَحتَفِلُ كُلُّ البِلادِ العَرَبِيَّةِ بالأعيادِ الإسْلامِيَّة، لكِنَّ بَعضَ البِلادِ العَرَبِيَّةِ تَحْتَفِلُ بالأعيادِ المَسيحيَّةِ أيْضاً، ويَكونُ هذا في سوريةَ ولُبنانَ وفِلَسطينَ والأردُنِّ والعِراقِ ومِصْرَ.

## عيدان إسلاميّان

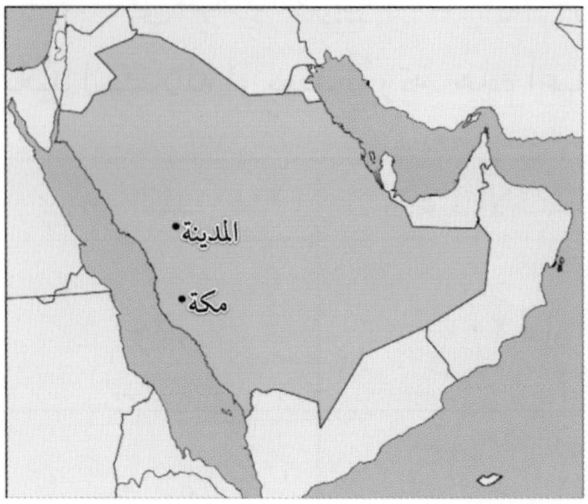


مِن الأعيادِ الإسلاميَّة عيدُ الفِطْرِ ويَأتي بَعدَ شَهرِ رَمَضان. في شَهرِ رَمَضانَ يَصومُ المُسْلِمونَ عَنِ الأكْلِ والشُرْبِ مِن الفَجْرِ حَتّى المَغرِب. بَعدَ رَمَضانَ كُلُّ المُسلِمينَ يَحتَفِلونَ بِعيدِ الفِطْرِ ثَلاثَةَ أيّام، يَأكُلونَ كُلَّ أنواعِ الطَعامِ والحَلْوى ويَشرَبونَ القَهْوة.

العيدُ الثاني هُوَ عيدُ الأضْحى ويَأتي في شَهرِ ذي الحِجَّةِ بَعدَ الحَجِّ. ويَكونُ الحَجُّ في مَكّةَ في السُعوديّة. يَحتَفِلُ المُسلِمونَ بِهذا العيدِ أربَعَةَ أيّام (بَعضُهُم يَحتَفِلُ بِهِ يوماً أو يومَينِ فَقَط).

بَعضُ البِلادِ الإسلامِيَّةِ تَحتَفِلُ بِعيدِ ميلادِ رَسولِ الله مُحَمَّد صلّى اللهُ عَلَيهِ وسَلَّمَ وبَعضُ البِلادِ لا تَحتَفِلُ بِهِ، ويُسَمَّى هذا العيدُ «عيدُ المَوْلِد.»

## عيدان مَسيحِيّان

عيدُ الميلادِ يَعني ميلادُ السَيِّدِ المَسيحِ عيسى عَلَيْهِ السلام ويَحتَفِلُ بِهِ المَسيحيّون في ٢٥ كانون الأوَّل.

**شَجَرَةُ عيدِ الميلاد**

**عيدُ الفِصْح**

العيدُ المسيحيُّ الثاني هُوَ عيدُ الفِصْحِ ويُحْتَفَلُ بِهذا العيدِ في يَومِ أحَد في فصل الربيع (في آذار أو نيسان أو أيار).

# أعْياد أمريكيّة

## عيدُ الشُكْر

ديك حَبَش

يَحتَفِلُ الأمريكيّونَ بِعيدِ الشُكْرِ في رابِعِ يَومِ خَميس مِن شَهرِ تِشرينَ الثاني. يَأكُلُ الأمريكيّونَ في هذا اليَومِ ديكَ حَبَش (ديك رومي) وحَلوى تُسَمّى فَطيرةَ القَرْع.

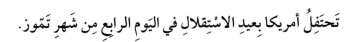

## عيدُ الاسْتِقلال

تَحتَفِلُ أمريكا بِعيدِ الاسْتِقلالِ في اليَومِ الرابِعِ مِن شَهرِ تَمّوز.

## عيدُ العُمّال

تَحتَفِلُ أمريكا بِعيدِ العُمّالِ في أوَّلِ يَومِ إثنين مِن شَهرِ أيلول.

## عيدُ مارتِن لوثَر كِنغ

تَحتَفِلُ مُعظَمُ الوِلاياتِ الأمريكيّةِ بِهذا العيدِ في ثالِثِ يَومِ إثنين مِن شَهرِ كانونَ الثاني.

# سُعاد ريماوي

سُعاد ريماوي فَتاةٌ عِراقيّةٌ مِن مَدينةِ بَغداد. تَدرُسُ التِجارةَ في جامِعةِ بَغدادَ وتَسكُنُ مَعَ أبيها وأُمِّها وثَلاثةِ إخْوةٍ في بَيتٍ كبيرٍ في شارِعِ دِجلة.

وُلِدَتْ سُعاد في مَدينةِ بَغدادَ وعيدُ ميلادِها في ٢٠ آذار. هي أكبَرُ إخوَتِها. دَرَسَتْ في مَدارِسِ بَغدادَ مِن الصَفِّ الأوَّلِ الابْتِدائيّ إلى الصَفِّ الثامِنِ المُتَوَسِّط. حينَ كانَتْ في سِنِّ الرابِعةِ عَشْرةَ اِنتَقَلَتْ مَعَ أبيها وأُمِّها مِن بَغدادَ إلى مَدينةِ المَوصِلِ لأنَّ أباها صارَ مُديرَ التَربيةِ والتَعليمِ فيها. دَرَسَت هُناكَ في مَدارِسِ المَوصِلِ ثَلاث سَنَوات. بَعدَ ذلِكَ رَجَعوا إلى بَغدادَ. حينَ تَخَرَّجَتْ مِن المَدرَسةِ الثانَويّةِ ذَهَبَتْ إلى جامِعةِ بَغداد.

سُعاد في سنِّ العِشرينَ الآن. تَقولُ سُعاد إنَّها حينَ تَتَخَرَّجُ مِنَ الجامِعةِ بَعدَ سَنَتَينِ سَوفَ تَرجِعُ إلى المَوصِلِ وتَعمَلُ هُناكَ لأنَّها تُحِبُّ تِلكَ المَدينة.

## تمرين ٤

**A. Listen and select:** Check the box that matches the information as expressed in the main passages for this lesson.

١- عيدُ الثَورةِ في مِصْرَ في __________ .

☐ ٤ تَمّوز ☐ ١٧ تَمّوز ☐ ٢٤ تَمّوز

٢- عيدُ __________ عيدٌ إسلاميّ.

☐ الفِصْح ☐ الفِطر ☐ الثَورة

٣- عيدُ اِستِقلالِ سورية في __________ .

☐ ١٧ نيسان ☐ ٨ آذار ☐ ٢٢ أيّار

٤- يُحتَفَلُ بِعيدِ __________ في شَهرِ كانون الأوّل.

☐ الفِصْح ☐ الأضْحى ☐ الميلاد

٥- سَكَنَتْ سُعاد ريماوي في المَوصِل __________ .

☐ سَنةً واحِدةً ☐ ثَلاثَ سَنَوات ☐ خَمسَ سَنَوات

٦- رَجَعَتْ سُعاد إلى بَغدادَ حينَ كانتْ في سِنِّ ______________ .

☐ الثالِثةَ عَشْرةَ ☐ السابِعةَ عَشْرةَ ☐ الثامِنةَ عَشْرةَ

٧- تَدرُسُ سُعاد ______________ في جامِعةِ بَغداد.

☐ التِجارة ☐ الطِبَّ ☐ اللُغَةَ الإنكليزيّةَ

٨- تَسكُنُ سُعاد ______________ .

☐ في شَقَّةٍ ☐ مَعَ أسرتِها ☐ في سَكَنِ الطالِبات

B. صواب أو خطأ: On a separate sheet of paper, mark the following sentences صواب or خَطأ according to the information in the main reading passage and correct any false statements.

٩- تَحتَفِلُ الجزائِرُ بالأعْيادِ الإسلاميَّةِ والمَسيحيَّة.

١٠- يُحْتَفَلُ بِعيدِ الفِصْحِ في ٢٢ آذار.

١١- يَأكُلُ الأمريكيونَ ديك حَبَش في عيدِ الفِصْح.

١٢- تَحتَفِلُ كُلُّ الوِلاياتِ الأمريكيَّةِ بِعيدِ مارتِن لوثَر كِنغ.

١٣- سُعاد أكبَرُ مِن إخوتِها الثَلاثة.

١٤- سَوفَ تَتَخَرَّجُ سُعادُ مِنَ الجامِعَةِ بَعدَ سَنةٍ واحِدة.

## تمرين ٥

**Conversation about a holiday:** In pairs, take turns describing a holiday that you remember well. Among the things that you may wish to express are:

1. what happened (to you) on that day
2. whom you were with
3. what you talked about with your friends or family
4. what you did on that day

If you cannot remember any certain holiday really well, create a fictional description emulating the main passages of this lesson and integrating the new vocabulary. As always, be creative with the language.

Upon completion of the exercise, report your neighbor's story to the class.

## تمرين ٦

**Sentence construction:** On a separate sheet of paper, rearrange the words in each item to make meaningful sentences.

١- يَحتَفِلُ - ميلادِه - بِعيدِ - أخوكَ - مَتى؟

٢- شَهر - أختي - آب - وُلِدَتْ - في

٣- جِدّاً - أستراليا - كَبيرةٌ - جَزيرةٌ

٤- في - إلى - الخَريف - هذِهِ - اِنتَقَلتُ - فَصْلِ - الشَقَّة

## تمرين ٧

**Paragraph construction:** On a separate sheet of paper, construct a meaningful paragraph by rearranging the following sentences. Do not change the position of the first sentence. Practice your script by writing the entire paragraph.

١- وُلِدَ مازِن المُدَرِّس في مَدينةِ حَلَب،

ثُمَّ رَجَعَ إلى حَلَب ودَرَسَ في جامِعَةِ حَلَبَ في السَنةِ الأولى.

بَعدَ ذلِكَ دَرَسَ في مَدرَسَةٍ ثانَويّةٍ في مَدينةِ دِمَشق.

يَقولُ مازِن إنّه سَوفَ يَرجِعُ إلى حَلَبَ حينَ يَتَخَرَّج.

دَرَسَ في مَدارِسِ حَلَبَ الابْتِدائيّةِ والمُتوَسِّطة.

ثُمَّ اِنتَقَلَ إلى جامِعَةِ دِمَشق في السَنةِ الثانية.

## تمرين ٨

**Find out from your neighbors:** Ask your neighbors the following questions in Arabic. Be prepared to report what your classmate said upon completion of the exercise.

اسألوا جيرانكُم:

١- كَيْفَ تَحْتَفِل(ين) بِعيدِ ميلادِك؟

٢- كَيْفَ يَحْتَفِلُ المَسيحيونَ بِعيدِ الميلاد؟

٣- كَيْفَ يَحْتَفِلُ المُسْلِمونَ بِعيدِ الفِطْر؟

٤- كَيْفَ اِحْتَفَلْت بِعيدِ رأسِ السَّنة؟

## تمرين ٩

**Composition about a festive event:** Select any holiday or festive event that was not covered in this lesson and describe it emulating your favorite passage from the main text. Provide information about when, how, and by whom it is celebrated. You may, if you wish, read your composition to your class. Again, if nothing comes to mind, feel free to take poetic license and create your own story.

### 1. The Five Nouns Revisited الأَسْماءُ الخَمْسة

The third of the five nouns that we will cover is **ذو** 'of, with, owner of'. You may recognize it as we learned it in Lesson 11 as the first part of the names of the eleventh ذو **القِعْدة** and twelfth months ذو **الحِجّة** (*the month of pilgrimage*) of the lunar calendar. Taking the twelfth month as an example, **ذو الحِجّة** takes the form **ذي** in the phrase **شَهر** ذي **الحجة**. Reflect for a moment on why this noun's last radical has changed from a **واو** to a **ياء**.

Because it is the second part of an **إضافة** structure, **شَهرُ** ذي الحِجّة is in the genitive case **مَجرور**. As with all of these five special nouns, case is indicated by long rather than short vowels occupying their final radical.

The remaining two nouns are **حَمو** 'father-in-law' and **فو / فَم** 'mouth'. A table illustrating the five nouns in the nominative, accusative, and genitive cases is presented here:

| حَمو | فو | ذو | أخو | أبو | مَرفوع |
| --- | --- | --- | --- | --- | --- |
| حما | فا | ذا | أخا | أبا | مَنصوب |
| حمي | في | ذي | أخي | أبي | مَجرور |

- **Remember** that nominative مَرفوع is the case of agents (doers of the action), subjects, and predicates; genitive مَجرور is the case of objects of prepositions and the second part of إضافة structures; and accusative مَنصوب is the case of objects of verbs and several other grammatical categories that we will cover as we progress on our journey learning Arabic.

- **Note:** ذو has a feminine form, ذات, and both the masculine and feminine have dual and plural forms which change with respect to case. As you can see upon close inspection of the following table, the accusative مَنصوب and genitive مَجرور forms of ذو in the dual and plural are identical.

| Forms of ذو | | | |
| --- | --- | --- | --- |
| مَجرور | مَنصوب | مَرفوع | |
| ذَوَيْ | ذَوَيْ | ذَوا | Dual masculine |
| ذَواتَيْ | ذَواتَيْ | ذَواتا | Dual feminine |
| ذَوي | ذَوي | ذَوو | Plural masculine |
| ذَواتِ | ذواتِ | ذَواتُ | Plural feminine |

- **Note:** ذو takes the same case as the noun to which it refers.

Some examples might shed some light on the meaning of the previous note. Turn your attention to examples 1–4 below. (Note that ذو عِلْم should be translated as "of intelligence," or simply "intelligent"—cases have no bearing on the meaning here.)

١ رَجُلٌ ذو عِلْمٍ / الرَجُلُ ذو عِلْمٍ

٢ امرأةٌ ذاتُ عِلْمٍ / المَرأةُ ذاتُ عِلْمٍ

Notice how ذو has taken on the nominative case with the long vowel واو occupying the final radical in example 1. As well, notice how neither *definiteness* nor *indefiniteness* has an effect on ذو; rather, it is the *gender* in examples 1 and 2 that causes ذو to change morphologically.

٣ شاهَدتُ رَجُلاً ذا عِلْمٍ.

Example 3 illustrates how ذو changes morphologically into ذا when the word it modifies is مَنصوب. It is in مَنصوب because رَجُل is the direct object of شاهَدتُ.

٤ تَكَلَّمْتُ مَعَ رَجُلٍ ذي عِلْمٍ

Example 4 shows ذو in the genitive case as ذي, because رَجُل is the object of the preposition مَعَ.

## تمرين ١٠

**The five nouns in practice:** Using the tables presented on the previous page, supply the appropriate form of the noun found between the parentheses.

١- ما اسمُ (أب + كَ)؟ ________________

٢- اِشتَرَيتُ بَيْتاً (ذو) أربَعِ غُرَف. ________________

٣- (أخ + ها) طالِبٌ في هذِهِ الجامِعَة. ________________

٤- (أب) أحْمَد رَجُلٌ مِن مَدينَةِ دُبَيّ. ________________

٥- هَل هذِهِ السَيّارَةُ لـ (أخ + ك)؟ ________________

٦- (ذو) الحِجّة اسْمُ شَهرٍ مِن الأشْهُرِ العَرَبيّة. ________________

٧- أتَتْ سامية إلى هذِهِ الجامِعةِ لأنَّ (أخ + ها) يَدرُسُ فيها. ________________

٨- أينَ (أب + كِ) يا مَها؟ ________________

## 2. Not Fully Inflected Nouns المَمْنوعُ مِنَ الصَرف (Diptotes)

Certain words in Arabic take only two of the three short vowels—the ضَمّة and the فَتحة; such words are known as diptotes. One such diptote occurred in our main reading passage—the name مكّة, which took a فَتحة on its final radical. Grammatically speaking, it should have taken a كَسرة because it is the second part of an إضافة structure. The فَتحة appears on the final radical because some proper nouns (names) and plurals do not inflect fully (i.e., they are indeclinable) when they are indefinite. These nouns differ from regular nouns (triptotes—words that take all three short vowels) in two respects:

1. They never take تَنوين when they are indefinite.
2. They take a فَتحة for both the accusative منصوب and the genitive مجرور cases.

Consider the cases markers of دِمَشق and شوارِع and their adjectives in the following examples:

| | | | | |
|---|---|---|---|---|
| ٥ | مَرفوع | هذِهِ دِمَشقُ الفَيحاءُ. | ٨ | هذِهِ شَوارِعُ نَظيفةٌ. |
| ٦ | مَنصوب | وَصَلتُ دِمَشقَ الفَيحاءَ | ٩ | أعرِفُ شَوارِعَ نَظيفةً. |
| ٧ | مَجرور | في دِمَشقَ الفَيحاءِ. | ١٠ | في شَوارِعَ نَظيفةٍ. |

Turn your attention to the case endings for the adjectives in examples 7–10. Can you come up with a rule that accounts for the differences between the diptote's short vowels and those of its modifying adjective?

From the preceding table, we can deduce the following rule:

- Adjectives modifying diptotes agree with what the case ending on the noun is supposed to be, not with what it actually is.

The name دِمَشق and the plural noun شوارِع are diptotes; therefore they are indeclinable, which means that they invariably take فَتحة in the مَنصوب and مَجرور, whereas their modifying adjectives take فَتحة and كَسرة, respectively. In other words, an adjective modifying a diptote acquires its case as though the diptote were a fully inflected triptote.

- **Note:** When the diptotes are definite, they fully inflect just like regular triptotes and their adjectives agree with them completely.

١١ هذِهِ الشَوارِعُ النَظيفةُ.

١٢ أعرِفُ الشَوارِعَ النَظيفةَ.

١٣ في الشَوارِعِ النَظيفةِ.

## SUMMARY

- Some proper names and indefinite plurals do not fully inflect, that is, they are marked by a فَتحة in both the accusative and genitive cases.
- Diptotes do not take تَنوين when they are indefinite.
- Adjectives modifying diptotes are fully inflected.

❋ الممنوعُ مِن الصرف لا يُنوَّن ويُنصَبُ ويُجَرُّ بالفتحة ❋

## تمرين ١١

**In search of diptotes:** Seven proper nouns that were mentioned in the main reading passage of this lesson are diptotes (one of which we have already mentioned). Identify these diptotes and write them down in the space provided below.

______________________________________________

______________________________________________

## تمرين ١٢

**Providing short vowels:** Provide the appropriate inflections (short vowels) on the final radical of nouns and adjectives:

١- دَرَسَتْ سامية في مَدارِس مِصْريَّة.

٢- في مَدينة الرِياضِ شَوارِع حَديثة.

٣- يَحُجُّ المُسلِمونَ إلى مَكَّة والمَدينة.

٤- ذَهَبنا في شَهر نيسان الماضي إلى لُبنان والأردُن بِالحافِلة.

## 3. The Passive Voice

A verb in the passive voice is generally formed from a transitive verb (= a verb that takes a direct object, e.g., to break, to buy, to read). Intransitive verbs, such as كان and ذَهَبَ, cannot be passive because they do not take an object. Unlike the English passive which is made with a form of the verb "to be" and the past participle of the verb (e.g., has been bought), the Arabic passive is formed by changing the short vowels.

### A. Past-Tense Passive

To make a past-tense **sound verb** passive, simply place a ضمّة on the first consonant of the verb and a كسرة on the second, resulting in the following form:

فُعِلَ

| | Passive | | | Active | |
|---|---|---|---|---|---|
| *was born* | وُلِدَ | ← | *to give birth* | وَلَدَ | ١٤ |

Apart from adding a ضمّة on the first consonant and a كسرة on the second, no other changes take place regardless of the conjugation.

**Hollow verbs** (الفعل الأجوَف), those that have a long vowel as the middle radical such as قال, take the long vowel equivalent of the كسرة = a ياء in the passive, as in example 15:

قيلَ ← قالَ ١٥

**Defective verbs** (الفعل الناقص), those that end with an ألف, are made passive just like regular verbs (i.e., by placing a ضمّة on the first consonant and a كسرة on the second) in addition to changing the final ألف into a ياء:

سُمِّيَ ← سَمّى ١٦

### B. Present-Tense Passive

The present-tense **sound verb** (الفعل الصحيح) is also made passive by internal changes. A ضمّة immediately follows the present-tense prefixes (أ، نـ، يـ، تـ), while a فتحة is placed after the middle consonant of the verb, resulting in the following form:

يُفْعَل

١٧ يَكتُبُ ← يُكتَبُ

:الفعل المثال — In active verbs that begin with a consonantal و, such as وَلَدَ 'to give birth,' the present passive is made with the long vowel و following the present-tense prefix and a فَتحة on the middle consonant, as in example 18:

١٨ يَلِدُ ← يُولَدُ

:الفعل الأجوف — Hollow present-tense verbs with a long vowel (أَلِف or ياء) as the middle radical are made passive with a ضَمّة on the present-tense prefix and a regular أَلِف replacing the long vowel.

١٩ يَقولُ ← يُقالُ

:الفعل الناقص — Present tense verbs ending in a long vowel (أَلِف or ياء) are made passive with an أَلِف مَقْصورة (ى) replacing the long vowel.

٢٠ يُسَمّي ← يُسَمّى

## C. Agent فاعل and Deputy Agent نائب فاعل

The noun that follows a passive verb is actually the object of an active sentence, but it occupies the subject (or agent) position in the passive sentence and therefore assumes its case: مَرفوع (nominative). It is called نائب فاعل in Arabic (literally, "deputy agent").

- **Note:** The verb must agree with the gender of the نائب فاعل.

٢١ تُسَمّى مَدينةُ نيويورك «التُفّاحةَ الكَبيرة.»

In example 21, it can be seen that the verb تُسَمّى is third-person feminine, which agrees with the نائب فاعل (مَدينةُ).

## SUMMARY

**The passive past-tense verb**

- A sound verb is made passive by placing a ضَمّة on the first consonant and a كَسرة on the second, resulting in the فُعِلَ form.
- A hollow verb's middle long vowel changes into a ياء—its only change.
- A defective verb's last letter is a long vowel, which changes into a ياء in addition to the normal short vowel changes of a sound verb.

**The passive present-tense verb**

- A sound verb is made passive by placing a ضَمّة after the present-tense prefix and a فَتحة on the middle consonant, resulting in the يُفْعَلُ form.
- If the first letter is a consonantal واو, the vowel و follows the prefix.
- A hollow verb's middle long vowel changes into an ألِف.
- A defective verb's final long vowel changes into an ألِف مَقْصورة.

**Agent and deputy agent**

- The noun that follows the passive verb is known in Arabic as نائِب فاعل, which is in the nominative case رَفع because it assumes the subject position in the passive sentence.

# تمرين ١٣

**Making the passive voice:** In order to form a passive sentence in the following five items, the subject of the sentence located between the parentheses has to be dropped. Then the verb must undergo changes to its short vowels. Provide full voweling for the verb and the deputy agent, as in the example:

**مِثال:** **(كَتَبَ سامي) رِسالةً مِن باريس.** **كُتِبَتْ رِسالةٌ مِن باريس.**

١- (يَقولُ أَصْدِقائي) إنَّ باريس مَدينةٌ جَميلة.

٢- (وَلَدَتْ أمّي) هالَة في بَيروت سَنَةَ ١٩٨٥.

٣- (يُسَمّي الأمريكيّونَ) وِلايَةَ نيويورك «إمباير ستيت.»

٤- (يَشرَبُ الناسُ) القهوةَ بَعدَ الطعامِ عادةً.

٥- (سَمّى العَرَبُ) بَغدادَ «مَدينةَ السلام.»

## 4. The Verb صارَ

Although the verb صارَ 'to become' has a meaning different from the verb كانَ 'was, were,' it shares with it the same grammatical function. Both of them belong to the same category of verbs known as sisters of كانَ (أخَواتُ كانَ), which makes the predicate of a nominal sentence مَنصوب (accusative):

٢٠ صارَ الطَقسُ جَيِّداً.

In example 20, the subject الطَقسُ is مَرفوع, and the predicate جيّداً is مَنصوب marked by تَنوين.

# تمرين ١٤

**Using صارَ in translation:** Translate the following sentences using the appropriate voweling.

1. The sky was cloudy, but it cleared up (became clear).

   ______________________________

2. The weather was cold in February, but it has become much warmer.

   ______________________________

3. She was a girl, but she has become a woman.

   ______________________________

4. The city turned (became) beautiful.

   ______________________________

5. That man became famous!

   ______________________________

# تمرين ١٥

**Past-tense conjugation:** Conjugate the parenthetical verbs in the past tense.

١- مَن __________ في عُطْلة الشِّتاء يا أحْمَد. (زارَ)

٢- هَل (أَنْتَ) __________ في شَهْرِ رَمَضان؟ (صامَ)

٣- مَتى __________ مِن الجامِعة يا مَها؟ (تَخَرَّجَ)

٤- كَم مَرّة __________ اليَوْم يا مايكل؟ (صَلَّى)

٥- مَتى __________ سَيِّدُنا المَسيح؟ (وَلَدَ)

## تمرين ١٦

**A. Fill in the blank:** Complete these sentences with information from the listening passage.

١- اِسمُ زَوْجَةِ مَحْمود ______________ .

٢- مَحمود لَهُ صَديقٌ أمريكيّ اِسمُهُ ______________ .

٣- يَعمَلُ صَديقُ مَحمود في مَدينةِ ______________ .

٤- تَخَرَّجَ مَحمود وصَديقُهُ مِنَ الجامِعَةِ في ______________ .

**B. Comprehension questions:** Answer these questions according to the listening passage.

٥- كَم مَدينةً أمريكيّةً زارَها مَحمود وزَوْجَتُه؟ ما هِيَ؟

______________________________

٦- ماذا يَعمَلُ صَديقُ مَحمود؟

______________________________

٧- في أيِّ يَومٍ وشَهرٍ احْتَفَلَ الأَصْدِقاءُ الأربَعَة بِعيدِ الشُكْر؟

______________________________

٨- ماذا أكلوا في عيدِ الشُكْر؟

______________________________

**C. صواب أو خطأ:** Mark the following sentences صواب or خَطأ according to the information in the listening passage and correct any false statements.

٩- يَسكُنُ مَحمود وزَوجَتُهُ في الوِلاياتِ المُتَّحِدَةِ الأمريكيّة.

______________________________

١٠- كانَ مَحمود وصَديقُهُ طالِبَينِ في جامِعَةٍ واحِدة.

______________________________

١١- يَسكُنُ صَديقُ مَحمود في بَيتٍ مَعَ زَوجَتِهِ كارلا.

______________________________

١٢- أَحَبَّتْ زَوجَةُ مَحمود الطَعامَ كَثيراً في بَيتِ صَديقِ مَحمود.

____________________

## تمرين ١٧

VIDEO

**تَمرينُ المُشاهَدة: شاهِدوا الدَرْسَ الخامس عَشَر على القُرْص الرَقْميّ.**

**المَشْهَدُ الأَوَّل**

1. Draw a circle around the Islamic holidays and underline Christian holidays according to the DVD passage:

| | |
|---|---|
| عيد الميلاد | عيد المَوْلِد النبَويّ |
| عيد رأْس السَنة الهِجْريَّة | عيد الفِصْح |
| عيد الفِطْر | عيد الأَضْحى المُبارَك |

٢- ما الأعيادُ الخاصّةُ بِسوريَّة؟ ____________________

____________________

____________________

٣- ما العِباراتُ الخاصةُ بالمُناسِبات؟ ____________________

____________________

____________________

**المَشْهَدُ الثاني**

٤- كَم يَوْماً يَحتَفِلُ المُسلِمون بعيد الفِطْر وبعيد الأَضْحى المُبارَك؟ ____________________

____________________

٥- كَيْفَ يَصومُ المُسلِمون في شَهرِ رَمَضان؟ ____________________

____________________

٦- كَيْفَ يُزَيِّنُ المَسيحيّون بُيوتَهُم لِعيدِ الميلاد؟ ____________________

____________________

٧- ما الأعيادُ المُهِمّةُ في أمريكا؟ ____________________

____________________

## المُفْرَدات

Listen to the vocabulary items on the CD and practice their pronunciation.

| | |
|---|---|
| to celebrate | اِحْتَفَلَ (يَحْتَفِلُ) اِحْتِفال بـِ (v.) |
| independence | اِسْتِقلال (n., m.) |
| Islam | إسلام (n., m.) |
| to move, to relocate | اِنتَقَلَ (يَنتَقِلُ) اِنْتِقال (v.) |
| country | بَلَد ج بِلاد (n., m.) |
| to graduate | تَخَرَّجَ (يتخرَّجُ) تَخَرُّج (v.) |
| education, upbringing | تَرْبِية (n., f.) |
| instruction, education | تَعليم (n., m.) |
| revolution | ثَوْرة ج ثورات (n., f.) |
| pilgrimage | حَجّ (n., m.) |
| dessert, sweets | حَلْوى ج حَلوَيات (n., f.) |
| special, particular (to) | خاصّ (adj.) |
| cock, rooster | ديك ج دِيَكة (n., m.) |
| turkey | ديك حَبَش (n., m.) |
| with, of, owner of | ذو ج ذَوو (n., m.) |
| head | رأس ج رُؤوس (n., m.) |
| Ramadan, the month of fasting | رَمَضان (n., m.) |
| to adorn, to decorate | زَيَّنَ (يُزَيِّنُ) تزيين (v.) |
| square, courtyard | ساحة ج ساحات (n., f.) |
| to save, to protect | سَلَّمَ (يُسَلِّمُ) تَسْليم (v.) |
| age of a person | سِنّ (n., m.) |
| to become | صارَ (يَصيرُ) صَيْر، صَيْرورة، مَصير (v.) |
| to fast | صامَ (يَصومُ) صَوْم (v.) |
| to pray, to bless | صَلّى (يُصَلّي) (v.) |
| to manufacture, to make | صَنَعَ (يَصنَعُ) صِناعة (v.) |

food . . . . . . . . . . . . . . . . . . . . . . . . . . (n., m.) طَعام ج أطْعِمة

phrase . . . . . . . . . . . . . . . . . . . . . . . . . (n., f.) عِبارة ج عِبارات

to be off from work . . . . . . . . . . . . . . . (v.) عَطَّلَ (يَعَطِّلُ) تَعْطيل

Feast of Immolation/sacrifice (after Haj), Greater Bairam . . . . (n., m.) عيدُ الأضْحى

Thanksgiving . . . . . . . . . . . . . . . . . . . . . (n., m.) عيدُ الشُكْرِ

Easter . . . . . . . . . . . . . . . . . . . . . . . . . (n., m.) عيدُ الفِصْحِ

feast of breaking the Ramadan fast . . . . . . . . . (n., m.) عيدُ الفِطْرِ

Christmas . . . . . . . . . . . . . . . . . . . . . . . (n., m.) عيدُ الميلاد

dawn, daybreak . . . . . . . . . . . . . . . . . . . (n., m.) فَجْر

pie . . . . . . . . . . . . . . . . . . . . . . . . . . . (n., f.) فَطيرة ج فَطائِر

pumpkin . . . . . . . . . . . . . . . . . . . . . . . . (n., m.) قَرْع

blessed . . . . . . . . . . . . . . . . . . . . . . . . . (n., m.) مُبارَك

intermediate . . . . . . . . . . . . . . . . . . . . . (adj., m.) مُتَوَسِّط

director, manager . . . . . . . . . . . . . . . . . . (n., m.) مُدير ج مُدَراء

Muslim, one of the Islamic faith. . . . . . . (n., m.) مُسْلِم ج مُسْلِمون

Christ . . . . . . . . . . . . . . . . . . . . . . . . . (n., m.) المَسيح

teacher . . . . . . . . . . . . . . . . (active participle) مُعَلِّم ج مُعَلِّمون

information . . . . . . . . . . . . . . . . . . . . . (n., f.) مَعلومة ج مَعلومات

sunset . . . . . . . . . . . . . . . . . . . . . . . . . (n., m.) مَغْرِب

occasion . . . . . . . . . . . . . . . . . . . . . . . (n., f.) مُناسَبة ج مُناسَبات

region . . . . . . . . . . . . . . . . . . . . . . . . . (n., f.) مِنْطَقة ج مَناطِق

birthday, birthplace . . . . . . . . . . . . . . . . (n., m.) مَوْلِد

birth, birthday. . . . . . . . . . . . . . . . . . . . (n., m.) ميلاد ج مَواليد

prophet. . . . . . . . . . . . . . . . . . . . . . . . . (n., m.) نَبيّ ج أنْبياء

هَنَّأَ (يُهَنِّئُ) تَهنئة (v.) . to congratulate, to felicitate (on the occasion of)

وُلِدَ (يولَدُ) وِلادة / مَوْلِد (v.) . . . . . . . . . . . . . to be born (passive)

# الدرسُ السادِسَ عشَرَ

## Objectives

- Describing people, activities, and past events
- The secrets of the language: Arabic verb forms
- Revisiting ordinal numbers

## رُكنُ المُفْرَداتِ الجَديدة

| | |
|---|---|
| *to occur; to start (war)* | قامَ (يَقومُ) قِيامٌ |
| *to elect* | اِنْتَخَبَ (يَنْتَخِبُ) اِنْتِخاب |
| *to assassinate* | اِغْتال (يَغتالُ) اِغتيال |
| *to pass away* | تُوُفِّيَ |
| *discrimination* | التَميز العُنْصُريّ |
| *to enter* | دَخَلَ (يَدْخُلُ) دُخول |
| *to be sent into exile* | نُفيَ (يُنْفى) نَفْيٌ |

## تمرين ١

**Odd word out:** Underline the word that does not belong to each set and explain your choice if needed.

| | | | | |
|---|---|---|---|---|
| ١- | وُلِدَ | نُفِيَ | تُوفِّيَ | أُغْتيلَ |
| ٢- | شاعِر | جَيْش | ضابِط | قائِد |
| ٣- | أمير | زَعيم | رَئيس | مُحامٍ |
| ٤- | كاتِب | حَصَلَ | قِسّيس | خَطيب |
| ٥- | مَدينة | قَرْية | بَلْدة | فَلْسَفة |

## تمرين ٢

**Matching:**

وافِقْ بَيْنَ الكَلِماتِ في العَمودَين.

| | | | |
|---|---|---|---|
| ١ | حَرْب | | خَرَجَ |
| ٢ | كِتاب | | الأندَلُس |
| ٣ | تُوُفِّيَ | | مَلِك |
| ٤ | قانون | | اجْتِماع |
| ٥ | غَرْناطة | | سَلام |
| ٦ | دَخَلَ | | مُقَدِّمة |
| ٧ | رَئيس | | وُلِدَ |
| | | | مُحامٍ |

## تمرين ٣

**Select the best choice:** Select the choice that correctly (or best) completes the sentence.

١- والت ويتمان ____________ أمريكيّ مَشْهور.

☐ شاعِرٌ ☐ زَعيمٌ ☐ رَئيسٌ

٢- ____________ رونالد ريغن رئيساً مَرَّتَين.

☐ تُوُفِّيَ ☐ وُلِدَ ☐ أُنْتُخِبَ

٣- أفلاطون أشْهَر ____________ في العالَم. * Plato

☐ مَلِكٍ ☐ فَيْلَسوفٍ ☐ مُحامٍ

٤- مَتى صارَتْ إليزابث الثانية ____________ بريطانيا؟

☐ قَريَةَ ☐ جائِزَةَ ☐ مَلِكَةَ

٥- فِرساي بَلْدَةٌ صَغيرةٌ ____________ باريس.

☐ قُرْب ☐ حَرْب ☐ جَيْش

٦- كانَ هوميروس أوَّلَ ____________ كَتَبَ التاريخ. * Homer

☐ مُؤَرِّخٍ ☐ قِسّيسٍ ☐ قائِدٍ

## تمرين ٤

**Sentence construction:** Rearrange the words in each item to make meaningful sentences.

١- شاعِرةً - كانَتْ - إميلي دِكَنسَن - مَشْهورةً - أمريكيّةً

---

٢- مَكتَبِ - أختي - مُحامٍ - تَخَرَّجَتْ - عَمِلَتْ - مِنَ - في - ثُمَّ - الجامِعةِ

---

٣- الأمريكيّةِ - مَرَّتَيْنِ - بِل كلنتَن - المُتَّحِدةِ - رَئيساً - أُنْتُخِبَ - لِلوِلاياتِ

---

٤- سَنَةَ - كِنيدي - في - دالاس - أُغْتيلَ - بِمَدينةِ - ١٩٦٣ - الرَّئيسُ

---

## تمرين ٥

**Paragraph construction:** On a separate sheet of paper, construct a meaningful paragraph by rearranging the following sentences. Do not change the position of the first sentence. Practice your script by writing the entire paragraph.

١- مُحَمَّد بن موسى الخوارِزمي عالِمُ رِياضِيّاتٍ مُسْلِمٌ مَشْهور.
وكَتَبَ كِتاباً في حِسابِ الجَبْرِ وتُرْجِمَ إلى اللاتينيّة.
عَرَفَتْ أوروبا عِلْمَ الجَبْرِ مِن هذا الكِتاب.
تُوُفِّيَ الخُوارِزمي سَنَةَ ٨٤٠ ميلاديّة.
كَلِمةُ *algorithm* مأخوذةٌ مِن اسْمِه.
وكَتَبَ أيْضاً عَن الصِفْر في الرِياضِيّات.
وُلِدَ الخُوارِزمي في مَدينةِ خُوارِزم.
أسَّسَ الخُوارِزمي عِلْمَ الجَبْر.

# شَخْصِيّاتٌ أمريكيّةٌ وعَرَبِيّةٌ

قائدُ الجَيْش

## جورج واشنِطَن
## ١٧٩٩-١٧٣٢

هُوَ أوّلُ رَئيسٍ لِلوِلاياتِ المُتَّحِدةِ الأمريكيّة. وُلِدَ في وِلايةِ فِرجينيا وتُوُفِّيَ فيها. كانَ قائِدَ الجَيشِ في الثَوْرةِ الأمريكيّةِ وحارَبَ البريطانيّينَ بَينَ سَنَتَيْ ١٧٧٦ و١٧٨١. صارَ رَئيسَ الجُمهوريّةِ في سَنَةِ ١٧٨٩ وأُنْتُخِبَ رَئيساً مَرّةً ثانِيَةً في ١٧٩٣، لكِنَّهُ رَفَضَ في المَرّةِ الثالِثةِ ورَجَعَ إلى دارِه في «ماونت ڤِرنَن» في فِرجينيا في سَنةِ ١٧٩٧ حَيْثُ تُوُفِّيَ بَعدَ سَنَتَيْن.

## إبراهام لِنكَن
## ١٨٦٥-١٨٠٩

هُوَ رَئيسُ الجُمْهوريَّةِ الأمريكيُّ السادِسَ عَشَر. وُلِدَ في وِلايَةِ كِنتكي سَنةَ ١٨٠٩. اِنتَقَلَ إلى وِلايةِ إلينوي في سَنةِ ١٨٣١. دَرَسَ لِنكَن القانونَ، وفي سَنةِ ١٨٣٦ صارَ مُحامِياً ثُمَّ صارَ رَئيسَ الجُمْهوريَّةِ في سَنةِ ١٨٦٠. بعدَ ذلِكَ قامَت الحَربُ الأهْليّةُ الأمريكيّة. أُنْتُخِبَ مَرّةً ثانيةً في سَنةِ ١٨٦٤. أُغْتيلَ إبراهام لِنكَن في واشِنطَن العاصِمة في شَهرِ نيسانَ سَنةَ ١٨٦٥.

## مارتِن لوثَر كِنغ

**١٩٢٩-١٩٦٨**

زَعيمٌ أمريكيٌّ أسْوَد. وُلِدَ في مَدينةِ أتلانتا في وِلايةِ جورجة. كانَ قِسّيساً وخَطيباً وحارَبَ التَميزَ العُنْصُريّ. حَصَلَ على جائِزَةِ نوبِل لِلسَلام سَنةَ ١٩٦٤. أُغْتيلَ في مَدينةِ مِمْفِس في وِلايةِ تِنيسي سَنةَ ١٩٦٨. تَحتَفِلُ مُعظَمُ الوِلاياتِ الأمريكيّةِ بِعيدِ مارتِن لوثَر كِنغ في ثالِثِ يَوْم إثنين مِن شَهرِ كانونَ الثاني.

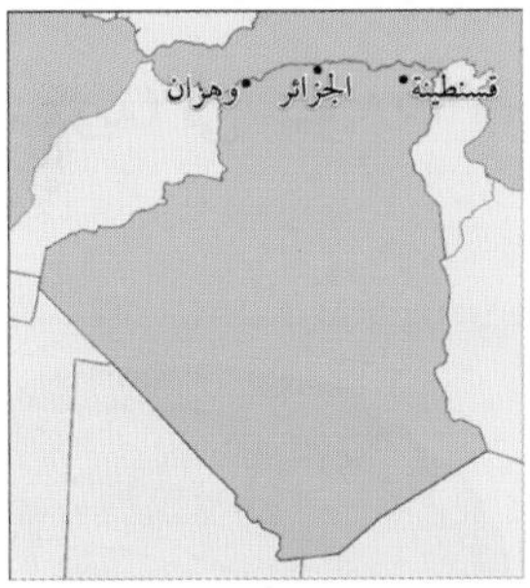


## عَبدُ القادِر الجَزائِري

**١٨٠٧-١٨٨٣**

أميرٌ وزَعيمٌ جَزائِريّ. وُلِدَ في قَريةٍ قُرْبَ «وَهْران» في الجَزائِر. حينَ دَخَلَتْ فَرَنسا الجَزائِرَ في سَنةِ ١٨٤٣ حارَبَ الأميرُ عَبدُ القادِرِ الفَرَنسيّينَ خَمسَ عَشْرَةَ سَنَةً ثُمَّ نُفِيَ إلى طولون. وفي سَنةِ ١٨٦٨ انتَقَلَ إلى دِمَشقَ حَيْثُ سَكَنَ وتُوُفِّيَ فيها في سَنةِ ١٨٨٣. كانَ الأميرُ عَبدُ القادِرِ كاتِباً وشاعِراً أيْضاً.

## يوسُف العَظْمة

**١٨٨٤-١٩٢٠**

قائِدٌ سوريٌّ وُلِدَ في مَدينةِ دِمَشق في سَنةِ ١٨٨٤. كانَ ضابِطاً في الجَيْشِ العُثْمانيّ ثُمَّ صارَ ضابِطاً في الجَيْشِ السوريّ. حينَ دَخَلَ الفَرَنسيّونَ سورية في سَنةِ ١٩٢٠ كانَ وَزيرَ الدِفاعِ وخَرَجَ على رَأْسِ جَيْشٍ صَغيرٍ وحارَبَهُم في «مَيْسَلون» قُرْبَ دِمَشق واسْتُشْهِدَ هُناك.

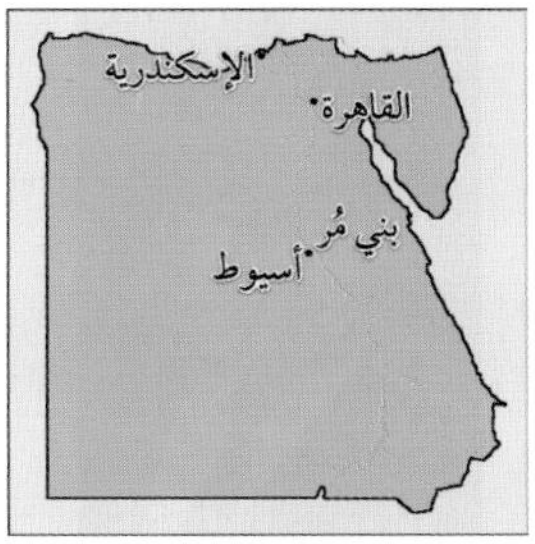

جَمال عَبْدُ النّاصِر

١٩١٨–١٩٧٠

زَعيمٌ عَرَبيٌّ مِن مِصْرَ وُلِدَ في قَرْيةِ «بَني مُرّ» قُرْبَ مَدينةِ «أسْيوط» في مِصْر. انْتَقَلَ إلى القاهِرةِ وهُوَ في سِنِّ الثامِنةِ وسَكَنَ مَعَ عَمِّهِ خَليل ودَرَسَ بها ثُمَّ بالإسْكَنْدَريّةِ. دَرَسَ بالكُلِّيّةِ الحَرْبيّةِ وتَخَرَّجَ مِنها وصارَ ضابِطاً بالجَيْشِ المِصْريِّ. حارَبَ في فِلَسْطينَ سَنَةَ ١٩٤٨ حَيْثُ جُرِحَ في الحَرْبِ. في سَنَةِ ١٩٥٢ قامَ بثَوْرةٍ على المَلِكِ وصارَتْ مِصْرُ جُمْهوريّةً. صارَ رَئيسَ الجُمْهوريّةِ المِصْريّةِ في سَنَةِ ١٩٥٦ ثُمَّ رَئيسَ الجُمْهوريّةِ العَرَبيّةِ المُتَّحِدةِ (مِصْر وسورية) في سَنَةِ ١٩٥٨. تُوُفِّيَ بالقاهِرةِ في سَنَةِ ١٩٧٠.



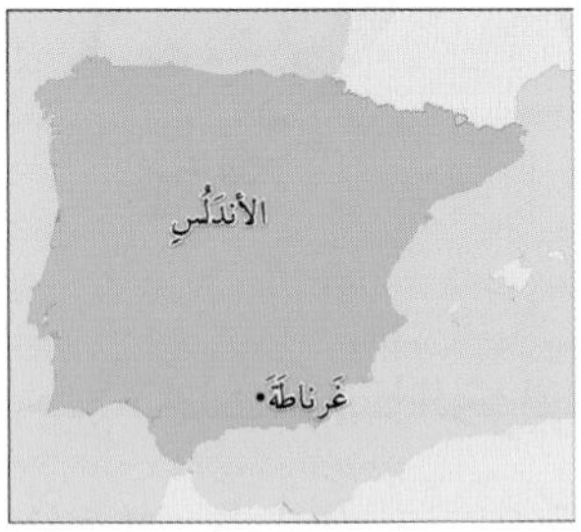

عَبْدُ الرَّحْمن بن خَلْدون

١٣٣٢–١٤٠٦

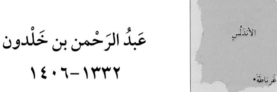

مُؤَرِّخٌ وفَيْلَسوفٌ وعالِمُ اجْتِماع عَرَبيّ. وُلِدَ في تونِسَ وتُوُفِّيَ بالقاهِرةِ. كَتَبَ كُتُباً في التاريخِ والاجْتِماعِ والفَلْسَفةِ والأدَب. أسَّسَ عِلْمَ الاجْتِماع في مُقَدِّمَتِهِ المَشْهورةِ لِكِتابِهِ «العِبَرِ.» عَمِلَ وسَكَنَ في مَدينةِ غَرناطَةَ في الأنْدَلُسِ وفي فاسَ في المَغْرِبِ وفي تِلِمْسانَ في الجَزائِرِ وفي القاهِرةِ في مِصْرَ حَيْثُ دَرَّسَ في الجامِعِ الأزْهَر.

## تمرين ٦

**A. Listen and select:** Check the box that matches the information as expressed in the main passages for this lesson.

١- تُوُفِّيَ الأميرُ عَبْدُ القادِرِ الجَزائِريّ في سَنَةِ ________ .

☐ ١٨٤٣ ☐ ١٨٦٨ ☐ ١٨٨٣

٢- كانَ يوسُف العَظْمة ضابِطاً في الجَيْشِ ________ .

☐ العُثمانيّ ☐ الفَرَنسِيّ ☐ الجَزائِريّ

٣- دَرَسَ جَمال عَبدُ الناصِر ________ .

☐ بِجامِعَةِ القاهِرة ☐ بِالجَيْشِ المِصْريّ ☐ بِالكُلِّيَّةِ الحَرْبيّة

٤- أَسَّسَ ابنُ خَلدون عِلْمَ ________ .

☐ الاجْتِماع ☐ الفَلْسَفَة ☐ التاريخ

٥- صارَ جورج واشِنطَن رَئيساً ________ .

☐ مَرَّةً واحِدةً ☐ مَرَّتَيْنِ ☐ ثَلاثَ مَرّاتٍ

٦- أُنْتُخِبَ إبراهام لِنكَن رَئيساً لِلوِلاياتِ المُتَّحِدةِ أوَّلَ مَرَّةٍ في سَنَةِ ________ .

☐ ١٨٣٦ ☐ ١٨٦٠ ☐ ١٨٦٤

٧- حَصَلَ مارتِن لوثَر كِنغ على جائِزَةِ نوبِل لِلسلامِ في سَنَةِ ________ .

☐ ١٩٦٠ ☐ ١٩٦٤ ☐ ١٩٦٨

**B. Fill in the blank:** Complete the following sentences with information from the main passages.

٨- نُفِيَ الأميرُ عَبدُ القادِرِ الجَزائِريّ إلى ________ .

٩- حارَبَ يوسُف العَظْمة الفَرَنسِيّينَ في ________ .

١٠- كانَ ________ رَئيسَ الجُمْهوريّةِ العَرَبيّةِ المُتَّحِدة.

١١- دَرَّسَ ________ في الجامِعِ الأزهَر.

١٢- وُلِدَ ________ في سَنَةِ ١٧٣٢.

١٣- صارَ ________ مُحامِياً في سَنَةِ ١٨٣٦.

١٤- حارَبَ مارتِن لوثَر كِنغ ________ .

C. **صواب أو خطأ:** Mark the following sentences **صواب** or **خطأ** according to the information in the main reading passage and correct any false statements.

١٥- سَكَنَ الأميرُ عَبدُ القادِرِ الجزائريّ مَدينة دِمَشق بَعدَ سَنَةِ ١٨٦٨.

١٦- كانَ يوسُف العَظْمة رَئيس سورية حينَ دَخَلَها الفرَنسيّون.

١٧- وُلِدَ يوسُف العَظْمة في دِمَشق سَنَةَ ١٨٨٤.

١٨- حارَبَ جَمال عَبد الناصِر البريطانيّينَ في مِصْرَ.

١٩- كانَ ابنُ خَلدون شاعِراً.

٢٠- تُوُفِّيَ جورج واشِنطَن في مَدينةِ واشِنطَن.

٢١- قامَت الحَرْبُ الأهْليّةُ الأمريكيّةُ قَبْلَ سَنَةِ ١٨٦٠.

٢٢- وُلِدَ مارتِن لوثَر كِنغ في مَدينةِ مِمفِس.

## تمرين ٧

**Biographical sketch and 20-questions:** Choose a figure from history that you find interesting and write a biographical sketch about that person, emulating the style of our main reading passages. Do some research on the Web to find some information about the personality of your choice.

As a follow-up exercise, play 20-questions with your classmates to see if they can guess the historical figure you chose. The questions and answers should be in Arabic. Some questions are not allowed in our game of 20-questions, like "What is your name?" or "Who are you?"

## تمرين ٨

**Ask your neighbor:** On a separate sheet of paper, write down the people in your class who . . .

1. were elected president of their high school class
2. are philosophers
3. know a lawyer
4. were officers in the army
5. have studied law
6. are writers
7. are poets
8. like strong personalities

Be prepared to report your findings to the class.

## 1. Secrets of the Language: Forms of the Arabic Verb

We have titled other sections in this textbook "Secrets of the Language," but, in truth, learning and understanding this section will provide you with the keys to unlocking the way Arabic, as a language, is structured and how you can exploit that structure to both deduce and create meaning. Arabic is a root derivational language—meaning that for every root, nearly 90 potential derivations exist, each of which shades the root in a different nuance. In the most basic sense, if you know the root of a word, you can create from it all tenses of the verb, ten different forms of the verb, nouns, active and passive participles, locations, gerunds, verbal nouns, as well as other word types.

You may have noticed that the verbs we have learned thus far differ in their form with respect to the number of consonants and the short and long vowels associated with them. Consider the following verbs:

| | | | | | | |
|---|---|---|---|---|---|---|
| اسْتَحَمَّ | انْتَقَلَ | تَكَلَّمَ | أرادَ | حارَبَ | دَرَّسَ | سَكَنَ |

Despite the fact that these verbs are third-person masculine singular in the past tense, they vary in their form. Variation in the verb form pertains to a characteristic of Arabic morphology (i.e., the structure of the word) whereby a given base verb acquires additional consonants and/or vowels to express shades of meaning or completely different meanings. A description of the so-called morphological patterns **الميزان الصَرْفي** should prove to be extremely useful, because an understanding of the system of patterns can serve as a road map to achieving the ability to use and understand the precise sense of words.

Knowledge of the forms of the Arabic verb not only allows one to determine the type and function of a given word, but it also facilitates the process of looking up words in a dictionary, because words are arranged by their roots (the base form). Some Arabic dictionaries, however, classify entries according to the stem of a word, or in alphabetical order (an excellent example is *al-Mawrid* by R. Baalbaki).

## A. Patterns الأوزان and the Root System

The basic word pattern in Arabic is a combination of three letters that represent the three root letters of the basic Arabic verb (the triliteral verb). As we described in Lesson 11 (section 5), but it bears repeating here, the letters ف، ع، ل act as a model for determining or creating patterns.

The فـ always stands for the first letter of a word, the ـعـ represents the second, or middle, letter, and the ـل denotes the third, or last, letter. So, the pattern for the verb سَكَن is فَعَل where the three letters of the pattern correspond to those that make up the word.

١ سَكَنَ ← فَعَلَ

- **Note:** All the short vowels of the word are represented *exactly* in the pattern except for the final short vowel, which is not important for this purpose. Any letters added to the triliteral root are also represented in the pattern. Let's turn our attention to the word إِنْتَقَل 'to move, to relocate' to consider its pattern:

٢ إِنْتَقَلَ ← اِفْتَعَلَ

When you read the word and its pattern aloud, they should, for lack of a better word, "rhyme." In other words, the two words should have the same syllable pattern and the same cadence. The way we use this knowledge and understanding of the patterns of root derivations is explained here, using example 2 as a model:

1. **Patterns determine word type:** Example 2 is an instance of a verb—a conclusion that can be arrived at because اِفْتَعَل is a verb pattern (as you can tell by referring to the verb measure chart in part 1B of this lesson).

2. **Patterns identify the root:** After stripping the word of any added letters, its basic form (i.e., its root) can be identified, which is, in the case of example 2, نَقَل.

3. **Patterns determine verb form:** This verb has had two letters (an أَلَف and a تاء) added to its root ن ق ل; therefore, it is a Form VIII verb (explained in full in part 1B of this lesson).

4. **Patterns are useful for looking up words:** As noted earlier, words in most Arabic dictionaries are classified according to their roots. You can identify the root by recognizing the added letters and eliminating them.

- To identify the root of a verb or a word, simply match the form of any nouns to the patterns on the noun chart on the following page, and any verbs to the patterns on the verb chart presented in part 1B of this lesson. Once you have matched the word with its pattern, then you have to eliminate any letters that do not correspond with the ف ع ل letters of the pattern. The three letters that remain are the root, or base form, of your word.

In this lesson, we first present the noun chart and then the verb chart. We strongly encourage you to memorize both charts along with the meanings and roman numerals that correspond to the ten forms. Do not be overwhelmed. Study the charts every day saying the past-tense verb, present tense, and the verbal noun *out loud* and memorize every verb you encounter from now on in this manner.

| NOUNS | | | | | |
|---|---|---|---|---|---|
| NOUN OF PLACE & TIME اِسْمُ المَكان والزَمان | RECIPIENT (Passive Participle) اِسْمُ المَفْعول | AGENT (Active Participle) (Doer) اِسْمُ الفاعِل | VERBAL NOUN (Masdar) المَصْدَر | FORM الوَزْن | MEANING, USE, AND RELATIONSHIP المعنى والاستعمال والعلاقة |
| مَفْعَلٌ (ة) | مَفْعولٌ | فاعِلٌ | فَعْلٌ فُعُولٌ فِعالَةٌ إلخ | I | REGULAR |
| مُفَعَّلٌ | مُفَعَّلٌ | مُفَعِّلٌ | تَفْعِيلٌ | II | CAUSATIVE OR INTENSIVE |
| مُفاعَلٌ | مُفاعَلٌ | مُفاعِلٌ | مُفاعَلَةٌ فِعالٌ | III | RECIPROCAL (Mutual Action) |
| مُفْعَلٌ | مُفْعَلٌ | مُفْعِلٌ | إفْعالٌ | IV | CAUSATIVE |
| مُتَفَعَّلٌ | مُتَفَعَّلٌ | مُتَفَعِّلٌ | تَفَعُّلٌ | V | REFLEXIVE OF II |
| مُتَفاعَلٌ | مُتَفاعَلٌ | مُتَفاعِلٌ | تَفاعُلٌ | VI | REFLEXIVE OF III |
| مُنْفَعَلٌ | ——— | مُنْفَعِلٌ | اِنْفِعالٌ | VII | PASSIVE OF I (No Agent) |
| مُفْتَعَلٌ | مُفْتَعَلٌ | مُفْتَعِلٌ | اِفْتِعالٌ | VIII | REFLEXIVE OF I |
| ——— | ——— | مُفْعَلٌّ | اِفْعِلالٌ | IX | COLORS OR PHYSICAL DEFECTS |
| مُسْتَفْعَلٌ | مُسْتَفْعَلٌ | مُسْتَفْعِلٌ | اِسْتِفْعالٌ | X | TO SEEK I |

Every word of Arabic origin has a pattern—meaning foreign and borrowed words generally do not hold to these forms. Patterns are representations of words that can be nouns, adjectives, or verbs; thus they may be singular, dual, plural, masculine, or feminine and can display the prefixes and suffixes of verbs. Let's take طالِب and see if we can locate it on the noun chart on the previous page.

We find that طالِب is a Form I active participle, or the *-er* form in English (swimmer, biker, runner). It follows that the translation of طالِب should have an *-er* in it. In fact, it does. The root of طالِب is طَلَبَ, meaning "to request, seek." So, طالِب actually means "requester/seeker," as in "requester or seeker of knowledge" طالِب العِلْم.

What this means for us is that for any three-letter verb we know, we can exchange its letters with wherever فعل occurs in both the noun and the verb charts to create meaning. Let's do another example. Take the three letters كَتَبَ and create the Form I active participle.

٣ كَتَبَ ← كاتِب

So if كَتَبَ means "to write," كاتِب (= the *-er* form) means "writer."

## تمرين ٩

**Active participles:** Create nouns from verbs with which we are familiar.

1. drinker ____________________
2. studier ____________________
3. worker ____________________
4. cleaner (one who cleans) ____________________
5. tenant (one who resides) ____________________
6. fighter ____________________

Take some time now and choose some three-letter verbs that you know and plug their letters into the Form I (or otherwise) active participle form to try to create meanings. Write your words down on a sheet of paper along with your guess as to what the word would mean. Your instructor will tell you if the word that you created does indeed exist and if you used the correct form.

Now we will try to identify the roots of some words with which we are familiar. Take the word مُسْلِمونَ, for instance. Our first task is to strip the word of any added letters before trying to find it on the noun chart. Our word before us, as you have already gathered, is plural—the ون combination at the end of words is a dead giveaway for sound masculine plurals. Now we know two things about the word: it has two added letters, and it is a noun. Therefore, we need to take our stripped-down version of the word مُسْلِم and see if we can't locate it on the noun chart.

٤    مُسْلِمونَ    ←    مُسْلِم = مُفْعِل

The answer to our search is that the word مُسْلِمونَ is a Form IV active participle.

Let's try another example: مَشْغولاتٌ. Once again, our first task is to strip the word of any added letters, and this time we have the ات ending, meaning that we are dealing with a sound feminine plural. But, the form is different this time.

٥    مَشْغولات    ←    مَشْغول = مَفْعول

We found out that مَشْغول was in fact a Form I passive participle, meaning "occupied, preoccupied, or busy."

## تمرين ١٠

**Pattern construction:** Construct patterns for the following words which occurred in this and previous lessons and identify the root of each one, as in the example:

| Form | Root | |
|---|---|---|
| نَظَفَ | تَفْعيل | ← مِثال: تَنْظيف |
| ______ | ______ | ١- اِسْتِحْمام |
| ______ | ______ | ٢- مُحَضِّرون |
| ______ | ______ | ٣- كِتابة |
| ______ | ______ | ٤- جامِعة |
| ______ | ______ | ٥- مُخْتَبَر |
| ______ | ______ | ٦- مَسْبَح |
| ______ | ______ | ٧- مَكْتَبة |
| ______ | ______ | ٨- مَلْعَب |

٩- تَفاضُل ______________ ______________

١٠- جالِسات ______________ ______________

**B. Verb Forms أوزان الفِعل**

The majority of Arabic verbs are triliteral, that is, they have a three-letter root; for example, كَتَبَ 'to write'. This is the base form (Form I) of the Arabic verb, which is known in Arabic as الفِعْل المُجَرَّد 'stripped verb' because it has no additional letters. Certain letters can be added to the base form, resulting in verb patterns known as الفِعْل المَزيد 'increased, or augmented, verb', which may have one, two, or three letters prefixed, infixed, or a combination of both (e.g., تَكاتَبَ 'to correspond with' is an example of a verb pattern that has a prefixed تاء and an infixed أَلَف).

- **Note:** It is rare for triliteral roots to have more than four to five derivative forms; most only have one or two.

Each increased form (Forms II–X) imbues the root form with a specific nuance. Some forms have more than one meaning. Form II فَعَّل, for example, has several meanings: *causative*, *intensive*, and *transitive*.

## Form II

Let's take a look at a Form I verb that we know and see what happens to its meaning when we double its second radical (= Form II). We know that دَرَس means "to study," but what does it mean when we double the middle radical, as in دَرَّس?

٦ دَرَس ← دَرَّس = فَعَّل

As we have mentioned, Form II has three possible meanings. In the case of example 6 it indicates *causation*, or "to cause someone to 'do the root meaning' = to cause someone 'to study'," which means "to teach." So, دَرَّس means "to teach." An example of a Form II verb that has an intensive meaning is exemplified by the verb كَسَر (Form I), which means "to break." What would you suppose كَسَّر to mean in terms of intensifying the root or intensifying "breaking"?

كَسَّر Form II means "to smash, to break into pieces." Take a couple of minutes to look over the Verb Chart on the following page. In the pages that follow the chart, we will explain each of the meanings of the forms (how they affect the base meaning), using example verbs taken from our previous reading passages.

Since we have already explained Form II, we will be covering Forms III–X in the order in which they usually occur in Western grammars of Arabic. The roman numerals that accompany the forms are a modern convention that have to be memorized to be able to use Western grammars and dictionaries. As well, we should memorize the patterns, which is the way native speakers learn these derivations.

| **VERBS** | | | | | FORM | MEANING, USE, AND RELATIONSHIP |
|---|---|---|---|---|---|---|
| PASSIVE | | IMPERA-TIVE (Command) | ACTIVE | | | |
| IMPERFECT (Present) المُضارِع | PERFECT (Past) الماضي | الأمْر | IMPERFECT (Present) المُضارِع | PERFECT (Past) الماضي | الوَزَن | المعنى والاستعمال والعلاقة |
| يُفْعَلُ | فُعِلَ | افعلْ | يَفْعُلُ | فَعُلَ | I | REGULAR |
| يُفَعَّلُ | فُعِّلَ | فَعِّلْ | يُفَعِّلُ | فَعَّلَ | II | CAUSATIVE; INTENSIVE; TRANSITIVE |
| يُفَاعَلُ | فُوعِلَ | فَاعِلْ | يُفَاعِلُ | فَاعَلَ | III | RECIPROCAL (Mutual Action) |
| يُفْعَلُ | أُفْعِلَ | أَفْعِلْ | يُفْعِلُ | أَفْعَلَ | IV | CAUSATIVE |
| يُتَفَعَّلُ | تُفُعِّلَ | تَفَعَّلْ | يَتَفَعَّلُ | تَفَعَّلَ | V | REFLEXIVE OF II |
| يُتَفَاعَلُ | تُفُوعِلَ | تَفَاعَلْ | يَتَفَاعَلُ | تَفَاعَلَ | VI | REFLEXIVE OF III |
| ——— | ——— | اِنْفَعِلْ | يَنْفَعِلُ | اِنْفَعَلَ | VII | PASSIVE OF I (No Agent) |
| يُفْتَعَلُ | اُفْتُعِلَ | اِفْتَعِلْ | يَفْتَعِلُ | اِفْتَعَلَ | VIII | REFLEXIVE OF I |
| ——— | ——— | اِفْعَلَّ | يَفْعَلُّ | اِفْعَلَّ | IX | ACQUISITION OF AN ATTRIBUTE |
| يُسْتَفْعَلُ | اُسْتُفْعِلَ | اِسْتَفْعِلْ | يَسْتَفْعِلُ | اِسْتَفْعَلَ | X | TO SEEK I |

## Form III فاعَلَ (يُفاعِلُ) مُفاعَلَة

This form is used not just to involve someone or something else in an action, but to cause a response from that person or thing. Think, for a moment, of actions that you could do to someone else that demand a reaction. What domains are included? In fact, conversation, sports (competition), and fighting/wrestling are themes in which Form III is necessarily involved.

| Form III | | | Form I | |
|---|---|---|---|---|
| *to talk* | حادَثَ | ← | *to happen* | حَدَثَ |
| *to share a drink with someone* | شارَبَ | ← | *to drink* | شَرِبَ |
| *to fight* | حارَبَ | ← | *a war* | حَرْبٌ |

## Form IV أفْعَلَ (يُفْعِلُ) إفْعال

Like Form II, Form IV has a causative sense. Sometimes Forms II and IV have similar meanings when they have the same root, but other times they do not.

| Form IV | | | Form II | | | Form I | |
|---|---|---|---|---|---|---|---|
| *to make a mistake* | أخْطأَ | ← | *to accuse s.o. of a mistake* | خَطَّأَ | ← | *to be mistaken* | خَطِئَ |
| *to oust* | أخْرَجَ | ← | *to take out* | خَرَّجَ | ← | *to exit* | خَرَجَ |
| *to admit into* | أدْخَلَ | ← | *to insert* | دَخَّلَ | ← | *to enter* | دَخَلَ |

## Form V تَفَعَّلَ (يَتَفَعَّلُ) تَفَعُّل

The reflexive of Form II, this form removes the agent (the doer of the action) from Form II's sense and is sometimes translated as the English "to be." Form V can be thought of as doing Form II's action to itself. As you can see, Form V is the same pattern as Form II with the addition of a **تاء** occupying the first position.

| Form V | | | Form II | | | Form I | |
|---|---|---|---|---|---|---|---|
| *to learn* | تَعَلَّمَ | ← | *to educate* | عَلَّمَ | ← | *to know* | عَلِمَ |
| *to graduate* | تَخَرَّجَ | ← | *to take out* | خَرَّجَ | ← | *to exit* | خَرَجَ |
| *to absorb* | تَشَرَّبَ | ← | *to give s.o. a drink* | شَرَّبَ | ← | *to drink* | شَرِبَ |
| *to blossom* | تَفَتَّحَ | ← | *to unfold* | فَتَّحَ | ← | *to open* | فَتَحَ |

## Form VI تَفاعَلَ (يَتَفاعَلُ) تَفاعُل

The reflexive of Form III, this form can be thought of as Form III's sense happening to itself. An additional meaning that we should keep in mind is that of "to feign," or "to pretend." Form VI is the same pattern as Form III with the addition of a تاء occupying the first position.

| Form VI | | | Form I | |
|---|---|---|---|---|
| *to write to each other* | تَكاتَبَ | ← | *to write* | كَتَبَ |
| *to fall individually (one by one)* | تَساقَطَ | ← | *to fall* | سَقَطَ |
| *to feign sickness* | تَمارَضَ | ← | *to become sick* | مَرِضَ |

## Form VII اِنْفَعَلَ (يَنْفَعِلُ) اِنْفِعال

This form has the same meaning as the فُعِلَ form that we learned to express the passive. If you need a blameless verb form, then this is the one that you will use—as in "I was hit" (not "who hit me") or "the glass broke" (not "who broke the glass").

| Form VII | | | Form I | |
|---|---|---|---|---|
| *to be hit* | اِنْضَرَبَ | ← | *to hit* | ضَرَبَ |
| *to be broken* | اِنْكَسَرَ | ← | *to break* | كَسَرَ |

## Form VIII اِفْتَعَلَ (يَفْتَعِلُ) اِفْتِعال

This form places the subject "inside" of the verb action. The Form I word "party" becomes "to celebrate" in Form VIII or "to put oneself inside the party." For the verb "to gather," Form VIII is "to put oneself in the gathering," or "to meet." Form VIII does not always adhere to the sense of placing the subject "inside" the root. In fact, at times it holds the same meaning as Form I, while at others it has seemingly little to no relation to Form I's sense, as in قَرْحة 'ulcer', which in Form VIII اِقْتَرَحَ means "to suggest."

| Form VIII | | | Form I | |
|---|---|---|---|---|
| *to meet with* | اِجْتَمَعَ | ← | *to gather* | جَمَعَ |
| *to move* | اِنْتَقَلَ | ← | *to transport s.t.* | نَقَلَ |
| *to celebrate* | اِحْتَفَلَ | ← | *to gather, assemble* | حَفَلَ |
| *to elect* | اِنْتَخَبَ | ← | *to choose* | نَخَبَ |

## Form IX اِفعَلَّ (يَفعَلُّ) اِفْعِلال

Used as a way to show the acquisition of a color or physical defect, Form IX is not frequently used. In terms of physical defects, this form gives meanings such as "to become bug-eyed," or "to become cross-eyed." In terms of color, this form is used to express the acquisition of a color, "to became pale," or "to blush."

| | | |
|---|---|---|
| *to become white* | اِبْيَضَّ | Colors |
| *to become red* | اِحْمَرَّ | |
| *to become bug-eyed* | اِجحَظَّ | Physical Defects |
| *to become cross-eyed* | اِحْوَلَّ | |
| *to be crooked* | اِعْوَجَّ | |

## Form X اِسْتَفْعَلَ (يَسْتَفْعِلُ) اِسْتِفْعال

This form is generally used to mean "to seek" Form I's meaning. Some examples include "to seek a bath," meaning "to bathe"; "to seek to serve," meaning "to utilize"; or "to seek to work," meaning "to use."

| Form X | | | Form I | |
|---|---|---|---|---|
| *to use* | اِسْتَعْمَلَ | ← | *to work* | عَمِلَ |
| *to utilize* | اِسْتَخْدَمَ | ← | *to serve* | خَدَمَ |
| *to bathe* | اِسْتَحَمَّ | ← | *bath* | حَمَّ |

**C. Special Cases**

**Verbs with doubled letters:** Words that seem to have only two letters, such as مَرَّ 'to pass through', are in fact triliteral, as indicated by the final doubled consonant. This word is represented by فَعَلَ, where the ع in the pattern stands for the first instance of ر in the verb and ل stands for the second ر.

| | | |
|---|---|---|
| ـل | ـعـ | فـ |
| ر | ر | مـ |

**Verbs with a long vowel:** If a verb is defective (= contains a long vowel in its root), it is represented in the pattern as a consonant. For example, the verb زار 'to visit' is represented by the pattern فَعَلَ, where the letter ع in the pattern stands for the long vowel أَلَف in the verb (which is originally و in the root).

| | | |
|---|---|---|
| ـل | ـعـ | فـ |
| ر | ا | ز |

**Quadriliteral verbs:** Verbs that have four original letters are represented with a pattern that has the final ل repeated:

٧ بَرْمَج ← فَعْلَل

We will revisit and elaborate on the root derivational system in following chapters.

# تمرين ١١

**Creating verb forms: (**1) Create a verb by substituting the root letters in the appropriate places, as in the example. (2) Guess the meaning of the verb based on your knowledge of its root and the Verb Form system.

| | | | | | | |
|---|---|---|---|---|---|---|
| **مِثال: ك ت ب** | + | **تَفاعَل** | = | **تكاتَب** | *Writing back and forth?* |
| ١ - دخ ل | + | تَفَعَّل | = | ________ | ________ |
| ٢ - ك ب ر | + | فَعُل | = | ________ | ________ |
| ٣ - ع م ل | + | اِسْتَفْعَل | = | ________ | ________ |
| ٤ - نَ س ي | + | فَعِل | = | ________ | ________ |
| ٥ - م ر ض | + | تَفاعَل | = | ________ | ________ |
| ٦ - ر س ل | + | أَفْعَل | = | ________ | ________ |
| ٧ - ن هـ ي | + | اِفْتَعَل | = | ________ | ________ |
| ٨ - ن ظ ف | + | فَعَّل | = | ________ | ________ |
| ٩ - ح ف ل | + | اِفْتَعَل | = | ________ | ________ |
| ١٠ - ط ب خ | + | فَعَل | = | ________ | ________ |
| ١١ - س ف ر | + | فاعَل | = | ________ | ________ |
| ١٢ - ج م ع | + | اِفْتَعَل | = | ________ | ________ |

## تمرين ١٢

**Pattern identification:** Identify each of the following verbs (most of which you have encountered in this and previous lessons) by pattern and roman numeral. Then identify its root by eliminating its added letters, as in the example:

| Meaning | Root | Number | Pattern | Verb | |
|---|---|---|---|---|---|
| *to like/love* | حَبّ | IV | أفْعَل | أحَبّ | مِثال |
| | | | | اِحْتَفَل | ١ |
| | | | | اِسْتَشْهَد | ٢ |
| | | | | دَرَس | ٣ |
| | | | | انْهَزَم | ٤ |
| | | | | تَكَلَّم | ٥ |
| | | | | اِشْتَرى | ٦ |
| | | | | تَخَرَّج | ٧ |
| | | | | حارَب | ٨ |
| | | | | اِحْمَرّ | ٩ |
| | | | | تَراسَل | ١٠ |

### 2. Ordinal Numbers Revisited

You may have noticed that lesson numbers in this textbook are ordinal (i.e., first, second, etc.). As we have mentioned, the ordinal number **أوَّل** differs in form from the cardinal number **واحِد**. All the rest are, in fact, formed from cardinal numbers based on the pattern **فاعِل**. So, **ثَلاث**, for example, becomes **ثالِث**, matching the **فاعِل** form. Ordinal numbers 1–10 take any of the three cases:

| | | |
|---|---|---|
| ٨ | هذا هُوَ الدَرسُ الثالِثُ. | Nominative |
| ٩ | قَرَأتُ الدَرْسَ الثالِثَ. | Accusative |
| ١٠ | في الدَرْسِ الثالِثِ. | Genitive |

Ordinals greater than the number 10 have two important characteristics:

1. Ordinal numbers 11–19 are invariable in that they do not inflect in case:

| | | |
|---|---|---|
| ١١ | هذا هُوَ الدَرْسُ الثالِثَ عَشَرَ. | Nominative |
| ١٢ | قَرَأتُ الدَرْسَ الثالِثَ عَشَرَ. | Accusative |
| ١٣ | في الدَرْسِ الثالِثَ عَشَرَ. | Genitive |

In examples 11–13, the noun **الدَرس** appears in three different cases, while the modifying phrase **الثالِثَ عَشَرَ** remains the same, with a **فتحة** appearing on the final radical of both constituents of the number.

2. Unlike cardinal numbers, both words of ordinal numbers 11–19 agree in gender with the modified noun:

١٤ الدَرْسُ الثالِثَ عَشَرَ

١٥ الصورةُ الثالِثةَ عَشْرَةَ

Forming the ordinal numbers 20, 30, 40, etc., is not a complex matter. Simply prefix the definite article **الـ** and you get an ordinal number

١٦ عِشْرونَ دَرْساً *20 lessons* ← الدَرْسُ العِشْرونَ *the 20th lesson*

Ordinal numbers 20–29, 30–39, etc., are declinable in that they agree with the case of their modified noun (highlighted in blue), as you can see in these sentences:

| | | |
|---|---|---|
| ١٧ | هذا هُوَ الدَرْسُ الثالِثُ والعِشْرونَ. | Nominative |
| ١٨ | قَرَأتُ الدَرْسَ الثالِثَ والعِشْرينَ. | Accusative |
| ١٩ | في الدَرْسِ الثالِثِ والعِشْرينَ. | Genitive |

The first part of the number (**الثالِث**) inflects to agree with the noun **الدَرس**, so does the second part **العشرون**, which has only two forms, **العشرون** for the nominative and **العشرين** for both the accusative and genitive.

Ordinal numbers over 100 are written with the hundred(s) separated from the tens by the preposition **بَعْدَ** 'after', as in the example:

٢٠ الدَرْسُ الخامِسَ عَشَرَ بَعدَ المِئة *the fifteenth lesson after the hundredth (115th)*

# تمرين ١٣

**A. Select the best choice:** Select the choice that correctly (or best) completes the sentence.

١- الصورةُ ____________ في هذا الدَرسِ هي صورةُ جورج واشِنطَن.

☐ الأوَّلُ ☐ الأولى ☐ الواحِدةُ

٢- قَرَأنا عَن هالَة بُستاني في الدَرسِ ____________.

☐ عَشْرة ☐ عاشِر ☐ العاشِر

٣- دَرسُ الكيمياء في الساعةِ ____________ والنِصْف.

☐ الثانيةُ عَشْرَةُ ☐ الثانيةَ عَشْرَةَ ☐ الثانيةِ عَشْرَةِ

٤- سَيَكونُ الدَرسُ ____________ عَن الدِراسةِ والمَواعيد.

☐ الثالِثِ والعِشْرينَ ☐ الثالِثَ والعِشْرينَ ☐ الثالِثُ والعِشْرونَ

٥- كانَ لِنكَن في السَنَةِ ____________ حينَ أُغْتيلَ في واشنطَن العاصِمة.

☐ الرابعةِ والخَمْسينَ ☐ الرابعةَ والخَمْسينَ ☐ الرابَعةُ والخَمْسونَ

**B. Forming the ordinal:** Form ordinal numbers and provide the short vowels on the final radical.

مِثال: الرَجُلُ ١٥ **الرَجُلُ الخامِسَ عَشَر**

٦- البِنتُ ٩ ____________

٧- الكِتابُ ١٨ ____________

٨- في السَنَةِ ٢٥ ____________

٩- في عيدِ الثَورةِ ١٠٥ ____________

١٠- على الصَفحةِ ١٢٢ ____________

١١- الطالِبُ ١ ____________

## تمرين ١٤

**A. Fill in the blanks:** Complete these sentences with information from the listening passage.

١- كانَتْ هٰذِهِ الشَخْصيّةُ زَوْجَةَ رَئيسِ ________________ .

٢- أُغْتيلَ زَوْجُها في ________________ .

٣- اِسمُ الزَوْجِ الثاني هُوَ ________________ .

**B. Listen and select:** Check the box that matches the information as expressed in the listening passage.

٤- صارَتْ هٰذِهِ الشَخْصيّةُ زَوْجةً ________________ .

☐ مَرّةً واحِدةً ☐ مَرّتَيْنِ ☐ ثَلاثَ مَرّاتٍ

٥- اِسْمُ هٰذِهِ الشَخْصيّةِ ________________ .

☐ أمريكيّ ☐ فَرَنسيّ ☐ عَرَبيّ

٦- بَعدَ وَفاةِ زَوْجِها الثاني سَكَنَتْ في ________________ .

☐ مَدينةِ نيويورك ☐ مَدينةِ واشِنطَن ☐ وِلايةِ تكساس

**C. صواب أو خطأ:** Mark the following sentences **صواب** or **خطأ** according to the information in the listening passage and correct any false statements.

٧- هٰذِهِ الشَخْصيّةُ فِرَنسيّةٌ.

______________________________

٨- صارَتْ زَوْجةً مَرّةً ثانيةً في سَنَةِ ١٩٦٨.

______________________________

٩- الزَوْجُ الثاني أمريكيّ.

______________________________

## تمرين ١٥

VIDEO

**تَمرينُ المُشاهَدة: شاهِدوا الدَرْسَ السادس عَشَر على القُرْص الرَقْميّ.**

**المَشْهَدُ الأوَّل**

١- مَن عَبد القادِر الجَزائري وماذا فَعَلَ؟ ________________________________

________________________________

________________________________

٢- ماذا قالَ ستيف عن جَمال عَبد الناصِر؟ ________________________________

________________________________

٣- أيّ عِلمٍ أَسَّسَهُ ابن خَلدون؟ ________________________________

٤- لماذا يَستطيعُ ستيف أن يَتكَلَّمَ اللغةَ العربيَّةَ جَيِّداً؟ ________________________________

________________________________

**المَشْهَدُ الثاني**

١- ما أنواعُ العَصيرِ لَدى أبي سمير؟ ________________________________

________________________________

________________________________

٢- ماذا طَلَبَ مايكل؟ ________________________________

٣- كَم دَفَعَ كُلٌ من مايكل وسامِر وستيف؟ ________________________________

________________________________

## المُفْرَدات

Listen to the vocabulary items on the CD and practice their pronunciation.

social gathering . . . . . . . . . . . . . (n., m.) اِجْتِماع ج اِجْتِماعات

to use, to utilize, to employ . . . . . . (v.) اِستَخدَمَ (يَستَخدِمُ) اِستِخدام

to become a martyr. . . . . . . (passive v.) أُسْتُشْهِدَ (يُستَشْهَدُ) اِسْتِشهاد

to establish, to found . . . . . . . . . . . . (v.) أَسَّسَ (يُؤَسِّسُ) تأسيس

black . . . . . . . . . . . . . . . . . . . . . . . . (n., m.) أَسْوَد ج سود

to be assassinated . . . . . . . . . . . . (passive v.) أُغْتيلَ (يُغتالُ) اِغتِيال

prince . . . . . . . . . . . . . . . . . . . . . . (n., m.) أمير ج أُمَراء

to elect . . . . . . . . . . . . . . . . . . . . . (v.) اِنْتَخَبَ (يَنتَخِبُ) اِنتِخاب

Andalusia, Muslim Spain . . . . . . . . . . . . . . (n., f.) الأَنْدَلُس

history . . . . . . . . . . . . . . . . . . . . . . (n., m.) تاريخ ج تَواريخ

discrimination . . . . . . . . . . . . . . . . . . (verbal n., m.) تَمييز

to pass away . . . . . . . . . . . . . . . . (passive v.) تُوُفِّيَ (يُتَوَفّى) وَفاة

mosque . . . . . . . . . . . . . . . . . . . . . . . (n., m.) جامِع ج جَوامِع

prize, award . . . . . . . . . . . . . . . . . . . . . . (n., f.) جائِزة ج جَوائِز

algebra . . . . . . . . . . . . . . . . . . . . . . . . . . . (n., m.) جَبْر

to be wounded, to be hurt . . . . . . . (passive v.) جُرِحَ (يُجرَحُ) جَرح

republic . . . . . . . . . . . . . . . . . . . . . (n., f.) جُمهوريّة ج جُمهوريّات

army . . . . . . . . . . . . . . . . . . . . . . . . . . (n., m.) جَيْش ج جُيوش

to fight . . . . . . . . . . . . . . . . . . . . (v.) حارَبَ (يُحارِبُ) حَرْب / مُحارَبة

war . . . . . . . . . . . . . . . . . . . . . . . . . . . (n., f.) حَرْب ج حُروب

account . . . . . . . . . . . . . . . . . . . . . . (n., m.) حِساب ج حِسابات

to acquire, to obtain, to get . . . . . . . . (v.) حَصَلَ (يَحصُلُ) حُصول

to tell a story; to talk . . . . . . . . . . . . . (v.) حَكَى (يَحْكي) حِكاية

to go out, to exit. . . . . . . . . . . . . . . . . (v.) خَرَجَ (يَخرُجُ) خُروج

orator, preacher, speaker . . . . . . . . . . . (n., m.) خَطيب ج خُطَباء

to enter. . . . . . . . . . . . . . . . . . . . . . (v.) دَخَلَ (يَدخُلُ) دُخول

to pay. . . . . . . . . . . . . . . . . . . . . . . . . (v.) دَفَعَ (يَدْفَعُ) دَفْع

defense. . . . . . . . . . . . . . . . . . . . . . (n., m.) دِفاع ج دِفاعات

head . . . . . . . . . . . . . . . . . . . . . . . (n., m.) رأس ج رُؤوس

to reject . . . . . . . . . . . . . . . . . . . . . (v.) رَفَضَ (يرفُضُ/ يَرفِضُ) رَفْض

leader, president. . . . . . . . . . . . . . . . (n., m.) رَئيس ج رُؤَساء

leader (popular). . . . . . . . . . . . . . . . . (n., m.) زَعيم ج زُعَماء

young man. . . . . . . . . . . . . . . . . . . . (n., m.) شابّ ج شَباب

poet. . . . . . . . . . . . . . . . . . . . . . . . (n., m.) شاعِر ج شُعَراء

personality, character. . . . . . . . . . . (n., f.) شَخصِيّة ج شَخصِيّات

ranking officer. . . . . . . . . . . . . . . . . (n., m.) ضابِط ج ضُبّاط

to request, to order (i.e., in a restaurant) . . . . (v.) طَلَبَ (يطْلُب) طَلَب

Toulon (a town in southern France) . . . . . . . . . . (n., f.) طولون

scholar, scientist. . . . . . . . . . . . . . . . (n., m.) عالِم ج عُلَماء

sociologist . . . . . . . . . . . . . . . . . . . . (n., m.) عالِم اجْتِماع

sociology. . . . . . . . . . . . . . . . . . . . . .(n., m.) عِلْم اجْتِماع

to introduce someone to someone else (v.) (على) عَرَّفَ (يُعَرِّف) تَعريف

race, element . . . . . . . . . . . . . . . . . (n., m.) عُنصُر ج عَناصِر

racial . . . . . . . . . . . . . . . . . . . . . . . . . (adj.) عُنصُريّ

philosophy. . . . . . . . . . . . . . . . . . . (n., f.) فَلْسَفة ج فَلسَفات

philosopher . . . . . . . . . . . . . . . . . . (n., m.) فَيْلَسوف ج فَلاسِفة

to do, to perform . . . . . . . . . . . . . . . . . (v.) قامَ (يَقومُ) قِيام

law . . . . . . . . . . . . . . . . . . . . . . . . (n., m.) قانون ج قَوانين

leader (military) . . . . . . . . . . . . . . (n., m.) قائد ج قُوّاد/ قادة

nearby, close . . . . . . . . . . . . . . . . . . . . . . . . . (adv.) قُرْب

village . . . . . . . . . . . . . . . . . . . . . . . . (n., f.) قَرية ج قُرى

priest . . . . . . . . . . . . . . . . . . . . . . . (n., m.) قِسّيس ج قِسّاوِسة

writer, scribe. . . . . . . . . . . . . . . . . . . (n., m.) كاتِب ج كُتّاب / كَتَبة

for the sake of (Syrian colloquial) . . . . . . . . . . كرمال

generous . . . . . . . . . . . . . . . . . . . . . . . . (adj.) كَريم ج كُرَماء

necessary . . . . . . . . . . . . . . . . . . . . (active participle) لازِم

lawyer, attorney-at-law, counsel . . . . . . . (n., m.) مُحامٍ ج مُحامون

mixed . . . . . . . . . . . . . . . . . . . . . . (passive participle) مُشَكَّل

introduction . . . . . . . . . . . . . . . . . . . . . (n., f.) مُقَدِّمة ج مُقَدِّمات

place, location . . . . . . . . . . . . . . . . . . . (n., m.) مَكان ج أمْكِنة

king. . . . . . . . . . . . . . . . . . . . . . . . . . . (n., m.) مَلِك ج مُلوك

جَيِّد (Syrian colloquial) . . . . . . . . . . . . . . . (adj.) مْنيح ج امْناح

historian . . . . . . . . . . . . . . . . . . . . . . (n., m.) مُؤَرِّخ ج مُؤَرِّخون

to be sent into exile, to be expelled . . . . (passive v.) نُفِيَ (يُنْفى) نَفْيٌ

now (Syrian colloquial) . . . . . . . . . . . . . . . . . . . هَللأ / هَلَّق

minister . . . . . . . . . . . . . . . . . . . . . . . . (n., m.) وَزير ج وُزَراء

# الدرسُ السابعَ عشَر

## Objectives

- Making appointments and schedules, and describing festivities
- Learning how to make dual and plural nouns in إضافة structures
- Expressing frequency with كُلّ – مَرَّة – مَرَّتين
- Expressing exception using ما عدا
- Explaining reason using لِـ and its case المُضارِع المَنصوب (the subjunctive)
- Introduction to active and passive participles (اسمُ الفاعِل واسمُ المَفعول)
- Using لَم to negate the past, creating المُضارِع المجزوم
- Introduction to weak verbs الفِعلُ المعتلّ

## رُكنُ المُفْرَداتِ الجَديدة

| | |
|---|---|
| أَخَذ (يَأخُذُ) أخْذ | *to take* |
| أرْسَلَ (يُرْسِلُ) إرْسال | *to send* |
| اِنْتَهى (يَنْتَهي) اِنْتِهاء | *to end* |
| بَدَأَ (يَبْدَأُ) بِداية | *to begin* |
| رأى (يَرى) رأي / رؤية | *to see* |
| سَاعَدَ (يُساعِدُ) مُساعَدة | *to help* |
| عَلِمَ (يَعْلَمُ) عِلْم | عَرَفَ (يَعْرِف) مَعْرِفة |
| وَجَدَ (يَجِدُ) وُجود | *to find* |
| ما عَدا | إلاّ |
| بَعْضُهُم بَعْضاً / بَعْضُهم البَعْض | *each other* |
| عامٌ | سَنَةٌ |

## تمرين ١

**اختَر الكَلِمةَ الّتي لا تُناسِب باقي الكَلِماتِ في كُلِّ مَجْموعةٍ وبَيِّن السَبَب.**

**Odd word out:** Underline the word that does not belong to each set and explain your choice if needed.

| | | | | |
|---|---|---|---|---|
| ١- | لأنَّ | بِسَبَب | ما عَدا | لِماذا |
| ٢- | عَرَب | رَمَضان | صامَ | غُروب |
| ٣- | عيد | الشام | مُعايَدة | حَلوى |
| ٤- | اِلتِهاب | طائِرة | مَطار | بَوّابة |
| ٥- | عِيادة | حَبّة | صَديق | طَبيب |
| ٦- | رَأى | جالِس | زارَ | اِستَقبَلَ |
| ٧- | طَبيب | مُدَرِّس | مُدير | طالِب |

## تمرين ٢

**Matching:**

**وافِقْ بَيْنَ الكَلِماتِ في العَمودَين.**

| | | | |
|---|---|---|---|
| ١ | أخَذَ | | نَسِيَ |
| ٢ | ألِمَ | | فَقير |
| ٣ | بَدَأَ | | طَبيب |
| ٤ | عَلِمَ | | اِنتَهى |
| ٥ | غَنيّ | | أعطى |
| | | | أسبِرين |

## تمرين ٣

**اسألوا جيرانكُم:** **Ask your neighbor:** Report your findings to the class.

١- متى بدأت تَتكَلّم(ينَ)؟

٢- أيّ لُغةٍ بدأت تَتكَلَّم(ينَ) بِها أولاً . . . ثانياً؟

٣- مَتى يَبْدأ ويَنْتَهي دَرْسُ اللُغةِ العَربيّةِ ؟

٤- مَن يُساعِدُك وكَيْف؟

٥- لِماذا تُحِبّ(ينَ) أو لا تُحِبّ(ينَ) زيارةَ طَبيبِ الأسنان؟

## تمرين ٤

**أعِدْ تَرتيبَ الكَلِماتِ في كُلِّ مَجموعةٍ لِتُشَكِّل جُمَلاً مُفيدة.** **Sentence construction:**

١- المُسلِمونَ - رَمَضان - في - شَهْرِ - يَصومُ.

٢- عاصِمةِ - ما - تَعلَمُ - هَلْ - اِسمُ - الأرْدُن؟

٣- الخَميس - المَكتَبَةِ - في - كُلَّ - ما عَدا - أدرُسُ - يومٍ - يومَ.

٤- شَهرِ - الدِراسةُ - حَزيران - تَنتَهي - الجامِعةِ - في - في.

٥- بَعدَ - السينَما - وَصَلتُ - الفيلم - دارِ - إلى - بِدايَةِ.

# عيدُ الفِطْرِ

AUDIO

مايكِل براون، كما تَعلَمونَ، مَوْجودٌ الآنَ في القاهِرةِ لِدِراسةِ العَرَبيّة. يَذهَبُ كُلَّ يومٍ إلى دُروسِهِ في الجامِعةِ ما عَدا يومَ الجُمعةِ لأنَّ هذا اليَومَ عُطلَةُ نِهايَةِ الأسبوعِ في مِصرَ وفي مُعظَمِ البِلادِ العَرَبيّةِ. كَتَبَ مايكِل في يَومِيّاتِهِ هذِهِ الكَلِمات:

**الثُلاثاء ٢٠ فِبْراير (شُباط) ٢٠٠٦**

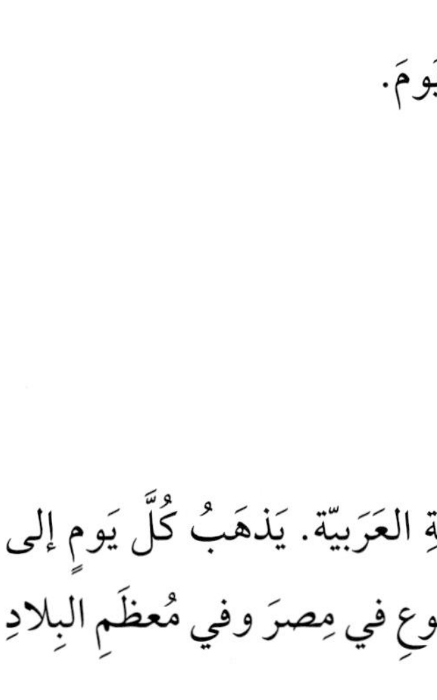

اليَومُ عُطلةٌ بِسبَبِ عيدِ الفِطر، وهو عيدٌ يَأتي بَعدَ شَهرِ رَمَضان. صامَ مُعظَمُ زُمَلائي المِصريّينَ في رَمَضان. فَفي هذا الشَهرِ يَصومُ الناسُ عَنِ الطَعامِ والشَرابِ مِنَ الصَباحِ حَتّى غُروبِ الشَمس. أمّا في العيدِ فَيَزورُ الناسُ بَعضُهُم بَعضاً عادةً ويَأكُلونَ كَثيراً مِنَ الطَعامِ والحَلوى ويَشرَبونَ الشايَ والقَهوة.

بِطاقَتا مُعايَدةٍ

أرسَلتُ أمسِ بِطاقاتِ مُعايَدةٍ لِبَعضِ أصدِقائي المِصريّين. وَجَدتُ في المَكتَبةِ بِطاقاتٍ مَكتوبٌ علَيْها «كُلَّ عامٍ وأنتُم بِخَير» وبِطاقات مَكتوبٌ علَيْها «عيدٌ مُبارَك.» اِشْتَرَيْتُ مِنَ النَوعِ الأوَّلِ، أمّا الناسُ فَيَقولُ بَعْضُهُم لِبَعْضٍ «كُلَّ سَنَةٍ وأنتَ طَيِّب.» وقالَ لي سَمير إنّ الناسَ في بِلادِ الشام يَقولونَ «كُلَّ سَنَةٍ وأنتَ سالِم.»

كُلَّ سَنةٍ وأنتَ سالِم يا سَمير!
وأنتِ سالِمة!


**الجُمْعة ١ مارِس (آذار) ٢٠٠٦**

**آلَمَني ضِرسي**

أمسِ كانَ عِندي مَوعِدٌ عِندَ طَبيبِ الأسْنانِ في الساعةِ الثانيةِ والنِصْف. آلَمَني ضِرسي كَثيراً في الليلةِ الماضِيةِ وأخَذتُ حَبّتَي أسبِرين دونَ فائدةٍ كَبيرة. لَمْ أنَمْ تِلكَ اللَيْلة مِن ألَمي.

وَصَلتُ إلى عِيادةِ الطَبيبِ قَبلَ مَوعِدي بِخَمسِ دَقائقَ فَقَط، لكِنَّ الطَبيبَ لَمْ يَرَني حَتّى الساعةِ الثالِثةِ وعَشْرِ دَقائق. قالَ لي إنَّ هُناكَ اِلْتِهاباً في الضِرْس. أعطاني حُبوباً ضِدَّ الالْتِهاب. سَأرجِعُ إلى الطَبيبِ بَعدَ ثَلاثةِ أيّام.

# عامٌ دِراسيٌّ جَديدٌ

كَتَبَ عَدنان مارتيني هذِهِ اليَوْمِيّات حينَ كانَ طالِباً في جامِعةِ وِلايةِ أوهايو يَدرُسُ عِلمَ الحاسوب، وكانَت هذِهِ هِيَ بِدايةُ السَنةِ الثانِيةِ لَهُ في كَلَمبَس.

**السَبت ٢١ أيلول ٢٠٠٦**

بَعدَ ثَلاثةِ أيّامٍ يَبدَأُ العامُ الدِراسيُّ الجَديد. في فَصلِ الصَيفِ الماضي لَمْ أرجِعْ إلى سوريَّة بَل دَرَستُ ثَلاثَ مَوادَّ وهِيَ عِلمُ الحاسوبِ والرياضِيّاتُ والكيمياء. اِنتَهَت الدِراسةُ في الشَهرِ الماضي وذَهَبتُ إلى نيويورك وفلوريدا وزُرتُ كَندا أيضاً. رَجَعتُ إلى كَلَمبَس في الأسبوعِ الماضي.

اليَومَ وغَداً سَأذهَبُ بِسيّارتي إلى مَطارِ كَلَمبَس الدَوْليِّ ثَلاثَ مَرّاتٍ لأستَقبِلَ بَعضَ الطُلاّبِ العَرَبِ الجُدُد. أنا لا أعرِفُهُم لكِنّي عَلِمتُ أسماءَهُم مِن مَكتَبِ الطُلاّبِ الأجانِبِ في الجامِعة. اليَومَ سَأستَقبِلُ هِشام تَميمي وخَديجة عَبد السلام. ولا أعرِفُ عَنْهُما شَيْئاً الآن. سَتَصِلُ طائِرةُ هِشام في الساعةِ الحادِيةَ عَشْرةَ والرُبعِ صَباحاً، أمّا مَوعِدُ طائِرةِ خَديجة فَهُوَ في الساعةِ الرابِعةِ والنِصْفِ بَعدَ الظُهر.

**الإثنين ٢٣ أيلول ٢٠٠٦**

يحمِلُ حَقيبة

ذَهَبتُ أمسِ وأمسِ الأوَّل إلى المَطار. اِسْتَقْبَلْتُ هِشام تَميمي وخَديجة عَبد السَلام أمسِ الأوَّل. وَصَلَت طائِرةُ هِشام مُتأخِّرةً عِشرينَ دَقيقة. كانَ مَعَهُ حَقيبَتان. حَمَلنا الحَقيبَتَينِ إلى السَيّارةِ ثُمَّ أخَذْتُهُ إلى سَكَنِ الطُلاّبِ حَيثُ سَيسكُنُ هذِهِ السَنة.

رَجَعتُ مَرَّةً ثانِيةً إلى المَطارِ بَعدَ الظُهرِ لأَسْتَقبِلَ خَديجة. وَصَلَت طائِرَتُها في مَوعِدِها. وَجَدْتُ خَديجة جالِسةً بِجانِبِ البَوّابَةِ رَقْم تِسعة. كانَ مَعَها حَقيبَتانِ أيضاً. أخَذتُها بِالسَيّارةِ بَعدَ ذلِكَ إلى سَكَنِ الطالِباتِ حَيثُ سَتسكُنُ هذِهِ السَنَة.

عَرَفتُ مِن هِشام أنَّهُ مِن مَدينةِ الخَليل في فِلَسطين. أتى إلى الوِلاياتِ المُتَّحِدةِ

هشام تَميمي

لِيدرُسَ الهَندَسةَ الكَهرَبائيّة. هُوَ مِن أُسرةٍ مُتَوسِّطة. أبوهُ مُديرُ مَدرسةٍ ثانَويةٍ وأمُّهُ مُدَرِّسَةُ عُلومٍ في مَدرَسةٍ مُتَوسِّطةٍ لِلبَنات. عِندَهُ أربَعةُ إخْوة: اِثنان في المَدرَسةِ الابتِدائيّة، واحِدٌ في الصَفِ الرابِعِ والثاني في السادِس، والأخُ الثالِثُ في الصَفِّ الثامِنِ في المَدرَسةِ المُتَوَسِّطة، والأخُ الرابِعُ في الصَفِّ الحادي عَشَر في المَدرَسَةِ الثانَويّة. لَهُ أختان، واحِدةٌ تَسكُنُ في مَدينةِ القُدْسِ والثانيةُ طالِبةٌ في جامِعَةِ «بير زَيْت».

خديجة عبد السلام

عَرَفْتُ مِن خَديجة أنَّها تونسيّةٌ مِن مَدينةِ تونِس أتَتْ إلى جامِعةِ وِلايةِ أوهايو لِتَدرُسَ الأدَبَ الأمريكيّ. عِندَ خَديجة أخَوان وأختٌ واحِدة. أخوها الكَبيرُ مُنير يَسكُنُ ويَعمَلُ في باريس. وأخوها الصَغيرُ في المَدرَسةِ الثانَويةِ في تونِس. أمّا أختُها فَهِيَ مُتَزَوِّجةٌ وتَسكُنُ مَعَ زَوْجِها في تونِس. قالَت خَديجة إنَّها فَقيرة، لكِنَّ أخاها الكَبيرَ يُساعِدُها.

ساعي بَريد

اِستَقبَلتُ طالِبَينِ أمسِ وهُما فُؤاد عَبدُ الرَحيم وسامِر العاني. فُؤاد مِن مِصرَ وأتى مِنَ القاهِرةِ لِيَدرُسَ عِلمَ الحاسوب. يَقولُ إنَّه مِن أسرةٍ لَيسَت غَنيّةً، فأبوهُ ساعي بَريد وأمُّه رَبّةُ بيت، لكنَّه حَصَلَ على مِنحةٍ دِراسيّةٍ مِن حُكومَتِه.

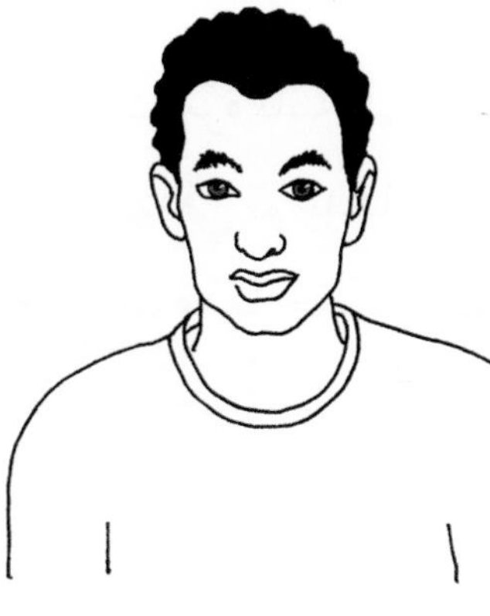

فؤاد عبد الرحيم

سامِر العاني

أمّا سامِر فَهُوَ عِراقيٌّ، لكِنَّهُ لَمْ يَأتِ مِن العِراق بَل مِن دُبَيْ حَيثُ يَعمَلُ أبوه وتَسكُنُ أسرتُه. يُريدُ سامِر دِراسةَ الطِبِّ لأنَّ أباهُ طَبيبٌ، لكِنَّهُ لَيسَ في كُلِّيَّةِ الطِبِّ الآن. سَيسكُنُ سامِر وفُؤاد في سَكَنِ الطُلاّبِ في فَصلِ الخَريف، لكِنَّهُما يُريدانِ السَكَنَ في شَقّةٍ بَعدَ ذلِك.

## تمرين ٥

**اختَرِ التكْمِلةَ المُناسِبةَ حَسَبَ النَص.**

Check the box that matches the information as expressed in the main passages for this lesson.

١- يَأتي عيدُ الفِطرِ ____________ شَهرِ رَمَضان.

☐ قَبْلَ ☐ بَعْدَ ☐ مَعَ

٢- عُطلَةُ نِهايَةِ الأسبوعِ في مُعظَمِ البِلادِ العَرَبيّةِ هِيَ يَومُ ____________ .

☐ الجُمْعة ☐ السَبت ☐ الأحَد

٣- ____________ المُسلِمونَ في شَهرِ رَمَضان من الصباح إلى المساء.

☐ يَأكُلُ ☐ يَصومُ ☐ يَشرَبُ

٤- ____________ الناسُ بَعْضُهُم بَعْضاً في العيد.

☐ يَأخُذُ ☐ يَنتَهي ☐ يَزورُ

٥- وَجَدَ مايكِل براون بِطاقاتِ ____________ في المَكتَبَة.

☐ حَلْوى ☐ مُعايَدة ☐ قَهْوة

٦- وَصَلَ مايكِل إلى عِيادَةِ طَبيبِ الأسنانِ ____________ .

☐ مُتأخِّراً ☐ في مَوعِده ☐ قَبْلَ مَوْعِده

٧- عَدنان مارتيني طالِبٌ في السَنَةِ ____________ .

☐ الأولى ☐ الثانية ☐ الثالِثة

٨- دَرَسَ عَدنان ____________ في فَصْلِ الصَيف.

☐ مادّةً ☐ مادّتَيْنِ ☐ ثَلاثَ مَوادّ

٩- اِنتَهَت الدِراسةُ في جامِعةِ عَدنان في شَهرِ ____________ .

☐ تَمّوز ☐ آب ☐ أيلول

١٠- اِستَقبَلَ عَدنان ____________ طُلاّبٍ عَرَبٍ في المَطار.

☐ ثَلاثَة ☐ أربَعَة ☐ خَمسَة

١١- وَصَلَت طائِرةُ خَديجة إلى المَطار ____________ .

☐ في مَوعِدِها ☐ مُتَأخِّرةً ☐ قَبْلَ مَوْعِدِها

١٢- أبو هِشام تَميمي ____________ .

☐ مُدَرِّسُ عُلوم ☐ ساعي بَريد ☐ مُديرُ مَدرَسة

١٣- كانَت خَديجة جالِسةً بِجانِبِ ____________ في المَطار.

☐ البَوّابةِ ☐ الكُرسيِّ ☐ الطائِرةِ

١٤- تُريدُ خَديجة دِراسةَ ____________ .

☐ الأدَبِ الأمريكيّ ☐ عِلمِ الحاسوب ☐ الطِبِّ

١٥- فُؤاد عَبد الرِحيم طالِبٌ ____________ .

☐ عِراقيّ ☐ سوريّ ☐ مِصريّ

## تمرين ٦

**املأ بِطاقةَ المُعايَدةِ هذِهِ بِعِبارةٍ مُناسِبةٍ ووَقِّعْ اسمَكَ عليها.**

**Holiday card:** Fill out this blank greeting card with an appropriate phrase and sign it in Arabic.

## تمرين ٧

**أجِبْ عَن هذِهِ الأسئلةِ حَسَبَ النَصّ.**

**Listening comprehension:** On a separate sheet of paper, answer the following questions according to the information that was presented in the main listening passage:

١- لِماذا لا يَذهَبُ مايكِل إلى الجامِعةِ في القاهِرةِ يَومَ الجُمْعة؟

٢- لِماذا ذَهَبَ مايكِل إلى طَبيبِ الأسنانِ؟

٣- أيّةَ بِلادٍ زارَ عَدنان مارتيني في الصَيف؟

٤- مِن أينَ حَصَلَ عَدنان على أسماءِ الطُلاّبِ العَرَب الجُدُد؟

٥- لِماذا يُريدُ سامِر دِراسَةَ الطِبِّ؟

## تمرين ٨

**أكتُبْ «خَطَأ» أو «صَواب» جانِبَ كُلِّ جُمْلَةٍ وصَحِّح الجُمَلَ الخَطأ.**

On a separate sheet of paper, mark the following sentences **صواب** or **خطأ** according to the information in the main reading passage and correct any false statements.

١- سَيَرى مايكِل طَبيبَ الأسنانِ مَرَّتَين.

٢- رَجَعَ عَدنان إلى سوريَّة في عُطلةِ الصَيف.

٣- مَدينةُ الخَليل في تونِس.

٤- تَدرُسُ أختُ خَديجة في جامِعةِ «بير زَيت».

٥- وَصَلَ سامِر إلى كَلَمبَس مِن بَغداد.

## تمرين ٩

**عَرِّف هؤلاءِ الأشْخاص كَما في المِثال حَسَبَ النَص.**

**Character identification:** Identify the following people according to the information in the reading passage, as in the example.

مِثال: رَبّةُ بَيت — هِيَ أمُّ الطالِب المِصريّ فُؤاد عَبد الرَحيم.

١- طَبيب الأسنان ________________

٢- مُدَرِّسةُ عُلوم ________________

٣- ساعي بَريد ________________

٤- أختُها مُتَزَوِّجة ________________

٥- طَبيب ________________

## تمرين ١٠

**وافِق بَيْنَ هؤلاءِ الأشخاصِ وبِلادِهِم واكتُب اسْمَ بَلَدِ كُلٍّ مِنهُم على الخَريطة.**

**Geography:** Match these people with their countries and write a sentence in Arabic about each person, according to the information presented in the main passage.

١- سامِر ٢- خَديجة ٣- هِشام ٤- فُؤاد ٥- عَدنان

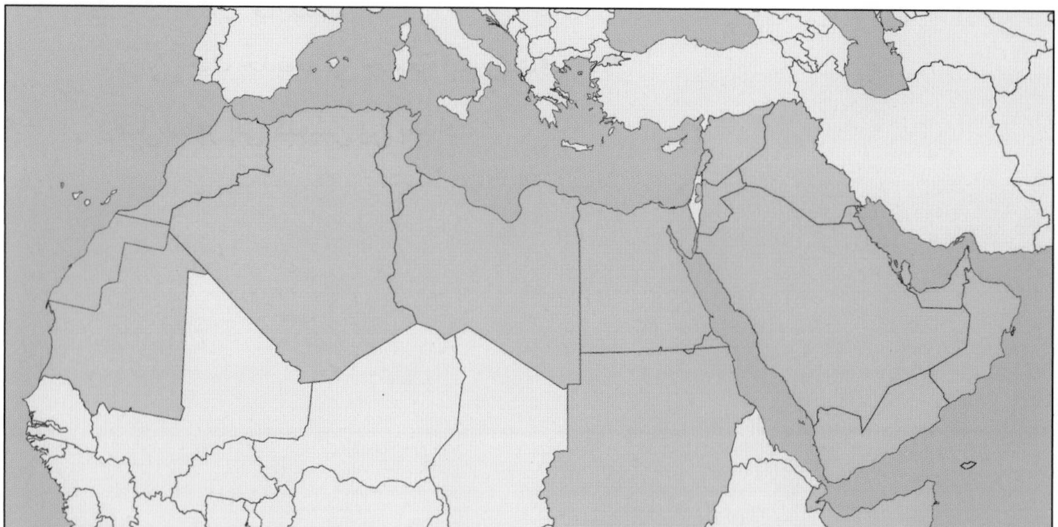

## 1. Dual and Plural Nouns in إضافة Structures (المُضاف (مُثَنّى وجَمْع

Dual nouns, as we have mentioned, are formed by suffixing an انِ to them if they are nominative and an ـَيْنِ if they are accusative or genitive. However, if a dual noun happens to be مُضاف, or the first word of an إضافة structure, the final ن in the suffix is dropped. Consider examples 1 and 2:

| | | | | | |
|---|---|---|---|---|---|
| ١ | حَبَّتان | *two pills* | + أسبِرين | ← | حَبَّتا أسبِرين |
| ٢ | بِطاقتانِ | *two cards* | + مُعايَدة | ← | بِطاقتا مُعايَدةٍ |

Similarly, some sound masculine plural nouns are formed by the suffixes ون and ين. If such plurals serve as مُضاف in an إضافة structure, the ن in the suffix is also dropped:

| | | | | | |
|---|---|---|---|---|---|
| ٣ | مُدَرِّسونَ | *teachers* | + العُلوم | ← | مُدَرِّسو العُلوم |

## 2. Expressing Frequency كُلّ، مَرّة

The two words كلّ and مرّة express frequency. The word كُلّ 'every, each' is considered a noun. Therefore, when it modifies another noun, as in كُلّ يومِ خميسٍ 'every Thursday', it forms an إضافة with the word or words that follow.

- **Remember:** Since كُلّ is مُضاف, it can be in any of the three cases, whereas the words following it (which are known as مُضاف إليهِ) must be in the genitive case مَجرور.
- **Note:** However, when the word مَرّة 'one time, instance' is used to express frequency, it is invariably in the accusative case مَنصوب.

٤ زُرْتُ دِمَشقَ مَرّةً.

٥ زُرتُ دِمَشقَ مَرَّتَين.

٦ زُرتُ دِمَشقَ ثَلاثَ مَرّاتٍ.

The form of مَرّة in examples 4, 5, and 6 is called مَفعول مُطلَق, or absolute object, which is the grammatical reason for being in the accusative case.

## 3. Expressing Exception ما عَدا

The combination of ما and عَدا means "except" (though عَدا by itself may also be used with no difference in meaning). The noun following ما عَدا (or عَدا) is always accusative مَنصوب

٧ اِسْتَقبَلَ عَدنان في المَطارِ كُلَّ الطُلاّبِ الجُدُدِ ما عَدا طالِبَين.

٨ كَتَبتُ إلى كُلِّ أصدِقائي ما عَدا ثَلاثةً مِنهُم.

## 4. Explaining Reason Using لِـ and Its Case المضارع المنصوب (Subjunctive)

**A. Reminder**

We have already learned to explain reason using لأنَّ 'because'. If you recall, لأنَّ must be followed by a subject and a predicate forming a nominal sentence. The subject (or topic) of لأنَّ is accusative مَنصوب, and its predicate (or comment) is nominative مَرفوع. (Note that لأنّ can also have its subject suffixed to it as an attached pronoun, e.g., لأنّها 'because she . . .'.)

٩ لا نَسبَحُ في البُحَيرةِ لأنَّ المَاءَ بارِدٌ.

*We don't swim in the lake because the water is cold.*

In sum, لأنَّ must be followed by a *nominal* sentence.

**B.** In this lesson, another word is used to explain reason: بِسَبَب 'because of'. This word is a combination of a preposition بِـ and a noun سَبَب, meaning 'reason, cause'. Together they mean 'by reason of'. بِسَبَب must be followed by a noun, which is genitive because it forms an إضافة structure with it.

- **Error Prevention:** بِسَبَب must be followed by a noun or a noun phrase—*it cannot be followed by a complete sentence.*

١٠ اليَومُ عُطلةٌ بِسَبَبِ العيدِ.

**C.** Another way of explaining reason involves the use of the particle لِـ with a form of the present-tense verb called المُضارِع المَنصوب (subjunctive). Note that لـ can only be a prefix. The table in section 7 of this lesson illustrates the three forms of المُضارِع (see Appendix C for conjugations of selected verbs).

- Remember that with the particle لِـ (among other particles that share this function حَتّى، كَي), the verb must be مُضارِع مَنصوب, marked by either a فَتحة on the end of singular verb forms (as in example 11) or the deletion of ن in the second-person feminine singular (example 12) and in dual (example 13) and plural masculine forms (example 14).

١١ ذَهَبَتْ أختي إلى المَطارِ لِتَأخُذَ أوَّلَ طائرةٍ إلى تونِس.

١٢ جئتِ إلى هذِه المدينةِ لِتَزوري صَديقتَكِ.

١٣ أتى سامِر وفؤاد إلى الولاياتِ المُتَّحِدَةِ لِيَدرُسا في الجامِعة.

١٤ ذَهَبوا إلى المَطعَمِ لِيَحتَفِلوا بِعيدِ ميلادِ صَديقِهِم.

## تمرين ١١

**Ask your neighbor:** **اسألوا جيرانكُم:**

Try to use the words between parentheses in your answers.

١- لِماذا تُرْسِل(ينَ) بِطاقاتِ مُعايَدة؟ (لِـ . . .)

٢- إلى مَن أَرْسَلْت بِطاقاتِ مُعايَدة؟ (كُلّ . . . ما عَدا)

٣- مَن اِستَقْبَلْت في المَطارِ ومِن أينَ أتى المُسافِر؟

٤- إلى أينَ سافَرْت ولماذا سافَرت إلى ذلك البَلَد؟ (بِسَبَب)

٥- كَمْ مَرّةً زُرت بَلَداً أَجْنَبِيّاً؟

Be prepared to report your findings.

## 5. Derived Forms: Active and Passive Participles إسمُ الفاعِل واسمُ المَفعول

As the Arabic terms indicate, **إسمُ الفاعِل واسمُ المَفعول** are nouns that are formed according to their respective patterns **فاعِل** and **مَفعول** in Form I **الفعل المُجَرَّد**.

The **active participle** **فاعل** may either refer to the agent (doer of the action), as in example 15:

١٥ هُوَ طالِبٌ في هذِهِ الجامِعة.

or it may refer to the action, as in example 16:

١٦ هُوَ ذاهِبٌ إلى المَكتَبة.

Like regular nouns, an active participle has dual **المُثَنّى** and plural **الجَمْع** forms which may be sound (requiring a plural suffix with no change in the order of letters, as in example 17) or broken (internal changes, as in example 18).

| | المُفْرَد | المُثَنّى | الجَمْع |
|---|---|---|---|
| ١٧ | ذاهِبٌ | ذاهِبان | ذاهِبونَ |
| ١٨ | طالِب | طالِبانِ | طُلاّب |

**The passive participle** refers to the recipient or "experiencer" of the action and has sound (as in example 19) or broken plural forms (as in example 20):

١٩ مَشهور ج مَشهورونَ / مَشاهير

٢٠ مَعْجون ج مَعاجين

It should be noted that the passive participle is formed only from transitive verbs (those that take objects).

### SUMMARY

Memorize and apply the following rules.

1. **All** active and passive participles for verb Forms II–X begin with a مُـ prefix.
2. **The Active Participle:** The ع, or middle letter, invariably takes a **كَسرة** (e.g., **مُدَرِّس** 'teacher').
3. **The Passive Participle:** The ع, or middle letter, invariably takes a **فَتحة** (e.g., **مُدَرَّس** 'taught' or 'someone receiving instruction').

| Example Passive Participle | Passive Participle Form | Example Active Participle | Active Participle Form | Example Verb | Verb Form | Roman Numeral |
|---|---|---|---|---|---|---|
| مِثال | اِسمُ المَفعول | مِثال | اِسمُ الفاعِل | مِثال | وَزن الفِعل | |
| مُدَرَّس *taught* | مُفَعَّل | مُدَرِّس *teacher* | مُفَعِّل | دَرَّس | فَعَّل | **II** |
| مُحارَب *fought, resisted* | مُفاعَل | مُحارِب *warrior* | مُفاعِل | حارَب | فاعَل | **III** |
| مُعْطى *given* | مُفْعَل | مُعْطِي *giver* | مُفْعِل | أعْطى | أفْعل | **IV** |
| مُتَعَلَّم *learnable* | مُتَفَعَّل | مُتَعَلِّم *educated* | مُتَفَعِّل | تَعَلَّم | تَفَعَّل | **V** |
| مُتَقاسَم *shared* | مُتَفاعَل | مُتَقاسِم *sharer* | مُتَفاعِل | تَقاسَم | تَفاعَل | **VI** |
| ------ | ------ | مُنْكَسِر *broken; defeated* | مُنفَعِل | اِنْكَسَر | اِنفَعَل | **VII** |
| مُحتَفَل *celebrated* | مُفْتَعَل | مُحْتَفِل *celebrator* | مُفْتَعِل | اِحْتَفَل | اِفتَعَل | **VIII** |
| مُخْضَرّ *colored green* | مُفْعَلّ | ----- | ----- | اِخْضَرّ | اِفْعَلّ | **IX** |
| مُسْتَقْبَل *received* | مُسْتَفْعَل | مُسْتَقْبِل *receiver* | مُسْتَفْعِل | اِسْتَقْبَل | اِسْتَفْعَل | **X** |

## تمرين ١٢

**Translation:** Use the appropriate Arabic active and passive participles.

1. The people celebrating the occasion brought several desserts.
2. She put the refrigerated foods on the kitchen table.
3. The receiving party met him at the gate.
4. The sent books were returned.
5. Her experience (**تجربة**) at work was painful.

## 6. Negating Past-Tense Verbs with لَمْ (المُضارِعُ المَجزوم)

Thus far we have used the particle **ما** to negate the past-tense verb. As you may recall, **ما** does not cause any changes either in the form of the verb or in word order:

٢١ زُرنا بَيروت. *We visited Beirut.* ← ما زُرنا بَيروت. *We didn't visit Beirut.*

We have at our disposal another particle to negate the past-tense verb: **لَمْ**, which provides a formal, emphatic negation. Unlike **ما**, however, **لَمْ** has an effect on the following verb. It changes a past-tense verb into a form of the present tense called **المضارع المَجزوم**, or the **jussive**. This mood is marked by a **سُكون** on the final radical of singular verb forms and the deletion of the **ن** in the second-person feminine singular and in dual and plural masculine forms. Although the verb form is called **مُضارِع**, the sentence still retains a sense of the past tense by virtue of **لَم**.

٢٢ زُرنا بَيروت. *We visited Beirut.* ← لَمْ نَزُرْ بَيروت. *We didn't visit Beirut.*

| | | | | |
|---|---|---|---|---|
| تَصريفُ الفِعْلِ (كَتَبَ) بالمَضارِع (المَرفوع، المَنصوب، المَجزوم) | | | | |
| **Conjugations of the Present-Tense Verb "to write" in the Indicative, Subjunctive, Jussive** | | | | |
| | المَجزوم | المَنصوب | المَرفوع | الضَمير |
| | أكْتُبْ | أكْتُبَ | أكْتُبُ | أنا |
| | نَكْتُبْ | نَكْتُبَ | نَكْتُبُ | نَحْنُ |
| | تَكْتُبْ | تَكْتُبَ | تَكْتُبُ | أنتَ |
| | تَكْتُبي | تَكْتُبي | تَكْتُبينَ | أنتِ |
| | تَكْتُبا | تَكْتُبا | تَكْتُبانِ | أنتُما |
| silent **ألِف** | تَكْتُبوا | تَكْتُبوا | تَكْتُبونَ | أنتُم |
| no change | تَكْتُبْنَ | تَكْتُبْنَ | تَكْتُبْنَ | أنتُنَّ |
| | يَكْتُبْ | يَكْتُبَ | يَكْتُبُ | هُوَ |
| | تَكْتُبْ | تَكْتُبَ | تَكْتُبُ | هِيَ |
| | يَكْتُبا | يَكْتُبا | يَكْتُبانِ | هُما |
| | تَكْتُبا | تَكْتُبا | تَكْتُبانِ | هُما |
| silent **ألِف** | يَكْتُبوا | يَكْتُبوا | يَكْتُبونَ | هُمْ |
| no change | يَكْتُبْنَ | يَكْتُبْنَ | يَكْتُبْنَ | هُنَّ |

## 7. Weak Verbs الفعل المُعتَلّ

There are verbs that contain either **و** or **ي** as one of their original letters. Such verbs conjugate in a special manner in **المُضارِع المَجزوم** as compared to the other two cases. Let's use two verbs as examples: **زارَ** 'to visit', which contains a long vowel in the **ع** position (originally **و**), and **مَشى** 'to walk', which contains a long vowel in the **ل** position (originally **ي**).

Notice how in some conjugations the long vowel (و in this example) changes into its short counterpart ضَمّة ( ـُ ), as in examples 21 and 23 (see Appendix C for conjugations of selected verbs):

٢٣ يَزورُ يَزُرْ

| تَصريفُ الفِعْلِ (زارَ) بِالمُضارِعِ المَرفوعِ والمَنصوبِ والمَجزومِ | | | | |
|---|---|---|---|---|
| **Conjugations of the Present-Tense Verb "to visit" in the Indicative, Subjunctive, Jussive** | | | | |
| | المَجزوم | المَنصوب | المَرفوع | الضَمير |
| | أزُرْ | أزورَ | أزورُ | أنا |
| | نَزُرْ | نَزورَ | نَزورُ | نَحْنُ |
| | تَزُرْ | تَزورَ | تَزورُ | أنتَ |
| | تَزوري | تَزوري | تَزورينَ | أنتِ |
| | تَزورا | تَزورا | تَزورانِ | أنتُما |
| silent أَلِف | تَزوروا | تَزوروا | تَزورونَ | أنتُم |
| no change | تَزُرْنَ | تَزُرْنَ | تَزُرْنَ | أنتُنَّ |
| | يَزُرْ | يَزورَ | يَزورُ | هُوَ |
| | تَزُرْ | تَزورَ | تَزورُ | هِيَ |
| | يَزورا | يَزورا | يَزورانِ | هُما |
| | تَزورا | تَزورا | تَزورانِ | هُما |
| silent أَلِف | يَزوروا | يَزوروا | يَزورونَ | هُمْ |
| no change | يَزُرْنَ | يَزُرْنَ | يَزُرْنَ | هُنَّ |

A similar conjugation occurs with verbs ending with a long vowel, such as مَشى:

| تَصريفُ الفِعْلِ (مَشى) بِالمُضارِعِ المَرفوعِ والمَنصوبِ والمَجزومِ | | | | |
|---|---|---|---|---|
| **Conjugations of the Present-Tense Verb "to walk" in the Indicative, Subjunctive, Jussive** | | | | |
| الضَمير | المَرفوع | المَنصوب | المَجزوم | |
| أنا | أمشي | أمشِيَ | أمشِ | |
| نَحْنُ | نَمشي | نَمشِيَ | نَمشِ | |
| أنتَ | تَمشي | تَمشِيَ | تَمشِ | |
| أنتِ | تَمشينَ | تَمشي | تَمشي | |
| أنتُما | تَمشِيانِ | تَمشِيا | تَمشِيا | |
| أنتُم | تَمشونَ | تَمشوا | تَمشوا | silent **ألِف** |
| أنتُنَّ | تَمشينَ | تَمشينَ | تَمشينَ | no change |
| هُوَ | يَمشي | يَمشِيَ | يَمشِ | |
| هِيَ | تَمشي | تَمشِيَ | تَمشِ | |
| هُما | يَمشِيانِ | يَمشِيا | يَمشِيا | |
| هُما | تَمشِيانِ | تَمشِيا | تَمشِيا | |
| هُمْ | يَمشونَ | يَمشوا | يَمشوا | silent **ألِف** |
| هُنَّ | يَمشينَ | يَمشينَ | يَمشينَ | no change |

## تمرين ١٣

**أعِدْ تَرتيبَ الجُمَلِ لِتُشكِّلَ فِقرةً مُفيدة.** **Paragraph construction:**

١- لَمْ أذْهَب (= ما ذَهَبتُ) اليَومَ إلى المَدرَسةِ بِسَبَبِ عيدِ الاستِقلال.

سَبَحنا في البَحْرِ ساعَتين.

ثُمَّ أخَذنا القِطارَ في الساعةِ الرابِعةِ والنِصْفِ ورَجَعنا إلى بُيوتِنا.

لِهذا السَبَبِ ذَهَبتُ أنا وأصدِقائي إلى شاطِئِ البَحْر.

بَعدَ الظُهرِ سَبَحنا قَليلاً مَرّةً ثانية.
ذَهَبنا إلى الشاطِئِ بِالقِطار.
بَعدَ ذلِكَ أكَلنا الغَداءَ في مَطعَمٍ صَغيرٍ على الشاطِئ.
وَصَلنا إلى الشاطِئِ في الساعةِ العاشِرةِ والنِصْفِ صَباحاً.

## تمرين ١٤

**Select the best choice:** Select the choice that correctly (or best) completes the sentence according to the grammatical explanations.

١- عِندي __________ كَبيرتانِ.
☐ دَرّاجتانِ ☐ دَرّاجتا ☐ دَرّاجَتَيْنِ

٢- يَعمَلُ في الشَرِكةِ __________ سَيّاراتٍ مِن بِلادٍ عَديدة.
☐ سائِقونَ ☐ سائِقو ☐ سائِقَيْنِ

٣- يَأكُلُ مازِن العَشاءَ مَعَ زَوجَتِهِ في المَطعَمِ __________ يَومِ جُمْعة.
☐ كُلَّ ☐ مَرَّةً ☐ ما عَدا

٤- زُرْتُ مَدينةَ باريس __________.
☐ مَرّتانِ ☐ مَرَّتَيْنِ ☐ مَرَّتا

٥- تَدرُسُ هالَةَ في المَكتَبَةِ كُلَّ يَوم __________ يَومَ الجُمْعة.
☐ ما عَدا ☐ كُلَّ ☐ مَرَّة

٦- يَسكُنُ مايكِل براون القاهِرَةَ الآنَ بِسَبَبِ __________.
☐ يُريدُ أن يدرسَ العَرَبيّة ☐ دِراسةِ العَرَبيّة

٧- عَندَ سالي سَيّارةُ تويوتا لأنَّ __________.
☐ السَيّاراتِ اليابانيّةَ جَيِّدةٌ ☐ تُحِبُّ اليابان

# تمرين ١٥

1. Locate one instance of اسم فاعِل in the paragraph next to which a picture of خديجة appears, and another instance in Adnān's Monday journal entry.

____________________________________________

2. Locate اسم مفعول in the first paragraph on p. 336.

____________________________________________

3. Locate two instances of مضارع مجزوم in Michael Brown's Friday journal entry and one instance of both مضارع منصوب and ومضارع مجزوم in Adnān's Saturday journal entry.

____________________________________________

4. Locate a simple and a compound ordinal number in the paragraph next to which a picture of هشام appears.

____________________________________________

5. From the third paragraph on p. 336, copy verbs that match these forms: افتَعَل، أفعَل ، فَعَل.

____________________________________________

6. Locate two instances of فِعْل مُعتلّ in the reading passage on p. 335 and one instance in the passage on p. 336 and list them in the third-person masculine singular in the past and present.

____________________________________________

7. In Michael's Friday journal entry, locate an إضافة structure where the مُضاف is dual and write it down.

____________________________________________

## تمرين ١٦

**Select the correct conjugation:** **اخترِ التَصْريفَ المُناسِبَ لِلفِعلِ لِتُكمِلَ الجُمَلَ التالية:**

١- أتى سامِر إلى أمريكا لِـ ____________ الطِبّ.

☐ يَدرُسُ ☐ يَدرُسَ ☐ يَدرُسْ

٢- لَمْ ____________ الطَبيبُ هذا الشَيء.

☐ يَقولُ ☐ يَقولَ ☐ يَقُلْ

٣- ما ____________ هاوائي حَتّى الآن.

☐ زُرنا ☐ نَزورَ ☐ نَزُرْ

٤- لَمْ ____________ بِعيدِ ميلادِ ابنَتِهم هذا العام.

☐ يَحتَفِلونَ ☐ اِحتَفَلوا ☐ يَحتَفِلوا

٥- ذَهَبَ عَدنان إلى كاليفورنيا لِـ ____________ ديزني لاند.

☐ يَرى ☐ يَرَ ☐ رأى

٦- لَمْ ____________ الفَتاةُ في اللَيلِ بِسَبَبِ الألَم.

☐ تَنامُ ☐ تَنامَ ☐ تَنَمِ

## تمرين ١٧

**A. Listen and select:** **آ -أكمِلِ الجُمَلَ بِالخِيارِ المُناسِب:**

Check the information as expressed in the listening passage.

١- الشَخْصُ في هذا التَمرينِ هُوَ ____________ .

☐ أُم ☐ أب ☐ طَبيب

٢- «اللاذِقيةُ» هُوَ اسمُ ____________ .

☐ بَحْرٍ ☐ عِيادَةٍ ☐ مَدينة

٣- لَمْ تَنَمِ البِنتُ بِاللَيلِ بِسَبَبِ ____________ .

☐ البَطْنِ ☐ الألَمِ ☐ الأسْبِرين

٤- سَوفَ تَنامُ البِنتُ في النَهارِ بِسَبَبِ ____________ .

☐ الإبْرَةِ ☐ الألَمِ ☐ حَبّاتِ الأسبِرين

**B. Fill in the blank:** ب- أكمِل الجُمَلَ التاليةَ بِعِباراتٍ مِنَ النَص:

Complete the following sentences with the appropriate phrases from the listening passage.

٥- اسمُ أبي البِنت ______________ .

٦- يَعمَلُ أبو البِنتِ ______________ .

٧- أعطى الطَبيبُ لِلبِنتِ ______________ في العِيادة.

٨- اسْمُ البِنتِ ______________ .

ت- **اكتُبْ «خَطأ» أو «صَواب» جانِبَ كُلِّ جُمْلَةٍ وصَحِّحِ الجُمَلَ الخَطأ.**

٩- الأمُّ لا تَعمَل.

١٠- لَم تَنَم الأمُّ كَثيراً بِسَبَبِ ألَمٍ في بَطنِها.

١١- أخَذَتِ البِنتُ الإبرةَ في عِيادَةِ الطَبيب.

١٢- سَتَأخُذُ البِنتُ حَبّةَ أسبِرين بَعدَ كُلِّ طَعام.

**D. Short answer:** ث- أجِبْ عَن هذِه الأسئِلةِ حَسَبَ النَصّ:

١٣- كَم وَلَداً في هذِهِ العائِلة؟

١٤- ماذا فَعَلَت الأمُّ في اللَيلِ لِتُساعِدَ ابنَتَها؟

١٥- إلى أينَ أخَذَت الأمُّ ابنَتَها في الصَباح؟

١٦- ما سَبَبُ ألَمِ البِنت؟

17. In the listening passage, there are three vocabulary items that we have not encountered before. Take a moment to write these words down and examine them in terms of their roots and their forms. Try to see if you can deduce their meanings, using context as a guide.

18. The name of a certain body of water occurs in the passage. Write it down in Arabic and list its English equivalent.

VIDEO

## تمرين ١٨

**تَمرينُ المُشاهَدة: شاهِدوا الدَرْسَ السابع عَشَر على القُرْص الرَقْميّ.**

١- لِماذا قالَتْ أمّ سامِر العِبارةَ «البيت بيتك»؟ ____________________

____________________

٢- لماذا لا يُريدُ مايكل أنْ يشربَ؟ ____________________

____________________

٣- أيْنَ يَدرُسُ هاني وهنادي؟ ____________________

____________________

٤- ماذا تَدرُسُ هنادي؟ ____________________

٥- لِماذا يَذهَبُ مايكل وستيف إلى باب توما؟ ____________________

____________________

____________________

## تَذَوَّقْ الثَقافة العَرَبيّة

Um Sāmir used the following expression when she first met Michael: **نَوَّرت الشام** which can be loosely translated as "you are the light of Damascus," or more literally as "you have illuminated Damascus." We also use the expression **نَوَّرت البَيْت** when someone enters our home. The location following **نَوَّرت** can be changed as the situation requires. A polite response to this phrase could be: **النور بوجودك** (i.e., "the light is from your presence"), but this is not the only response.

# المُفْرَدات

Listen to the vocabulary items on the CD and practice their pronunciation.

أَجْنَبِيّ ج أَجانِب (n., m.) . . . . . . . . . . . . . . . . . . . . . foreigner

أَجْنَبِيّ / أَجْنَبِيَّة (adj.) . . . . . . . . . . . . . . . . . . . . . foreign

أَخَذَ (يَأْخُذُ) أَخْذ (v.) . . . . . . . . . . . . . . . . . . . . . to take

أَرْسَلَ (يُرسِلُ) إِرْسال (v.) . . . . . . . . . . . . . . . . . . . . . to send

اِسْتَقبَلَ (يَسْتَقبِلُ) اِستِقبال (v.) . . . . . . . . . . . . to receive (someone)

اِعتَقَدَ (يعتَقِدُ) اِعتِقاد (v.) . . . . . . . . . . . . . . . . . . . . . to believe.

اِلْتِهاب ج اِلتِهابات (n., m.) . . . . . . . . . . inflammation, infection

أَلَم ج آلآم (n., m.) . . . . . . . . . . . . . . . . . . . . . pain.

آلَمَ (يُؤلِمُ) (v.) . . . . . . . . . . . . . . . . . . . . . to hurt

أمّا (particle) . . . . . . . . . . . . . . . . as for, but, yet, however

اِنْتَهى (يَنْتَهي) اِنتِهاء (v.) . . . . . . . . . . to finish, to come to an end

بَدَأَ (يبدَأُ) بَدْء (v.) . . . . . . . . . . . . . . . . . . . . . to begin

بِداية ج بِدايات (n., f.) . . . . . . . . . . . . . . . . . . . . . beginning

بَسّ . . . . . . . . . . . . . . . . only (Syrian colloquial)

بَوّابة ج بَوّابات (n., f.) . . . . . . . . . . . . . . . . . . . . . gate

جالِس ج جالِسون (n., m.) . . . . . . . . . . . . . . . . . . . . . sitting

حَبّة ج حَبّات (n., f.) . . . . . . . . . . . . . . . . . . . . . pill

حُكومة ج حُكومات (n., f.) . . . . . . . . . . . . . . . . . . . . . government

حَمَلَ (يَحْمِلُ) حَمْل (v.) . . . . . . . . . . . . . . . . . . . . . to carry.

رَأى (يَرى) رُؤية (v.) . . . . . . . . . . . . . . . . . . . . . to see

رَبّةُ بَيْت ج رَبّات بُيوت (n., f.) . . . . . . . . . . . . . . . . housewife

رَح . . . . . . . . . future marker (= *will* in Syrian colloquial)

زَميل ج زُمَلاء (n., m.) . . . . . . . . . . . . . . colleague, coworker.

mail carrier . . . . . . . . . . . . . . (n., m.) ساعٍ ج سُعاة (ساعي بَريد)

to help, to assist . . . . . . . . . . . . . . . (v.) ساعَدَ (يُساعِدُ) مُساعَدة

safe, secure; healthy. . . . . . . . . . . . . . (n., m.) سالِم ج سالِمون

reason, cause . . . . . . . . . . . . . . . . . (n., m.) سَبَب ج أَسْباب

Syria, Damascus, Greater Syria . . . . . . . . . . . . . . (n., f.) الشام

drink, beverage, sherbet . . . . . . . (n., m.) شَراب ج أَشْرِبة، شَرابات

opposite, anti-, adversary, opponent . . . . . (n., m.) ضِدٌّ ج أَضْداد

molar tooth . . . . . . . . . . . . (n., m.) ضِرْس ج أَضْراس، ضُروس

physician, doctor . . . . . . . . . . . . . . . (n., m.) طَبيب ج أَطِبّاء

good . . . . . . . . . . . . . . . . . . . . . . . . . (n., m.) طَيِّب ج طَيِّبون

year. . . . . . . . . . . . . . . . . . . . . . . . . (n., m.) عام ج أَعْوام

crowded (Syrian colloquial) . . . . . . . . . . . . . . . .(n., f) عَجْقة

to know . . . . . . . . . . . . . . . . . . . . . . . (v.) عَلِمَ (يَعْلَمُ) عِلْم

sunset . . . . . . . . . . . . . . . . . . . . . . . . . . . (n., m.) غُروب

rich, wealthy. . . . . . . . . . . . . . . . . . . . . . (n., m.) غَنيّ ج أَغنِياء

and, then, so. . . . . . . . . . . . . . . . . . . (coordinating particle) فَـ

benefit, use, advantage . . . . . . . . . . . . . . . (n., f.) فائِدة ج فَوائِد

poor . . . . . . . . . . . . . . . . . . . . . . . . . . (n., m.) فَقير ج فُقَراء

to worry . . . . . . . . . . . . . . . . . . . . . . . . . (v.) قَلِقَ (يَقْلَق) قَلَق

as . . . . . . . . . . . . . . . . . . . . . . . . . . . . . . . . (particle) كَما

electricity . . . . . . . . . . . . . . . . . . . . . . . . . . . (n., f.) كَهْرَباء

not (particle used to negate past-tense verbs) . . . . . . (particle) لَمْ

(a) night . . . . . . . . . . . . . . . . . . . . . . . . . . (n., f.) لَيْلة ج لَيالٍ

except . . . . . . . . . . . . . . . . . . . . . . . . . . . . . . (particle) ما عَدا

previous, last, past . . . . . . . . . . . . . . . . . . . (adj.) ماضٍ (الماضي)

blessed . . . . . . . . . . . . . . . . . . . . . . . . . . . . . . (n., m.) مُبارَك

مَدْرَسة ج مَدارِس (n., f.) . . . . . . . . . . . . . . . . . . . . school

مُعايَدة ج مُعايَدات (n., f.) . . . . . . . . . . . . . . . . . . . . greeting

مَكْتوب (n., m.) . . . . . . . . . . . . . . . . . . . . . . . . written

مِنْحة ج مِنَح (n., f.) . . . . . . . . . . . . . . . . scholarship, grant, gift

مَوْجود ج مَوْجودون (n., m.) . . . . . . . . . . . . . . existing, present

نَوْع ج أنْواع (n., m.) . . . . . . . . . . . . . . . . . . . . kind, sort

وَجَدَ (يَجِدُ) وُجود (v.) . . . . . . . . . . . . . . . . . . . . . to find

# الدرسُ الثامِن عشَر

## Objectives

- Describing activities in the past and present
- Reading newspaper advertisements
- Describing floor plans, house fixtures, and furniture
- Describing neighborhood businesses and their locations
- Expressing intention using the أريدُ أنْ + المُضارِع المَنصوب structure
- Introduction to the noun of instrument اِسمُ الآلة
- Reviewing prepositions and relational concepts
- Revisiting adverbs and prepositions of place

## المُفرداتُ الجَديدةُ في صُوَرٍ عَديدةٍ:

مَوْقِدٌ

بَرّادٌ / ثَلاّجةٌ

خِزانةُ كُتُبٍ

مِصْباحٌ

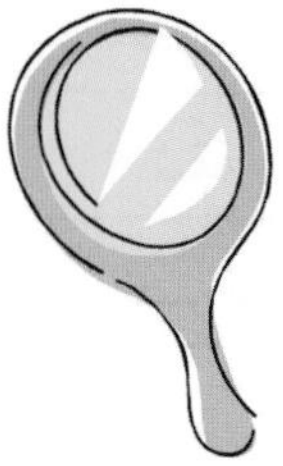

مِرآةٌ

حَوْضٌ

مِرحاضٌ

مَغسَلةٌ

## رُكنُ المُفْرَداتِ الجَديدةِ:

| | |
|---|---|
| to rent | اِسْتَأجَرَ (يَسْتَأجِرُ) اِسْتِئجار |
| it pleases | أعْجَبَ (يُعْجِبُ) إعْجاب |
| announcement; advertisement | إعلان ج إعلانات |
| rent | إيجار ج إيجارات |
| part(s) | جُزء ج أجْزاء |
| company | شَرِكة ج شَرِكات |
| to place | وَضَعَ (يَضَعُ) وَضْع |
| to fall; to be located | وَقَعَ (يَقَعُ) وُقوع |
| there is; there are | يُوجَدُ |

## تمرين ١

**Matching:**

وافِقْ بَيْنَ الكَلِماتِ في العَمودَيْنِ.

| | | | |
|---|---|---|---|
| ١ | بَرّاد | | مِترو |
| ٢ | خُبْز | | تَليفون |
| ٣ | مَحَطّة | | ثَلاّجة |
| ٤ | عِيادة | | خَلْفَ |
| ٥ | بِنايَة | | عَيْش |
| ٦ | بَنْك | | دُكّان |
| ٧ | هاتِف | | طَبيب |
| ٨ | بَقّال | | شَقّة |
| | | | مَصْرِف |

## تمرين ٢

**اختَرَ الكَلِمةَ الّتي لا تُناسِب باقي الكَلِماتِ في كُلِّ مَجْموعةٍ وبَيِّن السَبَب.** **Odd word out:**

| | | | | |
|---|---|---|---|---|
| ١- | خَبّاز | بَقّال | نَوْع | خُضَريّ |
| ٢- | مِرحاض | غَسّالة | بَرّاد | جَلاّية |
| ٣- | مَغسَلة | حَوْض | هاتِف | مَجلى |
| ٤- | فَوْق | شارِع | تَحتَ | أمامَ |
| ٥- | غُرفة | شَقَّة | مَوْقِف | بِناية |

## تمرين ٣

**أكمِلِ الجُمَلَ التالِيَةَ بِأفضَلِ كَلِمةٍ مُناسِبَة:** **Select the best choice:**

١- ________ مايكِل إلى شَقَّةٍ جَديدة.

☐ اِستَأجَرَ ☐ اِنتَقَلَ ☐ أعْجَبَ ☐ أحَبَّ

٢- أتَكَلَّمُ مَعَ أصدِقائي بِـ________ .

☐ البَرّاد ☐ المِصْباح ☐ المِرآة ☐ الهاتِف

٣- أجلِسُ ________ التِلفاز.

☐ أمامَ ☐ خَلْفَ ☐ تَحْتَ ☐ فَوْقَ

٤- تَضَعُ هالَةَ مَلابِسَها في ________ .

☐ الثَلاّجةِ ☐ الخِزانةِ ☐ المِرحاضِ ☐ السَريرِ

٥- يَعمَلُ أبو هِشام في ________.

☐ مَصرِف ☐ مَوقِف ☐ مَجلى ☐ خِزانَة

٦- يَجلِسُ صَديقي أحمَد إلى ________ .

☐ نَوْمي ☐ يَميني ☐ مَلابِسي ☐ خِزانَتي

٧- ________ مايكِل سَيّارَةً لِيَومَينِ حينَ كانَ في الإسكَندَرِيَّة.

☐ اِشتَرى ☐ باعَ ☐ اِسْتَأجَرَ ☐ اِنْتَقَلَ

# 🔊 شَقَّةُ مايكِلِ الجَديدةُ



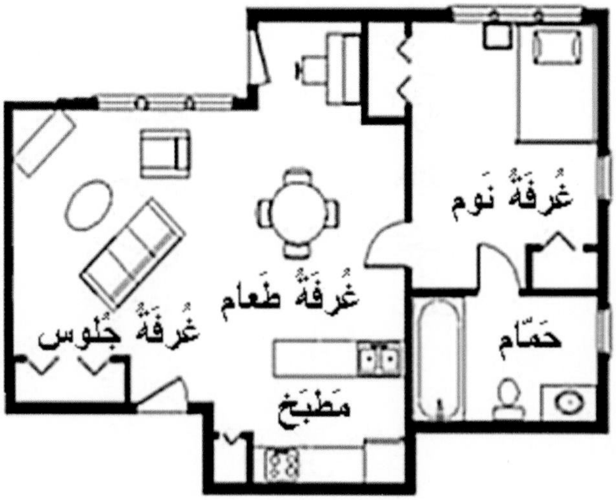

## مُخَطَّطُ شَقَّةِ مايكِلِ

يَسكُنُ مايكِلِ براون، كَما تَعلَمُ، في القاهِرةِ الآنَ لأنَّهُ يَدرُسُ اللُّغَةَ العَرَبيَّةَ في الجامِعةِ الأمريكيَّةِ بِالقاهِرة. أرادَ مايكِل أنْ يَنتَقِلَ مِن شَقَّتِهِ القَديمَةِ إلى شَقَّةٍ أُخرى أقْرَبَ إلى الجامِعةِ فيها هاتِفٌ وبَرّاد. قرأ في الجَريدةِ هذا الإعلانَ عَن شَقَّةٍ لِلإيجار:

للإيجار
شقة ٧٠ م، ش الأندلس،
غرفة نوم وجلوس بالتليفون،
الطابق الثالث. قرب مطعم
العمدة.

رَأى مايكِل تِلكَ الشَّقَّةَ، وهِيَ تَقَعُ في «بابِ اللُّوقِ» وأعجَبَتهُ، فاستَأجَرَها مِن سَيِّدةٍ عَلِمَ أنَّها عَمِلَتْ في الكُويتِ عِدَّةَ سَنَوات. أُجرةُ الشَّقَّةِ الشَهريَّةِ ٧٠٠ جُنَيهٍ مِصريٍّ بِالإضافةِ إلى الماءِ والكَهرَباء. تُوجَدُ غُرفةُ جُلوسٍ واحِدةٌ في الشَّقَّةِ لكِنَّ هذِهِ الغُرفةَ واسِعةٌ. هُناكَ طاوِلَةٌ وأربَعةُ كَراسٍ في جُزءٍ مِنَ الغُرفةِ يَستَعمِلُها مايكِل لِلطَعام ولِلدِراسةِ أيضاً، وفي الجُزءِ الآخَرِ أريكةٌ كَبيرةٌ لِلجُلوسِ يُوجَدُ مُقابِلَها تِلفازٌ وخِزانةٌ

كُتُبٍ صَغيرةٌ وَضَعَ مايكِل فيها كُتُبَهُ وعَلّقَ على الجِدارِ صورةَ أُسرتِه. إلى جانِبِ الأريكَةِ هُناكَ مِصْباحٌ وهاتِف.

غُرفَةُ طَعامٍ

غُرفَةُ جُلوسٍ

أمّا في غُرفَةِ النَومِ فَهُناكَ سَريرٌ وطاوِلَةٌ صَغيرَةٌ علَيْها مِصْباحٌ كَهْرَبائِيٌّ وخِزانَةُ مَلابِس. إلى جانِبِ غُرفَةِ النَومِ يُوجَدُ الحَمّامُ وفيهِ حَوْضُ الاسْتِحْمامِ ومِرْحاضٌ أوروبِيٌّ ومَغْسَلة. فَوْقَ المَغْسَلةِ هُناكَ مِرْآة.

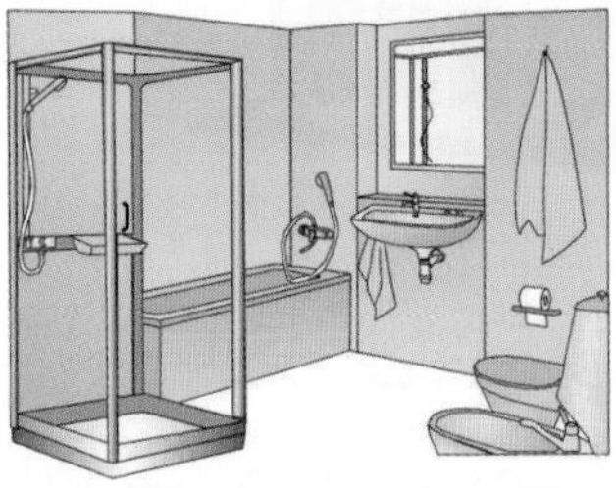

حَمّامٌ

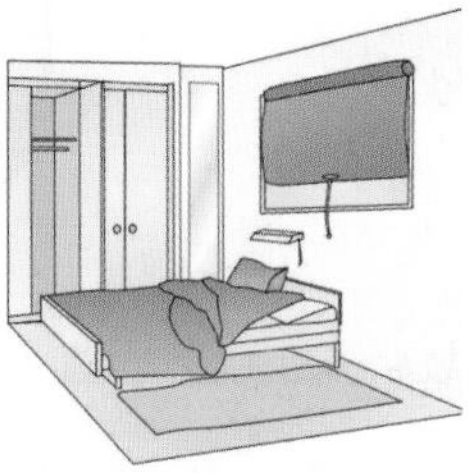

غُرفَةُ نومٍ

المَطبَخُ لَيْسَ واسِعاً. فيهِ ثَلاّجَةٌ ومَوْقِدٌ يَعمَلُ بِالغازِ ومَجْلى، لكِنْ لَيْسَ فيهِ غَسّالَةٌ ولا جَلاّيَةٌ كَهْرَبائِيَّة. مَطبَخُهُ هذا أكبَرُ مِن مَطبَخِهِ القَديم. يَستَعمِلُ مايكِل المَطبَخَ كُلَّ يومٍ لأَنَّهُ يأكُلُ فَطورَه في البَيتِ وأحْياناً يَأكُلُ الغَداءَ والعَشاءَ أيضاً.

حينَ انتَقَلَ مايكِل مِن شَقَّتِهِ القَديمَةِ إلى شَقَّتِهِ الجَديدةِ أتى صَديقاهُ المِصريّانِ سَمير عَبدُ الفَتّاح وحُسَيْن أحْمَد لِيُساعِداهُ في الانتِقال. حَمَلوا كُتُبَ مايكِل وحَقائِبَهُ ثُمَّ اسْتأجَروا شاحِنَةً صَغيرةً وذَهَبوا إلى الشَقَّةِ الجَديدة. لَمْ يَذهَبوا في ذلِكَ اليَومِ إلى الجامِعة.

شاحِنة

في مَساءِ يَومِ الخَميسِ مِنَ الأسبوعِ التالي زارَهُ في شَقَّتِهِ الجَديدةِ أصدِقاؤُهُ سَمير وحُسَين وجِنِفَر وهِبة. قالَت هِبة إنَّ الشَّقَّةَ أعْجَبَتها لأنَّها مُطِلَّةٌ على شارِعٍ كَبيرٍ، وقال حُسَين إنَّها تُعجِبُهُ لأنَّها في بِنايَةٍ نَظيفَة، وقال سَمير إنَّ الشَّقَّةَ تُعجِبُهُ لأنَّها قَريبةٌ مِنَ السوق. أمَّا جِنِفَر فقالَت إنَّها لا تُريدُ أَنْ تَسكُنَ في شَقَّةٍ لأنَّها لا تُحِبُّ أَنْ تُنَظِّفَها كُلَّ يَومٍ. لكِنَّ مايكِل قال لها إنَّ خادِمةً تأتي مَرَّتَينِ في الأسبوعِ لتُنَظِّفَ الشَّقَّةَ، وإنَّها تُساعِدُه أحْياناً في تَحضيرِ الطَعام.



شَقَّةُ مايكِل

طَبيبُ أسنان          مُحامٍ

شَرِكةُ تَأمين          شَرِكةُ تَأجيرِ سَيّارات

مَطعَمُ الصِحة          بَنكُ مِصر

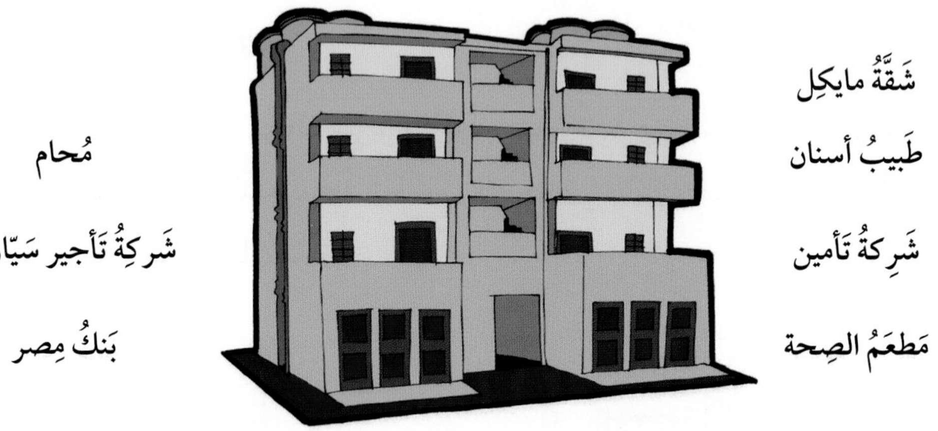

تَقَعُ شَقَّةُ مايكِل في بِنايَةٍ في بابِ اللّوقِ قَريبةٍ مِن وَسَطِ المَدينة. هُناكَ مَصرِفٌ في الطابَقِ الأرضِيِّ هُوَ «بَنكُ مِصرَ» ومَطعَمٌ صَغيرٌ يُسَمّى «مَطعَمُ الصِحّة». وفي الطابَقِ الأوَّلِ تُوجَدُ شَرِكةُ تَأجيرِ سَيّاراتٍ وشَرِكةُ تَأمين. أمّا في الطابَقِ الثاني فَهُناكَ عِيادةُ طَبيبِ أسنانٍ ومَكتَبُ مُحامٍ.

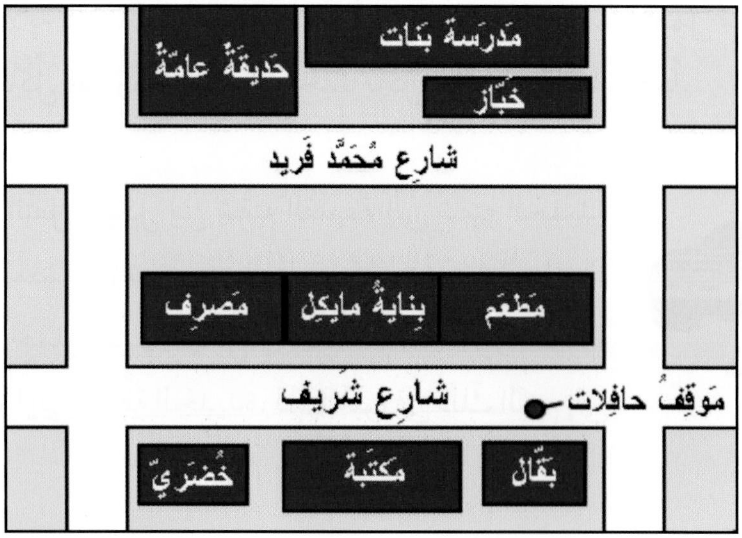

أمامَ البِنايَةِ هُناكَ مَوقِفُ حافِلات، ويُوجَد مُقابِلَها مَكتَبة. إلى يَمينِ المَكتَبة هُناكَ دُكّانُ بَقّال وإلى يَسارِها دُكّانُ الخُضَريّ. مَحطّةُ المِترو «سَعْد زَغلول» لَيْسَتْ بَعيدةً جِدّاً عَنِ البِنايَة. في الشارِعِ التالي بَعدَ شارِعِ شَريف، ويُسَمّى شارِعَ مُحَمّد فَريد، يُوجَدُ مَخبَزٌ يَبيعُ أنواعاً مِنَ الخُبزِ العَرَبيّ. اِشترى مايكِل مِنَ الخَبّازِ الخُبزَ الشاميَّ والعَيْش البَلَديَّ وأعجَبَهُ النَوعانِ جِدّاً. هُناكَ أيضاً حَديقَةٌ عامَّةٌ في ذلِكَ الشارِعِ تَقَعُ خَلفَها مَدرَسةُ بَناتٍ ابتِدائيّة.

## تمرين ٤

آ- **أجِبْ عن هذِهِ الأسئِلةِ حَسَبَ نَصِّ القِراءَة:** **A. Short answer:**

١- لِماذا اِنتَقَلَ مايكِل مِن شَقَّتِه القَديمة؟
٢- في أيِّ طابَقٍ تُوجَدُ شَقَّةُ مايكِل الجَديدة؟
٣- ما مَعنى الحَرفَينِ (م) و (ش) في الإعْلان؟
٤- مَن ساعَدَهُ في الانْتِقالِ مِن الشَقَّةِ القَديمةِ إلى الجَديدة؟
٥- في أيِّ مَكانٍ مِن القاهِرةِ تُوجَدُ الشَقّةُ الجَديدة؟
٦- هَل تُعجِبُ الشَقَّةُ الجَديدةُ حُسَين؟ لِماذا؟

ب- **أكتُبْ «خَطَأ» أو «صَواب» بِجانِبِ كُلِّ جُملَةٍ وصَحِّح الجُمَلَ الخَطَأ:** **B. True or false:**

٧- هُناكَ هاتِفٌ وبَرّادٌ في الشَقَّةِ الجَديدة.
٨- عَمِلَتْ هِبة عِدّةَ سَنواتٍ في الكُوَيت.
٩- عَلَّقَ مايكِل على الجِدارِ صورَةَ صَديقَتِه.
١٠- لا يَسْتَعمِلُ مايكِل المَطبَخَ كَثيراً.
١١- اِنتَقَلَ مايكِل إلى الشَقَّةِ الجَديدةِ بِالحافِلة.
١٢- يَعمَلُ المَوقِدُ في الشَقَّةِ الجَديدةِ بِالكَهرَباء.
١٣- المَخبَزُ في شارِعِ الأندلُس.
١٤- اِنتَقَلَ مايكِل إلى الشَقَّةِ الجَديدةِ يَوم الجُمْعة.

ت- اكتُبْ أسئِلَةً لِهذِهِ الإجاباتِ كَما في المِثال: **C. Jeopardy:**

مِثال: لأنَّهُ يَدرُسُ اللُغةَ العَرَبيّةَ بِالقاهِرة. ← لِماذا يَسكُنُ مايكِل بِالقاهِرة؟

١٥- بِشاحِنةٍ صَغيرةٍ. ________________

١٦- لأنَّها قَريبةٌ مِنَ السوق. ________________

١٧- في الطابَقِ الثاني. ________________

١٨- تَقَعُ خَلْفَ الحَديقَةِ العامَّة. ________________

## تمرين ٥

اسألوا جيرانَكُم: **Ask your neighbor:** Report your findings to the class.

١- مَتى اِسْتَأجَرْتَ شقةً أو سَيّارةً ؟ (ماضٍ)

٢- لِماذا يُعْجِبُك بَيْتُك / شَقّتُك أو لِماذا لا تعجِبُك؟

٣- أينَ يَقَعُ بَيْتُك / شَقَّتُك؟ (مُقابِلَ، أمامَ، خَلْفَ، يَسار، يَمين)

٤- ما مُخَطَّطُ بَيْتِك / شَقَّتِك؟

٥- مَن مِن أصْدقائك يَعْمَلُ في شَرِكةٍ وما اسمُها؟

## تمرين ٦

أكمِل الجُمَلَ التاليةَ بِالكَلِمَةِ المُناسِبَةِ حَسَبَ النَصّ. **Listen and select:**

١- شَقَّةُ مايكِل الجَديدةُ في الطابَقِ ________________ .

☐ الأوَّل ☐ الثاني ☐ الثالِث

٢- عَلِمَ مايكِل عَنِ الشَقّةِ مِن ________________ .

☐ حُسَين ☐ الجَريدة ☐ المَجَلّة

٣- أجرَةُ الشَقَّةِ السَنَويّةُ ________________ جُنَيهٍ مِصريّ.

☐ ٧٠٠ ☐ ٤٨٠٠ ☐ ٨٤٠٠

٤- الهاتِفُ في غُرفَةِ ________________ .

☐ الجُلوسِ ☐ النومِ ☐ الطَعامِ

٥- يَأكُلُ مايكِل طَعامَ ____________ دائِماً في البَيت.

☐ الفَطورِ ☐ الغَداءِ ☐ العَشاءِ

٦- المِرآةُ فَوقَ ____________ .

☐ المَجلى ☐ المَغسَلة ☐ الأريكة

٧- أصدِقاءُ مايكِل زاروه ____________ .

☐ صَباحاً ☐ ظُهراً ☐ مَساءً

٨- شَرِكةُ التَأمينِ في الطابَقِ ____________ .

☐ الأوَّلِ ☐ الثاني ☐ الثالِث

٩- يُوجَدُ ____________ مُقابِل بِنايَةِ مايكِل.

☐ مَكتَبَةٌ ☐ مَدرَسَةٌ ☐ مَحَطّةُ مِترو

١٠- اِشتَرى مايكِل العَيشَ البَلَديّ مِن ____________ .

☐ الخُضَريّ ☐ البَقّال ☐ الخَبّاز

## تمرين ٧

**أعطِ مُقابِلَ هذِهِ الكَلِمات:** **Antonyms:**

١- يَمين ____________ ٢- فَوْق ____________

٣- أمامَ ____________ ٤- واسِع ____________

## تمرين ٨

**أعِدْ تَرتيبَ الكَلِماتِ في كُلِّ مَجموعةٍ لِتُشَكِّلَ جُمَلاً مُفيدة.** **Sentence construction:**

١- بَيتي – اِبتِدائية – هُناكَ – خَلفَ – مَدرَسة

٢- التِلفاز – الكَبيرة – وَضَعْتُ – مُقابِلَ – الأريكة

٣- أصدِقائي – سَيّارَتي – مِن – في – ساعَدَني – غَسْلِ – اِثنانِ

٤- لِلإيجار – اليَوم – قَرَأتُ – شَقَّةٍ – إعلاناً – في – عَن – جَريدةٍ

## تمرين ٩

**Paragraph construction:** **أعِدْ تَرتيبَ الجُمَلِ لِتُشكِّلَ فِقرةً مُفيدة.**

١- مَرحبا. أنا مُنى الأسوَد وأعمَلُ مُدَرِّسَةً في وَسَطِ المَدينة.
لأنَّ فيها غُرفةَ مَكتَبٍ لَهُ وغُرفةَ طَعامٍ ومَطبَخاً واسِعاً.
قالوا إنَّ الشَقّةَ أعجبَتْهُم لأنَّها مُطِلّةٌ على حَديقَةٍ جَميلة.
اِنتَقَلْتُ وعائِلَتي في الشَهرِ الماضي إلى شَقَّةٍ كَبيرة.
لِذلِكَ أركَبُ الحافِلَةَ كُلَّ يومٍ إلى المَدرَسة.
تَقعُ شَقَّتي الجَديدة في شارِعٍ بَعيدٍ عَن وَسَطِ المَدينة.
زارَنا أمسِ بَعضُ أصدِقائِنا لِيُشاهِدوا الشَقَّةَ الجَديدة.
تُعجِبُني شَقّتي كَثيراً وتُعجِبُ زَوْجي كَذلِكَ.

## تمرين ١٠

**Storyboard:** Form a sentence for each picture or a short story based on the sequence of events.

١- 

______________________________
______________________________
______________________________
______________________________

٢- 

______________________________
______________________________
______________________________
______________________________

٣- 

٤- 

٥- 

٦- 

٧- 

## تمرين ١١

إقرأ هذَينِ الإعلانَينِ ثُمَّ أجِبْ عَنِ الأسئِلةِ التالية: **Newspaper articles:**

| | |
|---|---|
| دار في شارع الجلاء مع هاتف وبراد وغسالة وجلاية وتلفزيون. ثلاث غرف نوم وحمامان. غرفة جلوس واسعة وغرفة طعام مع طاولة طعام وستة كراس. مطلة على حديقة المدفع. الإيجار السنوي ٦٤٠ ألف ليرة سوريَّة. | شقة فاخِرة في شارع الخليج مطلة على البحر. غرفتا نوم وغرفة جلوس وطعام وغرفة للخادِمة، دون أثاث. مع هاتف. الإيجار الشهري ٥٨٠ دينار كويتي. |

١- في أيِّ بَلَدٍ تُوجَدُ كُلٌّ مِنَ الدارِ والشَقَّةِ؟

٢- كَمْ غُرفَةً في الشَقَّة؟

٣- ما عُمْلات (currencies) كُلٍّ مِن مِصرَ وسوريَّة والكُويْت؟

٤- اِقرأ الإعلانَينِ في هذا التَمرين والإعلانَ في أوَّلِ الدَرسِ والإعلانَ في الدَرسِ ١١ تَمرين ١٢ مَرّةً ثانيةً ثُمَّ اكتُب إعلاناً مِثلَ هذِه الإعلانات في جَريدةٍ عَرَبيّةٍ عَن غُرفتِك أو شَقّتِك أو بيتِك.

### ١. Expressing Intention: أرادَ أنْ + المضارع المنصوب

One way of expressing intention, want, or need is by using the verb **أراد** or other verbs of volition, followed by the particle **أنْ**. As a rule, when **أنْ** is followed by a present-tense verb, the verb will be **المضارع المنصوب**, as in example 1:

١ أرادَ مايكِل أنْ يَنتَقِلَ. *Michael wanted to move.*

- **Error Prevention:** Since the particle **أنْ** is loosely translated into English as the infinitive (as in example 1, "to move"), many students of Arabic make the mistake of using third-person past tense after it. Think of **أنْ** as meaning, quite literally, "that," as in "Michael wanted that he moves."
- Do not confuse **أنْ** (which is always followed by verbs) with **إنَّ** and **أنَّ**, which are used with nouns and pronouns.

أحَبَّ and أعجَبَ fall into the category of verbs that are used to express preference. When these verbs are followed by أنْ, the following verb must be in المضارع المنصوب, just as with أراد. Consider examples 1 and 2:

٢ أُحِبُّ أنْ آكُلَ عَشائي في المَطعَم. *I like to eat my dinner in the restaurant.*

In Arabic this أنْ is known as the أنْ المَصدَريّة because it is equivalent in meaning and is interchangeable with the verbal noun. Thus, أنْ ينتَقِلَ in example 1 may be replaced with the verbal noun الانتِقالَ, while in example two أنْ آكُلَ can be replaced with أكْلَ. In both of these cases, the verbal noun that follows the first verb is definite. Replacing أن آكُلَ with أكْلَ may seem to make أكْلَ indefinite, but أكْلَ is made definite by virtue of being in a definite إضافة structure (= أكْلَ عَشائي).

٣ يُعْجِبُه أنْ يَدرُسَ اللُغَةَ العَرَبِيَّة. *He likes to study Arabic.*

It may prove beneficial if we translate أعجَبَ in our minds literally when we use it so that the English and Arabic sentence structures match. A literal translation of example 3 reads: *[It] pleases him to study Arabic.* If you will notice, this literal translation includes the direct object, which is characteristic of sentences involving أعجَبَ (more on this in the section on the verb أعْجَبَ below).

If we attempt to substitute the مَصدَر for the أنْ المَصدَريّة in example 3, a structural change must occur in that the verb must agree in gender with the مَصدَر. Example 4 illustrates this substitution. Notice that the verbal noun دِراسة is feminine, hence the use of the feminine conjugation تُعْجِبُ.

٤ تُعجِبُه دِراسةُ اللُغةِ العَرَبِيَّة.

Notice that the مَصدَر and the following noun form an إضافة structure in example 4.

### The Verb أعْجَبَ

Note that this verb translates as "to like," but literally it means "to please." This might be a little confusing because in a sentence with أعجب, the agent, or subject, seems to occupy the position of the direct object. Compare these two sentences, which have a similar meaning:

٥ أُحِبُّ الطَعامَ العَرَبيَّ.

٦ يُعْجِبُني الطَعامُ العَرَبيّ.

In example 5, الطعامَ is the direct object of the verb أحبُّ, while الطعامُ is the agent in example 6. This sentence may be rephrased as follows to show its structure:

٧ يُعْجِبُ الطَعامُ العَرَبيُّ (أنا).

Example 7 clearly shows that الطعامُ is the agent, or subject, of the sentence and that the pronoun أنا is the direct object. If we substitute the object أنا with a noun, the case can be indicated, as in example 8:

٨ الطَعامُ العَرَبيُّ يُعْجِبُ الطالِبَ.

> **SUMMARY**
>
> Certain verbs, such as أراد and أحَبَّ, may be followed by a phrase starting with the particle أنْ, which is, in turn, followed by المضارع المنصوب.

## تمرين ١٢

**Translation:** Write two sentences for each of these five items. Use أحَبَّ أنْ for one and يُعْجِبُ + المَصدَر for the other, as in the example.

**Example:** *I like to swim.* أُحِبُّ أنْ أسْبَحَ / تُعْجِبُني السِباحةُ.

1. Rāmī wants to write to all his friends.
2. My friends like going to the beach.
3. Hāla enjoys helping your younger brother with his studies.
4. My sister likes to sleep late.
5. Living in this city pleases me.
6. Rānya likes reading before going to sleep.
7. Hanān wants to travel to Cairo.

## تمرين ١٣

Identify the following items from the main reading passages.

1. Four instances of نِسبة ______________________
2. Two instances of مَصْدر ______________________
3. Two instances of مُضارع منصوب ______________________
4. One instance of مُضارع مجزوم ______________________
5. Two comparative nouns اسم تَفضيل ______________________

### 2. The Noun of Instrument اسْمُ الآلة

There are patterns in Arabic that are used to derive names for instruments. The most common of these are the following patterns listed with examples, three of which (9, 10, 12) you already know:

| | | | |
|---|---|---|---|
| ٩ | مِفعال | مِفْتاح | |
| ١٠ | مِفْعَلة | مِسْطَرة | |
| ١١ | مِفْعَل | مِقَصّ | *scissors* |
| ١٢ | فاعول | حاسوب | |

However, with the need in the modern world to coin words for new devices, other patterns are also used to denote instrument. Six of these patterns are listed with examples from material covered so far in this textbook:

| Example | Pattern |
|---|---|
| هاتِف | فاعِل |
| حاسِبة | فاعِلة |
| مُحَرِّك | مُفعِّل |
| مُسَجِّلة | مُفعِّلة |
| بَرّاد | فَعّال |
| غَسّالة | فَعّالة |

# تمرين ١٤

**Pattern identification**: List the nouns below under their appropriate patterns.

| | | | | | | |
|---|---|---|---|---|---|---|
| مِرحاض | حاسِب | مِبراة | حافِلة | دَرّاجة | بَرّاد | ثلاّجة |
| جَلاّية | هاتِف | شاحِنة | خَلاّط | مِسْطَرة | مِصْباح | حاسِبة |

| فاعِل | فاعِلة | فَعّالة | فَعّال | مِفْعَلة | مِفْعال |
|---|---|---|---|---|---|
| | | | | | |
| | | | | | |
| | | | | | |

## 3. Prepositions حُروف الجَرّ: Relational Concepts

The meaning of a preposition is largely determined by the context in which it occurs. The preposition في, for example, may have several meanings depending on the context and purpose of the sentence, as in the following examples:

| | | |
|---|---|---|
| ١٣ | يَدرُسُ الطِبَّ في جامِعَةِ بِرِنْسْتَن. | *at (signifying a place)* |
| ١٤ | سَأستَقبِلُهُ في الساعةِ الثانِيَةِ. | *at (signifying a time)* |
| ١٥ | نَحنُ في الصَفِّ. | *in (place)* |
| ١٦ | زُرتُهُ في يَومِ الخَميسِ. | *on (time)* |

### A. Two Categories of Prepositions

Prepositions covered thus far fall into two categories: those prefixed to the noun they modify and those that stand independent of it. They include the following, starting with attached prepositions, each listed with an example. Remember that a noun modified by a preposition is in the genitive case مَجرور:

| | | | |
|---|---|---|---|
| (write) with | أَكْتُبُ بِالقَلَمِ. | بِ | ١٧ |
| in (place) | أَسْكُنُ بِبَيْروت. | | ١٨ |
| for ($50) | اِشْتَرَيْتُ الكِتابَ بِخَمْسينَ دولاراً. | | ١٩ |
| by (plane) | وَصَلْنا بِالطائِرة. | | ٢٠ |
| in (Arabic) | تَكَلَّمْتُ بِاللُّغةِ العَرَبيَّةِ. | | ٢١ |
| as (you know) | الأُستاذُ، كَما تَعْلَم، لُبْنانيّ. | كَـ | ٢٢ |
| has | لِساميّة أَرْبَعةُ أَوْلادٍ. | لِـ | ٢٣ |
| to (all of my friends) | كَتَبْتُ لِجَميعِ أَصْدِقائي. | | ٢٤ |
| from (the city of Baghdad) | هِيَ مِنْ مَدينةِ بَغْداد. | مِنْ | ٢٥ |
| to (the library) | ذَهَبْتْ إلى المَكْتَبةِ. | إلى | ٢٦ |
| about (his family) | تَكَلَّمَ عَنْ أُسْرَتِه. | عَنْ | ٢٧ |
| on (the table) | الكِتابُ على الطاوِلةِ. | على | ٢٨ |
| in (his room) [see examples 12–15] | هُوَ في غُرْفَتِه. | في | ٢٩ |
| till (two) | دَرَسْتُ حَتّى الساعةِ الثانيّةِ. | حَتّى | ٣٠ |
| by God (I swear) | وَاللهِ | وَ | ٣١ |
| except (Friday) | نَعْمَلُ كُلَّ يَوْمٍ عَدا يَوْمِ الجُمعة. | عَدا | ٣٢ |

The last example (32) is of عَدا as a preposition. It can, however, have a verbal meaning when used with ما, whereby the following noun is منصوب

٣٣   زارَني أَصْدِقائي ما عَدا واحِداً.

**B. Adverbs and Prepositions of Place**

Some grammarians consider a number of adverbs and nouns as prepositions. These nouns and adverbs describe the relationship between things in terms of location. The pictures below illustrate meanings of some of these items.

في

خَلْفَ

أمامَ

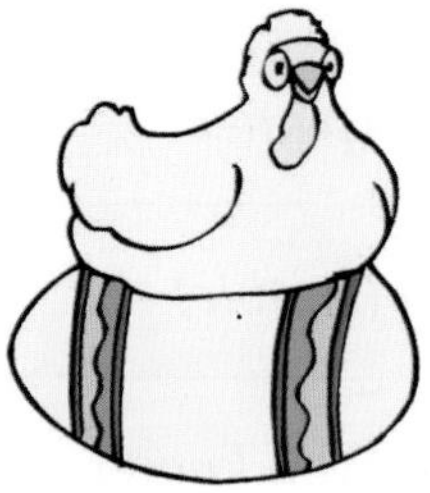
على

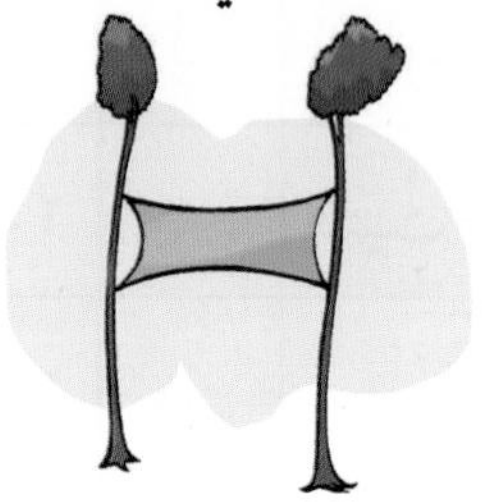
بَيْنَ

فَوْقَ

تَحْتَ

Preposition-like items (also considered adverbs of time and place) that we have learned so far are listed in the chart below. Note that these items are nouns in the accusative case منصوب and that they form an إضافة structure with the modified noun, which is, therefore, genitive مجرور.

| | | | |
|---|---|---|---|
| *at the door* | سَأراكَ عِندَ بابِ المَكتَبة. | عِندَ | ٣٤ |
| *in front of* | هُناكَ شَجَرةٌ أمامَ بابِ داري. | أمامَ | ٣٥ |
| *before the park (place)* | المَخبزُ قَبْلَ الحَديقةِ. | قَبْلَ | ٣٦ |
| *before (time)* | سَأراكَ قَبْلَ المَغرِبِ. | | ٣٧ |
| *after (the station)* | دُكّانُ البَقّالِ بَعدَ المَحَطّةِ. | بَعْدَ | ٣٨ |
| *after (the break)* | سَتَزورُنا بَعدَ العُطلةِ. | | ٣٩ |

| | | | |
|---|---|---|---|
| between | الحَديقةُ بَينَ دارِ جاري ودارِك. | بَيْنَ | ٤٠ |
| behind | هُناكَ مَصرِفٌ خَلْفَ بَيتي. | خَلْفَ | ٤١ |
| by, next to | أُحِبُّ أنْ أجلِسَ جانِبَ الشُبّاكِ. | جانِبَ | ٤٢ |
| by, next to | أُحِبُّ أنْ أجلِسَ بِجانِبِ الشُبّاكِ. | بِجانِبِ | ٤٣ |
| under | هُناكَ مَطعَمٌ تَحْتَ شَقَّتي. | تَحْتَ | ٤٤ |
| over | المِصباحُ فَوْقَ الطاوِلةِ. | فَوْقَ | ٤٥ |
| without | أشرَبُ الشاي دونَ سُكّرٍ. | دونَ | ٤٦ |
| across from | مَحطّةُ القِطارِ مُقابِلَ المَخبَزِ. | مُقابِلَ | ٤٧ |
| at (night) | وَصَلَتِ الطائِرةُ مَعَ اللَيلِ. | مَعَ | ٤٨ |
| with | سَكَنتُ مَعَ طالِبَةٍ لُبنانيّة. | مَعَ | ٤٩ |

## تمرين ١٥

**Ask your neighbor:** Find out who in your class . . .

1. rents an apartment or house
2. lives close to/far from campus
3. lives on the ground floor of their apartment building
4. likes their coffee with/without sugar
5. has a garden in front/back/on the side of their house
6. lives across from a bank

Write your answers down on a separate sheet of paper and be prepared to report them.

## تمرين ١٦

**أكمِلِ الجُمَلَ التاليةَ بِحرفِ الجرِّ المُنفَصِلِ أو الظَرْف المُناسِب.**

| في | إلى | حتّى | مِن | على | مَعَ | عَن |
|---|---|---|---|---|---|---|

١- وَصلَتِ الطائِرةُ ____________ مَوعِدِها.

٢- ذَهَبنا ____________ الجَزائِرِ بِالطائِرة.

٣- وَجدتُ كِتابي ____________ طاوِلَةِ الأستاذ.

٤- سَأدرُسُ في المَكتَبةِ ____________ الساعةِ الرابِعة.

٥- تَسكُنُ أمّي ____________ القُدسِ.

٦- قَرَأنا ____________ الأميرِ عَبدِ القادِرِ الجَزائِريِّ في هذا الكِتابِ.

٧- هذِهِ الأزهارُ ____________ صَديقي.

٨- ذَهَبتُ إلى السينَما ____________ ثَلاثةٍ مِن أصدِقائي.

**أكمِلِ الجُمَلَ التاليةَ بأحَدِ حُروفِ الجَرِّ المُتَّصِلةِ (لَ - بِ - كَ).**

٩- اِشتَرَتْ هالَة هذا الكِتابَ ____________ خمسينَ دولاراً.

١٠- هِيَ، ____________ ما تعلَم، مَغرِبِيَّة.

١١- هَل تَسكُنينَ ____________ هذِهِ الشَقَّة؟

١٢- هَل ____________ك إخوة؟

## تمرين ١٧

**اختَرِ الكَلِمةَ المُناسِبةَ لِتُكمِلَ الجُمَلَ التالية.**

١- هَل شَقّتُك ____________ عِيادةِ الطَبيب؟

☐ إلى ☐ بَيْنَ ☐ فَوْقَ ☐ عِنْدَ

٢- جَلَسْتُ في سَيّارةِ الأجرةِ ____________ السائِق.

☐ خَلْفَ ☐ بَيْنَ ☐ مُقابِل ☐ أمامَ

٣- هَل تَشرَبينَ القَهوةَ ____________ سُكَّر؟

☐ بَعْدَ ☐ قَبْلَ ☐ دونَ ☐ جانِبَ

٤- لَم يَرجِعْ أحمَد إلى المَدرَسةِ ________ الغَداء.

☐ أمامَ ☐ خَلْفَ ☐ تحتَ ☐ بَعْدَ

٥- تَقَعُ بَلَدَتي ________ مَدينَتَينِ كَبيرتَينِ.

☐ مُقابِل ☐ دونَ ☐ بَيْنَ ☐ خَلْفَ

٦- عَلَّقتُ صورةَ أمّي ________ صورةِ أبي.

☐ جانِبَ ☐ عِنْدَ ☐ دونَ ☐ بَعْدَ

٧- هَل هُناكَ مَوقِفُ حافِلةٍ ________ بابِ الشَرِكة؟

☐ خَلْفَ ☐ أمامَ ☐ فَوْقَ ☐ تَحتَ

٨- هُناكَ مَخبَزٌ ________ دُكّانِ البَقّالِ.

☐ بَيْنَ ☐ مُقابِلَ ☐ فَوْقَ ☐ مَعَ

## تمرين ١٨

**Giving directions:** Your Arab friend has just arrived in town and would like to stop by for a visit. Tell your friend when you will get home from **العَمَل**, and what time he/she should stop by. Now, with your partner, work through the following complications, trying to use as many prepositions as you can in this exercise. Use the apartment blueprint to form your answers.

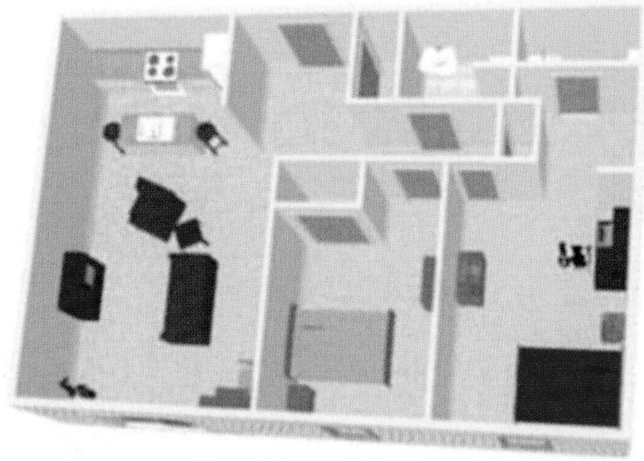

1. You and your friend are in **غُرفة الجُلوس** and he/she needs to use the bathroom to take a shower and brush his/her teeth. Give him/her specific instructions on how to get to the bathroom, what it is next to, in front of, etc.
2. You are in **المَطبَخ** and your friend needs a place to put his/her luggage. Tell him/her where the guest room is and where to put the luggage.
3. Give your friend a tour of your apartment, explaining in detail where everything is located.

## تمرين ١٩

**Short answer:**

**استَمِع إلى النَصِّ الأوَّلِ ثُمَّ أَجِبْ عَنِ الأسئِلة التالية:**

١- لِماذا انْتَقَلَتِ العائِلةُ إلى شَقّةٍ جَديدة؟

٢- لِماذا تُعْجِبُ الشَقَّةُ الجَديدةُ الزَوجة؟

٣- أينَ تَقَعُ الشَقّةُ الجَديدة؟

**اكتُبْ «خَطأ» أو «صَواب» جانِبَ كُلِّ جُمْلَةٍ وصَحِّحِ الجُمَلَ الخَطأ.**

٤- الشَقّةُ القَديمةُ أكبَرُ مِنَ الجَديدة.

٥- تَعمَلُ الزَوجةُ في شَرِكة.

٦- اِشتَرَت الزَوجةُ تِلفازاً.

## تمرين ٢٠

**Listen and select:**

**أكمِلِ الجُمَلَ بِالكَلِماتِ المُناسِبةِ حَسَبَ نَصِّ الاستِماع.**

١- الزَوجةُ والزَوجُ لَهُما ____________ .

☐ وَلَدٌ واحِد ☐ وَلَدانِ ☐ ثَلاثَةُ أولاد ☐ أربَعَةُ أولاد

٢- في الشَقّةِ الجديدةِ ____________ نَوم.

☐ غُرفةُ ☐ غُرفتا ☐ ثَلاثُ غُرَف ☐ أربَعُ غُرَف

٣- الشَقّةُ الجَديدةُ قَريبَةٌ مِن ____________ .

☐ عَمَلِ الزَوج ☐ بَيتِ أسرةِ الزَوجة

☐ بَيتِ أسرةِ الزَوج ☐ الجامِعة

٤- سَوفَ تَشتَري هذِهِ العائِلةُ ____________ .

☐ غَسّالةً ☐ بَرّاداً ☐ جَلاّيةً ☐ أريكةً

٥- الشَقّةُ الجَديدةُ مَوجودةٌ في الطابَقِ ____________ .

☐ الأوَّل ☐ الثاني ☐ الثالِث ☐ الرابع

## تمرين ٢١

**Speaking**: Working in groups of two, one person gives to the other directions to his/her place of residence from the classroom. The person listening is to draw a map based on what he/she understands from the directions without letting the speaker see the map. The person listening is allowed to ask questions if something is vague. Once you have completed the exercise, the listener is to show the speaker the map and then compare it to "reality." Switch roles once you are through.

## تمرين ٢٢

AUDIO

استَمِعْ إلى النَصِّ الثاني ثُمَّ اكتُبْ أسماءَ الشوارِعِ والأماكِنِ على المُخَطَّطِ حَسَبَ النَصِّ.

Fill out this map according to the second listening passage:

## تمرين ٢٣

VIDEO

**تَمرينُ المُشاهَدة: شاهِدوا الدَرْسَ الثامن عَشَر على القُرْص الرَقْميّ واكتبوا ما يقولون.**

سامر: تَفَضَّل. هُنا أرْضُ الديار ____________ فيها بَحْرةٌ وشَجَرةُ النارنج وفي ____________ العُلْوي ____________ غُرفةُ ____________ أبي وأمّي وتِلكَ غُرفةُ ____________ هَنادي، وهذِه غُرفةٌ ____________ فَقَط، هذا هوَ ____________ ____________ فيهِ ____________ ____________ ومايكرويف و____________ و____________ وطاولةُ طَعام نَجتَمِعُ حَوْلَها وهو **مُشتَرَكٌ** ____________ ستيف أيضاً وهذِه الغُرفَةُ هيَ غُرفةُ ____________ ____________ فيها ____________ كَبيرةٌ وتِلفازٌ وطاوِلةٌ في وَسَطِ الغُرفة.

هذِه غُرفتي وهذِه غُرفةُ ستيف تعالَ لأُريكَ إياها هذِه غُرفةُ ستيف فيها سَريرٌ و____________ أدراجٍ وفَوْقَها ____________ وبِجانِبِها كُرسيٌ مِن الخَشَبِ وطاوِلةٌ ____________ و____________ كَبيرةٌ وقُرْبَ الغُرفةِ ____________ ____________ خاصٌّ بِستيف ____________ فيه سَخّان للماءِ ودُوش و____________ مع ____________.

## المُفْرَدات

Listen to the vocabulary items on the CD and practice their pronunciation.

أثاث (n., m.) . . . . . furniture

اِجْتَمَعَ (يَجْتَمِع) اِجْتِماع (v.) . . . . . to meet; to gather

أَجَّر (يؤجِّر) تأجير (v.) . . . . . to lease, to let

أُجْرة ج أُجور (n., f.) . . . . . rent, wage, fare

آخَر ج آخَرون (n., m.) . . . . . other

أرض ج أراضٍ (n., f.) . . . . . ground, land.

أريكة ج أرائِك (n., f.) . . . . . couch.

استأجَرَ (يَستأجِرُ) استِئجار (v.) . . . . . to rent, to hire.

اِستَخدَمَ (يَستَخدِمُ) اِستِخدام (v.) . . . . . to use, to utilize, to employ

أَعْجَبَ (يُعْجِبُ) إعْجاب (v.) . . . . . to please

إعْلان ج إعْلانات (n., m.) . . . . . advertisement

أمامَ (prep.) . . . . . in front of

أنْ (particle) . . . . . to (infinitive)

أوروبا (n., f.) . . . . . Europe

إيجار ج إيجارات (n. m.) . . . . . rent

باعَ (يَبيعُ) بَيْع (v.) . . . . . to sell.

بَرّاد ج بَرّادات (n., m.) . . . . . refrigerator (Syria)

بَعيد (adv.) . . . . . far.

بَقّال ج بَقّالون (n., m.) . . . . . grocer

بَلَديّ (adj.) . . . . . local, popular

بَنْك ج بُنوك (n., m.) . . . . . bank (colloquial)

تَأخَّرَ (يَتأخَّرُ) تَأخُّر (v.) . . . . . to be late

تأمين ج تأمينات (n., m.) . . . . . insurance

telephone (colloquial) . . . . . . . . . . . تَليفون ج تَليفونات (n., m.)

refrigerator (Egypt) . . . . . . . . . . . . . ثَلاّجة ج ثَلاّجات (n., f.)

part . . . . . . . . . . . . . . . . . . . . جُزْء ج أَجْزاء (n., m.)

dishwasher . . . . . . . . . . . . . . . . . جَلاّية ج جَلاّيات (n., f.)

[Egyptian] pound . . . . . . . . . . . . . . جُنَيه ج جُنَيْهات (n., m.)

park, garden . . . . . . . . . . . . . . . . حَديقة ج حَدائِق (n., f.)

[bath] tub . . . . . . . . . . . . . . . . . حَوْض ج أَحْواض (n., m.)

servant . . . . . . . . . . . . . . . . . . . خادِم ج خَدَم (n., m.)

baker . . . . . . . . . . . . . . . . . . . . خَبّاز ج خَبّازون (n., m.)

closet, cupboard . . . . . . . . . . . . . . خِزانة ج خَزائِن / خِزانات (n., f.)

wood, lumber, timber . . . . . . . . . . . . خَشَب ج أَخْشاب (n., m.).

greengrocer . . . . . . . . . . . . . . . . . خُضَريّ ج خُضَريّون (n. m.)

behind . . . . . . . . . . . . . . . . . . . . خَلْفَ (prep.)

shop, store . . . . . . . . . . . . . . . . . دُكّان ج دَكاكين (n., f.)

dinar (currency in Algeria, Bahrain, Iraq, Kuwait) . . . . . . . . . . دينار ج دَنانير (n., m.)

water heater . . . . . . . . . . . . . . . . سَخّان لِلماء

truck . . . . . . . . . . . . . . . . . . . . شاحِنة ج شاحِنات (n. f.)

company . . . . . . . . . . . . . . . . . . . شَرِكة ج شَرِكات (n., f.)

health . . . . . . . . . . . . . . . . . . . . صِحّة (n.)

floor, storey, flat . . . . . . . . . . . . . . طابَق ج طَوابِق (n., m.)

in general, generally . . . . . . . . . . . . على العُموم

to hang . . . . . . . . . . . . . . . . . . . عَلَّقَ (يُعَلِّقُ) تَعْليق (v.)

doctor's practice, clinic . . . . . . . . . . . عِيادة ج عِيادات (n., f.)

bread (Egypt) . . . . . . . . . . . . . . . . عَيش (n., m.)

[butane] gas . . . . . . . . . . . . . . . . غاز ج غازات (n., m.)

washing machine . . . . . . . . . . . . . . . غَسّالة ج غَسّالات (n., f.)

deluxe, fancy, excellent, luxurious . . . . . . . . . . . . فاخِر (adj.)

[Syrian] pound; lira. . . . . . . . . . . . . . . . . لَيْرة ج لَيْرات (n., f.)

meter. . . . . . . . . . . . . . . . . . . . . . م (مِتْر) ج أمْتار (n., m.)

metro. . . . . . . . . . . . . . . . . . . . . . . . . . . . . مِترو (n., m.)

kitchen sink . . . . . . . . . . . . . . . . . . . . مَجْلى ج مَجالٍ (n., m.)

bakery . . . . . . . . . . . . . . . . . . . . . . . . مَخْبَز ج مَخابِز (n., m.)

[floor] plan, map . . . . . . . . . . . . . . . . . مُخَطَّط ج مُخَطّطات (n., m.)

mirror . . . . . . . . . . . . . . . . . . . . . . . . . . مِرْآة ج مَرايا (n., f.)

toilet . . . . . . . . . . . . . . . . . . . . . . . . مِرْحاض ج مَراحيض (n., m.)

elevated . . . . . . . . . . . . . . . . . . . . . . . . . مُرْتَفِع (active participle)

comfortable . . . . . . . . . . . . . . . . . . . . . . . . . . . . مُريح (adj.)

lamp . . . . . . . . . . . . . . . . . . . . . . . . . . مِصْباح ج مَصابيح (n., m.)

bank . . . . . . . . . . . . . . . . . . . . . . . . . . مَصْرِف ج مَصارِف (n., m.)

overlooking . . . . . . . . . . . . . . . . . . . . . . . . . . مُطِلٌّ (verbal noun)

washbasin, bathroom sink. . . . . . . . . . . . مَغْسَلة ج مَغاسِل (n., f.)

opposite, across from. . . . . . . . . . . . . . . . . . . . . . . مُقابِل (adv.)

clothes . . . . . . . . . . . . . . . . . . . . . . . . مَلبَس ج مَلابِس(n., m.)

[cooking] range . . . . . . . . . . . . . . . . . . . . . . مَوْقِد ج مَواقِد (n., m.)

[bus] stop, parking lot . . . . . . . . . . . . . . . مَوْقِف ج مَواقِف (n., m.)

spacious, large. . . . . . . . . . . . . . . . . . . . . . . . . . . . واسِع (adj.)

there is/are, to exist. . . . . . . . . . . . . . . . . وُجِدَ (يوجَدُ) (passive of وَجَد)

to put. . . . . . . . . . . . . . . . . . . . . . . . . . . وَضَعَ (يَضَعُ) وَضْع (v.)

to be located; fall down. . . . . . . . . . . . . . . . وَقَعَ (يَقَعُ) وُقوع / وَقْع (v.)

left . . . . . . . . . . . . . . . . . . . . . . . . . . . . . . . . . . . . يَسار (n., m.)

right . . . . . . . . . . . . . . . . . . . . . . . . . . . . . . . . . . يَمين (n., m.)

# الدَرسُ التاسِعَ عَشَر

## Objectives

- Describing activities in the past and present
- Writing postcards and letters
- Using terms of address in written communication
- Introduction to adverbs of time and place
- Negating future time
- Learning how to use relative nouns such as الَّذي والَّتي
- Revisiting prepositions
- Introduction to the possessive إضافة

## المُفرداتُ الجَديدةُ في صُوَرٍ عَديدةٍ:

رَكِبَ (يَرْكَبُ) رُكوب

سألَ (يسألُ) سُؤال

اِلتَقَطَ (يَلْتَقِطُ) اِلْتِقاط

اِمْتَحَنَ (يَمْتَحِنُ) اِمْتِحان

حَيوان ج حَيوانات

خِزانةُ مَلابِس

تَذْكَرتان

## رُكنُ المُفْرَداتِ الجَديدةِ:

| | |
|---|---|
| to answer | أجابَ (يُجيبُ) إجابة |
| to be able | اِسْتَطاعَ (يَسْتَطِيعُ) اِسْتِطاعة |
| to enjoy | اِسْتَمْتَعَ (يَسْتَمْتِعُ) اِسْتِمْتاع (بِـ) |
| to meet | اِلْتَقَى (يَلْتَقي) اِلْتِقاء (بِـ) |
| to eat, take | تَناوَلَ (يَتَناوَل) تَناوُل |
| like, similar to | مِثْلُ ج أمْثال |
| to pass by | مَرَّ (يَمُرُّ) مُرور |
| place | مَكان ج أماكِن |
| since | مُنْذُ |
| مُهِمّ | هامّ |
| أب | والِد |

## تمرين ١

**Odd word out:** اختَرِ الكَلِمةَ الّتي لا تُناسِب باقي الكَلِماتِ في كُلِّ مَجْموعةٍ وبَيِّنِ السَبَب.

| | | | | | |
|---|---|---|---|---|---|
| ١- | قِطار | سَيّارة | حَديقَة | قارِب | طائِرة |
| ٢- | شَلاّل | نَهر | بُحَيرة | مَبنى | ماء |
| ٣- | طَيِّب | دافِئ | حارّ | بارِد | مُعتَدِل |
| ٤- | اِستَحَمَّ | أعجَبَ | أحَبَّ | اِستَمتَعَ | هوِيَ |
| ٥- | دِراسة | اِمتِحان | مَحَطّة | سُؤال | مَدرَسة |

# تمرين ٢

**وافِقْ بَيْنَ الكَلِماتِ في العَمودَين.** **Matching:**

| | | | |
|---|---|---|---|
| ١ | شاهَدَ | | أحَبَّ |
| ٢ | مَشى | | شَلاّل |
| ٣ | بِنايَة | | رَأى |
| ٤ | طَريق | | مَيْدان |
| ٥ | ساحَة | | دُكّان |
| ٦ | دافِئ | | سارَ |
| ٧ | طَيِّب | | حَتّى |
| ٨ | أَعْجَبَ | | شارِع |
| ٩ | مَحَلٌّ تِجاريّ | | مَبنى |
| ١٠ | إلى أنْ | | جَيِّد |
| | | | حارّ |

# تمرين ٣

**أكمِلِ الجُمَلَ التالِيَةَ بِأفضَلِ كَلِمَةٍ مُناسِبَة:** **Select the best choice:**

١- ___________ أخي سَيّارةً حينَ زارَ سان فرانسيسكو.

☐ اِسْتَأْجَرَ ☐ اِسْتَقبَلَ ☐ اِسْتَمتَعَ

٢- أريدُ أنْ أزورَ مَدينَةَ المَلاهي ___________ تَبدأَ الدِراسة.

☐ مَعَ أنَّ ☐ إلى أنْ ☐ قَبلَ أنْ

٣- تَقَعُ شَقَّتي ___________ مَحَطّةِ القِطار.

☐ قُرْبَ ☐ شَمالاً ☐ أطوَلَ

٤- ___________ عَشَراتِ الصُوَرِ في حَديقَةِ الحَيَوانات.

☐ اِنتَقَلتُ ☐ اِلتَقَطتُ ☐ اِحتَفَلتُ

٥- هَل ________ الغَداءَ.

☐ شاهَدتُم ☐ زُرتُم ☐ تناوَلتُم

٦- ________ نَهرَ النيلِ أطوَلُ نَهرٍ في العالَم.

☐ لَنْ ☐ إنَّ ☐ أنْ

٧- ________ تُشاهِدْ أختي فيلمَ «عيدِ الاستِقلال» حَتّى الآن.

☐ لَم ☐ لَن ☐ أنْ

٨- تَناوَلْتُ ________ عَرَبيّاً في مَطعَمٍ مَرّاكِشيّ.

☐ طَعاماً ☐ موسيقا ☐ فِرقَةً

٩- ________ الفيلمُ التِلفزيوني في الساعةِ الحادِيَةَ عَشْرَةَ.

☐ أعجَبَ ☐ اِلتَقَطَ ☐ اِنتَهى

١٠- ________ أدرُسَ الرِياضيّاتِ في الفَصلِ المُقبِل.

☐ لَم ☐ لَنْ ☐ لا

## مايكِل براون في القاهِرَةِ والإسكَندَريَّة

**القاهِرةَ، الجُمْعَة ١٣ سِبتَمبر ٢٠٠٦**

أكتُبُ هذِهِ اليَوميّاتِ كَجُزءٍ مِن دَرسِ اللُغَةِ العَرَبيَّةِ، وأنا أَستَمْتِعُ بِكِتابَتِها كَثيراً. وَصَلتُ إلى القاهِرةِ مُنذُ أسابيعَ وأعجَبَتْني هذِهِ المَدينةُ مَعَ أَنَّها مَدينةٌ كَبيرةٌ جِدّاً فيها أَكثَرُ مِن ١٤ مِليون نَسَمة. بَعدَ وُصولي إلى القاهِرةِ بِمُدّةٍ قَصيرةٍ ذَهَبتُ مَعَ أصدِقائي إلى «الجيزة» قُرْبَ القاهِرةِ لِمُشاهَدةِ الأهْراماتِ، والأهراماتُ مَبانٍ عَظيمةٌ بَناها الفَراعِنةُ مُنذُ آلافِ السِنين. اِلتَقَطتُ صُوَراً كَثيرةً بِآلةِ تَصويري الجَديدة. ورَكِبتُ هُناكَ على الجَمَل. لَم أرَ جِمالاً إلاّ عِندَ الأهراماتِ وفي حَديقةِ الحَيَواناتِ الّتي زُرتُها في عُطلةِ عيدِ الأضحى. شاهَدتُ هُناكَ عَدَداً كَبيراً مِن الحَيَواناتِ مِن كُلِّ بِلادِ العالَم.

آلةُ تَصوير

جَمَل

القاهِرة، السَبت ٢١/٩/٢٠٠٦

شاطئ البحر

سافَرْتُ أَوَّلَ أَمسِ الخَميسِ إلى الإسكَندَريّةِ بالقِطارِ مَعَ بَعضِ الأَصْدِقاء. الإسكَندَريّة ميناءٌ هامٌّ على البَحرِ الأَبْيَضِ المُتَوَسِّطِ وهِيَ أَقدَمُ مِن القاهِرةِ بِمِئاتِ السِنين. أَخَذنا القِطارَ مِن مَحَطّةِ رَمْسيس في مَيْدانِ رَمْسيس في الساعةِ الثامِنةِ والنِصْفِ صَباحاً. اِشْتَرَيتُ تَذكَرةً ذَهاباً وإياباً بِعِشرينَ جُنَيهاً. مَرَرْنا في الطَريقِ إلى الإسكَندَريّةِ بِمَدينةِ طَنطا ثالِثِ أَكبَرِ مُدُنِ مِصرَ. وَصَلنا إلى الإسكَندَريّةِ بَعدَ الظُّهرِ. ذَهَبنا أَوَّلاً إلى مَطعمٍ قَريبٍ مِنَ الشاطِئِ حَيثُ تَناوَلْنا طَعاماً مِصرِيّاً وشَرِبنا القَهوةَ.

الكورنيش

مَشَينا قَليلاً في شارِعٍ طَويلٍ وجَميلٍ بِجانِبِ الشاطِئِ يُسَمّى «الكورنيش» ثُمَّ نَزَلنا إلى الشاطِئِ وسَبَحنا ساعَتَينِ أَو ثَلاث. كانَ الطَقسُ دافِئاً وجَميلاً والشَمسُ ساطِعةٌ. نَزَلنا تِلكَ اللَيلةَ في فُندُقٍ صَغيرٍ لكِنَّهُ نَظيف. وفي اليَومِ التالي ذَهَبنا إلى الشاطِئِ مَرَّةً ثانِيّةً، ثُمَّ رَكِبنا القِطارَ ورَجَعنا إلى القاهِرةِ مَساءً. لَمْ أَنسَ أَنْ أَكتُبَ بِطاقةً بَريدِيّةً لأِستاذَتي. أَعْجَبَتْني الإسكَندَريّةُ كَثيراً واسْتَمتَعتُ بِهذِهِ الزيارةِ بِسَبَبِ المَناظِرِ الجَميلةِ ولأِنَّ الإسكَندَرانيّينَ طَيِّبونَ ويُحِبّونَ أَنْ يُساعِدوا الناسَ الآخَرين.

قارِبٌ في البَحرِ المُتوَسِّط

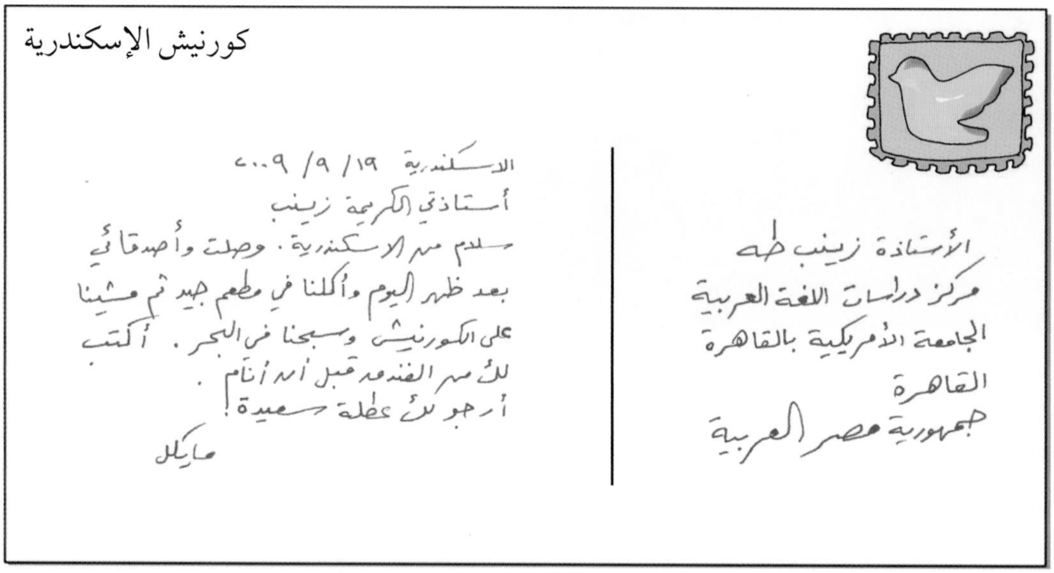

كورنيش الإسكندرية

الإسكندرية ١٩/ ٩/ ٢٠٠٩

أستاذتي الكريمة زينب

سلام من الإسكندرية. وصلت وأصدقائي بعد ظهر اليوم وأكلنا في مطعم جيد ثم مشينا على الكورنيش وسبحنا في البحر. أكتب لك من الفندق قبل أن أنام.

أرجو لك عطلة سعيدة!

مايكل

الأستاذة زينب طه

مركز دراسات اللغة العربية

الجامعة الأمريكية بالقاهرة

القاهرة

جمهورية مصر العربية

See Appendix E for typed version of postcard.

**القاهِرة، الجُمعة ٢٢ نوفَمبر ٢٠٠٦**

إنَّ الشَيءَ الَّذي أعْجَبَني في القاهِرةِ كَثيراً هو السَماءُ الزَرقاءُ ونَهرُ النيلِ العَظيمِ الَّذي يَبدَأُ مِن وَسَطِ أفريقيا في« بُروندي ». يَسيرُ النيلُ شَمالاً إلى الخُرطومِ عاصِمةِ السودانِ حَيثُ يَلتَقي نَهرا النيلِ الأبيَضِ والنيلِ الأزرَق، ومِن هُناكَ يَسيرُ النيلُ شَمالاً إلى القاهِرةِ ثُمَّ إلى البَحرِ الأبيَضِ المُتَوَسِّط. نَهرُ النيلِ أطوَلُ نَهرٍ في العالَم، وطولُهُ ٦٦٩٥ كيلومِتراً، لِذلِكَ فَهُوَ أطوَل مِن نَهرِ أوهايو ونَهرِ الميسيسيبي.

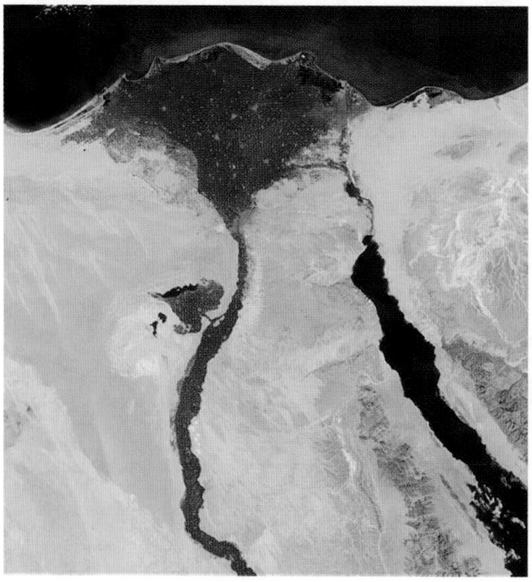

نَهرُ النيل

**القاهِرة، السَبت ٢١ ديسمبر ٢٠٠٦**

**المُتْحَف المِصريّ**

في كُلِّ عُطلةِ نِهايةِ أسبوعٍ أزورُ مَكاناً جَديداً. ذَهَبتُ صَباحَ أمسِ إلى المُتْحَفِ المِصريّ ووَجَدتُ فيهِ عَدَداً كَبيراً مِنَ الآثارِ الفِرعَونيَّةِ القَديمةِ وكَذلِكَ آثاراً إسلامِيَّةً وعَرَبيَّة. إنّه مُتْحَفٌ جَيِّدٌ جِدّاً وسَأزورُهُ مَرّةً ثانيَةً إنْ شاءَ الله. اِشتَريتُ مِنَ المُتْحَفِ بَعضَ الصُوَرِ وكِتاباً عَن آثارِ مِصر. ومِن هُناكَ ذَهَبتُ إلى مَسجِدِ مُحَمَّد عَليّ والتَقَطتُ بَعضَ الصُوَر. في الأسبوعِ المُقبِلِ سَوفَ أزورُ بَعضَ المَساجِدِ القَديمةِ في القاهِرة، لكِنّي لَنْ أسافِرَ إلى مُدُنٍ أخرى في ذَلِكَ الأسبوع.

## عَدنان مارتيني في نيويورك وكَنَدا وفَلوريدا

**كَلَمبَس، الأربعاء ٢٨ آب ٢٠٠٦**

أخَذتُ أمسِ آخِرَ امتِحانٍ في هذا الفَصلِ الدِراسيِّ وكانَ في مادّةِ الرِياضِيّات. أظُنُّ أنّي أجَبْتُ عَنِ الأسئِلَةِ جَيِّداً، وأنا سَعيدٌ أنَّ الدِراسةَ انتَهَت. أسْتَطيعُ الآنَ أنْ أسافِرَ لِزيارةِ الأماكِنِ الجَميلةِ في الوِلاياتِ المُتَّحِدةِ وكَنَدا الَّتي أريدُ زِيارتَها.

اِشْتَرَيتُ في الشَهرِ الماضي تَذْكَرَةَ طائِرةٍ إلى نيويورك ذَهاباً وإياباً بِمِئَتَيْنِ وثلاثينَ دولاراً. أرَدْتُ زيارةَ نيويورك مُنذُ أشهُرٍ فَأنا لا أعرِفُها، مَعَ أنَّ لي صَديقاً يَسكُنُ هُناكَ ويَدرُسُ الهَندَسةَ الصِناعِيَّةَ في جامِعةِ نيويورك. سَوفَ يَستَقبِلُني غَسّان في المَطار. لَن أنزِلَ في فُندُقٍ، بَل في شَقَّةِ غَسّان.

**نيويورك، السَبت ٣١ آب ٢٠٠٦**

وَصَلَتْ طائِرتي إلى مَطارِ «لاغوارديا» في مَوعِدِها وكانَ غَسّان أمامَ البَوّابةِ وأخذَني إلى شَقَّتِه حَيثُ وَضَعتُ حَقيبَتي وأشيائي. مَشَينا في الشَوارِعِ حَتّى وَصَلنا إلى ساحَةٍ مَشهورةٍ تُسَمّى «تايمز سكوير». ثُمَّ زُرْنا بَعدَ ذلِكَ مَحَلاّتٍ تِجارِيّةٍ مِثلَ «ساكْس فيفث أفِنيو » و«ماسيز»، لكِنَّنا لَم نَشتَرِ أيَّ شَيءٍ.

مَشَينا في الشارِعِ الخامِسِ لِزيارةِ مَبْنى «إمبايَر ستيت» الَّذي يَقَعُ بَينَ الشارِعِ الثالِثِ والثَلاثينَ والشارِعِ الرابِعِ والثَلاثين والَّذي بُنِيَ مُنذُ أكثَرَ مِن ثَمانيةٍ وسَبعينَ عاماً. أخَذنا المِصْعَدَ إلى الطابَقِ

١٠٢ وشاهَدْنا مَدينةَ نيويورك مِن فَوق. كانَ هذا المَبْنى أطولَ مَبنىً في العالَمِ إلى أنْ بُنِيَ مَبنى «سِيَرز» في شيكاغو وغيره في كولا لامبور ودُبَي.

شلاّلات

بَعدَ ذلِكَ تَناوَلنا طَعامَ العَشاءِ في مَطعَمٍ فَرَنسيٍّ جَيِّدٍ قَريبٍ مِن مَسْرَحِ «راديو سيتي». كانَ الطَعامُ جَيِّداً لكِنَّهُ كانَ غالياً جِدّاً. شاهَدنا فيلماً في راديو سيتي. لَن أستَطيعَ أن أزورَ جامِعةَ نيويورك غَداً لأنّنا سَنُسافِرُ بِالقِطارِ صَباحاً إلى شَلاّلاتِ نَياغَرا.

**شَلاّلاتُ نَياغَرا، الإثنين ٢ أيلول ٢٠٠٦**

وَصَلنا أمسِ ظُهراً إلى الشَلاّلاتِ الّتي يَقَعُ جُزءٌ مِنها في الوِلاياتِ المُتَّحِدَةِ والجُزءُ الآخَرُ في كَندا. ذَهَبنا أوَّلاً إلى الجانِبِ الكَنَديّ، وقالَ غَسّانُ إنَّ الشَلاّلاتَ على الجانِبِ الكَنَديِّ أجْمَل. لَم أرَ أعْظَمَ مِن هذِهِ الشَلاّلاتِ مِن قَبل. أعْجَبَتْني الحَدائِقُ والأزهارُ الجَميلةُ في الجانِبِ الكَنَديّ.

تِمثالُ الحُريَّة

في اليَومِ التالي ذَهَبنا إلى الجانِبِ الأمريكيِّ ورَكِبنا قارِباً مَعَ ناسٍ آخَرينَ سارَ بِنا تَحتُ الشَلاّلات. كانَ مَنظَرُ الشَلاّلاتِ مِن تَحت عَظيماً جِدّاً، والتَقَطتُ صُوَراً كَثيرةً مِنَ القارِب.

سَنَرجِعُ غَداً إلى نيويورك حَيثُ سأزورُ تِمثالَ الحُريَةِ و«ستاتن آيلاند». شاهَدتُ صُوَرَ التِمثالِ في المَجلاّتِ والأفلامِ وقَرَأتُ عَنهُ كَثيراً مُنذُ كُنتُ صَغيراً، لكِنّي لَمْ أرَهُ إلى الآن.

القِمار

سَنُسافِرُ أنا وغَسّان إلى «أتلانتِك سيتي» لِيَومٍ واحِدٍ فَقَط بِالقِطارِ، وهذِهِ المَدينةُ مِثلُ مَدينةِ «لاس فيغاس» فيها أماكِنُ كَثيرةٌ لِلقِمارِ بأنواعِه. بَعدَ ذلِكَ سَأسافِرُ وَحدي إلى فَلوريدا بِالطائِرةِ لِزيارةِ «ديزني وُرلد» في «أورلاندو».

**أورلاندو، السَبت ٧ أيلول ٢٠٠٦**

وَصَلتُ إلى هُنا أَوَّلَ أمسِ بَعدَ الظُهرِ. نَزَلتُ في فُندُقِ «رامادا» وهُوَ قَريبٌ مِن«ديزني وُرلد». في ذلِكَ المَساءِ ذَهَبتُ إلى العَشاءِ في مَطعَمٍ يُقَدِّمُ أطعِمَةً مِن الغَربِ الأمريكيّ. لَم يُعجِبْني الطَعامُ أبَداً.

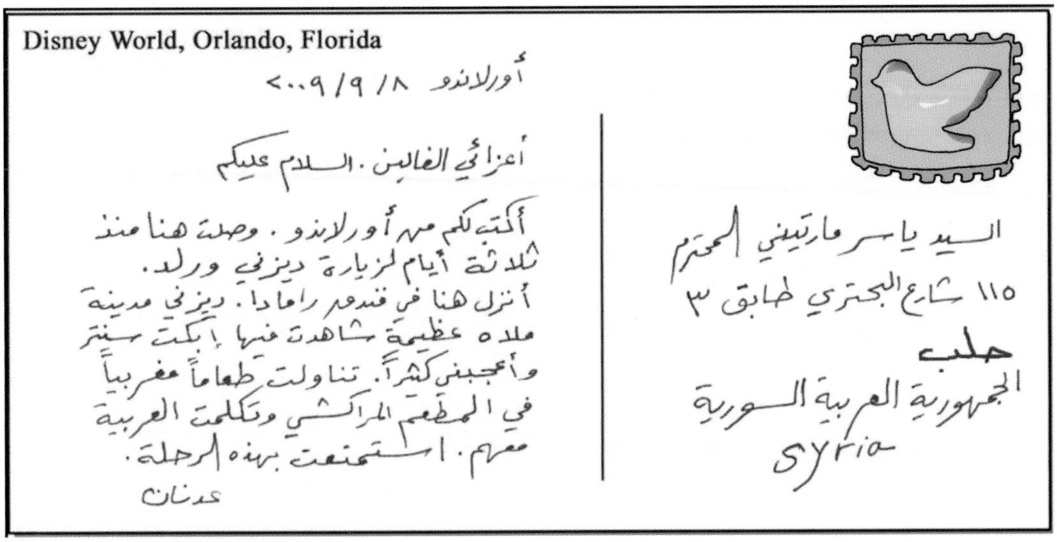


See Appendix E for typed version of postcard.

في صَباحِ اليَومِ التالي ذَهَبتُ مِنَ الفُندُقِ مَعَ بَعضِ الناسِ الآخَرينَ في حافِلَةٍ صَغيرةٍ إلى ديزني وُرلد، وهِيَ مَدينةُ مَلاهٍ واسِعةٌ جِدّاً فيها عَدَدٌ كَبيرٌ مِن العُروضِ والألعابِ والمَطاعِمِ والمَحلاّتِ التِجاريّةِ مِن كُلِّ بَلَدٍ في العالَم. أعْجَبَني «إبكَت سِنتَر» كَثيراً وكَذلِكَ «ماجك كِنغدَم». لَم أرَ كُلَّ شَيءٍ في اليَومِ الأوَّلِ، لِذلِكَ رَجَعتُ في اليَومِ التالي وشاهَدتُ الأشياءَ الّتي لَم أشاهِدْها وزُرتُ «إبكَتْ» مَرَّةً ثانِيَة. تَناوَلتُ العَشاءَ مَساءً في ديزني وُرلد في المَطعَمِ المَرّاكِشيّ الّذي يُقَدِّمُ أطعِمةً مَغرِبيّة. أعجَبَني المَطعَمُ والموسيقا العَرَبيّة الّتي قَدَّمَتْها فِرقةٌ مَغرِبيّة. لَم يَكُنِ الطَعامُ غالياً.

## رِسالةُ عَدنانَ إلى صَديقِهِ مازِن

كلمبس في ١٢ أيلول ٢٠٠٩

أخي العزيز مازن، سلام حار لك من كلمبس.

كيف حالك يا أخي؟ لم تصلني منك أية رسالة منذ مدة طويلة. كتبت لك رسالة في شهر آذار الماضي ولم يصلني منك أي شيء لذلك ظننت أنك انتقلت من عنوانك القديم في حلب. علمت من مروان بعد ذلك أنك انتقلت إلى جامعة دمشق وهو الذي أعطاني عنوانك الجديد. هل يعجبك السكن والدراسة في دمشق؟

أنا كما تعلم أدرس علم الحاسوب في جامعة ولاية أوهايو. بعد أيام سيبدأ العام الدراسي الجديد، وهذه هي سنتي الثانية هنا. أنا سعيد في كلمبس وأستمتع بالسكن فيها وبالدراسة كذلك.

في الأسابيع الثلاثة الماضية زرت مدينة نيويورك وأتلانتك سيتي وشلالات نياغرا في كندا وكذلك «ديزني ورلد» وهي مدينة ملاهٍ كبيرة جداً في مدينة أورلاندو في فلوريدا. استمتعت بهذه الزيارات كثيراً. أرجو أن أزور ولاية كاليفورنيا في السنة المقبلة إن شاء الله ولاس فيغاس أيضاً.

أرجو أن تكتب لي عنك وعن دراستك. لك مني أطيب السلام وإلى لقاء قريب في حلب.

أخوك المخلص
عدنان

See Appendix E for typed version of letter.

## تمرين ٤

**اسألوا زملاءكم:**

١- لِماذا أو لِماذا لا تُحِبّ(ينَ) زيارةَ شَلاّلات نياغراً؟

٢- أيّ مكانٍ في العالَم تُريد(ين) الذَهاب إليه؟

٣- بِأيّ نوعٍ من الموسيقا تَسْتَمْتِع(ينَ) ومتى تَستَمِع(ينَ) إليه؟

٤- متى تَلتَقِط(ينَ) صوراً وماذا تُحِب(ينَ) أنْ تُصَوِّر(ي)؟

٥- ماذا يُعْجِبُك أن تَفعَل(ي) في عُطْلَة نِهاية الأسْبوع ؟

## تمرين ٥

**أجِب عَن هذِهِ الأسئِلَةِ حَسَبَ النَصِّ:**

١- مَتى زارَ مايكِل الأهراماتِ وفي أيِّ مَكانٍ تَقَعُ؟

٢- ماذا يُعجِبُ مايكِل في القاهِرةِ؟

٣- مِن أينَ اِشترى مايكِل كِتاباً عَن آثارِ مِصرَ؟

٤- ما اسمُ المَحطَّةِ الَّتي سافَرَ مِنها مايكِل إلى الإسكَندَريّة؟

٥- لِماذا أعجَبَتِ الإسكَندَريَّة مايكِل؟

٦- مَتى كَتَبَ مايكِل البِطاقَةَ البَريديّةَ لأستاذَتِهِ؟

٧- في أيِّ يومٍ أخَذَ عَدنان امتِحانَ الرِياضِيّاتِ؟

٨- أينَ تَناوَلَ عَدنان طَعامَ العَشاءِ في نيويورك ومَعَ مَن؟

٩- في أيِّ يَومٍ زارَ عَدنان تِمثالَ الحُرِيَّة؟

١٠- مَعَ مَن سافَرَ عَدنان إلى أورلاندو؟

١١- أينَ تَكَلَّمَ عَدنان العَرَبيّةَ في أورلاندو؟

١٢- أينَ يَدرُسُ مازِن الآن؟

## تمرين ٦

AUDIO

**اختَر التَكْمِلةَ المُناسِبةَ حَسَبَ النَص.** **Listen and select:**

١- يَومِيّاتُ مايكِل جُزءٌ مِن ____________.

☐ رَسائلِهِ ☐ دِراستِهِ ☐ زيارتِهِ

٢- رَأى مايكِل الجَملَ في ____________.

☐ حَديقَةِ الحَيَواناتِ ☐ كُلِّ مَكانٍ ☐ شَوارِعِ القاهِرةِ

٣- الإسكَنْدَريّة ____________.

☐ مَدينةٌ حَديثةٌ ☐ أقدَمُ مَدينةٍ ☐ ميناءٌ هامّ

٤- الناسُ في الإسكَندَريّةِ ____________.

☐ جَميلونَ ☐ يُحِبّونَ ☐ طَيِّبونَ

٥- يلتَقي النيلانُ الأبيَضُ والأزرَقُ في ____________ .

☐ الخُرطوم ☐ القاهِرَةِ ☐ الإسكَندَريَّةِ

٦- عَدنان سَعيدٌ لأنّ ____________ .

☐ الفَصلَ الدِراسيِّ الجَديدَ بَدَأَ ☐ الدِراسَةَ انتَهَتْ

☐ تذكِرة الطائرة بمئتين وثلاثين دولاراً

٧- نَزَلَ عَدنان في نيويورك في ____________ .

☐ فُندُقِ رَمادا ☐ إمبايَر ستيت ☐ شَقّةِ صَديقِهِ

٨- بُنِيت «إمباير ستيت» مُنذُ أكثَرِ مِن ____________ عاماً.

☐ ٥٥ ☐ ٧٨ ☐ ٩٥

٩- كانَ الطَعامُ في المَطعَمِ الفِرَنسيِّ ____________ .

☐ غالِياً ☐ طَويلاً ☐ جَميلاً

١٠- لَم يَزُرْ عَدنان جامِعَةَ نيويورك بِسَبَبِ ____________ .

☐ العُطلَةِ السَنَويةِ ☐ زِيارَتِهِ لِلشَلّالاتِ ☐ الطَقسِ

١١- التَقَطَ عَدنان صُوَراً لِلشَلّالاتِ مِن ____________ .

☐ الجانِبِ الكَنَديّ ☐ القارِبِ ☐ الحَدائِقِ

١٢- سافَرَ عَدنان إلى أتلانتيك سيتي ____________ .

☐ بِالقِطارِ ☐ بِالسَيّارَةِ ☐ بِالطائِرَةِ

١٣- لَم يُعجِبْ مايكِلِ الطَعامُ ____________

☐ الفَرَنسيّ ☐ المُرّاكِشيّ ☐ الأمريكيّ الغَربيّ

١٤- تَسكُنُ أسرةُ عَدنان في ____________ .

☐ دِمَشقَ ☐ حَلَبَ ☐ عَمّان

١٥- يُريدُ عَدنان زِيارةَ ____________ في السَنةِ المُقبلة.

☐ فَلوريدا ☐ كَندا ☐ كاليفورنيا

# تمرين ٧

**أكتُبْ «خطأ» أو «صَواب» بِجانبِ كُلِّ جُملَةٍ وصَحِّح الجُمَلَ الخَطأ.**

١– اِشتَرى مايكِل صُوَراً عِندَ الأهرامات.

٢– يَسيرُ النيلُ شَمالاً مِنَ القاهِرةِ إلى الخُرطوم.

٣– الإسكَندَريّة أقدَمُ مِنَ القاهِرةِ بِمِئاتِ السِنين.

٤– نامَ مايكِل وأصدِقاؤهُ على الشاطِئِ في الإسكَندَريّة.

٥– لَم يرَ عَدنان تِمثالَ الحُريّةِ مِن قَبل.

٦– ذَهَبَ عَدنان إلى مَبنى إمباير ستيت بِالسَيّارة.

٧– يَظُنُّ غَسّان أنَّ الشَلاّلاتِ على الجانِبِ الأمريكيِّ أجمَل.

٨– زارَ عَدنان «ديزني وُرلد» لِيَومٍ واحِدٍ فَقَط.

٩– اِنتَقَلَ مازِن صَديقُ عَدنان مِن جامَعةِ دمشق إلى حَلَب.

# تمرين ٨

**وافِقْ بَيْنَ الكَلِماتِ في العَمودَين.** **Matching:**

| | | | |
|---|---|---|---|
| ١ | شَلاّلات | | حَيَوانات |
| ٢ | بِطاقة | | المَلاهي |
| ٣ | آلَةُ | | طائِرة |
| ٤ | حَديقةُ | | نَياغَرا |
| ٥ | عيدُ | | تِجاريّ |
| ٦ | تَذْكَرةُ | | تَصوير |
| ٧ | مَحَلٌّ | | تَأمين |
| ٨ | مَدينةُ | | بَريديّة |
| | | | الأضحى |

## تمرين ٩

**أعِدْ تَرتيبَ الكَلِماتِ في كُلِّ مَجموعةٍ لِتُشَكِّلَ جُمَلاً مُفيدة.** **Sentence construction:**

١- لُغاتٍ - جَيِّداً - أختي - أنْ - ثَلاثَ - تَتَكَلَّمَ - تَستَطيعُ

٢- العِشرينَ - المِصعَدَ - الطابَقِ - يَأخُذُ - إلى - الناسُ

٣- فيلماً - بِهِ - واستَمتَعتُ - في - السينَما - شاهَدْتُ - دارِ

٤- آلافِ - بُنِيَتْ - السِنين - الأهراماتُ - مُنْذُ

٥- الإسكَندَريّةِ - رَمسيس - إلى - رَكِبْنا - مِن - القِطارَ - مَحَطّةِ

٦- تَسْتَمتِعوا - لِمَدينَتِنا - بِزيارتِكُم - أنْ - أرجو

٧- تَصويري - صورةً - بِآلَةِ - لأصدِقائي - الجَديدة - التَقَطتُ

## تمرين ١٠

**أعِدْ تَرتيبَ الجُمَلِ لِتُشكِّلَ فِقرةً مُفيدة.** **Paragraph construction:**

١- أرَدتُ أنا وعائلَتي زِيارةَ مَدينةِ اللاذِقيّة في عُطلةِ الرَبيع.

في الطَريقِ إلى اللاذِقيّةِ مَرَرْنا بِمَدينتَيْ حِمصَ وطَرطوس.

في اليَومِ التالي ذهَبنا إلى الشاطِئِ وسَبَحْنا

سارَتِ الحافِلةُ في الثامِنةِ صَباحاً.

ذَهَبنا أوّلاً إلى الفُندُقِ حَيثُ وَضَعنا حَقائِبَنا.

واللاذِقيّةُ ميناءُ سوريةَ الأوّلُ على البَحرِ الأبيضِ المُتَوسِّط.

بَعدَ الغَداءِ رَكِبنا قارِباً صَغيراً لِساعةٍ أو أكثَر.

عِندي عائِلةٌ كَبيرةٌ مِن أربعَةِ أبناءٍ وثَلاثِ بنات.

ثُمَّ ذَهَبنا إلى شاطِئِ البَحرِ حَيثُ تَناوَلنا الغَداء.

اسْتَمتَعنا كَثيراً بِهذِهِ الزِيارة.

وجَلَسْتُ أنا وزَوجَتي خَلفَ السائِق.

وَصَلنا إلى اللاذِقيّةِ في الثانِيةِ بَعدَ الظُهر.

جَلَسَ ابني الكَبير إلى جانِبِ السائِق.

لِذلِكَ اسْتَأجَرنا حافِلةً صَغيرةً مَعَ سائِقِها.

## 1. Terms of Address in Written Communication

When writing postcards, letters, and the like, we need to address the person to whom we are writing appropriately. For this purpose certain terms of address, or salutations, are used, such as عَزيز 'dear' حَبيب 'loved one, darling,' and variations thereof. In addition, to add formality to a letter, for example, one might use the noun والِد instead of أب and والدة for أم. Therefore, a letter to a father, for instance, may be started as follows:

١ والِدي الحَبيب or والِدي العَزيز

A friend may be addressed in this manner:

٢ أخي العَزيز فُلان

٣ أختي العَزيزة فُلانة

Note: فُلان is a generic term that stands for a person's name (e.g., "so-and-so").

However, a man addressing a woman may not use الحبيبة or حَبيبَتي unless she is his wife, fiancée, sister, daughter, etc.

Generally, the writer signs off, referring to oneself by one of these terms:

| | | |
|---|---|---|
| ٤ | المُخلِص / المُخلِصة | *sincerely* |
| ٥ | المُشتاق / المُشتاقة | *missing you* |
| ٦ | المُحِبّ / المُحِبّة | *lovingly* |

## تمرين ١١

**اكتُبْ بِطاقةً بَريديّةً إلى صَديقٍ عَرَبيٍّ مِن مَدينةٍ زُرتَها في الوِلاياتِ المُتَّحِدةِ أو في مَكانٍ آخَر.**

Write a postcard to an imaginary Arab pen pal from a real or fictitious town. Address the person properly, provide the date, and a plausible address. Describe the town briefly, say where you are staying, what you have seen, what you plan to do in the near future, when you are returning home, and whether or not you enjoyed this visit and why. Use the postcard illustration on the next page so that you do not exceed customary length. A word bank follows with words that might be useful for completing this exercise:

| | | | | | |
|---|---|---|---|---|---|
| حفلة | احتفلتُ بـ | زيارة | أحْبَبْتُ | عيد | إجازة |
| اِسْتطاع | اِلْتقى | مَرَّة | مُنْذُ | اِلْتقَطَ | تناوَلَ |
| سَيِّد | مع | تَكَلَّمْتُ | سَهِرْتُ | اِسْتَمْتَعْتُ بِـ | أصْدِقائي |

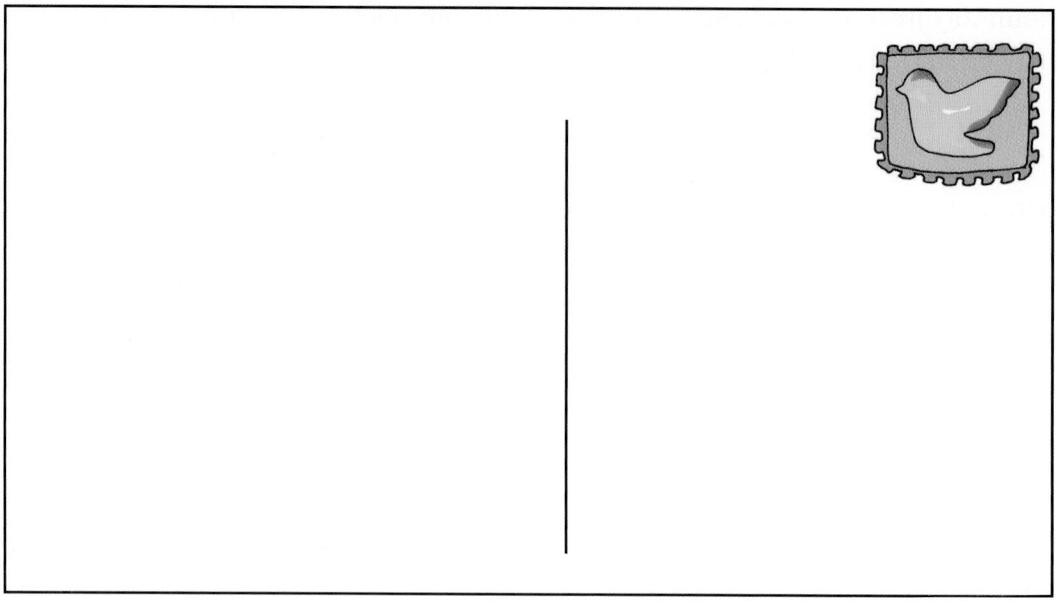

## 2. Adverbs of Time and Place ظَرف الزَمان والمَكان

Simply by English convention do we use the word "adverb" here, as no true adverbs exist in Arabic. These are, in fact, nouns in the accusative case **منصوب** that function as indicators of the time or place of an action. The Arabic term **ظَرف** signifies that these adverbs are the vessels or containers in which an action occurs. **Adverbs of time** denote the time when an action occurs, as in example 7:

٧ وَصَلَتِ الطائِرةُ مَساءً.

Some frequently occurring adverbs of time are:

| | | | | | | | | | | |
|---|---|---|---|---|---|---|---|---|---|---|
| مُنذُ | حينَ | زَمان | عام | سَنَة | شَهر | أُسبوع | ليلة | يَوم | ساعة | دَقيقة |

٨ وُلِدْتُ عامَ ١٩٥٢.

Similarly, **adverbs of place** denote the place where an action takes place:

٩ مَشَيْتُ شَمالاً.

١٠ شَقَّتي تَحتَ عِيادةِ الطَبيب.

Some commonly used adverbs of place include directions:

| | | | | | | | | | |
|---|---|---|---|---|---|---|---|---|---|
| أمامَ | خلفَ | تحتَ | فوقَ | شمالَ | غربَ | يمينَ | يسارَ | جنوبَ | شرقَ |

١١ تَقَعُ الإسكَندَرِيَّةُ شَمالَ القاهِرةِ.

١٢ الأهراماتُ في الجيزةِ قُرْبَ القاهِرَةِ.

- **Note:** These adverbs of time and place also function as regular nouns, acquiring the case of their particular syntactic contexts:

١٣ وُلِدْتُ في عامِ ١٩٥٢.

١٤ مَشَيْتُ إلى الشَّمالِ.

In examples 13 and 14, **عامِ** and **الشَّمالِ** are objects of prepositions; therefore, they display the **كَسرة** indicating the genitive case. As you may have noticed, when the adverb acts as a noun, it is placed in a prepositional phrase. A generality can be made here concerning the adverb-noun relationship: adverbs of noun and place have a prepositional phrase counterpart—both of which have the same meaning, as in **صَباحاً** and **في الصباحِ**.

## 3. Negating Future Time (لَنْ)

You already know that future time is expressed by using the particles **سَـ** (which is a prefix) and **سَوفَ** (which is an independent word) immediately before a present-tense form of the verb:

١٥ سَأسافِرُ إلى مُدُنٍ أخرى.

١٦ سَوفَ أزورُ جامِعَةَ نيويورك.

As you may have noticed in Michael Brown's and Adnān Martini's journals, future time is negated by using the particle **لَن**:

١٧ لَنْ أسافِرَ إلى مُدُنٍ أُخرى.

١٨ لَنْ أزورَ جامِعَةَ نيويورك.

Reflect for a moment on the changes that occurred to the verbs in examples 15–16 and 17–18 above. What rule(s) can you come up with concerning the effect of **لَن** on the verbs that follow it?

We find that أسافرُ and أزورُ, which are مضارع مرفوع in examples 15–16, have changed to أسافرَ and أزورَ, which are مضارع منصوب marked by a فَتحة.

> ## SUMMARY
>
> When we use لَن, two changes need to be made to the following verb:
>
> 1. The future markers سَـ or سَوفَ are dropped.
> 2. The مضارع مرفوع (indicative) is changed into مضارع منصوب (subjunctive).
>
> - **Error Prevention:** Reread rule 1 and apply it. Do not place سَـ or سَوفَ after لَن.

## تمرين ١٢

**اِنْفِ (negate) الجُمَلَ التاليّة:**

١- سَوفَ أدرُسُ اللُغةَ العَرَبِيَّةَ في جامُعةِ دِمَشق.

٢- سَتزورُني أمّي في الشَهرِ المُقبِل.

٣- سَوفَ أشاهِدُ فيلمَينِ في عُطلةِ الأسبوعِ هذِه.

٤- سَأستَمتِعُ بِالسِباحةِ في هذا الطَقس.

## 4. Relative Nouns (الّذي، الّتي) الأسْماءُ المَوصولة

In the English sentence structure, a relative clause has a modifying function which is similar to that of an adjective. A relative clause is, in fact, a sentence modifying a noun phrase. Examine the following example:

19 *The student who speaks Arabic lived in Damascus for two years.*

The clause "speaks Arabic" modifies the noun (the student), but unlike the noun-adjective pattern in Arabic, a relative clause *follows* its modified noun phrase in exactly the same order as in English. An Arabic sentence parallel to example 19 is:

٢٠ الطالِبُ الّذي يَتكَلَّمُ العَرَبيَّةَ سَكَنَ في دِمَشقَ سَنَتَين.

The sentence يَتَكَلَّمُ العَرَبية modifies (refers back to) the head noun الطالب, which is called the antecedent. If the antecedent is definite, the relative sentence is introduced by a relative noun. In example 20, the relative noun is الذي (pronounced: *al-laḏī*). Its role is to link the antecedent to the relative clause.

### A. Restrictive Relative Nouns الأسماء الموصولة الخاصة

There are Arabic relative nouns which are restricted to a specific noun, that is, they modify a noun and agree with this modified noun (antecedent) in number and gender.

| الأسماءُ المَوصولةُ الخاصّة | | | | |
|---|---|---|---|---|
| الجَمْع | المُثنى المَنصوب والمَجرور | المُثَنى المَرفوع | المُفْرَد | |
| الّذينَ | اللّذَيْنِ | اللّذانِ | الّذي | المُذكَّر |
| اللاتي/ اللواتي | اللّتَيْنِ | اللّتانِ | الّتي | المؤنَّث |

Dual relative nouns vary according to case. Thus, the relative noun assumes different forms, depending on the form of the antecedent. Notice how the relative noun (highlighted in blue) varies as the antecedent (the first word in the sentences below) changes in examples 21–25:

| مَرفوع | | |
|---|---|---|
| Feminine singular | الطالِبةُ الّتي تتكلَّمُ العَرَبِيَّةَ . . . | ٢١ |
| Masculine dual | الطالِبانِ اللّذانِ يَتكلَّمانِ العَرَبِيَّةَ . . . | ٢٢ |
| Feminine dual | الطالِبَتانِ اللّتانِ تَتكلَّمانِ العَرَبِيَّةَ . . . | ٢٣ |
| Masculine plural | الطُلاّبُ الّذينَ يَتكلَّمونَ العَرَبِيَّةَ . . . | ٢٤ |
| Feminine plural | الطالِباتُ اللاتي يَتكلَّمْنَ العَرَبِيَّةَ . . . | ٢٥ |

The middle أَلِف in examples 22 and 23 changes into ي when the antecedent is منصوب (accusative) or مجرور (genitive). Compare examples 22 and 23 with 26 and 27.

| منصوب | | |
|---|---|---|
| Masculine dual | أعرِفُ الطالِبَينِ اللذَينِ يَتكَلَّمانِ العَرَبيَّةَ . . . | ٢٦ |
| Feminine dual | أعرِفُ الطالِبَتَينِ اللتَينِ تتكَلَّمانِ العَرَبيَّةَ . . . | ٢٧ |

**B. Agreement with Non-Rational Plurals**

Just like adjectives, non-rational plural antecedents are treated as third-person feminine singular regardless of the gender of the singular noun (see Noun–Adjective Agreement in Lesson 10, section 4).

٢٨ هذِهِ هِيَ الكُتُبُ الّتي اشتَرَيتُها.

٢٩ أعْطِني المَجَلاّتِ الّتي قَرَأتها.

In example 28, the noun **الكُتُب** is the plural of the masculine singular noun **كِتاب**, and in 29, the noun **المَجَلاّت** is the plural of the feminine singular noun **مَجَلّة**. Notice that both are modified by **الّتي**, a third-person feminine singular relative noun.

## تمرين ١٣

**Use the appropriate relative noun.** **اسْتَخدِم الاسمَ المَوصولَ المُناسِبَ في الجُمَلِ التالِيةِ.**

١- هَل قَرَأتِ المَجَلَّةَ ____________ اشتَرَيتُها أمس؟

٢- هَؤلاءِ هُنَّ الطالِباتُ ____________ يَسكُنَّ في سَكَنِ الطالِبات.

٣- أحمَد وأيمَن هُما الطالِبانِ ____________ يَدرُسانِ الرِياضِيّاتِ.

٤- مَن هُوَ الأستاذُ ____________ كَتَبَ هذا الكِتاب؟

٥- أعرِفُ الرَجُلَينِ ____________ يَعمَلانِ في هذِهِ الشَرِكة.

٦- مَن هُم أصدِقاؤكَ ____________ زاروا مِصرَ؟

٧- كَتَبتُ إلى السَيِّدَتَينِ ____________ تَسكُنانِ في تِلكَ البِناية.

٨- سَلمى وهَنا هُما ____________ تَعمَلانِ في هذِهِ الدُكّان.

## C. Non-Restrictive Relative Nouns مَن and ما

There are a number of relative nouns used for antecedents that vary in number and gender. That is to say, the same relative noun can be used with masculine, feminine, singular, dual, and plural antecedents. We are already familiar with one of them, مَنْ, which we have used thus far for asking questions about the identity of a person or persons:

٣٠   مَنْ زَارَ الإسكَنْدَرِيَّة؟

When we use مَن as a question particle, as in example 30, it is non-restrictive in the sense that we may be asking about a man, a woman, or two or more people. Similarly, مَن can be used as a non-restrictive relative noun in a statement. Consider example 31:

٣١   أَعْجَبَتِ الإسكَنْدَرِيَّةُ مَنْ زارَها.

- Bear in mind that مَنْ is generally used with rational nouns (humans). Its non-restrictive counterpart that generally refers to non-rational nouns is ما:

٣٢   إقرأي مِن تِلكَ الكُتُبِ / المَجَلّاتِ ما تُريدينَ.

A translation of example 32 could be: "Read what[ever] you like of those books/magazines."

- ما does not change with the gender of the antecedent. Both كُتُب, which is masculine in its singular, and مَجَلّات, which is feminine in its singular, are modified by ما.

## D. Combining Relative Nouns with Prepositions

When preceded by certain prepositions, the relative nouns مَن and ما combine with them to form single words:

٣٣   كَتَبَ عَدنان عَمّا فَعَلَ في العُطلةِ الصَيفِيَّة.   (عَن + ما)

*Adnān wrote about what he did in the summer break.*

٣٤   تَكَلَّمَ عَدنان عَمَّن استَقبَلَ مِن الطُلّابِ الجُدُد.   (عَن + مَن)

*Adnān talked about whom he met of the new students.*

٣٥   هَل تُريدُ أَنْ تَشرَبَ مِمّا أَشرَب؟   (مِن + ما)

*Would you like to drink of what I'm drinking?*

٣٦ وَصَلَتْني رَسائِلُ مِمَّن كَتَبتُ لَهُم. (مِن + مَن)

*I have received letters from those to whom I wrote.*

٣٧ قَرَأتُ فيما قَرَأتُ يومِيّاتِ طالِبٍ في القاهِرة. (في + ما)

*Part of what I have read are the journals of a student in Cairo.*

٣٨ عَرَفتُ فيمَن عَرَفتُ في الجامِعةِ طالِبَةً تونسيَّة. (في + مَن)

*Among those whom I knew at the university was a Tunisian female student.*

**E. Indefinite Antecedents**

In the examples cited so far in this lesson, the antecedent—or the noun modified by the relative noun—has been definite by virtue of a prefixed definite article الـ, a suffixed possessive pronoun, or a proper name. Consider the antecedents that have been used so far as examples in this section:

| | | | | | |
|---|---|---|---|---|---|
| الإسكَندَريّة | سَلمى وهَنا | أصدِقاؤك | المَجَلاّت | الكُتُب | الطالِب |

Antecedents can be indefinite, in which case no relative noun is used. In Michael's journal we read:

٣٩ الأهرامات مُبانٍ عَظيمةٌ بَناها الفَراعِنةُ.

*The pyramids are great buildings [that] the pharaohs built.*

- Although there is no relative noun in the Arabic sentence, the English translation requires one because the sentence **بناها الفراعنة** is still a relative clause. The relative pronoun is not used because the head noun **مبانٍ** is indefinite.

### F. The Referent as Object in the Relative Clause

Another feature which you may have noticed in example 39 is the suffix **ها** attached to the verb **بَنى**. This suffix, which refers back to the antecedent **مَبانٍ**, is the object of the verb **بنى**. According to the rules of Arabic sentence structure, if the referent in the relative clause is an object of a verb or a preposition, or if it forms an **إضافة** with a noun, it must be used. It is, however, omitted in a similar English structure. Compare the Arabic and English examples:

٤٠ خَديجةُ هِيَ الطالِبةُ الّتي استَقبَلَها عَدنان في المَطار.

*Khadīja is the student whom Adnān met (her) at the airport.*

The verb in the Arabic relative sentence translates: "he met her," whereas in the English translation no such pronoun is needed. Consider examples 41–43, in which the referent is the object of a verb (41), the object of a preposition (42), and an **إضافة** (43), respectively:

| | |
|---|---|
| ٤١ هذِهِ هِيَ السَيّارةُ الَّتي اشتَرَيتُها. | *This is the car which I bought (it).* |
| ٤٢ هذِهِ هِيَ السَيّارةُ الَّتي رَكِبتُ فيها. | *This is the car which I rode in (it).* |
| ٤٣ هذِهِ هِيَ السَيّارةُ الَّتي أعرِفُ سائِقَها. | *This is the car whose driver I know.*<br>*(lit.) This is the car which I know its driver.* |

In examples 41–43, the object pronoun **ها** refers to **السيارة** in the main sentence. **ها** functions as the object of the verb in example 42, as the object of the preposition in 43, and forms an **إضافة** with the noun **سائق** in 43.

With the relative nouns **مَن** and **ما**, however, the object pronoun is not needed:

| | |
|---|---|
| ٤٤ اشتَرَيتُ مِن الكُتُبِ ما أريدُ. | *I bought books I want.* |
| ٤٥ زُرتُ مِن الأصدِقاءِ مَن أُحِبُّ. | *I visited friends I like.* |

## SUMMARY

**When to use a referential pronoun:**

If the subject of the sentence is not the subject of the verb, then a referential pronoun is needed.

خَديجةُ هِيَ الطالِبةُ الّتي استَقبَلَها عَدنان في المَطار.

Subject of the sentence: خَديجةُ
Subject of the verb: عَدنان

You may apply this rule in any situation in which these conditions are met.

**When a referential pronoun is not needed:**

If the subject of the sentence is the subject of the verb, then no referential pronoun is needed. (Another way of putting this is that the referential pronoun is not needed in this case because the pronoun is included in the verb itself.)

خَديجةُ هِيَ الطالِبةُ الّتي كانَت في المَطار.

Subject of the sentence: خَديجةُ
Subject of the verb: خَديجةُ

## تمرين ١٤

Fill in the blanks with the appropriate relative nouns (restrictive or non-restrictive) in the sentences that require one. In the sentences that do not require a relative noun (i.e., when the antecedent is indefinite), place an 'x'.

١- أعرِفُ طالِباً ____________ يَدرُسُ اللُغتَينِ العَرَبيّةَ والصينيّةَ.

٢- أعطِني الكِتابَ ____________ كُنتُ أقرأ فيه.

٣- هَل تُريدينَ أنْ تقرأي ____________ كَتَبتُ؟

٤- أينَ الرِجالُ ____________ وَصَلوا بِالطائرةِ المِصْريّةِ.

٥- أعرِفُ ____________ يُحِبُّ هذا النوعَ مِن الطَعام.

٦- استَقبَلتُ في المَطارِ طالِبَتَينِ ____________ سَتَدرُسانِ عِلمَ الحاسوب.

٧- هَل شاهَدتَ الحَيواناتِ ____________ وَصَلتْ إلى الحَديقَةِ مِن كينيا؟

٨- هَؤلاءِ هُنَّ الأمّهاتُ ____________ أتَينَ لِمُشاهَدَةِ أبنائِهِنَّ على المَسرَح؟

## تمرين ١٥

**اسألوا جيرانَكُم:**

١- مَتى تَركَب(ينَ) الحافِلَةَ الّتي تَمُرُّ أمام هذه البِناية؟

٢- أين تَناوَلت الطعام الذي أكَلْته اليوم؟

٣- مَتى شاهَدْت المُسَلْسَل الّذي ظَهَرَ في التِلْفاز ليلة أمس؟

٤- كَم مَرّةً زُرتَ حَديقةَ الحيواناتِ الّتي يَذهب إليها عددٌ كبيرٌ مِن الناس؟

٥- بكَم اِشتَريَت السَيّارة/ الدَرّاجة الّتي تسوقُها الآن؟

## 5. Prepositions Revisited

In our main reading passages for this lesson, we encountered prepositions in combination with other prepositions, particles, adverbs, and demonstrative nouns. While the resulting meanings are straightforward and predictable in most cases, some combinations have special new meanings. Consider this table:

| | | | | |
|---|---|---|---|---|
| | preposition + adverb of place | *from above* | مِن فَوق | ٤٦ |
| | preposition + adverb of place | *from below* | مِن تَحت | ٤٧ |
| | preposition + adverb of time | *until now* | إلى الآنَ | ٤٨ |
| Must be followed by verb | preposition + particle | *till; until* | إلى أنْ | ٤٩ |
| Must be followed by noun or attached pronoun | preposition + particle | *although* | مَعَ أنَّ | ٥٠ |
| | preposition + demonstrative noun | *likewise* | كَذلِكَ | ٥١ |
| | preposition + demonstrative noun | *therefore* | لِذلِكَ | ٥٢ |

## تمرين ١٦

**أكمِل الجُمَلَ التالية بِكَلِماتٍ مُناسِبةٍ مِن الجَدوَل أعلاه.**

**A.** Complete the following sentences with prepositional combinations from the preceding table.

١– اشترى سالِم بَيتاً جَديداً و ____________ سَيّارةً جديدةً.

٢– عِصام رَجُلٌ فقيرٌ، ____________ لا يَستَطيعُ أنْ يَشتَريَ بَيتاً.

٣– لَم تَزُرْ سامية بَيروت ____________ صَديقتَها تَسكُنُ هُناكَ.

٤– جَلَسنا على شاطِئِ البَحرِ ____________ غابَتِ الشَمسُ.

**B.** Express these meanings in Arabic.

5. So far, I haven't been able to visit the Grand Canyon.
6. The view of the city is beautiful from above.
7. He is not happy although he is rich.
8. We studied at the library until my friends wanted to go to the movies.
9. I like to travel, as does my wife.

## 6. Possessive إضافة

We are already familiar with one way of rendering nouns possessive: by suffixing attached pronouns to them (e.g., كتابي، سيارتُهُم). Making an إضافة phrase possessive is based on the same principle in that the pronoun, in the majority of cases, should be suffixed to the final member of the إضافة structure. Reflect on the following examples:

| | | |
|---|---|---|
| *my camera* | آلَةُ تَصويري | ٥٣ |
| *his apartment address* | عُنوانُ شَقَّتِهِ | ٥٤ |
| *the key to the door of her car* | مِفتاحُ بابِ سَيّارَتِها | ٥٥ |

## تمرين ١٧

Express these meanings in Arabic, using إضافة structures with possessive suffixes.

1. my bedroom
2. her (male) friend's car
3. his wife's mother
4. their house floor plan
5. our grocer's store
6. my weekend

## تمرين ١٨

**استمِعْ إلى النَصّ المُسَجَّل ثُمَّ أجِبْ عَن الأسئِلة:**

١- كَم وَلَداً في هذِه العائِلة؟

٢- أينَ هذِهِ العائِلَةُ الآنَ؟

٣- أيُّ فَصلٍ مِن السَنةِ في هذا النَصّ؟

**أكمِل الجُمَلَ التاليةَ حَسَبَ النَصّ:**

٤- لِلأردُن ____________ .

☐ ميناءٌ واحدٌ ☐ ميناءانِ ☐ ثَلاثةُ مَوانِئ

٥- سافَرَتِ العائِلَةُ إلى العَقَبةِ ____________ .

☐ بِالسَيّارةِ ☐ بِالطائِرةِ ☐ بِالقِطارِ

٦- زارَتْ عائِلةُ مَيساء العَقَبةَ لِمُدَّةِ ____________ أيّام.

☐ ثَلاثةِ ☐ أربَعةِ ☐ خَمسةِ

٧- كانَ الطَقسُ في العَقَبةِ ____________ .

☐ حارّاً ☐ مُعتَدِلاً ☐ بارِداً

٨- سَبَحوا في البَحرِ ____________ في اليَوم.

☐ مَرَّتَينِ ☐ ساعَتَينِ ☐ يومَينِ

٩- اسْتأجَرَتِ العائِلةُ ____________ في الفُندُق.

☐ غُرفةً ☐ غُرفتَينِ ☐ ثَلاثَ غُرَف

**اكتُبْ «خَطَأ» أو «صَواب» بِجانبِ كُلِّ جُملَةٍ وصَحِّح الجُمَلَ الخَطأ.**

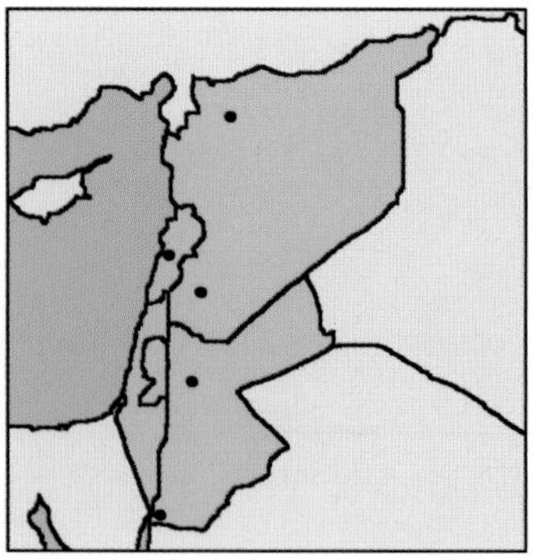

١٠- المرأةُ في النَصِ مُتَزَوِّجةٌ واسمُ زَوجِها هِشام.

١١- تَناوَلَت مَيساء وعائِلَتُها العَشاءَ في مَطعَمِ «نَخيل».

١٢- العَقَبةُ ميناءٌ على البَحرِ الأبيَضِ المُتَوَسِّط.

١٣- الفُندُقُ في شارِعٍ قَريبٍ مِن الشاطِئ.

١٤- سَتركَبُ العائِلَةُ قارِباً بَعدَ الظُهر.

١٥- اكتبْ على الخَريطةِ اسمَ البَلَدِ المَوجودِ في النَصِّ واسمَ المَدينتَينِ واسمَ البَحرِ.

## تمرين ١٩ VIDEO

**تَمرينُ المُشاهَدة: شاهِدوا الدَرْسَ التاسع عَشَر على القُرْص الرَقْميّ.**

١- لِماذا ستيف لَيسَ مَوجوداً في البَيْتِ عِندَ الفَطور مع باقي الأسرة؟ ______________

______________________________

______________________________

٢- كَيفَ حياة مايكل في القاهِرةِ في رأيه؟ ______________________________

______________________________

______________________________

٣- ماذا شاهَدَ مايكل في الجيزة وماذا فَعَلَ هُناك؟ ______________________________

______________________________

______________________________

٤- إلى أين سَيَذهَب سامِر ومايكل بَعدَ شُربِ القهوة؟ ______________________________

______________________________

______________________________

٥- مَنِ الحَكَواتيّ؟ ______________________________

______________________________

______________________________

٦- مَن عَدنان؟ ______________________________

______________________________

______________________________

## المُفْرَدات

Listen to the vocabulary items on the CD and practice their pronunciation.

| | |
|---|---|
| to return | آبَ (يؤوبُ) إياب (v.) |
| white | أبيَض ج بيض (n., m.) |
| ruin, antiquity, artifact, relic | أثَر ج آثار (n., m.) |
| to respond, to answer | أجابَ (يُجيبُ) إجابة (v.) |
| then, therefore | إذاً |
| to be able, can | استَطاعَ (يَستَطيعُ) استِطاعة (v.) |
| to enjoy | استَمتَعَ (يَستَمتِعُ) استِمتاع (v.) |
| until | إلى أنْ |
| apparatus, device, gadget, machine | آلة ج آلات (n., f.) |
| to meet, converge, encounter | التَقى (يَلتَقي) التِقاء (v.) |
| to take, make (a picture) | التَقَطَ (يَلتَقِطُ) التِقاط (v.) |
| who, that | الَّتي (n., f.) |
| who, that | الَّذي (n., m.) |
| to examine, to test | امتَحَنَ (يَمتَحِنُ) امتِحان (v.) |
| early | باكِراً (adverbial) |
| mail, post | بَريد (n., m.) |
| to remain, to stay | بَقِيَ (يَبْقى) بَقاء (v.) |
| to build, to construct | بَنى (يَبني) بِناء (v.) |
| to wander about, to tour | تَجَوَّلَ (يَتَجَوَّلُ) تَجَوُّل (v.) |
| ticket | تَذكِرة ج تَذاكِر (n., f.) |
| statue | تِمثال ج تَماثيل (n., m.) |
| to eat; to take; to reach for something | تَناوَلَ (يَتَناوَلُ) تَناوُل (v.) |
| camel | جَمَل ج جِمال (n., m.) |

حُرِّيّة ج حُرِّيّات (n., f.) . . . . . . . . . . . . . . . . liberty, freedom

حَيَوان ج حَيَوانات (n., m.) . . . . . . . . . . . . . . . . . . animal

دائماً (adverbial) . . . . . . . . . . . . . . . . . . . . . . . . . always

دَخَّنَ (يُدَخِّنُ) تَدْخين (v.) . . . . . . . . . . to smoke (e.g., a cigarette)

راح (يروح) على (v.) . . . . . . . . . . . . (Syrian colloquial) ذهب

رَجا (يَرجو) رَجاء (v.) . . . . . . . . . . . . . . . . . . . . . . to hope

رَكِبَ (يَركَبُ) رُكوب (v.) . . . . . . . . . . . . . . . . . to ride, to mount

ساحة ج ساحات (n., f.) . . . . . . . . . . . . . . . square, courtyard

سادة . . . . . . . . . . . . . . . . . . . . . . . . . unsweetened coffee

سارَ (يَسيرُ) سَيْر (v.) . . . to move, to walk, to travel, to march, to flow

سَعيد ج سُعَداء (adj., m.) . . . . . . . . . . . . . happy, pleased, joyful

سُؤال ج أسئِلة (n., m.) . . . . . . . . . . . . . . . . . . question, query

شاهَدَ (يُشاهِدُ) مُشاهَدة (v.) . . . . . . . . . . to witness, to see, to watch

شَلاّل ج شَلاّلات (n., m.) . . . . . . . . . . . . . . . . . . . . waterfall

شَمال (n., m.) . . . . . . . . . . . . . . . . . . . . . . . . . . . north

شَيْء ج أشياء (n., m.) . . . . . . . . . . . . . . . . . . thing, object

صَحّة وهَنا . . . . . . . . . . . . . bon appétit (Syrian colloquial)

صِناعة ج صِناعات (n., f.) . . . . . . . . . . . . . . . . . . . . industry

صَوَّرَ (يُصَوِّرُ) تَصوير (v) . . to make a picture, to portray, to illustrate

طَريق ج طُرُق، طُرُقات (n., f.) . . . . . . . . . . . . . . . . way, road.

عَدَد ج أعْداد (n., m.) . . . . . . . . . . . . . . . number (quantity)

عَرْض ج عُروض (n., m.) . . . . show, demonstration, performance

عَزيز ج أعِزّاء (n., m.) . . . . . . . . . . . dear, esteemed, beloved

عَظيم ج عُظَماء (adj./n., m.) . . . . . . . great, important, imposing

غالٍ (n., m.) . . . . . . . . . . . . . . . . . . . . . . expensive, dear

غالِباً (adv.) . . . . . . . . . . . . . . . . . . often, mostly, generally.

west . . . . . . . . . . . . . . . . . . . . . . . . . غَرْب (n., m.)

pharaoh . . . . . . . . . . . . . . . . . . . . . فِرعَون ج فَراعِنة (n., m.)

band, company, troupe . . . . . . . . . . . . فِرقة ج فِرَق، أفْرِقة (n., f.)

boat . . . . . . . . . . . . . . . . . . . . . . . قارِب ج قَوارِب (n., m.)

to gamble . . . . . . . . . . . . . . . . . . . . قامَرَ (يُقامِرُ) مُقامَرة، قِمار (v.)

to serve, to provide . . . . . . . . . . . . . . قَدَّمَ (يُقَدِّمُ) تَقديم (v.)

also, as well . . . . . . . . . . . . . . . . . . كَذلِكَ

kilometer . . . . . . . . . . . . . . . . . . . . كيلومِتر ج كيلومِترات (n., m.)

عِنْدَ . . . . . . . . . . . . . . . . . . . . . . . . لَدى (prep.)

game, play, ride . . . . . . . . . . . . . . . لُعبة ج لُعبات، ألعاب (n., f.)

building, construction . . . . . . . . . . . . مَبنى ج مَبانٍ (n. m.)

museum . . . . . . . . . . . . . . . . . . . . . مُتحَف ج مَتاحِف (n., m.)

loving . . . . . . . . . . . . . . . . . . . . . . مُحِبّ ج مُحِبّون (n.)

sincere, faithful, (sincerely yours) . . . . مُخلِص ج مُخلِصون (n., m.)

period, duration . . . . . . . . . . . . . . . . مُدّة ج مُدَد (n., f.)

to pass, to go by . . . . . . . . . . . . . . . . مَرَّ (يَمُرُّ) مُرور (v.)

mosque . . . . . . . . . . . . . . . . . . . . . مَسجِد ج مَساجِد (n., m.)

theater, stage . . . . . . . . . . . . . . . . . مَسرَح ج مَسارِح (n., m.)

one who is longing, yearning . . . . . . . . مُشْتاق ج مُشْتاقون (n.)

elevator, lift . . . . . . . . . . . . . . . . . . مِصعَد ج مَصاعِد (n., m.)

though, although . . . . . . . . . . . . . . . . مَعَ أنَّ

coming, next, following . . . . . . . . . . . مُقبِل ج مُقبِلون (n., m.)

place, location . . . . . . . . . . . . . . . . . مَكان ج أمْكِنة (n., m.)

million . . . . . . . . . . . . . . . . . . . . . . مِليون (n., m.)

since, for . . . . . . . . . . . . . . . . . . . . مُنْذُ (prep.)

square, field, arena . . . . . . . . . . . . . . مَيدان ج مَيادين (n., m.)

port. . . . . . . . . . . . . . . . . . . . . . . . . (n., m.) ميناء ج مَوانِئ

person (used in population counts). . . . . . (n., f.) نَسَمة ج نَسَمات

important, significant . . . . . . . . . . . . . (n./adj.) هامٌّ ج هامّون

pyramid . . . . . . . . . . . . . . . . . . . (n., m.) هَرَم ج أهرام / أهرامات

father, parent . . . . . . . . . . . . . . . . (n., m.) والِد ج والِدون

# الدَرسُ العِشرونَ

## Objectives

- Discussing sports and food
- Expressing uncertainty using رُبَّما
- Expressing preference using فَضَّل (يُفَضِّلُ) تَفضيل
- Expressing frequency using مَرّةً – أحياناً – دائماً – غالِباً – يوميّاً – أبَداً
- Expressing degree using قَليلاً – كَثيراً – جَيِّداً – جِدّاً
- Introduction to the habitual and progressive past
- Introduction to colors
- Introduction to comparative nouns with doubled consonants
- Revisiting the weak verbs الفِعل المُعتلّ

## رُكنُ المُفْرَداتِ الجَديدةِ:

| | |
|---|---|
| *to use* | اِسْتَخْدَمَ (يَسْتَخْدِمُ) اِسْتِخْدام |
| *to stay* | بَقِيَ (يَبْقى) بَقاء |
| *almost* | تَقْريباً |
| *especially* | خُصوصاً (= خِصّيصاً أو خاصّةً) |
| مُمْكِن | رُبَما |
| *to understand* | فَهِمَ (يَفْهَمُ) فَهْم |
| *to play* | لَعِبَ (يَلْعَبُ) لُعْب |
| *match, game* | مُباراة ج مُبارَيات |
| *to prefer* | فَضَّلَ (يُفَضِّلُ) تَفْضيل |
| *time* | وَقْت ج أوْقات |
| *to explain* | شَرَحَ (يَشْرَحُ) شَرْح |

## المُفرداتُ الجَديدةُ في صُوَرٍ عَديدةٍ:

جَرى (يَجْري) جَري

مُتَفَرِّج ج مُتَفَرِّجون

فازَ (يَفوزُ) فَوْز

فَريق ج فِرَق

## تمرين ١

**وافِق بين كلماتٍ مِنَ العَمودِ الأيْمَن وكلِماتٍ مِنَ العَمودِ الأيْسَر واكتُب الكَلِمَتين في الوسط.**

**Matching:**

| | | | |
|---|---|---|---|
| ١ | إجّاص | | عَرَبية |
| ٢ | حِصان | | سودانيّ |
| ٣ | مَوعِد | | وَقت |
| ٤ | طابَق | | مُفَضَّل |
| ٥ | فُلَيفُلة | | بَقَر |
| ٦ | لَحْم | | تِجاري |
| ٧ | فول | | فاكِهة |
| ٨ | مَحَلّ | | أرضيّ |
| ٩ | بِلاد | | خَضْراء |
| | | | خَيل |

تمرين ٢

اخْتَرِ الكَلِمةَ الَّتي لا تُناسِب باقي الكَلِماتِ في كُلِّ مَجْموعةٍ وبَيِّنِ السَبَب.     Odd word out:

| | | | | |
|---|---|---|---|---|
| ١- | مَصْنوع | بَقِيَ | سَكَنَ | جَلَسَ | نَزَلَ |
| ٢- | مَلْعَب | مُتَفَرِّج | شاطِئ | مُباراة | فَريق |
| ٣- | سَميط | لُبّ | مِياه غازية | عَصا | شاي |
| ٤- | دائِماً | أحياناً | عادة | غالِباً | تَقريباً |
| ٥- | قَرْنَبيط | توت | باذِنْجان | بامية | خَسّ |
| ٦- | لَذيذ | جَيِّد | شَرَح | مُفَضَّل | مَشْوِيّ |

# 🔊 رِياضاتٌ وأطعِمةٌ مُفَضَّلةٌ

**مِن يَومِيّاتِ عَدنان مارتيني**

كُرةُ السَلّةِ

حينَ كُنتُ في المَدرسةِ الثانويةِ في حَلَبَ لَعِبتُ كُرةَ السَلّةِ مع فَريقٍ المَدرسةِ من الصَفِّ العاشِرِ حَتّى الثاني عَشَر. كانت كُرةُ السَلّةِ في ذلِكَ الوَقتِ رياضَتي المُفَضَّلةَ. كُنتُ ألعَبُها كُلَّ يومٍ تَقريباً. كُنتُ أذهبُ مع أصدِقائي إلى مُبارَياتِ كُرةِ السَلّةِ دائِماً وأشاهِدُها على التِلفاز.

كُرةُ الطاوِلةِ

أمّا هُنا في أمريكا فَلا ألعَبُ كُرةَ السَلّةِ كَثيراً، مَرَّتَينِ أو ثَلاثَ مَرّاتٍ فَقَط في الشَهرِ بِسَبَبِ الدِراسة. صِرتُ ألعَبُ الآنَ كُرةَ الطاوِلة. هُناكَ مَكانٌ واسِعٌ لِلألعابِ في الطابِقِ الأرضيِّ حَيثُ تُوجَدُ شَقَّتي. أنزِلُ إلى هذا المَكانِ مَساءً وفي صَباحِ يومِ السَبتِ وألعَبُ مع أصدِقائي أو مع بَعضِ السُكّانِ الآخَرين. تُعجِبُني كُرةُ الطاوِلةِ كَثيراً.

عصا وكُرةٌ

مُنذُ ثَلاثةِ شُهورٍ أخَذَني صَديقي تِم نِكلز إلى مُباراةٍ في لُعبةٍ تُسَمّى هُنا «بيسبول». لا أعرِفُ لَها اسماً بالعَربيّةِ رُبَّما لأنَّنا لا نَلعَبُها في البِلادِ العَربيّة. يُحِبُّ الأمريكيّونَ هذهِ اللُعبةَ جِدّاً، وهي تُلعَبُ

بِعَصا طَويلةٍ وكُرةٍ صَغيرةٍ بَيضاء اللَون. شَرَحَ لي تِم كيفَ تُلعَب البيسبول، لكنّي لَم أفهَمْ قَواعِدَ اللُعبةِ مِن أوَّلِ مَرّة. لكِنَّني الآن أفهَمُها أكثر وبدَأتْ تُعجِبُني.

نَقانِق

بَقِينا في المَلعَبِ أربعَ ساعاتٍ تَقريباً. شَرِبنا كولا وأكلنا شَطائِرَ «هَط ضَغ»، وهذا النَوعُ مِن الطعامِ مَشهورٌ جِدّاً في أمريكا ويأكلُه الناسُ في كُلِّ وَقْتٍ تَقريباً. الـ«هَط ضَغ» مِثلُ النَقانِق في بِلاد الشام، لكِنّها أكبَر ومَصنوعة من لَحْمِ البَقَر. صِرتُ أُحِبُّ أنْ آكلَ شطائِرَ الهط ضَغ الآنَ وكذلك شَطائِرَ الـ«هامبَرغر»، لكنّ النَقانِقَ ألَذُّ من الهَط ضغ لأنَّ فيها تَوابِل كَثيرة.

السِباحةُ من الرياضاتِ الَّتي أُفَضِّلُها كَثيراً بالإضافةِ إلى كُرةِ السَلّةِ وكُرةِ الطاوِلة. هُناكَ مَسْبَحٌ في الجامِعةِ أذهَبُ إليه دائِماً قَبلَ دُروسي في الصَباحِ ثَلاثَ مَرّاتٍ أو أكثَر في الأسبوع.

أفَضِّلُ السِباحةَ في البَحْرِ في فَصلِ الصَيفِ وكَلَمبَس لَيسَتْ على شاطئِ البَحر، لكِنَّها قَريبةٌ مِن عَدَدٍ مِن البُحَيراتِ الكَبيرةِ الَّتي يُوجَدُ على شواطِئِها حَدائِقُ عامّة واسِعة. سَبَحتُ في بَعضِها في الصَيفِ حينَ ذَهَبتُ إلى هُناكَ مع بَعضِ الأصدِقاء. كان في تِلكَ الحَدائق عائلاتٌ كَثيرة، وكان الكِبارُ والصِغارُ يَلعَبونَ الكُرةَ الطائِرةَ وكُرةَ القَدَمِ الأوروبيّةَ وغَيرَهُما مِن الألعاب. لَم أرَ أحَداً يَلعَبُ كُرةَ القَدَمِ الأمريكيّة.

كُرةُ القَدَمِ الأمريكيّة

كُرةُ القَدَمِ الأوروبيّة

الكُرةُ الطائِرةُ

مِشْواةٌ في حَديقة

يوجَدُ أيْضاً في هذهِ الحَدائِقِ مَشاوٍ عامّةٌ يَستَخدِمُها الناسُ لِشَيِّ اللَحْمِ و«الهَط ضَغ»، واللَحمُ المَشويُّ هو الطعامُ المُفَضَّلُ للناسِ في الحَدائق. هذه الحَدائقُ نَظيفةٌ غالِباً وفيها الكَثيرُ من الأشجارِ وأماكِنُ واسِعةٌ لِلَّعب. وَصَلنا إلى الحَديقةِ عِندَ الظُهرِ تَقريباً وبَقِينا فيها حَتّى الساعةِ التاسِعةِ مَساءً. استَمتَعتُ كَثيراً في ذلك اليوم.

# من يوميّاتِ مايكل براون

سميط بالشكولاتة

الرياضةُ المُفَضَّلةُ عِندَ المِصريّينَ هي كُرَةُ القَدَم، لكِنَّها لَيسَت كُرَةَ القَدمِ الّتي نَعرِفُها في أمريكا، بَل كُرَةَ القَدَمِ الأوروبيّة. هُناكَ فِرَقٌ كَثيرةٌ لِكُرةِ القَدَمِ في مِصر، لكنَّ الفَريقَينِ المَشهورَينِ في القاهِرة هُنا «الأهلي» و«الزمالِك». ذَهبتُ إلى إحدى المُبارَياتِ بَينَهُما مع سَمير في مَلعَبِ القاهِرة الدَوْلي الّذي يَتَّسِعُ لِمِئةٍ وعِشرينَ ألفَ مُتَفَرِّج. وكان هُناكَ عَشرات الآلاف من المُتفَرِّجين، رِجالاً ونِساءً وأولاداً وبَناتاً. يأكُلُ الناسُ في المَلعَبِ عادةً «السَميط» ويَشرَبونَ الشايَ والقهوةَ والمِياهَ الغازيّة. يأكُلُ كَثيرٌ من الناسِ اللُبَّ (أو اللِبّ كما يَقولون) وهو بُذور البِطّيخ المُحَمَّصة، وكذلك الفولَ السودانيّ.

قال لي سَمير إنّه يَلبَسُ قَميصاً أحمرَ لأنّ اللونَ الأحمَر هو لونُ «الأهلي»، أمّا لون «الزمالِك» فَهو الأبيَض. وقال إنّ لِكُلِّ فَريقٍ بالقاهِرة مَلعَبَه، لكنّ الفِرَق الكَبيرة تَلعَبُ في مَلعَبِ القاهِرةِ الدَولي عادةً. شَرَحَ لي سَمير قَواعِدَ اللُعبةِ وفهِمتُها واستمتَعتُ بالمُباراةِ جِدّاً. وكان سَمير سَعيداً جِداً لأنّ فَريقَهُ «الأهلي» فازَ بالمُباراة. صِرتُ أشاهِدُ مُبارَياتِ كُرةِ القَدَمِ على التِلفاز وأذهَبُ أحياناً إلى المَلعَبِ حينَ يكونُ عِندي وقت.

المَشي في شَوارِعِ القاهِرة

صار عِندي في القاهِرة رِياضةٌ مُفَضَّلةٌ أخرى وهي المَشي. هُنا في القاهِرة أمشي إلى كُلِّ مَكان. أكثَر الناس يَمشونَ ولا يَركَبونَ السيّارات أو الحافِلات دائماً. أُفَضِّلُ أنْ أمشيَ مَساءً خُصوصاً في الصَيف. أمّا في الفُصولِ الأخرى فَأيُّ وَقتٍ مِن اليَومِ مُناسِبٌ لِلمَشي. وبِسَبَبِ المَشي يَومياً صِرتُ أعرِف شَوارِعَ القاهِرة جَيِّداً ومَكانَ مُعْظَم المَحلاّت التِجاريّة القَريبة والشَركات وغَيرِها. لا تَجِدُ ناساً يَجرونَ في شَوارِع القاهِرة كَما في أمريكا. الجَري هُنا رِياضةٌ يَلعَبُها بَعضُ الناسِ في المَلعَبِ فَقَط وليس في الشارِع. جَميعُ الألعابِ الّتي نَعرِفُها مَوجودةٌ في مِصرَ وكذلكَ في البِلادِ العربيّة الأخرى كَكُرةِ المَضرِب وكُرةِ الماء ورُكوبِ الخَيل ورُكوبِ الدَرّاجاتِ وغَيرِ ذلك.

| | | | |
|---|---|---|---|
|  |  |  |  |
| رُكوبُ الدرّاجاتِ | رُكوب الخَيلِ | كُرةُ الماءِ | كُرةُ المَضربِ |

الخُضَرُ والفَواكِه في مِصرَ لَذيذةٌ جداً. صِرتُ آكلُ الآنَ الكَثيرَ من الخُضَرِ كَالفاصولية والبازِلاء والخَسِّ والبامية والباذِنجانِ والكوسا والفُلَيفُلة الخَضراء وغَيرِها. أفَضِّلُ الباذِنجانَ من الخُضَر.

## الخُضَر

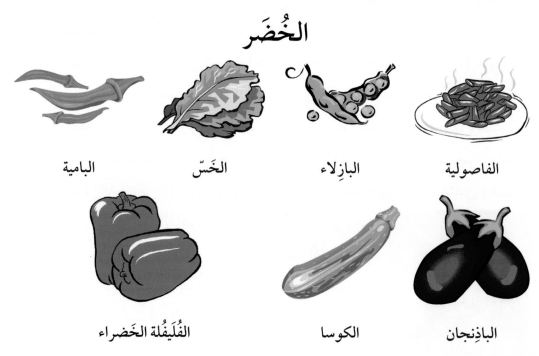

| | | | |
|---|---|---|---|
| 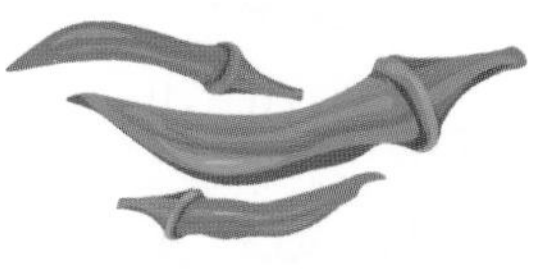 |  |  |  |
| البامية | الخَسّ | البازِلاء | الفاصولية |
| 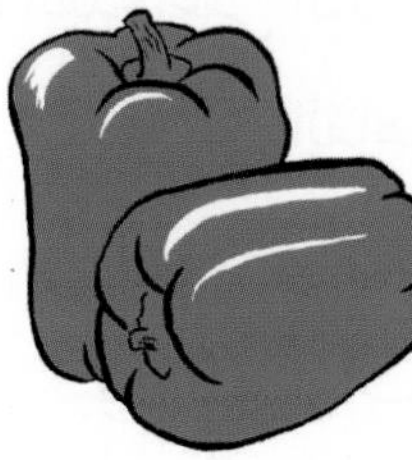 | | 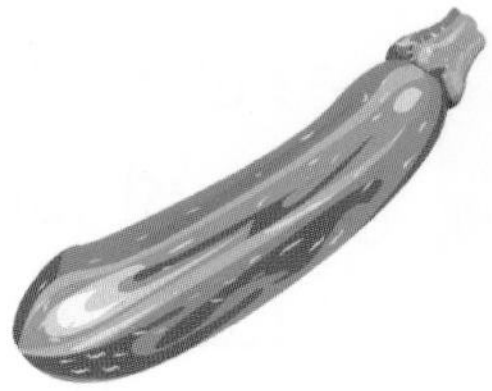 | 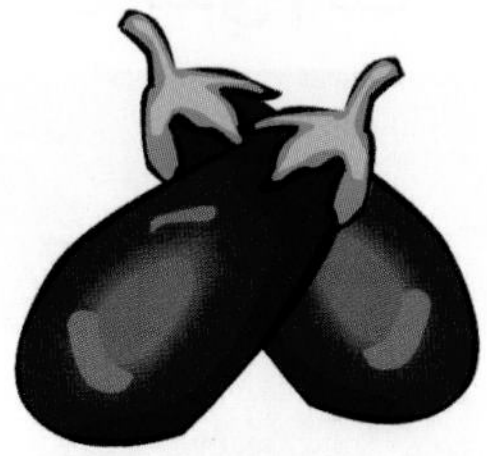 |
| الفُلَيفُلة الخَضراء | | الكوسا | الباذِنجان |

لا يوجدُ تُفّاح كَثير في مِصر، لكِن هُناكَ فَواكِهُ كَثيرةٌ أخرى كَالبُرتُقالِ والعِنَبِ والمَوْزِ والتوتِ والبِطّيخ والمَنجةِ والإجّاص. فاكِهَتي المُفَضّلة في مِصرَ هي المَنجة المِصريّة لأنَّها لَذيذةٌ وأكبَرُ من أيِّ نَوعٍ آخَر أعرِفُه.

# الفَواكِه

التُفّاح

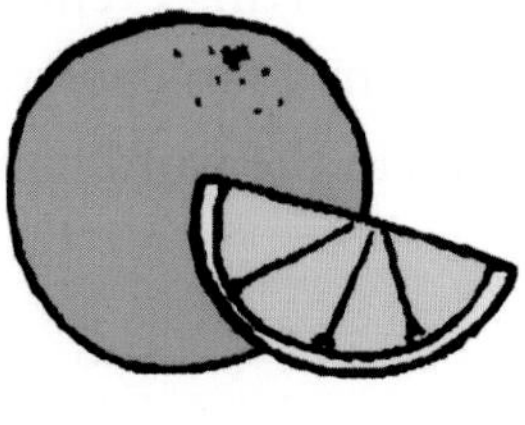

البُرتُقال

العِنَب

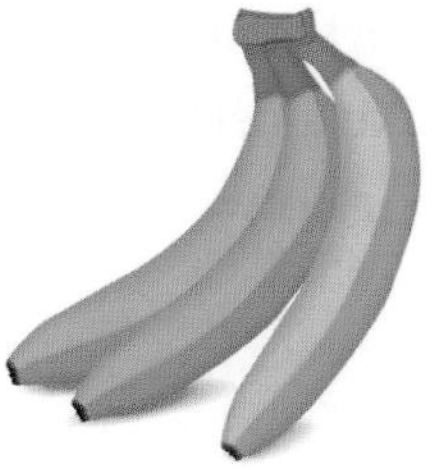

المَوْز

التوت

البِطّيخ

المَنجة

الإجّاص

ومِن الأطعِمةِ المِصريّةِ أفضَلُ الطَعميّة والكُشَري. أجِدُ هذه الأطعِمةَ لَذيذةً بِسَبَبِ التَوابِلِ المَوجودةِ فيها. لَم أكُنْ آكلُ طَعاماً فيه تَوابِل كَثيرة، لكِن بَعدَ أنْ تَناوَلتُه في مِصرَ صارَ يُعْجِبُني.

## تمرين ٣

**أجِبْ عن الأسئلةِ التالية حَسَبَ النَصِّ.**

١– ما الرِياضةُ المُفَضَّلةُ الّتي كانَ يَلعَبُها عَدنان حينَ كانَ في المدرسة الثانوية؟

٢– ماذا يوجَد تَحتَ شَقّةِ عَدنان؟

٣– ماذا يَأكُلُ الأمريكيّونَ في مُباراةِ البيسبول؟

٤– أينَ يَسبَحُ عَدنان في الصَيف أحياناً؟

٥– ماذا يأكُلُ الناسُ ويَشرَبون في مَلاعِبِ كُرَةِ القَدَمِ في القاهِرة؟

٦– ما الرياضاتُ الأخرى في البِلادِ العربيّة؟

٧– لِماذا صارَ مايكل يَعرِفُ شَوارِعَ القاهِرةِ جيّداً؟

٨– ما فاكِهةُ مايكل المُفَضَّلة في مِصر؟ لِماذا يُفَضِّلُها؟

## تمرين ٤

**Conversation:** Describe a sporting event that you attended, or a sport's team that you participated on, or talk from a fan's perspective about why you like a certain sport. Use as many of the words in the word bank as you can during your conversation.

| | | | | | | | |
|---|---|---|---|---|---|---|---|
| فازَ | خَسِرَ | اِسْتَخْدَمَ | خُصوصاً | تَقريباً | مُفَضَّل | مُباراة | فَريق |
| الّذي | الّتي | الّذين | أعْجَبَ | اِسْتَطاعَ | فَهِمَ | أَسْتَمْتِعُ بِـ | |

## تمرين ٥

**أكتُبْ «خَطَأ» أو «صَواب» بِجانبِ كُلِّ جُملَةٍ وصَحِّحِ الجُمَلَ الخَطَأ.**

١- يَلعَبُ عَدنان كُرَةَ الطاوِلَةِ في الجامِعة.

٢- لَيسَ لِرياضةِ البيسبول كَلِمةٌ عَرَبيّةٌ لأنّ العَرَبَ لا يَلعَبونَها.

٣- النَقانِقُ مَصنوعةٌ مِن اللَحم.

٤- يوجَد في كَلَمبَس بُحَيراتٌ كَبيرة.

٥- شاهَدَ مايكل مُباراةَ كُرةِ قَدَم في مَلعَبِ فَريق «الأهلي».

٦- كان مايكل يَلعَبُ رِياضَةَ الجَري في شَوارِعِ القاهِرة.

٧- لا يوجَدُ تُفّاح وبِطّيخ كَثير في مِصر.

٨- الكُشَري من أطعِمَة مايكل المُفَضَّلة لأنَّ مايكل صارَ يأكُلُ كثيراً من الخُضَر.

## تمرين ٦

**اختَرِ التَكمِلةَ المُناسِبةَ حَسَبَ النَص.**

١- لَعِبَ عَدنان كُرَةَ السَلّةِ في أمريكا ____________ .

☐ يَومِيّاً ☐ مَرّةً في الأسبوع ☐ مَرّتين أو ثلاث مرّات في الشَهر

٢- لُعبةُ عَدنان المُفَضَّلةُ في أمريكا هي ____________ .

☐ كُرةُ السَلّة ☐ كُرةُ الطاوِلة ☐ البيسبول

٣- لَم ____________ عَدنان رياضةَ البيسبول مِن أوَّلِ مَرّة.

☐ يَفهَمْ ☐ يُشاهِدْ ☐ يُعْجِبْ

٤- أكل عَدنان في المَلعَب ______________ .

☐ هامبرغر ☐ هَط ضَغ ☐ نَقانِق

٥- يَظُنُّ عَدنان أنَّ النَقانِق ______________ مِن الهَط ضَغ.

☐ ألَذّ ☐ أصغَر ☐ أكبَر

٦- يَسبَحُ عَدنان في أيّام الدِراسة في ______________ .

☐ البُحيرة ☐ المَسبَح ☐ البَحر

٧- طَعامُ الناسِ المُفَضَّل في الحَدائق العامة هو اللَحم ______________ .

☐ المَشويّ ☐ المُحَمَّص ☐ الحارّ

٨- بَقِيَ عَدنان في الحَديقةِ العامّةِ حَتّى ______________ .

☐ الظُهر ☐ المَساء ☐ اللَيل

٩- يتَّسِعُ مَلعَب القاهِرة الدَولي لـ______________ ألف مُتَفَرِّج.

☐ ٢٠ ☐ ٦٠ ☐ ١٢٠

١٠- يأكلُ المِصريّونَ في المَلعَب ______________ .

☐ اللَحمَ المَشويّ ☐ النَقانِق ☐ السَميط

١١- الوَقتُ المُناسِبُ لِلمَشي بالقاهِرة في الصَيف هو ______________ .

☐ الظُهر ☐ المَساء ☐ أيّ وَقت

١٢- يُفَضِّلُ مايكل مِن الخُضَر ______________ .

☐ الباذِنجان ☐ المَنجة ☐ الفاصولية

١٣- تُعْجِبُ المَنجةُ مايكل لأنّها ______________ .

☐ صَغيرة ☐ مِصريّة ☐ لَذيذة

١٤- صارَ مايكل يُحِبُّ أنْ يَتَناوَلَ طَعاماً فيه ______________ .

☐ كُشَري ☐ تَوابِل ☐ طَعميّة

# تمرين ٧

**اختَر التكمِلةَ المُناسِبةَ لِتُكمِلَ الجُمَلَ التالية.**

١- ________ كُرةَ الطاوِلة في المدرسة.

☐ أُعجِبُ ☐ ألعَب ☐ أشترَي ☐ أُنزِل

٢- في المَبنى حَيثُ أسكُنُ، هُناك ________ مِن عَدَدٍ مِن بِلادِ العالَم.

☐ سُكّان ☐ شَطائِر ☐ مَلاعِب ☐ نَقانِق

٣- شَرَحَ لي صَديقي كَيفَ ________ كُرةُ القَدَمِ الأمريكيّة.

☐ تُشاهَدُ ☐ تُؤكَلُ ☐ تُفهَمُ ☐ تُلعَبُ

٤- أحِبُّ الفلافِل لأنّ فيها ________ .

☐ خُضَراً ☐ تَوابِل ☐ شَطائِر ☐ فَواكه

٥- ألعبُ ________ السَلّةِ في المدرسة.

☐ عَصا ☐ كُرَةَ ☐ ملَعبَ ☐ طابَقَ

٦- ________ ناديا اللغةَ الفَرَنسيّة وتتكلّمُها جَيِّداً.

☐ تَلعَبُ ☐ تَضَعُ ☐ تَنزِلُ ☐ تفهَمُ

٧- تُعجِبُ أخي السيّاراتُ اليابانيّةُ ________ تويوتا.

☐ أحياناً ☐ دائِماً ☐ خُصوصاً ☐ جِدّاً

٨- أكلتُ ________ جُبن مع فِنجان شاي صَباحاً.

☐ شَطيرة ☐ لَذيذة ☐ فُليفُلة ☐ أطعِمة

٩- ما طَعامُك ________ .

☐ اللَذيذ ☐ المَشوي ☐ النَظيف ☐ المُفَضَّل

١٠- ما اسمُ ________ كُرةِ السَلّةِ المَشهور في لوس أنجِلس؟

☐ جَري ☐ رِياضةِ ☐ فَريقِ ☐ لُعبةِ

١١- هَل تَفهمينَ ________ لُعبة كُرةِ القَدَمِ الأمريكيّة؟

☐ فِرَقَ ☐ قَواعَدَ ☐ رِياضات ☐ مُبارَيات

١٢- حَضَّرنا طَعامَ الغَداءِ على ________ في حَديقةِ داري.

☐ مِشواةٍ ☐ عَصا ☐ كُرةٍ ☐ بَقَرةٍ

## تمرين ٨

**أعد ترتيب الكلمات لتشكّلَ جملاً مفيدة.**

١- بِسَبَبِ - تَوابِلِها - العَرَبيّةِ - أحِبُّ - الأطعِمةِ - بَعْضَ

٢- الوَطَنِ - هي - العربيِّ - القَدَمِ - اللُعبةُ - في - كُرةُ - المُفَضَّلةُ

٣- لَذيذةٌ - أنَّ - عَدنان - النَقانِقَ - يَظُنُّ

٤- في - المَشاوي - العامّةِ - تُستَخدَم - الحَدائقِ - اللَحمِ - لِشَيِّ

٥- على - أنْ - حُسين - الجَديد - المُبارَيات - تِلفازه - يَستَطيعُ - يُشاهِدَ

## تمرين ٩

**أعد ترتيب الجمل لتشكّل فِقرة.**

١- أرَدتُ أنْ أشاهِدَ مُباراةَ كُرةِ القَدَمِ مع أصدِقائي في المَلعَب.

بَدأتِ المُباراةُ في الثالِثة والنِصف.

لأنَّ فَريقَنا فازَ بِالمُباراة.

لِذلك اشتَرَيتُ تَذاكِرَ المُباراةِ قَبلَ يومَين.

وكانَ في المَلعَبِ آلافُ المُتَفَرِّجين.

وَصَلنا أنا وأصدِقائي إلى المَلعَبِ في الساعةِ الثالِثةِ إلاّ رُبعاً.

بَقِينا في المَلعَبِ ساعتَينِ حَتّى انتَهتِ المُباراة.

رَجَعنا إلى بُيوتِنا سُعَداء في الساعةِ السادِسةِ مَساءً.

الّذينَ كانوا يأكلونَ الفولَ السودانيَّ ويَشرَبونَ المياهَ الغازية.

## تمرين ١٠

صِفْ مُباراةً رياضِيّة شاهَدتها في المَلعَبِ أو على التِلفاز. أيّةُ لُعبةٍ كانت؟ بَينَ أيّ فَريقَين؟ ماذا أكلت وشرِبت أثناء المُباراة؟ هل استمتعت بها؟ مَن فاز بِالمُباراة؟

**Composition:** Describe a sporting event you have watched either in person or on television. Mention which game it was, who the two teams were, what you did while watching it, whether you enjoyed it, and who won the game.

# تمرين ١١

**Using words of frequency:** Find out who in your class . . .

| | | | | | | | | | | |
|---|---|---|---|---|---|---|---|---|---|---|
| جداً | جيّداً | كثيراً | قليلاً | كلّ | أبداً | يوميّاً | غالباً | دائماً | أحياناً | مرّة |

1. plays soccer a lot
2. has never played tennis
3. always goes to football games
4. studies most of the time
5. sometimes eats hot peppers
6. eats an apple a day (daily)
7. plays table tennis every weekend
8. calls his/her mother on the telephone three times a month
9. has eaten at a very expensive restaurant
10. did not sleep much last night (slept a little)

## ١. Habitual and Progressive Past

The habitual past (e.g., "I used to" + present-tense verb) is expressed in Arabic by using two verbs in succession. The first verb is set in the past, while the second verb is in the present, just as in English. Consider example 1, which is taken from your main reading passage:

١ كُنتُ ألعَبُ كُرةَ السَلّةِ كُلَّ يوم.

*I used to play basketball every day.*

The sequence of the two verbs **كنتُ ألعبُ** 'I used to play' in example 1 differs from the single verb **لعِبتُ** 'I played', which can only express the simple past.

٢ كُنتُ أمشي في الطَريق حينَ رأيتُ صَديقتي.

*I was walking down the street when I saw my friend.*

Example 2 illustrates that if there is a second clause, the verb involved in the second clause must be in the past (= **رأيت**), paralleling the English sentence structure.

The verb **صار** differs from the sense of **كانَ** in that **صار** refers to the present when used in combination with another verb. In his journal, Michael Brown writes:

٣ صِرتُ أعرِفُ شَوارعَ القاهِرةِ جَيِّداً.

*I now know (have come to know) the streets of Cairo well.*

Verbs that refer to the senses can also convey a progressive meaning:

٤    رَأَى سامي هالَة تَمشي على شاطِئِ البَحر.

*Sāmī saw*
*Hāla* <u>*walking/walk*</u> *on the beach.*

## تمرين ١٢

**Translation:** Express these meanings in Arabic, using sequences of past and present verbs.

1.   Hāla used to play tennis twice a week.
2.   I saw Adnān riding a bicycle.
3.   I now know the names of all my classmates.
4.   We watched the two teams play a basketball match.

## تمرين ١٣

اسألوا جيرانَكُم:

١–    أَيّ طعامٍ كُنْت لا تُحِبُّه/ تُحِبِينه ولكِنّك صِرْت تُحِبُّه/ تُحِبِّينَه الآن؟

٢–    أَيَّةَ لُعبةٍ كُنْت تَلْعَبُها/ تَلْعَبِينَها كَثيراً في الماضي ولا تَستَطيعُ/ ينَ لُعبَها الآن؟

٣–    أَيّ مُسَلْسَلٍ تَلَفِزيونيّ كُنْت تُشاهِدُه/ تُشاهِدينَه في طُفولتِك؟

٤–    هل صِرْت تَعْرِف/ تَعْرِفينَ كَيْفَ تَتَكَلَّمُ/ تَتَكَلَّمينَ باللغة العربية؟ (حقيقةً)

٥–    ما هو العَمَلُ الّذي كُنْت تُريد/ تُريدينَ أَنْ تَعمَلَ/ تَعمَلي فيه في الماضي؟

## تمرين ١٤

املأ الفَراغات بالتَصريفِ المُناسِبِ حَسَبَ السِياق.

١–    كانوا _____ مُشاهَدةَ الأفلام الأمريكيّة. (أَحَبَّ)

٢–    كُنْتُ _____ جَريدةَ الصَباح يَومياً. (قَرَأَ)

٣–    مَتى كانَ _____ إلى عَمَلِه؟ (أتى)

٤–    كانت هالة _____ أنَّها تَفهَمُ الدَرس. (ظَنَّ)

٥–    ماذا كُنْتِ _____ على الفُطور يا شَهيرة؟ (أَكَلَ)

## 2. Colors

The six basic colors function as nouns and adjectives; therefore, they change morphologically with respect to number and gender. When forming the color dual (by adding ان), the هَمزة changes into و. The same process applies when forming the color plural of feminine nouns (by adding ات). Consider example 5:

| الجمع | | المُثنّى | | المُفرَد | |
|---|---|---|---|---|---|
| بيض | ← | بَيْضاوان | ← | بَيْضاء | ٥ |

The table below lists the six basic colors as adjectives, in the singular, dual, and plural in the masculine and feminine.

| المُؤنّث | | | المُذكَّر | | | |
|---|---|---|---|---|---|---|
| الجَمع | المُثنى | المُفرَد | الجَمع | المُثنى | المُفرَد | اللَون |
| بِيض | بَيْضاوانِ | بَيْضاء | بِيض | أبْيَضانِ | أبْيَض | *white* |
| سود | سَوداوانِ | سَوداء | سود | أسْوَدانِ | أسْوَد | *black* |
| خُضْر | خَضْراوانِ | خَضْراء | خُضْر | أخْضَرانِ | أخْضَر | *green* |
| زُرْق | زَرْقاوانِ | زَرْقاء | زُرْق | أزْرَقانِ | أزْرَق | *blue* |
| حُمْر | حَمْراوانِ | حَمْراء | حُمْر | أحْمَرانِ | أحْمَر | *red* |
| صُفر | صَفراوانِ | صَفراء | صُفر | أصْفَرانِ | أصْفَر | *yellow* |

- **Note:** Feminine and masculine plurals are identical (e.g., بنات/ أولاد بيض).

## تمرين ١٥

**Translation:** Colors in a story. Translate the following paragraph.

Two white clouds moved slowly (ببُطءٍ) in the blue sky. I sat on the white beach and watched them above the blue water and the white boats. A girl wearing a red shirt and white shorts was watching the volleyball game next to a small park on the beach. She had green eyes and black hair. Her mother, wearing green shorts and a white shirt, came to take her daughter to their hotel room located across from the public park. One of the teams was wearing yellow shirts and the other was wearing green shirts. It appeared that (على ما يبدو) the green team was winning, but everyone was happy.

## 3. Comparative Nouns with Doubled Consonants

A comparative (and superlative) noun is formed on the pattern **أفْعَل**, such as **أكْبَر**, which is derived from the adjective **كَبير**. We have dealt with making the **أفعَل** pattern from adjectives like **كَبير** that are comprised of a triliteral root. If, however, an adjective has a doubled consonant, such as **جديد**, **قليل**, and **لذيذ**, in which the second radical is repeated, the two like consonants are collapsed into one doubled consonant. Let's take a close look at the table below for some examples:

| | | | | |
|---|---|---|---|---|
| ٦ | جَديد | سَيّارتي أجَدُّ مِن سَيّارتك. | *newer than* | not أجْدَد |
| ٧ | قَليل | عَدَدُ سُكّانِ الإسكَندَريّةِ أقَلُّ مِن عَدَد سُكّانِ القاهِرة. | *less than* | not أقْلَل |
| ٨ | لَذيذ | النَقانِقُ ألَذُّ مِن الهَط ضَغ. | *more delicious than* | not ألْذَذ |

For a review of the formation of comparative and superlative nouns, refer to Lesson 11, section 5.

## تمرين ١٦

**اشتقّ** (derive) **اسمَ تَفضيلٍ مِن الصِفة بَينَ القَوسين.**

**مِثال: بِنايةُ «سيرز» (طَويل) مِن بِنايةِ إمبايَر «سَتيت».** أطْوَل

١– ما (صَغير) وِلاية في الوِلاياتِ المُتّحِدة الأمريكيّة؟ ________

٢– هذِهِ (لَذيذ) حَلوى أكلتُها حَتّى الآن. ________

٣– تَظُنُّ رانية أنَّ زَوجَةَ سامي (جَميل) فَتاةٍ في البَلدة. ________

٤– عَدَدُ دَفاتِري (قَليل) مِن عَدَدِ دَفاتِرِك. ________

٥– يَسكُنُ أحمَد في (جَديد) شَقّةٍ في البِناية. ________

## 4. Weak Verbs Revisited (الفعل المعتلّ)

In Lesson 13, section 3, and Lesson 17, section 7, we introduced two types of verbs (defective and hollow) that contain a long vowel as one of their root letters. So far we have encountered three types of weak verbs:

a. **المِثال:** This type is known as "assimilated" and has the vowel in the ف position:

٩ وَضَعَ، وَجَدَ، وَسِعَ، وَصَلَ

b. **الأجوَف:** This type is known as "hollow" because it contains a vowel in the ع position:

١٠ قالَ، فازَ

c. **الناقص:** This type is known as "defective" in English and is characterized by a vowel (و or ي) occupying the ل position:

١١ مَشى، جرى، بَقِيَ، نَسِيَ

We will now take a close look at type a, **المِثال**, which is known in English as "assimilated," and for good reason. When verbs of this type are in Form VIII **افتَعَل**, the initial **و** changes to **ت** because it assimilates into the **ت** of the pattern. Let's take a look at this process as illustrated by the verbs **وَسِع** 'to hold, to contain' and **وَصَل** 'to arrive, to connect, to establish contact'.

| **Conversion to Form VIII افتَعَل of an Assimilated Verb** | | | | | |
|---|---|---|---|---|---|
| Assimilated form | | Theoretical form | | فَعَل | |
| اِتَّسَعَ | ← | اِوتَسَعَ | ← | وَسِع | ١٢ |
| اِتَّصَل | ← | اِوتَصَل | ← | وَصَل | |

- **Note:** The ت of Form VIII اِفتَعَل and the ت from the converted و are spelled as a doubled تّ with a **شَدّة**.

**All weak verbs share three common characteristics:**

1. In the present-tense conjugation, the long vowel is replaced with its short equivalent when the mood changes from **مرفوع** to **مجزوم** (from indicative to jussive):

| مجزوم | | مرفوع | |
|---|---|---|---|
| يَقُلْ | ← | يَقول | ١٣ |
| يَجرِ | ← | يَجري | |
| يَبقَ | ← | يَبقى | |

2. The **و** is omitted in the present and the imperative:

| الأمر | | المُضارِع | | الماضي | |
|---|---|---|---|---|---|
| صِلْ | ← | يَصِلُ | ← | وَصَلَ | ١٤ |

3. For defective verbs, the final vowel is dropped when it is an indefinite (active participle) **اسم الفاعل** , but it is restored when definite:

| | اسمُ الفاعِل | | | | | |
|---|---|---|---|---|---|---|
| | **Definite** | | **Indefinite** | | **Verb** | |
| *to remain* | الباقي | ← | باقٍ | ← | بَقِيَ | ١٥ |
| *to run* | الجاري | ← | جارٍ | ← | جَرى | ١٦ |
| *to walk* | الماشي | ← | ماشٍ | ← | مَشى | ١٧ |
| *to forget* | الناسي | ← | ناسٍ | ← | نَسِيَ | ١٨ |

## تمرين ١٧

**Using لَم and المُضارِع المَجزوم:** Negate these sentences with لَم, taking into account the changes that take place in weak verbs:

**انفِ الجُمَلَ التالية باستِعمال (لَم).**

١- بَقِيتُ في المَكتَبةِ أكثَرَ مِن ساعتَين.

٢- مَشى رياض إلى المَدرَسة.

٣- فَهِمَتْ سَلمى الدرسَ كُلَّه.

٤- نَسِيتُ أنْ أكتُبَ رِسالةً لِصَديقي.

٥- سَكنوا في الدارِ البَيضاء.

## تمرين ١٨

آ- **أجِبْ عن هذِهِ الأسئلة حَسَبَ نَصِّ الاستِماع.**

١- أينَ شاهَدَ رِياض مُباراةَ كُرةِ القَدَم؟

٢- لِماذا لَم يَكُنْ سُهَيل سَعيداً في نِهايةِ المُباراة؟

٣- مَن حَضَّرَ الحَلوى؟

ب- **أكتُبْ «خَطَأ» أو «صَواب» بِجانبِ كُلِّ جُملَةٍ وصَحِّحِ الجُمَلَ الخَطَأ.**

٤- حَضَّرَ سُهَيل الشايَ والحِمَّص.

٥- اِستَمتَعَ رِياض وأصدِقاؤه بالمُباراة.

٦- لَم يَكُنْ والِدا سُهَيل في البَيتِ في وَقتِ المُباراة.

ت- **اختَرِ التَكمِلةَ المُناسِبةَ حَسَبَ النَص.**

٧- في وَقتِ المُباراةِ كانَ هُناكَ ____________ أشْخاصٍ في بَيتِ سُهَيل.

☐ أربعةُ　☐ خَمسةُ　☐ سِتّةُ　☐ سَبعةُ

٨- أكَلَ الأصدِقاءُ الحِمَّص مع ____________ .

☐ الشاي　☐ الحَلوى　☐ أم سُهَيل　☐ الفُلَيفُلة

٩- لَم يَكُنِ الأصدِقاءُ سُعَداء في نِهايةِ المُباراةِ لأنّ ____________ لَم يَفُزْ.

☐ صَديقَهُم سُهَيل ☐ فريقَهُم

☐ والِدَ سُهَيل ☐ رِياض

١٠- شاهَدَ الأصدِقاء ____________ المُباراةِ على التِلفاز.

☐ كُلَّ ☐ بَعْضَ ☐ جُزءاً مِن ☐ مُعْظَم

١١- شاهَدَ رِياض المُباراةَ في ____________ .

☐ دارِه ☐ بَيتِ صَديقِه ☐ المَلعَبِ ☐ المَدرَسةِ

١٢- شَرِبَ الأصدِقاءُ الشايَ ____________ أنْ أكَلوا الحِمَّص.

☐ قَبْلَ ☐ بَعْدَ ☐ مع ☐ عِندَ

## تمرين ١٩

VIDEO

**تَمرينُ المُشاهَدة: شاهِدوا الدَرْسَ العشرين على القُرْص الرَقْميّ.**

١- ما الأمكِنَةُ الّتي زارَها عَدنان في مَدينةِ نيويورك؟ ____________

____________

____________

٢- لِماذا لا يَلْعَبُ عَدنان كُرةَ السَلّةِ كَما كانَ يَفْعَلُ في حَلَب؟ ____________

____________

____________

٣- ما الرياضَتانِ اللّتانِ يَقومُ بِهِما عَدنان في مدينَتِهِ؟ ____________

____________

____________

٤- في رأيِ عَدنان، ما أجمَلُ شيءٍ في مدينَتِهِ؟ ____________

____________

____________

٥- أيْنَ سَيَذهَبُ سامِر ومايكل بَعْدَ هذا الاجْتِماعِ في الفُندُق؟ ____________

____________

____________

## المُفْرَدات

Listen to the vocabulary items on the CD and practice their pronunciation.

never, not at all . . . . . . . . . . . . . . . . . . . . . (adv.) أبداً

to hold, to contain . . . . . . . . . . . . . . . . (v.) اتَّسَعَ (يَتَّسِعُ) اتِّساع

to contact . . . . . . . . . . . . . . . . . . (v.) (بـ) اِتَّصَلَ (يَتَّصِلُ) اِتِّصال

to agree (with someone) . . . . . . . . . . . (v.) (مَعَ) اِتَّفَقَ (يَتَّفِقُ) اِتِّفاق

pear . . . . . . . . . . . . . . . . . . . . . . . . . . . (n., m.) إجّاص

red. . . . . . . . . . . . . . . . . . . . . . . . . (adj.) أحمَر ج حُمْر

to notify, to inform . . . . . . . . . . . . . . . . (v.) أخْبَرَ (يُخْبِرُ) إخْبار

blue . . . . . . . . . . . . . . . . . . . . . . . . . (adj.) أزرَق ج زُرْق

to use, to utilize, to employ . . . . . . . . . . . . (v.) استَخدَمَ (يَستَخدِمُ) استِخدام

yellow . . . . . . . . . . . . . . . . . . . . . . . . (adj.) أصْفَر ج صُفْر

eggplant . . . . . . . . . . . . . . . . . . . . . . . . (n., m.) باذِنجان

green peas. . . . . . . . . . . . . . . . . . . . . . . . (n., f.) بازِلاء

ochra . . . . . . . . . . . . . . . . . . . . . . . . . . (n., f.) بامْية

slowly . . . . . . . . . . . . . . . . . . . . . . . . . . . (adv.) بِبُطءٍ

seed, kernel . . . . . . . . . . . . . . . . . . . . (n., f.) بِذرة ج بُذور

watermelon . . . . . . . . . . . . . . . . . . . . . . . . (n., m.) بِطّيخ

cow, cattle . . . . . . . . . . . . . . . . . . . (n., f.) بَقَرة ج أبْقار / بَقَر

to remain, to stay . . . . . . . . . . . . . . . . . . . (v.) بَقِيَ (يَبْقى) بَقاء

tomato . . . . . . . . . . . . . . . . . (n., f.) بَنَدورة (طَماطِم في مصر)

white . . . . . . . . . . . . . . . . . . . . . . (n./adj., f.) بَيضاء ج بيض

spice, condiment, seasoning . . . . . . . . . . . (n., m.) تابِل ج تَوابِل

approximately, about, nearly, roughly . . . . . . . . . . (adv.) تَقريباً

berry . . . . . . . . . . . . . . . . . . . . . . . . . . . . (n., m.) توت

garlic . . . . . . . . . . . . . . . . . . . . . . . . (n., m.) ثوم

to run, to flow, to hurry, to rush, to happen, to occur . . . . . . . . . . . (v.) جَرى (يَجري) جَري

horse . . . . . . . . . . . . . . . . . . . . . (n., m.) حِصان ج أحْصِنة

lettuce . . . . . . . . . . . . . . . . . . . . . . . . . (n., m.) خَسّ

especially, particularly . . . . . . . . . . . . . . . . . (adv.) خُصوصاً

party . . . . . . . . . . . . . . . . . . . . . (n., f.) حَفْلة ج حَفَلات

corn . . . . . . . . . . . . . . . . . . . . . . . . . . (n., f.) ذُرة

perhaps, probably. . . . . . . . . . . . . . . . . . . (adv.) رُبَّما

basket . . . . . . . . . . . . . . . . . . . . . (n., f.) سَلّة ج سِلال

a kind of toasted thin bread . . . . . . . . . . . . . . . (n., m.) سَميط

to explain, to expound, to illustrate . . . . . . . . . . . . (v.) شَرَحَ (يَشرَحُ) شَرْح

sandwich . . . . . . . . . . . . . . . . . . . . (n., f.) شَطيرة ج شَطائِر

to grill, to broil . . . . . . . . . . . . . . . . . (v.) شَوى (يَشوي) شَي

to laugh . . . . . . . . . . . . . . . . . (v.) ضَحِكَ (يَضْحَكُ) ضِحْك

public . . . . . . . . . . . . . . . . . . . . . . . . . (adj.) عامّ

stick, rod, cane . . . . . . . . . . . . . . . . . (n., f.) عَصا ج عُصِيّ

it seems; it appears . . . . . . . . . . . . . . . . . على ما يَبْدو (أنّ)

grape . . . . . . . . . . . . . . . . . . . . . . . . . (n., m.) عِنَب

non-, un-, other than, different from. . . . . . . . . . . (n., m.) غَيْر

to win . . . . . . . . . . . . . . . . . . . . . (v.) فازَ (يفوزُ) فَوز

green beans . . . . . . . . . . . . . . . . . . . . . . (n., f.) فاصولية

team, company, band, troupe. . . . . . . . . . . . (n., f.) فَريق ج فِرَق

to think, to reflect, to ponder (not to believe) . . . . . . . . . (v.) فَكَّرَ (يُفَكِّرُ) تَفْكير

green (bell) pepper . . . . . . . . . . . . . . . . . . (n., f.) فُلَيفُلة

to understand, to comprehend, to realize . . . . . . . . . . . (v.) فَهِمَ (يَفْهَمُ) فَهْم

peanuts . . . . . . . . . . . . . . . . . . . (n., m.) فول (سوداني)

rule, principle, basis, foundation, base . . . . (n., f.) قاعِدة ج قَواعِد

cauliflower . . . . . . . . . . . . . . . . . . . (n., m.) قَرنَبيط

like, as . . . . . . . . . . . . . . . . . . . . . . . . (prep.) كَـ

sufficient . . . . . . . . . . . . . . (active participle) كافٍ (الكافي)

ball, sphere . . . . . . . . . . . . . . . . . . . (n., f.) كُرة ج كُرات

basketball . . . . . . . . . . . . . . . . . . . كُرةُ السَلّة

table tennis . . . . . . . . . . . . . . . . . . كُرةُ الطاولة

volleyball . . . . . . . . . . . . . . . . . . . الكُرةُ الطائرة

football/soccer . . . . . . . . . . . . . . . . كُرةُ القَدَم

water polo. . . . . . . . . . . . . . . . . . . . كُرةُ الماء

tennis . . . . . . . . . . . . . . . . . . . . . . . كُرةُ المَضرِب

zucchini . . . . . . . . . . . . . . . . . . . . . . (n., m.) كوسا

kernel, seed . . . . . . . . . . . . . . . . . . (n., m.) لُبّ ج لُبوب

delicious, delightful, tasty . . . . . . . . . . . . . . (adj., m.) لَذيذ

to play . . . . . . . . . . . . . . . . . . . . . . (v.) لَعِبَ (يَلعَبُ) لُعْب

no longer . . . . . . . . . . . . . . . . . . . . . . لَمْ يَعُدْ

soda . . . . . . . . . . . . . . . . . . (n., f.) ماء غازيّ ج مِياه غازيّة

match, game . . . . . . . . . . . . . . . . . (n., f.) مُباراة ج مُبارَيات

spectator . . . . . . . . . . . . . . . . . . . . (n., m.) مُتَفَرِّج ج ون

roasted, toasted . . . . . . . . . . . . . . . . . (n./adj., m.) مُحَمَّص

grill, gridiron . . . . . . . . . . . . . . . . . (n., f.) مِشواة ج مَشاوٍ

grilled . . . . . . . . . . . . . . . . . . . . . . . . . . . . (adj.) مَشويّ

preferred, favorite. . . . . . . . . . . . . . . . . . (n./adj., m.) مُفَضَّل

banana . . . . . . . . . . . . . . . . . . . . . . (n., m.) مَوْز

small, spicy mutton sausage . . . . . . . . . . (n., pl.) نَقانِق (أو مَقانِق)

time . . . . . . . . . . . . . . . . . . . . . . . . . . (n., m.) وَقْت ج أوْقات

# الدَرسُ الحادي والعِشرونَ

## Objectives

- Describing countries, populations, and products
- Describing geographical directions and features
- Introduction to the noun كِلتا / كِلا (both of)
- Expressing exception with إلاّ and غَير

## رُكنُ المُفْرَداتِ الجَديدةِ:

| | |
|---|---|
| *to overlook* | أطَلَّ (يُطِلُّ) إطلال (على) |
| *to consider* | اِعْتبَرَ (يَعْتَبِرُ) اِعْتِبار |
| *to produce* | أنْتجَ (يُنْتِجُ) إنْتاج |
| *to consist (of)* | تَألَّف (مِن) |
| *device* | جِهاز ج أجْهِزة |
| *to border* | حَدَّ / يَحُدُّ / حَدّ |
| *to form* | شَكَّلَ (يُشَكِّلُ) تَشْكيل |
| *to flow into; to pour* | صَبَّ (يَصُبُّ) صَبّ |
| *to make* | صَنَعَ (يَصْنَعُ) صِناعة |
| *outlet* | مَنفَذ |
| *to spring from, to flow from* | نَبَعَ (يَنبَعُ) نَبع |
| *oil, petroleum* | نِفْط |

## المُفرداتُ الجَديدةُ في صُوَرٍ عَديدةٍ:

جَبَل ج جِبال

زَرَعَ (يَزْرَعُ) زِراعة

سِلْسِلة ج سَلاسِل

ساحِل ج سَواحِل

سَهْل ج سُهول

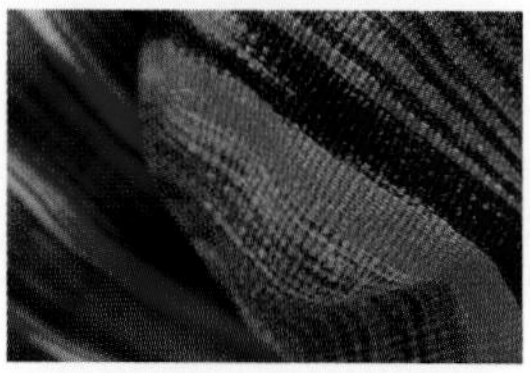

نَسيج ج أنْسِجة

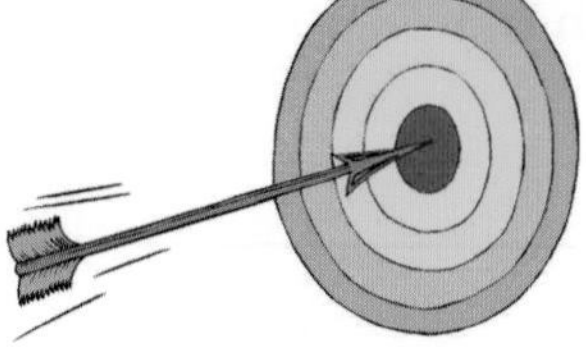

وَسَط ج أوساط

## تمرين ١

وافِق بين كُلِّ كَلِمة ومُضادِتها واكتُب الكَلِمَتين في الوسط.

**Antonyms:**

| | | | |
|---|---|---|---|
| ١ | واسِع | | فَقير |
| ٢ | كَبير | | صَبَّ |
| ٣ | طَويل | | تَحْتَ |
| ٤ | غَنيّ | | ضَيِّق |
| ٥ | بَعيد | | جَميل |
| ٦ | كَثير | | قَصير |
| ٧ | نَبَعَ | | صَغير |
| ٨ | فَوق | | قَريب |
| | | | قَليل |

# تمرين ٢

**وافِق بين كُلِّ كَلِمة وما يناسبها واكتُب الكَلِمَتين في الوسط.** **Matching:**

| | | | |
|---|---|---|---|
| ١ | عَلَم | | بَحر |
| ٢ | بَلَد | | ميناء |
| ٣ | جَزيرة | | شِعار |
| ٤ | سَفينة | | زِراعة |
| ٥ | صِناعة | | رِياضة |
| ٦ | نِفْط | | قُطْر |
| | | | غاز |

# تمرين ٣

**اختَر الكَلِمَةَ الّتي لا تُناسِب باقي الكَلِمات في كُلِّ مَجْموعةٍ وبَيِّن السَبَب.**

| | | | | | |
|---|---|---|---|---|---|
| ١- | مُحيط | بَحر | وَطَن | بُحَيرة | نَهر |
| ٢- | صِناعة | ساحِل | جَبَل | صَحراء | سَهْل |
| ٣- | قُطْن | تبغ | قَمْح | خُضار | نَسَمة |
| ٤- | ذُرة | شَمال | شَرْق | غَرْب | جَنوب |
| ٥- | خَليج | سُكّان | ميناء | بَحر | سَفينة |

## تمرين ٤

**أكمل الجُمَلَ بِالاختِيارِ المُناسِبِ.**

١- كوبا ________ تَقَعُ في البَحرِ الكاريبي.

☐ مَنفَذٌ ☐ جَزيرةٌ ☐ مُحيطٌ ☐ ميناءٌ

٢- ________ الوِلاياتُ المُتَّحِدةُ الأمريكيّةُ مِن ٥٠ وِلاية.

☐ تُطِلُّ ☐ تقَعُ ☐ تُشكِّلُ ☐ تتألَّفُ

٣- زُرْتُ بِلادَ شَمالِ إفريقية ________ تونِس.

☐ إلاّ ☐ إلى ☐ بِـ ☐ لِذلِكَ

٤- يوجَدُ مَصارِفُ ________ في مَدينةِ نيويورك.

☐ ضَيِّقةٌ ☐ خَصيبةٌ ☐ عَديدةٌ ☐ شَرقيّةٌ

٥- كَم ________ في العَلَمِ الأمريكيّ؟

☐ نَجمةً ☐ جَزيرةً ☐ وادِياً ☐ قُطْراً

٦- ماذا ________ كَندا مِن الشَمال؟

☐ يوجَدُ ☐ يَقَعُ ☐ يَتألَّفُ ☐ يَحُدُّ

٧- الجُبنُ مِن ________ الحَليب.

☐ صِناعاتِ ☐ مُنتَجاتِ ☐ أجهِزةِ ☐ مِساحاتِ

٨- هُناكَ ________ كَثيرةٌ في الدُكّان.

☐ رُكّابٌ ☐ سُكّانٌ ☐ حُدودٌ ☐ بَضائِعُ

# جُغرافِيَّةُ الوَطَنِ العَرَبيّ والوِلاياتِ المُتَّحِدةِ الأمريكيّة

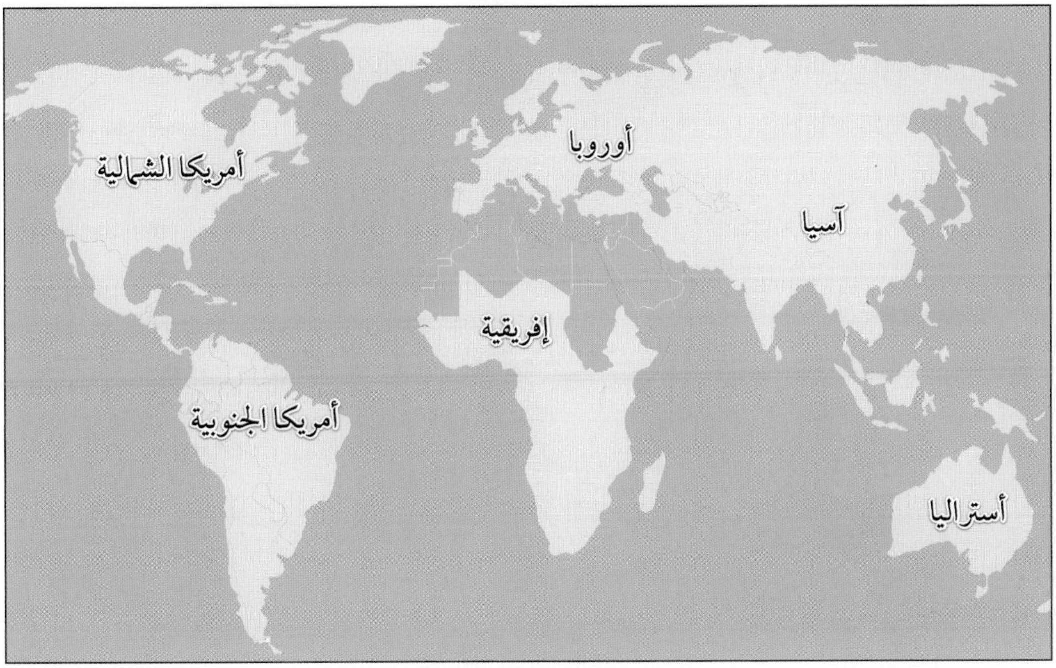


**خريطة الوطن العربي والعالم**

يَقَعُ الوَطَنُ العَرَبيُّ في قارّتَينِ هُما آسيا وإفريقية. تَقَعُ تِسعةُ أقطارٍ عَرَبيّةٍ في إفريقية واثنا عَشَرَ قُطْراً في آسيا. يَتألَّفُ الوَطَنُ العربيّ مِن خَمسةِ أقاليمَ جُغرافيَّةٍ هي بِلادُ الشامِ وما بَينَ النَهرَينِ (العِراق) وشِبْهُ الجَزيرةِ العَربيّةِ ووادي النيل وشَمالُ إفريقية.

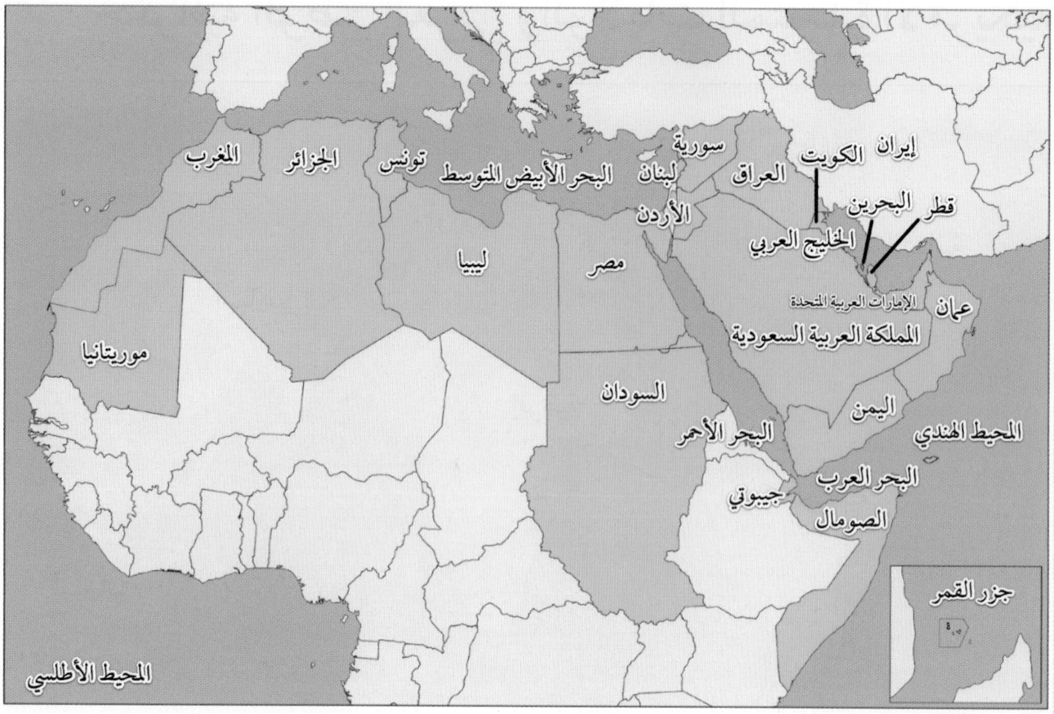


خريطة الوطن العربي

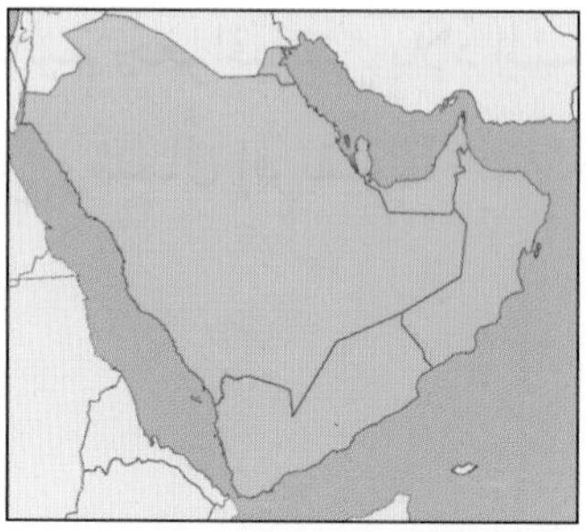

شِبْهُ الجِزيرةِ العَرَبيّةِ

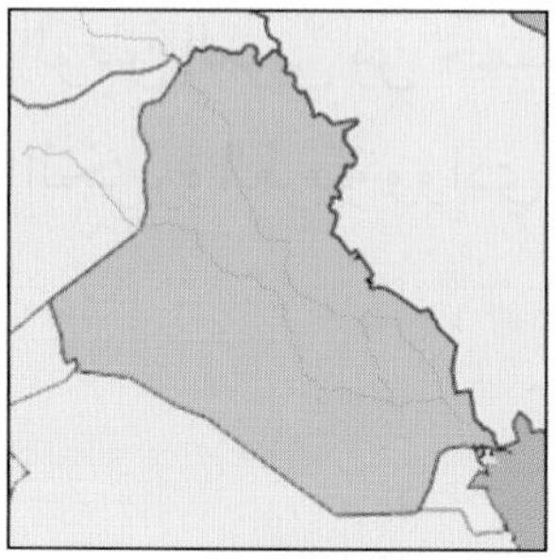

العِراق

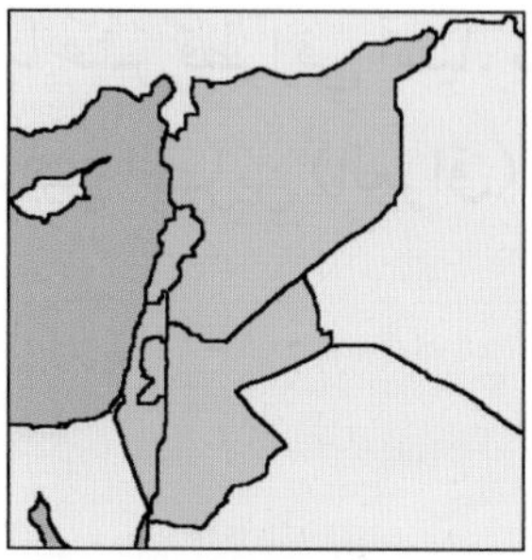

بِلادُ الشام

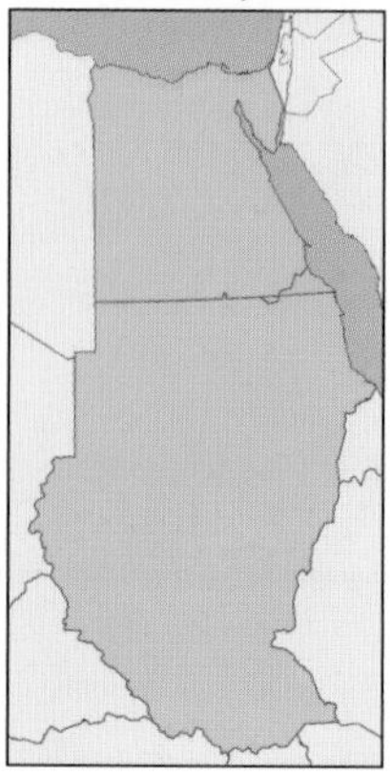

مِصْر والسودان

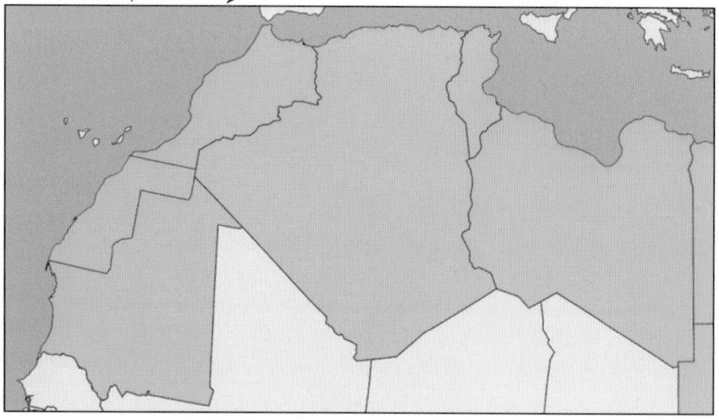

شَمالُ إفريقية

تُطِلُّ بَعضُ الأقطارِ العربيّةِ على البَحرِ الأبْيَضِ المُتَوَسِّطِ مِثلُ سورية ولُبنان وفِلَسطين ومِصرَ وليبيا وتونس والجزائِر والمَغرِب.

يُطِلُّ المَغرِبُ وموريتانيا على المُحيطِ الأطلَسيّ، وتُطِلّ خمسةُ بُلْدانٍ على البَحرِ الأحمَرِ هي مِصرُ والسودانُ واليَمَنُ والمَملكةُ العربيّةُ السُعوديّةُ والأردُنّ. لكِنَّ الأردُنَّ لَهُ مَنفَذٌ ضَيِّقٌ فَقَط على البَحرِ الأحمَرِ هو ميناءُ العَقَبة.

يُطِلُّ على الخَليجِ العربيِّ الكويتُ والمَملَكةُ العربيّةُ السُعوديّةُ وقَطَرُ والإماراتُ العربيّة، ولِلعِراقِ مَنفَذٌ ضَيِّقٌ على الخَليج. أمّا البَحرين فَهو جَزيرةٌ صَغيرةٌ تَقَعُ في الجُزءِ الغَربيِّ مِن الخَليجِ العَربيّ وهو أصْغَرُ بَلَدٍ عَربيّ. ويُطِلّ اليَمَنُ وعُمانُ على بَحرِ العَرَب. أمّا الصومالُ وجيبوتي فَيُطِلاّنِ على بَحر العَربِ والمُحيطِ الهِنْديّ.

يَحُدُّ الوَطَنَ العَربيَّ مِن الشَمالِ تُركيّا والبَحرُ الأبْيَضُ المُتَوَسِّط، ومِن الشَرقِ إيرانُ وبَحرُ العَرَب، ومِن الجَنوبِ المُحيطُ الهِنديُّ والصَحراءُ الكُبرى، ومِن الغَربِ المُحيطُ الأطلَسيّ.

# الوِلاياتُ المُتَّحِدةُ الأمريكيّةُ

تَقَعُ الوِلاياتُ المُتَّحِدةُ الأمريكيّةُ في أمريكا الشَماليّة إلاّ وِلايةَ هاوائي. يَحُدُها مِن الشَرقِ المُحيطُ الأطْلَسيّ، ومِن الغَربِ المُحيطُ الهادي، ومِن الشَمالِ كَندا، ومِن الجَنوبِ المِكسيك وخَليجُ المِكسيك.

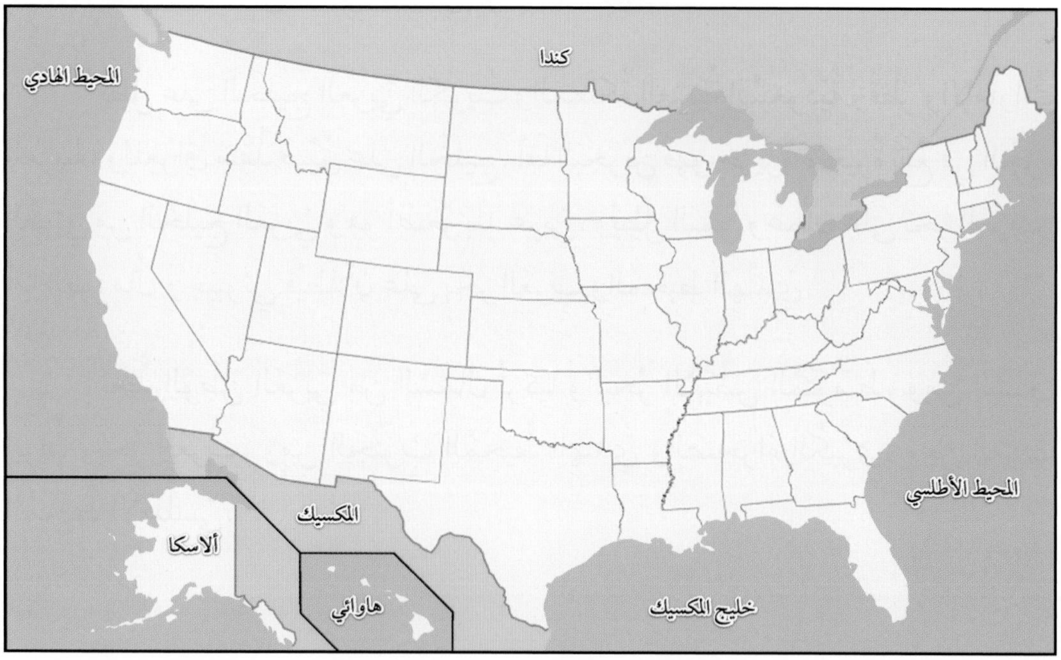


خَريطةُ الولاياتِ المتحدةِ الأمريكيّة

أمّا وِلايةُ ألاسكا فَتَقَعُ شَمالَ غَربِ كَندا، ووِلايةُ هَوائي في وَسَطِ المُحيطِ الهادي. أصغرُ وِلايةٍ أمريكيّةٍ مِن حيثُ المِساحةُ هي "رود آيلاند" في شَرقِ الوِلاياتِ المُتَّحِدةِ على المُحيطِ الأطلَسيّ، وأكبرُها ألاسكا، لكِنَّها أقَلُّ الوِلاياتِ بِعَدَدِ السُكّان.

# سوريَة

تَقَعُ سورية في شَمالِ الوَطَنِ العَربيّ. يَحُدُّها مِن الشَمالِ تُركِيّا ومِن الشَرقِ العِراقُ ومِن الجَنوبِ الأردُنُّ ومِن الجَنوب الغَربيّ لُبنانُ وفِلَسطينُ ومِن الغَربِ البَحرُ الأبْيَضُ المُتَوَسِّط.

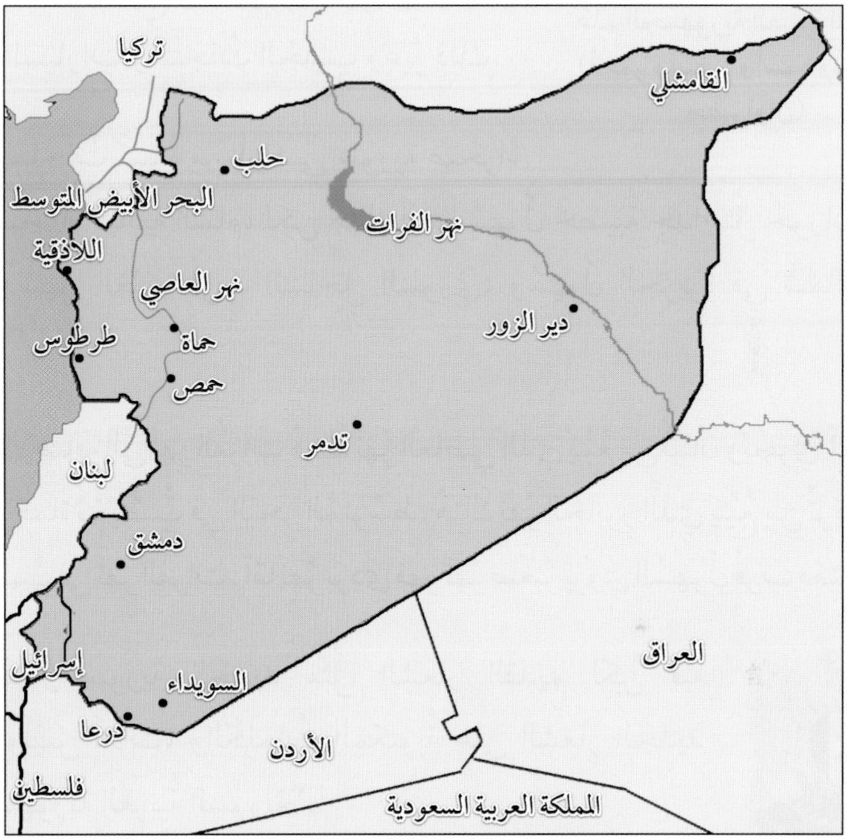


**خريطة الجُمهورية العربية السورية**

عاصِمةُ سورية هي دِمَشقُ وتَقَعُ في جَنوبِها الغَربيّ وهي أكبَرُ مُدُنِها وأقدَمُ مَدينةٍ في العالَمِ سُكِنَت دونَ انقِطاع.

ثاني أكبَرِ مَدينةٍ هي حَلَب وتَقَعُ في الشَمال. هُناكَ صِناعاتٌ عَديدةٌ في كِلتا المَدينتَينِ وبِالقُربِ مِنهُما. تَقَعُ مَدينتا حِمْصَ وحماة بَينَ حَلَبَ ودِمَشق. اللاذِقيّةُ ميناءُ سوريةَ الأوّل، وطَرطوس ميناءٌ آخَرُ على الساحِلِ السوريّ. أمّا بانياسُ فهي ميناءٌ نِفطيّ. تَقَعُ السُوَيداء في جَنوبِ سورية والقامِشلي في شَمالِها الشَرقي. أمّا مَدينةُ دَيرِ الزَوْرِ فتَقَعُ على نَهرِ الفُراتِ الّذي يَنْبُعُ مِن تُركِيّا ويمُرُّ بِسورية ثُمَّ بِالعِراق.

عَلَم الجمهورية العربية السورية (أحمَر وأبْيَض وأسود ونَجمتان خَضراوان)

مِساحَةُ سورية ١٨٥١٠٠ كيلومِتراً مُربَّعاً (٧١٤٦٧ ميلاً مُربّعاً) وعَدَدُ سُكّانِها ٢١ مِليون نَسَمة تَقريباً. يوجَدُ في سورية زِراعَةُ الحُبوبِ والزيتون والفَواكِهِ والخُضَرِ والقُطْنِ والتَبْغ. هُناكَ أيْضاً صِناعاتُ النَسيجِ والأجهِزةِ الكَهرَبائيَّةِ والنِفْطِ وتجميعُ السياراتِ ومُنتَجاتُ الحَليبِ وغيرُ ذلِك.

مِساحاتٌ كَبيرةٌ مِن أراضي سورية صَحْراءُ أو شِبهُ صَحْراءَ كَباديةِ الشام، لكِنْ هُناكَ أيْضاً سُهولٌ خَصيبةٌ جِدّاً مِثْلُ حَورانَ جَنوبيِّ دِمَشق، وسَهْلُ الغابِ قُربَ الساحِلِ السوريّ، وسُهولُ الجزيرةِ في شَمالِ شَرقيِّ سورية.

بالإضافةِ إلى نَهرِ الفُراتِ هُناكَ نَهرُ العاصي الذي يَنبُعُ مِن لُبنانَ ويَجري شَمالاً إلى حِمصَ وحَماةَ ثُمَّ يَصُبُّ في البَحرِ المُتَوّسِّط. هُناكَ نَهرُ الخابورِ الَّذي يَنبُعُ مِن تُركيّا ويَسيرُ جَنوباً لِيَصُبَّ في نَهرِ الفُرات. أمّا نَهرُ بَردى فهو نَهرٌ صَغيرٌ يَروي السُهولَ قُربَ دِمَشق.

شِعار سورية الجديد

شِعارُ سورية الجَديد مِثلُ الشِعارِ القَديمِ لكِنَّ فيه نَجمَتَينِ ولَيْسَ ثَلاث، والكَلِماتُ المَكتوبةُ على الشِعارِ الجَديد هي "الجُمهوريةُ العَربيّةُ السورية".

يوجَدُ جِبالٌ عاليةٌ في سورية كَجَبَلِ الشَيْخ في جَنوبِ غَربِ دِمَشق الَّذي يَصِلُ إلى ٢٨١٤ متراً (٩٢٣٢ قَدَماً) وهو جُزءٌ مِن سِلسِلةِ جِبالِ لُبنانَ الشَرقيّةِ ويُعْتَبَرُ أعلى جَبَلٍ فيها. هُناكَ جِبالُ العَلَويّين على طولِ الساحَلِ السوريّ، وجَبَلُ العَرَبِ في الجَنوب.

# وِلايةُ أوهايو

AUDIO

تَقَعُ وِلايةُ أوهايو في الجُزءِ الشَرقيِّ مِن الوِلاياتِ المُتَّحِدة، وتُعْتَبَرُ أيْضاً واحِدةً مِن وِلاياتِ الغَربِ الأوسَط. يَحُدُّها مِن الشَمالِ بُحَيرةُ إيري، ومِن الشَمالِ الغَربيّ وِلاية ميشِغَن، ومِن الغَربِ وِلايةُ إندِيانا، ومِن الجَنوبِ وِلايةُ كِنتكي، ومِن الجَنوبِ الشَرقيِّ وِلايةُ فِرجينيا الغَربيّة (وِسْت فِرجينيا)، ومِن الشَرقِ وِلايةُ بِنْسِلفانيا.

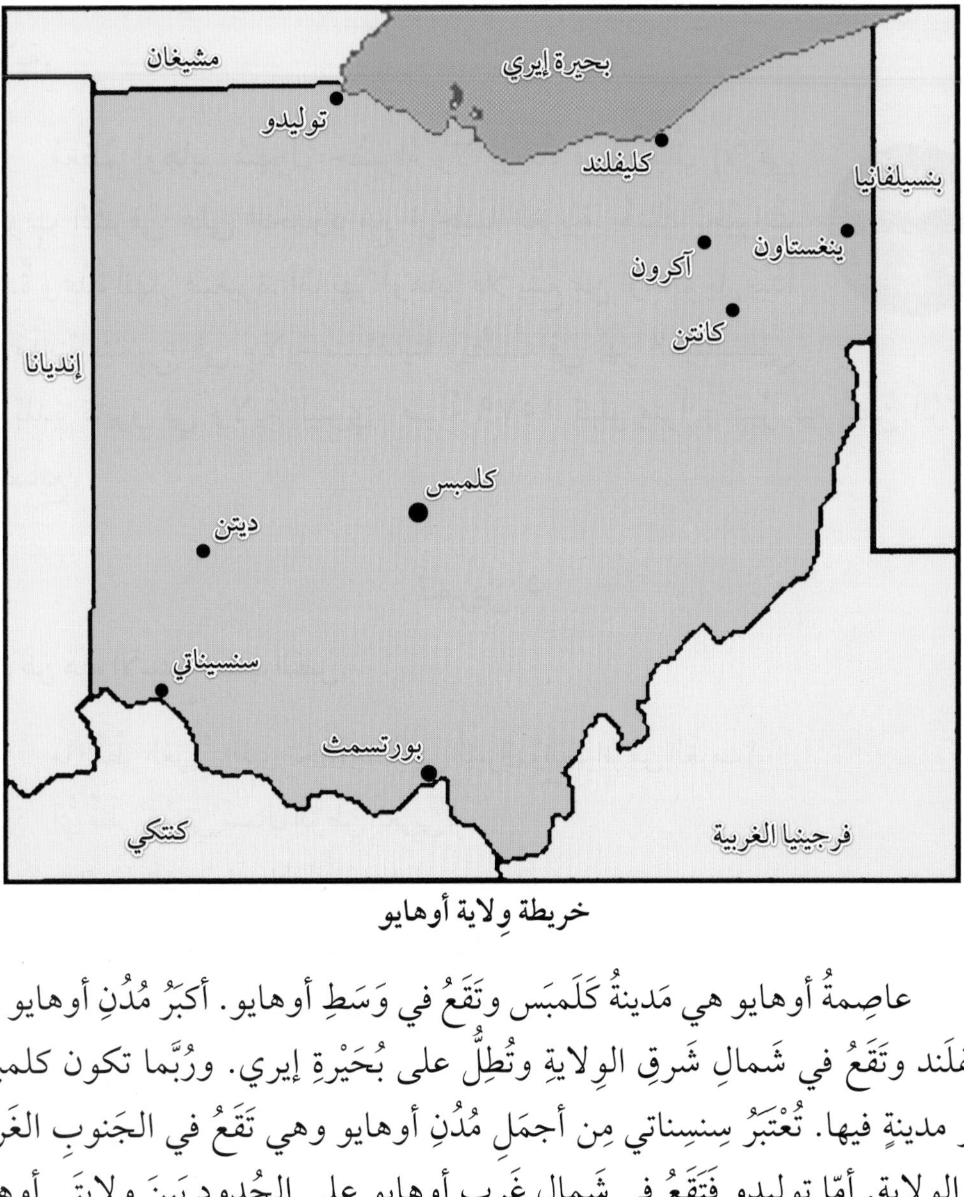


**خريطة وِلاية أوهايو**

عاصِمةُ أوهايو هي مَدينةُ كَلَمبَس وتَقَعُ في وَسَطِ أوهايو. أكبَرُ مُدُنِ أوهايو هي كليفلَند وتَقَعُ في شَمالِ شَرقِ الوِلايةِ وتُطِلُّ على بُحَيْرةِ إيري. ورُبَّما تكون كلمبس أكبر مدينةٍ فيها. تُعْتَبَرُ سِنسِناتي مِن أجمَلِ مُدُنِ أوهايو وهي تَقَعُ في الجَنوبِ الغَربيِّ مِن الوِلاية. أمّا توليدو فَتَقَعُ في شَمالِ غَربِ أوهايو على الحُدودِ بَينَ وِلايتَي أوهايو وميشِغَن، وهي مَدينةٌ صِناعيّة. وهُناكَ آكرَن وكانتَن في شَمالِ شَرقِ أوهايو وكِلتاهُما مَدينتانِ صِناعيَّتانِ كَذلكِ.

مِساحةُ أوهايو ١٠٦٧٦٥ كيلومِتراً مُرَبَّعاً (٤١٢٢٢ ميلاً مُرَبَّعاً) وعَدَدُ سُكّانِها ١١ مِليونَ نَسَمةٍ تَقريباً. أوهايو وِلايةٌ صِناعِيّةٌ تأتي في إنتاجِها الصِناعِيّ بَعدَ وِلايَتي نيويورك وكاليفورنيا، وهي زِراعِيَّةٌ كَذلِكَ وتُنتِجُ الذُرَةَ والقَمحَ ومُنتَجاتِ الحَليبِ والأبقار.

لأوهايو ميناءانِ هامّانِ على بُحَيْرَةِ إيري هُما كليفلَند وتوليدو. وتُعْتَبَرُ سِنسِناتي ميناءً هامّاً أيْضاً على نَهرِ أوهايو الّذي يُشَكِّلُ الحُدودَ الجَنوبِيَّةَ ونِصفَ الحُدود الشَرقيّةِ لِلوِلاية.

مُعظَمُ أوهايو سُهولٌ خَضراءُ ولا يوجَدُ فيها جِبالٌ إلاّ في الجَنوبِ الشَرقيِّ على الحُدودِ مع فِرجينيا الغَربيّة. هُناكَ بُحَيْرات عَديدةٌ وعِدّةُ أنهار صَغيرة. أمّا نَهرُ أوهايو فَلا يَنْبُعُ مِن أوهايو بَل يَبْدَأُ عِندَ مَدينةِ بِتسبرغ في وِلايةِ بِنسِلفانِيا ويَصُبُّ في نَهرِ الميسيسيبي عِندَ بَلدةِ كايرو في وِلايةِ إلينوي. طولُهُ ١٥٧٩ كيلو مِتراً وتَسيرُ فيهِ سُفُنُ الرُكّابِ والبَضائِع.

## تمرين ٥

**أجِب عَن هذه الأسئِلةِ حَسَبَ النَص.**

١- ما القُطرُ العَرَبيُّ الّذي تَحُدُّهُ مِصرُ مِن الشَرقِ والجَزائِرُ مِن الغَرب؟

٢- أيُّ قُطرٍ يَقَعُ في شَمالِ الوَطَنِ العَربيّ؟

٣- ما البَحْرُ الّذي يُطِلُّ الأردُنُّ عَليه؟

٤- ماذا يَحُدُّ الوِلاياتِ المُتَّحِدةَ مِن الغَرب؟

٥- أيُّ بَلَدٍ غيرِ عَرَبيّ لَهُ حُدودٌ مع سورية؟

٦- ما بَعضُ مُنتَجاتِ سورية؟

٧- كَم وِلايةً تَحُدُّ وِلايةَ أوهايو؟

٨- هَل الإنتاجُ الصِناعِيُّ في أوهايو كَبير؟ اشْرَحْ ذلِك.

## تمرين ٦

**أكتُبْ «خَطأ» أو «صَواب» بِجانبِ كُلِّ جُملةٍ وصَحِّح الجُمَلَ الخَطأ.**

١- تُطِلُّ البَحْرَين على الخَليجِ العَرَبيّ.

٢- أكبَرُ الوِلاياتِ الأمريكيّةِ بِالمِساحَةِ هي تِكساس.

٣- يَنْبُعُ نَهرُ العاصي مِن تُركِيّا ويَصُبُّ في الخَليجِ العَرَبيّ.

٤- كانتَن ميناءٌ هامٌ على بُحَيْرةِ إيري.

## تمرين ٧

**اكتُبْ أسئِلةً مُناسِبةً لِهذِهِ الإجابات.** **Jeopardy:**

١- ثَلاثَةُ أقطارٍ عَرَبيَّةٍ تُطِلُّ على هذا البَحر.

٢- هُما تُركِيّا وإيران.

٣- خَليجُ المِكسيك والمِكسيك.

٤- هو مَدينةُ بانياس.

٥- أحَدَ عَشَرَ مليون نَسَمة.

## تمرين ٨

**اختَرِ التَكْمِلةَ المُناسِبةَ حَسَبَ النَص.**

١- تَقَعُ ________ أقطارٍ عَرَبيَّةٍ في إفريقية.

☐ ٩ ☐ ١٢ ☐ ٢٠ ☐ ٢٢

٢- يُطِلُّ الأردُنُّ على ________ .

☐ البَحرِ المُتوَسِّط ☐ البَحرِ الأحْمَر

☐ الخَليجِ العَرَبيّ ☐ بَحرِ العَرَب

٣- ________ أصغَرُ قُطرٍ عَرَبيّ.

☐ عُمان ☐ قَطَر ☐ البَحرَين ☐ لُبنان

٤- تَقعُ وِلايَةُ ألاسكا في__________.

☐ المُحيطِ الهادي ☐ المُحيطِ الأطلَسيّ

☐ أمريكا الشَماليّة ☐ كَندا

٥- تُعْتبَرُ __________ أصغرَ وِلايةٍ أمريكيّةٍ مِن حَيثُ عَدَدِ السُكّان.

☐ رود آيلاند ☐ ديلاوير ☐ ألاسكا ☐ هَوائي

٦- أقدَمُ مَدينةٍ في العالَم سُكِنَتْ دونَ انقِطاع هي __________ .

☐ دِمَشق ☐ حَلَب ☐ القاهِرة ☐ بَغداد

٧- __________ مِن المُنتَجات السورية.

☐ النِفط ☐ التبْغ ☐ القُطْن ☐ كُلُّ ما سَبَقَ

٨- تَقعُ جِبالُ العَلَوِيّين __________ سورية.

☐ في جَنوبِ ☐ على ساحِلِ ☐ في شَرقِ ☐ في وَسَطِ

٩- يَحُدُّ أوهايو مِن الشَمال __________ .

☐ كَندا ☐ ميشِغَن ☐ أيوا ☐ بِنسلفانيا

١٠- يُشَكِّلُ نَهرُ أوهايو __________ .

☐ أكبَرُ أنهارِ الوِلاية ☐ الحُدودَ الجَنوبيّةَ الشَرقيّةَ والجنوبيّة

☐ حُدودَ الوِلاية ☐ ميناءً هامّاً

١١- __________ مِن أجمَلِ مُدُنِ أوهايو.

☐ سِنسِناتي ☐ كَلَمبَس ☐ كليفلَند ☐ توليدو

١٢- لا يوجَدُ __________ في وَسَطِ وشَمالِ أوهايو.

☐ صِناعاتٌ ☐ جِبالٌ ☐ سُهولٌ ☐ مَوانِئُ

تمرين ٩

أعِدْ تَرتيبَ الكَلِماتِ في كُلِّ مَجموعةٍ لِتُشَكِّلَ جُمَلاً مُفيدةً.

١- ساحِلِ – على – تَقَعُ – مِلبورن – الجَنوبيّ – أستراليا

٢- العَربيّ – ضَيِّقٌ – على – مَنفَذٌ – الخَليجِ – لِلعِراقِ

٣- الوَطَنِ – مِنَ – واحِدَةٌ – الأقاليم – الشام – العَرَبيِّ – في – بِلادُ – الجُغرافية

٤- النِفطَ – الزِراعيَّةَ – تُنتِجُ – والمَنتوجاتِ – الجَزائِرُ

تمرين ١٠

١- اقرأ النَصَّ التالي ثُمَّ اكتُب على الخَريطةِ المَوجودةِ فوقَهُ اسمَ البَلَدِ الَّذي يَصِفُهُ النَصُّ وأسماءَ مُدُنِهِ وأنهارِهِ وجِبالِهِ وصَحرائِهِ والأقطارَ الَّتي تَحُدُّهُ. بَيِّنْ بَعضَ الصِناعاتِ والزِراعاتِ حَسَبَ مَكانِها.



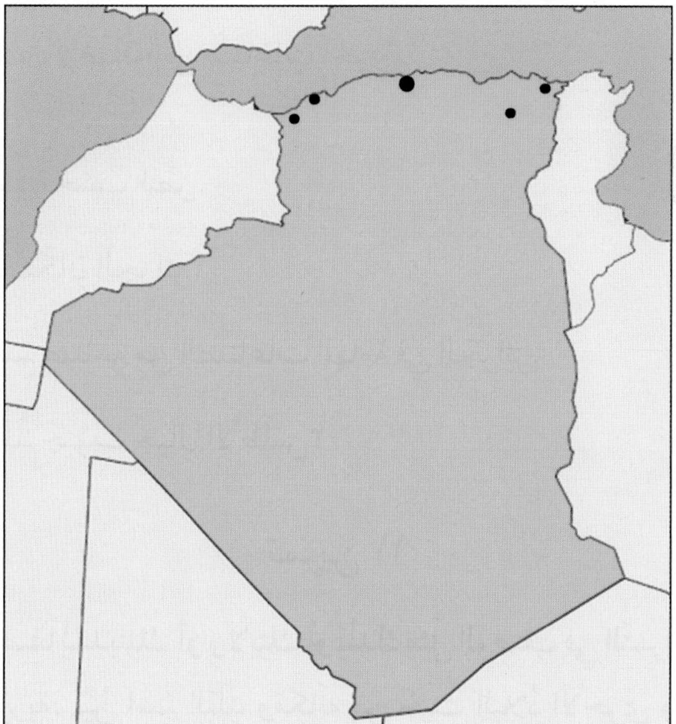

يَحُدُّ القُطرَ الجَزائِريَّ مِنِ الشَمالِ البَحرُ الأبْيَضُ المُتَوَسِّط ومِنِ الغَربِ المَغرِبُ ومِنِ الجَنوبِ الغَربِيِّ موريتانيا ومالي، ومِنِ الجَنوبِ

الشَرقيِّ النيجَر، وتَحُدُّه مِن الشَرقِ ليبيا وتونِس. عاصِمةُ الجَزائِر هي مَدينةُ الجَزائِر وتَقَعُ في شَمالِ البِلادِ على ساحِلِ البَحرِ المُتوَسِّط، وهي ميناءٌ هامٌّ وفيها صِناعةُ النِفطِ والسَيّارات. ومِن أهمِّ المُدُنِ الأخرى وَهرانُ وتَقَعُ على الساحِلِ في غَربيِّ الجَزائِر، وتَقَعُ تِلمسان في الشَمالِ الغَربيِّ مِن البِلاد لكِنَّها لَيسَتْ على الساحِل. أمّا مَدينةُ عَنّابة فتَقَعُ في الشَمالِ الشَرقيِّ على ساحِلِ البَحر، وقَسَنطينة في الشَمالِ الشَرقيّ أيْضاً، لكِنَّها إلى الجَنوبِ الغَربيّ مِن عَنّابة.

تَقَعُ جِبالُ الأطْلَسِ على طولِ الساحِلِ إلى الجَنوبِ مِنه قَليلاً، ويَقَعُ بَينَ هذِهِ الجِبالِ والبَحرِ المُتَوَسِّطِ سُهولٌ خَصيبةٌ تُسْتَخدَمُ لِلزِراعة. مُعظَمُ الأراضي جَنوبَ جِبالِ الأطلَسِ صَحْراويّة.

عَدَدُ سُكّانِ الجَزائِر ٣٣ مليون نَسَمة تَقريباً. يَعمَلُ نِصْفُ السُكّانِ في الزِراعةِ ويُنتِجونَ العِنَبَ والبُرتُقالَ والحُبوبَ والفَواكِه. تُنتِجُ الجَزائِرُ أيْضاً النِفطَ والغاز. ويوجَدُ إلى جانِبِ الزِراعةِ صِناعةُ السَيّاراتِ بِالإضافةِ إلى صِناعاتٍ أخرى.

**أجِب عَن هذِهِ الأسئِلةِ حَسَبَ النَصّ.**

٢- كَم عَدَدَ سُكّانِ الجزائر؟

٣- اكتُب اسمَ صِناعَةٍ مِن الصِناعاتِ الهامّة في الجَزائِر.

٤- ماذا يوجَدُ جَنوبَ جِبالِ الأطلَس؟

## تمرين ١١

**اكتب وصفاً لِمَدينتِك أو وِلايتِك أو بَلَدِك مِثلَ الوَصفِ في التَمرين السابق (١٠) وفي وَصفِ سورية. بَيِّنْ اسمَ البَلَدِ ومَكانَه مِن حَيثُ البِلادُ الأخرى والمدُنُ والأنهارُ والبُحَيراتُ والزراعةُ والصِناعةُ والسُكّان.**

## تمرين ١٢

**صِفِ القُطرَ العِراقيَّ حَسَبَ المَعلوماتِ المَوجودةِ على الخَريطة. استَخدِمِ النَصَّ في التَمرين ١٠ والنَصّينِ عَن سورية وأوهايو كأمثِلة.**

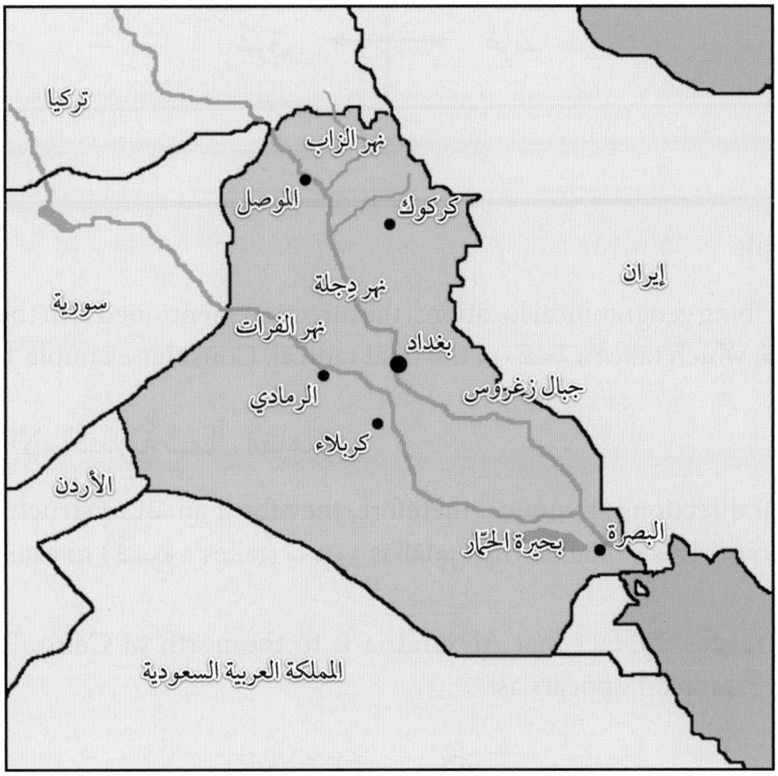


## تمرين ١٣

**اسألوا جيرانَكُم:**

١- صِفْ لي مَدينتَك.

٢- أيْنَ تَقْعُ سِلْسِلة جِبال روكي وهل تُريد(ين) زيارتها؟

٣- ما الأجمَل في رأيك، الساحِل الأمريكيّ الغَرْبيّ أم الشَرْقيّ ولِماذا؟

٤- أيْنَ تُنْتَجُ السيّارات في أمريكا؟

٥- أيّةُ وِلايةٍ تَقْعُ في وَسَط أمْريكا ؟

## 1. Geographical Directions

The cardinal directions can be used either as adverbials or in a prepositional phrase.

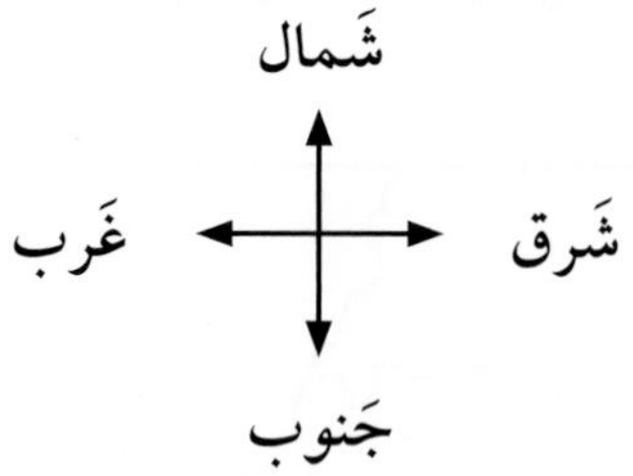


### A. Adverbials

When describing geographical locations, the direction mentioned is in the accusative case مَنصوب, which takes a فَتحة on the final radical. Consider example 1:

١ تَقَعُ الإسكَندَريّةُ شَمالَ القاهِرةِ.

The cardinal directions are nouns; therefore, they form an إضافة structure with the following noun. This explains why القاهِرة is مَجرور (takes a كَسرة) in example 1.

Example 1 relates the fact that Alexandria is to the north of Cairo. Represented graphically, example 1 appears as:

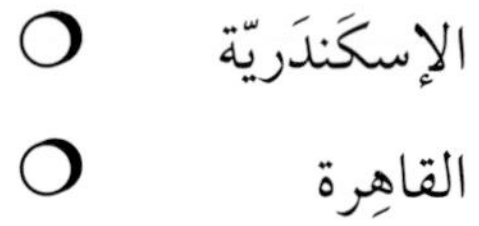


### B. Prepositional Phrases

When we mention geographical directions in positional phrases, the spatial relationship is different. Read example 2 and then consider its graphic:

٢ تَقَعُ الإسكَندَريّةُ في شَمالِ مِصر. أو . . .
تَقَعُ الإسكَندَريّةُ في شَماليِّ مِصر.

The relationship in example 2 is inclusive; that is, we are told that Alexandria is in northern Egypt, not to the north of something. Graphically, this relationship may be represented as follows:

The word شَماليّ in the alternative sentence in example 2 is a *nisba* noun.

## تمرين ١٤

**Conversation:** Interview a classmate concerning a country in which he/she has resided, or a country he/she has visited in his/her lifetime. The person listening should try to draw a map of this area. The person describing the location should try to use as many directions and details as possible, as well as utilizing the cardinal and intercardinal (e.g., northwest, southeast) directions.

| | | | | | | | |
|---|---|---|---|---|---|---|---|
| عاصِمة | وَسَط | سِلْسِلة | صَنَعَ | أَنْتَجَ | يَحُدُّ | اِعْتَبَرَ | وَقَعَ |
| جَنوب | شَمال | غَرْب | شَرْق | حُدود | اِسْتَطاع | اِسْتَمْتَعَ بِـ | أَعْجَبَ |

## 2. The Noun كِلا / كِلتا (both of)

The words كِلا (masculine) and كِلتا (feminine) are singular nouns that have a dual meaning. These two words usually form an إضافة structure with the following noun and are invariable (i.e., they do not change form) regardless of their grammatical position:

٣ كِلا الكِتابَين كُتِبَ بِالعَرَبِيَّة.

٤ كِلتا السَيّارتَين أَتَتْ مِن ديترويت.

- **Note:** The verbs that reference كِلا or كِلتا are in the singular because this noun is treated as singular despite its dual meaning.

| | | | |
|---|---|---|---|
| مَنصوب | قَرَأتُ كِلا الكِتابَين. | مُذَكَّر | ٥ |
| | زُرْنا كِلتا المَدينتَين. | مُؤَنَّث | ٦ |
| مَجرور | كَتَبْتُ إلى كِلا الطالِبين. | مُذَكَّر | ٧ |
| | أعْرِفُ طُلاّباً مِن كِلتا الجامِعَتَين. | مُؤَنَّث | ٨ |

In the منصوب ومجرور cases, the final *alif* in كِلا and كِلتا changes into ي (كِلَي، كِلتَي) when an attached pronoun is suffixed to them. We use كِلَي and كِلتَي in reference to a noun that is either the object of a verb (as in example 9) or the object of a preposition (as in example 10):

٩ قَرَأتُ الكِتابَينِ كِلَيْهما.

١٠ اِسْتَمتَعنا بِالزيارتَينِ كِلتَيْهما.

## تمرين ١٥

Convey these meanings in Arabic, using appropriate forms of كِلا.

1. Arabic and Hebrew are Semitic (ساميّ) languages, and both of them are written from right to left.
2. Both his sisters study medicine at this university.
3. I read both his letters.
4. There is a telephone in both houses.

## 3. Expressing Exception with إلاّ and غَيْر

We are familiar with three ways of expressing exception using ما عَدا، إلاّ، غَيْر.

### A. The Particle ما عَدا

When we use ما عَدا, the following noun (its object) is مَنصوب (for review of ما عَدا see Lesson 17):

١١ أتى جَميعُ الطُلاّبِ ما عَدا واحِداً.

### B. The Article إلاّ

إلاّ has no grammatical effect on the excepted noun if: (1) the sentence in which it is used is negative; and (2) the noun from which exception is made is not mentioned.

The case of the excepted noun is determined strictly by context:

| | | |
|---|---|---|
| ١٢ | ما وَصَلَ إلاّ أحْمَدُ. | مَرفوع |
| ١٣ | لا تُحِبُّ أختي إلاّ الحِمَّصَ. | مَنصوب |
| ١٤ | لا يُطِلُّ الأرْدُنُّ إلاّ على البَحرِ الأحْمَر. | مَجرور |

The excepted noun in example 12 is **مَرفوع** because it is the doer of the action. In example 13, **الحِمَّص** is the object of the verb and, therefore, **مَنصوب**. In example 14, the excepted noun is **مَجرور** because it is the object of a preposition.

In an affirmative sentence, the particle **إلاّ** causes the excepted noun, which follows it immediately, to be **منصوب** regardless of its position in the sentence.

١٥ وَصَلَ الطُلاّبُ إلاّ خالِداً.

١٦ نَظَّفَ الرَجُلُ كُلَّ السَيّاراتِ إلاّ سَيّارَتَك.

١٧ كَتَبْتُ إلى كُلِّ أصْدِقائي إلاّ واحِداً مِنهُم.

### C. The Noun غَيْر

Since **غَيْر** is a noun, it forms an **إضافة** with its excepted noun, which follows it. The case of **غَير** is determined just as the case of the excepted noun after **إلاّ** is determined; that is, **غَير** is **مَنصوب** in affirmative sentences (example 18) and takes the appropriate case based on context in negative sentences (examples 19–21):

١٨ وَصَلَ الطُلاّبُ غَيرَ خالِدٍ (= إلاّ خالِداً).

١٩ ما وَصَلَ طُلاّبٌ غَيْرُ خالِدٍ.

٢٠ لا تَعْرِفُ أُمّي غَيرَ العَرَبيّةِ.

٢١ ما كَتَبْتُ لِغَيرِ خالِدٍ.

In example 19, **غَيْر** is the doer of the action, in 20 it is the object of the verb, and in 21 it is the object of the preposition **لـ**.

# تمرين ١٦

**Using exception:** Find out who in your class . . .

1. has traveled to every continent except Antarctica ( قارّة القُطْبِ الجَنوبيّ)
2. has seen all but one of Johnny Depp's movies
3. has read all but the last lesson of this book
4. has watched nothing but reality television (البَرامِج الواقِعِيّة)
5. has visited a country that borders Saudi Arabia
6. was born in a state that borders Ohio
7. has lived on a peninsula
8. has visited both the East and West Coasts of America
9. has swum in both the Atlantic and Pacific Oceans
10. has walked in a desert

# تمرين ١٧

AUDIO

١- اسْتَمِعْ إلى النَصّ ثُمَّ اكتُبْ على الخَريطَة اسمَ البَلَد الَّذي يَصِفُهُ النَصُّ وأسماءَ مُدُنِهِ وجِبالِه وسُهولِهِ والبِلادَ الّتي تَحُدُّه مِن كُلِّ جانِب.

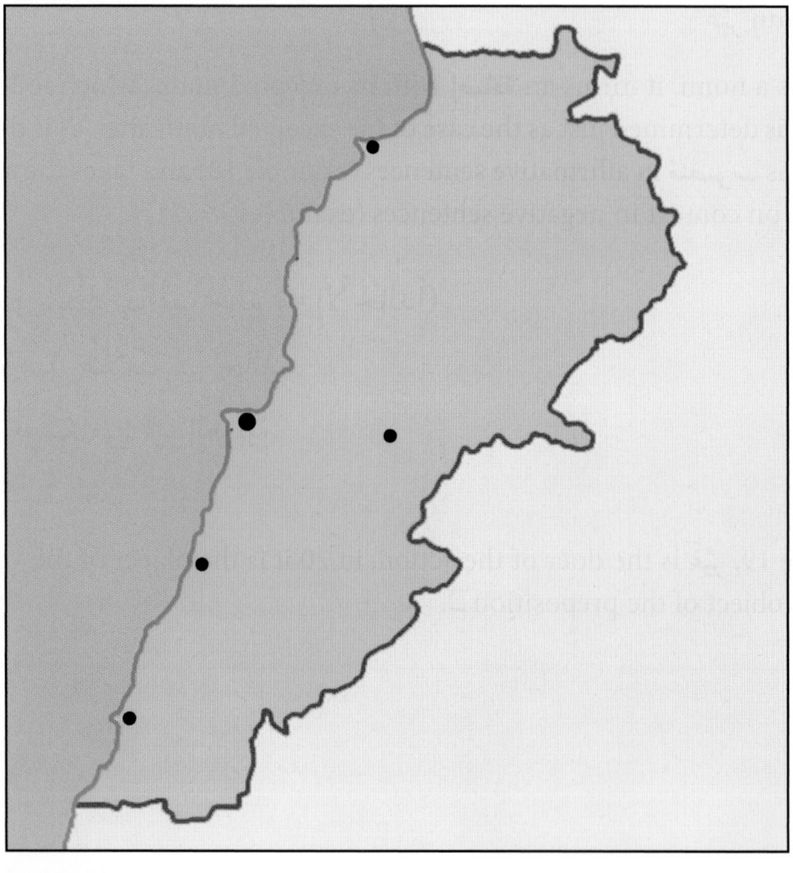

أجب عَن الأسْئِلَةِ التالية.

٢- لِماذا تُعْتبَرُ عاصِمَةُ هذا البَلَدِ العاصِمةَ التِجارِيَّةَ لِلشَرقِ الأوسَط؟

٣- ما المُنتَجاتُ الزِراعِيَّةُ في هذا البَلَد؟

٤- آلسُهولُ (أ+السُهولُ) أكثَرُ في هذا القُطرِ أمِ الجِبال؟

## تمرين ١٨

تَمرينُ المُشاهَدة: شاهِدوا الدَرْسَ الحادي والعشرين على القُرْص الرَقْميّ.

١- ما صِفاتُ سوقِ الحَمَيدية؟ ____________________

____________________

____________________

٢- لِماذا يُوجَدُ ثُقوبٌ في سَقْفِ السوق؟ ____________________

____________________

____________________

٣- ما المدينَتانِ اللتان تَقَعانِ على الساحِلِ السوريّ؟ ____________________

____________________

____________________

٤- إذا زُرت سورية أيها الطالب العزيز، أيَّةَ مُدُنٍ تُريد/ ين أن تَزور/ ي ولِماذا؟ __________

____________________

____________________

____________________

____________________

____________________

____________________

٥- ضَع دائرةً حَولَ المُدُنِ الّتي زارَها سامِر:

| | | | | | | |
|---|---|---|---|---|---|---|
| حمص | اللاذقية | حماة | دير الزور | بانياس | طرطوس | حلب |

## المُفْرَدات

Listen to the vocabulary items on the CD and practice their pronunciation.

during . . . . . . . . . . . . . . . . . . . . . . . . . . . . أثْناء

Asia . . . . . . . . . . . . . . . . . . . . . . . . . (n., f.) آسيا

to overlook (s.t.) . . . . . . . . . . . . . . . . . . (v.) أطَلَّ (يُطِلُّ) إطْلال

Atlantic . . . . . . . . . . . . . . . . . . . . . . . . (adj.) أطلَسيّ

to discharge a firearm, to shoot; to dispatch . . . . . . . . . . . . . (v.) أطْلَقَ (يُطْلِق) إطْلاق

to consider . . . . . . . . . . . . . . . . . . . . . . (v.) اِعتبَرَ (يَعتَبِرُ) اِعتِبار

top, highest point, upper . . (n., m., superlative form) أعْلى ج أعالٍ

Africa . . . . . . . . . . . . . . . . . . . . . . . . (n., f.) إفريقية

region . . . . . . . . . . . . . . . . . . . . . . . (n., m.) إقليم ج أقاليم

to produce . . . . . . . . . . . . . . . . . . . . . . (v.) أنتَجَ (يُنتِجُ) إنتاج

to be interrupted, to be severed . . . . . . . . . . . . . . . . . (v.) اِنقَطَعَ (يَنقَطِعُ) اِنقِطاع

Iran . . . . . . . . . . . . . . . . . . . . . . . . . . . . إيران

semi–arid desert . . . . . . . . . . . . . . . . . . . (n., f.) بادِية ج بَوادٍ

merchandise, goods . . . . . . . . . . . . . . (n., f.) بِضاعة ج بَضائِع

ice cream . . . . . . . . . . . . . . . . . . . . . . . (n., f.) بوظة

to consist of, to comprise . . . . . . . . . . . (v.) تَألَّفَ (يَتَألَّفُ) تَألُّف

traditional. . . . . . . . . . . . . . . . . . . . . . (adjective) تَقْليديّ

date (fruit) . . . . . . . . . . . . . . . . . . . . . (n., m.) تَمْر ج تُمور

hole . . . . . . . . . . . . . . . . . . . . . . . . .(n., m.) ثَقْب ج ثُقوب

mountain . . . . . . . . . . . . . . . . . . . . . . (n., m.) جَبَل ج جِبال

to test, to try (≠ to attempt). . . . . . . . . . (v.) جَرَّبَ (يُجَرِّبُ) تَجْرِبة

island . . . . . . . . . . . . . . . . . . . . . . . . (n., f.) جَزيرة ج جُزُر

جغرافية (n., m.) . . . geography

جَنوب (n., m.) . . . south

جِهاز ج أجهِزة (n., m.) . . . device, apparatus, appliance

حَدَّ (يَحُدُّ) حَدّ (v.) . . . to border, to demarcate, to limit

حَدّ ج حُدود (n., m.) . . . border, edge, boundary, borderline

حِذاء ج أحْذية (n., m.) . . . shoe

خَريطة ج خَرائِط (n., f.) . . . map

خَصيب (adj.) . . . fertile

خَليج ج خُلجان (n., m.) . . . gulf, bay

راكِب ج رُكّاب (n., m.) . . . passenger, rider

رِحْلة ج رِحلات (n., f.) . . . trip, journey, flight

رَصاص (n., m.) . . . bullets; lead

رَوى (يَروي) رَيّ (v.) . . . to irrigate, to water

زَرَعَ (يزرَعُ) زَرْع، زِراعة (v.) . . . to plant, to cultivate

ساحِل ج سَواحِل (n., m.) . . . coast, shore

سَقْف ج سُقوف (n., m.) . . . ceiling

سِلسِلة ج سَلاسِل (n., f.) . . . range, series, chain

سَهل ج سُهول (n., m.) . . . plain

شِبْه ج أشباه (n., m.) . . . semi-, quasi, similarity

شِعار ج شِعارات، أشعِرة (n., m.) . . . emblem, sign, slogan

شَكَّلَ (يُشَكِّلُ) تَشكيل (v.) . . . to form, to constitute

صَبَّ (يصُبُّ) صَبّ (v.) . . . to flow into

صَحْراء ج صَحاري (n., f.) . . . desert

صَنَعَ (يَصنَعُ) صِناعة (v.) . . . to manufacture, to make

صِفة ج صِفات (n., f.) . . . characteristic

narrow, tight . . . . . . . . . . . . . . . . . . . . (adj.) ضَيِّق

capital city . . . . . . . . . . . . . . . . (n., f.) عاصِمة ج عَواصِم

high, elevated . . . . . . . . . . . . . . . . (adj.) (العالي) عالٍ

several, multiple . . . . . . . . . . . . . . . . . . . (adj.) عَديد

throughout, all the way . . . . . . . . . . . . . . . . على طُول

flag, banner . . . . . . . . . . . . . . . . . (n., m.) عَلَم ج أعْلام

pistachio . . . . . . . . . . . . . . . . . . . . . .(n., m.) فُسْتُق

continent . . . . . . . . . . . . . . . . . . (n., f.) قارّة ج قارّات

country . . . . . . . . . . . . . . . . . . . (n., m.) قُطْر ج أقْطار
(almost exclusively used for Arab countries)

cotton . . . . . . . . . . . . . . . . . . . . . . . . . (n., m.) قُطْن

wheat . . . . . . . . . . . . . . . . . . . . . . . . . (n., m.) قَمْح

both . . . . . . . . . . . . . . . . . . . . . . . . . . . . (n.) كِلا

what . . . . . . . . . . . . . . . . . . . . . (adverbial particle) ما

ocean . . . . . . . . . . . . . . . . . . . (n., m.) مُحيط ج مُحيطات

square . . . . . . . . . . . . . . . . . . . . . . . . . . (adj.) مُرَبَّع

area . . . . . . . . . . . . . . . . . . . . (n., f.) مِساحة ج مِساحات

made (of /from) . . . . . . . . . . .(passive participle) (مِن) مَصْنوع

covered (with) . . . . . . . . . . . . . (passive participle) (بـ) مُغَطًّى

Mexico . . . . . . . . . . . . . . . . . . . . . . . (n., f.) المِكسيك

product . . . . . . . . . . . . . . . . . . (n., m.) مُنتَج ج مُنتَجات

outlet . . . . . . . . . . . . . . . . . . . . (n., m.) مَنْفَذ ج مَنافِذ

to spring, to originate, to flow . . . . . . . . . . . (v.) نَبَعَ (يَنبُعُ) نَبْع

section, manner, mode, fashion . . . . . . . . (n., m.) نَحْو ج أنْحاء

textile, tissue, fabric. . . . . . . . . . . . . . . . . . (n., m.) نَسيج

petroleum, crude oil . . . . . . . . . . . . . . . . . . (n., m.) نِفْط

الهادي (adj.) . . . . . . . . . . . . . . . . . . . . . . . . . . . Pacific

وَسَط ج أوساط (n., m.) . . . . . . . . . . . . . . . . . middle, central

# الدرسُ الثاني والعِشرونَ

## Objectives

- Describing events (television and radio programs)
- Expressing obligation with على . . . أن
- Expressing possibility with the verb يُمْكِنُ
- Introduction to the structure لَمْ يَعُدْ
- Introduction to the relative noun ما
- Introduction to the particle أنْ after adverbs of time
- Introduction to the noun بِضْع

## رُكنُ المُفْرَداتِ الجَديدةِ:

| | |
|---|---|
| *broadcasting station* | إذاعة ج إذاعات |
| *to listen (to)* | اِسْتَمَعَ (يَسْتَمِعُ) اِسْتِماع (إلى) |
| *to participate (in)* | اِشْتَرَكَ (يَشْتَرِكُ) اِشْتِراك (في) |
| *to be possible* | أمْكَنَ (يُمْكِنُ) إمْكان |
| *to guess* | حَزَرَ (يَحْزِرُ) حَزْر |
| *to improve (s.t.)* | حَسَّنَ (يُحَسِّنُ) تَحْسين |
| *during, through* | خِلالَ |
| *person* | شَخْص ج أشْخاص |
| *of course; naturally* | طَبْعاً (مِن طَبيعة) |
| *to appear* | ظَهَرَ (يَظْهَرُ) ظُهور |
| رَجَعَ (يَرجِعُ) رُجوع | عادَ (يَعودُ) عَوْد |
| *to die* | ماتَ (يَموتُ) مَوْت |

| | |
|---|---|
| *free of charge* | مَجّاني |
| *for the sake of* | مِن أجْل (+ مَصدَر) |
| *via (by means of)* | مِن خِلالِ |
| *system* | نِظام ج أنْظِمة |
| *including* | بِما في ذلِكَ |

## المُفرداتُ الجَديدةُ في صُوَرٍ عَديدةٍ:

شَريط ج أشْرِطة

غَنّى (يُغَنّي) غِناء

رَقَصَ (يَرْقُص) رَقْص

طِفْل ج أطْفال

الفَضاء

قَمَر ج أقْمار

مُتزَوِّج ج مُتزَوِّجون

مُمَثِّل ج مُمَثِّلونَ

## تمرين ١

**اختَر الكَلِمةَ الّتي لا تُناسِب باقي الكَلِماتِ في كُلِّ مَجْموعةٍ وبَيِّن السَبَب.**

١- بَرنامَج مُسَلسَل أخبار لُغة

٢- بَثّ مَجّاني قَناة مَوجة

٣- عَودة موسيقا أغنية مُغنّية

٤- حَيَوان طَبيعة تِجارة أشجار

٥- مَوْجة إذاعة مَحطّة طِفْل

## تمرين ٢

**وافِق بين كلماتٍ مِنَ العَمودِ الأيْمَن وكلِماتٍ مِنَ العَمودِ الأيْسَر واكتُب الكَلِمَتين في الوسط.**

| | | | |
|---|---|---|---|
| ١ | إذاعة | | مُمتاز |
| ٢ | قناة | | سوق |
| ٣ | إعلانات | | أكثر |
| ٤ | تُوُفِّيَ | | بَثّ |
| ٥ | مُغَنٍّ | | مَوجة |
| ٦ | جَيِّد | | عاميّة |
| ٧ | فَصيحة | | أغنية |
| ٨ | مُعظَم | | تِجارة |
| | | | ماتَ |

## تمرين ٣

**اختَر التكمِلةَ المُناسِبةَ حَسَبَ النَص.**

١- أشاهِدُ مُسَلسَلي المُفَضَّل على __________ سِت.

☐ المَحَطّة ☐ القَناة ☐ اللاسِلكي ☐ المَوجَة

٢- تُريدُ أختي أنْ تَعمَلَ __________ بَعدَ تَخَرُّجِها.

☐ فَصيحة ☐ عاميّة ☐ أُغنية ☐ مُذيعة

٣- شاهَدتُ __________ على التِلفاز مع المُغَنّية مَيّادة حِنّاوي.

☐ مُقابَلة ☐ موسيقا ☐ مُمتازة ☐ مُسَلسَلاً

٤- __________ إلى الأغاني مِن مُسَجِّلتي.

☐ أستَمِعُ ☐ أشاهِدُ ☐ أفهَمُ ☐ أُحَسِّنُ

٥- أختي الكَبيرة __________ مِن رَجُل جَزائريّ.

☐ مُغَنّية ☐ مُمَثِّلة ☐ مُتَزَوِّجة ☐ موسيقيّة

# الإذاعةُ والتِلفاز

## في الوِلاياتِ المُتَّحِدةِ والوَطنِ العربيّ

مِن يَومِيّاتِ عَدنان مارتيني

مُنذُ أنْ أتَيتُ إلى الولاياتِ المُتَّحِدةِ لَمْ أعُدْ أشاهِدُ التِلفازَ كَما كُنتُ أشاهِدُهُ في حَلَب، رُبَّما لأنَّني الآنَ مَشغولٌ بِدراسَتي ولَيْسَ عِندي الوَقتُ لِمُشاهَدةِ البَرامِجِ والمُسَلسَلاتِ الكَثيرة. لكِنَّني أشاهِدُ الأخبارَ كُلَّ يَومٍ صَباحاً قَبلَ أنْ أذهَبَ إلى الجامِعةِ ومَساءً بَعدَ عَودَتي مِنها. وأشاهِدُ كَذلِكَ بَعضَ المُسَلسَلاتِ أحياناً.

أشاهِدُ غالِباً بَرنامَجَ «صَباحُ الخَيْرِ يا أمريكا» على القناةِ سِتّ في الساعةِ السابِعةِ صَباحاً مِن مَحَطّةِ «إي بي سي». نَشْرَةُ الأخبارِ في هذِه المَحطَّةِ مُدّتُها نِصفُ ساعةٍ لكِنَّها سَريعة. يَقرَأُ المُذيعُ أو المُذيعةُ الخَبَرَ في بِضعِ دَقائِقَ ثُمَّ تَظهَرُ الإعلاناتُ التِجاريّة. وهذِه الإعلاناتُ تَظهَرُ في أيِّ وَقتٍ خِلالَ المُسَلسَلاتِ والأفلامِ والبَرامِجِ، وهذا شَيءٌ لا يُعجِبُني.

في المَساءِ أشاهِدُ الأخبارَ أوّلاً على القَناةِ ٣٤ مِن مَحَطّةِ «پي بي إس»، ونَشْرةُ الأخبارِ في هذِه المَحطّةِ طَويلةٌ وفيها أخبارٌ مِن أمريكا والعالَمِ وكَذلِكَ مُقابَلاتٌ مع أشْخاصٍ عَديدينَ. تَبُثُّ هذِهِ المَحطّةُ بَرامِجَ عِلميّةً مُمتازة عَن الحَيَواناتِ والطَبيعة، وهي مَحَطّةٌ عامَّةٌ ولَيْسَتْ تِجاريّة. حينَ يكونُ عِندي وَقتٌ أُفَضِّلُ أنْ أشاهِدَ هذِهِ البَرامِج.

في الساعةِ السادِسةِ والنِصفِ أشاهِدُ الأخبارَ على إحدى القَنَواتِ الّتي تَبُثُّ علَيها المَحطّاتُ التِجاريَّةُ «إن بي سي» و«سي بي إس». أشاهِدُ أحياناً بَعضَ المُسَلسَلاتِ مِثلَ «ساينفِلد» و«فريجر» و«فريندز»، أي «الأصدِقاء». يُعجِبُني أيْضاً بَرنامَجي «عِشرين على عِشرين» و«سِتّونَ دَقيقة».

يوجَدُ في أمريكا نِظامانِ لِلبَثِّ التِلفزيوني واحِدٌ لاسِلكيّ وهو مَجّانيّ والآخَرُ سِلكيّ (ويُسَمّى كيبل هُنا) ويُمْكِنُ أنْ تَحصُلَ عليهِ مُقابِلَ اشتِراكٍ شَهريّ. يَحْصُلُ الناسُ من النِظامِ اللاسِلكيّ على المَحطّاتِ الكَبيرةِ الثَلاث: «سي بي إس»، «أي بي سي»، «إن بي سي» بالإضافةِ إلى «پي بي إس» (المَحَطّةِ العامّة) وكَذلِكَ مَحَطّةِ «فوكس».

أمّا النِظامُ السِلكيُّ ففيهِ عَشَراتُ القَنَواتِ لِلأفلامِ السينَمائيّةِ والأطفالِ والتاريخِ والعُلومِ والموسيقا وبَيعِ البَضائعِ التِجاريّةِ وغَيْرِ ذلِكَ كَثير. شاهدتُ مَرّةً قَناةَ «ديسكفري» وأعجَبَتْني جِداً بِسَبَبِ البَرامِجِ العِلمِيَّةِ الَّتي تَبُثُّها يَومِيّاً.

حينَ أقرأُ دُروسي مَساءً في الشَقَّةِ أحِبُّ أنْ أسْتَمِعَ إلى الإذاعةِ وهُناكَ عَدَدٌ كَبيرٌ مِن المَحطّات. أستَمِعُ عادةً إلى ما يُعجِبُني مِن الأغاني والموسيقا مِن مَحطّاتٍ على المَوجةِ «إف إم» لكِنْ هُناكَ أيْضاً مَحطّاتٌ كَثيرةٌ على المَوجَةِ المُتَوَسِّطة. إذاعَتي المُفَضَّلةُ هي الإذاعةُ العامّة «إن پي آر» لأنَّ فيها أخباراً وبَرامِجَ مُمتازة. في الشُهورِ الأولى حينَ أتَيْتُ إلى الوِلاياتِ المُتَّحِدةِ كُنتُ أستَمِعُ إلَيها عِدّةَ ساعاتٍ كُلَّ يَوم وساعَدَتني كَثيراً في تَحسينِ لُغَتي الإنكليزيّة.

أمّا مِن أجلِ الأغاني والموسيقا فأستَمِع إلى عِدّةِ مَحطّات. تُعجِبُني الموسيقا الحَديثة وأغاني «ستيفي وَنِدَر» و«مادونا» و«غلوريا إستِفان» وغيرِهِم. لكِنْ عِندي أيْضاً أشْرِطةٌ لِمُغَنينَ عَرَبٍ مِثلِ فيروز وصَباح فَخري ووَديع الصافي وراغِب علامة ومُحَمّد عَبدُه. وَصَلَتني هذِه الأشرِطةُ من أخي رامي.

وَديع الصافي

راغِب عَلامة

فَريد الأطرَش

## من يَومِيّات مايكل براون

صِرتُ الآنَ أفهَمُ كَثيراً مِمّا أسمَعُ في الإذاعةِ والتِلفاز. أشاهِدُ التِلفاز ساعةً أو ساعتَينِ كُلَّ يوم مَساءً ويُساعِدُني هذا كَثيراً في تَحسينِ لُغَتي العربيّة، الفَصيحةِ والعامِيّة. هُناكَ بَرامِجُ بالعَرَبيّةِ الفَصيحةِ كَالأخبارِ والمُقابَلاتِ والبَرامِجِ العِلميّة وغَيرِها. أمّا المُسَلسَلاتُ الإذاعيّةُ والتِلفزيونيّةُ فَمُعظَمُها بِالعامِيَّة، وأنا أريدُ تَحسينَهُما كِلتَيْهِما.

في شَهرِ رَمَضان بَثَّ التِلفزيون المِصريّ بَرنامَجاً غِنائيّاً أحَبَّه مُعظَمُ المِصريّينَ اسمُهُ «فَوازير رَمَضان»، وعَلِمتُ أنَّهُ يُبَثُّ أيْضاً في أقطارٍ عَرَبيّةٍ أُخرى. قَدَّمَتْ هذا البَرنامَج اليَوميّ مُمَثِّلةٌ ومُغَنِّيَّةٌ اسمُها «نيللي»، كانَت تَرقُصُ وتُغَنّي أُغنيةً تَصِفُ فيها شَيئاً وكان على مُشاهِدي البَرنامَج أنْ يَحزِروا هذا الشَيء. لكِنّي لَم أحْزِرْ أيَّ شَيءٍ وَصَفَته.

مُعظَمُ المِصرّيينَ يُحِبّونَ أمَّ كُلثوم ويَسمَعونَها كُلَّ يوم. كانَت أمُّ كُلثوم مُغَنّيَةً مَشهورةً جِدّاً في مِصرَ وفي كُلِّ الوَطَنِ العَرَبيّ. بَدَأت الغِناءَ في العِشرينات وغَنَّتْ دونَ انقِطاع في مِصرَ وفي عَدَدٍ مِن الأقطارِ العَرَبيّةِ حَتّى تُوُفِيَت في عامِ ١٩٧٥.

أمُّ كُلثوم

عبد الحليم حافظ

ومن المُغَنّينَ المَشهورينَ الَّذينَ ماتوا ولا يَزالُ الناسُ يَسمَعونَ أغانيهِم ويُحِبّونَها مُحَمَّد عَبدُ الوَهّاب وفَريدُ الأطْرَش وعَبدُ الحَليم حافِظ وفايزة أحمَد وغَيرُهُم.

طَبعاً هُناكَ عَدَدٌ كَبيرٌ من المُغَنّينَ الأحياء، ومن أشهَرِهم اليَوم وَردَة الجَزائِرية ومَيّادة حِنّاوي وعَمْرو دياب ونانسي عجرم. الأولى أتَتْ إلى القاهِرة من الجَزائر في السِتّينات، والثانية من سوريَّة، والثالث من مِصر، أما الرابعة والأخيرة فهي لبنانية.

ميّادة حِنّاوي

وردة الجزائرية

عمرو دياب

نانسي عجرم

هُناكَ طَبعاً مُغَنّونَ ومُغَنيّات في الأقطارِ العَرَبيّةِ الأخرى. مُغَنيَتي المُفَضَّلَة من غَيرِ المِصريّات هي فَيروز. لا تُسمَع أغانيها في مِصر كَثيراً لكِنَّها مُسَجَّلَةٌ على أشرِطة ومَوجودةٌ في السوق. بَدَأتْ فَيروزُ الغِناءَ في لُبنانَ وسوريَّة في خَمسيناتِ القَرنِ العِشرين وهي لاتَزالُ تُغَنّي إلى الآن. صَوتُ فَيروز جَميلٌ جِدّاً ويُحِبُّهُ اللُبنانيّونَ والسوريّونَ خُصوصاً. كانَت مُتَزَوِّجةً من عاصي الرَحباني الّذي كانَ موسيقِيّا مُمْتازاً، ولَها ابنٌ منهُ اِسمُه زِياد الرَحباني وهو موسيقيّ ومُغَنٍّ أيْضاً. غَنَّتْ فَيروزُ في مُعظَمِ الأقطارِ العَرَبيّةِ وفي أوروبا وأوستراليا والوِلاياتِ المُتَّحِدةِ حَيثُ كانَت أوَّلَ مُغَنِيَةٍ عَرَبيَّةٍ تُغَنّي في قاعَةِ «كارنِغي» في نيويورك وكانَ ذلِكَ في ٢٩ أيلول ١٩٧٢.

فَيروز

# بَرامِجُ إذاعة وتلفزيون

**من الجرائِدِ العربية**

هُناكَ مَحَطّةُ إذاعةٍ أو أكثَر، ومَحَطّةُ تِلفزيونٍ أو أكثَر في كُلِّ قُطْرٍ عَربيّ. يوجَدُ اليَومَ أيْضاً مَحطّاتٌ فَضائيّة، أيْ بَرامِجُ تِلفزيونيّة من عِدّة أقطارٍ عَرَبيّة تُبَثُّ من خِلالِ القَمَرِ الصِناعيِّ العربيّ «عَرَبسات» وغيره من الأقمار.

قَمَرٌ صِناعيٌّ

| الفضائية المغربية | |
|---|---|
| ١٢,١٥ | نور الإيمان، صلاة الجمعة، الأخبار |
| ١,٣٠ | السلسلة العربية التاريخية «ميراث السنين» |
| ٢,٣٠ | النشرة الجوية |
| ٣,٠٠ | «مرايا» برنامج عن المرأة |
| ٣,٣٠ | الفلم العربي «القانون واللعبة» |
| ٥,٣٠ | الأخبار الدولية |
| ٥,٥٥ | ألعاب القوى من مدينة كولوينا |
| ٨,٣٠ | الجريدة المتلفزة الرئيسية |
| ٩,١٠ | ركن المفتي |
| ٩,٣٥ | السهرة السينمائية العربية «لعبة الانتقام» |
| ١١,٠٠ | منوعات غنائية |
| ١١,١٠ | الأخبار الأخيرة |
| ١١,٣٠ | حفلات أقيمت بالمغرب |
| ١,٢٠ | ما تيسر من الذكر الحكيم |
| ١,٣٠ | ختام البرامج |

| تلفزيون | |
|---|---|
| ١٠,٠٠ | صور وموسيقا |
| ٣,٣٠ | برنامج أجنبي |
| ٤,٠٠ | لبنان هذا النهار |
| ٤,٣٠ | رسوم متحركة |
| ٥,٠٠ | ستاديوم |
| ٥,٣٠ | رياضة من حول العالم |
| ٦,٠٠ | الأرض الطيبة |
| ٦,٣٠ | برنامج عربي |
| ٧,٣٠ | أخبار لبنان والعالم هذا المساء |
| ٨,٠٠ | برنامج أجنبي |
| ٨,٣٠ | فيلم أجنبي |
| ١٠,٠٠ | أوتوغراف |
| ١١,٠٠ | خليك بالبيت |
| ١٢,٠٠ | أخبار آخر السهرة |

يُمكِنُكَ أنْ تَقرَأَ بَرامِجَ الإذاعةِ والتِلفزيون في مُعظَمِ الجَرائِد العربيّة، بِما في ذلِكَ بَرامِجُ المَحطّاتِ الفَضائيّة. في ما يَلي بَعضُ هذِهِ البَرامِج من جَرائِدَ عَربيّة. اقرأها وحاوِل أنْ تَعرِفَ من أيّ قُطرٍ عَربيّ كُلٌّ من هذِه البَرامِج، وهَل هي بَرامِجُ إذاعيةٌ أو تِلفزيونيّة.

| القناة الأولى | |
|---|---|
| ٧,٠٠ | صباح الخير يا مصر والقرآن الكريم |
| ١٠,١٣ | سينما الأطفال |
| ١١,٠٧ | نشرة الأخبار |
| ١١,٢٧ | مجلة المرأة |
| ١٢,٢٠ | إذاعة خارجية |
| ١,٣٠ | مسلسل سر الأرض |
| ١,٤٩ | اللقاء الأسبوعي للشيخ الشعراوي |
| ٢,٣٥ | مع النجوم |
| ٢,٤٦ | فلم الزهور الفاتنة |
| ٤,٥٨ | لقاء الأجيال |
| ٥,٢٨ | صندوق الدنيا |
| ٦,٠٠ | الأخبار وحدث في مثل هذا اليوم |
| ٦,٣٠ | رسالة مهرجان القراءة للجميع |
| ٧,٣٠ | مسلسل من الذي لا ينساك |
| ٨,٣٠ | حديث الروح |
| ٩,٠٠ | الأخبار |
| ٩,٥٣ | فكّر ثواني واكسب دقائق |
| ١١,٣٦ | حلقتان من مسلسل الفرسان |
| ١٢,٠٠ | آخر الأنباء |
| ١,١٠ | مسلسل ألف ليلة وليلة |
| ١,٤٢ | فوازير أم العريف |
| ٢,٠٨ | ابتسامة آخر الليل |
| ٢,٣٣ | القرآن الكريم |

| برامج الإذاعة | |
|---|---|
| ٥,٢٧ | الافتتاح |
| ٦,١٥ | الأخبار الأولى |
| ٦,٤٥ | معكم على الهواء |
| ١١,٣٠ | مسابقة الأغاني المحلية |
| ١,٠٠ | قصص من العالم |
| ١,٣٠ | الشرطة في خدمة الشعب |
| ٢,١٥ | الأخبار الثالثة |
| ٣,٠٠ | برنامج قصة في تمثيلية |
| ٤,١٥ | المجلة الاقتصادية |
| ٥,٠٠ | المسلسل اليومي |
| ٥,٣٠ | صوت القوات المسلحة |
| ٦,٠٠ | في رحاب اللغة |
| ٨,٠٠ | حكاية شاعر |
| ١٠,٠٠ | سوريَّة اليوم |
| ١٢,٠٠ | الشعر والليل موعدنا |
| ١٢,٣٠ | معالم من الوطن العربي الكبير |
| ١,١٥ | الأخبار السابعة |
| ١,٣٠ | شخصيات روائية |
| ٢,١٥ | آخر المشوار |

## تمرين ٤

**أجِب عن هذه الأسئِلة حَسَبَ النَصّ.**

١- ما الّذي ساعدَ عَدنان على تَحسين لُغَتِهِ الإنكليزيّة؟

٢- أين شاهَدَ عَدنان بَرامِجَ عن الحَيَوانات؟

٣- اكتُب اسمَ أحدِ البَرامِجِ التلفزيونيّةِ في رَمَضان بِمِصر.

٤- مَن المُغَنّي المَشهور من المُغَنّينَ الأحياء في مِصر؟

٥- كَم نَشرةَ أخبارٍ يَبُثُّ التلفزيون المِصريّ؟

٦- في أيِّ وَقتٍ تَبدأ بَرامِجُ الإذاعةِ السوريّةِ ومَتى تَنتَهي؟

٧- ما اسمُ بَرنامَجِ المرأةِ في التلفزيون المَغربيّ؟

٨- ما الكَلِمةُ المُستعمَلَةُ في المَغرِب بَدَلاً مِن «مُسَلسَل»؟

٩- مَتى يُمكِنُ أنْ تَسمَعَ الموسيقا والأغاني في تلفزيون لُبنان؟

١٠- ما البَرنامَجُ الّذي يُبَثُّ مِن مِصرَ في الساعةِ السادِسَةِ مَساءً؟ اشرحْه كَما تَفهَمُه بِالعَرَبيّةِ أو الإنكليزيّة.

**اكتُب اسم الشَخصِ أو الشيءِ الّذي تَصِفُهُ الجُمَلَ التالية:**

١١- هي مِن الجَزائِر.

١٢- يُشاهِدُهُ عَدنان مِن مَحَطّةِ «إن بي سي».

١٣- هي بِالعاميَّةِ المِصريّة.

١٤- يُحِبُّها اللُبنانيّونَ والسوريّون.

**اكتُبْ «خَطَأ» أو «صَواب» بِجانبِ كُلِّ جُملَةٍ وصَحِّح الجُمَلَ الخَطأ.**

١٥- كانَ عَدنان يُشاهِدُ التِلفزيون في حَلَبَ أكثَرَ مِن أمريكا.

١٦- لا تُعجِبُ عَدنان الإعلاناتُ التِجاريّة.

١٧- على مُشاهِدي بَرنامَج «فَوازير رَمَضان» أنْ يُغَنّوا مع المُغَنِّية.

١٨- تُوفِيَت فايزة أحمَد عامَ ١٩٧٥.

١٩- يُبَثُّ مُسَلسَلُ «ألف لَيلة ولَيلة» مِن التِلفزيون المَغربيّ.

٢٠- «ابتسامةُ آخِرِ اللَيل» هي آخِرُ فِقرةٍ في التلفزيون المِصريّ.

## تمرين ٥

**Define these phrases according to the text:** **عَرِّف العِبارات التالية حَسَبَ النَصّ:**

١- التِلفاز السِلكيّ

٢- اللُغَة العَربيّة الفَصيحة

٣- فَوازير رَمَضان

٤- زِياد الرَحباني

٥- مَعالِم من الوَطَنِ العربيّ الكَبير

٦- رِياضة مِن حَولِ العالَم

## تمرين ٦

**Conversation:** Pair up with someone in class and converse with each other about your favorite television or radio programs, detailing why you like the program, who is on it, what their personalities are like, when you listen to it, with whom you listen to it, how long you have been a fan, and anything else you think is relevant about the program. Try to use all of the words in the word bank in your conversation, and be prepared to report your conversation to the class:

| | | | | | | | |
|---|---|---|---|---|---|---|---|
| اِعْتَبَر | وَصَفَ | يَبْدو | يَظْهَرُ | اِسْتَمْتَعَ بِـ | اِسْتَمَعَ (إلى) | اِشْتَرَكَ | مَوجة |
| يُمْكِنُني | طَبْعاً | أَسْتَطيعُ أنْ | مُسَلْسَل | على أنْ | يُعْجِبُني | شَخْص ج أَشْخاص | إذاعة |

## تمرين ٧

**اختَرِ التكمِلةَ المُناسِبةَ حَسَبَ النَصّ.**

١- يُشاهِدُ عَدنان الأخبارَ ______________.

☐ صَباحاً ☐ مَساءً

☐ صَباحاً وظُهراً ☐ صَباحاً ومَساءً

٢- نَشرةُ الأخبارِ في المَحطّاتِ التِجاريّةِ الأمريكيّة ____________ .

☐ طَويلة ☐ سَريعة ☐ جَميلة ☐ قَصيرة

٣- تَظهَرُ الإعلاناتُ التِجاريّةُ ____________ الأخبارِ في أمريكا.

☐ دونَ ☐ قَبْلَ ☐ بَعْدَ ☐ خِلالَ

٤- مَحَطّةُ «پي بي إس» ____________ .

☐ طَويلة ☐ تِجاريّة ☐ عامّة ☐ عِلميّة

٥- نِظامُ البَثِّ التلفزيوني اللاسلكي ____________ .

☐ مَجّاني ☐ عِلميّ ☐ عَديد ☐ عاميّ

٦- المُغَنّية المُفضّلة في مِصر هي ____________ .

☐ فَيروز ☐ أمّ كُلثوم ☐ مادونا ☐ فايزة أحمد

٧- غَنَّت فَيروز في قاعةِ ____________ .

☐ لُبْنان ☐ كِندي ☐ كارنِغي ☐ الرَحباني

٨- هُناكَ ____________ نَشَراتِ أخبارٍ في الإذاعة السوريَّة.

☐ أربعُ ☐ خَمسُ ☐ سِتُّ ☐ سَبعُ

٩- يُمكِنُ أنْ يُشاهَدَ التلفزيون المَغربيّ في لُبنان مِن خِلالِ ____________ .

☐ القَمَرِ الصِناعيّ العَرَبيّ ☐ مَحَطّةٍ تلفزيونيّةٍ مَغربيّةٍ

☐ البَثِّ التلفزيونيّ المِصريّ ☐ الإذاعةِ المَغربيّةِ

## تمرين ٨

**صَنِّف كَلِماتٍ مِن هذا الدَرسِ تَحتَ الفِئاتِ التالية:**

Categorize words from the main reading passages that fall under these headings:

| ١ | مَحَطّات تلفزيون | ٢ | مُسَلسَلات | ٣ | برامِج | ٤ | إذاعة | ٥ | مُغَنّون ومُغَنيات | ٦ | لُغة |
|---|---|---|---|---|---|---|---|---|---|---|---|
| | | | | | | | | | | | |
| | | | | | | | | | | | |
| | | | | | | | | | | | |

| ١ | مَحطّات تلفزيون | ٢ | مُسَلسَلات | ٣ | برامِج | ٤ | إذاعة | ٥ | مُغَنّون ومُغَنيات | ٦ | لُغة |
|---|---|---|---|---|---|---|---|---|---|---|---|
| | | | | | | | | | | | |
| | | | | | | | | | | | |
| | | | | | | | | | | | |
| | | | | | | | | | | | |

## تمرين ٩

**أعِدْ تَرتيبَ الكَلِمات في كُلِّ مَجموعةٍ لِتُشَكِّلَ جُمَلاً مُفيدة.**

١– مِن – إلى – المُفَضَّلة – المُسَجِّلة – أغانيَّ – أستَمِعُ

٢– دِمَشقَ – صَباحاً – إذاعةُ – الخامِسة – بَثَّها – تَبدَأ – الساعةِ – في

٣– مُذيعةً – إذاعةِ – أختُ – مَحطّةِ – في – حَلَب – تَعمَلُ – صَديقي

## تمرين ١٠

**أعِدْ تَرتيبَ الجُمَلِ لِتُشَكِّلَ فِقرةً مُفيدةً دونَ تغييرِ مَكانِ الجُملةِ الأولى.**

١– أوّلُ شَيءٍ أفعَلُهُ صَباحاً هو الذَهاب إلى الحَمّام.

٢– بَعدَ مُشاهَدةِ مُسَلسَلي المُفَضَّل أنامُ نِصفَ ساعةٍ فَقَط.

٣– في الساعةِ الثامِنةِ صَباحاً أذهَبُ إلى عَمَلي.

٤– في المَساءِ أشاهِدُ أنا وزَوجي فيلماً مِن التِلفاز أو مِن شَريط مُسَجَّل.

٥– بَعدَ ذلِكَ أجلِسُ أمامَ التِلفاز وأشاهِدُ الأخبارَ خِلالَ تَناوُلِ الفَطور.

٦– حينَ أعودُ إلى البَيتِ بَعدَ الظُهرِ أشاهِدُ مُسَلسَلي المُفَضَّل.

٧– خِلالَ العَمَلِ استَمِعُ إلى الإذاعة.

### 1. Expressing Obligation with على . . . أن (have to)

In this lesson, we introduced the structure **على . . . أن**, which is one of the multiple ways to express obligation in Arabic. Functionally speaking, **على . . . أن** starts with a preposition; theoretically, however, the verb **يجب** is understood to precede **على**, but it is omitted in practice.

When على . . . أن is used, the preposition على is immediately followed by a noun, a noun phrase, or an attached pronoun. Let's take a look at an example from the main reading passage:

١ على مُشاهِدي البَرنامَج أنْ يَحزِروا هذا الشَيء.

*The program's viewers have to guess what it is.*

In example 1, على is followed by the noun phrase مشاهدي البرنامج, which is a plural إضافة (refer to Lesson 11, section 6). مشاهدي البرنامج acts as the agent, or the doer, of the action and is in the genitive case (مجرور) because it follows the preposition على. The particle أنْ introduces verbs, and in this case it introduces يَحزِروا. Verbs following أنْ must be in المُضارِع المَنصوب, a mood of the present tense (refer to Lesson 18, section 1).

When the preposition على is followed by an attached pronoun, the final ألَف in على changes into a ياء. We will use the sentence in example 1 to illustrate this process. If we substitute an attached pronoun in the place of مشاهدي البرنامج, we have the following result:

٢ علَيْهِم أنْ يَحزِروا هذا الشَيء.

As always, we may substitute a definite مَصدر in place of the أنْ المَصدريّة:

٣ علَيْهِم حَزْرُ هذا الشَيء.

- **Note:** Using the past tense with على أنْ is no more than placing the verb كان in front of على:

٤ كانَ علَينا أنْ نَحزِرَ هذا الشَيء.

If we wish to use first-person singular "I must . . . ," the final ياء takes a شَدّة:

٥ كانَ علَيَّ أنْ أحزِرَ هذا الشَيء.

## تمرين ١١

**Translation:** Express this paragraph in Arabic, using على . . . أن.

*What do we have to do today?* I have to have a cup of coffee after I get up in the morning! Likewise, my father has to read the paper while he eats breakfast. After that, he has to go to work, and I have to go to school. I had to do my homework last night before I went to sleep, but I didn't finish it, so now I have to do it before I get to school. I have to get to school early today to talk to Sāmī about our football game tonight. We have to get to the field at 7:00 p.m. for our big game. After the game, Sāmī told me that he has to watch his favorite TV program, so I might watch it with him . . . , but I don't have to.

## 2. Expressing Possibility with the Verb أمكنَ

One way of expressing possibility is with the verb أمكنَ 'to be possible', whose conjugation is somewhat similar to يُعْجِبُ in that it can take an attached suffixed pronoun, as in example 6. The difference between the two verbs lies in the fact that the suffixed pronoun for يُعْجِبُ is its direct object, whereas for أمكنَ the suffixed pronoun serves as the subject:

٦ هَلْ يُمكِنُكَ مُساعَدتي؟ *Can you help me?*

The direct object of أمْكَنَ can be a verbal noun like مُساعَدَتي in example 6, or, as with all verbs, أنْ المَصدريّة may be substituted, as in example 7:

٧ هَلْ يُمكِنُكَ أنْ تُساعِدَني؟ *Can you help me?*

The فاعِل in examples 6 and 7 takes the form of the attached pronoun (ك). The فاعل can also be a noun, as in example 8:

٨ هَلْ يُمكِنُ أحمَدُ أنْ يُساعِدَني؟ *Can Ahmed help me?*

Certain verbs, like أمْكَنَ, can take a direct object either as an attached pronoun (the ك in example 7) or as a noun (أحمَد in example 8). Another verb of this type is ساعَدَ 'to help'. The pronominal suffixes that are attached to verbs are the same pronominal suffixes that are attached to nouns *except* for first-person singular.

The difference in spelling and usage for the first-person singular attached pronoun can be seen in examples 6 and 7. In example 6, a ي has been attached to the verbal noun مُساعَدة, resulting in مُساعَدَتي, denoting 'my help'. In example 7, ني is attached to the verb تُساعِدُ, resulting in تُساعِدُني, denoting 'you help me'. The ن that separates the verb and the ي has no grammatical function and is sometimes referred to as a "buffer نون."

## SUMMARY

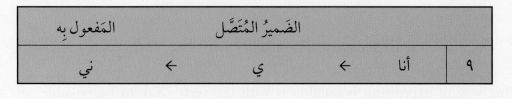

- The first-person singular pronoun attached to nouns is ي (e.g., بَيتي).
- The first-person singular pronoun attached to verbs is ني (e.g., شاهَدَني).

| المَفعول به | | الضَميرُ المُتَّصَل | | | |
|---|---|---|---|---|---|
| ني | ← | ي | ← | أنا | ٩ |

## 3. The Structure لَمْ يَعُدْ

This structure uses the verb عادَ (يَعودُ) 'to return'. Its meaning, however, is equivalent to the English phrase "no longer," as in:

١٠ لَمْ يَعُدْ أحمَدُ يَسكُنُ هُنا. — *Ahmed no longer lives here.*

Note that the verb in the phrase لَمْ يَعُدْ is مُضارِع مَجزوم (jussive). It is followed by a present-tense verb, which provides the present-tense reference. Both verbs have the same agreement with the فاعِل. That is, both verbs are third-person masculine singular. If the فاعِل were سلمى, for example, both verbs would have to be feminine:

١١ لَمْ تَعُدْ سَلمى تَسكُنُ هُنا.

## تمرين ١٢

**Ask your neighbor:** Find out who in your class . . . Be prepared to report your findings.

1. no longer watches a lot of TV
2. no longer likes to watch *The Simpsons*
3. no longer listens to American music, but prefers to listen to Arabic music
4. no longer has time to play sports, but has to study
5. is able to watch Arabic programs on TV
6. is able to cook Arabic food
7. is able to listen to an Arabic broadcasting station
8. has free cable
9. was able to meet a famous actor or actress

## 4. The Relative Noun ما

The relative noun ما generally refers to inanimate (= non-rational) objects. In this sense, it is similar to the way "what" is used in English. Consider example 12:

| | |
|---|---|
| *I eat what I want.* | ١٢ آكُلُ ما أريد. |

In example 12, ما stands for الشَيء الَّذي (refer to section 4 in Lesson 19 for a discussion of relative nouns).

Prepositions may be prefixed to ما:

| | |
|---|---|
| *I didn't like what I heard.* | ١٣ لَمْ يُعجِبْني شَيءٌ مِمّا سَمِعتُ. |

مِمّا, in example 13, is a combination of مِن and ما. Similar examples include:

| | |
|---|---|
| *I don't know what they are talking about.* | ١٤ لا أعرِفُ عَمّا يَتكَلَّمونَ. |

The word عَـمّا in example 14 is made up of عَن and ما:

١٥ يَمكِنُكَ أنْ تَأتيَ إلى هُنا بِما عَلَيْكَ مِن مَلابِس.

*You could come here in whatever clothes you are wearing.*

### تمرين ١٣

**Translation using ما.** تَرجِم إلى العربية ما يلي بِاسْتِعمالِ (ما).

1. Write down in Arabic what you heard on the news.
2. I like what I see (what I see pleases me).
3. She is happy with what she has.
4. You may purchase these Arabic books with whatever U.S. dollars you have on you.

## 5. The Particle أنْ after Adverbs of Time

In English, you may use a sentence immediately after an adverb of time or place:

16 *We had dinner after we had gone to the movies.*

In Arabic, أَنْ is used to separate verbs that follow بَعدَ and قَبلَ.

١٧    تَناوَلنا العَشاءَ بَعدَ أَنْ ذَهَبْنا إلى السينَما.

If we do not wish to use a verb after بَعدَ and قَبلَ, we have the option of using a definite مَصدَر.

١٨    تَناوَلنا العَشاءَ بَعدَ ذهابِنا إلى السينَما.

One difference exists between بَعدَ and قَبلَ when they are used with verbs. قَبلَ أَنْ must be followed by the present tense, while بَعدَ أَنْ can be followed by either past or present. For an American speaker, applying this rule is more difficult than memorizing it. Consider the following statement:

19    _Before_ I _traveled_ to Egypt, I began studying Arabic.

In English, we can use past tense after "before"; not so in Arabic. Reflect on example 20 and try to integrate this rule into your functional vocabulary:

٢٠    قَبْلَ أَنْ أُسافِرَ إلى مِصرَ، بَدَأْتُ أَدرُسُ اللُغةَ العَرَبيّةَ.

---

### SUMMARY

- Only a present-tense verb can follow قبل أَنْ; whereas a present- or past-tense verb can follow بعد أَنْ.

- Only use أَنْ when separating the adverb from a verb; if the adverb of time is followed by a noun, it will not take the أَنْ (قبل ذهابي).

---

الدَرسُ الثاني والعِشرونَ                                                            ٤٩٢

## تمرين ١٤

**Fill in the blank:** Choose the appropriate adverb of time according to the context.

| | | | |
|---|---|---|---|
| قَبْلَ | قَبْلَ أنْ | بَعْدَ | بَعْدَ أنْ |

١- عُدْتُ إلى البيت ____________ تكلمتُ مع أصدِقائي.

٢- لا يُمْكِنُ مَها أنْ تُسافِرَ إلى مِصرَ إلاّ ____________ تَحْصُلَ على تأشيرة.

٣- شاهَدَ مُصطَفى المُسَلسَلَ ____________ ينام.

٤- لَمْ يخرُجْ أحَدٌ مِن الحَفلةِ إلاّ ____________ نهايتها.

٥- يَشرَبُ العَرَبُ عادةً فِنجانَ قَهوةٍ ____________ الأكل.

٦- ركِبتُ الحافلةَ ____________ انتَظَرتُها طَويلاً.

٧- يقولُ الأطِباء لا تأكُلْ ____________ السِباحة.

## 6. The Noun بِضْع

بِضع can be roughly translated as "a few," but it is generally restricted to referring to a small number of things: from three to about five. Coincidently, it behaves in a manner similar to the numbers 3 to 10 in that it has reverse gender agreement with the singular of the modified noun. That is, singular masculine nouns are modified by بِضْعة and singular feminine nouns by بِضع. The case of بِضع is context dependent. Note that its modified noun must be *indefinite*:

٢١ عِندي بِضْعُ صَديقات في الدارِ البَيضاء.

٢٢ قَرَأتُ بِضْعَةَ كُتُبٍ عِن تاريخ أوروبا.

## تمرين ١٥

**Translation:** Express the following meanings in Arabic.

1. I read a few newspapers on the plane.
2. I spent a few weeks in Beirut.
3. My friend bought a few books on the Arab world when she was in Syria.
4. I stayed in the hotel for a few days.

## تمرين ١٦

**اكتُبْ «خَطَأ» أو «صَواب» بِجانبِ كُلِّ جُملَةٍ وصَحِّح الجُمَلَ الخطَأ.**

١- السَيِّدةُ الّتي تَتكَلّمُ على الشَريطِ المُسَجَّلِ مُتزَوِّجةٌ.

٢- مُسَلسَلُ «الجَوارِح» مِن دَولَةِ الإمارات.

**أجِب عَن هذه الأسئلةِ حَسَبَ النَصِّ المُسَجَّل.**

٣- لِماذا يُعجِبُ هذِه السَيِّدة مُسَلسَلُ الجَوارِح؟

٤- أينَ تُشاهِدُ السَيِّدةُ البَرامِجَ التونِسيّة والمَغربيّة؟

**اختر التكملةَ المُناسِبة حَسَبَ النَصِّ المُسَجَّل.**

٥- صُوِّرَ مُسَلسَلُ «الجَوارِح» في ______________.

☐ الصَحراء ☐ سوريَّة ☐ المَغرِب

٦- مَوعِدُ مُسَلسَلِ «الجَوارِح» ______________.

☐ التاسِعةُ صَباحاً ☐ التاسِعةُ مَساءً ☐ الحادية عَشرَةَ

٧- لُغةُ مُسَلسَلِ «الجَوارِح» ______________.

☐ العامِيّةُ السوريَّة ☐ العامِيّةُ المِصريّة ☐ العَربيةُ الفَصيحة

٨- تُشاهِدُ السَيِّدةُ المُسَلسَلاتِ العامِيَّةَ مِن تلفزيون ______________.

☐ تونِس ☐ المَغرِب ☐ دِمَشق وعَمّان

**أكمِلِ الجُمَلَ التاليةَ مِن النَصِ المُسَجَّل.**

٩- يَبُثُّ التلفزيون هذِه الأيّام مُسَلسَلاً ______________.

١٠- هُناكَ طَبعاً مُسَلسَلاتٌ أُخرى لكِنَّها لَيسَتْ تاريخِيّةً ______________.

## تمرين ١٧ VIDEO

**تَمرينُ المُشاهَدة: شاهِدوا الدَرْسَ الدرسَ الثاني والعشرين على القُرْص الرَقْميّ.**

١- مَن مِن المُطربينَ العَرَب يَسْتَمِعُ إليهم الناسُ في مِصر؟ ______________

______________________________

______________________________

٢- املأ الفراغات في الحوار التالي:

مايكل: من هو ________ العربي ________ أو ________ العربية ________ ستيف؟

ستيف: أنا أحب فيروز جداً و________ إليها كل يوم في الصباح وأحب أيضاً ماجدة الرومي.

مايكل: وأنت سامر؟

سامر: طبعاً ________ فيروز وأحب ________ إلى عبد الحليم حافظ.

مايكل: وأنت عدنان؟

عدنان: طبعاً فيروز و________ ________ ________ ________ ________ وديع الصافي ومحمد عبده وصباح فخري وراغب علامة وعمرو دياب فأنا عندي ________ لهم.

سامر: وأنت مايكل من هو ________ العربي ________ أو ________ العربية ________؟

مايكل: أنا بصراحة ________ ________ ________ فيروز كثيراً وأحب أن ________ عمرو دياب وراغب علامة.

ستيف: ومن هو ________ الغربي ________ عدنان؟

٣- ماذا يَفعَلُ عَدنان ليُحَسِّنَ لُغَتَهُ الإنكليزية؟ ______________

______________________________

______________________________

## المُفْرَدات

Listen to the vocabulary items on the CD and practice their pronunciation.

for the sake of, because of . . . . . . . . . . . . . . . أجْل (مِن أجْلِ)

broadcasting station . . . . . . . . . . . . . (n. f.) إذاعَة ج ات

to listen . . . . . . . . . . . . . . . . . . . . (v.) اِسْتَمَعَ (يَسْتَمِعُ) اِسْتِماع

to enroll in, to subscribe to. . . . . . . . . . (v.) اِشْتَرَكَ (يَشْتَرِكُ) اِشْتِراك

song . . . . . . . . . . . . . . . . . . . . . . . (n., f.) أُغنية ج أغانٍ

to be possible . . . . . . . . . . . . . . . . . (v.) أمْكَنَ (يُمكِنُ) إمْكان

to broadcast. . . . . . . . . . . . . . . . . . . (v.) بَثَّ (يَبُثُّ) بَثّ

a few. . . . . . . . . . . . . . . . . . . . . . . . . (n.) بِضْع

to guess . . . . . . . . . . . . . . . . . . . . . (v.) حَزَرَ (يحْزِرُ) حَزْر

to improve, to make better . . . . . . . . . (v.) حَسَّنَ (يحَسِّنُ) تَحْسين

a living person . . . . . . . . . . . . . . . . (n., m.) حَيّ ج أحْياء

during, through. . . . . . . . . . . . . . . . . . (prep.) خِلال

to dance . . . . . . . . . . . . . . . . . . . . . (v.) رَقَصَ (يرقُصُ) رَقْص

wire . . . . . . . . . . . . . . . . . . . . . . . (n., m.) سِلْك ج أسْلاك

to hear. . . . . . . . . . . . . . . . . . . . . . (v.) سَمِعَ (يَسْمَع) سَمْع

tape . . . . . . . . . . . . . . . . . . . . . . . (n., m.) شَريط ج أشْرِطة

person. . . . . . . . . . . . . . . . . . . . . . (n., m.) شَخْص ج أشْخاص

honestly, candidly . . . . . . . . . . . . . . (n., f.) صَراحةً (بِصَراحة)

of course . . . . . . . . . . . . . . . . . . . . . . (adv.) طَبْعاً

nature . . . . . . . . . . . . . . . . . . . . . . . . (n., f.) طَبيعة

child. . . . . . . . . . . . . . . . . . . . . . . (n., m.) طِفْل ج أطْفال

to appear, to become visible . . . . . . . . . . (v.) ظَهَرَ (يَظهَرُ) ظُهور

to go back, to return . . . . . . . . . . . . . (v.) عادَ (يعودُ) عَوْد

colloquial, vulgar, dialectal . . . . . . . . . . . . . . . . (adj.) عاميّ

to sing . . . . . . . . . . . . . . . . . . . . . (v.) غَنّى (يُغَنّي) غِناء

riddle . . . . . . . . . . . . . . . . . . . . . (n., f.) فَزّورة ج فوازير

pure, good, clear, standard, or literary, Arabic . . . . . . . . . . . . . . . . . . (adj.) فَصيح

space . . . . . . . . . . . . . . . . . . . . . . . . . (n., m.) فَضاء

moon, satellite . . . . . . . . . . . . . . . . . . (n. m.) قَمَر ج أقْمار

channel . . . . . . . . . . . . . . . . . . . . . . (n., f.) قَناة ج قَنَوات

cable. . . . . . . . . . . . . . . . . . . . . . . . . . (n., m.) كيبِل

what . . . . . . . . . . . . . . . . . . . . . . (relative pronoun) ما

to die . . . . . . . . . . . . . . . . . . . . . . . . (v.) ماتَ (يموتُ) مَوْت

married man . . . . . . . . . . . . . . . . . . . . (n., m.) مُتَزَوِّج ج ون

free of charge . . . . . . . . . . . . . . . . . . . . . . (adj.) مَجّانيّ

announcer . . . . . . . . . . . . . . . . . . . . . (n., m.) مُذيع ج ون

series, serial . . . . . . . . . . . . . . . . . (n., m.) مُسَلسَل ج مُسَلسَلات

entertainer . . . . . . . . . . . . . . . . . . . (n., m.) مُطْرِب ج مُطْرِبون

singer . . . . . . . . . . . . . . . . . . . . . . . . (n., m.) مُغَنٍّ ج ون

interview . . . . . . . . . . . . . . . . . . . . . . . (n. f.) مُقابَلة ج ات

excellent. . . . . . . . . . . . . . . . . . . . . . . . (adj.) مُمْتاز ج ون

actor, representative . . . . . . . . . . . . . . . (n., m.) مُمَثِّل ج ون

by means of, via. . . . . . . . . . . . . . . . . . . . . . . . مِن خِلالِ

wave. . . . . . . . . . . . . . . . . . . . . . . . . . . . (n., f.) مَوْجة ج ات

bulletin, report . . . . . . . . . . . . . . . . . . (n., f.) نَشْرة ج نَشَرات

system. . . . . . . . . . . . . . . . . . . . . . . . (n., m.) نِظام ج أنْظِمة

# الدَرسُ الثالِثُ والعِشرونَ

## Objectives

- Describing professions
- Describing travel-related activities
- Introduction to the particle فَـ
- Learning the function of the particle قَدْ
- Introduction to البَدَل, known in English as the permutative
- Introduction to the particle إنْ

## رُكنُ المُفْرَداتِ الجَديدةِ:

| | |
|---|---|
| *to rise* | اِرْتَفَعَ (يَرْتَفِعُ) اِرْتِفاع |
| *to insist* | أَصَرَّ (يُصِرُّ) إصرار |
| *to think (that)* | اِعْتَقَدَ (يَعْتَقِدُ) اِعْتِقاد (أنَّ) |
| *to wait* | اِنْتَظَرَ (يَنْتَظِرُ) اِنْتِظار |
| *to become acquainted (with)* | تَعَرَّف (يَتَعَرَّفُ) تَعَرُّف (على) |
| *to be accustomed (to)* | تَعَوَّدَ (يَتَعَوَّدُ) تَعَوُّد (على) |
| *to attend* | حَضَرَ (يَحْضُرُ) حُضور |
| *outside; abroad* | خارِج |
| *to cross (a street)* | عَبَرَ (يَعبُرُ) عُبور |
| *to leave* | غادَرَ (يُغادِرُ) مُغادَرة |
| *means of transportation* | مُواصَلات |

## المُفرداتُ الجَديدةُ في صُوَرٍ عَديدةٍ:

ضَحِكَ (يَضْحَكُ) ضِحْك

دَفَعَ (يَدْفَعُ) دَفْع

عَكْس

صَحَفيّ ج ون

مُزْدَحِم (بِـ)

مُلَوَّث

هَدية ج هَدايا

مَصْنَع ج مَصانِع

## تمرين ١

**اخترَ الكَلِمةَ الّتي لا تُناسِب باقي الكَلِماتِ في كُلِّ مَجْموعةٍ وبَيِّن السَبَب.**

١- صَحَفِيّ مَجلّة عاصِمة جَريدة

٢- مَصرِف عائِلة أسرة أقرِباء

٣- مُواصلات قِطار طائِرة حَلوى

٤- نامَ تَجَوَّلَ سافَرَ مَشى

## تمرين ٢

**وافِق بين كلماتٍ مِنَ العَمودِ الأيْمَن وكَلِماتٍ مِنَ العَمودِ الأيْسَر واكتُب الكَلِمَتين في الوسط.**

| | | | |
|---|---|---|---|
| ١ | صَحيفة | | رياضة |
| ٢ | شَريط | | أسرة |

| | | | |
|---|---|---|---|
| ٣ | لاعِب | | نادِل |
| ٤ | تأشيرة دُخول | | اِسْتَضاف |
| ٥ | عائِلة | | مَصرِف |
| ٦ | مَطعَم | | جَريدة |
| ٧ | نُقود | | مَنزِل |
| ٨ | دار | | مُسَجِّلة |
| | | | جَواز سَفَر |

## عَدنان في مَدينةِ دِنْـڤر

في عُطلةِ فَصلِ الرَبيعِ سافَرَ عَدنان مارتيني بِالطائِرةِ مِن مَدينةِ كَلمبَس في أوهايو حَيثُ يَدرُسُ عِلمَ الحاسوبِ في جامِعةِ وِلايةِ أوهايو إلى مَدينةِ دِنْـڤر عاصِمةِ وِلايةِ كولورادو. نَزَلَ في دِنْـڤر في مَنزِلِ عائِلةٍ أمريكيّةٍ هي عائِلةُ السَيِّدِ والسَيِّدةِ آلَن. تَسْتَضيفُ عائِلةُ آلَن الطُلاّبَ الأجانِبَ خِلالَ العُطلاتِ لِمُدّةِ أسبوعٍ أو أسبوعَينِ.

مَنزِل عائِلةُ آلَن

أوهايو وكولورادو على خريطةِ الوِلاياتِ المُتَّحِدةِ

يَعمَلُ السَيِّدُ تشارلز آلَن صَحَفِيّاً ويَكتُبُ لِمَجلّةٍ في دِنْـڤر ولِصُحُفٍ ومَجلاّتٍ أُخرى في الوِلاياتِ المُتَّحِدةِ، وتَعمَلُ زَوجَتُهُ آليس مُحاسِبةً في مَصْرِفٍ. تشارلز وآليس لَهُما اِبنٌ وابنة. الابنُ، واسمُهُ پول، طالِبٌ في جامِعةِ كولورادو في بولدَر حَيثُ يَدرُسُ العُلومَ السِياسِيّةَ وهُو لاعِبُ كُرةِ قَدَمٍ أيْضاً. أمّا ابنَتُهُما هِذَر فَهي تَدرُسُ التِجارةَ في جامِعةِ كاليفورنيا في سانتا كروز وتَعمَلُ أيْضاً نادِلةً في مَطعَمٍ هُناكَ ثَلاثَ ساعاتٍ كُلَّ يَوم.

يول آلن لاعِبُ كُرةِ قدم

السَيِّدُ تشارلز آلن صَحفيّ

السَيِّدة آلَن مُحاسِبة

هِذَر آلن نادِلة

زارَ عَدنان وَسَطَ المَدينةِ وعَدَداً مِن البُيوتِ القَديمةِ هُناك. وفي يَومِ السَبتِ حَضَرَ مع عائِلةِ آلَن مُباراةَ كُرةِ قَدَمٍ في مَلعَبِ المَدينةِ الَّذي يُسمّيهِ أهلُها «المَلعَبَ العالي» لأَنَّهُ يَرتَفِعُ ميلاً عَن سَطحِ البَحرِ.

في اليَومِ التالي ذَهَبوا بِالسَيّارةِ إلى جِبالِ «الروكي» وتَناوَلوا طَعامَ الغَداءِ في مَطعَمٍ قَديمٍ في الجِبالِ وقَد أعجَبَهُ ذلِكَ جِدّاً. في طَريقِ العَودَةِ مَرّوا بمَصنَعِ بيرَةِ «كورز» وهو مَصْنَعٌ كَبيرٌ يَعمَلُ فيهِ مِئاتُ العُمّالِ.

لَقَد اسْتَمتَعَ عَدنان بِهذِهِ الزِيارةِ اسْتِمتاعاً كَبيراً، وفي نِهايَتِها شَكَرَ السَيِّدَ والسَيِّدةَ آلَن على كَرَمِهما واسْتِضافَتِهما لَهُ. قَدَّمَ لَهُما هَديَّةً وهي شَريطٌ مُسَجَّلٌ عَلَيْهِ موسيقا وأغانٍ عَربيّة. وقَدَّمَ كَذلِكَ مِفْرَشاً جَميلاً لِطاوِلةِ الطَعامِ مَصنوعاً في دَمَشق. عادَ عَدنان إلى كَلَمبَس كَما أتى مِنها بِالطائِرة.

## تمرين ٣

**أكمِلِ الجُمَلَ التالِيةَ مِن نَصِّ القِراءة.**

١- سافَرَ عَدنان إلى دِنْـفَر بِـ ______________.

٢- تَعمَلُ هِذَر ______________.

٣- تَستَضيفُ عائِلةُ السَيِّد آلَن الطُلاّبَ ______________.

٤- شاهَدَ عَدنان في جِبالِ الروكي مَصنَعَ ______________.

٥- يُسَمّي الناسُ في دِنْـفَر مَلعَبَ المَدينةِ «المَلعَبَ العالي» لأَنَّهُ ______________.

**أكتُبْ «خطأ» أو «صَواب» بِجانبِ كُلِّ جُملَةٍ وصَحِّحِ الجُمَلَ الخَطأ.**

٦– مَدينةُ دِنْـفَر عالية.

٧– يوجَدُ خَمسةُ أشخاصٍ في عائِلةِ آلَن.

٨– يَدرُسُ پول آلَن التِجارةَ في جامِعةِ كولورادو.

٩– قَدَّمَ عَدنان هَديّةً لِلسَيِّدِ والسَيِّدَةِ آلَن.

**أجِب عَن هٰذِه الأسئلةِ حَسَبَ النَصّ.**

١٠– مَن يَعمَلُ مُحاسَباً؟

١١– ماذا يَعمَلُ السَيِّدُ آلَن؟

١٢– ماذا فَعَلَ عَدنان يَومَ السَبت؟

١٣– أينَ صُنِعَ مِفرَشُ الطاوِلة؟

## تمرين ٤

**وافِق بين كلماتٍ مِنَ العَمودِ الأيْمَن وكلِماتٍ مِنَ العَمودِ الأيْسَر واكتُب الكَلِمَتين في الوسط.**

| | | | |
|---|---|---|---|
| ١ | جُنَيه | | أسرة |
| ٢ | مَقعَد | | أُجرة |
| ٣ | قَرية | | انتَظَرَ |
| ٤ | اعتَقَدَ | | كُرسيّ |
| ٥ | مِثل | | عَكْس |
| ٦ | قَريب | | ظَنَّ |
| ٧ | مُلَوَّث | | وَصَلَ |
| ٨ | غادَرَ | | بَلدة |
| ٩ | سَيّارة | | نَقِيّ |
| | | | لَيرة |

## تمرين ٥

**أعِدْ تَرتيبَ الكَلِماتِ في كُلِّ مَجموعةٍ لِتُشكِّلَ جُمَلاً مُفيدةً.**

١- الأجانِبَ - آلَن - الطُلاّبَ - عائلةُ - تَستَضيفُ

٢- جُنَيهاً - القِطار - عَشَرَ - تَذكِرةَ - بِأرْبَعةَ - اشتَرَيتُ

٣- مُزدَحِمةٌ - القاهِرةِ - مُلَوَّث - شَوارِعُ - وهَواؤُها - بِالناسِ

٤- العيدِ - لالينيا - في - المِنيا - مَدينةَ - زارَتْ

# لالينيا تزورُ المِنيا

لالينيا غولدزبري طالِبةٌ أمريكيّةٌ تَدرُسُ اللُغَةَ العَرَبيّةَ في جامِعةِ وِلايةِ أوهايو، وقَد ذَهَبَتْ إلى الجامِعةِ الأمريكيّةِ في القاهِرةِ لِمُدَّةِ سَنَةٍ دِراسيّةٍ لِدِراسةِ العَرَبيّةِ هُناك. في العُطلاتِ زارَتْ لالينيا أماكِنَ عَديدَةً في مِصرَ وخارِجِها. هذا ما كَتَبَتْهُ إلى أستاذِها عَن رِحلَتِها إلى المِنيا.

**في اليَوم الأَوَّلِ مِن عيد الفِطْر رَكِبتُ سَيّارة أجرةٍ مِن حَيّ العَجوزة إلى مَحَطَّةِ الجيزة لِلقِطارات ودَفَعْتُ لِلسائقِ ثَلاثةَ جُنَيهاتٍ أجْرَةَ السَيّارة. كانَت المَحَطّةُ مُزدَحِمةً بِالناس، رُبَّما بِسَبَبِ العيد. أعتَقِدُ أنَّ مَحَطّةَ رَمسيس كانت مُزدَحِمةً أيْضاً، لكِنَّني لَمْ أذْهَبْ إليها في ذلِكَ اليَوم. اشتَرَيتُ تَذكِرةً بِالدَرَجَةِ الثانية بِأرْبَعةَ عشَرَ جُنَيهاً، وتَدافَعتُ مع مِئاتِ الرُكّابِ لِلحُصولِ على مَقعَدٍ مع أنَّ لي مَقعَداً مَحجوزاً. أظُنُّ أنَّ الناسَ تَعَوَّدوا على التَدافُعِ في المُواصَلاتِ العامّة.**

**مَرَّ القِطارُ بِقُرى عَديدَةٍ ووَصَلتُ المِنيا بَعدَ ثَلاثِ ساعاتٍ ونِصف حَيثُ كانَ أخو صَديقي في استِقبالي في المَحَطّة. رَكِبتُ معهُ سَيّارَتَهُ الّتي ساقَها في شَوارِعِ البَلَدَةِ لأَتَعَرّفَ عليها. المنيا بَلدَةٌ لَيْسَت كَبيرةً ولا أعرِفُ عَدَدَ سُكّانِها تَماماً. كانَ فيها الكَثيرُ مِن الأشجارِ الخَضراءِ وكانَ الهَواءُ نَقيّاً غَيْرَ مُلَوَّثٍ والشَوارِعُ هادئةٌ بِعَكسِ القاهِرة، حَتّى أنّني شاهَدْتُ عَدَداً كَبيراً مِن النُجومِ في السَماءِ في اللَيل.**

مَرَرْنا بِشارِعٍ يُسَمّى الكورنيش تَقَعُ على أَحَدِ جانِبَيْهِ حَديقةٌ عامّةٌ واسِعةٌ كانَ فيها عَدَدٌ كَبيرٌ مِن النّاسِ بَعْضُهُم يَمْشي وبَعْضُهُم يَلْعَبُ ويَتَنَزَّهُ. قالَ لي أخو صَديقي إنَّ الحَديقةَ لا يوجَدُ فيها هذا العَدَدُ مِن النّاسِ عادةً، لكِنَّها كانَت مُزْدَحِمةً في ذلِكَ اليَوم بِسَبَبِ العيد. عَبَرْنا إلى الجانِبِ الآخَرِ مِن نَهرِ النيلِ حَيْثُ توجَدُ مَزارِعُ المَوزِ، وشاهَدْنا أنواعاً مُخْتَلِفةً مِن النّاسِ مُعْظَمُهُم مِن الفَلّاحين.

بَقيتُ مع أُسْرةِ صَديقي ثَلاثةَ أَيّام وهي أَيّامُ العيد. كُلُّ شَيءٍ في المَنزِلِ كانَ يَدُلُّ على العيدِ، الحَلْوى الّتي تُسَمّى «كَعْكَ العيدِ» وبَرامِجِ الإذاعةِ والتِلفازِ الخاصّة والزِياراتُ إلى بُيوتِ الأصدِقاء والأقرِباء.

في نِهايةِ عُطلةِ العيدِ رَجَعْتُ إلى القاهِرة. كانَ مَوعِدُ القِطارِ في الساعةِ السادِسةِ صباحاً وأخَذَني الأبُ إلى المَحَطّةِ بِسَيّارتِه وانتَظَرَني هُناكَ حَتّى غادَرَ القِطارُ المَحَطّة.

جَلَسْتُ في القِطارِ إلى جانِبِ شابٍّ، وقَد قَدَّمَ لي حَلْوى وهي كَعكُ العيدِ فَرَفَضْتُ، لكِنَّهُ أَصَرَّ فَأخَذْتُ واحِدة. ثُمَّ مَرَّ بائِعُ الشاي فَسَأَلَني إِنْ كُنْتُ أَريدُ كَأْسَ شايٍ فَقُلْتُ لا. بَعْدَ قَليل سَأَلَني إِنْ كُنْتُ مِن القاهِرةِ أم مِن المِنيا، فَضَحِكْتُ بَيْني وبَيْنَ نَفْسي مِن هذا السُؤال السَخيف لأنَّهُ لا شَكْلي ولا كَلامي يَدُلّانِ على أنّي مِصريّة، لكِنَّني كُنْتُ سَعيدةً أنَّهُ ظَنَّ أنّي مِصريّة. قالَ لي هذا الشابُّ إنَّهُ مِن أسوان وتَكَلَّمنا عَن الدِراسة، وسَرَّهُ كَثيراً أنّي كُنْتُ أَدْرُسُ العَرَبيّة. كانَ يَقرأُ كِتاباً خِلالَ الرِحلةِ وأَصَرَّ أنْ يُقَدِّمَهُ لي كَهَديّة. كانَ الكِتابُ عَن الخَليفةِ الرابِع. لَقَد استَمْتَعْتُ بِهذِه الرِحلةِ أَيّما استِمتاع وقَد أزورُ المِنيا ثانِية.

## تمرين ٦

**أكمِلِ الجُمَلَ التالية مِن نَصِّ القِراءةِ الثاني.**

١- كَتبَتْ لالينيا إلى أستاذِها عَن ________________.

٢- تَسكَنُ لالينيا في حَيّ ________________.

٣- كانتَ المَحَطّةُ ________________ بِسَبَبِ العيد.

٤- تَقَعُ مَزارِعُ المَوزِ ________________.

٥- تَستَغرِقُ الطَريقُ مِن القاهِرةِ إلى المِنيا ________________.

٦- كانَ الشابُّ في القِطارِ يَقرَأُ كِتاباً عِن ________________.

## تمرين ٧

**أكتُبْ «خطَأ» أو «صَواب» بِجانبِ كُلِّ جُملَةٍ وصَحِّحِ الجُمَلَ الخَطَأ.**

١- تَدافَعَ الناسُ لِلحُصولِ على مَقعَدٍ في القِطارِ لأنَّ المقاعِدَ قَليلة.

٢- لالينيا طالِبةٌ مِصريّة.

٣- استَقبَلَ لالينيا في المَحَطّةِ أخو صَديقِها.

٤- جَلَسَتْ لالينيا في طَريقِ العَودَةِ إلى جانِبِ سَيِّدةٍ مِصريّة.

٥- حَصَلَتْ لالينيا على هَدِيّةٍ مِن عائِلةِ صَديقِها.

٦- هَواءُ القاهِرةِ مُلَوَّث.

## تمرين ٨

**Conversation:** Talk to your neighbor about how holidays differ from normal work days. You may wish to touch upon:

1. **Foods:** What foods are special for the holidays, who prepares the food in your home, are the grocery stores and restaurants busier or less busy?
2. **Transportation:** Are the streets in your city busier or less busy, what type of holiday travel do you prefer, do you pay more for tickets or the same?
3. **People:** Do people want to help more, are they happier, do they offer presents to those they do not know or just to people they know?

Once you are finished, compare your experiences to Lalaynia's holiday experience in Egypt. With the class, talk about holiday experiences at home and abroad.

تمرين ٩

صَنِّف كَلِماتٍ مِن هذا الدَرسِ تَحتَ الفِئاتِ التالية.

Categorize words from our main reading passages that fall under these headings:

| | ١ عيد | | ٢ بيئة | | ٣ مواصَلات | | ٤ زِراعة |
|---|---|---|---|---|---|---|---|
| | | | | | | | |
| | | | | | | | |
| | | | | | | | |
| | | | | | | | |
| | | | | | | | |
| | | | | | | | |

تمرين ١٠

أعِدْ تَرتيبَ الجُمَلِ لِتُشَكِّلَ فِقرةً مُفيدة:

١-    أرادَ برِتْ آدَمز أنْ يَزورَ المَغرِب.

كانَتِ الرِحلةُ طَويلةً واستَغرَقَت ١٥ ساعةً تَقريباً.

رَكِبَ برِتْ سَيّارةَ أجرةٍ مِن المَطارِ إلى الفُندُق.

اتَّصَلَ بِأُمِّهِ بِالهاتِفِ مِن الفُندُقِ وأخبَرَها بِوصولِهِ إلى المَغرِب.

ثانياً اشتَرى تَذكِرةَ طائِرةٍ على الخُطوطِ المَلِكِيّةِ المَغرِبيّة.

في يَومِ السَفَرِ أخَذَتْهُ أُمُّهُ إلى المَطارِ بِسَيّارتِها.

وحَصَلَ في الفُندُقِ على غُرفةٍ بِسَريرٍ واحِدٍ مع حَمّامٍ بِداخِلِها.

أوَّلاً كانَ عَليهِ أنْ يَحصُلَ على تأشيرةِ دُخول.

فَقَد وَصَلَ إلى مَطارِ الدارِ البَيضاءِ في اليَومِ التالي.

لِذلِكَ أرسَلَ جَوازَ سَفَرِهِ إلى السِفارةِ المَغرِبيّةِ بِواشِنطَن.

## 1. The Use of the Particle فَـ

This particle فَـ functions as a conjunction and gains its meaning through context. As with all one-letter particles in Arabic, it is prefixed to the word that follows it.

### A. When Prefixed to Nouns

The particle فـ has two meanings when prefixed to nouns:

1. It signifies a gradual process, as can be seen in example 1:

١ يَوماً فيَوماً *day by day*

شَيئاً فَشَيْئاً *bit by bit*

2. It can be used to describe a sequence of locations, as in example 2:

٢ مَرَرْنا بِحَلَبَ فَحماةَ فَحِمصَ فَدِمَشق.

*We passed through Aleppo, Hama, Hims, and then Damascus.*

### B. When Prefixed to Verbs

The semantic range of فَـ when prefixed to verbs is too great to enumerate here, but its primary meanings are "then," "thus," and "so." In this lesson, فَـ occurred four times in two consecutive sentences—a stylistically acceptable feature of written discourse in Arabic:

٣ قدّمَ لي حَلوى وهي كَعكُ العيدِ فَرفضتُ، لكِنَّهُ أصَرَّ فَأخَذتُ واحِدة.
ثُمَّ مَرَّ بائِعُ الشاي فَسَألَني إنْ كُنتُ أريدُ كأسَ شاي فَقُلتُ لا.

- **Integration into our daily speech:** One of the meanings of فَـ is "so," which has a function similar to, if not exactly like, its English counterpart. For example, when we need some compiling time to think, we string out both words (*faaaaaaaaa*; *soooooo*), and when we come back from an interrupted conversation, we restart the conversation with this particle. In order to immediately integrate this particle into our speech, we can simply rely on our English sense of how we use "so" in our discourse.

## 2. Functions of the Particle قَدْ

There are two main functions for **قَدْ**, depending on whether the verb following it is past or present.

**A. With Past-Tense Verbs (Perfect)**

**قَدْ** denotes completed action similar to the use of the perfective in English (present and past perfect):

٤ أرجو أنْ يَكونَ الكِتابُ قَدْ أعجَبَك. — *I hope the book has pleased you.*
More idiomatically: *I hope you liked the book.*

Note that while **قَدْ** does not have an exact English counterpart, certain translation practices can be used to account for its presence in the Arabic sentence (i.e., "have," "had," or an intensive meaning like "indeed"). For instance, when a sentence contains two past-tense verbs, **قَدْ** denotes that the verb following it occurred first. The use of **قَدْ** in this instance is similar to that of the English past perfect:

٥ وَصَلتُ إلى الصَفِّ في التاسِعةِ والرُبع وكانَ الدَرسُ قد بَدَأ.

*I arrived in the classroom at 9:15 and the lesson had already started.*

The sense of **قَدْ** in example 5 is not the only way it can function in a sentence containing two past-tense verbs. Example 6 illustrates that **قَدْ** can be used to simply emphasize the second verb:

٦ تَناوَلتُ الغَداءَ في مَطعَمٍ قَديمٍ وقد أعجَبَني. — *I had lunch in an old restaurant and I indeed enjoyed it.*

Example 6 shows us that in some sentences containing two past-tense verbs, the particle **قَدْ** provides emphasis, but does not have a bearing on how a sequence of events played out.

Certain particles may be prefixed to **قَدْ** such as the **لَـ** (**لَقد**), the **وَ** (**وَقد**), and the **فَـ** (**فَقد**), a process which might entail some changes in meaning:

٧ لَقد دَرَسَ العَرَبيَّةَ في المَغرِب. — *He has studied Arabic in Morocco.*

٨ شاهَدتُ فيلماً مُمتازاً وقد نَسيتُ اسمَهُ الآن. — *I saw an excellent movie, and/but I have forgotten its title now.*

| | |
|---|---|
| ٩ لَمْ أشتَرِ كِتابَ غسّان كَنفاني فَقَد قَرَأتُهُ مِن قبل. | *I didn't buy Kanafani's book because I had read it before.* |

**B. With Present-Tense Verbs**

If the following verb is in the present tense (imperfect), the use of قَدْ denotes possibility. No change in the verb form takes place:

| | |
|---|---|
| ١٠ قد أسافِرُ إلى عَمّانَ غَداً. | *I might travel to Amman tomorrow.* |

## SUMMARY

**قَدْ used with past-tense verbs:**

- The particle قَدْ, when followed by a past-tense verb, denotes either completed action or emphasis.
- When used in a sentence containing two past-tense verbs, the particle قَدْ may denote an order of events by indicating that the verb following it happened earlier, or it may indicate emphasis.

**قَدْ used with present-tense verbs:**

- When the particle قَدْ is followed by a present-tense verb, it denotes possibility (e.g., *may*, *might*).

## تمرين ١١

Express these meanings in Arabic, using قَدْ with reference to the section above.

1. They (m., pl.) may travel to Damascus by plane.
2. I saw her house and I really liked it.
3. When we got to our friends' house, they had already had dinner.

## 3. البَدَل (Substitution or the Permutative)

The permutative is a noun or noun phrase that stands for another noun that immediately precedes it. **البَدَل** can function as a full substitute for the modified noun (e.g., the Big Apple, the City of Lights). Let's examine some instances of **البَدَل** that occurred in our lesson:

١١ سافَرَ عَدنان إلى مَدينةِ دِنفَر عاصِمةِ وِلايةِ كولورادو.

*Adnān traveled to the city of Denver, capital of the state of Colorado.*

In example 11, the phrase **عاصِمةِ ولايةِ كولورادو** stands for the noun phrase **مَدينةِ دَنفِر**. As you can see, if we omit **مَدينة دَنفِر**, the sentence retains the same meaning because the permutative is its natural subsitute. Note that **البَدَل** has the same case as the modified noun or noun phrase (compare **مَدينةِ** and **عاصِمةِ**).

Example 12 illustrates the case of **البَدَل** when its modified noun is a diptote. Remember that diptotes **المَمنوع من الصَرف** take a **فَتحة** in both **المَجرور** (genitive) and **المَنصوب** (accusative) (refer to Lesson 15, section 2):

١٢ سافَرَ رامي إلى عَمّانَ عاصِمةِ الأردُن.

Since **عَمّان** is a diptote, it cannot take a **كَسرة** even though it is functionally in the genitive case. Instead, **عَمّان** takes a **فَتحة** on its final radical, but the grammatical reality (i.e., being in the genitive case) is reflected in the **كَسرة** that graces the final radical of its **البَدَل**.

## تمرين ١٢

Underline **البَدَل** in the following sentences and provide the appropriate inflectional ending.

١- دَفَعتُ لِلسائِقِ ثَلاثةَ جُنَيهاتٍ أجرة السَيّارة.

٢- زُرنا القاهِرةَ أكبَر مُدُنِ إفريقيا.

٣- وَصَلنا صَباحاً إلى الرباط عاصِمة المَغرِب.

٤- سَكَنَتْ لَيلى في «بيز ووتر» حَيّ العَرَب في لَندَن.

**A Reminder about إضافة**

The first word of an إضافة structure (i.e., المُضاف) can *never* have:

1. the definite article الـ;
2. nor تَنوين;
3. the final نون of the dual and plural suffixes.

In the last passage of this lesson, we read the following sentence:

١٣ أَرَدتُ أنا وصَديقتايَ آن ورينا أن نَزورَ سورية.

The noun صَديقتايَ is a combination of the dual noun صديقتان plus the possessive suffix ي, which forms an إضافة with the noun. Since صديقتان is the مُضاف, it loses the final نون of the dual suffix.

## 4. The Particle إنْ

The particle إنْ is a conditional particle (like "if" in English) that introduces a plausible condition—meaning a condition that is not hypothetical, but rather something that could actually happen. The sentence introduced by إنْ is known as الجُملة الشرطيّة. This sentence is comprised of two clauses: (1) the conditional clause الشَرط; and (2) the result clause الجَواب. Each clause has to contain a verb. The two verbs can be in either the present tense, past tense, or a combination of the two tenses. Read and contemplate the following examples:

١٤ إنْ تَزُرْ حَلَبَ تُعجِبْك. *If you visit Aleppo, you'll like it.*

١٥ إنْ زُرتَ حَلَبَ أعجَبَتْك.

١٦ إنْ تَزُرْ حَلَبَ أعْجَبَتْك.

١٧ إنْ زُرتَ حَلَبَ تُعجِبْك (أو تُعجِبُك).

As you can see, we have four possible structures from which we can choose. The rules that govern these four structures differ somewhat. Let's take a closer look at our examples.

When the verb immediately following إنْ is in the present tense, it must be مُضارع مَجزوم (jussive), as in examples 14 and 16.

When the verb in the "answer" is in present tense (example 17), it can be either a regular present (indicative مَرفوع) or jussive (مَجزوم).

The oft-used إنْ شاءَ الله (God willing) is an example of a conditional phrase; in fact, it follows the structure of example 17.

The conditional clause will contain a past-tense verb (i.e., كنتُ أريدُ) when the answer clause is omitted, as was the case in our main reading passage:

١٨ سألَني إنْ كُنتُ أريدُ كأسَ شاي.

## تمرين ١٣

**Ask your neighbor:** Find out who in your class . . .

1. might travel to Syria this summer
2. might study abroad this summer
3. might work in Washington, the capital of America
4. would enjoy swimming, if they traveled to Alexandria
5. would buy train tickets, if they were cheaper than plane tickets
6. might read a book, if they had time

## تمرين ١٤

AUDIO

**أجِب عَن الأسئِلةِ حَسَبَ نَصِّ الاستِماع.**

١- إلى أيِّ بَلَدٍ سَتكونُ الرِحلة؟

٢- كَم يَوماً سَتَبقى الصَديقات في القاهِرة؟

٣- هَل سَتُسافِرُ المُتَكَلِّمةُ مع صَديقاتِها؟ لِماذا؟

**أكتُبْ «خَطَأ» أو «صَواب» بِجانبِ كُلِّ جُملَةٍ وصَحِّح الجُمَلَ الخَطَأ.**

٤- مَسجِدُ مُحَمَّد عليّ في الإسكَندَريّة.

٥- مُدَّةُ الرِحلةِ إلى الإسكَندَريّةِ ثَلاثَةُ أيّام.

٦- سَيكونُ السَفَرُ إلى الأقصُر بِالحافِلة.

٧- لَن تُسافِرَ الفَتاةُ مع صَديقاتِها لأنَّها تَعرِفُ مِصر.

**أكمِلِ الجُمَلَ بِالاختيارِ المُناسِبِ حَسَبَ نَصِّ الاستِماع.**

٨- سَتَزورُ الصَديقاتُ في القاهِرةِ ____________.

☐ المَكتبات الكُبرى ☐ المُتحَفَ المِصريّ ☐ البَحرَ المُتوَسِّط

٩- الأهرامات مَوجودةٌ ____________.

☐ قُربَ القاهِرة ☐ في الأقْصُر ☐ في جَنوبِ مِصر

١٠- سَتأخُذُ الصَديقاتُ رِحلةً ____________.

☐ خاصّة ☐ عامّة ☐ جامِعيّة

١١- لَيْسَ عِندَ الفَتاةِ ____________.

☐ وَقتٌ ☐ هُويّةٌ ☐ صَديقاتٌ

١٢- الآثارُ الفِرعَونيّةُ مَوجودَةٌ ____________.

☐ في الطَريق إلى الأقْصُر ☐ في الإسكَندَريّة

☐ في مَسجِدِ مُحَمَّد عليّ

## تمرين ١٥

VIDEO

**تَمرينُ المُشاهَدة: شاهِدوا الدرسَ الثالثَ والعشرين على القُرْص الرَقْميّ.**

١- ما رأي عَدنان في أمريكا؟ ____________

____________

٢- كَيْفَ ساعَدَ هِشام صَديقَه عَدنان في التَعوُّدِ على الحياةِ في أمريكا؟ ____________

____________

____________

٣- لِماذا أحَبَّ مايكل زيارتَه إلى الشام؟ ____________

____________

____________

٤- ما هو الاخْتِلافُ بَيْنَ فِكْرةِ ستيف الّتي جاءَ بِها إلى سوريَّة وفِكرتِه الآن؟ ____________

____________

____________

## المُفْرَدات

Listen to the vocabulary items on the CD and practice their pronunciation.

| | |
|---|---|
| اِخْتَلَفَ (يَخْتَلِفُ) اِخْتِلاف (عَن) (v.) | to differ (from) |
| اِرتَفَعَ (يرتَفِعُ) اِرتِفاع (v.) | to rise, to be higher |
| اِستَضافَ (يستَضيفُ) استِضافة (v.) | to host |
| اِشْتاقَ (يَشْتاقُ) اِشْتِياق (لِـ/ إلى) (v.) | to long (for), to yearn |
| أصَرَّ (يُصِرُّ) إصْرار (v.) | to insist |
| اِعتَقَدَ (يَعتَقِدُ) اِعتِقاد (v.) | to believe |
| اِقْتَرَبَ (يَقْتَرِبُ) اِقْتِراب (مِن) (v.) | to draw near, get close (to) |
| إنْ (particle) | if |
| اِنتظَرَ (يَنْتَظِرُ) اِنتِظار (v.) | to wait |
| أيَّما (n.) | immensely, greatly (intensifies the following noun) |
| بَسيط ج بُسطاء (adj.) | simple |
| تأشيرة دُخول (n., f.) | visa |
| تَدافَعَ (يَتَدافَعُ) تَدافُع (v.) | to push, shove one another |
| تَعَرَّفَ (يَتَعَرَّفُ) تَعَرُّف (على) (v.) | to be acquainted with |
| تَعَوَّدَ (يَتَعَوَّدُ) تَعَوُّد (على) (v.) | to be accustomed to |
| تَنَزَّهَ (يَتَنَزَّهُ) تَنَزُّه (v.) | to stroll; to have a good time; to go on a picnic |
| جَواز (سَفَر) (n., m.) | passport |
| حَضَرَ (يحْضُرُ) حُضور (v.) | to attend, to be present |
| خارِج (n.) | outside |
| خَفَّفَ (يُخَفِّفُ) تَخْفيف (عَن) (v.) | to diminish the difficulty of |
| خَليفة ج خُلَفاء (n., m.) | caliph, successor |
| دَرَجة ج دَرَجات (n., f.) | class, step, level, degree |

دَفَعَ (يَدْفَعُ) دَفْع (v.) . . . to pay

رِحْلة ج رِحلات (n., f.) . . . trip, journey, flight

ساقَ (يَسوقُ) سِياقة (v.) . . . to drive

سَخيف ج سُخَفاء (n./adj.) . . . silly, absurd, foolish

سَرَّ (يَسُرُّ) سُرور (v.) . . . to please, to be glad

سَطْح ج سُطوح (n., m.) . . . surface, level

سِياسيّ (adj.) . . . political

شَيِّق (adj.) . . . interesting, thrilling

صَحَفِيّ ج ون (n., m.) . . . journalist

صَحيفة ج صُحُف (n., f.) . . . newspaper

ضَحِكَ (يَضْحَكُ) ضِحْك (v.) . . . to laugh

عَبَرَ (يعبُرُ) عُبور (v.) . . . to cross

عَكْس (n.) . . . opposite, reverse, contrary

غادَرَ (يُغادِرُ) مُغادَرة (v.) . . . to leave

فَلاّح ج ون (n., m.) . . . peasant, farmworker

قَد (particle) . . . no meaning, denotes completed action, emphasis, or possibility

قَريب ج أقارِب (n., m.) . . . a relative

قَلْب ج قُلوب (n., m.) . . . heart

كَـ (prep.) . . . as, like

كَرَم (n., m.) . . . hospitality, generosity

كَلام (n., m.) . . . speech, speaking

لاعِب ج ون (n., m.) . . . player

لَقَد (particle) . . . a variation of *qad*

مُجْتَمَع ج مُجْتَمَعات (n., m.) . . . society, community

مُحاسِب ج ون (n., m.) . . . accountant

crowded . . . . . . . . . . . . . . . . . . . . مُزدَحِم (adj.)

farm . . . . . . . . . . . . . . . . . . . . مَزْرَعة ج مَزارِع (n., f.)

recorded . . . . . . . . . . . . . . . . . . . . مُسَجَّل (n./adj.)

factory, plant . . . . . . . . . . . . . . . . مَصْنَع ج مَصانِع (n., m.)

tablecloth . . . . . . . . . . . . . . . . مَفرَش ج مَفارِش (n., m.)

seat, bench, armchair . . . . . . . . . . . . مَقْعَد ج مَقاعِد (n., m.)

enjoyable . . . . . . . . . . . . . . . . . . مُمْتِع (active participle)

polluted . . . . . . . . . . . . . . . . . . . . مُلَوَّث (adj.)

house, residence . . . . . . . . . . . . . . . مَنزِل ج مَنازِل (n., m.)

view, panorama . . . . . . . . . . . . . . . . مَنْظَر ج مَناظِر (n., m.)

means of transportation . . . . . . . . مُواصَلة ج مُواصَلات (n., f.)

waiter . . . . . . . . . . . . . . . . . . . . نادِل ج نُدُل (n., m.)

mint, peppermint . . . . . . . . . . . . . . . . . . نَعناع (n., m.)

pure . . . . . . . . . . . . . . . . . . . . . . . . نَقيّ (adj.)

quiet, serene . . . . . . . . . . . . . . . . . . . . هادِئ (adj.)

present, gift . . . . . . . . . . . . . . . . هَدِيّة ج هَدايا (n., f.)

# الدَرْسُ الرابِعُ والعِشرونَ

## Objectives

- Revisiting family members and relations
- Describing professions
- Using the terms of address أبو and أم
- Revisiting the comparative and superlative degrees
- Expressing reason with كَي and لِـ
- Revisiting verbal nouns المَصدَر
- Learning details about the *hamza* and how to write it

## رُكنُ المُفْرَداتِ الجَديدةِ:

| | |
|---|---|
| *to choose* | اِخْتارَ (يَخْتارُ) اِختِيار |
| *to import* | اِسْتَوْرَدَ (يَسْتَوْرِدُ) اِسْتِيراد |
| *to care for* | اِعْتَنى (يَعْتَني) اِعْتِناء (بِـ) |
| *to reside* | أقامَ (يُقيم) إقامة |
| *to appear* | بَدا (يَبدو) بُدو / بَداء |
| *to retire* | تَقاعَدَ (يَتَقاعَدُ) تَقاعُد |
| *to respond* | رَدَّ (يَردُّ) رَدّ |
| *to register* | سَجَّلَ (يُسَجِّلُ) تَسْجيل |
| *to issue* | صَدَرَ (يَصدُرُ) صُدور |
| *note; observation* | مُلاحَظة ج مُلاحَظات |
| *occupation; profession* | مِهْنة ج مِهَن |
| *comprised of* | مُؤَلَّف (مِن) |
| *same* | نَفْس ج أَنْفُس |

## تمرين ١

**وافِق بين كلماتٍ مِنَ العَمودِ الأيْمَن وكلِماتٍ مِنَ العَمودِ الأيْسَر واكتُب الكَلِمَتين في الوسط.**

| | | | |
|---|---|---|---|
| ١ | كُبرى | | نَهار |
| ٢ | اِلْتَقَطَ | | بَحر |
| ٣ | يَمين | | بَنات |
| ٤ | سَفينة | | صُغرى |
| ٥ | مَحَلٌّ تَجاري | | يَسار |
| ٦ | بَنون | | واسِع |
| ٧ | لَيْل | | صَوَّرَ |
| | | | دُكّان |

## تمرين ٢

**أعِدْ تَرتيبَ الكلِماتِ في كُلِّ مَجموعة لِتُشَكِّلَ جُملاً مُفيدة.**

١- لِلبَنين - في - مَروانُ - بَحَلَب - ثانوِيَّةٍ - يَدرُسُ - مَدرسَةٍ

٢- لِبيعِ - السَيّاراتِ - أبي - غِيارِ - عِندَ - واسِعٌ - عَدنان - قِطَعِ - مَحَلٌّ

٣- كَيْ - عَدنان - بِعائِلَتِها - عَمَلِها - تَقاعَدَت - تَعتَنيَ - أُمُّ - عَن

٤- مارتيني - ومُحاسِبٌ - في - ياسِر - عُمّالٍ - ثَلاثَةُ - وبائِعان - يَعمَلُ - مَحَلِّ

## تمرين ٣

**أعِدْ ترتيبَ الجُمَلِ لِتُشَكِّلَ فِقرةً مُفيدة. لا تُغَيِّر مَكانَ الجُمْلةِ الأولى.**

١- دَرَسَتْ هالة الصيدَلة في جامِعَةِ دِمشق. *pharmacy, pharmacology**

اشتَريا داراً كَبيرةً في دِمشق مُؤَلَّفةً مِن ثَلاثةِ طوابِق.

تَعَرَّفَتْ في المُستَشفى على زَوجِها مازِن الّذي كانَ يَعمَلُ طَبيباً. *hospital**

أمّا الطابَقُ الثاني فَسَكنوا فيه.

وتَخَرَّجَتْ مِنَ الجامِعَةِ في العامِ ٢٠٠٢.

حينَ صارَ أولادُهُما في سِنِّ المَدرَسة انتَقَلا إلى دِمشق.

بَعدَ تَخَرُّجِها عَمِلَت صَيدلانِيّةً في مَشفى في مَدينةِ الكُوَيت. * pharmacist

والطابَقُ الأوَّل صارَ عِيادَةً لمازِن.

صارَ لِهالة ومازِن بِنتان ووَلَدان.

في الطابَقِ الأرضِيِّ مَحَلٌّ تِجاريٌّ واسِعٌ فَتَحَتْهُ هالة صَيْدَلِيّة. * pharmacy

## تمرين ٤

**اختَرِ الكَلِمةَ الّتي لا تُناسِب باقي الكَلِماتِ في كُلِّ مَجْموعةٍ وبَيِّن السَبَب.**

| | | | | |
|---|---|---|---|---|
| ١- | استيراد | صورة | التَقَطَ | ظَهَرَ |
| ٢- | عام | سَنة | عَمّ | عُمُر |
| ٣- | رِسالة | طِبٌّ | تِجارة | عِلْمُ الحاسوب |
| ٤- | بِضاعة | دُكّان | مُدَرِّس | مَحَلّ تِجاري |
| ٥- | كَيْ | أَيُّ | لِذلِكَ | لِـ |
| ٦- | جَواز سَفَر | عامِل | مُحاسِب | مُوَظَّف |

# أُسرَةُ عَدنان مارتيني

### القِصّة

هذِهِ صورةُ أُسرةِ عَدنان مارتيني. لَقَد أرسَلَ أبو عَدنان صورةَ العائلةِ مَعَ رسالةٍ إلى ابنِهِ عَدنان الَّذي يَدرُسُ عِلمَ الحاسوبِ في جامِعةِ ولايةِ أوهايو في الولايّاتِ المتحدةِ الأمريكيّة. يَظهَرُ في الصورةِ أبو عَدنان في أعْلى الصورةِ إلى اليَمين وتَظهَرُ أمُّ عَدنان إلى جانبِهِ إلى يَسارِ الصورة. تَظهَرُ في أسفَلِ الصورةِ إلى اليَمينِ أختُ عَدنان

الصُغرى أماني، وعُمُرُها إحدى عَشْرةَ سَنةً وهي في الصَفِّ السادِسِ الابتدائي. إلى جانبِ أماني تبدو أختُها أمينة، وعُمُرُها خَمسَ عَشْرَةَ سَنة. أمينة في الصَفِّ العاشِر وهي تَذهَبُ إلى المَدرسةِ الثانَوِيّةِ الجَديدةِ لِلإناثِ في مَدينةِ حَلَبَ في سورية. يَجلِسُ مَروان إلى جانِبِ أمينة، وهو طالِبٌ في الصَفِّ الثاني عَشَر العِلمِيّ في المَدرسةِ الثانَويّةِ لِلبَنين وعُمرُهُ سَبعةَ عَشَرَ عاماً. لا يَظهَرُ أخوهُم رامي في الصورةِ وكذلِكَ أيمَن لأَنَّهُما ما كانا في حَلَبَ حينَ التُقِطَت الصورة.

ياسِر مارتيني

أبوعَدنان، واسمُهُ ياسِر مارتيني، تاجِرٌ في الخامِسةِ والخَمسين من عُمرِه. لَهُ مَحَلٌّ تِجاريٌّ في حَلَبَ فَتَحَهُ مُنذُ خَمسةٍ وعشرين عاماً يَبيعُ فيهِ قِطَعَ غِيارٍ لِبعْضِ السيّاراتِ الألمانيّة كَفولكسفاكن وأوبِل. مَحَلُّ أبي عَدنان واسِعٌ وهو مُؤَلَّفٌ مِن دُكّانٍ لبَيعِ قِطَعِ الغِيارِ ومَكتَبٍ لَهُ وآخَرَ لِلمُحاسِب، وهُناكَ مَخزَنٌ كَبيرٌ لِتَخزينِ البِضاعة. يَعملُ عِندَهُ في المَحَلِّ مُحاسِبٌ واحِدٌ وبائعانِ وثَلاثةُ عُمّالٍ لِنَقلِ البِضاعةِ مِن المَحَلِّ وإليه. يستَوردُ السَيِّد ياسِر مارتيني بِضاعتَه مِن ألمانيا وتَصِلُه إلى حَلَبَ بالشاحِناتِ غالِباً وأحياناً بالبَحْرِ عَن طريقِ ميناءِ اللاذِقيّة، لكنَّها تَتَأخَّرُ عادةً بِهذه الطَريق. لِذلِكَ فَهو يُسافِرُ إلى ميونيخ وكولون وفرانكفورت ليشتريَ البِضاعةَ بِنَفسِه مِن ألمانيا.

سامية كَحّال

أمُّ عَدنان، واسمُها سامية كَحّال، عُمُرُها خَمسونَ عاماً. هي رَبَّةُ بَيتٍ الآن ولا تَعمَل، لكِنَّها كانَت مُدَرِّسَةَ لُغةٍ فَرَنسيّةٍ في إحدى مَدارِسِ الإناثِ الثانِويّةِ في حَلَب. تَقاعَدَتْ السَيِّدةُ سامية كَحّال عَن العَمَلِ مُنذُ ثَماني سَنواتٍ كَي تَعتَنيَ بوالِدَتِها المَريضةِ وبِمَنزِلِها وزَوجِها وأولادِها. فَكانت تَعمَلُ في المنزِلِ في النَهارِ وتَزورُ صديقاتِها مَساءً وفي اللَيلِ تَبقى مَعَ عائِلَتِها.

الجمهورية العربية السورية
RÉPUBLIQUE ARABE SYRIENNE

وزارة الداخلية
MINISTÈRE DE L'INTÉRIEUR

إدارة الهجرة والجوازات
DÉPARTEMENT DE L'IMMIGRATION & DES PASSEPORTS

صدر بمدينة: حلب: Fait à: Alep

في اليوم: السادس من شهر نيسان ٢٠٠٧
Le 6 avril ٢٠٠٧

وينتهي مفعوله بتاريخ ٥ نيسان ٢٠١٣
Et expire le 5 avril ٢٠١٣

رقم التسجيل ٣٦١٧٣٥٤٢

الاسم والشهرة: ياسِر مارتيني
اسم الأب: عَبد الغَني
اسم الأم: رُقيَّة
مكان الإقامة الحالي: حلب
تاريخ ومكان الولادة: حلب ١٥ آب ١٩٥٥
المِهنة: تاجِر
الشعر: أسوَد
الطول: ١٧١ سنتيمتر
اللون: أسمَر
العينان: بُنيتان

التوقيع: ياسر مارتيني

**صفحتان من جواز سفر السيد ياسر مارتيني**

سافَرَتْ أمُّ عَدنان خارجَ سورية مَرَّةً واحِدةً مَعَ زَوجِها إلى ألمانيا مُنذُ سَنَتَين ومَرَّةً أخرى إلى الوِلاياتِ المتحِّدة لِزيارةِ ابنِها عَدنان، لكنَّها سافَرَتْ وَحدَها ومَعَ زَوجِها عِدّةَ مَرّاتٍ إلى دِمشقَ واللاذِقيّة وكَذلِكَ إلى لُبنانَ والأردُن.

كَتَبَ أبو عَدنان الرِسالةَ التالية إلى ابنِهِ عَدنان في أمريكا وأرسَلَ لَهُ مَعَها صورةَ العائِلة. يُخبِرُ أبو عَدنان ابنَه في الرِسالةِ أنَّ والِدَتَهُ سَتَزورُهُ في الولايات المتحدةِ في الصيفِ المُقبِلِ وأنَّهُ لَن يَستَطيعَ أنْ يَكونَ مَعَها في هذِه الزِيارة.

## تَذَوّقِ الثَقافة العَرَبيّة

**مُلاحَظة ثقافية حَولَ الدِراسة في سورية. . .** حينَ يَصِلُ الطالِبُ إلى الصفِّ الحادي عَشَر يَختارُ الفَرْعَ العِلمِيَّ أو الفَرعَ الأدبِيَّ ويَبقى فيهِ سَنَتَين. في الفرعِ العِلمِيِّ يَدْرُسُ الرياضيّات والكيمياء والفيزياء وعِلمَ الأحْياء والجيولوجيا. أمّا في الفَرعِ الأدبِيِّ فيَدرُسُ لُغتَينِ أجنَبِيَّتَينِ والأدَبَ والشِعْرَ العَرَبيَّ والفَلسَفَةَ والتاريخَ والجُغرافيا وعِلمَ الاجتِماع.

# تمرين ٥

**Conversation:** **مُحادَثة :تفعيلُ المفرداتِ**

Bring in some of your family photographs from home to describe to your classmates. Now, work in groups of two and see if you can use every word in the word bank:

| | | | | | | |
|---|---|---|---|---|---|---|
| يَظهَرُ | يَبدو | إلى يَمين | إلى يَسار | أعْلى | أسْفل | أكْبَر مِن |
| أصْغَر مِن | كي / لِـ | مُؤلَّف مِن | تَقاعَدَ عن | أقامَ | اِلْتَقَطَ | |

# التمرين ٦

**Ask your neighbor:** Find out if your partner . . . **محادثة: إسأل جيرانَك**

1. has a passport
2. has traveled abroad
3. has lived abroad
4. has relatives abroad
5. knows where Aleppo is
6. has written a letter in Arabic
7. can read Arabic handwriting

. . . and now report your findings to class, using as much detail and being as creative as possible concerning what you learned about your classmates' lives.

# رسالةُ ياسر مارتيني إلى ابنِهِ عَدنان

حلب في ٢٢ أيار ٢٠٠٨

ابني الحبيب عدنان، السلامُ عليكَ ورحمةُ اللّٰه.

أرجو أن تصلكَ رسالتي هذه وأنت في أحسن حال. كُلُّنا بخير والحمد للّٰه. كتبت لكَ رسالة في الشهر الماضي وما وصلني منك ردٌّ عليها. أما وصلتكَ رسالتي؟ آخر رسالة منكَ كان تاريخها ٧ كانون الثاني. أرجو أن تكتب لنا دون تأخير.

أكتب هذه الرسالة لأخبرك أن والدتكَ تريد أن تسافر إليكَ في شهر آب. لن أستطيع أن أسافر معها هذه المرّة لأني مشغول جداً. يجب أن أسافر إلى ألمانيا في آب المقبل من أجل استيراد بضاعة لمحلي.

اشتريتُ تذكرة طائرة لوالدتكَ على الخطوط الجوية الهولندية. تغادر طائرتها مطار دمشق في يوم الخميس ١٤ آب وتصل إلى شيكاغو في اليوم نفسه. أرجو أن تستقبلها في المطار لأنها كما تعلم لا تتكلم الإنكليزية ولا تعرف أحداً على الطائرة.

والآن إليكَ أخبار الأسرة. أخوكَ أيمن كلّمنا بالهاتف من دمشق وهو بخير ويرسل لكَ سلامه. أخوكَ رامي لا يزال يدرس في الجامعة ويعمل سائقاً في شركة البرادات، وهو سعيد بذلكَ. خالكَ أحمد انتقل في الشهر الماضي وعائلته إلى دمشق حيث سيعمل مدرساً للفيزياء في إحدى المدارس الثانوية. تقاعد عمكَ زهير من عمله في وزارة التربية، وهو يقول إن حياة المتقاعد تعجبه كثيراً. جدتكَ أم ياسر ترسل لكَ سلامها وتشكركَ على الهدية التي أرسلتها لها. أكتب لنا عن أخباركَ وإلى اللقاء.

والدكَ

See Appendix E for typed version of letter.

## تمرين ٧

آ- **أجِب عن الأسئلة التالية حَسَبَ النَص:**

١- في أيِّ صَفٍ أمينة؟

٢- ما اسْم أختِ عَدنان الصُغرى؟

٣- أينَ يَجلِسُ مَروان في الصورة؟

٤- مِن أينَ يَستَوْرِدُ ياسِر مارتيني بِضاعَتَهُ؟

٥- كَمْ مُوَظَّفاً يَشتَغِلُ في مَحَلِّ أبي عَدنان؟

٦- لماذا يُسافِرُ أبو عَدنان إلى ألمانيا؟

٧- ماذا كانَت تعمَلُ أمُّ عَدنان؟

٨- مَتى تَقاعَدَت عن العَمَل ولِماذا؟

٩- مَتى كَتَبَ عَدنان آخِرَ رِسالةٍ إلى أسرَته؟

١٠- مَن أمُّ ياسِر؟

**ب - أكتُبْ «خَطَأ» أو «صَواب» بِجانبِ كُلِّ جُملَةٍ وصَحِّحِ الجُمَلَ الخَطَأ.**

١١- تَذهَبُ أمينة إلى مَدرَسةٍ ثانوِيَّةٍ لِلبَنين.

١٢- يَدرُسُ رامي عِلمَ الحاسوبِ في أمريكا.

١٣- مَروان أصْغَر إخوَةِ عَدنان وهو في السابِعةَ عَشْرَةَ مِن عُمرِه.

١٤- تَصِلُ بِضاعَةُ السَيِّد مارتيني إلى ميناءِ اللاذِقيّةِ دائماً.

١٥- لَمْ تَزُرْ أمُّ عَدنان أمريكا.

١٦- خالُ عَدنان مُتَقاعِدٌ الآن.

**ج - اختَرِ التكمِلةَ المُناسِبةَ حَسَبَ النَصّ.**

١٧- ياسِرمارتيني لَهُ . . .

☐ مَحَلٌّ تِجاريّ ☐ سَيّارة ألمانية

☐ سَيّارة فولكسفاكن ☐ مَحَلٌّ في ألمانيا

١٨- يَستَوْرِدُ ياسِر مارتيني بِضاعَتَه مِن . . .

☐ حَلَب ☐ الشاحِنات

☐ البَحْر ☐ ألمانيا

١٩- مَحَلُّ أبي عَدنان مَوجودٌ في . . .

☐ دِمَشق ☐ حَلَب

☐ اللاذِقيّة ☐ ألمانيا

٢٠- أوبِل اسمُ . . .

☐ سَيّارةٍ ألمانية ☐ مَحَلِّ ياسِر مارتيني

☐ قِطَعِ غِيارِ السَيّاراتِ ☐ مَخْزَنِ سَيّارات

٢١- يَستورِدُ أبو عَدنان بِضاعَتَهُ غالِباً عَن طَريقِ . . .

☐ البَحْرِ ☐ الشاحِناتِ

☐ الجَوِّ ☐ القِطاراتِ

٢٢- أمُّ عَدنان . . . الآن.

☐ مُدَرِّسةُ لُغَةٍ فَرَنسيّة ☐ رَبَّةُ بيت

☐ جَدّة ☐ مُوَظَّفة

٢٣- أحمَد هو . . . عَدنان.

☐ خالُ ☐ عَمُّ

☐ جَدُّ ☐ أخو

٢٤- سَتُسافِرُ أمُّ عَدنان إلى أمريكا على الخُطوطِ الجَوِيّة . . .

☐ السوريّة ☐ الألمانيّة

☐ الهولنديّة ☐ الأردنيّة

## تمرين ٨

**اكْتُبْ في كلِّ عَمود (column) كَلِمات مِن النَص تُناسِب الكَلِمات في أعلاه.**

| ١ جواز سَفَر | ٢ عائِلة | ٣ تِجارة | ٤ مَدارِس | ٥ مِهَن | ٦ بِلاد |
|---|---|---|---|---|---|
| | | | | | |

# تَذَوَّق الثَّقافة العَرَبِيّة

**Terms of Address:** As is the case in many languages, there are several ways in which people address one another. You have already learned that men may be addressed by أخ، سيّد، أستاذ، دكتور and women by أخت، آنسة، سيّدة، سِت، أستاذة، and دكتورة. However, in many parts of the Arab world, the use of أبو and أم followed by the name of the eldest son is a common practice. Addressing a man by أبو سليم rather than by his first name, for example, may be interpreted as a sign of respect, an indication of solidarity, or a manifestation of a formal situation. It is not uncommon that someone may only be known by their nickname (e.g., أبو سامر، أم هشام). Not all communities, though, assign positive interpretations to the use of these two terms. In urban centers in Egypt, for instance, the use of أبو and أم as terms of address is almost restricted to the lower working class.

## تمرين ٩

تَصوَّر أنَّ هذه الصورةَ تُمَثِّلُ اجتماعَ أساتِذةٍ وطُلابٍ مِن قِسْمِ اللُغةِ العَربية. أعطِ لِكلِّ شَخصٍ في الصورةِ اسماً مِن عِندك ثمَّ اكتُب وَصْفاً كالوَصفِ المَوجودِ في الفِقرةِ الأولى مِن الدَرسِ مُستَخدِماً أفعالاً وكلِماتٍ مثل:

| | | | | | |
|---|---|---|---|---|---|
| يَظهَرُ | يَجلِسُ | يَقِفُ | يَبدو | إلى جانِبِ | إلى يَمينِ |
| إلى يَسارِ | أعلى | أسفَل | أمامَ | خَلفَ | |

The picture on the next page represents a meeting of the Arabic department. First, try to describe the events that are taking place in the picture. Then try to create a story about what could be happening in the lives of the characters that are represented (real or imagined stories are fine, just as long as they are humorous). Use as many of the words as you can from the word bank.

## 1. Comparative and Superlative Degrees Revisited

As you may recall, the comparative form (e.g., longer than) is formed based on the pattern أفْعَل and followed by the preposition مِن (e.g., أنا أطوَل مِن عدنان). The superlative form (e.g., the longest) is formed using the same pattern as the comparative, but it is followed not by مِن, but rather by another noun which possesses the superlative attribute. Together, the two forms create an *iḍāfa* structure (e.g., أطْوَل رجل). The superlative may also have the definite article الـ prefixed to it (e.g., أخي الأكبر). This construction is known as اسم تَفضيل.

| اسم التفضيل | | | | |
|---|---|---|---|---|
| **Feminine Plural** | **Feminine Superlative** | **Masculine Plural** | **Masculine Superlative** | **Adjective** |
| كُبرَيات | كُبرى | أكابِر | أكْبَر | كَبير |
| صُغرَيات | صُغرى | أصاغِر | أصْغَر | صَغير |
| ----- | عُليا | أعالي | أعلى | عالٍ |
| سُفلَيات | سُفلى | أسافِل | أسْفَل | سافِل |
| يُمنَيات | يُمنى | ----- | أيمَن | يَمين |
| يُسْرَيات | يُسرى | ----- | أيْسَر | يَسار |

- **Note:** Remember that adjectives change form based on gender and number. كَبير, for example, may be كبيرة، كبيران، كبيرتان، كِبار or كبيرات based on the context.

The Arabic comparative and superlative are nouns, most of which are masculine, but there are some feminine counterparts as well. In this lesson, we came across the following phrase:

١ أُخْتُ عَدنان الصُغرى *Adnān's youngest sister*

Example 1 illustrates the feminine superlative pattern, which is فُعْلى. Other adjectives from which feminine superlative nouns are derived are listed in the preceding table.

## 2. The Particles كَيْ and لِـ

The particles كَيْ and لِـ 'in order to' are two of a group of particles used to express reason. They can be used independent of each other (as in example 2) or in combination لِكَي (as in example 3). There is no difference in meaning between the two choices.

٢ حَضَرَتْ أمُّ عَدنان إلى أمريكا كَيْ تزورَ ابنَها. *Umm Adnān came to America in order to visit her son.*

٣ ذَهَبَ الطّلاب إلى دِمشقَ لِكَيْ يَدرُسوا العَربيّة. *The students went to Damascus to study Arabic.*

## تمرين ١٠

**Ask your neighbor:** Answers must include لِـ or كَيْ. **محادثة: تفعيل القواعد**

1. why he/she chooses to study at this university/college/school
2. why he/she chooses to study Arabic
3. why he/she has a car/bike
4. why he/she does/doesn't have a job
5. why he/she will/will not stay home this weekend
6. why he/she will/will not do his/her homework tonight
7. why he/she wants to graduate.

- **Note:** Remember that we have come across other such particles that cause the verb that follows them to be in المضارع المنصوب. These particles include

لَن (used to negate verbs denoting future time) and أنْ ('to', which follows certain verbs, such as أراد). المضارع المنصوب, as you may recall, is marked by a فَتحة on the final radical (e.g., لن يكتبَ) or by the deletion of the final ن in the suffix in dual and plural forms (e.g., لَنْ يَكتُبا).

## تمرين ١١

**Fill in the blank:** Write the appropriate form of المضارع المنصوب of the verb found between parentheses. The verb is listed in the past tense. Please indicate the correct vowel or ending.

**مِثال: أظُنُّ أنَّني لَنْ (زار) أزورَ فلوريدا هذا الشِتاء.**

١- يُريدُ هِشام وأماني أنْ (سَكَنَ) ________ في مَدينةٍ كبيرة.

٢- أظُنُّ أنَّ أصدقائي لَنْ (أتى) ________ إلى الصَفِّ اليَوم.

٣- هَل تُحِبُّ أنْ (شَرِبَ) ________ الشايَ مَعَ السُكَّر؟

٤- حَضَرْتُ إلى هذِه الجامِعةِ كَيْ (دَرَسَ) ________ العَرَبيَّة.

٥- مَنْ يُريدُ أنْ (اِعتَنى) ________ بِقِطَّتي حينَ أسافِر؟

٦- ذَهَبْنا إلى مَطعَمٍ عَرَبيّ لِـ (أَكَلَ) ________ الفَلافِل.

### 3. Verbal Nouns Revisited المَصْدَر

**A Short Note on Verbal Patterns:** In section 3 of Lesson 10 we introduced different patterns of المَصدَر. Since that point, we have become aware that each verb form has a different verbal noun pattern. It is worth noting that of Forms I–X, only the Verb Form I فَعَلَ has more than two verbal noun patterns. All the rest have either one or two patterns of المَصدَر (refer to section 1 of Lesson 16 for Verb Form tables).

In this lesson, several instances of المَصدَر are used with the preposition لِـ and are therefore مَجرور, because they are objects of a preposition:

| | | |
|---|---|---|
| ٤ | لِبَيْعِ قِطَعِ الغِيار | *for selling spare parts* |
| | لِتَخزينِ البِضاعة | *for storing the merchandise* |

Because words that are مَصدَر are nouns, they can function as subjects of sentences (as in example 5) and objects of verbs (as in example 6):

٥ تُعْجِبُني دِراسةُ الأدَب.

٦ أريد بَيْعَ سَيّارَتي القديمة.

## تمرين ١٢

**Identifying the مَصْدَر and its root:** (1) Underline verbal nouns المَصْدَر in these sentences; (2) write their grammatical function (i.e., subject, object) directly above them; and (3) write down the root of each مَصْدَر in the blank next to the sentence, as in the example. Note that there may be more than one مَصْدَر in each sentence.

**مِثال: ذَهَبَت الزَوجَةُ إلى عَمَلِها بَعدَ تَحضيرِ الفَطور.** عمل، حضر

١- يُريدُ أحمَد بَيْعَ سَيّارتِه القَديمةِ لِيَشتَرِيَ سَيّارةً جَديدة. ____________________

٢- لَم أرَ أختي مُنذُ كِتابةِ هذِه الكلِمات. ____________________

٣- أعرِفُ اللُغةَ الألمانيةَ لكِنْ لا يُمكِنُني التَكلُّمُ بِها. ____________________

٤- سَوفَ أعمَلُ في شَرِكةٍ تِجاريّةٍ بَعدَ تَخَرُّجي. ____________________

٥- اسْتِضافَتُكُم في بَيْتي تَسُرّني جِدّاً. ____________________

٦- يُعجِبُني التَنَزُّهُ على شاطِئِ البَحر. ____________________

### 4. Writing the *Hamza*

Rules for writing the letter *hamza* are quite numerous and are characterized by exceptions. There are two types of the *hamza*: همزة الوَصل *hamzatu-l-waṣl* (literally, the *hamza* of connection, or the conjunctive *hamza*) and همزة القطع *hamzatu-l-qaṭ'* (the disjunctive *hamza*).

#### A. *Hamzatu-l-waṣl* همزة الوَصل (The Conjunctive *Hamza*)

This type of *hamza* serves a phonetic need. For example, Arabic does not allow two consonants in a row, as in جْلِس. In order to break it, an initial *hamza* with a following short vowel is added: اِجْلِس. It is spelled on an *alif* without the diacritic (ء) and can only occupy the initial position in certain words which include the following:

٧ جْلِس ← اِجْلِس

1. **The definite article الـ** is pronounced (*al*) if the word modified by it is in the initial position (i.e., no other words or particles precede it). Thus, the word for "house" البَيت is pronounced *al-bayt* when it occurs independently. Taking البَيت as an example, if it were preceded by a noun with which it forms an *iḍāfa*, the *hamza* would be dropped. In fact, the *hamza* will be dropped if البَيت is preceded by any prefix. Consider the three phonetic items in example 8:

| | | |
|---|---|---|
| ٨ | وَالبَيْت | *wa-l-bayt* |
| | بِالبَيْت | *bi-l-bayt* |
| | بابُ البَيْت | *bābu-l-bayt* |

- **Pronunciation note:** In all three examples, the *alif* of الـ is not pronounced, though it remains graphically represented.

2. **A restricted class of nine nouns** starts with *Hamzatu-l-waṣl*. Of these, the most common nouns are the following: اِبن، اِبنة، اِسم، اِثنان، اِثنتان، اِمرأة، اِمرُؤ. We have already encountered all of them except for اِمرؤ (man, one, person). Example 8 is illustrative of the phonetic changes that occur when these nine nouns do not independently start a sentence.

٨ اِسمُهُ (*ismuhu*) ← واسمُهُ (*wa-smuhu*) wherein the *i* is dropped

3. **Some augmented verbs (الفِعْلُ المَزيد) and their derivatives:**

   The imperative of Form I verbs, such as اُكتُب (*uktub*) or اِجلِسْ (*ijlis*), will lose the initial sound of their *hamza* (i.e., *a-*, *u-*, *i-*) when preceded by any article. Note that the *alif* is retained in writing (e.g., واجلِسْ *wa-jlis*, واكتُبْ *wa-ktub*). A list of verbs that lose their initial *hamza* when preceded by any article follows:

   a. The past tense and verbal noun of Form VII, e.g., اِنْكَسَرَ، اِنْكِسار.

   b. The past tense, imperative, and verbal noun of Form VIII, e.g., اِنتَظَرَ، اِنتَظِرْ، اِنتِظار.

   c. The past tense and verbal noun of Form IX, e.g., اِحْمَرّ، اِحْمِرار

   d. The past tense, imperative, and verbal noun of Form X, e.g., اِستَخدَمَ، اِستَخدِمْ، اِستِخدام.

   A phonetic representation of this form is illustrated in example 9.

٩ اِستَخدَمَ *istakhdama* ← واستَخدَمَ *wa-stakhdama*

**B. *Hamzatu-l-qaṭ'* همزة القطع (The Disjunctive *Hamza*)**

This is the type of *hamza* that is pronounced (and spelled) in *all* word positions. It occurs in particles, nouns, and verbs. Examples of particles include:

١٠ أ (interrogative particle used with yes/no questions) أتَدرُسين في المَكْتَب؟

أ (used as a vocative to call the attention of someone—archaic) أمَروان!

أ (the first-person singular indicative prefix—I) أكْتُبُ

إلى (preposition)، أينَ (question particle)

- **Note:** The spelling of *hamzatu-l-qaṭ'* in the initial position is *not* affected by prefixes:

  ١١ لأنَّ، سَأكتبُ، لِأسْكُنَ

  However, there are three exceptions: (1) when the preposition لـ is prefixed to ألاّ 'not to', the combination is spelled لِئلاّ 'in order not to'; (2) when the letter هـ is prefixed to the demonstrative أولاءِ 'these, those', it is spelled هؤلاء; and (3) when the particle لَـ is prefixed to the particle إنْ 'if', the word is spelled لَئِنْ.

  Examples of nouns that have همزة القطع include: أحمَد, فُؤاد, and مَساء.

  Examples of verbs that have همزة القطع (first-person singular prefix I) include: أساعِدُ، أعْمَلُ.

The rules for the initial position of the *hamza* can be summarized as follows:

1. **In the initial position:** The *hamza* is spelled over a silent *alif*, which serves exclusively as a seat. If the *hamza* is followed by a *kasra*, it may be written either over the *alif* with a *kasra* indicated below it or, more frequently, below the *alif* with no *kasra*:

   أَ        أُ        إِ

2. **In the medial position:** Spelling the *hamza* correctly involves determining its seat by the vowels immediately preceding and following it. Four possible seats for the *hamza* exist, three of which are the three long vowels, while the last possible seat is the *hamza* lying flush on the line.

   ء        ئ        ؤ        أ

   The seat for the *hamza* is determined on the basis of the more powerful vowel adjacent to it. Each short vowel has a corresponding long vowel that serves as a seat: a *fatḥa* and an *alif* correspond to an *alif*, a *ḍamma* and a *wāw* correspond to a *wāw*, and a *kasra* and a *yā'* correspond to a *yā'*.

The weighting system is relatively uncomplicated. The *sukūn*, or absence of a vowel, is the weakest. The *fatḥa* and the *alif* are more powerful than the *sukūn*, but weaker than the *ḍamma* and the *wāw*. The most powerful vowels are the *kasra* and the *yā'*. Reflect on the following illustration:

| Most Powerful | | | | | | | Least Powerful |
|---|---|---|---|---|---|---|---|
| Seat | Vowel | Seat | Vowel | Seat | Vowel | Seat | Vowel |
| ي | ِ / ي | و | ُ / و | ا | َ / ا | ـ | ْ |

If the preceding vowel is a *fatḥa* and the following vowel is a *kasra*, for example, the *hamza* should be seated on a dummy *yā'* (with no dots) because the *kasra* prevails. Now let's look at instances of the *hamza* in the medial position classified according to the vowel preceding it.

- **Note:** The *hamza* is placed on the line medially when it is preceded by a long *alif* and followed by a *fatḥa* (e.g., سَاءَلَ). Keep in mind that a suffix renders a final *hamza* a medial one.

**a.** **A *sukūn* preceding:** In the absence of a preceding vowel (marked with a *sukūn*), the seat corresponds to the vowel that follows (note that the *yā'* loses its dots when used as a seat):

- It is placed above an *alif* because the *fatḥa* is more powerful than the *sukūn*: ١٢ مَسْأَلَة
- The *wāw* is more powerful; therefore the *hamza* is placed on the *wāw*: ١٣ مَسْؤول
- The *kasra* prevails and the *hamza* is placed on the *yā'*: ١٤ مَرْئِيّ

A preceding *yā'*, be it a long vowel or a semivowel, causes the *hamza* to be seated on a *yā'*:

١٥ بيئة شَيْئُك شَيْئِك شَيْئان هَيْئة بَذيئون

b. **A *fatḥa* preceding:** When the *hamza* is preceded by a *fatḥa* and followed by a *sukūn*, a *fatḥa*, or an *alif*, the seat is an *alif*; when the following vowel is a *ḍamma* or a *wāw*, the seat is a *wāw*; and when the next vowel is a *yā'* or a *kasra*, the seat is a *yā'*.

١٦ رَأس سَأَلَ بَؤُسَ سَئِمَ رَئِيس رَؤُوف

c. **A *ḍamma* preceding:** The *hamza* followed by vowels that are weaker than a *ḍamma* is seated on a *wāw*. But a following *kasra* or a *yā'* requires a *yā'* for the *hamza* as a seat.

١٧ لُؤلُؤ بُؤَر سُؤال سُئِلَ

d. **A *kasra* preceding:** Since the *kasra* is the most powerful vowel, all instances of a medial *hamza* following a *kasra* are seated on a *yā'*.

١٨ بِئْر مِئَة مِئات مِئتان

e. **An *alif* (ا) or a *wāw* (و) preceding:** If the long vowel preceding is either *alif* (ا) or *wāw* (و) and the *hamza* is followed by a *fatḥa*, *ḍamma*, or an *alif*, the medial *hamza* is placed flush on the line:

١٩ ساءَل قِراءَة ضَوْءُك يَسوءُك مَملوءان مَملوءاً

f. **A *yā'* (ي) preceding**. If the preceding long vowel is *yā'* (as either a vowel or a semivowel) and the *hamza* is followed by a *fatḥa*, *ḍamma*, or an *alif*, a medial *hamza* is spelled on the letter *yā'* (without the dots):

٢٠ شَيْئاً شَيْئان شَيْئُك شَيْئَك بذيئان بيئات

g. **An *alif* (ا) preceding:** A *hamza* after an *alif* is spelled according to the rule of the more powerful vowel if it has a *ḍamma*, *kasra*, *wāw*, or *yā'* following it:

٢١ تَساؤُل عائِلة مُراؤون مُرائين

h. **A *wāw* (و) preceding:** A *hamza* after a *wāw* is spelled according to the rule of the more powerful vowel if it has a *ḍamma*, *kasra*, *wāw*, or *yā'* following it:

٢٢ يَنوءون تَسوئين يَسوؤُكم سوئِل

i. **A *yā'* (ي) preceding:** Since the *yā'* is the most powerful vowel, all instances of a medial *hamza* following a *yā'* are seated above *yā'* regardless of the following vowel.

٢٣ بيئَة بيئات يَجيئان يَجيئون شَيْئَين

3. **In the final position:** A *hamza* in the final position is placed on a letter that corresponds to the short vowel preceding it:

٢٤ يَقرَأُ لُؤلُؤ سَيِّئ

If a *sukūn* or a long vowel precedes the final *hamza*, then it is placed on the line:

٢٥ شَيْء جُزْء ماء سوء بريء

**Placement of double *fatḥa* (*tanwīn*) and other suffixes on a final *hamza*:** As you know, a double *fatḥa* requires an *alif* seat. However, there are two cases in which an *alif* is not required as a seat for the *tanwīn*:

a. If the final *hamza* follows a long *alif* (e.g., مساءً).

b. If the final *hamza* is placed above an *alif* (e.g., مَرْفَأً).

In all other cases an *alif* seat is required for a double *fatḥa*. This *alif* may either be connected to the *hamza* or not:

a. If the letter preceding the final *hamza* is a non-connector, the *alif* should be independent, unconnected (e.g., جُزْءاً).

b. If the letter preceding the final *hamza* is a connector, the *alif* should be connected (e.g., عِبْئاً).

## SUMMARY

- There are two types of *hamza*, *waṣl* and *qaṭ'*:
  - *hamzatu-l-waṣl* only occurs in the initial position and is spelled on an *alif* without the diacritic (ء)—serving a phonetic purpose.
  - *hamzatu-l-qaṭ'* occurs in all word positions and is spelled with the diacritic (ء).
- In the initial position, the *hamza* is placed above or below an *alif* (أب، إلى).
- In the medial position, it is placed on a silent long vowel corresponding to the stronger of two vowels preceding and following it, or it may be placed on the line.
- In the final position, it is placed on a silent long vowel, corresponding to the preceding vowel, or it may be placed on the line.

# تمرين ١٣

**Identifying the *hamza***: Check the correct spelling of each item below and explain your choice in English if necessary.

١- ☐ المَرأَة ☐ المَرْءَة ☐ المَرْئَة

٢- ☐ لُأيّ ☐ لُئَيّ ☐ لُؤَيّ

٣- ☐ تَوْأم ☐ تَوْءَم ☐ تَوْئَم

٤- ☐ مَوْءِل ☐ مَوْإِل ☐ مَوْئِل

٥- ☐ آباء ☐ ءَاباء ☐ أاباء

٦- ☐ يجيئون ☐ يَجيْؤونَ ☐ يَجيْءونَ

# تمرين ١٤

**Spelling the *hamza***: Provide the correct spelling of the following combinations, where the *hamza* in the items is spelled with an independent *hamza*.

١- مَ + رْ + ء + و + س = ____________________

٢- مُ + ء + ا + مَ + ر + ة = ____________________

٣- ج + ا + ءَ = ____________________

٤- ح + ا + ءِ + ل = ____________________

٥- فَ + ءْ + س = ____________________

٦- رِ + ءَ + ة = ____________________

٧- ءَ + ثَ + ر = ____________________

٨- بَ + ذ + ي + ء = ____________________

٩- مَ + س + ا + ء + ً = ____________________

١٠- ذِ + ءْ + ب = ____________________

١١- وَ + طْ + ء + ً = ____________________

١٢- ن + ا + ء + ي = ____________________

١٣- س + ا + ءِ + ل = ____________________

١٤- دَ + و + ا + ءِ + يّ = ________________

١٥- يَ + ب + و + ء + و + نَ = ________________

١٦- دَ + ء + و + ب = ________________

## تمرين ١٥

**أجِب عن السؤالَين حَسَبَ نصّ الاستماع**

١- أينَ تَسكُنُ الفَتاة ووالِداها ؟

٢- مَنْ يَعمَلُ ويَسكُنُ في الدارِ البَيْضاء ؟

**أكتُبْ «خَطأ» أو «صَواب» بِجانبِ كُلِّ جُملَةٍ وصَحِّحِ الجُمَلَ الخَطأ.**

٣- تَدرُسُ الفَتاةُ الهَنْدَسةَ الكَهْرُبائية.

٤- لِلفَتاةِ أخٌ يَدرُسُ في أمريكا.

**أكمِلْ الجُمَلَ بالاخْتيار المُناسِب حَسَبَ نَصّ الاستِماع.**

٥- سَتَصِلُ أسرةُ نِزار إلى فيلادلفيا على طائرةٍ . . .

☐ سورية ☐ مَغربية ☐ أمِريكية

٦- اشترى الوالِدُ . . . . . . . . . سَفَر.

☐ تَذكِرةَ ☐ تَذكِرَتي ☐ ثلاثَ تَذاكِرَ

**أكمِلْ الجُمَلَ التاليّة حَسَبَ نَصّ الاستِماع.**

٧- تُريدُ الفَتاةُ أنْ تَرى ________________

٨- سَتبقى الفَتاةُ ووالِداها في الدارِ البَيضاء مُدّةَ ________________.

## تمرين ١٦

VIDEO

تَمرينُ المُشاهَدة: شاهِدوا الدَرْسَ الرابع والعشرين على القُرْص الرَقْميّ.

١- ماذا يَعمَلُ أبو عَدنان؟ ______

______

______

٢- لِماذا تقاعَدَت أم عَدنان عن العَمَل؟ ______

______

______

٣- مَتى ستَزور والدة عَدنان أمريكا؟ ______

______

______

٤- لماذا لا يستَطيعُ والِدُ عدنان أن يأتي إلى أمريكا مع زوجتِهِ؟ ______

______

______

## تَذَوّق الثَقافة العَربيّة

In our DVD scene, we heard Adnān respond to Sāmir's question about how his family members were doing by saying:

كلهم بخير ويسلمون عليكم كثيراً.

Whenever someone asks about the condition of someone close to us, we usually respond by answering the question and then saying that that person is also thinking of them by using the phrase

وفُلان الفُلاني يسَلِّم عليك.

## المُفْرَدات

Listen to the vocabulary items on the CD and practice their pronunciation.

| | |
|---|---|
| اِخْتارَ (يَخْتارُ) اِخْتِيار (v.) | to select |
| آخِر (adj.) | last, latest |
| إدارة ج إدارات (n., f.) | department |
| اِسْتَوْرَدَ (يَسْتَوْرِدُ) اِسْتِيراد (v.) | to import |
| أسْفَل ج أسافِل (n., m., superlative form) | bottom, lowest point, lower |
| أشْبَهَ (يُشْبِهُ) شَبَه (v.) | to resemble |
| اِعْتَنى (يَعْتَني) اِعتِناء (بِـ) (v.) | to take care of, to tend |
| أعْلى ج أعالٍ (n., m., superlative form) | top, highest point, upper |
| أقام (يُقيم) إقامة (v.) | to reside in |
| اِلْتَقَطَ (يَلْتَقِطُ) اِلْتِقاط (v.) | to pick up; to take (a picture) |
| أُنْثى ج إناث (n., f.) | female |
| بائِع ج بائعون (n., m.) | salesperson |
| بَدا (يبدو) بُدُوٌّ / بَداء (v.) | to appear, to seem |
| بُنّيّ (adj.) | brown |
| تاجِر ج تُجّار (n., m.) | merchant, businessman |
| تَأَخَّرَ (يَتَأَخَّرُ) تَأَخُّر (v.) | to be late |
| تَقاعَدَ (يَتَقاعَدُ) تَقاعُد (عن) (v.) | to retire (from work) |
| تَوْقيع (n., m.) | signature |
| جَدّ ج جُدود (n., m.) | grandfather |
| جيولوجيا (n., f.) | geology |
| خال ج أخْوال (n., m.) | maternal uncle |
| خَزَّنَ (يُخَزِّنُ) تَخْزين (v.) | to store |

| | |
|---|---|
| guide | دَليل ج أدِلاّء (n., m.) |
| to refer to, to review | راجَعَ (يُراجِعُ) مُراجعَة (v.) |
| to respond, to answer | رَدَّ (يَرُدُّ) رَدّ (v.) |
| to register, to record | سَجَّلَ (يُسَجِّلُ) تَسْجيل (v.) |
| tourist | سياحيّ (adj.) |
| hair | شَعْر ج شُعور / أشْعار (n., m.) |
| poetry, poem | شِعْر ج أشْعار (n., m.) |
| last name, surname | شُهْرة (n., f.) |
| to issue | صَدَرَ (يَصْدُرُ) صُدور (v.) |
| youngest, smallest | صُغرى superlative of صَغيرة, |
| pharmacist | صَيدلانيّة (n., f.) |
| pharmacy | صَيْدَليّة (n., f.) |
| height | طول (n., m.) |
| paternal uncle | عَمّ ج أعْمام (n., m.) |
| age | عُمُر ج أعْمار (n., m.) |
| eye | عَيْن ج عُيون (n., f) |
| spare part, change | غِيار ج غيارات (n., m) |
| branch, subdivision | فَرْع ج فُروع (n., m.) |
| to talk to, to speak with | كَلَّمَ (يُكَلِّمُ) (v.) |
| expresses completed action with a perfect tense verb | لَقَد (particle) |
| retired person | مُتَقاعِد ج مُتَقاعِدون (n., m.) |
| store, shop; place, location | مَحَلّ ج مَحَلات (n., m.) |
| store, warehouse | مَخْزَن ج مَخازِن (n., m.) |
| teacher | مُدَرِّس ج مُدَرِّسون (n., m.) |
| sick, ill, patient | مَريض ج مَرْضى (adj., m) |

hospital . . . . . . . . . . . . . . . . . . . . . . . (n., m.) مُسْتَشْفى

effectiveness, validity . . . . . . . . . . . (passive participle) مَفعول

note, observation . . . . . . . . . . . . (n., f.) مُلاحَظة ج مُلاحظات

occupation, profession . . . . . . . . . . . . . (n., f.) مِهْنة ج مِهَن

consisting of, comprising. . . . . . (passive participle) مُؤَلَّف (مِن)

same. . . . . . . . . . . . . . . . . . . . . . . . . . (n., f.) (. . .الـ) نَفْس ج أَنْفُس

ministry, department in an administration . . . . . . . . . . . . (n., f.) وِزارة ج وِزارات

# Appendix A

## Arabic Alphabet and Diacritical Marks

## حروف الهجاء العربية
وعلامات التشكيل

| الرمز | أشكال الحرف في مواضع الكلمة | | | اسم الحرف | الحرف |
|---|---|---|---|---|---|
| **Symbol** | **Final** | **Medial** | **Initial** | **Name** | **Letter** |
| **ā** | ـا | ـا | ا | ألف | ا |
| **b** | ـب | ـبـ | بـ | باء | ب |
| **t** | ـت | ـتـ | تـ | تاء | ت |
| **ṯ** | ـث | ـثـ | ثـ | ثاء | ث |
| **j** | ـج | ـجـ | جـ | جيم | ج |
| **ḥ** | ـح | ـحـ | حـ | حاء | ح |
| **ḳ** | ـخ | ـخـ | خـ | خاء | خ |
| **d** | ـد | ـد | د | دال | د |
| **ḏ** | ـذ | ـذ | ذ | ذال | ذ |
| **r** | ـر | ـر | ر | راء | ر |
| **z** | ـز | ـز | ز | زاي | ز |
| **s** | ـس | ـسـ | سـ | سين | س |

| | | | | | |
|---|---|---|---|---|---|
| **š** | ـش | ـشـ | شـ | شين | ش |
| **ṣ** | ـص | ـصـ | صـ | صاد | ص |
| **ḍ** | ـض | ـضـ | ضـ | ضاد | ض |
| **ṭ** | ـط | ـطـ | طـ | طاء | ط |
| **ẕ** | ـظ | ـظـ | ظـ | ظاء | ظ |
| ʿ | ـع | ـعـ | عـ | عين | ع |
| **ġ** | ـغ | ـغـ | غـ | غين | غ |
| **f** | ـف | ـفـ | فـ | فاء | ف |
| **q** | ـق | ـقـ | قـ | قاف | ق |
| **k** | ـك | ـكـ | كـ | كاف | ك |
| **l** | ـل | ـلـ | لـ | لام | ل |
| **m** | ـم | ـمـ | مـ | ميم | م |
| **n** | ـن | ـنـ | نـ | نون | ن |
| **h** | ـه | ـهـ | هـ | هاء | ه |
| **w/ū** | ـو | ـو | و | واو | و |
| **y/ī** | ـي | ـيـ | يـ | ياء | ي |
| **ā** | ـى | | | أَلِف مَقصورة | ى |

| | | | | | |
|---|---|---|---|---|---|
| **t** | ـة | | | تاء مربوطة | ة |
| ʾ | ـأـؤـئ | ـأـؤـئـ | أإ | هَمزة | ء |
| **a** | *fatḥa* | | | فَتحة | ـَ |
| **u** | *ḍamma* | | | ضَمّة | ـُ |
| **i** | *kasra* | | | كَسرة | ـِ |
| **-an** | *tanwīn* | | | تَنوين بالفَتح | ـً |
| **-un** | *tanwīn* | | | تَنوين بالضَمّ | ـٌ |
| **-in** | *tanwīn* | | | تَنوين بالكَسْر | ـٍ |
| *sakūn* signifies the absence of a short vowel | | | | سُكون | ـْ |
| *šadda* indicates a doubled consonant | | | | شَدّة | ـّ |
| *madda* denotes a *hamza* and a long *alif* | | | | مَدّة | آ |

# Appendix B

A Key to the Arabic Sound System
and the Transliteration System Used in the Textbook

| الحرف | الرمز | |
|---|---|---|
| **Arabic Letter** | **Roman Symbol** | **Example/Description** |
| ا | *ā* | *a* as in *far* and *bad* |
| ب | *b* | *b* as in *bet* |
| ت | *t* | *t* as in *two* |
| ث | *ṯ* | *th* as in *three* |
| ج | *j* | *j* as in *judge* |
| ح | *ḥ* | *h*-like sound produced with constriction |
| خ | *ḳ* | *ch* as in Scottish *loch* or German *Bach* |
| د | *d* | *d* as in *dip* |
| ذ | *ḏ* | *th* as in *then* |
| ر | *r* | *r* as in Spanish *pero* (trilled *r*) |
| ز | *z* | *z* as in *zip* |
| س | *s* | *s* as in *sad* |
| ش | *š* | *sh* as in *show* |
| ص | *ṣ* | *s* as in *sod* |
| ض | *ḍ* | *d* as in *dark* |
| ط | *ṭ* | *t* as in *tar* |

| | | |
|---|---|---|
| ظ | *ẓ* | *th* as in *thine* |
| ع | ʿ | a fricative sound produced in the throat |
| غ | *ġ* | roughly similar to the German *r*; a gargling sound |
| ف | *f* | *f* as in *fit* |
| ق | *q* | roughly similar to the *c* in *cot*, but further back |
| ك | *k* | *k* as in *kit* |
| ل | *l* | *l* as in *leak* |
| م | *m* | *m* as in *mint* |
| ن | *n* | *n* as in *nill* |
| ه | *h* | *h* as in *hat* |
| و | *ū* | *oo* as in *pool* |
| و | *w* | *w* as in *wet* |
| ي | *ī* | *ee* as in *feel* |
| ي | *y* | *y* as in *yet* |
| ى | *ā* | *a* as in *dad* (a form of *alif* in the final position) |
| ة | *t* | see the discussion on *tāʾ marbūṭa* in Unit 3 (Workbook) |
| ء | ʾ | glottal stop; the stop before *a* in *above* |
| ـَ | *a* | roughly similar to *u* as in *but* |
| ـُ | *u* | *u* as in *pull* |
| ـِ | *i* | *i* as in *bill* |

# Appendix C

## Verb Conjugations

This appendix contains a representative sample of verb conjugation paradigms. At the top of each table, الماضي (past) with المضارع (present) are listed next to each other followed by the pattern of the verb and its roman numeral, the المصدر (verbal noun), اسم الفاعل (active participle), and اسم المفعول (passive participle). Each table has separate pronouns in the right-hand column followed by the conjugations of المضارع: المرفوع والمنصوب والمجزوم (indicative, subjunctive, jussive) in that order, and الأمر (imperative). All are in the active voice. The conjugations are classified according to person: first, second, and third. Only one conjugation for the second-person dual masculine and feminine (أنتما) is provided. Feminine pronouns follow masculine pronouns.

# ظَنَّ (يَظُنُّ) (فَعَل I) (ظَنّ – ظانّ – مَظنون)

*to think, to presume*

| Imperative | Jussive | Subjunctive | Indicative | Past | Pronoun |
|---|---|---|---|---|---|
| الأمر | المضارع المجزوم | المضارع المنصوب | المضارع المرفوع | الماضي | الضمير |
| | أَظُنَّ | أَظُنَّ | أَظُنُّ | ظَنَنْتُ | أنا |
| | نَظُنَّ | نَظُنَّ | نَظُنُّ | ظَنَنَّا | نَحنُ |
| ظُنَّ | تَظُنَّ | تَظُنَّ | تَظُنُّ | ظَنَنْتَ | أنتَ |
| ظُنِّي | تَظُنِّي | تَظُنِّي | تَظُنِّينَ | ظَنَنْتِ | أنتِ |
| ظُنَّا | تَظُنَّا | تَظُنَّا | تَظُنَّانِ | ظَنَنْتُما | أنتما |
| ظُنّوا | تَظُنّوا | تَظُنّوا | تَظُنّونَ | ظَنَنْتُمْ | أنتُم |
| اظْنُنَّ | تَظْنُنَّ | تَظْنُنَّ | تَظْنُنَّ | ظَنَنْتُنَّ | أنتُنَّ |
| | يَظُنَّ | يَظُنَّ | يَظُنُّ | ظَنَّ | هُوَ |
| | تَظُنَّ | تَظُنَّ | تَظُنُّ | ظَنَّتْ | هِيَ |
| | يَظُنَّا | يَظُنَّا | يَظُنَّانِ | ظَنَّا | هُما |
| | تَظُنَّا | تَظُنَّا | تَظُنَّانِ | ظَنَّتا | هُما |
| | يَظُنّوا | يَظُنّوا | يَظُنّونَ | ظَنّوا | هُم |
| | يَظْنُنَّ | يَظْنُنَّ | يَظْنُنَّ | ظَنَنَّ | هُنَّ |

# تَكَلَّمَ (يَتَكَلَّمُ) (تَفَعَّل V) (تَكَلُّمٌ – مُتَكَلِّم – مُتَكَلَّم)

*to talk, to speak*

| Imperative | Jussive | Subjunctive | Indicative | Past | Pronoun |
|---|---|---|---|---|---|
| الأمر | المضارع المجزوم | المضارع المنصوب | المضارع المرفوع | الماضي | الضمير |
| | أَتَكَلَّمْ | أَتَكَلَّمَ | أَتَكَلَّمُ | تَكَلَّمْتُ | أنا |
| | نَتَكَلَّمْ | نَتَكَلَّمَ | نَتَكَلَّمُ | تَكَلَّمْنا | نَحنُ |
| تَكَلَّمْ | تَتَكَلَّمْ | تَتَكَلَّمَ | تَتَكَلَّمُ | تَكَلَّمْتَ | أنتَ |
| تَكَلَّمي | تَتَكَلَّمي | تَتَكَلَّمي | تَتَكَلَّمينَ | تَكَلَّمْتِ | أنتِ |
| تَكَلَّما | تَتَكَلَّما | تَتَكَلَّما | تَتَكَلَّمانِ | تَكَلَّمْتُما | أنتما |
| تَكَلَّموا | تَتَكَلَّموا | تَتَكَلَّموا | تَتَكَلَّمونَ | تَكَلَّمْتُم | أنتُم |
| تَكَلَّمْنَ | تَتَكَلَّمْنَ | تَتَكَلَّمْنَ | تَتَكَلَّمْنَ | تَكَلَّمْتُنَّ | أنتُنَّ |
| | يَتَكَلَّمْ | يَتَكَلَّمَ | يَتَكَلَّمُ | تَكَلَّمَ | هُوَ |
| | تَتَكَلَّمْ | تَتَكَلَّمَ | تَتَكَلَّمُ | تَكَلَّمَتْ | هِيَ |
| | يَتَكَلَّما | يَتَكَلَّما | يَتَكَلَّمانِ | تَكَلَّما | هُما |
| | تَتَكَلَّما | تَتَكَلَّما | تَتَكَلَّمانِ | تَكَلَّمَتا | هُما |
| | يَتَكَلَّموا | يَتَكَلَّموا | يَتَكَلَّمونَ | تَكَلَّموا | هُم |
| | يَتَكَلَّمْنَ | يَتَكَلَّمْنَ | يَتَكَلَّمْنَ | تَكَلَّمْنَ | هُنَّ |

# كانَ (يَكونُ) (فَعَلَ I) (كَوْنٌ – كائِن – مَكون)

*to be*

| Imperative | Jussive | Subjunctive | Indicative | Past | Pronoun |
|---|---|---|---|---|---|
| الأمر | المضارع المجزوم | المضارع المنصوب | المضارع المرفوع | الماضي | الضمير |
| | أكُنْ | أكونَ | أكونُ | كُنْتُ | أنا |
| | نَكُنْ | نكونَ | نكونُ | كُنّا | نَحنُ |
| كُنْ | تَكُنْ | تكونَ | تكونُ | كُنْتَ | أنتَ |
| كوني | تكوني | تكوني | تكونينَ | كُنْتِ | أنتِ |
| كونا | تكونا | تكونا | تكونانِ | كُنْتُما | أنتما |
| كونوا | تكونوا | تكونوا | تكونونَ | كُنْتُم | أنتُم |
| كُنَّ | تَكُنَّ | تَكُنَّ | تَكُنَّ | كُنْتُنَّ | أنتُنَّ |
| | يَكُنْ | يَكونَ | يَكونُ | كانَ | هُوَ |
| | تَكُنْ | تكونَ | تكونُ | كانَتْ | هِيَ |
| | يَكونا | يَكونا | يَكونانِ | كانا | هُما |
| | تكونا | تكونا | تكونانِ | كانتا | هُما |
| | يَكونوا | يَكونوا | يَكونونَ | كانوا | هُم |
| | يَكُنَّ | يَكُنَّ | يَكُنَّ | كُنَّ | هُنَّ |

## أعطى (يُعْطي) (أَفْعَل IV) (إعْطاء – مُعْطٍ – مُعْطىً)

*to give*

| Imperative | Jussive | Subjunctive | Indicative | Past | Pronoun |
|---|---|---|---|---|---|
| الأمر | المضارع المجزوم | المضارع المنصوب | المضارع المرفوع | الماضي | الضمير |
| | أُعْطِ | أُعْطِيَ | أُعْطي | أَعْطَيْتُ | أنا |
| | نُعْطِ | نُعْطِيَ | نُعْطي | أَعْطَيْنا | نَحنُ |
| أعْطِ | تُعْطِ | تُعْطِيَ | تُعْطي | أَعْطَيْتَ | أنتَ |
| أعْطي | تُعْطي | تُعْطي | تُعْطينَ | أَعْطَيْتِ | أنتِ |
| أعْطِيا | تُعْطِيا | تُعْطِيا | تُعْطِيانِ | أَعْطَيْتُما | أنتما |
| أعْطوا | تُعْطوا | تُعْطوا | تُعْطونَ | أَعْطَيْتُم | أنتُم |
| أعْطينَ | تُعْطينَ | تُعْطينَ | تُعْطينَ | أَعْطَيْتُنَّ | أنتُنَّ |
| | يُعْطِ | يُعْطِيَ | يُعْطي | أَعْطى | هُوَ |
| | تُعْطِ | تُعْطِيَ | تُعْطي | أَعْطَتْ | هِيَ |
| | يُعْطِيا | يُعْطِيا | يُعْطِيانِ | أَعْطَيا | هُما |
| | تُعْطِيا | تُعْطِيا | تُعْطِيانِ | أَعْطَتا | هُما |
| | يُعْطوا | يُعْطوا | يُعْطونَ | أَعْطَوْا | هُم |
| | يُعْطينَ | يُعْطينَ | يُعْطينَ | أَعْطَيْنَ | هُنَّ |

# أَحَبَّ (يُحِبُّ) (أَفْعَل IV) (حُبّ – مُحِبّ – مُحَبّ)
## *to like, to love*

| Imperative | Jussive | Subjunctive | Indicative | Past | Pronoun |
|:---:|:---:|:---:|:---:|:---:|:---:|
| الأمر | المضارع المجزوم | المضارع المنصوب | المضارع المرفوع | الماضي | الضمير |
| | أُحِبَّ | أُحِبَّ | أُحِبُّ | أَحْبَبْتُ | أنا |
| | نُحِبَّ | نُحِبَّ | نُحِبُّ | أَحْبَبْنَا | نَحنُ |
| أَحْبِبْ | تُحِبَّ | تُحِبَّ | تُحِبُّ | أَحْبَبْتَ | أنتَ |
| أَحِبِّي | تُحِبِّي | تُحِبِّي | تُحِبِّينَ | أَحْبَبْتِ | أنتِ |
| أَحِبَّا | تُحِبَّا | تُحِبَّا | تُحِبَّانِ | أَحْبَبْتُما | أنتما |
| أَحِبُّوا | تُحِبُّوا | تُحِبُّوا | تُحِبُّونَ | أَحْبَبْتُمْ | أنتم |
| أَحْبِبْنَ | تُحْبِبْنَ | تُحْبِبْنَ | تُحْبِبْنَ | أَحْبَبْتُنَّ | أنتنَّ |
| | يُحِبَّ | يُحِبَّ | يُحِبُّ | أَحَبَّ | هُوَ |
| | تُحِبَّ | تُحِبَّ | تُحِبُّ | أَحَبَّتْ | هِيَ |
| | يُحِبَّا | يُحِبَّا | يُحِبَّانِ | أَحَبَّا | هُما |
| | تُحِبَّا | تُحِبَّا | تُحِبَّانِ | أَحَبَّتا | هُما |
| | يُحِبُّوا | يُحِبُّوا | يُحِبُّونَ | أَحَبُّوا | هُم |
| | يُحْبِبْنَ | يُحْبِبْنَ | يُحْبِبْنَ | أَحْبَبْنَ | هُنَّ |

## أرادَ (يُريدُ) (أفْعَل IV) (إرادة – مُريد – مُراد)

*to want*

| Imperative | Jussive | Subjunctive | Indicative | Past | Pronoun |
|---|---|---|---|---|---|
| الأمر | المضارع المجزوم | المضارع المنصوب | المضارع المرفوع | الماضي | الضمير |
| | أُرِدْ | أُريدَ | أُريدُ | أَرَدْتُ | أنا |
| | نُرِدْ | نُريدَ | نُريدُ | أَرَدْنا | نَحنُ |
| أَرِدْ | تُرِدْ | تُريدَ | تُريدُ | أَرَدْتَ | أنتَ |
| أريدي | تُريدي | تُريدي | تُريدينَ | أَرَدْتِ | أنتِ |
| أريدا | تُريدا | تُريدا | تُريدانِ | أَرَدْتُما | أنتما |
| أريدوا | تُريدوا | تُريدوا | تُريدونَ | أَرَدْتُمْ | أنتُم |
| أَرِدْنَ | تُرِدْنَ | تُرِدْنَ | تُرِدْنَ | أَرَدْتُنَّ | أنتُنَّ |
| | يُرِدْ | يُريدَ | يُريدُ | أَرادَ | هُوَ |
| | تُرِدْ | تُريدَ | تُريدُ | أَرادَتْ | هِيَ |
| | يُريدا | يُريدا | يُريدانِ | أَرادَا | هُما |
| | تُريدا | تُريدا | تُريدانِ | أَرادَتا | هُما |
| | يُريدوا | يُريدوا | يُريدونَ | أَرادوا | هُم |
| | يُرِدْنَ | يُرِدْنَ | يُرِدْنَ | أَرَدْنَ | هُنَّ |

## عَنى (يَعْني) (فَعَل I) (عَني – عانٍ – مَعْنيّ)

*to mean*

| Imperative | Jussive | Subjunctive | Indicative | Past | Pronoun |
|---|---|---|---|---|---|
| الأمر | المضارع المجزوم | المضارع المنصوب | المضارع المرفوع | الماضي | الضمير |
| | أَعْنِ | أَعْنِيَ | أَعْنِي | عَنَيْتُ | أنا |
| | نَعْنِ | نَعْنِيَ | نَعْني | عَنَيْنا | نَحنُ |
| اِعْنِ | تَعْنِ | تَعْنِيَ | تَعْني | عَنَيْتَ | أنتَ |
| اِعْني | تَعْني | تَعْني | تَعْنينَ | عَنَيْتِ | أنتِ |
| اِعْنِيا | تَعْنِيا | تَعْنِيا | تَعْنِيانِ | عَنَيْتُما | أنتما |
| اِعْنوا | تَعْنوا | تَعْنوا | تَعْنونَ | عَنَيْتُمْ | أنتُم |
| اِعْنينَ | تَعْنينَ | تَعْنينَ | تَعْنينَ | عَنَيْتُنَّ | أنتُنَّ |
| | يَعْنِ | يَعْنِيَ | يَعْني | عَنى | هُوَ |
| | تَعْنِ | تَعْنِيَ | تَعْني | عَنَتْ | هِيَ |
| | يَعْنِيا | يَعْنِيا | يَعْنِيانِ | عَنَيا | هُما |
| | تَعْنِيا | تَعْنِيا | تَعْنِيانِ | عَنَتا | هُما |
| | يَعْنوا | يَعْنوا | يَعْنونَ | عَنَوْا | هُم |
| | يَعْنينَ | يَعْنينَ | يَعْنينَ | عَنَيْنَ | هُنَّ |

## اِشْتَرى (يَشْتَري) (اِفْتَعَل VIII) (اِشتِراء – مُشْتَرٍ – مُشْتَرى)

*to buy*

| Imperative | Jussive | Subjunctive | Indicative | Past | Pronoun |
|---|---|---|---|---|---|
| الأمر | المضارع المجزوم | المضارع المنصوب | المضارع المرفوع | الماضي | الضمير |
| | أَشْتَرِ | أَشْتَرِيَ | أَشْتَري | اِشْتَرَيْتُ | أنا |
| | نَشْتَرِ | نَشْتَرِيَ | نَشْتَري | اِشْتَرَيْنا | نَحنُ |
| اِشْتَرِ | تَشْتَرِ | تَشْتَرِيَ | تَشْتَري | اِشْتَرَيْتَ | أنتَ |
| اِشْتَري | تَشْتَري | تَشْتَري | تَشْتَرينَ | اِشْتَرَيْتِ | أنتِ |
| اِشْتَرِيا | تَشْتَرِيا | تَشْتَرِيا | تَشْتَرِيانِ | اِشْتَرَيْتُما | أنتما |
| اِشْتَروا | تَشْتَروا | تَشْتَروا | تَشْتَرونَ | اِشْتَرَيْتُمْ | أنتُم |
| اِشْتَرينَ | تَشْتَرينَ | تَشْتَرينَ | تَشْتَرينَ | اِشْتَرَيْتُنَّ | أنتُنَّ |
| | يَشْتَرِ | يَشْتَرِيَ | يَشْتَري | اِشْتَرى | هُوَ |
| | تَشْتَرِ | تَشْتَرِيَ | تَشْتَري | اِشْتَرَتْ | هِيَ |
| | يَشْتَرِيا | يَشْتَرِيا | يَشْتَرِيانِ | اِشْتَرَيا | هُما |
| | تَشْتَرِيا | تَشْتَرِيا | تَشْتَرِيانِ | اِشْتَرَتا | هُما |
| | يَشْتَروا | يَشْتَروا | يَشْتَرونَ | اِشْتَرَوا | هُم |
| | يَشْتَرينَ | يَشْتَرينَ | يَشْتَرينَ | اِشْتَرَيْنَ | هُنَّ |

## وَصَلَ (يَصِلُ) (فَعَل I) (وُصول – واصِل – مَوْصول)

*to arrive*

| Imperative | Jussive | Subjunctive | Indicative | Past | Pronoun |
|---|---|---|---|---|---|
| الأمر | المضارع المجزوم | المضارع المنصوب | المضارع المرفوع | الماضي | الضمير |
| | أَصِلْ | أَصِلَ | أَصِلُ | وَصَلْتُ | أنا |
| | نَصِلْ | نَصِلَ | نَصِلُ | وَصَلْنا | نَحنُ |
| صِلْ | تَصِلْ | تَصِلَ | تَصِلُ | وَصَلْتَ | أنتَ |
| صِلي | تَصِلي | تَصِلي | تَصِلينَ | وَصَلْتِ | أنتِ |
| صِلا | تَصِلا | تَصِلا | تَصِلان | وَصَلْتُما | أنتما |
| صِلوا | تَصِلوا | تَصِلوا | تَصِلونَ | وَصَلْتُم | أنتُم |
| صِلْنَ | تَصِلْنَ | تَصِلْنَ | تَصِلْنَ | وَصَلْتُنَّ | أنتُنَّ |
| | يَصِلْ | يَصِلَ | يَصِلُ | وَصَلَ | هُوَ |
| | تَصِلْ | تَصِلَ | تَصِلُ | وَصَلَتْ | هِيَ |
| | يَصِلا | يَصِلا | يَصِلانِ | وَصَلا | هُما |
| | تَصِلا | تَصِلا | تَصِلانِ | وَصَلَتا | هُما |
| | يَصِلوا | يَصِلوا | يَصِلونَ | وَصَلوا | هُم |
| | يَصِلْنَ | يَصِلْنَ | يَصِلْنَ | وَصَلْنَ | هُنَّ |

## اِتَّصَلَ (يَتَّصِلُ) (اِفْتَعل VIII) (اِتِّصال - مَتَّصِل - مُتَّصَل)

*to contact, to connect*

| Imperative | Jussive | Subjunctive | Indicative | Past | Pronoun |
|---|---|---|---|---|---|
| الأمر | المضارع المجزوم | المضارع المنصوب | المضارع المرفوع | الماضي | الضمير |
| | أَتَّصِلْ | أَتَّصِلَ | أَتَّصِلُ | اِتَّصَلْتُ | أنا |
| | نَتَّصِلْ | نَتَّصِلَ | نَتَّصِلُ | اِتَّصَلْنا | نَحنُ |
| اِتَّصِلْ | تَتَّصِلْ | تَتَّصِلَ | تَتَّصِلُ | اِتَّصَلْتَ | أنتَ |
| اِتَّصِلي | تَتَّصِلي | تَتَّصِلي | تَتَّصِلينَ | اِتَّصَلْتِ | أنتِ |
| اِتَّصِلا | تَتَّصِلا | تَتَّصِلا | تَتَّصِلانِ | اِتَّصَلْتُما | أنتما |
| اِتَّصِلوا | تَتَّصِلوا | تَتَّصِلوا | تَتَّصِلونَ | اِتَّصَلْتُم | أنتُم |
| اِتَّصِلْنَ | تَتَّصِلْنَ | تَتَّصِلْنَ | تَتَّصِلْنَ | اِتَّصَلْتُنَّ | أنتُنَّ |
| | يَتَّصِلْ | يَتَّصِلَ | يَتَّصِلُ | اِتَّصَلَ | هُوَ |
| | تَتَّصِلْ | تَتَّصِلَ | تَتَّصِلُ | اِتَّصَلَتْ | هِيَ |
| | يَتَّصِلا | يَتَّصِلا | يَتَّصِلانِ | اِتَّصَلا | هُما |
| | تَتَّصِلا | تَتَّصِلا | تَتَّصِلانِ | اِتَّصَلَتا | هُما |
| | يَتَّصِلوا | يَتَّصِلوا | يَتَّصِلونَ | اِتَّصَلوا | هُم |
| | يَتَّصِلْنَ | يَتَّصِلْنَ | يَتَّصِلْنَ | اِتَّصَلْنَ | هُنَّ |

## عَلَّق (يُعَلِّقُ) (فَعَّل II) (تَعْليق – مُعَلِّق – مُعَلَّق)

*to hang*

| Imperative | Jussive | Subjunctive | Indicative | Past | Pronoun |
|---|---|---|---|---|---|
| الأمر | المضارع المجزوم | المضارع المنصوب | المضارع المرفوع | الماضي | الضمير |
| | أُعَلِّقْ | أُعَلِّقَ | أُعَلِّقُ | عَلَّقْتُ | أنا |
| | نُعَلِّقْ | نُعَلِّقَ | نُعَلِّقُ | عَلَّقْنا | نَحنُ |
| عَلِّقْ | تُعَلِّقْ | تُعَلِّقَ | تُعَلِّقُ | عَلَّقْتَ | أنتَ |
| عَلِّقي | تُعَلِّقي | تُعَلِّقي | تُعَلِّقينَ | عَلَّقْتِ | أنتِ |
| عَلِّقا | تُعَلِّقا | تُعَلِّقا | تُعَلِّقانِ | عَلَّقْتُما | أنتما |
| عَلِّقوا | تُعَلِّقوا | تُعَلِّقوا | تُعَلِّقونَ | عَلَّقْتُمْ | أنتُم |
| عَلِّقْنَ | تُعَلِّقْنَ | تُعَلِّقْنَ | تُعَلِّقْنَ | عَلَّقْتُنَّ | أنتُنَّ |
| | يُعَلِّقْ | يُعَلِّقَ | يُعَلِّقُ | عَلَّقَ | هُوَ |
| | تُعَلِّقْ | تُعَلِّقَ | تُعَلِّقُ | عَلَّقَتْ | هِيَ |
| | يُعَلِّقا | يُعَلِّقا | يُعَلِّقانِ | عَلَّقا | هُما |
| | تُعَلِّقا | تُعَلِّقا | تُعَلِّقانِ | عَلَّقَتا | هُما |
| | يُعَلِّقوا | يُعَلِّقوا | يُعَلِّقونَ | عَلَّقوا | هُم |
| | يُعَلِّقْنَ | يُعَلِّقْنَ | يُعَلِّقْنَ | عَلَّقْنَ | هُنَّ |

## اِنْتَقَلَ (يَنْتَقِلُ) (اِفْتَعَل VIII) (اِنْتِقال – مُنْتَقِل – مُنْتَقَل)

*to move, to relocate*

| Imperative | Jussive | Subjunctive | Indicative | Past | Pronoun |
|---|---|---|---|---|---|
| الأمر | المضارع المجزوم | المضارع المنصوب | المضارع المرفوع | الماضي | الضمير |
| | أَنْتَقِلْ | أَنْتَقِلَ | أَنْتَقِلُ | اِنْتَقَلْتُ | أنا |
| | نَنْتَقِلْ | نَنْتَقِلَ | نَنْتَقِلُ | اِنْتَقَلْنا | نَحنُ |
| اِنْتَقِلْ | تَنْتَقِلْ | تَنْتَقِلَ | تَنْتَقِلُ | اِنْتَقَلْتَ | أنتَ |
| اِنْتَقِلي | تَنْتَقِلي | تَنْتَقِلي | تَنْتَقِلينَ | اِنْتَقَلْتِ | أنتِ |
| اِنْتَقِلا | تَنْتَقِلا | تَنْتَقِلا | تَنْتَقِلانِ | اِنْتَقَلْتُما | أنتما |
| اِنْتَقِلوا | تَنْتَقِلوا | تَنْتَقِلوا | تَنْتَقِلونَ | اِنْتَقَلْتُمْ | أنتُم |
| اِنْتَقِلْنَ | تَنْتَقِلْنَ | تَنْتَقِلْنَ | تَنْتَقِلْنَ | اِنْتَقَلْتُنَّ | أنتُنَّ |
| | يَنْتَقِلْ | يَنْتَقِلَ | يَنْتَقِلُ | اِنْتَقَلَ | هُوَ |
| | تَنْتَقِلْ | تَنْتَقِلَ | تَنْتَقِلُ | اِنْتَقَلَتْ | هِيَ |
| | يَنْتَقِلا | يَنْتَقِلا | يَنْتَقِلانِ | اِنْتَقَلا | هُما |
| | تَنْتَقِلا | تَنْتَقِلا | تَنْتَقِلانِ | اِنْتَقَلَتا | هُما |
| | يَنْتَقِلوا | يَنْتَقِلوا | يَنْتَقِلونَ | اِنْتَقَلوا | هُم |
| | يَنْتَقِلْنَ | يَنْتَقِلْنَ | يَنْتَقِلْنَ | اِنْتَقَلْنَ | هُنَّ |

## اِسْتَخْدَمَ (يَسْتَخْدِمُ) (اِسْتَفْعَلَ X) (اِسْتِخْدام – مُسْتَخْدِم – مُسْتَخْدَم)

*to use*

| Imperative | Jussive | Subjunctive | Indicative | Past | Pronoun |
|---|---|---|---|---|---|
| الأمر | المضارع المجزوم | المضارع المنصوب | المضارع المرفوع | الماضي | الضمير |
| | أَسْتَخْدِمْ | أَسْتَخْدِمَ | أَسْتَخْدِمُ | اِسْتَخْدَمْتُ | أنا |
| | نَسْتَخْدِمْ | نَسْتَخْدِمَ | نَسْتَخْدِمُ | اِسْتَخْدَمْنا | نَحنُ |
| اِسْتَخْدِمْ | تَسْتَخْدِمْ | تَسْتَخْدِمَ | تَسْتَخْدِمُ | اِسْتَخْدَمْتَ | أنتَ |
| اِسْتَخْدِمي | تَسْتَخْدِمي | تَسْتَخْدِمي | تَسْتَخْدِمينَ | اِسْتَخْدَمْتِ | أنتِ |
| اِسْتَخْدِما | تَسْتَخْدِما | تَسْتَخْدِما | تَسْتَخْدِمانِ | اِسْتَخْدَمْتُما | أنتما |
| اِسْتَخْدِموا | تَسْتَخْدِموا | تَسْتَخْدِموا | تَسْتَخْدِمونَ | اِسْتَخْدَمْتُمْ | أنتُم |
| اِسْتَخْدِمْنَ | تَسْتَخْدِمْنَ | تَسْتَخْدِمْنَ | تَسْتَخْدِمْنَ | اِسْتَخْدَمْتُنَّ | أنتُنَّ |
| | يَسْتَخْدِمْ | يَسْتَخْدِمَ | يَسْتَخْدِمُ | اِسْتَخْدَمَ | هُوَ |
| | تَسْتَخْدِمْ | تَسْتَخْدِمَ | تَسْتَخْدِمُ | اِسْتَخْدَمَتْ | هِيَ |
| | يَسْتَخْدِما | يَسْتَخْدِما | يَسْتَخْدِمانِ | اِسْتَخْدَما | هُما |
| | تَسْتَخْدِما | تَسْتَخْدِما | تَسْتَخْدِمانِ | اِسْتَخْدَمَتا | هُما |
| | يَسْتَخْدِموا | يَسْتَخْدِموا | يَسْتَخْدِمونَ | اِسْتَخْدَموا | هُم |
| | يَسْتَخْدِمْنَ | يَسْتَخْدِمْنَ | يَسْتَخْدِمْنَ | اِسْتَخْدَمْنَ | هُنَّ |

# Appendix D

## Answer Key

The answer key provides answers to most of the exercises in the textbook, including listening and comprehension exercises. Exercises that have variable answers are not included here.

### الدرس الأول

**تمرين ١**

١- دِمَشْق　　٢- جامِعة　　٣- صورة، ساعة　　٤- كُرْسيّ

٥- صورة　　٦- رياضيّات

**تمرين ٢**

١- لوح/ صورة　　٢- غُرْفة/ صَفّ　　٣- أسْتاذ/ طالِب　　٤- جِدار/ باب

٥- هُنا/ هُناكَ　　٦- على/ في

**تمرين ٥**

١- هذا هاتِف.　　٢- هذه وَرَقة.　　٣- هذا قَلَم.　　٤- هذا تِلْفاز.

٥- هذا لَوْح.　　٦- هذه دَرّاجة.　　٧- هذه حَقيبة.

**تمرين ٦**

١- صورَةُ هالَة عَلى الجِدار لكنَّ صورَتَكِ عَلى الباب.

٢- دِمَشقُ في سورية لكنَّ عَمّانَ في الأُرْدُن.

٣- أنتِ مِصريَّةٌ لكنَّني سودانيٌّ.

٤- حاسوبُ الأستاذِ أمريكيٌّ لكِنَّ حاسوبَ الطالِبِ يابانيٌّ.

٥- جامِعتي في وِلايَةِ تكْساس لكنَّ جامِعتَكِ في وِلايةِ فلوريدا.

٦- ساعَةُ الأسْتاذِ سُويسْريَّةٌ لكِنَّ ساعَةَ الطالِبِ أمريكيَّةٌ.

٧- جَريدَةُ نيويورك تايمز أمريكيّةٌ لكِنَّ جَريدَةَ الأهْرام مِصريَّةٌ.

٨- مِفْتاحي عَلى الكِتاب لكِنَّ مِفْتاحَكَ بِجانِبِ التِلْفاز.

٩- صورَةُ مونا ليزا إيطاليّةٌ لكِنَّ صورَةَ بابلو بيكاسو إسْبانيّةٌ.

١٠- قَلَمُ الأسْتاذِ عَلى الطاوِلةِ لكَنَّ حَقيبَةَ الأسْتاذِ عَلى القَلَمِ.

**تمرين ٧**

١- أسْتاذُنا مِصْريٌّ.　　- أسْتاذُنا لَيسَ مِصْريّاً.

٢- الحَقيبةُ عَلى الطاوِلةِ.　　- الحَقيبةُ لَيسَتْ على الطاوِلةِ.

٣- نَحْنُ سوريّون.　　- نَحْنُ لَسْنا سوريّينَ.

٤- أنا أُستاذٌ. - أنا لَسْتُ أُستاذاً.
٦- هذِه السَيّارَةُ أمريكيَّةٌ. - هذه السَيّارةُ لَيسَتْ أمريكيّةً.
٧- جامِعةُ هارفرد في وِلايةِ مِشيغان - جامِعةُ هارفرد لَيسَتْ في وِلايةِ مِشيغان.
٨- أنا في الصَفِّ. - أنا لَسْتُ في الصَفِّ.
٩- سوزانُ أوسْتَراليّةٌ. - سوزانُ لَيسَتْ أوسْتَراليّةً.
١٠- الدَفْتَرُ بِجانِبِ الهاتِفِ. - الدَفْتَرُ لَيسَ بِجانِبِ الهاتِفِ.

تمرين ٨

١- مَدْرَسَتُك في دِمَشْق لكِنَّ مَدْرَسَته في القاهِرة.
٢- لَيس عِنْدَها دَرّاجةٌ لكِنْ سَيّارة.
٣- لَيسَ هُناكَ جَريدةٌ في حَقيبتي لكِنَّ هُناكِ كِتاباً على طاوِلتي.
٤- هذِه مُسَجِّلَةٌ لكِنَّ هذا تِلفاز.
٥- لَيسَ هَناكَ حاسِبةٌ على الطاوِلةِ لكِنَّ هُناكَ مُمحاةً ومِسْطَرة.
٦- سَيّارتُه أمريكيّةٌ لكِنَّ حاسوبَه يابانيّ.

تمرين ٩

| | | | |
|---|---|---|---|
| ١- الطاوِلة - شَمسيّ | ٢- الجَريدة - قَمَريّ | ٣- المِفتاح - قَمَريّ | ٤- الساعة - شَمسيّ |
| ٥- القَلَم - قَمَريّ | ٦- الباب - قَمَريّ | ٧- النافِذة - شَمسيّ | ٨- الكُرسيّ - قَمَريّ |

تمرين ١٠

| | | | |
|---|---|---|---|
| ١- جَريدَتي | ٢- نَظّارَتُه | ٣- حاسوبُكِ | ٤- عِنْدَها |
| ٥- طاوِلة | ٦- صَفُّكُم | ٧- كُرْسيّ | |

تمرين ١١

| | | | |
|---|---|---|---|
| ١- سَيّارَتُكَ D | ٢- هاتِفٌ I | ٣- كِتابي D | ٤- الجامِعةُ D |
| ٥- دَرّاجَتُها D | ٦- مُسَجِّلَةٌ I | ٧- جَريدَتُه D | ٨- لَوْحٌ I |
| ٩- المِفْتاحُ D | ١٠- غُرْفةٌ I | | |

## الدرس الثاني

تمرين ١

| | | |
|---|---|---|
| الاسم: هَيْثَم نَجّار | الكُلّيّة: كُلّيّة العُلوم | الجامِعة: جامِعة دِمَشْق |
| الاسم: راغِب طبّاع | الكُلّيّة: كُلّيّة العُلوم | الجامعة: الجامِعة الأردُنيّة |

| | | |
|---|---|---|
| ١- عِدّةٌ | ٢- مَلعَبٌ رياضيٌّ ومسبح | ٣- مُخْتَبرٌ لُغَويّ |
| ٤- أستاذٌ | ٥- رِياضِيّات | ٦- كُلّيّةِ العُلوم |
| ٧- هاتِفٌ | ٨- الأرْضِ | |

تمرين ٤

١- جانِب – not related to school
٢- هَندَسة – not a location
٣- عِدّة – not part of a classroom
٤- رِياضيّ – not a demonstrative

تمرين ٥

١- رِياضة/ مَلعَب
٢- مُختبَر/ لُغويّ
٣- ذلِكَ/ تِلك
٤- كُلّيّة/ طِبّ
٥- كِتاب/ مَكتَبة

تمرين ٦

١- جَريدَةٌ رِياضيّةٌ
٢- كِتابٌ طِبّيٌّ
٣- غُرْفَةٌ مَدْرَسيّةٌ
٤- صَفٌّ صَباحيٌّ
٥- طالِبةٌ جامِعيّةٌ
٦- سَيّارةٌ يابانيّةٌ
٧- الجامِعةُ الأرْدُنيّةُ
٨- اللُغَةُ العَرَبيّةُ
٩- كُلّيّةٌ أمريكيّةٌ
١٠- كِتابٌ عِلْميٌّ

تمرين ٧

١- كُلّيّة العُلوم
٢- جامِعة دِمَشْق
٣- عِدّة كُلّيّاتٍ
٤- كُلّيّة الهَنْدَسَةِ
٥- كُلّيّة الآداب
٦- كُلّيّة العُلوم
٧- كُلّيّة الطِبِّ
٨- كُلّيّة التِجارة
٩- كُلّيّة الحُقوق
١٠- بجانِبِ كُلّيّتي
١١- كُلّيّة الآداب
١٢- كُلّيّة الحُقوق
١٣- أسْتاذ رِياضيّات
١٤- غُرْفة مَكتَبي
١٥- بجانِب الطاوِلة
١٦- كُلّيّة العُلوم

تمرين ٨

١- مَكْتَبُ الأستاذِ
٢- صورةُ المَدينةِ
٣- كُلّيّةُ العُلومِ
٤- غُرْفَةُ الصَفِّ
٥- جامِعَةُ حَلَب
٦- كِتابُ الطِبِّ

تمرين ٩

١- كُلّيّةُ الطِبِّ
٢- نافِذةُ غُرْفَتي
٣- مِفْتاحُ السَيّارةِ
٤- نَظّارةُ طالِبةٍ
٥- أستاذةُ ساندي
٦- دَرّاجةُ طالِبٍ
٧- صورةُ حَلَبَ
٨- بابُ غُرْفةِ الصَفِّ
٩- جَريدَةُ أحْمَد
١٠- جامِعةُ وِلايةِ أوهايو

تمرين ١٠

١- نِسْبة
٢- إضافة
٣- إضافة
٤- إضافة
٥- نِسْبة
٦- إضافة
٧- نِسْبة
٨- إضافة
٩- إضافة
١٠- نِسْبة

تمرين ١١

١- ذلِكَ لِنْكَن.
٢- تِلْكَ سَيّارةٌ.
٣- ذلِكَ بَيْتٌ.
٤- تِلْكَ دَرّاجةٌ.
٥- هذِه وَرَقةٌ.
٦- هذا تِلْفازٌ.
٧- هذِه نَظّارةٌ.
٨- هذا هاتِفٌ.

تمرين ١٢

١- سَمْهوري
٢- بير زَيْت
٣- الآداب
٤- القُدس

٥- خطأ، عِندَهُ حاسوب ٦- صواب ٧- صواب

تمرين ١٣

١- كُلّيّة الاقْتِصاد كُلّيّة الطِبّ كُلّيّة الهَنْدَسة كُلّيّة العُلوم

كُلّيّة الآداب كُلّيّة الحُقوق

٢- طاوِلة كُرْسيّ مَكْتَبة صَغيرة هاتِف

حاسوب نافِذة

## الدرس الثالث

تمرين ١

١- بَلْدة/ مَدينة ٢- عُنوان/ شارِع ٣- العَرَبيّة/ لُغة ٤- رَقْم/ ثَلاثة

٥- بِطاقة/ هُويّة ٦- شُكْراً/ عَفْواً

تمرين ٧

The University of Allepo; Identity Card; Name: Hala Bustānī; Father's name: Waḥīd; Address: ٢٥ el-Mansōr Street, Damascus; Telephone number: ٢٨٤٨٥٦٩; Identity number: ٩٧١٤٠٢

تمرين ٨

١- نِزار ٢- شَقّة ٣- سَيّارة ٤- ٦٠١٥٧٩٤

٥- بَلدة في سورية ٦- لا نَعْرِف ٧- ٥ شارِع ابن خَلْدون

تمرين ٩

١- أينَ تَسْكُنينَ؟

٢- أنا لا أسْكُنُ في شارِع لِنكَن.

٣- هَل تَسْكُنُ في شَقَّةٍ أم في بَيْتٍ؟

٤- تَسْكُنُ أسْتاذتي في مَدينةِ . . .

٥- أنا لا أعْرِفُ اللُغة الـ. . .

٦- أنا لا أعْرِف عُنوانَ أسْتاذي.

٧- ما رَقْمُ هاتِفِكَ؟

٨- ما عُنوانُكِ؟

تمرين ١١

١- دَرّاجةً ٢- مِفْتاحاً ٣- قَلَماً ٤- مُسَجِّلَةً

٥- هاتِفاً ٦- جامِعةً ٧- كَلِمةً ٨- أسْتاذاً

تمرين ١٣

١- تِسْعة – only number

٢- لَيسَ – not a question word

٣- عِلْميّ – not a language

٤- طاوِلة – only piece of furniture

تمرين ١٥

١- بَلْدَةِ الباب ٢- التِجارةِ ٣- هاتِفٌ

٤- خطأ، في سكن الطالِبات ٥- صواب ٦- خطأ، لُغتين

تمرين ١٧

المشهد الأول: ١- عِشرون (٢٠)

المشهد الثاني ١- (ج) سوريَّة ٢- يَسْكُنُ السَيِّد نبيل في شَقّةٍ صَغيرة

٣- (ب) ٦٦٢١٣٤ ٤- (أ) ٦٦٢٧٠٠٣

## الدرس الرابع

تمرين ١

١- كُلِّيَّةِ الطِبِّ ٢- شَقَّةٍ ٣- مَعَ ٤- مِن

٥- تِسْعَة ٦- التِجارَةَ

تمرين ٢

١- خطأ، ليسَت أستاذتَها. هي تَسكُن معها ٢- خطأ، لا نَعرِفُ مِن النَصّ

٣- صواب ٤- خطأ، تَدرُسُ هالَةُ الطِبَّ في جامِعةِ حَلَبَ ٥- صواب

تمرين ٣

١- مادّة/ أحْياء ٢- لُغة/ الإنكليزية ٣- كُرْسيّ/ سَرير ٤- بِناية/ شَقّة

٥- تَعرِف/ تَسكُن ٦- في/ مَعَ

تمرين ٤

١- الفَرَنْسيّة – the only language in the set ٢- كُلّيّة – not a residence

٣- دَرّاجة – not a piece of furniture

تمرين ٥

A. In my house (there are) three tables, and beside one of them there are four chairs. There is not just one computer on the table; in fact, there are three computers. There are also two televisions on the table. In my room there are three phones, ten books, seven notebooks, and six pairs of glasses.

ب - عِنْدي حَقيبَةٌ وفيها ثَلاثةُ أقْلامٍ وأرْبعةُ كُتُبٍ وهاتِفانِ وثَلاثُ بِطاقاتِ هُوِيّةٍ وحاسوبٌ وخَمْسَةُ مَفاتيح.

تمرين ٨

١- هذه حَقيبةٌ. ٢- تِلْكَ كَراسٍ. ٣- تِلْكَ ساعةٌ. ٤- هذه بُيوتٌ.

٥- هؤلاءِ طُلاّبٌ. ٦- هذا تِلْفازٌ. ٧- تِلْكَ مَفاتيحَ. ٨- هذه طالِبةٌ.

٩- تِلْكَ نَظّارةٌ. ١٠- هذِه سَيّاراتٌ.

تمرين ٩

١- عَبدُ الرَحيم ٢- الطِبّ ٣- وَجْدة ٤- سَريرانِ

٥- صَواب ٦- صَواب ٧- خطأ، أرْدُنّيّ ٨- صَواب

تمرين ١٠

١- سَريرانِ خِزانةٌ طاوِلة كُرسيّانِ ثَلاثُ نَوافِذُ ٢- ثَلاثُ بَناتٍ

٣- البِنْتُ الصَغيرةُ تَدرُسُ في كُلِّيَّةِ الطِبِّ والبِنْتُ الوُسطى تَدرُسُ في كُلِّيَّةِ الآدابِ والبِنْتُ الكَبيرةُ مُتَزَوِّجةٌ والوَلَدانِ في المَدرَسةِ الثانويّة.

## الدرس الخامِس

تمرين ١

١- اِبنٌ واحِدٌ ٢- الرابع ٣- لُبنانيّ ٤- مادَّتَيْنِ

٥- عِلمَ الحاسوب ٦- شَقَّةٍ ٧- أوهايو ٨-مازِن نَجّار

٩- زياد نابلُسي ١٠- زياد نابلُسي ووليد صايغ

١١- ثَلاثَ مَوادَّ ١٢- اللغُة الإنكليزيّة والفيزياء والتَفاضُل

تمرين ٢

١- صَواب ٢- خطأ، مازِن زَوْجُ ناديا ٣- صَواب ٤- خطأ، رِحاب اِبْنةُ مازِن

٥- صَواب ٦- خطأ، أحْمَد اِبنُ مازِن ٧- خطأ، أحْمَد ابنُ ناديا

تمرين ٤

١- أُخْت – not a school subject ٢- وَحيد – does not pertain to school

٣- أوَّل – not a family relation ٤- اِبنَة –not a preposition

تمرين ٧

أ)١ – هشام – man's name علي – father's name حافظ – grandfather's name

ب) الشيباني وهويدي

تمرين ٨

١- تَعرِفُ سَناء أربَعَ لُغاتٍ. ٢- أدرُسُ مادَّتَيْنِ في هذا الفَصْلِ.

٣- لا تَعرِفُ سامية عُنوانَ هالَة. ٤- تَدرُسُ هالَة مادَّةَ الأحْياءِ في جامِعَةِ القاهِرة.

تمرين ١٠

١- فِلَسطين/ لُبنان ٢- فَصْل/ دِراسيّ ٣- بِنْت/ وَلَد ٤- سِتَّة/ سادِس

٥- اِبن/ اِبنة ٦- ثَماني/ ثامِن ٧- خامِس/ خَمسة

تمرين ١١

١- تَدرُسُ هالَة مادَّةَ الرِياضِيّاتِ في هذا الفَصْل. ٢- كَمْ مادّةً عِندَكَ يا سالِم؟

٣- هَلْ أنتَ الابنُ الثاني في عائِلَتِكَ؟ ٤- أخي في الصَفِّ الرابع الابتِدائيّ

تمرين ١٢

١- هذِه هي المِبراة. ٢- الأستاذُ هو راغِب طَبّاع. ٣- أخي هو نِزار.

٤- هذا هو دَفتَرُ العائلَة. ٥- هذانِ هُما الطالِبانِ. ٦- هؤلاءِ هُم إخوَتي.

تمرين ١٣

اِسمُ الأب: مازِن نَجّار، اِسمُ الأم: ناديا الخولي، الوَلَدُ الأوَّل: أحمد مازِن النَجّار، الوَلَدُ الثانِي: لَيسَ هنُاك وَلَدٌ ثانٍ

البِنْتُ الأُولى:رِحاب، البِنْتُ الثانِية: رانية

تمرين ١٥

١- الفَرَنسيّة ٢- اِبنانِ ٣- سَميح ٤- السابع

٥- خطأ، تَسكُنُ مَعَ نَدى وسَميح. ٦- صواب

٧- خطأ، زَوجتُهُ أَسْتاذةٌ في مَدرسةِ بَنات. ٨- صَواب

تمرين ١٦

أ) ١- هي ٢- أَنْتِ ٣- أنا ٤- هي ٥- نَحْنُ

ب) أنا أَدْرُس، أَنْتَ تَدْرُسُ، نَحْنُ نَعْرِفُ، مايكل براون يَدْرُسُ، هالَة بُستاني وسَحَر حَلاّق تَدْرُسانِ، تَسْكُنُ هالَة وسَحَر، تَسْكُنانِ

تمرين ١٨

١- يَسكُنُ هاني مُحَمَّد مَعَ عائلتِه. ٢- يَدْرُسُ هاني الحُقوق.

٣- يَسْكُنُ أخو هاني في مدينةٍ أخرى مع عائلتِه. ٤- تَدْرُسُ أخْتُ هاني مادّةَ الطِبِّ.

٥- يَسْكُنُ عِماد حَسَن مع طالبين مِصْريِّين. ٦- يَدْرُسُ الطالِبانِ المِصريّانِ في كُلِّيَّةِ الآداب.

## الدرس السادِس

تمرين ١

١- الغُرفة رَقْم ٣٧ ٢- شَقَّةِ رَقْمُ ٩ ٣- نِداء خَيّاط ٤- لَيْسَ مَعَهُ كِتاب

٥- لا تَعرِفُ ٦- طالِبٌ

تمرين ٢

١- الأَسْتاذ وليد طَرَزي ٢- يا سَيِّد مَحمود! ٣- يا آنِسة ريم! ٤- السَيِّدة رَباب كَحّال

٥- السَيِّد عبد الرحيم حُسين ٦- دَكتور قدّورة ٧- الآنِسة زَيْنَب حَمدي

تمرين ٤

١- آسِف ٢- آسِفة ٣- آسِفانِ ٤- آسِفتان

٥- آسِفات ٦- آسِفونَ

**تمرين ٥**

١- جَيِّداً/ قَليلاً　　٢- آنِسة/ سَيِّدة　　٣- يَتكَلَّمُ/ لُغة　　٤- أمينَة/ مَكتبَة

٥- الله/ أعْلَم　　٦- سَيِّداتي/ سادتي

**تمرين ٦**

١- الآنسة　　٢- آسِف　　٣- الله أعْلَم　　٤- سَيِّداتي

٥- قَليلاً

**تمرين ٧**

١- لا تَعرِفُ الآنِسة أيْنَ كُلِّيَّةُ الحُقوق.

٢- عُنوان هالَة بُستاني هو ٤٥ شارع الكَواكبي/ شَقّة رَقم ٩/ حَلَب-سورية.

٣- سَيِّداتي وسادتي الأستاذ . . .　　٤- أتَكَلَّمُ اللُغَةَ العَرَبيّةَ قليلاً.

٥- الله أعْلَم　　٦- آسِفة　　٧- آسِف

**تمرين ٨**

١- حَيْثُ　　٢- جَيِّد　　٣- أمينَةُ　　٤- آسِف

٥- تَتكَلَّمُ

**تمرين ٩**

تَعرِفُ سَناء، تَتكَلَّمُها، يَتكَلَّمُ مايكل براون، هو يَعرِفُ، لكِنَّه يَتكَلَّمُ، هُوَ يَسكُنُ، هُوَ يَدرُسُ، لكِنَّهُما تَسكُنانِ

تَدرُسانِ، تَسكُنونَ، تَدرُسونَ

**تمرين ١٢**

١- الإسكندريّة　　٢- أخو　　٣- الإسكندرية　　٤- ثلاث أخَوات

٥- سَكَن الطالِبات　　٦- لَها أختان　　٧- زَينَب أختُ سامية

٨- هي في المدرسة الثانوية.

٩- تَهاني تسكن مع سامية وهي من مدينة المنصورة وتدرس الصيدلة.

ث) في الغُرفةِ مكتبَةٌ وتِلفازٌ وطاوِلةٌ كُرسيّان وسريران. هُناكَ أربَعُ صُوَرٍ على الجِدار.

**تمرين ١٣**

**المشهد الأول:** مكتبُ المُدير في الطابَق الثاني الغُرفة رقم ثلاثة بجانب غرفةِ المكتب.

**المشهد الثاني:** اسم الأستاذة سماح وهي من لبنان، من مدينة بعلبك ولكنّها تسكن في الولايات المتّحدة منذ عشرين سنة وهي تزور بعلبك كل ثلاث أو أربع سنوات.

## الدرس السابع

**تمرين ٢**

١- جَريدَةٌ ٢- مَجلاّتٌ وجَرائِدُ ٣- مَجَلَّةٌ ٤- يَعرِفونَ العَرَبيّة

٥- المَعرِفة ٦- الدُسْتور ٧- الرافِدين ٨- جَريدةً لُبنانيّةً

**تمرين ٣**

١- أيّة ٢- عادةً ٣- مِن فَضْلِك ٤- آسِفة

٥- تَقرَأ

**تمرين ٤**

١- جَريدةٌ/ مَجَلَّةٌ ٢- عادةً/ أحْياناً ٣- أعطِني/ تَفَضَّل ٤- يَقرأ/ يَكْتُبُ

٥- العَرَبي/ الأهْرام

**تمرين ٦**

١- الصَفِّ - مَجرور - مُضاف إليه

٢- السَيّارةُ - مَرفوع - مُبْتَدأ، الشارِعِ - مَجرور - حرف جر

٣- طالِباً - مَنصوب - تَمييز

٤- عُنوانَ - منصوب - مَفْعول به ٥- اللُغَةَ - مَنصوب - مَفْعول به

٦- الطالِبةُ - مَرفوع - فاعِل، وَرَقةٍ - مَجرور - حرف جر، دَفْتَرِها - مَجرور - حرف جر

٧- كِتاباً - مَنصوب - مَفعول به

٨- مِفتاحُ - مَرفوع - مُبْتَدأ، الأسْتاذِ - مَجرور - مُضاف إليه

**تمرين ٧**

١- عند ريما درّاجتان. ٢- لِبيتنا ثلاثة أبواب. ٣- مع أحمد سيّارة الآن. ٤- لي أخ وأخت.

٥- هل نظّارتك معك ؟ ٦- السيدة بستاني لها ابن وابنة.

**تمرين ٨**

١- أعرِفُها. ٢- أعْطانا جَريدةً. ٣- هُم يَعرِفونَ العَرَبيّةَ ويَتكَلّمونَها في البَيْت.

٤- أعْطِني تِلكَ المَجَلّةَ مِن فَضْلِكَ. ٥- يَعْرِفُنَني. ٦- هَل تَعرِفينَهُم؟

٧- أعْطيه رَقْمَ هاتِفِكِ.

**تمرين ٩**

١- جون كلارك غيبل – John Clark Gable ٢- كلايد وير – Clyde Wier

٣- جيم – Jim ٤- جيمس برولين – James Brolin

٥- ريتشارد راوندتري – Richard Roundtree

١- غراهم غرين - Graham Greene
٢- جون لو كاريه - John le Carré
٣- برلين - Berlin

تمرين ١٠

١- فاطِمة
٢- الأهرام
٣- ابن
٤- رانية وسميرة
٥- الشرق الأوسط
٦- الدستور
٧- خطأ. لا يقرأ أحمد مجلات.
٨- صواب
٩- خطأ. يسكنون في مدينة عَمّان.

تمرين ١١

١- يُحِبُّ قِراءة الجرائد العربية لأنّه يتعلّم مفردات جديدة.
٢- يقرأ جَريدة الشرق الأوسط.
٣- المحلّ الذي يبيع الجرائد العربية خلف الجامعة، قرب المطعم الهندي.

## الدرس الثامِن

تمرين ٣

١- المَطْعَم
٢- عَصيرَ بُرتُقالٍ
٣- البَيْضَ
٤- القَهوةَ العَرَبيّة
٥- دونَ سُكَّرٍ
٦- العَسَلَ
٧- مطعَم نِعْمة
٨- اللَحْم
٩- جَريدةً
١٠- البَيْتِ
١١- صَواب
١٢- صواب
١٣- صواب. تريد كاثي كأس عصير برتقال صباحا.
١٤- خطأ. تريد هادية فِنجانَ قهوة.
١٥- يَشرَبُ مايكل الشاي في القاهِرةِ صَباحاً.
١٦- عادةً تَشرَبُ هالَة الشاي في الصَباح.
١٧- تَأكُل كاثي قِطعةَ خُبزٍ مَعَ الزُبدةِ والعَسَلِ صَباحاً.
١٨- يأكُلُ مايكل في مَطْعَمٍ اسمُه نِعمة ظُهْراً.

تمرين ٤

١- مُرَبّى - only sweet food
٢- دونَ - does not pertain to time
٣- بُرتُقال - not a drink
٤- خُبْز - not a drink

تمرين ٥

١- شاي/ قَهوَة
٢- مُرَبّى/ عَسَل
٣- لَحْم/ خِنزير
٤- صَباحاً/ مَساءً
٥- مَعَ/ دونَ
٦- مَطْعَم/ مَقصَف
٧- يَشرَب/ يأكُل
٨-عَصير/ بُرتُقال

تمرين ٦

١- عَصير بُرتُقال
٢- مَطْعَم
٣- العَسَل
٤- الماءَ
٥- الحُبوب

تمرين ٧

١ - أريدُ كأسَ ماءٍ مِن فَضلِكَ.

٢ - يأكُل سَمير الخُبْزَ والجُبْنَ ويَشرَبُ الشايَ صَباحاً.

٣- يُحِبُّ مايكل الفَلافِلَ لكِنَّهُ لا يُحِبُّ اللَحْمَ.

تمرين ٩

١ - اِجلِسي مِن فَضْلِكِ. ٢ - اِجلِسوا مِن فَضْلِكُم. ٣ - اِجلِس مِن فَضْلِكَ. ٤ - اِجلِسنَ مِن فَضْلِكُنَّ.

٥ - اِجلِسوا مِن فَضْلِكُم.

تمرين ١٠

١ - السَيّاراتُ اليابانِيَّةُ سَيّاراتٌ جَيِّدةٌ. ٢ - هؤلاءِ طُلّابٌ ماليزيّونَ.

٣- هُناكَ بَناتٌ وأبناءٌ كثيرونَ في عائِلاتِ المِصريّينَ. ٤ - في كُلِّيَّتي حواسيبُ كَثيرة.

٥ - يأكُلُ السوريّونَ الجُبنَ والزَيتونَ صَباحاً. ٦ - مَن مَعَهُ أقلامٌ في حَقيبتِهِ؟

تمرين ١١

١ - عِندَنا ثلاث طالبات فرنسيات في صفنا. ٢ - معي ثلاثة أقلام.

٣- في هذه الغرفة خمسة هواتف. ٤ - هل تعرف أي طلاّب مصريين؟

٥ - هناك ثلاث طاولات وستّة كراسٍ في غرفة الأساتذة.

تمرين ١٣

١ - عصير برتقال ٢ - فنجان قهوة ٣- كأس ماء ٤ - فنجان شاي

٥ - جامعة أركانسو ٦ - قطعة خبز

تمرين ١٤

١ - قَهوة ٢ - الخبز والجبن ٣- الدجاج واللحم

٤ - خطأ. هي تأكل اللحم أو الدجاج. ٥ - خطأ. هي تأكل السلطة ظهراً. ٦ - صواب

تمرين ١٥

**المشهد الأول:**

١ - تريد الآنسة فنجان قهوة سكر خفيف وكأس ماء وجريدة.

٢ - تحب الآنسة قراءة الجرائد عندما تشرب القهوة.

**المشهد الثاني:**

١ - تريد الآنسة الأولى أن تشرب الشاي وتريد الآنسة الثانية فنجان قهوة.

٢ - ستحضّر الآنستان عشاءً خفيفاً من بيض مسلوق أو مقلي ولبنة وزبدة مع مربّى وزعتر.

٣- حَسَناً = very well, okay (a response denoting agreement)

**المشهد الثالث:**

١ - زعتر وبيض ولبنة ومربّى وزبدة وزيتون.

٢ - ستأكل الآنستان الخضروات واللحم والأرزّ مع الدجاج على الغداء.

# الدرس التاسِع

تمرين ١

١- الساعةُ السابعةُ إلاّ خمسَ دقائق
٢- الساعةُ السادسةُ والنصفُ وخمسُ دقائق
٣- الساعةُ الثالثةُ
٤- الساعةُ العاشرةُ والربع
٥- الساعةُ الرابعةُ والنصفُ إلاّ خمسَ دقائق
٦- الساعةُ الثالثةُ إلاّ ثلثا
٧- الساعةُ السابعةُ إلاّ ربعاً
٨- الساعةُ الثانيةَ عشرةَ إلاّ عشرَ دقائق
٩- الساعةُ التاسعةُ والثلث

تمرين ٣

١- دمشق
٢- مع طالبة
٣- اللغة الإنكليزية
٤- مقصف
٥- الواحدة بعد الظهر
٦- لين
٧- القاهرة
٨- سمير عبد الفتاح
٩- الهندسة
١٠- خطأ. عند سحر حلاق أربع مواد في هذا الفصل.
١١- تقرأ سحر الجرائد في المكتبة بعد درس الإنكليزية.
١٢- صواب
١٣- صواب
١٤- صواب

تمرين ٤

الساعة التاسعة: موعد درس الرياضيات، الساعة العاشرة: موعد درس اللغة الإنكليزية، الساعة الحادية عشرة: قراءة مجلات وجرائد إنكليزية في المكتبة، الساعة الثانية عشرة: تأكل في مقصف الجامعة، الساعة الواحدة: موعد درس المحاسبة، الساعة الثانية: ليس عندها درس، الساعة الثالثة: موعد درس الإحصاء، من الساعة الرابعة إلى السادسة: دراسة في المكتبة

تمرين ٥

جاك براون: الأب، مارثا براون: الأم، لين: الأخت، ريتشارد: الأخ

تمرين ٦

١- أول/ واحد
٢- الولايات المتحدة/ أمريكا
٣- ساعة/ دقيقة
٤- مادّة/ العلاقات الدولية
٥- نصف/ ثلث

تمرين ٧

١- كثير – not a fraction
٢- موعد – not food
٣- دقيقة – not a school subject
٤- واحد – not an ordinal number

تمرين ٩

١- برتقالة – an orange
٢- خبزة – a piece of bread
٣- زيتونة – an olive
٤- بيضة – an egg
٥- فولة – a fava bean
٦- سكّرة – a piece of sugar/candy

تمرين ١٠

١- تسعمئة وسبعة ٢- أربعةُ آلاف وسبعمئة وثلاثٌ وثمانون

٣- ثلاثةَ عشَرَ ألفاً وستّمئة وخمسٌ وثمانون ٤- ألفٌ وتسعمئة وأربعٌ وثمانون

٥- ألفان وعشر

تمرين ١١

١- متى تأكل سَحَر في المقصف؟ تأكل في المقصَفِ في الساعة الثانية عشرة ظهراً.

٢- في أية ساعةِ مَوعد درسِ سَحَر في الإحصاء؟ موعد درس الإحصاء في الساعة الثالثة.

٣- ما اسمُ أستاذةِ مايكل في مادّةِ اللغةِ العربية؟ اسمها الأستاذة زَينب طه.

٤- أين يسكن والِدا مايكل (أو: أبو مايكل وأمّه)؟ يسكنان في مدينة سنسناتي.

تمرين ١٢

١- عادِل ٢- الإنكليزيّ ٣- جزائريّ ٤- بريطانيا

٥- خطأ. في الجامعة الأردنية ٦- صواب

٧- خطأ. هو عربيّ من عمّان ٨- صواب ٩- الساعة التاسعة: مادّة اللغة الإنكليزية. الساعة الواحدة: مادّة الأدب الإنكليزيّ ١٠- الدكتور

تمرين ١٣

١- يستيقظ المتكلّم في الساعة السابعة والربع صباحاً. ٢- يذهب إلى الجامعة في الساعة الثامنة والنصف.

٣- تبدأ دروسه في الساعة التاسعة صباحاً وتنتهي في الساعة الواحدة ظهراً. ٤- ينام في الساعة الحادية عشرة ليلاً.

## الدرس العاشر

تمرين ١

١- الدَوحة عاصمةُ قَطَر. ٢- سيارةُ حسين بورش ألمانية.

٣- شارع حَمَد المُبارَك في الكويت.

تمرين ٢

١- قطر ٢- اللغة الإنكليزيّة ٣- المكتبة ٤- دار أسرتها

٥- ثلاث سيارات ٦- لندن ٧- الكويت ٨- ألمانية

٩- خطأ. سبع غرف. ١٠- صواب ١١- خطأ. في مكتبة الجامعة

١٢- خطأ. السيّارة جميلة والمحرك قويّ ١٣- ليس متزوِّجاً ويسكن لوَحدَهُ في شقّة.

تمرين ٣

١- محرِّك ٢- غرفة ٣- دار ٤- صديق

٥- سائقاً

**تمرين ٤**

١- قصير – nothing to do with books or reading

٢- صديق –not related to cars or driving  ٣- دراسة –not a country

٤- لبس – not a family member  ٥- فتاة – not an adjective

**تمرين ٥**

١- سيّارة/ سائق  ٢- كبير/ صغير  ٣- دار/ بيت  ٤- طويل/ قصير

٥- وسيم/ جميلة  ٦- قديم/ حديث  ٧- فتاة/ بنت  ٨- مكتبة/ مجلات

**تمرين ٧**

١- ذَهَبْنا  ٢- قَرَأتُ  ٣- تَكَلَّمْتُ  ٤- أكَلْتُ

٥- شَرِبْتُ  ٦- أكَلَتْ  ٧- أكَلَتْ  ٨- أكَلَ ٩- شَرِبَ

ب) ١- عيد الشكر بمعنى Thanksgiving  ٢- كلمة بطاطا بمعنى potatoes

٣- المتكلّم وأخوه  ٤- شربنا شاياً وكوكا كولا وماء  ٥- كلمة أرزّ بمعنى rice

**تمرين ٨**

١- أحِبُّ القِراءَ في الصباح.  ٢- يُريدُ صَديقي عُمَر دِراسةَ الرياضيات.

٣- أسكُنُ في سَكَنِ الطلاّب.  ٤- أنا وأصدقائي نُحِبُّ شُرْبَ القهوةِ دونَ سكَّر.

٥- تُحِبُّ أختي الصَغيرةُ الأكْلَ العربيّ.  ٦- يُحِبُّ حُسَين العَمَلَ في الكويت.

٧- يُحِبُّ أخوها لُبْسَ الكوفية.

**تمرين ٩**

١- عِندي هاتِفٌ يابانِيّة. - خطأ. هاتف يابانيّ  ٢- تَأكُلُ سَلمى في مَطعَمٍ صَغير.- صواب

٣- عِندَ أخي كُتُبٌ قَديمات. - خطأ. كُتُب قَديمة  ٤- إخْوَةُ مَحمود طِوال.- صواب

٥- هَل أولادُها الصَغيرُ مَعَها؟ - خطأ. أولادُها الصِغار

٦- في صَفِّنا كَراسٍ قَديم. - خطأ. كراسٍ قَديمة

**تمرين ١٠**

١- باريس مَدينةٌ فَرَنسيٌّ.- خطأ. مدينة فرنسيّة  ٢- عَدنان طالِبٌ سوريٌّ.- صواب

٣- مينيسوتا وِلايةٌ أمريكيَّةٌ. - صواب  ٤- جامِعَتُنا كَبيرٌ.- خطأ. جامعتنا كبيرة

٥- صَفُّنا صَغيرٌ.- صواب ٦- حُسَيْن رَجُلٌ قَطَرِيَّةٌ.- خطأ. رجل قطريّ

**تمرين ١١**

١- عِندي كِتابانِ جَديدَيْنِ. - خطأ. كِتابان جديدانِ  ٢- يَدرُسُ سامي لُغَةٌ جَديدةٌ. - خطأ. لغةً جَديدةً

٣- يَدرُسُ عَدنان في الجامِعَةِ الأمريكيَّةِ. - صواب  ٤- أعرِفُ رِجالاً وَسيمونَ.- خطأ. رِجالاً وسيمينَ

٥- هذِه شَقّةُ الطالِبَةِ السوريَّةُ. -خطأ. الطالبةِ السوريّةِ

تمرين ١٢

١- صوابphrase ٢- صوابphrase ٣- صوابsentence
٤- خطأ. سيارةٌ حديثةٌ phrase ٥- خطأ. صورةٌ جميلةٌ phrase
٦- صوابsentence ٧- صواب phrase ٨- خطأ. رجلٌ وسيمٌ phrase
٩- صوابphrase ١٠- خطأ. سيارتُك جديدةٌsentence
١١- صوابsentence ١٢- صواب phrase

تمرين ١٣

١- الجَديدةُ ٢- القَديمةُ ٣- القَديمَةَ ٤- فَرَنسيّتانِ
٥- الجَديدِ ٦- الجَديداتُ

تمرين ١٤

١- صغيرةٌ ٢- الصغيرةِ ٣- الصِغارَ ٤- صغيرتانِ
٥- صغيرةٌ ٦- صغيرتان ٧- صغيرٌ ٨- الصغيرِ

تمرين ١٥

١- تونِسيّ ٢- علم الحاسوب ٣- سكن الطلاّب ٤- أختانِ
٥- صواب ٦- خطأ. يريد دراسةَ الطبّ
٧- خطأ. هي أخت سعيد ٨- خطأ. هي لا تدرس. هي في البيت. ٩- صواب
١٠- خطأ. عنده درّاجة

## الدرس الحادي عشر

تمرين ١

١- شَهْر – the only noun ٢- غُرْفة – not an establishment
٣- أيلول – a month, not a day ٤- حينَ – does not pertain to a place
٥- ساعة – not related to sleeping

تمرين ٢

١- آب/ أغسطس ٢- مساءً/ ظُهراً ٣- نزل/ فُندُق ٤- شباط/ فبراير
٥- وسادة/ سرير ٦- فاهيتا/ المكسيك ٧- شهر/ أسبوع ٨- الأحد/ السبت
٩- كانون الثاني/ يناير ١٠- مطار/ طائرة

تمرين ٤

١- في الساعةِ السادِسة ٢- العاشِرةِ والنِصْف ٣- صَديقُ رامي ٤- المَطار
٥- غُرفَتا نَوْم ٦- شَقَّةِ هِشام ٧- قَميصاً ٨- ٢٧٦
٩- صواب ١٠- صواب
١١- خطأ ذهب عدنان إلى دروسه في الجامعة يوم الأربعاء.

١٢- خطأ يظنّ عدنان أنَّ جامعةَ ولايةِ أوهايو كبيرة جداً.

**تمرين ٦**

١- درس الرياضيات بعد درس اللغة الإنكليزية بثلاث ساعات وقبل الكيمياء بثلاث ساعات.

٢- درس الكيمياء بعد درس الرياضيات بثلاث ساعات وقبل الذهاب إلى السوق بساعتين.

**تمرين ٨**

١- أنَّ الجامِعةَ ٢- إنَّ سيّارتَها ٣- تَظُنّينَ أنّ الكِتابَينِ

٤- أظُنُّ أن مَدينةَ سان فَرانسيسكو ٥- يقولُ إنّ الطُلاّبَ

٦- تَقولُ إنّ السيّارتَينِ جَديدتانِ

**تمرين ١٠**

١- أجْمَل مِن ٢- أكْبَر ٣- أطول ٤- أقْدَم

٥- أكْبَر مِن ٦- أحْدَث ٧- أجْمَل ٨- أطْوَل مِنّي

**تمرين ١٢**

١- سائقي شاحنات ٢- شركة المطاحن ٣- مئتي دينار ٤- ثلاثمئة دينار

٥- شارع الجلاء ٦- ثلاث غرف نوم ٧- غرفتا جلوس ٨- غرفة طعام

٩- ألف ليرة

**تمرين ١٣**

١- سَيكونُ ٢- كانا ٣- كانَ ٤- كُنّا ٥- كانوا

٦- كانا ٧- كُنْتِ ٨- تَكونُ

**تمرين ١٥**

١- حَزيران ٢- نيسان ٣- حَزيران ٤- كانون الأوّل

٥- شَعْبان ٦- سبعة ٧- الجُمْعة ٨- الأحَد

٩- الجُمْعة ١٠- السَبْت والأحَد

**تمرين ١٦**

١- لأخيها ٢- اللُغةَ ٣- أبو ٤- الكِتابُ

٥- جامعةِ ٦- أبا

**تمرين ١٧**

١- دمشق ٢- ابن وبنت ٣- دار أبيه ٤- أربع غرف نوم

٥- خطأ. ذهب إلى دمشق بالطائرة مع عائلَتِه ٦- صواب

٧- خطأ. حَسّان أستاذ في مدرسة ثانوية في الرياض ٨- صواب

**تمرين ١٨**

١- يَذْهَبُ سامِر وستيف إلى مَطار دِمَشْق الدُوَليّ لمقابلة عدنان.

٢- وَصَلَ عَدنان إلى سوريَّة مساء أمس. ٣- سَيَصِلُ مايكل إلى دِمَشْق غداً.
٤- تعَرَّفَ سامِر على مايكل على الحاسوب ٥- مايكل سَيُقابِلُ عَدنان وستيف غداً.
٦- أكيد بمعنى certainly بالإنكليزيّة.

## الدرس الثاني عشر

**تمرين ١**

١- رَبيع/ خَريف ٢- حارّ/ بارد ٣- غائم/ صحوٍ ٤- شاطِئ/ بَحر
٥- ليل/ نهار ٦- ثلج/ مطر ٧- درجة/ مئوية

**تمرين ٢**

١- ثلج – not a plant ٢- بحيرة – not weather-related
٣- مطر – not a body of water ٤- فصل – does not pertain to temperature
٥- أسبوع – not a weather condition

**تمرين ٣**

١- فصول ٢- الخريف ٣- معتدل ٤- البحر
٥- أريزونا ٦- الخريف ٧- في فصلي الربيع والصيف
٨- في فصل الصيف ٩- variable answers ١٠- يكون الطقسُ حارّاً في فصل الصيف عادةً.
١١- خطأ. يسقط الثلج في الشتاء. ١٢- صواب
١٣- خطأ. تكون الشمس ساطعةً في الصيف ١٤- variable answers

**تمرين ٥**

١- وصلَتْ طائرةُ هاني في الساعةِ التاسعة والنصِف.
٢- وَصَلتُ إلى هذه المدينة في سنةِ ٢٠٠٦.
٣- تصِلُ درجةُ الحرارةِ في الصيف إلى ٤٠ دَرَجة مِئويّة في بَلَدَتي.
٤- وصلنا إلى الدرس الثاني عشر.
٥- ستصِل درجة الحرارة إلى ناقِص خمسة في الليل.

**تمرين ٦**

١- ما سبحتُ في تِلكَ البُحيرة. ٢- هذا مِفتاحُ بابِ شقَّةِ أختي.
٣- يأتي شهرُ حَزيران بعد شهرِ أيّار. ٤- سيكونُ الطقْسُ صحواً بعد غدٍ.
٥- يذهب الناسُ إلى شاطئ البحرِ في الصيفِ.
٦- قالت زينب لصديقاتها إنّها ستذهب إلى المغرب غداً.
٧- قال لي أستاذي إنّ لُغتي العربية جيّدةٌ.
٨-ذهبتُ من حلب إلى دمشق بالقطار في يوم السبت.

تمرين ٨

في كل عطلة نهاية أسبوع في الصيف نذهب أنا وبعض أصدقائي إلى الشاطئ. أمشي عادةً على الشاطئ يوم الجمعة بالليل مع صديقتي ليلى ونتكلّم عن كلِّ دروسِنا. يوم السبت أقرأ عادةً أو أسبح مُعظَمَ اليوم. لا يحبُّ بعضُ أصدقائي القراءةَ أو الدراسة على الشاطئ ولكني أحبها. مُعْظَمُ يومِ الأحد نكون في سيارتِنا في طريقنا إلى البيت. واللهِ، الصيف فصلٌ جميلٌ مِن فُصولِ السنة.

تمرين ٩

١ - ٣٨ مئوية = ١٠٠,٤ ٢ - ٨٤ فرنهايت = ٢٨,٨ ٣- ٣٢ فرنهايت = صفر

٤ - ٢٠ مئوية =٦٨ ٥ - ٩٢ فرنهايت = ٣٣,٣

تمرين ١٠

١ - معتدلاً ٢ - الربيع ٣- الخميس ٤ - حلب

٥ - خطأ. بالسيّارة. ٦ - صواب ٧- خطأ. تريد السكن في صافيتا.

٨- خطأ. بارد قليلاً

تمرين ١١

١ - يحبُّ فصل الصيف لأنّه يذهب إلى البحر للسباحة.

٢ - يحبُّ فصل الربيع لأنّ الأشجار مزهرة والطقس جميل ومعتدل.

٣- يحبُّ فصل الشتاء لأنّه يحبُّ المطر والثلج. ٤ - في السنة إثنا عشر شهراً.

## الدرس الثالث عشر

تمرين ١

١ - استحمّ/ غسل ٢ - فرشاة/ معجون أسنان ٣- نسي/ موعد

٤- سرير/ نوم ٥ - كباب/ فلافل ٦ - حلق/ ذقن ٧- مقصف/ مطعم

تمرين ٢

١ - فرشاة – not a drink ٢ - طبّ – not a meal

٣- حاسبة – not a means of transportation ٤ - صابون – not food

٥ - لبن – not a body part ٦ - مادّة – not a TV program

٧- مرّة – not a verb ٨- مشاهدة – has nothing to do with writing

تمرين ٤

١ - حلب ٢ - السابعة ٣- بالحافلة ٤ - غادة ٥ - الثالثة

٦ - الجبن ٧- في موعده ٨- مشغولة ٩- خمس عشرة ساعة

١٠ - برنامج ستّون دقيقة ١١ - صديقتها سحر ١٢ - الخامسة

١٣ - العاشرة والنصف ١٤ - في وقت مبكر جداً ١٥ - العشاء

١٦ - المكتبة ١٧ - خطأ. تأكل هالة بستاني الفول على الفطور يوم الجمعة.

١٨- خطأ تذهب هالة إلى النوم في الساعة العاشرة والنصف.

١٩- خطأ تنظّف هالة وجهها بالماء والصابون. ٢٠- صواب

٢١- خطأ تحبُّ هالة مشاهدة المسلسلات العربيّة والأمريكيّة وبرامج الأخبار.

٢٢- خطأ يحلق عدنان ذقنه بعد النوم. ٢٣- خطأ نسي عدنان موعد العشاء.

٢٤- خطأ تكلّمت ليسا أمس بالهاتف وقالت إنها مشغولة.

٢٥- صواب ٢٦- خطأ سيكتب عدنان رسالة يوم الخميس.

تمرين ٥

١- تأكل هالة الفول المدمّس على الغداء. ٢- أحبُّ مشاهدة برامج الأخبار صباحاً.

٣- يغسل زوجي السيّارةَ يوم السبت.

تمرين ٦

١- اسمي روضة قطان. ٢- أعمل أمينة مكتبة في الجامعة الأردنية في عمّان.

٣- أذهب إلى عملي في الساعة السابعة كلَّ يوم.

٤- لكنّني أنهض متأخّرةً في يوم الجمعة (في التاسعة أو العاشرة).

٥-أحضّر عادةً فطوراً كبيراً لي ولزوجي وأولادي. ٦- أحضّر أحياناً الفول المدمّس والبيض المقليّ.

٧- وأحياناً نأكل الحمّص إلى جانب الزيتون والجبن.

٨- بعد الفطور أنظّف الدار وأغسل القمصان.

٩- في الساعة الرابعة بعد الظهر أذهب وأولادي إلى دار أبي وأمي.

١٠- حيث أتكلّم معهما ومع أختي وأخي. ١١- نرجع إلى البيت في الساعة الثامنة مساءً.

تمرين ٨

١- الشاي ٢- الصابون ٣- الحلوى ٤- تنهضين

٥- المعجون ٦- تبولة

تمرين ١١

نهضتُ اليوم وبعد ذلك حضّرتُ الفَطور. على الفَطور أكلت بعض البيض وقطعة خبز وقطع جبن وشربت كأسي عصير برتقال وفنجان قهوة.

تمرين ١٢

١- لا تكتب/ تكتبوا على الجُدران. ٢- لا تنسَ موعدَ طائرتِك.

٣- لا تعطِه رقم هاتفكِ. ٤- لا تجلِس على ذلك الكرسيّ.

٥- لا تذهبا إلى الدرس اليوم.

تمرين ١٤

١- يدرسون ٢- وصلت ٣- عمل ٤- يسكنان

٥- انتقلوا ٦- يلبس ٧- تدرس

تمرين ١٥

١- الجمعة ٢- دار صديقه ٣- دمشق ٤- بريطانيا

٥- الصحّة ٦- خطأ. عند أبيه سيّارة. ٧- خطأ. يدرس الأدب الإنكليزيّ.

٨- خطأ. سيذهبون إلى المطعم بعد السينما. ٩- صواب

١٠- سيغسل سيّارة أبيه وسينظّف غرفته ويغسل قمصانَه.

١١- غسّان طالب في جامعة دمشق يدرس الأدب الإنكليزيّ وسوف يذهب في السنة المقبلة إلى بريطانيا ليدرس الأدب الإنكليزيّ.

تمرين ١٦

١- تَسْتَيْقِظُ في الساعةِ السابعةِ والنِصْفِ. ٢- تَغسِلُ وَجهَها وتُنَظِّفُ أسنانَها.

٣- تَستَمِعُ إلى الموسيقا وهي تَشرَبُ القهوة مع زَوْجِها.

٤- تُحَضِّرُ الفَطور. ٥- تَغسِلُ الصُحونَ ثمّ تُغَيِّرُ ملابِسَها.

٦- في الساعة الثالثة تَعودُ إلى البيت وتُحَضِّرُ الغداء.

٧- في المساء تَذهَبُ هي وزَوجُها لزيارة العائلة أو الأصدقاء.

٨- تَعودُ إلى البيت لِتُحَضِّرَ العَشاء وتُرَتِّبَ البيت.

٩- تُشاهِدُ التلفاز وتَنام في الساعةِ الثانيةَ عشرةَ ليلاً.

## الدرس الرابع عشر

تمرين ١

١- مشهور ٢- عطلة ٣- حيّ ٤- المُقبِل

٥- بصل – not weather-related ٦- سرير – not related to transportation

٧- طقس –not a kind of food ٨- عيد – not related to bodies of water

تمرين ٢

١- المسخّن أكلة فلسطينيّة مشهورة. ٢- زارَ مايكل براون مدينةَ الإسكندريّة.

٣- كان هناك ناس كثيرون على شاطئ البحر. ٤- وصلت سامية إلى محطةِ القطار مساءً.

تمرين ٣

١- أحْمَد حِجازي رَجُلٌ مِن مَدينَةِ حَلَب.

٢- أرادَ أحْمَدُ زِيارةَ مَدينَةِ طَرطوسَ مَعَ عائِلَتِه.

٣- وطَرطوسُ مَدينَةٌ صَغيرَةٌ على الشاطِئِ السورِيّ.

٤- لكِنَّ طَرطوسَ لَيْسَتْ قَريبَةً ولَيْسَ عِندَ أحْمَد سَيّارة.

٥- لِذلِكَ ذَهَبوا إلى هُناكَ بِالقِطار.

٦- كانوا في مَحَطَّةِ القِطارِ في حَلَبَ في الساعةِ السابِعَةِ صَباحاً.

٧- بَعدَ أربَعِ ساعاتٍ ونِصْفٍ وَصَلوا إلى طَرْطوس.

٨- نَزَلوا في طَرطوسَ في فُنْدُقٍ قَريبٍ مِن شاطِئِ البَحْر.
٩- بَعدَ خَمسةِ أيّامٍ رَجَعوا إلى حَلَبَ بِالقِطارِ أيْضاً.

**تمرين ٤**

١- مطعم ٢- مصريّة ٣- نظيفاً ٤- محطّة الجيزة
٥- المكتبة ٦- مَلاهٍ ٧- الإثنين ٨- تِم
٩- خطأ. ثلاث ساعات ونصف. ١٠- خطأ. في الساعة السابعة صباحاً
١١- خطأ. كان الطقس جميلاً جداً. ١٢- صواب

**تمرين ٧**

١- نَهْرُ النيلِ طَويلٌ أمّا نَهْرُ بَرَدى فَقَصيرٌ.
٢- يَسكُنُ نادِر في شَقّةٍ أمّا ناديا فَتَسكُنُ في سَكَنِ الطالِبات.
٣- أخي مُهَندِس أمّا أختي فَأستاذة. ٤- اِشتَرَيْتُ مِحْفَظَةً أمّا زَوْجَتي فِاشْتَرَتْ نَظّارةً.
٥- مَدينَةُ طَرابُلْسَ الشام في لُبنانَ أمّا مَدينَةُ طَرابُلْسَ الغَرْبِ فَفي ليبيا.
٦- أُحِبُّ عَصيرَ البُرتُقالِ أمّا أنْتِ فتُحِبّينَ الحَليب.

**تمرين ٨**

١- المَكتَبَةُ قَريبةٌ لِذلِكَ مَشَيْتُ إلَيْها. ٢- يُحِبُّ مَحْمودُ البيتزا كَثيراً لِذلِكَ يَأكُلُها كُلَّ يوم.
٣- سَحَر مِن دِمَشقَ وتَدرُسُ في جامِعَةِ حَلَبَ لِذلِكَ تَسكُنُ في شَقَّةٍ هُناك.
٤- ليس عندي سيّارة لِذلِكَ ذهبت بالقِطار.
٥- جلسنا في غرفة الصف نصف ساعة ولكن ما جاء الأستاذ لِذلِكَ ذهبنا إلى المكتبة.
٦- تحبّ سُهى السباحة لِذلِكَ تسكن على شاطئ البحيرة.

**تمرين ٩**

١- قالَ لي أستاذي إنّه سيكون في مكتبه في الساعة التاسعة.
٢- قالَ محمود لزوجتِه إنّه نزل في فندق شيراتون في دمشق.
٣- قالَ لَها أيضاً إنّه أكل في مطعم الشرق كلَّ يوم.
٤- يقولُ مروان إنّ أخاه سيصل إلى محطّة القِطار في الساعة الرابعة بعد الظُهر.

**تمرين ١٠**

١- هذا أستاذُنا. ٢- عطلتكِ هذه . . . ٣- أصدقائي هؤلاء . . . ٤- هذه سيارتي.
٥- نظّارة أمي هذِه . . .

**تمرين ١١**

١- أوروبيّ ٢- سَنَويّ ٣- سَماويّ ٤- شَتَويّ
٥- ميلاديّ ٦- مِئويّ ٧- خَريفيّ ٨- أسَرَويّ

تمرين ١٣

١- حِمْصَ ٢- سَيأكُلانِ غَداءً كَبيراً ٣- الحادِيَةَ عَشْرَةَ ٤- أطعِمةً لُبنانِيَّةً

٥- مُهَندِساً ٦- حِمص

٧- الربيع ٨- لبنان الأخضَر ٩- صواب ١٠- صواب

١١- خطأ. كان الطقسُ جميلاً والشمسُ ساطِعةً.

١٢- خطأ. بالسيّارة.

تمرين ١٤

**المشهد الأول:** ١- جاء مايكل إلى دِمَشق ليزورها وليرى صديقه.

٢- سيبقى أربعة أيام في دِمَشق وعليه أن يرجع لأن الدراسةَ تبدأ بعد أسبوع.

٣- في رأي مايكل مدينة القاهرة جميلة يوجد فيها النيل ولكن شوارعها مزدحمة جداً بالسيّارات.

٤- صديقه ستيف ينتظره عند قوس باب شرقي.

**المَشْهَدُ الثاني:** ١- يَدرُسُ سامِر التاريخ في كُلِّيَّة الآداب. ٢-يُفَضِّلُ مايكل الحديث بالفُصحى.

٣-سَيذهَبُ كُلٌّ مِن ستيف وسامِر ومايكل ليشربوا عصيراً.

## الدرس الخامس عشر

تمرين ١

١- فجر – nothing to do with education

٢- الجزيرة – not a festivity

٣- إسلاميّ – not a school level

٤- حلوى – not a time of day

تمرين ٢

١- إسلاميّ/ مسيحيّ

٢- عيد الشكر/ ديك حبش

٣- عيد الأضحى/ الحج

٤- عيد الميلاد/ المسيح

٥- عيد الفطر/ رمضان

٦- عيد استقلال أمريكا/ ٤ تمّوز

تمرين ٣

١- إسلاميّ ٢- لأنَّ ٣- وُلِدَ ٤- الاستقلال ٥- نَوع

٦- رمضان

تمرين ٤

١- ٢٤ تمّوز ٢- الفِطر ٣- ١٧ نيسان ٤- الميلاد

٥- ثلاث سنوات ٦- السابعة عشرة ٧- التجارة ٨- مع أسرتها

٩-خطأ. لا تَحتَفِلُ الجزائِرُ بِالأعْيادِ الإسلاميَّةِ والمَسيحيَّة.

١٠- خطأ. يُحْتَفَلُ بِعيدِ الفِصْحِ في يوم أحد بين ٢٢ آذار و٢٥ نيسان.

١١-خطأ. يَأكُلُ الأمريكيونَ ديكَ حَبَش في عيدِ الشكر.

١٢- خطأ. تَحتَفِلُ معظم الوِلاياتِ الأمريكيّةِ بِعيدِ مارتِن لوثَر كِنغ.

١٣- صواب ١٤-خطأ. سَوفَ تَتَخَرَّجُ سُعادُ مِنَ الجامِعَةِ بَعدَ سنتين.

تمرين ٦

١- مَتى يَحتَفِلُ أخوكَ بِعيدِ ميلادِه؟ ٢- وُلِدَتْ أختي في شَهر آب.

٣- أستراليا جَزيرةٌ كَبيرةٌ جِدّاً. ٤- اِنتَقَلتُ إلى هذِهِ الشَقَّة في فَصْلِ الخَريف.

تمرين ٧

١- وُلِدَ مازِن المُدَرِّس في مَدينةِ حَلَب. ٢- دَرَسَ في مَدارِسِ حَلَبَ الابْتِدائيّةِ والمُتَوَسِّطة.

٣- بَعدَ ذلِكَ دَرَسَ في مَدرَسَةٍ ثانَويّةٍ في مَدينةِ دِمَشق.

٤- ثُمَّ رَجَعَ إلى حَلَب ودَرَسَ في جامِعَةِ حَلَبَ في السَنةِ الأولى.

٥- ثُمَّ انتَقَلَ إلى جامعةِ دِمَشقَ في السنةِ الثانية.

٦- يَقولُ مازِن إنّه سَوفَ يَرجِعُ إلى حَلَبَ حينَ يَتَخَرَّج.

تمرين ١٠

| | | | |
|---|---|---|---|
| ١- أبيكَ | ٢- ذا | ٣- أخوها | ٤- أبو |
| ٥- لأخيك | ٦- ذو | ٧- أخاها | ٨- أبوكِ |

تمرين ١١

| | | | |
|---|---|---|---|
| ١- سوريّة | ٢- لبنان | ٣- فلسطين | ٤- مصر |
| ٥- رمضان | ٦- مكّة | ٧- بغداد | |

تمرين ١٢

١- مدارِسَ مِصريّةٍ ٢- شوارِعُ حديثةٌ ٣- مكّةَ والمدينةِ

٤- نيسانَ . . . لبنانَ والأردنِّ

تمرين ١٣

١- يُقالُ إنَّ باريس مَدينةٌ جَميلة. ٢- وُلِدَتْ هالَةَ في بَيروت سَنَةَ ١٩٨٥.

٣- تُسَمَّى وِلايةُ نيويورك إمباير ستيت. ٤- تُشرَبُ القهوةُ بَعدَ الطعامِ عادةً.

٥- تُسَمّى بَغْدادُ مدينةَ السلام.

تمرين ١٤

١- كانت السماء غائمةً لكن صارت صافيةً.

٢- كان الطقسُ بارداً في شهر شُباط، لكنّه صار حارّاً.

٣- كانت بنتاً لكنّها صارت امرأةً.

٤- صارت المدينةُ جميلةً.

٥- صار الرجلُ مشهوراً.

تمرين ١٥

١- زُرْتَ ٢- صُمْتَ ٣- تَخَرَّجْتِ ٤- صَلَيْتَ

٥- وُلِدَ

تمرين ١٦

١- أماني ٢- أندرو هارت ٣- أوستن ٤- مدينة أوستن

٥- زارا ستَّ مدن هي نيويورك وشيكاغو وسياتل وسان فرانسيسكو ولوس أنجليس وأوستن.

٦- يعمل مهندساً. ٧- يوم الخميس ٢٣ تشرين الثاني.

٨- ديك حبش وفطيرة القرع. ٩- خطأ. زارا الولايات المتّحدة.

١٠- صواب ١١- صواب ١٢- خطأ. ما أحبّت ديك الحبش.

تمرين ١٧

**المشهد الأول:**

| | |
|---|---|
| ١- عيد الميلاد | عيد الفِصْح |
| عيد المَوْلِد النَبَويّ | عيد رأْس السَنة الهِجْريَّة |
| عيد الفِطْر | عيد الأَضْحى المُبارَك |

٢- في سورية يحتفل الناس جميعاً بالأعياد الوطنية مثل عيد الجلاء يعني عيد الاستقلال، وعيد المعلّم وعيد الأمّ وعيد العمال وعيد الشهداء.

٣- كلَّ عام وأنتم بخير ويقول المسيحيون في عيد الفصح «المسيح قام» والرد «حقاً قام»

**المشهد الثاني:** ٤- يحتفل المسلمون بعيد الفطر ثلاثة أيّام وبعيد الأضحى أربعة أيّام.

٥- يصوم المسلمون عن الأكل والشرب من الفجر حتّى المغرب في شهر رمضان.

٦- ويزيّن المسيحيون بيوتهم بشجرة الميلاد وكذلك شوارع وساحات المناطق المسيحيّة.

٧- الأعياد المهمّة في أمريكا هي عيد الفصح وعيد الميلاد ورأس السنة الميلاديّة وعيد الشكر.

## الدرس السادس عشر

تمرين ١

١- نُفِيَ– not related to birth or death

٢- شاعِر – nothing to do with the army

٣- مُحامٍ – not a leader

٤- حَصَلَ – the only verb

٥- فَلْسَفَة – not a town

تمرين ٢

١- حرب/ سلام ٢- كِتاب/ مُقَدِّمة ٣- تُوُفِّي/ وُلِد ٤- قانون/ مُحامٍ

٥- غَرْناطة/ الأندلس ٦- دَخَلَ/ خَرَجَ ٧- رَئيس/ مَلِك

تمرين ٣

١- شاعِر ٢- أُنْتُخِبَ ٣- فيلسوف ٤- مِلِكة

٥- قُرْب ٦- مؤرِّخ

**تمرين ٤**

١- كانَتْ إميلي دِكَنسَن شاعِرةً أمريكيّةً مَشْهورةً.
٢- تَخَرَّجَتْ أختي مِنَ الجامِعةِ ثُمَّ عَمِلَتْ في مَكْتَبِ مُحام.
٣- أُنْتُخِبَ بِل كلنتَن رَئيساً لِلوِلاياتِ المُتَّحِدةِ الأمريكيّةِ مَرَّتَيْنِ.
٤- أُغْتيلَ الرَئيسُ كِنيدي بِمَدينةِ دالاس في سَنَةِ ١٩٦٣.

**تمرين ٥**

١- مُحَمَّد بن موسى الخوارِزمي عالِمُ رِياضِيّاتٍ مُسْلِمٌ مَشْهور.
٢- وُلِدَ الخُوارِزمي في مَدينةِ خُوارِزم.
٣- أَسَّسَ الخُوارِزمي عِلْمَ الجَبْر.
٤- وكَتَبَ كِتاباً في حِسابِ الجَبْرِ وتُرْجِمَ إلى اللاتينيّة.
٥- عَرَفَتْ أوروبا عِلْمَ الجَبْرِ مِن هذا الكِتاب. ٦- وكَتَبَ أيْضاً عَن الصِفْر في الرِياضيّات.
٧- تُوُفِّيَ الخُوارِزمي سَنَةَ ٨٤٠ ميلاديّة. ٨- كَلِمةُ *algorithm* مأخوذةٌ مِن اسْمِه.

**تمرين ٦**

| | | | |
|---|---|---|---|
| ١- ١٨٨٣ | ٢- العثمانيّ | ٣- بالكلّيّة الحربيّة | ٤- الاجتماع |
| ٥- مرتين | ٦- ١٨٦٠ | ٧- ١٩٦٤ | ٨- طولون |
| ٩- ميسلون | ١٠- جمال عبد الناصر | ١١- ابن خلدون | ١٢- جورج واشنطن |
| ١٣- إبراهيم لنكن | ١٤- التمييز العنصريّ | | ١٥- صواب |

١٦- خطأ. كان وزير الدفاع. ١٧- صواب
١٨- خطأ. حارب في فلسطين ١٩- خطأ. كان مؤرِّخاً وفيلسوفاً
٢٠- خطأ. في «ماونت فرنن» ٢١- خطأ. بعد سنة ١٨٦٠
٢٢- خطأ. اغتيل في مدينة ممفيس.

**تمرين ٩**

| | | | |
|---|---|---|---|
| ١- شارِب | ٢- دارِس | ٣- عامِل | ٤- مُنَظِّف |
| ٥- ساكِن | ٦- مُحارِب | | |

**تمرين ١٠**

١- اِستِحْمام - اِستِفْعال - حمم ٢- مُحَضِّرون - مُفَعِّلون - حضر
٣- كِتابة - فِعالة - كتب ٤- جامِعة - فاعِلة - جمع
٥- مُختَبَر - مُفْتَعَل - خبر ٦- مَسْبَح - مَفْعَل - سبح
٧- مَكْتَبة - مَفْعَلة - كتب ٨- مَلْعَب - مَفْعَل - لعب
٩- تَفاضُل - تفاعُل - فضل ١٠- جالِسات - فاعِلات - جلس

تمرين ١١

١- تَدَخَّل – to interfere
٢- كَبُر – to grow
٣- اِسْتَعمَل – to use
٤- نَسِي – to forget
٥- تَمارَض – to feign sickness
٦- أرْسَل – to send
٧- اِنْتَهى – to end
٨- نَظَّف – to clean
٩- اِحْتَفَل – to celebrate
١٠- طَبَخ – to cook
١١- سافَر – to travel
١٢- اِجْتَمَع – to meet

تمرين ١٢

| | Verb | Pattern | Number | Root | Meaning |
|---|---|---|---|---|---|
| ١- | اِحْتَفَل | اِفْتَعَل | VIII | حفل | to celebrate |
| ٢- | اِسْتَشْهَد | اِسْتَفْعَل | X | شهد | to cite |
| ٣- | دَرَس | فَعَل | I | درس | to study |
| ٤- | اِنْهَزَم | اِنْفَعَل | VII | هزم | to be defeated |
| ٥- | تَكَلَّم | تَفَعَّل | V | كلم | to talk |
| ٦- | اِشْتَرى | اِفْتَعَل | VIII | شرى | to buy |
| ٧- | تَخَرَّج | تَفَعَّل | V | خرج | to graduate |
| ٨- | حارَب | فاعَل | III | حرب | to fight |
| ٩- | اِحْمَرّ | اِفْعَلّ | IX | حمر | to turn red |
| ١٠ | تَراسَل | تَفاعَل | VI | رسل | to correspond |

تمرين ١٣

١- الأولى
٢- العاشِر
٣- الثانيةَ عَشرَةَ
٤- الثالثُ والعِشرونَ
٥- الرابعةِ والخَمسينَ
٦- البنتُ التاسِعةُ
٧- الكتابُ الثامِنَ عشرَ
٨- في السنةِ الخامسةِ والعشرين
٩- في عيد الثَورةِ الخامِسِ بعد المئةِ
١٠- على الصفحةِ الثانيةِ والعشرين بعد المئةِ
١١- الطالبُ الأولُ

تمرين ١٤

١- الولايات المتَّحدة الأمريكيّة
٢- سنة ١٩٦٣ في تكساس
٣- أرسطو أوناسيس
٤- مرّتين
٥- فرنسيّ
٦- مدينة نيويورك
٧- خطأ. هي أمريكيّة
٨- صواب
٩- خَطَأ. يونانيّ

**تمرين ١٥**

**المشهد الأول:** ١- كان عبد القادر الجزائريّ أميراً وزعيماً في الجزائر وحارب الفرنسيين.

٢- قال ستيف إن عبد الناصر كان رئيساً لمصر ثمّ رئيساً للجمهوريّة العربيّة المتّحدة.

٣- أسَّسَ ابن خلدون علم الاجتماع.

٤- يتكلّم ستيف اللغة العربيّة جيّداً لأنّه يستخدم العربيّة في كل مكان والناس في سورية يتكلّمون العربيّة فقط الفصحى أو العاميّة.

**المشهد الثاني:** ١- عند أبي سمير عصير موز وحليب وموز وفريز عصير تفّاح وعصير منجا وعصير عنب وكوكتيل فواكه مشكّلة: فريز وموز ومنجا وتفّاح وبرتقال وعنده أيضاً عصير جزر وبردقان أو جزر وتفّاح.

٢- طلب مايكل عصير بردقان وجزر وتفّاح فقط.

٣- ما دفعوا شيئاً لأن الحساب كان على أبي سمير.

## الدرس السابع عشر

**تمرين ١**

١- ما عدا – nothing to do with explaining reason

٢- عَرَب – not related to fasting

٣- الشام – not related to festivities

٤- التهاب – not related to airport

٥- صديق – nothing to do with illness

٦- جالس – not a verb

٧- طالِب – not a paid profession

**تمرين ٢**

١- أخَذ/ أعطى
٢- ألَم / أسبِرين
٣- بَدَأ/ انتهى
٤- عَلِمَ/ نَسيَ
٥- غَنيّ/ فَقير

**تمرين ٤**

١- يَصومُ المُسلِمونَ في شَهْرِ رَمَضان.

٢- هَلْ تَعلَمُ ما اِسمُ عاصِمةِ الأردُن؟

٣- أدرُسُ في المَكتَبةِ كُلَّ يَوم ما عَدا يَومَ الخَميس.

٤- تَنتَهي الدِراسةُ في الجامِعةِ في شَهرِ حَزيران.

٥- وَصَلتُ إلى دارِ السينَما بَعدَ بِدايَةِ الفيلم.

**تمرين ٥**

١- بعد
٢- الجمعة
٣- يصوم
٤- يزور ٥- معايدة
٦- قبل موعده
٧- الثانية
٨- ثلاث موادّ
٩- آب ١٠- أربعة
١١- في موعدها
١٢- مدير مدرسة
١٣- البوابة
١٤- الأدب الأمريكيّ
١٥- مصريّ

**تمرين ٧**

١- لأنَّ يومَ الجمعة عطلة ٢- لأنَّ ضرسه آلمه ٣- زار نيويورك وفلوريدا وكندا

٤- من مكتب الطلاّب الأجانب ٥- لأنّ أباه طبيبٌ.

**تمرين ٨**

١- خطأ. سيرى الطبيب مرّة واحدة ٢- خطأ. لم يرجع إلى سورية بل درس ثلاث موادّ

٣- خطأ. في فلسطين ٤- خطأ. أخت هشام في جامعة بير زيت ٥- من دبي

**تمرين ٩**

١- زاره مايكل براون لأن كان عنده ألم في ضرسه.

٢- أم هشام مدرِّسة علوم. ٣- أبو فؤاد عبد الرحيم ساعي بريد.

٤- أخت خديجة متزوِّجة. ٥- أبو سامر طبيب.

**تمرين ١٠**

١- سامر/ العراق ٢- خديجة/ تونس ٣- هشام/ فلسطين ٤- فؤاد/ مصر

٥- عدنان/ سورية

**تمرين ١٢**

١- أحضَرَ المحتَفِلون بالمُناسَبةِ بعضَ الحَلويات. ٢- وَضَعَت المأكولات المُثَلَّجة على طاوِلةِ المطبخ.

٣- قابله المُستَقبَلون عِندَ البوابة. ٤- أُرجِعَتِ/ أُعيدَتِ الكُتُبُ المُرْسَلة.

٥- كانت تَجرِبتُها في العَمَل مُؤلِمة.

**تمرين ١٣**

١- لَمْ أذْهَب اليَومَ إلى المَدرَسةِ بِسَبَبِ عيدِ الاستِقلال.

٢- لِهذا السَبَبِ ذَهَبتُ أنا وأصدِقائي إلى شاطِئِ البَحْر.

٣- ذَهَبنا إلى الشاطِئِ بِالقِطار.

٤- وَصَلنا إلى الشاطِئِ في الساعةِ العاشِرةِ والنِصْفِ صَباحاً.

٥- سَبَحنا في البَحْرِ ساعَتين.

٦- بَعدَ ذلِكَ أكَلنا الغَداءَ في مَطعَمٍ صَغيرٍ على الشاطِئ.

٧- بَعدَ الظُهرِ سَبَحنا قَليلاً مَرّةً ثانية.

٨- ثُمَّ أخذنا القِطارَ في الساعةِ الرابِعةِ والنِصْفِ ورَجَعنا إلى بُيوتِنا.

**تمرين ١٤**

١- درّاجتان ٢- سائقو ٣- كُلّ ٤- مرّتَينِ

٥- ما عدا ٦- دراسة العربيّة ٧- السيّارات اليابانيّة جيّدة

**تمرين ١٥**

١- اسم فاعل = متأخِّرة، متزوِّجة ٢- اسم مفعول = مكتوب

٣- **المضارع المجزوم** في يوميات مايكل = لَم أَنَمْ، لَم يَرَني، **المضارع المجزوم** في يوميات عدنان مارتيني لَم أرجِعْ، **والمضارع المنصوب** لأستقبلَ

٤- ثاني، رابع، سادس/ الحادي عشر ٥- أرسلتُ = أفعل، اشتريت = افتعل، قال = فعل

٦- قال، صام، وجد، زار ٧- حبتي أسبرين

تمرين ١٦

١- يدرسَ ٢- يَقُلْ ٣- زُرنا ٤- يحتفلوا

٥- يَرى ٦- تَنَمِ

تمرين ١٧

١- أمّ ٢- مدينة ٣- الألم ٤- الإبرة ٥- عصام

٦- مدرِّس رياضيات ٧- إبرة ٨- نادية ٩- خطأ. هي تعمل.

١٠- خطأ. بسبب ألم في بطن ابنتها. ١١- صواب

١٢- خطأ. ستأخذ حبتين كل ستّ ساعات بعد الطعام. ١٣- ثلاثة

١٤- أعطتها أربع حبات أسبرين للأطفال ١٥- إلى عيادة الطبيب ١٦- لا نعرف من النصّ

١٧- صبي boy، بطن abdomen، إبرة = shot ١٨- البحر الأبيض المتوسط = Mediterranean

تمرين ١٨

١- لأنَّها أرادت أن يعرفَ الضيوفُ أنّ بيتَها مفتوحٌ لهم. ٢- لأنّ ضرسه يؤلِمه.

٣- يدرس هاني في المدرسة الثانوية وتدرس هنادي في الجامعة.

٤- تدرس هنادي اللغة الإنكليزيّة. ٥- لأن ليذهبا إلى عيادة طبيب أسنان.

## الدرس الثامن عشر

تمرين ١

١- برّاد/ ثلاّجة ٢- خبز/ عيش ٣- محطّة/ مترو ٤- عيادة/ طبيب

٥- بناية/ شقة ٦- بنك/ مصرف ٧- هاتف/ تليفون ٨- بقّال/ دكّان

تمرين ٢

١- نوع- not a store ٢- مرحاض- not an appliance

٣- هاتف- not a house fixture ٤- شارع- not a location or direction

٥- موقف- not a residence

تمرين ٣

١- اِنتَقَلَ ٢- الهاتف ٣- أمام ٤- الخزانة

٥- مصرف ٦- يميني ٧- استأجر

**تمرين ٤**

١- يريد مايكل شقة قريبة من الجامعة فيها هاتف. ٢- الطابق الثالث ٣- م = متر، ش= شارع
٤- صديقاه سمير عبد الفتاح وحسين أحمد ٥- في باب اللوق
٦- نعم، لأنّها في بناية نظيفة. ٧- صواب
٨- خطأ. استأجر مايكل الشقة من سيّدة كانت تعمل في الكويت.
٩- خطأ. علّق صورة أسرته. ١٠- خطأ. يستعمله كلَّ يوم
١١- خطأ. بشاحنة استأجرها هو وصديقاه. ١٢- خطأ. يعمل بالغاز
١٣- خطأ. في شارع محمَّد فريد. ١٤- خطأ. انتقل في يوم فيه دروس في الجامعة.
١٥- كيف انتقل مايكل إلى شقته الجديدة؟ ١٦- لماذا تعجب سمير شقةُ مايكل الجديدة؟
١٧- أين توجد عيادة طبيب الأسنان ومكتب المحامي؟
١٨- أين تقع مدرسة البنات الابتدائية؟

**تمرين ٦**

١- الثالث ٢- الجريدة ٣- ٧٠٠ ٤- الجلوس
٥- الفطور
٦- المغسلة ٧- مساء ٨- الأوّل ٩- مكتبة
١٠- الخبّاز

**تمرين ٧**

١- يمين/ يسار ٢- فوق/ تحت ٣- أمام/ خلف ٤- واسع/ صغير

**تمرين ٨**

١- هناك مدرسة ابتدائية خلف بيتي. ٢- وضعتُ التلفاز مقابل الأريكة الكبيرة.
٣- ساعدني اثنان من أصدقائي في غسل سيّارتي. ٤- قرأت إعلاناً في جريدة عن شقّةٍ للإيجار.

**تمرين ٩**

١- مَرحباً. أنا مُنى الأسوَد وأعمَلُ مُدَرِّسَةً في وَسَطِ المَدينة. ٢- اِنتَقَلْتُ وعائِلَتي في الشَهرِ الماضي إلى شَقَّةٍ كَبيرة. ٣- تَقعُ شَقَّتي الجَديدة في شارِعٍ بَعيدٍ عَن وَسَطِ المَدينة. ٤- لِذلِكَ أركَبُ الحافِلَةَ كُلَّ يوم إلى المَدرَسة. ٥- تُعجِبُني شَقّتي كَثيراً وتُعجِبُ زَوْجي كَذلِكَ. ٦- لأنَّ فيها غُرفةَ مَكتَبٍ لَهُ وغُرفَةَ طَعامٍ ومَطبَخاً واسِعاً. ٧- زارَنا أمسِ بَعضُ أصدِقائِنا لِيُشاهِدوا الشَقَّةَ الجَديدة. ٨- قالوا إنَّ الشَقّةَ أعجبَتْهُم لأنَّها مُطِلَّةٌ على حَديقَةٍ جَميلة.

**تمرين ١١**

١- الدار في سورية والشقة في الكويت. ٢- خمس غرف
٣- الجنيه في مصر والليرة في سورية والدينار في الكويت.

تمرين ١٢

١- يريد رامي أن يكتب لكلّ أصدقائه. ٢- يحبُّ أصدقائي أن يذهبوا إلى الشاطئ.
٣- تعجب هالة مساعدة أخيها الصغير في دراسته. ٤- تحبُّ أختي أن تنام متأخّرةً. ٥- يعجبني السكن في هذه المدينة. ٦- تحبُّ رانية أن تقرأ قبل النوم. ٧- تريد حنان أن تسافر إلى القاهرة.

تمرين ١٣

١- النسبة: مصريّ، أوروبيّ، كهربائيّ، عربيّ ٢- المصدر: الانتقال، دراسة ٣- مضارع منصوب: أن ينتقلَ، ليساعداه ٤- مضارع مجزوم: لم يذهبوا ٥- اسم تفضيل: أقرب، أكبر

تمرين ١٤

| مِفْعال | مِفْعَلة | فَعّال | فَعّالة | فاعِلة | فاعِل |
|---|---|---|---|---|---|
| مِرحاض | مِسْطرة | بَرّاد | دَرّاجة | حافِلة | حاسِب |
| مِصْباح | | خَلاّط | ثَلاّجة | شاحِنة | هاتِف |
| مِمْحاة | | | جَلاّية | حاسِبة | |

تمرين ١٦

١- في ٢- إلى ٣- على ٤- حتّى
٥- بـ/ في ٦- عن ٧- من/ إلى ٨- مع
٩- بـ ١٠- كـ ١١- بِـ ١٢- لِـ

تمرين ١٧

١- فوق ٢- خلف ٣- دون ٤- بعد
٥- بين ٦- جانب ٧- أمام ٨- مقابل

تمرين ١٩

١- لأن العائلة عندها ثلاثة أطفال وتريد شقة أكبر. ٢- لأنّها مطلّة على الحديقة العامّة.
٣- تقع بين بيت أسرتها وبيت أسرة زوجها. ٤- خطأ. الجديدة أكبر.
٥- خطأ. هي ربّة بيت. ٦- خطأ. سوف تشتري تلفازاً.

تمرين ٢٠

١- ثلاثة أولاد ٢- ثلاث غرف ٣- عمل الزوج ٤- برّاداً
٥- الرابع

تمرين ٢٢

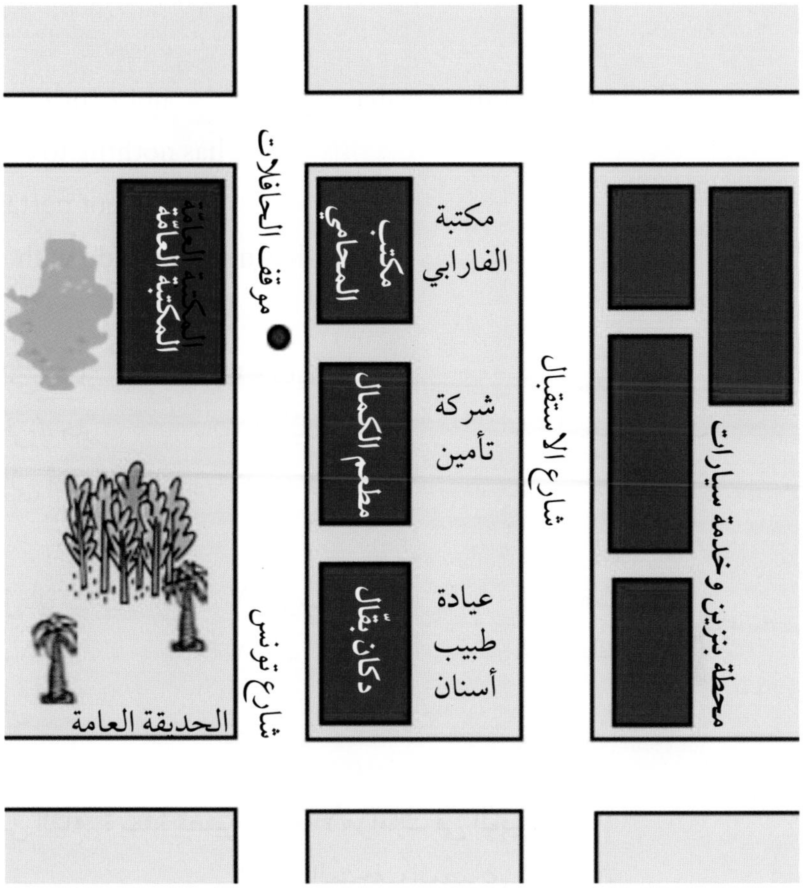


تمرين ٢٣

سامر: تفضّل. هنا أرض الديار ويوجد فيها بحرة وشجرة النارنج وفي الطابق العلوي يوجد غرفة نوم أبي وأمي وتلك غرفة أختي هنادي، وهذه غرفة للضيوف فقط، هذا هو المطبخ يوجد فيه موقد غاز ومايكرويف وبرّاد وثلاّجة وطاولة طعام نجتمع حولها وهو مشترك يستخدمه ستيف أيضاً. وهذه الغرفة هي غرفة الجلوس يوجد فيها أريكة كبيرة والتلفاز وطاولة في وسط الغرفة.

هذه غرفتي وهذه غرفة ستيف تعالَ لأريك إياها هذه غرفة ستيف فيها سرير وخزانة أدراج وفوقها مرآة وبجانبها كرسي من الخشب وطاولة للدراسة وخزانة كبيرة وقرب الغرفة يوجد حمّام خاصّ بستيف يوجد فيه سخّان للماء ودوش ومغسلة مع مرآة.

# الدرس التاسع عشر

**تمرين ١**

١- حديقة – not a means of transportation ٢- مبنى – not a body of water

٣- طيّب – has nothing to do with temperature

٤- استحمّ – does not pertain to enjoyment

٥- محطّة – has nothing to do with school and study

**تمرين ٢**

١- شاهد/ رأى ٢- مشى/ سار ٣- بناية/ مبنى ٤- طريق/ شارع

٥- ساحة/ ميدان ٦- دافئ/ حارّ ٧- طيّب/ جيّد ٨- أعجب/ أحبّ

٩- محلّ تجاريّ/ دكّان ١٠- إلى أنْ/ حتّى

**تمرين ٣**

١- استأجر ٢- قبل أنْ ٣- قُرب ٤- اِلتَقَطتُ

٥- تناولتم ٦- إنّ ٧- لَم ٨- طعاماً

٩- انتهى ١٠- لَنْ

**تمرين ٥**

١- زار الأهرامات بعد وصوله إلى القاهرة بمدة قصيرة وتقع الأهرامات في الجيزة.

٢- السماء الزرقاء ونهر النيل. ٣- من المتحف المصري.

٤- محطة رمسيس ٥- بسبب المناظر الجميلة ولأن الإسكندريانيين طيِّبون.

٦- كتب البطاقة قبل أن ينام. ٧- يوم الأربعاء ٢٨ آب (أغسطس)

٨- في مطعم فرنسيّ مع صديقه غسّان. ٩- يوم الثلاثاء ٣٠ أيلول (سبتمبر)

١٠- سافر لوحدَهُ ١١- في المطعم المراكشيّ

١٢- يدرس في جامعة دمشق.

**تمرين ٦**

١- دراسته ٢- حديقة الحيوانات ٣- ميناء هامّ ٤- طيّبون

٥- الخرطوم ٦- الدراسة انتهت ٧- شقّة صديقه ٨- ٧٨

٩- غالياً ١٠- زيارته للشلاّلات ١١- القارِب ١٢- بالقطار

١٣- الأمريكيّ الغربيّ ١٤- حلب ١٥- كاليفورنيا.

**تمرين ٧**

١- خطأ. من المتحف المصريّ ٢- خطأ. من الخرطوم إلى القاهرة

٣- صواب ٤- خطأ. في فندق صغير ٥- صواب

٦- خطأ. مشى إلى مبنى إمباير ستيت. ٧- خطأ. تظنّ أنّها أجمل على الجانب الكَنديّ.

٨- خطأ. زار أتلاتيك سيتي ليوم واحد. ٩- خطأ. انتقل من حلب إلى دِمَشق.

**تمرين ٨**

١- شلاّلات نياغرا ٢- بطاقة بريدية ٣- آلة تصوير ٤- حديقة حيوانات

٥- عيد الأضحى ٦- تذكرة طائرة ٧- محلّ تجاريّ ٨- مدينة الملاهي

**تمرين ٩**

١- تَستطيعُ أختي أنْ تتكَلَّمَ ثَلاثَ لُغاتٍ جَيِّداً. ٢- يَأخُذُ الناسُ المِصعَدَ إلى الطابَقِ العِشرينَ.

٣- شاهَدْتُ فيلماً في دارِ السينَما واستَمتَعتُ بِهِ. ٤- بُنِيَتْ الأهراماتُ مُنْذُ آلافِ السِنين.

٥- رَكِبْنا القِطارَ مِن مَحَطّةِ رَمسيس إلى الإسكَندَريّةِ. ٦- أرجو أنْ تَسْتَمتِعوا بِزيارتِكُم لِمَدينَتِنا.

٧- التَقَطتُ صورةً لأصدِقائي بِآلَةِ تَصويري الجَديدة.

**تمرين ١٠**

١- أَرَدتُ أنا وعائلَتي زِيارةَ مَدينةِ اللاذِقيّة في عُطلةِ الرَبيع.

٢- واللاذِقيّةُ ميناءُ سورية الأوَّلُ على البَحرِ الأبيضِ المُتَوَسِّط.

٣- عِندي عائلةٌ كَبيرةٌ مِن أربعَةِ أبناءٍ وثَلاثِ بِنات. ٤- لِذلِكَ اسْتَأجَرنا حافِلةً صَغيرةً مَعَ سائِقِها.

٥- جَلَسَ ابني الكَبير إلى جانِبِ السائِق. ٦- وجَلَسْتُ أنا وزَوجَتي خَلفَ السائِق.

٧- سارَتِ الحافِلةُ في الثامِنةِ صَباحاً.

٨- في الطَريقِ إلى اللاذِقيّةِ مَرَرْنا بِمَدينتَيْ حِمصَ وطَرطوس.

٩- وَصَلنا إلى اللاذِقيَّةِ في الثانِيةِ بَعدَ الظُهر. ١٠- ذَهَبنا أوّلاً إلى الفُندُقِ حَيثُ وَضَعنا حَقائِبَنا.

١١- ثُمَّ ذَهَبنا إلى شاطِئِ البَحرِ حَيثُ تَناوَلنا الغَداء. ١٢- بَعدَ الغَداءِ رَكِبنا قارِباً صَغيراً لِساعةٍ أو أكثَر.

١٣- في اليَومِ التالي ذهَبنا إلى الشاطِئِ وسَبَحْنا ١٤- اسْتَمتَعنا كَثيراً بِهذِهِ الزِيارة.

**تمرين ١٢**

١- لَنْ أدرسَ اللغةَ ... ٢- لَنْ تزورَني أمي ...

٣- لَنْ أشاهدَ فيلمَين ... ٤- لَنْ أستَمتِعَ بالسباحةِ ...

**تمرين ١٣**

١- الّتي ٢- اللاّتي ٣- اللّذان ٤- الّذي

٥- اللّذَيْنِ ٦- الّذينَ ٧- اللّتَيْنِ ٨- اللّتانِ

**تمرين ١٤**

١- x ٢- الّذي ٣- ما ٤- الّذينَ

٥- مَن ٦- x ٧- الّتي ٨- اللاّتي

**تمرين ١٦**

١- كذلك ٢- لذلك ٣- مع أنّ ٤- إلى أنْ

٥- لم أتمكّن حتى الآن من زيارة / أن أزور الوادي الكبير.

٦- منظر المدينة جميل من فوق. ٧- هو ليس سعيداً مع أنّه غَنيّ.
٨- درسنا في المكتبة إلى أنْ أراد أصدقائي أن يذهبوا إلى دار السنيما.
٩- أحبّ السفر وتحبُه زوجتي كذلك.

تمرين ١٧

١- غرفة نومي ٢- سيّارة صديقها ٣- أمّ زوجتي ٤- مخطّط بيتهم
٥- محلّ بقّالنا ٦- عطلة نهاية أسبوعي

تمرين ١٨

١- ولدان ٢- في العَقَبة ٣- فَصل الرَبيع ٤- ميناء واحد
٥- بالسيّارة ٦- أربعة ٧- مرّتين ٨- مُعتَدِلاً
٩- غرفتَين ١٠- خطأ. اسم الزوج نَديم
١١- خطأ. نَزَلوا في فندق نخيل ١٢- خطأ. على البحر الأحمر
١٣- خطأ. الفندق على الشاطئ. ١٤- صواب ١٥- see map

تمرين ١٩

١- ذهب ستيف إلى الجامعة باكراً لأن لديه دروس كثيرة. ٢- مايكل سعيد جداً لأنّه تعرّف على أصدقاء يدرسون معه في الجامعة. ٣- ذهب مايكل إلى الجيزة لمشاهدة الأهرامات وهناك ركب على الجمل وتجوّل فيها والتقط صوراً كثيرة للأهرامات ولأبي الهول. ٤- سيذهب سامر ومايكل إلى قهوة النوفرة قرب الجامع الأموي ليدخِّنا الأركيلة هناك ويستمعا إلى الحكواتي.
٥- يحكي الحكواتي حكايات قديمة إلى المستمعين. ٦- عدنان صديق سامر وهو يدرس في جامعة ولاية أوهايو.

## الدرس العشرون

تمرين ١

١- إجّاص/ فاكهة ٢- حصان/ خيل ٣- موعد/ وقت ٤- طابق/ أرضيّ
٥- فليفلة/ خضراء ٦- لحم/ بقر ٨- فول/ سودانيّ ٩- بلاد/ عربيّة

تمرين ٢

١- مصنوع - the only nonverb ٢- شاطئ - not related to games
٣- عصا -not food or drink ٤- تقريباً - not used to express frequency
٥- توت - not a vegetable ٦- شرح - the only verb in the set

تمرين ٣

١- كرة السلّة ٢- مكان واسع للألعاب ٣- شطائر هط ضغ وهامبرغر
٤- في بحيرات كبيرة ٥- يأكلون السميط واللُب ويشربون الشاي والقهوة والمياه الغازية
٦- كرة المضرب وكرة الماء وركوب الدرّاجات وركوب الخيل.

٧- لأنّه كان يمشي إلى كلِّ مكان.　　٨- المنجة لأنّها لذيذة وكبيرة.

**تمرين ٥**

١- خطأ. في الطابق الأرضي حيث توجد شقته.　　٢- صواب　　٣- صواب

٤- خطأ. هي قريبة من بحيرات كبيرة.　　٥- خطأ. في ملعب القاهرة الدوليّ.

٦- خطأ. كان يمشي في شوارع القاهرة.　　٧- خطأ. البطّيخ موجود في مصر.

٨- خطأ. يفضِّل الكشري بسبب التوابل الموجودة في ذلك الطعام.

**تمرين ٦**

١- مَرّتين أو ثلاث مرّات في الشَهر　　٢- كرة الطاولة　　٣- يفهم

٤- هط ضغ　　٥- ألذّ　　٦- المسبح　　٧- المشوي

٨- المساء　　٩- ١٢٠　　١٠- السميط　　١١- أيّ وقت

١٢- الباذِنْجان　　١٣- لَذيذة　　١٤- توابل

**تمرين ٧**

١- أشْتَري　　٢- سكّان　　٣- تُلعَب　　٤- توابل

٥- كرة　　٦- تفهم　　٧- خصوصاً　　٨- شطيرة

٩- المفضَّل　　١٠- فريق　　١١- قواعد　　١٢- مشواة

**تمرين ٨**

١- أحِبُّ بَعْضَ الأطعِمةِ العَرَبيّةِ بِسَبَبِ تَوابِلِها.

٢- كُرةُ القَدَمِ هي اللُعبةُ المُفَضَّلةُ في الوَطَنِ العربيِّ.　٣- يَظُنُّ عدنان أنَّ النَقانِقَ لَذيذةٌ.

٤- تُستَخدَمُ المَشاوي لِشَيِّ اللَحم في الحَدائقِ العامّةِ.

٥- يَستَطيعُ حُسين أنْ يُشاهِد المُبارَيات على تِلفازه الجَديد.

**تمرين ٩**

١- أرَدتُ أنْ أشاهِدَ مُباراةَ كُرةِ القَدَمِ مع أصدِقائي في المَلعَب.

٢- لِذلك اشتَرَيتُ تَذاكِرَ المُباراةِ قَبلَ يومَين.

٣- وَصَلنا أنا وأصدِقائي إلى المَلعَبِ في الساعةِ الثالِثةِ إلاّ رُبعاً.

٤- وكانَ في المَلعَبِ آلافُ المُتَفَرِّجين.

٥- الّذينَ كانوا يأكلونَ الفولَ السودانيَّ ويَشرَبونَ المياهَ الغازية.

٦- بَدأتِ المُباراةُ في الثالِثة والنِصف.

٧- بَقينا في المَلعَبِ ساعتَينِ حَتّى انتهتِ المُباراة.

٨- رَجَعنا إلى بُيوتِنا سُعَداء في الساعةِ السادِسةِ مَساءً.

٩- لأنَّ فَريقَنا فازَ بِالمُباراة.

تمرين ١٢

١- كانت هالة تلعب كرة المضرِب مرّتين في الأسبوع.

٢- رأيتُ عدنان يركب درّاجةً.

٣- صِرتُ أعرف أسماء كل طلاّب صفي.

٤- شاهدنا الفريقين يلعبان مباراة بكرة السلّة.

تمرين ١٤

١- يُحِبّون

٢- أقرأ

٣- يأتي

٤- تَظُنُّ

٥- تأكلين

تمرين ١٥

انسابَتْ (مشت) غيمتان بيضاوان ببطء في السماء الزرقاء. جلستُ على الشاطئ الأبيض أشاهدهما فوق الماء الأزرق والقوارب البيضاء. كان هناك بنت تلبس قميصاً أحمر وبنطلوناً قصيراً أبيض اللون وكانت تشاهد لعبة الكرة الطائرة في حديقة صغيرة بجانب الشاطئ. كان لها عينان خضراوان وشعر أسود. جاءت أمها وكانت تلبس بنطلوناً قصيراً أخضر اللون وقميصاً أبيض لتأخذ بنتها إلى غرفتهما في الفندق الموجود مقابل الحديقة العامة. كان يلبس أحَدُ الفريقين قمصاناً صفراءَ والآخرُ كان يلبس قمصاناً خضراء. على ما يبدو كان الفريق الأخضر فائزاً ولكنَّ كلَّ الناسِ كانوا سعداء.

تمرين ١٦

١- أصغر

٢- ألذّ

٣- أجمل

٤- أقَلّ

٥- أجَدّ

تمرين ١٧

١- لَمْ أبْقَ

٢- لِمْ يَمْشِ

٣- لَمْ تَفْهَمْ

٤- لَمْ أنْسَ

٥- لَمْ يَسْكُنوا

تمرين ١٨

١- في دار صديقه سُهَيل.

٢- لأنّ فريقَه لَم يَفُزْ.

٣- أمّ سُهَيل

٤- خطأ. حضّر سُهَيل الشاي، لكنَّ أمَّه حضّرت الحِمَّص

٥- صواب

٦- صواب

٧- سَبْعةُ

٨- الفليفلة

٩- فريقهم

١٠- كُلّ

١١- بيت صديقه

١٢- بعد

تمرين ١٩

١- زار تمثال الحريّة وأتلانتك سيتي وشلاّلات ناياغرا وديزني ورلد وكندا كذلك.

٢- فلم يعُد لدى عدنان الوقت الكافي ليلعبها.

٣- الرياضتان اللّتان يقوم بهما عدنان في مَدينَتِهِ هما السباحة وكرة الطاولة.

٤- في رأي عدنان أجمل شيء في مَدينَتِهِ هو الحدائق فهي واسعة ونظيفة وفيها أماكن للعب والشواء.

٥- سيذهب سامر ومايكل لزيارة سوق الحميدية والجامع الأموي وقهوة النوفرة.

# الدرس الحادي والعشرون

### تمرين ١

| | | | |
|---|---|---|---|
| ١- واسع/ ضيّق | ٢- كبير/ صغير | ٣- طويل/ قصير | ٤- غنيّ/ فقير |
| ٥- بعيد/ قريب | ٦- كثير/ قليل | ٧- نبع/ صبّ | ٨- فوق/ تحت |

### تمرين ٢

| | | | |
|---|---|---|---|
| ١- عَلَم/ شعار | ٢- بلد/ قُطْر | ٣- جزيرة/ بحر | ٤- سفينة/ ميناء |
| ٥- صناعة/ زراعة | ٦- نفط/ غاز | | |

### تمرين ٣

١- وطن – not a body of water

٢- صناعة – not a geographical feature

٣- نَسَمة – not a product

٤- ذرة – not a geographical direction

٥- سُكّان – not related to the sea

### تمرين ٤

| | | | |
|---|---|---|---|
| ١- جزيرة | ٢- تتألّف | ٣- إلاّ | ٤- عديدة |
| ٥- نجمة | ٦- يحُدّ | ٧- منتجات | ٨- بضائع |

### تمرين ٥

١- ليبيا

٢- سورية

٣- البحر الأحمر

٤- المحيط الهادي

٥- تركيا

٦- القطن والحبوب والفواكه والخضار والنفط

٧- خمس ولايات

٨- نعم، إنتاج أوهايو الصناعيّ كبير فهي تأتي بعد ولايتي نيويورك وكاليفورنيا.

### تمرين ٦

١- خطأ. البحرين في الخليج العربيّ

٢- خطأ. ألاسكا أكبر الولايات الأمريكية بالمساحة.

٣- خطأ. ينبع نهر العاصي من لبنان ويسير في سورية ثمّ يصبّ في البحر المتوسّط.

٤- خطأ. كليفلند ميناء هامّ.

### تمرين ٧

١- كم قطراً عربيّاً يطلّ على بحر العرب؟

٢- ما البَلَدانِ اللّذان يحدّان الوطن العربيّ من الشمال والشرق؟

٣- ماذا يحدّ الولايات المتَّحدة من الجنوب؟

٤- ما ميناءُ سورية النفطيّ؟

٥- ما عدد سكان أوهايو؟

**تمرين ٨**

١- ٩ ٢- البحر الأحمر ٣- البحرين ٤- أمريكا الشماليّة

٥- رود آيلاند ٦- دمشق ٧- كلّ ما سبق ٨- على ساحل

٩- ميشِغن ١٠- الحدود الحنوبيّة الشرقيّة والجنوبيّة ١١- سنسناتي

١٢- جبال

**تمرين ٩**

١- تَقَعُ مِلبورن على ساحِلِ أستراليا الجَنوبيّ. ٢- لِلعِراقِ مَنفَذٌ ضَيِّقٌ على الخَليجِ العَرَبيّ.

٣- بِلادُ الشام واحِدَةٌ مِنَ الأقاليم الجُغرافيّةِ في الوَطَنِ العَرَبِيِّ.

٤- تُنتِجُ الجَزائِرُ النِفطَ والمَنتوجاتِ الزِراعيّةَ.

**تمرين ١٠**

١-

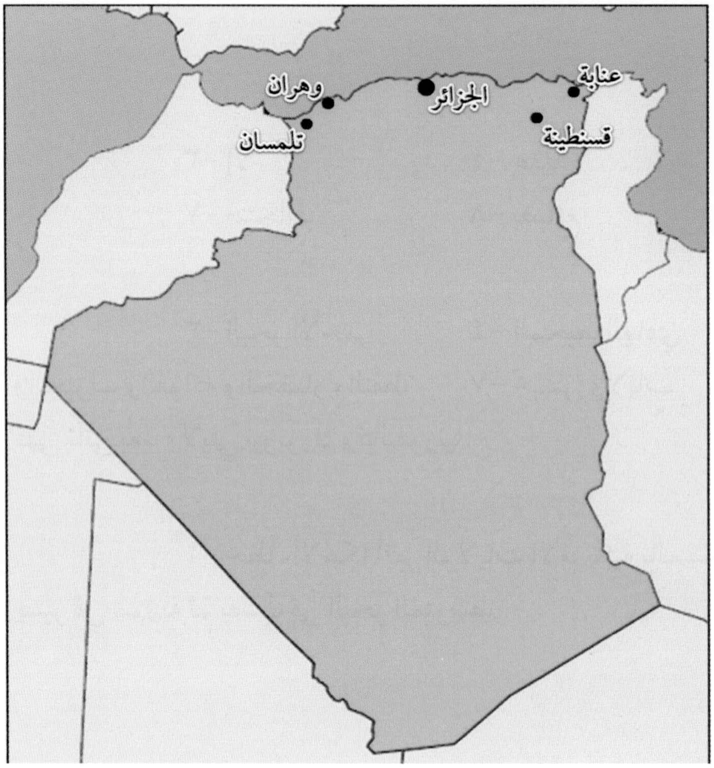


٢- ٣٣ مليون نسمة تقريباً ٣- صناعة النفط والسيّارات

٤- أراضٍ صحراوية

**تمرين ١٢**

يحدُّ العراق من الشمال تركيّا ومن الشرق إيران ومن الجنوب الشرقيّ الكويت ومن الجنوب المملكة العربيّة السعوديّة ومن الغرب سورية والأردن. عاصمة العراق بغداد وتقع في وسط البلاد. يدخل نهر دجلة العراق من الشمال ويسير جنوباً ويمرُّ ببغداد والبصرة ويصبّ في شَطِّ العرب. ينبع نهر الزاب من شمال شرق العراق ويسير نحو الجنوب ليصبَّ في دجلة جنوب بغداد. أمّا نهر الفرات فيدخل العراق من سورية

من الغرب ويسير إلى الجنوب الشرقي ويصبّ في شطِّ العرب عند البصرة. تقع بحيرة الحَمّار غرب البصرة. الرمادي مدينة على الفرات في غرب العراق، والموصل على دجلة في شماله. أمّا كركوك فهي في الشمال الشرقيّ. يوجد النفط في شمال شرق العراق وفي جنوبه. هناك زراعة الحبوب في جنوب العراق بين نهري دجلة والفرات، ويوجد كذلك التمر قرب البصرة.

تمرين ١٥

١- اللغتان العربيّة والعبريّة ساميتان وكلتاهما مكتوبتان من اليمين إلى اليسار.

٢- كلتا أختيه تدرسان الطبّ في هذه الجامعة.

٣- قرأتُ كلتا رسالتيه. ٤- يوجد هاتف في كلا البيتين.

تمرين ١٧

١-

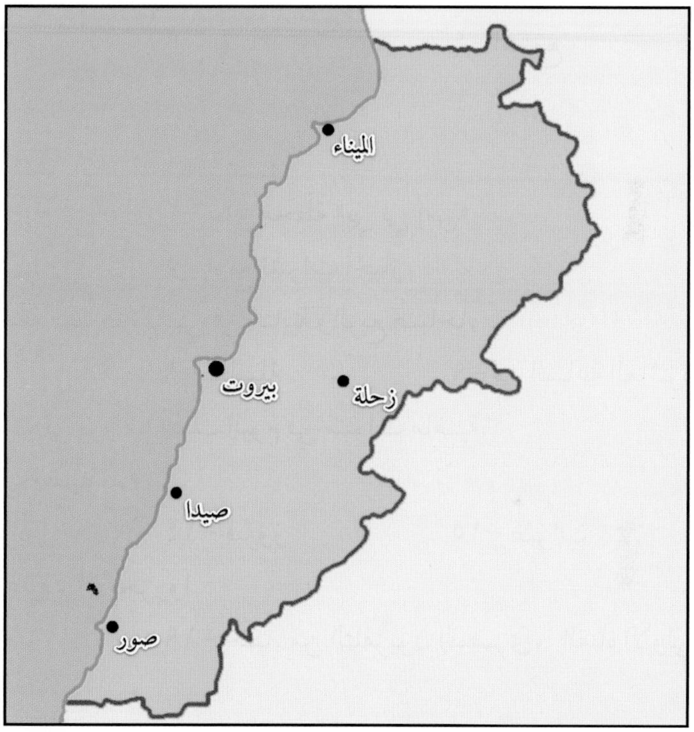


٢- بسبب المَصارِف والشركات التجارية العديدة الموجودة فيها.

٣- الحبوب والزيتون والبرتقال والخضار ٤- الجبال أكثر.

تمرين ١٨

١- سوق الحميدية من أقدم الأسواق في دمشق يوجد فيها محلات كثيرة وهي مغطاة بسقف.

٢- بعض الناس يقولون إن هناك ثُقوباً في السقف كي يدخل الضوء إلى السوق ويقال أيضاً إنها بسبب إطلاق الرصاص أثناء الثورة السورية ضد الفرنسيين.

٣- تقع مدينة اللاذقية على الساحل السوريّ ومدينة طرطوس أيضاً.

٤- زار سامر اللاذقية وطرطوس وحلب ودير الزور.

# الدرس الثاني والعشرون

**تمرين ١**

١- لغة – ليست برنامج ٢- مَجّاني – has nothing to do with programming

٣- عودة – has nothing to do with music ٤- تِجارة – has nothing to do with nature

٥- طفل – has nothing to do with broadcasting

**تمرين ٢**

١- إذاعة/ بثّ ٢- قناة/ موجة ٣- إعلانات/ تجارة ٤- توفّي/ مات

٥- مغنٍّ/ أغنية ٦- جيِّد/ ممتاز ٧- فصيحة/ عاميّة ٨- معظم/ أكثر

**تمرين ٣**

١- القناة ٢- مذيعة ٣- مقابلة ٤- أستمع

٥- متزوِّجة

**تمرين ٤**

١- الاستماع إلى الإذاعة العامّة «إن پي آر» ٢- على محطّة «پي بي إس»

٣-فَوازير رَمَضان ٤- عَمرو دياب ٥- أربع نشرات أخبار

٦- تبدأ في الخامسة وسبع وعشرين دقيقة صباحاً وتنتهي في الثانية والربع صباحاً.

٧- اسم برنامج المرأة «مَرايا». ٨- سلسلة ٩- في الساعة العاشرة

١٠- الأخبار وبرنامج يقدِّم أخباراً وقعت في يوم مثل ذلك اليوم في سَنَوات ماضية.

١١- وردة الجزائريّة ١٢- مسلسل «ساينفِلد»

١٣- مسلسلات إذاعيّة وتلفزيونيّة مصريّة ١٤- فيروز ١٥- صواب

١٦- صواب ١٧- خطأ. عليهم أن يحزروا.

١٨- خطأ. توفّيَت أم كلثوم عام ١٩٧٥. ١٩- خطأ. من التلفزيون المصريّ، القناة الأولى

٢٠- صواب.

**تمرين ٥**

١- اسمه «كيبل» ويحصل عليه الناس مقابل اشتراك شهريّ.

٢- تُستعمَل العربيّة الفصيحة في الأخبار والمقابلات والبرامج العلميّة.

٣- برنامج يُبَثُّ في رمضان تصف فيه الممثّلة شيئاً بالرقص وعلى الناس أن يحزروا هذا الشيء.

٤- ابن فيروز

٥- اسم برنامج من الإذاعة السوريّة يُبَثُّ في الساعة الثانية عَشْرة والنصف صباحاً.

٦- اسم برنامج يبثّه تلفزيون لبنان.

**تمرين ٧**

١- صباحاً ومساءً ٢- سريعة ٣- خِلال ٤- عامّة

٥- مجّانيّ ٦- أمّ كلثوم ٧- كارِنغي ٨- سبع
٩- القَمَر الصِناعيّ العربيّ

**تمرين ٨**

١- إن بي سي، سي بي إس، آي بي سي، فوكس، ديسكفري ٢- ساينفلد، فريجر، فريندز
٣- صباح الخير يا أمريكا، أخبار، ٢٠ دقيقة، فَوازير رَمَضان
٤- موجة، بَرامج، مُسَلَسَلات، أخبار، أغانٍ، مُقابلات ٥- غلوريا إستفان، مادونا، ستيفي وَندَر، فيروز، صباح فَخري، وديع الصافي، راغب علامة، فَريد الأطرش، نيللي، أمّ كلثوم، عبد الحَليم حافظ، محمّد عبد الوَهّاب، فائزة أحمَد، وَردة الجَزائريّة، مَيادة حِنّاوي، عَمرو دياب، زياد رَحَباني ٦- عاميّة، فَصيحة

**تمرين ٩**

١- أستَمِعُ إلى أغانيَّ المُفَضَّلة مِن المُسَجِّلة. ٢- تَبدَأ إذاعةُ دِمَشقَ بَثَّها في الساعةِ الخامِسة صَباحاً.
٣- تَعمَلُ أختُ صَديقي مُذيعةً في إذاعةِ مَحطّةِ حَلَب.

**تمرين ١٠**

١- أوَّلُ شَيءٍ أفعَلُهُ صَباحاً هو الذَهاب إلى الحَمّام.
٢- بَعدَ ذلِكَ أجلِسُ أمامَ التِلفاز وأشاهِدُ الأخبارَ خِلالَ تَناوُلِ الفَطور.
٣- في الساعةِ الثامِنةِ صَباحاً أذهَبُ إلى عَمَلي.
٤- خِلالَ العَمَلِ استَمِعُ إلى الإذاعة.
٥- حينَ أعودُ إلى البَيتِ بَعدَ الظُهرِ أشاهِدُ مُسلسَلي المُفَضَّل.
٦- بَعدَ مُشاهَدةِ مُسَلسَلي المُفَضَّل أنامُ نِصفَ ساعةٍ فَقَط.
٧- في المَساءِ أشاهِدُ أنا وزَوجي فيلماً مِن التِلفاز أو مِن شَريط مُسَجَّل.

**تمرين ١١**

ماذا علينا أن نفعل اليوم؟ عليَّ أن أشرب فنجان قهوة بعد أن أنهض في الصباح. كذلك، على أبي أن يقرأ الجريدة وهو يأكل الفطور. بعد ذلك عليه الذهاب إلى العمل، وعليّ الذهاب إلى المدرسة. كان عليّ أن أكتب واجباتي البيتية ليلة أمس قبل أن أنام، ولكنّني لم أنتهِ منها لذلك عليّ أن أكتبها قبل وصولي إلى المدرسة. عليّ أن أصل إلى المدرسة باكِراً اليوم لأتكلّم مع سامي عن مباراتنا بكرة القدم الأمريكيّة. علينا أن نصل إلى الملعب في الساعة السابعة مساءً لمباراتنا الكبيرة. وبعد اللعبة، قال لي سامي إن عليه مشاهدة برنامجه المفضَّل على التلفاز، وقد أشاهده معه، ولكن ليس بالضرورة.

تمرين ١٣

١- اكتب بالعربيةِ ما سمعتَ في نشرةِ الأخبار. ٢- يعجبني ما أرى. ٣- هي سعيدةٌ بِما عِندها.

٤- يمكنك أنْ تشتريَ هذه الكتب العربيّة بما معك من دولاراتٍ أمريكيّة.

تمرين ١٤

١- بعد أن ٢- بعد أن ٣- قبل أن ٤- بعد

٥- بعد ٦- بعد أن ٧- قبل

تمرين ١٥

١- قرأتُ بِضعَ جَرائد في الطائرة. ٢- قضَيْتُ بضعةَ أسابيعَ في بيروت.

٣- اشترَتْ صديقتي بضعةَ كُتُبٍ عربيةٍ عن الوطن العربي حين كانت في تونس.

٤- نزلتُ في فندقٍ بضعةَ أيّامٍ.

تمرين ١٦

١- صواب ٢- خطأ. هو سوريّ لكنّه صُوِّرَ في دولةِ الإمارات.

٣- لأنّهُ بالعربيّة الفَصيحة ٤- على التِلفاز من المحطّات الفضائيّة.

٥- الصحراء ٦- التاسعةَ مساءً ٧- العربيّة الفَصيحة ٨- دمشق وعمّان

٩- تاريخيّاً ١٠- وهي بالعاميّة السوريّة والمصريّة.

تمرين ١٧

١- الناس في مصر يحبّون الاستماع إلى أمّ كلثوم وعبد الحليم حافظ وفايزة أحمد.

٢- مايكل: من هو مطربك العربيّ المفضَّل أو مطربتك العربية المفضَّلة ستيف؟ ستيف: أنا أحبُّ فيروز جدّاً وأستمع إليها كلَّ يوم في الصباح وأحبُّ أيضاً ماجدة الرومي. مايكل: وأنت سامر؟ سامر: طبعاً أكيد فيروز وأحبُّ الاستماع إلى عبد الحليم حافظ. مايكل: وأنت عدنان؟ عدنان: طبعاً فيروز وأحبُّ أن أستمع أيضاً إلى وديع الصافي ومحمَّد عبده وصباح فخري وراغب علامة وعمرو دياب فأنا عندي أشرطة لهم. سامر: وأنت مايكل من هو مطربك العربيّ المفضَّل أو مطربتك العربيّة المفضَّلة؟ مايكل: أنا بصراحة أحبُّ أن أسمع فيروز كثيراً وأحبُّ أن أسمع عمرو دياب وراغب علامة. ستيف: ومن هو مطربك الغربيّ المفضَّل عدنان؟

٣- يشاهد التلفاز ويستمع إلى الإذاعة.

## الدرس الثالث والعشرون

تمرين ١

١- عاصِمة – not related to journalism ٢- مَصرِف – not related to families

٣- حَلوى – not a means of transportation ٤- نام – not related to travel

تمرين ٢

١- صحيفة/ جريدة ٢- شريط/ مسجّلة ٣- لاعِب/ رياضة

٤- تأشيرة دخول/ جواز سفر ٥- عائلة/ أسرة ٦- مطعم/ نادل
٧- نقود/ مصرف ٨- دار/ منزل

**تمرين ٣**

١- بالطائرة ٢- نادلة ٣- الأجانب ٤- بيرة «كورز»
٥- يرتفع ميلاً عن سطح البحر ٦- صواب ٧- خطأ. أربعة أشخاص
٨- خطأ. يدرس العلوم السياسيّة ٩- صواب ١٠- السيّدة آلن
١١- صحافياً ١٢- حضر مباراة كرة قدم ١٣- في دمشق

**تمرين ٤**

١- جنيه/ ليرة ٢- مقعد/ كرسيّ ٣- قرية/ بلدة ٤- اعتقد/ ظنّ
٥- مثل/ عكس ٦- قريب/ أسرة ٧- ملوّث/ نقيّ ٨- غادر/ وصل
٩- سيّارة/ أجرة

**تمرين٥**

١- تَستَضيفُ عائلةُ آلَن الطُلاّبَ الأجانِبَ. ٢- اشترَيتُ تَذكِرةَ القِطار بِأَربَعةَ عَشَرَ جُنَيهاً.
٣- شَوارِعُ القاهِرةِ مُزدَحِمةٌ بِالناسِ وهَواؤُها مُلَوَّث. ٤- زارَتْ لالينيا مَدينةَ المِنيا في العيدِ.

**تمرين ٦**

١- رحلتها إلى المنيا ٢- العجوزة ٣- مُزدحمة
٤- على الجانب الآخر من النيل ٥- ثلاث ساعات ونصف ٦- الخليفة الرابع

**تمرين ٧**

١- خطأ. لأنّ الناس رُبَّما تَعَوَّدوا على التدافُع ٢- خطأ. أمريكيّة ٣- صواب
٤- خطأ. إلى جانب شاب مصريّ ٥- خطأ. من الشاب في القطار ٦- صواب

**تمرين ٩**

١- عطلةالربيع، عيدالفِطر، لَعِبَ، تَنَزَّهَ، حَلوى، كعكالعيد، برامجتلفزيونخاصّة، زياراتللأقارب
٢- نقيّ، ملّوّث، هادئ، مزدحم ٣- طائرة، سيّارة، سيّارة أجرة، قطار
٤- شجرة، مزرعة، فلاّح، موز

**تمرين ١٠**

١- أرادَ برِتْ آدَمز أنْ يَزورَ المَغرِب.
٢- أوّلاً كانَ علَيهِ أنْ يَحصُلَ على تأشيرةِ دُخول.
٣- لِذلِكَ أرسَلَ جَوازَ سَفَرِه إلى السِفارةِ المَغربيّةِ بواشِنطَن.
٤- ثانياً اشتَرى تَذكِرةَ طائِرةٍ على الخُطوطِ المَلَكيّةِ المَغربيّة.
٥- في يَوم السَفَرِ أخَذَتْهُ أُمُّهُ إلى المَطارِ بِسَيّارتِها.
٦- كانَتِ الرِحلةُ طَويلةً واستَغرَقَت ١٥ ساعةً تَقريباً.

٧- فَقَد وَصَلَ إلى مَطارِ الدارِ البَيضاء في اليَوم التالي.
٨- رِكِبَ برِتْ سَيّارةَ أجرةٍ مِن المَطارِ إلى الفُندُق.
٩- وحَصَلَ في الفُندُقِ على غُرفةٍ بِسَريرٍ واحِدٍ مع حَمّام بداخِلِها.
١٠- اتَّصَلَ بِأمِّهِ بالهاتِفِ مِن الفُندُقِ وأخبرَها بِوصولِه إلى المَغرب.

تمرين ١١

١- قد يسافرون إلى دمشق بالطائرة.
٢- رأيتُ بيتَها وقد أعجبني كثيراً.
٣- حين وصلنا إلى بيت أصدقائنا كانوا قد تناولوا العشاء.

تمرين ١٢

١- دَفَعتُ لِلسائِقِ ثَلاثةَ جُنَيهاتٍ أجرةَ السَيّارةِ.
٢- زُرنا القاهِرةَ أكبَرَ مُدُنِ إفريقيا.
٣- وَصَلنا صَباحاً إلى الرِباط عاصِمةِ المَغرِب.
٤- سَكَنَتْ لَيلى في "بيز ووتر" حَيِّ العَرَبِ في لَندَن.

تمرين ١٤

١- إلى مصر
٢- ثلاثة أيّام
٣- لا، لأنّها مشغولة وليس عندها وقت وموعد الرحلة قريب.
٤- خطأ. في القاهرة.
٥- خطأ. يومان
٦- خطأ. بالقطار
٧- خطأ. لن تسافرَ لأنّها مشغولة.
٨- المتحف المصريّ
٩- قرب القاهرة
١٠- جامعيّة
١١- وقت
١٢- في الطريق إلى الأقصر

تمرين ١٥

١- في رأي عدنان أمريكا كبيرة جداً والحياة فيها ممتعة ولقد أصبح لديه أصدقاء هناك.
٢- عرّف هشام صديقه عدنان على المدينة وعلى الجامعة وساعده كثيراً.
٣- أحبّ مايكل الشام لأنها جميلة جداً وهي مدينة قديمة ولقد أخذه سامر إلى أماكن جميلة وإلى الجامع الأموي والأسواق القديمة.
٤- الاختلاف هو أنّ ستيف يعيش الآن التجربة بنفسه واقترب من الناس وتعرّف عليهم فأصبح يفهم كيف يفكّرون.

## الدرس الرابع والعشرون

تمرين ١

١- كُبرى/ صُغرى
٢- التقط/ صوّر
٣- يمين/ يسار
٤- سفينة/ بَحر
٥- محلّ تجاريّ/ دكّان
٦- بَنون/ بنات
٧- ليل/ نهار

تمرين ٢

١- يَدرُسُ مَروانُ بَحَلَب في مَدرسَةٍ ثانوِيَّةٍ لِلبَنين.
٢- عِندَ أبي عَدنان مَحَلٌّ واسِعٌ لِبَيعِ قِطَعِ غِيارِ السَيّاراتِ.
٣- تَقاعَدَتْ أُمُّ عَدنان عَن عَمَلِها كَيْ تَعتَنيَ بِعائِلَتِها.

٤- يعمَلُ ثَلاثَةُ عُمّالٍ وبائِعان ومُحاسِبٌ في مَحَلِّ ياسِر مارتيني.

**تمرين ٣**

١- دَرَسَتْ هالة الصيدَلة في جامِعَةِ دِمشق.
٢- وتَخرَّجَتْ مِنَ الجامِعةِ في العام ٢٠٠٢.
٣- بَعدَ تَخَرُّجِها عَمِلَت صَيدلانِيّةً في مَشفى في مَدينةِ الكُوَيت.
٤- تَعَرَّفَتْ في المُستَشفى على زَوجِها مازِن الَّذي كانَ يَعمَلُ طَبيباً.
٥- صارَ لِهالة ومازِن بِنتان ووَلَدان.
٦- حينَ صارَ أولادُهُما في سِنِّ المَدرَسة انتَقَلا إلى دِمشق.
٧- اشتَرَيا داراً كَبيرةً في دِمشق مُؤَلَّفةً مِن ثَلاثةِ طوابق.
٨- في الطابَقِ الأرضِيِّ مَحَلٌّ تِجاريٌّ واسِعٌ فَتَحَتْهُ هالة صَيْدَليّة.
٩- والطابَقُ الأوَّل صارَ عِيادَةً لمازِن.
١٠- أمّا الطابَقُ الثاني فَسَكنوا فيه.

**تمرين ٤**

١- استيراد – not related to photographs
٢- عَمّ – not related to age
٣- رِسالة – not a school subject
٤- مُدَرِّس – not related to business
٥- أيّ – not used to express reason
٦- جواز سَفَر – not related to personnel

**تمرين ٧**

١- في الصفّ العاشر
٢- أماني
٣- إلى جانب أمينة
٤- من ألمانيا
٥- ستّة موظَّفين
٦- ليشتريَ بضاعتَه
٧- مُدَرِّسة لغة فرنسية
٨- تقاعدتْ منذ ثماني سنوات لتعتنيَ بوالدتها وبمنزلِها وعائلتِها.
٩- في ٧ كانون الثاني.
١٠- هي جدّة عدنان.
١١- خطأ. تذهب إلى مدرسة ثانوية للإناث.
١٢- خطأ. عدنان يدرس علم الحاسوب.
١٣- صواب
١٤- خطأ. أحياناً
١٥- خطأ. زارتها مرّةً
١٦- خطأ. عمُّه تقاعد
١٧- محلّ تِجاريّ
١٨- ألمانيا
١٩- حلب
٢٠- سيّارة ألمانية
٢١- الشاحنات
٢٢- ربّة بيت
٢٣- خال
٢٤- الهولندية

**تمرين ٨**

١- وزارة
الداخلية، هجرة، صدر، مفعول، تسجيل، شهرة، إقامة، ولادة، مهنة، شَعر، توقيع، طول، لون
٢- والد، والدة، أب، أم، أخ، أخت، عَمّ، خال، جَدّ، جَدّة
٣- استيراد، بيع، مُحاسِب، بائع، عامِل، محلّ تِجاريّ
٤- ثانويّة، ابتدائيّة، صفّ، مُدَرِّس، طالِب، إناث، بَنين
٥- مُدَرِّس، تاجِر، رَبّة بَيت، سائق، مُتَقاعِد

٦- الجمهوريّة العربيّة السوريّة، الولايات المتَّحدة الأمريكيّة، ألمانيا، لبنان، الأردنّ

**تمرين ١١**

١- يَسْكُنا ٢- يأتوا ٣- تشربَ ٤- أدرسَ

٥- يعتنيَ ٦- نأكلَ

**تمرين ١٢**

| | | |
|---|---|---|
| ١- يُريدُ أحمَد بَيْعَ سَيّارته القَديمةِ لِيَشتَريَ سَيّارةً جَديدة. | **الجذر:** بيع | object of verb |
| ٢- لَم أرَ أختي مُنذُ كِتابةِ هذِه الكلِمات. | كتب | object of prep |
| ٣- أعرِفُ اللُغةَ الألمانِيةَ لكِنْ لا يُمكِنُني التكلُّمُ بِها. | كلم | subject of verb |
| ٤- سَوفَ أعمَلُ في شَرِكةٍ تِجاريّةٍ بَعدَ تَخرُّجي. | خرج | object of prep |
| ٥- اسْتِضافَتُكُم في بَيتي تَسُرّني جِدّاً. | ضيف | subject |
| ٦- يُعجِبُني التَنزُّهُ على شاطِئِ البَحر. | نزه | subject |

**تمرين ١٣**

١- المرأة ٢- لُؤي ٣- تَوْأم ٤- مَوْئِل

٥- آباء ٦- يجيئون

**تمرين ١٤**

١- مَرؤوس ٢- مُؤامَرة ٣- جاءَ ٤- حائِل

٥- فَأْس ٦- رِئة ٧- أَثر ٨- بَذيء

٩- مساءً ١٠- ذِئْب ١١- وَطْئاً ١٢- نائي

١٣- سائِل ١٤- دوائي ١٥- يبوؤون ١٦- دؤوب

**تمرين ١٥**

١- في دمشق ٢- عمّ الفَتاة ٣- خطأ. أخوها يدرس الهندسة الكهربائيّة.

٤- صواب ٥- أمريكيّة ٦- ثلاث تذاكر

٧- تريد الفتاةُ أن ترى أخاها والولايات المتّحدة الأمريكيّة كذلك ٨- أسبوعين

**تمرين ١٦**

١- عند أبي عدنان محلّ تجاريّ في حلب حيث يبيع فيه قطع غيار لبعض السيّارات الألمانيّة.

٢- تقاعدت أمّ عدنان عن العمل كي تعتني بوالدتها المريضة وبعائلتها.

٣- أمّ عدنان ستزوره في الصيف المقبل في شهر آب.

٤- لن يستطيع أبو عدنان أن يأتي معها لأنه لديه عمل ويجب أن يسافر إلى ألمانيا.

# Appendix E

## Texts of Postcards and Letters from Lessons 19 and 24

### ١ – بِطاقةُ مايكِل براون إلى أُستاذَتِه

الأستاذة زَيْنَب طَه

مَرْكِزُ دِراسةِ اللُغَة العَرَبيَّة

الجامِعةُ الأمريكيَّةُ بِالقاهِرة

القاهِرة

جُمهورِيَّةُ مِصْرَ العَرَبيَّة

الإِسْكَندَرِيَّة ١٩/ ٩/ ٢٠٠٨

أُسْتاذَتي الكَريمة زَيْنَب.

سَلامٌ مِنَ الإسكَندَرِيّة. وَصَلتُ وأصْدقائي بَعْدَ ظُهْرِ اليَوم وأكَلْنا في مَطْعَمٍ جَيِّدٍ ومَشَيْنا عَلى الكورنَيْش وَسَبَحنا في البَحرِ. أكتُبُ لَكِ مِنَ الفُندُق قَبْلَ أنْ أنامَ. أرجو لَكِ عُطلَةً سَعيدة.

مايكِل

٢- بِطاقةُ عَدنان مارتيني إلى أسرَتِه:

| | |
|---|---|
| أورلاندو ٨/ ٩/ ٠٨<br><br>أعزّائي الغالين، السلامُ عَلَيكُم<br>أكتُبُ لَكُم مِن أورلاندو. وَصَلتُ إلى هُنا<br>مُنْذُ ثَلاثَةِ أيّام لِزيارَةِ ديزني وُرلد.<br>أنزِلُ هُنا في فُندُق رامادا. ديزني<br>مَدينَةُ مَلاهٍ عَظيمة شاهَدْتُ فيها إبكَتْ<br>سِنتَر وأعجَبَني كَثيراً. تَناوَلْتُ طَعاماً<br>مَغرِبيّاً في المَطعَمِ المُراكِشيِّ وتَكَلَّمتُ<br>العَرَبيَّةَ مَعَهُم. استَمْتَعْتُ بِهذِهِ الرِحْلة.<br><br>عَدنان | السيِّد ياسِر مارتيني المُحْتَرَم<br>١١٥ شارِع البُحتُري، طابَق ٣<br>حَلَب، الجَمْهوريّة العَرَبيّة<br>السوريّة |

## ٣- رِسالَةُ عَدنان إلى صَديقِهِ مازِن (الدرس ١٩):

كَلمبَس في ٢١ أيلول ٢٠٠٨

أخي العَزيز مازِن، سَلامٌ حارٌ لَكَ مِن كَلمبَس.

كَيفَ حالُكَ يا أخي؟ لم تَصلْني مِنكَ أيّةُ رِسالةٍ مُنذُ مُدّةٍ طويلةٍ كَتَبتُ لَكَ رِسالةً في شَهرِ آذارَ الماضي ولَم يَصِلْني مِنكَ أيُّ شَيء، لِذلِكَ ظَنَنْتُ أنَّكَ انتَقَلتَ مِن عُنوانِكَ القَديم في حَلَب. عَلِمتُ مِن مَروان بَعدَ ذلِكَ أنَّكَ انْتَقَلْتَ إلى جامِعَةِ دِمَشق، وَهُوَ الّذي أعْطاني عُنْوانَكَ الجَديد. هَل يُعجِبُكَ السَكَنُ و الدِراسَةُ في دِمَشقَ؟

أنا كَما تَعْلَم أدرُسُ عِلمَ الحاسوبِ في جامِعَةِ وِلايَةِ أوهايو. بَعدَ أيّام سَيَبدَأُ العامُ الدراسِيُّ الجَديد، وهذِهِ هِيَ سَنَتي الثانِيَةُ هُنا. أنا سَعيدٌ في كَلَمبَس وأسْتَمْتِعُ بِالسَكَنِ فيها وبِالدِراسَةِ كَذلِك.

في الأسابيعِ الثلاثةِ الماضِيَةِ زُرتُ مَدينةَ نيويورك وأتلانتِك سيتي وشلّالاتِ نَياغَرا في كَندا وكذلِكَ «ديزني ورلد» وهِيَ مَدينَةُ مَلاهٍ كَبيرةٌ جِدّاً في مَدينةِ أورلاندو في فلوريدا. اِستَمتَعتُ بِهذِهِ الزِياراتِ كَثيراً. أرجو أنْ أزورَ وِلايَةَ كاليفونيا في السَنَةِ المُقبلَةِ إنْ شاءَ الله، و«لاس فيغاس» أيْضاً.

أرجو أنْ تَكتُبَ لي عَنكَ وعَن دِراسَتِك. لَكَ مِنّي أطيَبُ السَلامِ وإلى لِقاءٍ قَريبٍ في حَلَب.

أخوكَ المُخلِص

عَدنان

## ٤- رِسالةُ ياسِر مارتيني إلى ابنِهِ عَدنان (الدرس ٢٤):

حَلَب في ٢٢ أيّار ٢٠٠٨

ابني الحَبيب عَدنان، السلامُ عليكَ ورَحمَةُ الله.

أرجو أنْ تَصِلَكَ رِسالَتي هذِهِ وأنتَ في أحسَنِ حال. كُلُّنا بِخَير والحَمْدُ لله. كَتَبتُ لَكَ رِسالةً في الشَهرِ الماضي وما وَصَلَني مِنكَ رَدٌّ علَيْها. أما وَصَلتْكَ رِسالَتي؟ آخِرُ رِسالةٍ مِنكَ كانَ تاريخُها ٧ كانونَ الثاني. أرجو أنْ تَكتُبَ لَنا دونَ تَأخير.

أكتبُ لَكَ هذِهِ الرِسالةَ لأُخبِرَكَ أنّ والِدَتَكَ تُريدُ أنْ تُسافِرَ إلَيكَ في شَهرِ آب. لَن أستَطيعَ أنْ أسافِرَ مَعَها هذِهِ المرّة لأنّي مَشغولٌ جِدّاً. يَجِبُ أنْ أسافِرَ إلى ألمانيا في آبَ المُقبِلِ مِن أجلِ استيراد بِضاعَةٍ لِمَحَلّي.

اشتَرَيتُ تَذكِرةَ طائِرةٍ لِوالِدَتِكَ عَلى الخُطوطِ الجَوِيَّةِ الهولَنْدِيّة. تُغادِرُ طائِرتُها مَطارَ دِمَشقَ في يَومِ الخَميس ١٤ آب وتَصِلُ إلى شيكاغو في اليَومِ نَفسِه. أرجو أنْ تَستَقبِلَها في المَطارِ لأنَّها كَما تَعلَم لا تَتَكَلَّمُ الإنكليزيّةَ ولا تَعرِفُ أحداً عَلى الطائِرة.

والآنَ إليكَ أخبارَ الأُسْرَة. أخوكَ أيْمَن كَلَّمَنا بِالهاتِفِ مِن دِمَشقَ وهُوَ بِخَيْرٍ ويُرسِلُ لَكَ سَلامُه. أخوكَ رامي لا يَزالُ يَدْرُسُ في الجامِعةِ ويَعمَلُ سائِقاً في شَرِكةِ البَرّادات، وهُوَ سَعيدٌ بِذلِك. خالُكَ أحْمَد انتَقَلَ في الشَهرِ الماضي وعائِلَتُه إلى دِمَشقَ حَيْثُ سَيَعمَلُ مُدَرِّساً لِلفيزياءِ في إحدى المدارِس الثانَوِيَّة. تَقاعَدَ عَمُّكَ زُهَير مِن عَمَلِهِ في وِزارةِ التَربية، وهُوَ يَقولُ إنَّ حَياةَ المُتَقاعِدِ تُعجِبُهُ كَثيراً. جَدَّتُكَ أمّ ياسِر تُرسِلُ لَكَ سَلامَها وتَشكُرُكَ على الهَدِيَّةِ الّتي أرسَلتَها لَها. اكتُبْ لَنا عَن أخبارِكَ وإلى اللِقاء.

والِدُك

# Cumulative Vocabulary

## أ

| | |
|---|---|
| a question particle to form yes/no questions [3] | أ |
| father [5] | أب ج آباء (n., m.) |
| August [11] | آب (n., m.) |
| to return [19] | آبَ (يؤوبُ) إياب (v.) |
| elementary [5] | ابْتِدائيّ (adj.) |
| never, not at all [20] | أبَداً (adv.) |
| son [5] | ابْنٌ ج أبْناء (n., m.) |
| a 14th-century Arab historian and sociologist [3] | ابْنُ خَلْدون (proper noun) |
| daughter [5] | ابْنَة ج بَنات (n., f.) |
| Abu Dhabi (*abū ẓabī*) [4] | أبو ظَبي (n., f.) |
| white [19] | أبيَض ج بيض (n., m.) |
| to come [11] | أتى (يَأتي) إتيان (إلى) (v.) |
| to hold, to contain [20] | اتَّسَعَ (يَتَّسِعُ) اتِّساع (v.) |
| to contact [20] | اِتَّصَلَ (يَتَّصِلُ) اِتِّصال (بـ) (v.) |
| to agree (with someone) [20] | اِتَّفَقَ (يَتَّفِقُ) اِتِّفاق (مَعَ) (v.) |
| furniture [18] | أثاث (n., m.) |
| ruin, antiquity, artifact, relic [19] | أثَر ج آثار (n., m.) |
| during [21] | أثْناء |
| two [3] | اِثنان (n., m.) |
| Monday [11] | الإثْنَين (n., m.) |
| to respond, to answer [19] | أجابَ (يُجيبُ) إجابة (v.) |
| pear [20] | إجّاص (n., m.) |
| social gathering [16] | اِجْتِماع ج اِجْتِماعات (n., m.) |
| to lease, to let [18] | أجَّر (يؤجِّر) تأجير |
| rent, wage, fare [18] | أُجْرة ج أُجور (n., f.) |
| for the sake of, because of [22] | أجْل (مِن أجْلِ) |
| foreigner [17] | أَجْنَبيّ ج أَجانِب (n., m.) |
| foreign [17] | أجْنَبيّ / أجْنَبيَّة (adj.) |

| | |
|---|---|
| to meet, to gather [18] | اِجْتَمَعَ (يَجْتَمِع) اِجْتِماع (v.) |
| to like [7] | أَحَبَّ (يُحِبُّ) حُبّ، مَحَبّة (v.) |
| to celebrate [15] | اِحْتَفَلَ (يَحْتَفِلُ) اِحْتِفال (v.) |
| one [9] | أَحَد ج آحاد (n., m.) |
| Sunday [11] | الأَحَد (n., m.) |
| statistics [9] | إحْصاء (n., m.) |
| to bring [8] | أَحْضَرَ (يُحْضِرُ) إحْضار (v.) |
| red [20] | أحمَر ج حُمْر (adj.) |
| biology [4] | أحْياء (f., pl.) |
| sometimes [7] | أحياناً (adv.) |
| brother [5] | أَخ ج إخوة (n., m.) |
| to notify, inform [20] | أَخْبَرَ (يُخْبِرُ) إخْبار (v.) |
| sister [5] | أُخْت ج أَخَوات (n., f.) |
| to select [24] | اِخْتارَ (يَخْتارُ) اِخْتِيار (v.) |
| to differ (from) [23] | اِخْتَلَفَ (يَخْتَلِفُ) اِخْتِلاف (عَن) (v.) |
| to take [17] | أَخَذَ (يَأخُذُ) أخْذ (v.) |
| other [18] | آخَر ج آخَرون (n., m.) |
| last, latest [24] | آخِر (adj.) |
| green [12] | أَخْضَر ج خُضْر (adj., m.) |
| department [24] | إدارة ج إدارات (n., f.) |
| literature [2] | أَدَب ج آداب (n., m.) |
| proper noun (man's name) [2] | أديب (n., m.) |
| then, therefore [19] | إذاً |
| March [11] | آذار (n., m.) |
| broadcasting station [22] | إذاعَة ج ات (n., f.) |
| to want [7] | أرادَ (يُريدَ) إرادة (v.) |
| Wednesday [11] | الأَرْبِعاء (n., m.) |
| four [3] | أَرْبَعة (n., f.) |
| to rise, to be higher [23] | اِرتَفَعَ (يرتَفِعُ) اِرتِفاع (v.) |
| Jordan [4] | الأُرْدُنّ (n., f.) |
| rice [8] | أَرُزّ (n., m.) |
| to send [17] | أَرْسَلَ (يُرسِلُ) إرْسال (v.) |

| | |
|---|---|
| ground, land [2] | أرْض ج أراضٍ (n., f.) |
| Arizona [4] | أريزونا (n., f.) |
| couch [18] | أريكة ج أرائِك (n., f.) |
| blue [20] | أزرَق ج زُرْق (adj.) |
| week [11] | أُسْبوع ج أَسابيع (n., m.) |
| professor, teacher [1] | أسْتاذ ج أساتِذَة (n., m.) |
| to rent, to hire [18] | استأجَرَ (يَستأجِرُ) استِئجار (v.) |
| to bathe, to take a bath or shower [13] | اسْتَحَمَّ (يَستَحِمُّ) استِحْمام (v.) |
| to use, to utilize, to employ [16] | اِستَخدَمَ (يَستَخدِمُ) اِستِخدام (v.) |
| to become a martyr [16] | أُسْتُشْهِدَ (يُستَشْهَدُ) اِسْتِشهاد (passive v.) |
| to host [23] | اِستَضافَ (يستَضيفُ) استِضافة (v.) |
| to be able [6] | اِسْتَطاعَ (يَسْتَطيعُ) اِسْتِطاعة (v.) |
| to spend time [29] | اِسْتَغْرَقَ (يَسْتَغْرِقُ) اِسْتِغْراق (v.) |
| to receive (s.o.) [17] | اسْتَقبَلَ (يَسْتَقبِلُ) اسْتِقبال (v.) |
| independence [15] | اِسْتِقلال (n., m.) |
| to enjoy [19] | استَمتَعَ (يَستَمتِعُ) استِمتاع بـ (v.) |
| to listen [22] | اِسْتَمَعَ (يَسْتَمِعُ) اِسْتِماع (v.) |
| to import [24] | اِسْتَوْرَدَ (يَسْتَوْرِدُ) اِسْتِيراد (v.) |
| to wake up [9] | اِسْتَيْقَظَ (يَسْتَيْقِظُ) اِسْتِيقاظ (v.) |
| extended family [14] | أُسْرة ج أُسَر (n., f.) |
| to establish, to found [16] | أَسَّسَ (يُؤَسِّسُ) تأسيس (v.) |
| sorry [12] | آسِف (n., m.) / آسِفة (n., f.) |
| bottom, lowest point, lower [24] | أَسْفَل ج أسافِل (n., m., superlative) |
| Islam [15] | إسلام (n., m.) |
| name | اِسم ج أَسْماء (n., m.) |
| black [16] | أَسْوَد ج سود (n., m.) |
| Asia [21] | آسيا (n., f.) |
| to long (for), to yearn [23] | اِشْتاقَ (يَشْتاقُ) اِشْتِياق (لـ/ إلى) (v.) |
| to buy [11] | اِشتَرى (يَشتري) شِراء (v.) |
| to enroll in, to subscribe to [22] | اِشْتَرَكَ (يَشْتَرِكُ) اِشْتِراك (v.) |
| to become [14] | أَصْبَحَ (يُصْبِحُ) (v.) |
| to insist [23] | أَصَرَّ (يُصِرُّ) إصْرار (v.) |

| | |
|---|---|
| yellow [20] | أَصْفَر ج صُفْر (adj.) |
| to overlook (sth.) [21] | أَطَلَّ (يُطِلُّ) إطْلال (v.) |
| Atlantic [21] | أَطلَسيّ (adj.) |
| to discharge a firearm, to shoot; to dispatch [21] | أَطْلَقَ (يُطْلِق) إطْلاق (v.) |
| to consider [21] | اِعتبَرَ ( يَعتبِرُ) اِعتِبار (v.) |
| to believe [17] | اِعتَقَدَ (يَعتَقِدُ) اِعتِقاد (v.) |
| to take care of, to tend [24] | اِعْتَنى (يَعْتَني) اِعتِناء (بـ) (v.) |
| to please [18] | أَعْجَبَ يُعْجِبُ (v.) |
| to give [7] | أعطى (يُعطي) أَعْطِ (v.) (imperative) إعْطاء (verbal n.) |
| top, highest point, upper [21] | أَعْلى ج أعالٍ (n., m., superlative) |
| advertisement [18] | إعْلان ج إعْلانات (n., m.) |
| most knowledgeable [6] | أعلَم (n., superlative) |
| to be assassinated [16] | أُغْتيلَ (يُغتالُ) اِغتِيال (passive v.) |
| song [22] | أُغنِية ج أغانٍ (n., f.) |
| Africa [21] | إفريقية (n., f.) |
| to reside in [24] | أقام (يُقيم) إقامة (v.) |
| to draw near, to get close (to) [23] | اِقْتَرَبَ (يَقْتَرِبُ) اِقْتِراب (مِن) (v.) |
| region [21] | إقليم ج أقاليم (n., m.) |
| to eat [8] | أَكَلَ (يأكُلُ) أكْل (v.) |
| certainly, surely [11] | أكيد (exclamation) |
| Pakistan [10] | الباكِسْتان (n., f.) |
| good-bye | إلى اللقاء |
| until [19] | إلى أنْ |
| except, minus [9] | إلاّ (particle) |
| now [3] | الآن (n., m) |
| device, gadget, machine, apparatus [19] | آلة ج آلات (n., f.) |
| to meet, to converge, to encounter [19] | التَقى (يَلتَقي) التِقاء (v.) |
| to take, to make (a picture) [19] | التَقَطَ (يَلتَقِطُ) التِقاط (v.) |
| inflammation, infection [17] | اِلْتِهاب ج اِلتِهابات (n., m.) |
| who, that [19] | الَّتي (n., f.) |
| who, that [19] | الَّذي (n., m.) |
| the name of the letter alif | أَلِف (n., f.) |

| | |
|---|---|
| thousand [9] | أَلْف ج آلاف (n., m.) |
| God [3] | الله (n., m.) |
| God knows [6] | اللهُ أَعْلَم |
| pain [17] | أَلَم ج آلام (n., m.) |
| to hurt [17] | آلَمَ (يُؤلِمُ) (v.) |
| Germany [10] | ألمانيا (n., f.) |
| German [10] | ألمانيّ (adj.) |
| or (particle used in questions) [3] | أَمْ (conjunction) |
| mother [5] | أُمّ ج أُمَّهات (n., f.) |
| as for, but, yet, however [17] | أمّا (particle) |
| United Arab Emirates [4] | الإمارات (n., f.) |
| in front of [18] | أمامَ (prep.) |
| to examine, to test [19] | اِمتَحَنَ (يَمتَحِنُ) امتِحان (v.) |
| woman [3] | اِمرأة ج نِساء (n., f.) |
| yesterday [11] | أَمْسِ (adv.) |
| to be possible [22] | أَمْكَنَ (يُمكِنُ) إمْكان (v.) |
| prince [16] | أمير ج أُمَراء (n., m.) |
| librarian [6] | أمينُ/ أمينةُ مَكتَبةٍ (n., m./f.) |
| that (after verbs similar to "to think") [11] | أَنَّ (particle) |
| that (after the verb "to say") [11] | إنَّ (particle) |
| to (infinitive) [18] | أَنْ (particle) |
| if [23] | إنْ (particle) |
| hopefully (*lit.* "God willing") [11] | إنْ شاءَ الله (set phrase) |
| I | أنا (pron.) |
| you | أَنْتَ (pron., m. sg.) |
| you | أَنْتِ (pron., f. sg.) |
| to produce [21] | أَنتَجَ (يُنتِجُ) إنتاج (v.) |
| to elect [16] | اِنْتَخَبَ (يَنتَخِبُ) اِنتِخاب (v.) |
| to wait [14] | اِنتظَرَ (يَنْتَظِرُ) اِنتِظار (v.) |
| to move, to relocate [13] | اِنتقَلَ (يَنتَقِلُ) اِنْتِقال (v.) |
| you | أَنْتُمْ (pron., m. pl.) |
| you | أَنْتُما (pron., f./m. pl.) |

| | |
|---|---|
| you | أَنْتُنَّ (pron., f. pl.) |
| to end [9] | اِنْتَهى (يَنْتَهي) اِنْتِهاء (مِن) (v.) |
| female [24] | أُنْثى ج إناث (n., f.) |
| Andalusia, Muslim Spain [16] | الأَنْدَلُس (n., f.) |
| Indiana [4] | إنديانا (n., f.) |
| to be interrupted, to be severed [21] | اِنقطَعَ (يَنقَطِعُ) اِنقِطاع (v.) |
| English [5] | إِنْكليزيّ (adj., m.) |
| English (language) [3] | الإنكليزية (adj., f.) |
| hello, welcome (response to a greeting) | أَهْلاً (n., m.) |
| or (used with statements) [3] | أو (conjunction) |
| Europe [18] | أوروبا (n., f.) |
| first [5] | أَوَّل ج أوائِل (n., m.) |
| those [2] | أولائِكَ (pl., demonstrative) |
| which [7] | أيّ (n., m.) / أيّةُ (n., f.) |
| May [11] | أَيّار (n., m.) |
| rent [18] | إيجار ج إيجارات (n., m.) |
| Iran [21] | إيران (n., f.) |
| too, also [1] | أَيْضاً (adv.) |
| September [11] | أَيْلول (n., m.) |
| immensely, greatly (intensifies the following noun) [23] | أَيَّما (n.) |
| where | أَيْنَ (question particle) |

# ب

| | |
|---|---|
| on, in, by, with, for [1] | بِـ (prep.) |
| name of the letter *bā* | باء (n., f.) |
| door | باب (n., m.) |
| semi-arid desert [21] | بادِية ج بَوادٍ (n., f.) |
| eggplant [20] | باذِنجان (n., m.) |
| cold [12] | بارِد (adj., m.) |
| green peas [20] | بازِلاء (n., f.) |
| to sell [7] | باعَ (يَبيعُ) بَيْع (v.) |
| early [19] | باكِراً (adverbial) |

| | |
|---|---|
| ochra [20] | بامْية (n., f.) |
| salesperson [24] | بائِع ج بائعون (n., m.) |
| slowly [20] | ببُطءٍ |
| to broadcast [22] | بَثَّ (يَبُثُّ) بَثّ (v.) |
| of [13] in need | بِحاجةٍ (إلى) |
| sea [12] | بَحْر ج بِحار (n, m.) |
| lake [12] | بُحَيْرة ج بُحَيْرات (n., f.) |
| fine, well | بِخَيْر |
| to appear, to seem [24] | بَدا (يَبدو) بُدُوٌّ (v.) |
| to begin [9] | بَدَأ (يَبْدأُ) بِداية، بَدْء (v.) |
| beginning [17] | بِداية ج بِدايات (n., f.) |
| seed, kernel [20] | بِذرة ج بُذور (n., f.) |
| refrigerator (Syria) [18] | بَرّاد ج بَرّادات (n., m.) |
| orange [8] | بُرتُقال (n., m.) |
| program [6] | بَرْنامِج ج بَرامِج (n., m.) |
| mail, post [19] | بَريد (n., m.) |
| only (Syrian colloquial) [17] | بَسّ |
| because of [17] | سَبَب |
| simple [23] | بَسيط ج بُسطاء (adj.) |
| onion [14] | بَصَل (n., m.) |
| merchandise, goods [21] | بِضاعة ج بَضائِع (n., f.) |
| a few [22] | بِضْع (n.) |
| card [3] | بِطاقة ج بِطاقات (n., f.) |
| watermelon [20] | بِطّيخ (n., m.) |
| after [9] | بَعْدَ (prep.) |
| some [11] | بَعْض (n., m.) |
| far [11] | بَعيد (adv.) |
| grocer [18] | بَقّال ج بَقّالون (n., m.) |
| cow, cattle [20] | بَقَرة ج أَبْقار / بَقَر (n., f.) |
| to remain, to stay [19] | بَقِيَ (يَبْقى) بَقاء (v.) |
| rather, but [4] | بَلْ (particle) |
| country [15] | بَلَد ج بِلاد (n., m.) |

| | |
|---|---|
| small town [3] | بَلْدة ج بَلْدات (n., f.) |
| local, popular [18] | بَلَديّ (adj.) |
| to build, to construct [19] | بَنى (يَبني) بِناء (v.) |
| building [4] | بِناية ج بِنايات (n., f.) |
| girl [5] | بِنْت ج بَنات (n., f.) |
| tomato [20] | بَنَدورة (طَماطِم في مصر) (n., f.) |
| bank (colloquial) [18] | بَنْك ج بُنوك |
| brown [24] | بُنّيّ (adj.) |
| gate [17] | بَوّابة ج بَوّابات (n., f.) |
| ice cream [21] | بوظة (n., f.) |
| house, home [2] | بَيْت ج بُيوت (n., m.) |
| egg [8] | بَيْض (n., m.) |
| white [20] | بَيضاء ج بيض (n./adj., f.) |

## ت

| | |
|---|---|
| spice, condiment, seasoning [20] | تابِل ج تَوابِل (n., m.) |
| merchant, businessman [24] | تاجِر ج تُجّار (n., m.) |
| to be late [18] | تَأَخَّرَ (يَتَأَخَّرُ) تَأَخُّر (v.) |
| history [16] | تاريخ ج تَواريخ (n., m.) |
| ninth [5] | تاسِع (adj.) |
| visa [23] | تأشيرة دُخول (n., f.) |
| to consist of, to comprise [21] | تَأَلَّفَ (يَتَأَلَّفُ) تَأَلُّف (v.) |
| insurance [18] | تأمين ج تأمينات (n., m.) |
| those [2] | تانِكَ (dual, nom.; *rare*) |
| salad made with finely chopped parsley, cracked wheat, tomatoes, lemon juice, and olive oil [13] | تَبّولة (n., f.) |
| trade, business, commerce [2] | تِجارة (n., f.) |
| to wander about, to tour [19] | تَجَوَّلَ (يَتجَوَّلُ) تَجَوُّل (v.) |
| to graduate [15] | تَخَرَّجَ (يتخرَّجُ) تَخَرُّج (v.) |
| to push, to shove one another [23] | تَدافَعَ (يَتَدافَعُ) تَدافُع (v.) |
| ticket [19] | تَذكِرة ج تَذاكِر (n., f.) |
| education, upbringing [15] | تَرْبية (n., f.) |

| | |
|---|---|
| nine [3] | تِسْعة (n., f.) |
| October [11] | تِشرين الأوَّل (n., m.) |
| November [11] | تِشرين الثاني (n., m.) |
| come here! [8] | تَعال (imperative) |
| to be acquainted with [11] | تَعَرَّفَ (يَتعَرَّفُ) تَعَرُّف (على) (v.) |
| to learn [1] | تَعَلَّمَ (يَتعَلَّمُ) تَعَلُّم (v.) |
| instruction, education [15] | تَعليم (n., m.) |
| to be accustomed to [23] | تَعَوَّدَ (يَتعَوَّدُ) تَعَوُّد (على) (v.) |
| apple [8] | تُفّاح (n., m.) |
| differential equations [5] | تَفاضُل (n., m.) |
| if you please [7] | تَفَضَّلْ/ تَفَضَّلي (imperative) |
| to retire (from work) [24] | تَقاعَدَ (يَتَقاعَدُ) تَقاعُد (عن) (v.) |
| approximately, about, nearly, roughly [20] | تَقريباً (adv.) |
| traditional [21] | تَقْليديّ (adj.) |
| calendar [11] | تَقويم ج تَقاويم (n., m.) |
| my pleasure, with pleasure, gladly, at your service (colloquial) [16] | تِكرَم عَيْنك |
| to speak [6] | تَكَلَّمَ (يَتكَلَّمُ) تَكَلُّم (v.) |
| television | تِلْفاز (n., m.) |
| that [2] | تِلكَ (n., f. sg.) |
| telephone (colloquial) [18] | تَليفون ج تَليفونات (n., m.) |
| exactly | تماماً (adv.) |
| statue [19] | تِمثال ج تَماثيل (n., m.) |
| dates [21] | تَمْر ج تُمور (n., m.) |
| July [11] | تَمّوز (n., m.) |
| discrimination [16] | تَمييز (verbal n., m.) |
| to eat, to take, to reach for sth. [8] | تَناوَلَ (يَتَناوَلُ) تَناوُل (v.) |
| to stroll, to have a good time, to go on a picnic [23] | تَنَزَّهَ (يَتَنَزَّهُ) تَنَزُّه (v.) |
| *tanwīn* (diacritical mark signaling indefiniteness) | تَنوين (n., m.) |
| berry [20] | توت (n., m.) |
| to pass away [16] | تُوُفِّيَ (يُتَوَفّى) وَفاة (passive v.) |
| signature [24] | تَوْقيع (n., m.) |
| those [2] | تَيْنِكَ (dual, acc., gen.; *rare*) |

# ث

| | |
|---|---|
| third [5] | ثالِث (.adj) |
| eighth [5] | ثامِن (.adj) |
| second [5] | ثانٍ (الثاني) (.n., m) |
| secondary [10] | ثانَوِيّ (.adj) |
| hole [21] | ثُقْب ج ثُقوب (.n., m) |
| three [3] | ثَلاثة (.n., f) |
| Tuesday[11] | الثُلاثاء (.n., m) |
| refrigerator (Egypt) [18] | ثَلاّجة ج ثَلاّجات (.n., f) |
| a third [9] | ثُلْث ج أثْلاث (.n., m) |
| snow [12] | ثَلْج ج ثُلوج (.n., m) |
| then, and again [13] | ثُمَّ (conjunction) |
| eight [3] | ثَمانِية (.n., f) |
| revolution [15] | ثَوْرة ج ثَورات (.n., f) |
| garlic [20] | ثوم (.n., m) |

# ج

| | |
|---|---|
| sitting [17] | جالِس ج جالِسون (.n., m) |
| mosque [16] | جامِع ج جَوامِع (.n., m) |
| university [1] | جامِعَة ج جامِعات (.f) |
| side [1] | جانِب (.n., m) |
| to come [11] | جاء (يَجيءُ) مَجيء (.v) |
| prize, award [16] | جائِزة ج جَوائِز (.n., f) |
| algebra [16] | جَبْر (.n., m) |
| mountain [21] | جَبَل ج جِبال (.n., m) |
| name of a town in Syria [3] | جَبْلة (.n., f) |
| cheese [8] | جُبْن ج أجْبان (.n., m) |
| grandfather [24] | جَدّ ج جُدود (.n., m) |
| wall [1] | جِدار ج جُدْران (.n., m) |
| new [1] | جَديد (.adj) |
| to run, to flow; to hurry, to rush; to happen, to occur [20] | جَرى (يَجري) جَري (.v) |

| | |
|---|---|
| to test, to try (≠ to attempt) [21] | جَرَّبَ (يُجَرِّبُ) تَجْرِبة (v.) |
| to be wounded, to be hurt [16] | جُرِحَ (يُجرَحُ) جَرح (passive v.) |
| newspaper | جَريدة ج جرائد (n., f.) |
| part [18] | جُزْء ج أجْزاء (n., m.) |
| island [21] | جَزيرة ج جُزُر (n., f.) |
| abundant [6] | جَزيلاً |
| geography [21] | جغرافية (n., m.) |
| dishwasher [18] | جَلاّية ج جَلاّيات (n., f.) |
| to sit [8] | جَلَسَ (يَجلِسُ) جُلوس (اِجلِسْ) (imperative) (v.) |
| Islamic month (*Jumādī al-āḳira*) [11] | جُمادى الآخِرة (n., f.) |
| Islamic month (*Jumādī al-'ūlā*) [11] | جُمادى الأولى (n., f.) |
| Friday [11] | الجُمعة (n., m.) |
| camel [19] | جَمَل ج جِمال (n., m.) |
| republic [16] | جُمهوريّة ج جُمهوريّات (n., f.) |
| beautiful, good looking [10] | جَميل ج (ون) (adj.) |
| south [21] | جَنوب (n., m.) |
| [Egyptian] pound [18] | جُنَيه ج جُنَيْهات (n., m.) |
| device, apparatus, appliance [21] | جِهاز ج أجهِزة (n., m.) |
| to prepare [13] | جَهَّزَ (يُجَهِّزُ) تَجْهيز (v.) |
| passport [23] | جَواز (سَفَر) (n., m.) |
| good [6] | جَيِّد (adj.) |
| well [6] | جَيِّداً (adv.) |
| army [16] | جَيْش ج جُيوش (n., m.) |
| geology [24] | جيولوجيا (n., f.) |

## ح

| | |
|---|---|
| hot [12] | حارّ (adj., m.) |
| to fight [16] | حارَبَ (يُحارِبُ) حَرْب / مُحارَبة (v.) |
| calculator | حاسِبة ج حاسِبات (n., f.) |
| computer | حاسوب ج حَواسيب (n., m.) |
| ready, all set (polite expression) [8] | حاضِر (participle) |
| bus, tram [13] | حافِلة ج حافِلات (n., f.) |

| | |
|---|---|
| grain, cereal [8] | حَبّ ج حُبوب (n., m.) |
| pill [17] | حَبّة ج حَبّات (n., f.) |
| till, until [11] | حَتّى (particle) |
| pilgrimage [15] | حَجّ (n., m.) |
| to border, to demarcate, to limit [21] | حَدَّ (يَحُدُّ) حَدّ (v.) |
| border, edge, boundary, borderline [21] | حَدّ ج حُدود (n., m.) |
| conversation [9] | حَديث ج أحاديث (n., m.) |
| modern [10] | حَديث (adj.) |
| park, garden [18] | حَديقة ج حَدائِق (n., f.) |
| shoe [21] | حِذاء ج أحْذية (n., m.) |
| heat [12] | حَرارة (n., f.) |
| war [16] | حَرْب ج حُروب (n., f.) |
| campus; sacred possession [26] | حَرَم ج أحْرام (n., m.) |
| liberty, freedom [19] | حُرِّيّة ج حُرِّيّات (n., f.) |
| silk [23] | حَرير (n., m.) |
| to guess [22] | حَزَرَ (يحْزِرُ) حَزْر (v.) |
| June [11] | حَزيران (n., m.) |
| account [16] | حِساب ج حِسابات (n., m.) |
| to improve, to make better [22] | حَسَّنَ (يحَسِّنُ) تَحْسين (v.) |
| good [23] | حَسَن (adj.) |
| very well, okay (a response denoting agreement) [8] | حَسَناً (adv.) |
| horse [20] | حِصان ج أحْصِنة (n., m.) |
| to obtain, to get, to acquire [16] | حَصَلَ (يَحصُلُ) حُصول (v.) |
| to attend, to be present [23] | حَضَرَ (يحْضُرُ) حُضور (v.) |
| to prepare [8] | حَضَّرَ (يُحَضِّرُ) تَحضير (v.) |
| party [20] | حَفْلة ج حَفَلات (n., f.) |
| right, law [2] | حَقٌّ ج حُقوقٌ (n., m.) |
| bag; briefcase [4] | حَقيبة ج حقائب (n., f.) |
| to tell a story; to talk [16] | حَكَى (يَحْكي) حِكاية (v.) |
| government [17] | حُكومة ج حُكومات (n., f.) |
| Aleppo [1] | حَلَب (n., f.) |
| to shave [13] | حَلَقَ (يَحلِقُ) حَلْق (v.) |

| | |
|---|---|
| dessert, sweets [15] | حَلْوى ج حَلوَيات (n., f.) |
| ornament, jewelry [23] | حَلي ج حُليّ (n., m.) |
| milk [8] | حَليب (n., m.) |
| bathroom [13] | حَمّام ج حمّامات (n., f.) |
| dip prepared from chickpeas, sesame seed paste, lemon juice [9] | حِمَّص (n., m.) |
| to carry [17] | حَمَلَ (يَحْمِلُ) حَمْل (v.) |
| [bath] tub [18] | حَوْض ج أحْواض (n., m.) |
| around [23] | حَوْلَ (adj.) |
| neighborhood, borough [14] | حَيّ ج أحْياء (n., m.) |
| a living person [22] | حَيّ ج أحْياء (n., m.) |
| where, when [6] | حَيْثُ (adv.) |
| when [11] | حينَ (adv.) |
| animal [19] | حَيَوان ج حَيَوانات (n., m.) |

## خ

| | |
|---|---|
| servant [18] | خادِم ج خَدَم (n., m.) |
| outside [23] | خارِج (n.) |
| special, particular (to) [15] | خاصّ (بـ) (adj.) |
| maternal uncle [24] | خال ج أخْوال (n., m.) |
| fifth [5] | خامِس (adj.) |
| news story [13] | خَبَر ج أخْبار (n., m.) |
| bread [8] | خُبْز (n., m.) |
| baker [18] | خَبّاز ج خَبّازون (n., m.) |
| to stamp, to seal [23] | خَتَمَ (يَخْتِمُ) خَتْم (v.) |
| to go out, to exit [16] | خَرَجَ (يَخرُجُ) خُروج (v.) |
| map [21] | خَريطة ج خَرائِط (n., f.) |
| autumn [12] | خَريف (n., m.) |
| closet, cupboard [4] | خِزانة ج خَزائِن / خِزانات (n., f.) |
| to store [24] | خَزَّنَ (يُخَزِّنُ) تَخزين (v.) |
| lettuce [20] | خَسّ (n., m.) |
| wood, lumber, timber [18] | خَشَب ج أخْشاب (n., m.) |
| especially, particularly [20] | خُصوصاً (adv.) |

| | |
|---|---|
| fertile [21] | خَصيب (adj.) |
| vegetables [13] | خُضرة ج خُضَر (n., f.) |
| green [12] | خَضْراء ج خُضْر (adj., f.) |
| vegetables; greens [8] | خَضْراوات (n., f.) |
| greengrocer [18] | خُضَريّ ج خُضَريّون (n., m.) |
| orator, preacher, speaker [16] | خَطيب ج خُطَباء (n., m.) |
| to diminish the difficulty of [23] | خَفَّفَ (يُخَفِّفُ) تَخْفيف (عَن) (v.) |
| light [8] | خَفيف (adj.) |
| during, through [22] | خِلال |
| to disrobe, to take off [23] | خَلَعَ (يَخلَعُ) خَلْع (v.) |
| behind [18] | خَلْفَ (prep.) |
| to allow (s.o. to do sth.) (Syrian colloquial) [14] | خَلِّي + attached pron. |
| gulf, bay [21] | خَليج ج خُلجان (n., m.) |
| caliph, successor [23] | خَليفة ج خُلَفاء (n., m.) |
| five [3] | خَمْسة (n., f.) |
| Thursday [11] | الخَميس (n., m.) |
| pig, swine [8] | خِنزير ج خَنازير (n., m.) |
| horse [20] | خَيْل (n., m.) |

## د

| | |
|---|---|
| house [10] | دار ج دور (n., f.) |
| warm [12] | دافِئ (adj., m.) |
| always [19] | دائماً (adverbial) |
| chicken [8] | دَجاج (n., m.) |
| to enter [16] | دَخَلَ (يَدخُلُ) دُخول (v.) |
| bicycle | دَرّاجة ج دَرّاجات (n., f.) |
| study [10] | دِراسة ج دِراسات (n., f.) |
| of school, academic [5] | دِراسِيّ (adj.) |
| degree (temperature), step [12] | دَرَجة ج دَرَجات (n., f.) (درجة حرارة) |
| study [4] | دَرَسَ (يَدرُسُ) دِراسة / دَرْس (v.) |
| lesson [11] | دَرْس ج دُروس (n., m.) |
| defense [16] | دِفاع ج دِفاعات (n., m.) |

| | |
|---|---|
| notebook | دَفْتَر ج دَفاتِر (n., m.) |
| to pay [16] | دَفَعَ (يَدْفَعُ) دَفْع (v.) |
| minute [9] | دَقيقَة ج دَقائِق (n., f.) |
| shop, store [18] | دُكّان ج دَكاكين (n., f.) |
| to indicate, to point out [23] | دَلّ (يَدُلّ) دَلالة (v.) |
| guide [24] | دَليل ج أدِلاء (n., m.) |
| international [9] | دَوْلِيّ (n., m.) |
| without [8] | دونَ (prep.) |
| cock, rooster [15] | ديك ج دِيَكة (n., m.) |
| turkey [15] | ديك حَبَش (n., m.) |
| dinar (currency in Algeria, Bahrain, Iraq, Kuwait) [18] | دينار ج دَنانير (n., m.) |

## ذ

| | |
|---|---|
| corn [20] | ذُرة (n., f.) |
| chin (when used with "to shave," it signifies shaving one's beard) [13] | ذَقْن ج ذُقون (n., f.) |
| that [2] | ذلِكَ (n., m. sg.) |
| to go [10] | ذَهَبَ (يَذْهَبُ) ذَهاب (إلى) (v.) |
| with, of, owner of [15] | ذو ج ذَوو (n., m.) |
| Islamic month (*d̲ū al-ḥijja*) [11] | ذو الحِجّة (n., m.) |
| Islamic month (*d̲ū al-Qi'da*) [11] | ذو القِعدة (n., m.) |

## ر

| | |
|---|---|
| to see [17] | رَأى (يَرى) رُؤية (v.) |
| fourth [5] | رابع (adj.) |
| to refer to, to review [24] | راجَعَ (يُراجِعُ) مُراجعَة (v.) |
| ذهب (Syrian colloquial) [19] | راح (يروح) (v.) |
| head [15] | رأس ج رُؤوس (n., m.) |
| passenger, rider [21] | راكِب ج رُكّاب (n., m.) |
| wonderful; awesome [11] | رائع (active participle) |
| housewife [17] | رَبّةُ بَيْت ج رَبّات بُيوت (n., f.) |
| quarter [9] | رُبْع ج أرْباع (n., m.) |
| perhaps, probably [20] | رُبَّما (adv.) |

| | |
|---|---|
| spring [12] | رَبيع (n., m.) |
| Islamic month (*Rabīʻal-āḳir*) [11] | رَبيع الآخِر (n., m.) |
| Islamic month (*Rabīʻal-ʻawwal*) [11] | رَبيع الأوَّل (n., m.) |
| to organize [13] | رَتَّبَ (يُرَتِّبُ) تَرْتيب (v.) |
| to hope [19] | رَجا (يَرجو) رَجاء (v.) |
| Islamic month (*Rajab*) [11] | رَجَب (n., m.) |
| to return, to go back [13] | رَجَعَ (يَرْجِعُ) رُجوع (v.) |
| man [3] | رَجُل ج رِجال (n., m.) |
| future marker (= "will" in Syrian colloquial) [17] | رَح |
| trip, journey, flight [21] | رِحْلة ج رِحلات (n., f.) |
| cheap, inexpensive [23] | رَخيص (adj.) |
| to respond, to answer [24] | رَدَّ (يَرُدُّ) رَدّ (v.) |
| letter, message [13] | رِسالة ج رَسائِل (n., f.) |
| bullets; lead [21] | رَصاص (n., m.) |
| to reject [16] | رَفَضَ (يَرفُضُ) رَفْض (v.) |
| to dance [22] | رَقَصَ (يرقُصُ) رَقْص (v.) |
| number [3] | رَقْم ج أرْقام (n., m.) |
| to ride, to mount [19] | رَكِبَ (يَركَبُ) رُكوب (v.) |
| Islamic month (*Ramaḍān*) [11] | رَمَضان (n., m.) |
| to irrigate, to water [21] | رَوى (يَروي) رَيّ (v.) |
| Roman [23] | رومانيّ (adj.) |
| Riyadh (capital of Saudi Arabia) | الرياض (n., f.) |
| sport [2] | رِياضَة ج رِياضات (n., f.) |
| of sports; athletic [2] | رياضِيّ (adj.) |
| mathematics, calculus [1] | رياضِيّات (n., f.) |
| leader, president [16] | رَئيس ج رُؤَساء (n., m.) |
| wind [12] | ريح ج رِياح (n., f.) |

## ز

| | |
|---|---|
| to visit [11] | زارَ (يَزورُ) زِيارة (v.) |
| plus [3] | زائِد (n., m.) |
| butter [8] | زُبْدة (n., f.) |

| | |
|---|---|
| to plant, to cultivate [21] | زَرَعَ (يزرَعُ) زَرْع، زِراعة (v.) |
| wild thyme [8] | زَعتَر (n., m.) |
| leader (popular) [16] | زَعيم ج زُعَماء (n., m.) |
| alley, narrow street [23] | زُقاق ج أزِقّة (n., m.) |
| colleague, coworker [17] | زَميل ج زُمَلاء (n., m.) |
| flower [12] | زَهْرة ج زَهْرات / أزْهار (n., f.) |
| husband [5] | زَوْج ج أزْواج (n., m.) |
| wife [5] | زَوْجَة ج زَوْجات (n., f.) |
| olive [8] | زَيْتون (n., m.) |
| to adorn, to decorate [15] | زَيَّنَ (يُزَيِّنُ) تزيين (v.) |

# س

| | |
|---|---|
| shall, will [11] | سَـ (future particle) |
| seventh [5] | سابع (adj.) |
| square, courtyard [15] | ساحة ج ساحات (n., f.) |
| coast, shore [21] | ساحِل ج سَواحِل (n., m.) |
| sixth [5] | سادِس (adj.) |
| unsweetened (coffee) [19] | سادة (adj., f.) |
| to move, to walk, to travel, to march, to flow [19] | سارَ (يَسيرُ) سَيْر (v.) |
| brilliant, shining [12] | ساطِع (adj., m.) |
| mail carrier [17] | ساعٍ ج سُعاة (ساعي بَريد) (n., m.) |
| to help, to assist [17] | ساعَدَ (يُساعِدُ) مُساعَدة (v.) |
| o'clock, hour [9] | ساعَة ج ساعات (n., f.) |
| to travel [19] | سافَرَ (يُسافِرُ) سَفَر (v.) |
| to drive [23] | ساقَ (يَسوقُ) سِياقة (v.) |
| safe, secure, healthy [17] | سالِم ج سالِمون (n., m.) |
| to equal [3] | ساوى (يُساوي) مُساواة (v.) |
| to do (Syrian colloquial) [14] | ساوى (يساوي) (v.) |
| driver, chauffeur [10] | سائِق ج سائقون (n., m.) |
| reason, cause [17] | سَبَب ج أسْباب (n., m.) |
| Saturday [11] | السَبْت(n., m.) |

| | |
|---|---|
| to swim [12] | سَبَحَ (يَسْبَحُ) سِباحة (v.) |
| seven [3] | سَبْعة (n., f.) |
| six [3] | سِتّة (n., f.) |
| to register, to record [24] | سَجَّلَ (يُسَجِّلُ) تَسْجيل (v.) |
| prisoner [23] | سَجين ج سُجناء (n., m.) |
| water heater [18] | سَخّان لِلماء (m. sg.) |
| silly, absurd, foolish [23] | سَخيف ج سُخَفاء (n./adj.) |
| to please, to be glad [23] | سَرَّ (يَسُرُّ) سُرور (v.) |
| bed [4] | سَرير ج أسِرّة (n., m.) |
| surface, level [23] | سَطْح ج سُطوح (n., m.) |
| Saudi Arabia | السُعودية (n., f.) |
| happy, pleased, joyful [19] | سَعيد ج سُعَداء (n., m.) |
| embassy [23] | سِفارة ج سِفارات (n., f.) |
| to fall [12] | سَقَطَ (يَسْقُطُ) سُقوط (v.) |
| ceiling [21] | سَقْف ج سُقوف (n., m.) |
| sugar [8] | سُكَّر (n., m.) |
| to live, to reside [3] | سَكَنَ (يَسْكُنُ) سَكَن (v.) |
| (student) living, residence, dormitory [3] | سَكَنُ (الطُلاّبِ) (verbal n., m.) |
| basket [20] | سَلّة ج سِلال (n., f.) |
| range, series, chain [21] | سِلسِلة ج سَلاسِل (n., f.) |
| salad [8] | سَلَطة ج سَلَطات (n., f.) |
| wire, cable [22] | سِلْك ج أسْلاك (كيبِل) (n., m.) |
| to save, to protect [15] | سَلَّمَ (يُسَلِّمُ) تَسْليم (v.) |
| sky [12] | سَماء ج سَماوات (n., f.) |
| to hear [22] | سَمِعَ (يَسْمَع) سَمْع (v.) |
| a kind of toasted thin bread [20] | سَميط (n., m.) |
| tooth [13] | سِنٌّ ج أسْنان (n., f.) |
| age of a person [15] | سِنّ (n., m.) |
| year [11] | سَنة ج سَنَوات / سُنون (n., f.) |
| plain [21] | سَهل ج سُهول (n., m.) |
| question, query [19] | سُؤال ج أسئِلة (n., m.) |
| shall, will [11] | سَوْفَ (future particle) |

| | |
|---|---|
| market [10] | سوق ج أسْواق (n., f.) |
| tourist [24] | سياحيّ (adj.) |
| car | سَيّارة ج سَيّارات (n., f.) |
| political [23] | سِياسيّ (adj.) |

# ش

| | |
|---|---|
| want, will [3] | شاءَ (يَشاءُ) مَشيئة (v.) |
| young man [16] | شابّ ج شَباب (n., m.) |
| truck [18] | شاحِنة ج شاحِنات (n., f.) |
| street [3] | شارِع ج شَوارِع (n., m.) |
| beach [12] | شاطِئ ج شَواطِئ (n., m.) |
| poet [16] | شاعِر ج شُعَراء (n., m.) |
| empty [23] | شاغِر (adj.) |
| Syria, Damascus, Greater Syria [17] | الشام (n., f.) |
| to see, to watch, to witness [13] | شاهَدَ (يُشاهِدُ) مُشاهَدة (v.) |
| tea [8] | شاي (n., m.) |
| February [11] | شُباط (n., m.) |
| semi-, quasi, similarity [21] | شِبْه ج أشباه (n., m.) |
| winter [12] | شِتاء (n., m.) |
| tree [12] | شَجَرة ج شَجَرات (n., f.) |
| person [22] | شَخْص ج أشْخاص (n., m.) |
| personality, character [16] | شَخصِيّة ج شَخصِيّات (n., f.) |
| drink, beverage, sherbet [17] | شَراب ج أشْرِبة، شَرابات (n., m.) |
| to drink [8] | شَرِبَ (يَشرَبُ) شُرْب (v.) |
| to explain, to expound, to illustrate [20] | شَرَحَ (يَشرَحُ) شَرْح (v.) |
| bed sheet [11] | شَرْشَف ج شَراشِف (n., m.) |
| company [18] | شَرِكة ج شَرِكات (n., f.) |
| tape [22] | شَريط ج أشْرِطة (n., m.) |
| sandwich [20] | شَطيرة ج شَطائِر (n., f.) |
| emblem, sign, slogan [21] | شِعار ج شِعارات، أشعِرة (n., m.) |
| Islamic month (*ŝaʻbān*) [11] | شَعبان (n., m.) |
| hair [24] | شَعْر ج شُعور / أشْعار (n., m.) |

| | |
|---|---|
| poetry, poem, knowledge [24] | شِعْر ج أشْعار (n., m.) |
| apartment [3] | شَقّة ج شُقَق (n,. f.) |
| thank you [3] | شُكْراً |
| to form, to constitute [21] | شَكَّلَ (يُشَكِّلُ) تَشكيل (v.) |
| waterfall [19] | شَلاّل ج شَلاّلات (n., m.) |
| north [19] | شَمال (n., m.) |
| sun [12] | شَمْس ج شُموس (n., f.) |
| of the sun; solar [1] | شَمْسِيّ (adj.) |
| month [11] | شَهْر ج أشْهُر / شُهور (n., m.) |
| last name, surname [24] | شُهْرة (n., f.) |
| what (Syrian colloquial) [14] | شو (interrogative particle) |
| to grill, to broil [20] | شَوى (يَشوي) شَي (v.) |
| Islamic month (*ŝawwāl*) [11] | شَوّال (n., m.) |
| thing, object [1] | شَيء ج أشْياء (n., m.) |
| interesting, thrilling [23] | شَيِّق (adj.) |

## ص

| | |
|---|---|
| soap [13] | صابون (n., m.) |
| to become [15] | صارَ (يَصيرُ) صَيْر، صَيْرورة، مَصير (v.) |
| pure, clear, not cloudy [12] | صافٍ (adj., m.) صافِية (adj., f.) |
| to fast [15] | صامَ (يَصومُ) صَوْم (v.) |
| to flow into [21] | صَبَّ (يَصُبُّ) صَبّ (v.) |
| morning [8] | صَباح (n., m.) |
| journalism [14] | صِحافة (n., f.) |
| desert [21] | صَحْراء ج صَحاري (n., f.) |
| journalist [23] | صَحَفِيّ ج ون (n., m.) |
| plate [13] | صَحْن ج صُحون (n., m.) |
| health [18] | صِحّة (n., f.) |
| bon appétit (Syrian colloquial) [19] | صَحّة وهَنا |
| clear, fine (of weather) [12] | صَحْوٌ (adj., m.) |
| newspaper [23] | صَحيفة ج صُحُف (n., f.) |
| to issue [24] | صَدَرَ (يَصْدُرُ) صُدور (v.) |

friend [1] — صَديق ج أَصْدِقاء (n., m.)
honestly, candidly [22] — صَراحةً (بِصَراحة) (n., f.)
youngest, smallest [24] — صُغرى, superlative of صَغيرة
small; young [5] — صَغير (adj., m.)
class [1] — صَفّ ج صُفوف (n., m.)
zero [3] — صِفْر ج أَصْفار (n., m.)
Islamic month (*ṣafar*) [11] — صَفَر (n., m.)
characteristic [21] — صِفة ج صِفات (n., f.)
to pray; to bless [15] — صَلّى (يُصَلّي) (v.)
industry [19] — صِناعة ج صِناعات (n., f.)
to manufacture, to make [15] — صَنَعَ (يَصنَعُ) صِناعة (v.)
to make a picture, to portray, to illustrate [19] — صَوَّرَ (يُصَوِّرُ) تَصوير (v.)
picture — صورة ج صُوَر (n., f.)
pharmacology [6] — صَيْدَلَة (n., f.)
pharmacist [24] — صَيدلانِيّة (n., f.)
pharmacy [24] — صَيْدَلِيّة (n., f.)

## ض

ranking officer [16] — ضابِط ج ضُبّاط (n., m.)
to laugh [20] — ضَحِكَ (يَضْحَكُ) ضِحْك (v.)
opposite, anti-, adversary, opponent [17] — ضِدٌّ ج أَضْداد (n., m.)
molar tooth [17] — ضِرْس ج أَضْراس، ضُروس (n., m.)
guest [11] — ضَيْف ج ضُيوف (n., m.)
narrow, tight [21] — ضَيِّق (adj.)

## ط

floor, storey, flat [18] — طابَق ج طَوابِق
male student [1] — طالِب ج طُلاّب (n., m.)
female student [1] — طالِبة ج طالِبات (n., f.)
table — طاوِلة ج طاوِلات (n., f.)
airplane [11] — طائِرة ج طائِرات (n., f.)
medicine [2] — طِبّ (n., m.)

| | |
|---|---|
| of course [22] | طَبْعاً (adv.) |
| nature [22] | طَبيعة (n., f.) |
| physician, doctor [17] | طَبيب ج أَطِبّاء (n., m.) |
| way, road [12] | طَريق ج طُرُق، طُرُقات (n., f.) |
| food [15] | طَعام ج أطْعِمة (n., m.) |
| taste, flavor [23] | طَعْم ج طُعوم (n., m.) |
| patty made from ground beans and spices fried in oil (Egypt) [8] | طَعْمِيّة (n., f.) |
| child [5] | طِفْل ج أطْفال (n., m.) |
| weather [12] | طَقْس ج طُقوس (n., m.) |
| to request; to order (i.e., in a restaurant) [16] | طَلَبَ (يَطْلُب) طَلَب (v.) |
| height [24] | طول (n., m.) |
| Toulon (a town in southern France) [16] | طولون (n., f.) |
| tall [10] | طَويل ج طِوال (n., m.) |
| good [17] | طَيِّب ج طَيِّبون (n., m.) |
| bird [23] | طَيْر ج طُيور (n., m.) |

## ظ

| | |
|---|---|
| to think, to believe [11] | ظَنَّ (يَظُنُّ) (v.) |
| to appear, to become visible [22] | ظَهَرَ (يَظهَرُ) ظُهور (v.) |
| noon [8] | ظُهْر (n., m.) |

## ع

| | |
|---|---|
| to return [13] | عادَ (يَعودُ) عَوْدة (v.) |
| usually [7] | عادَةً (adv.) |
| tenth [5] | عاشِر (adj.) |
| capital city [21] | عاصِمة ج عَواصِم (n., f.) |
| high, elevated [21] | عالٍ (العالي) (adj.) |
| world [13] | عالَم ج عَوالِم (n., m.) |
| scholar, scientist [16] | عالِم ج عُلَماء (n., m.) |
| sociologist [16] | عالِم اجْتِماع (n., m.) |
| year [17] | عام ج أعْوام (n., m.) |
| public [20] | عامّ (adj.) |

| | |
|---|---|
| worker, laborer [12] | عامِل ج عُمّال (n., m.) |
| colloquial, vulgar, dialectal [22] | عاميّ (adj.) |
| colloquial [14] | عاميّة (active participle) |
| nuclear family [5] | عائِلَة ج عائِلات (n., f.) |
| phrase [15] | عِبارة ج عِبارات (n., f.) |
| to cross [23] | عَبَرَ (يَعبُرُ) عُبور (v.) |
| crowded (Syrian colloquial) [17] | عَجْقة (n., f.) |
| number (quantity) [19] | عَدَد ج أعْداد (n., m.) |
| lentils [14] | عَدَس (n., m.) |
| a number of, several [2] | عِدَّةُ (n., f.) |
| several, multiple [21] | عَديد (adj.) |
| Arab | عَرَبيّ (adj.) |
| Arabic (language) [3] | العَرَبيّة (n., f.) |
| show, demonstration, performance [19] | عَرْض ج عُروض (n., m.) |
| to know | عَرَفَ (يَعرِفُ) مَعْرِفة (v.) |
| to introduce someone to someone else [16] | عَرَّفَ (يُعَرِّف) تَعريف (على) (v.) |
| dear, esteemed, beloved [19] | عزيز ج أعِزّاء (n., m.) |
| honey [8] | عَسَل (n., m.) |
| dinner [13] | عَشاء ج أعْشِية (n., m.) |
| ten [3] | عَشَرة (n., f.) |
| stick, rod, cane [20] | عَصا ج عُصِيّ (n., f.) |
| juice [8] | عَصير (n., m.) |
| to be off from work [15] | عَطَّلَ (يُعَطِّلُ) تَعطيل (v.) |
| break; vacation [13] | عُطْلة ج عُطلات (n., f.) |
| weekend [14] | عُطْلة نِهاية الأسْبوع (n., f.) |
| great, important, imposing [19] | عَظيم ج عُظَماء (adj./n., m.) |
| you're welcome [1] | عَفْواً (adv.) |
| group of ten [6] | عَقْد ج عُقود (n., m.) |
| cord used to hold a male's headdress in place [10] | عِقال ج عُقُل (n., m.) |
| group of ten; decade [6] | عَقْد ج عُقود (n., m.) |
| opposite, reverse, contrary [23] | عَكْس (n., m.) |
| on [1] | عَلى (prep.) |

| | |
|---|---|
| in general, generally [18] | على العُموم |
| throughout, all the way [21] | على طُول |
| it seemed; it appeared [20] | على ما يَبْدو (أنّ) |
| relation [9] | عَلاقة ج عَلاقات (n., f.) |
| to hang [18] | عَلَّقَ (يُعَلِّقُ) تَعْليق (v.) |
| flag, banner [21] | عَلَم ج أعْلام (n., m.) |
| to know [17] | عَلِمَ (يَعْلَمُ) عِلْم (v.) |
| science, discipline [2] | عِلْم ج عُلوم (n., m.) |
| sociology [16] | عِلْم اجْتِماع (n., m.) |
| of science, scientific [2] | عِلميّ (adj.) |
| knowledgeable [6] | عَليم (adj.) |
| paternal uncle [24] | عَمّ ج أعْمام (n., m.) |
| mayor [14] | عُمْدَة ج عُمَد (n., m.) |
| age [1] | عُمُر ج أعْمار (n., m.) |
| to work [10] | عَمِلَ (يَعْمَلُ) عَمَل (v.) |
| to mean [9] | عَنى (يَعْني) (v.) |
| grape [20] | عِنَب (n., m.) |
| at (expressing possession) | عِنْدَ (prep.) |
| race, element [16] | عُنصُر ج عَناصِر (n., m.) |
| racial [16] | عُنصُريّ (adj.) |
| address [3] | عُنوان ج عَناوين (n., m.) |
| doctor's practice, clinic [18] | عِيادة ج عِيادات (n., f.) |
| celebration, festivity, feast day, day, holiday, *eid* [14] | عيد ج أعْياد (n., m.) |
| Feast of Immolation/sacrifice (after *Haj*), Greater Bairam [15] | عيدُ الأضْحى (n., m.) |
| Thanksgiving [15] | عيدُ الشُكْرِ (n., m.) |
| Labor Day [12] | عيد العُمّال (n., m.) |
| Easter [15] | عيدُ الفِصْحِ (n., m.) |
| feast of breaking the Ramadan fast [15] | عيدُ الفِطْرِ (n., m.) |
| Christmas [15] | عيدُ الميلاد (n., m.) |
| bread (Egypt) [18] | عَيش (n., m.) |
| eye [24] | عَيْن ج عُيون (n., f.) |

# غ

| | |
|---|---|
| to leave [23] | غادَرَ (يُغادِرُ) مُغادَرة (v.) |
| [butane] gas [18] | غاز ج غازات (n., m.) |
| expensive, dear [19] | غالٍ (n., m.) |
| often, mostly, generally [19] | غالِباً (adv.) |
| cloudy; overcast [12] | غائِم (adj., m.) |
| a male's headdress [10] | غُتْرة ج غُتَر/ غُترات (n., f.) |
| tomorrow [11] | غَداً (adv.) |
| lunch [13] | غَداء ج أغْدِية (n., m.) |
| west [19] | غَرْب (n., m.) |
| room [1] | غُرْفَة ج غُرَف (n., f.) |
| sunset [17] | غُروب (n., m.) |
| washing machine [18] | غَسّالة ج غَسّالات (n., f.) |
| to wash [13] | غَسَلَ (يَغْسِلُ) غَسْل (v.) |
| rich, wealthy [17] | غَنيّ ج أغنِياء (n., m.) |
| to sing [22] | غَنّى (يُغَنّي) غِناء (v.) |
| spare part; change [24] | غِيار ج غيارات (n., m) |
| non-, un-, other than, different from [20] | غَيْر (n., m.) |
| to change sth. [13] | غَيَّرَ (يُغَيِّرُ) تَغيير (v.) |
| rain cloud [12] | غَيْمة ج غُيوم (n., f.) |

# ف

| | |
|---|---|
| and, then, so [17] | فَـ (coordinating particle) |
| deluxe, fancy, excellent, luxurious [18] | فاخِر (adj.) |
| to win [20] | فازَ (يفوزُ) فَوز (v.) |
| green beans [20] | فاصولية (n., f.) |
| benefit, use, advantage [17] | فائِدة ج فَوائِد (n., f.) |
| girl, young woman [10] | فَتاة ج فَتَيات (n., f.) |
| dawn, daybreak [15] | فَجْر (n., m.) |
| brush [13] | فُرْشاة ج فَراشٍ (n., f.) |
| *lit.* "a happy opportunity," *meaning* "good to meet you" [9] | فُرْصَة سَعيدة |

| | |
|---|---|
| branch, subdivision [24] | فَرْع ج فُروع (n., m.) |
| pharaoh [19] | فِرعَون ج فَراعِنة (n., m.) |
| band, company, troupe [19] | فِرقة ج فِرَق، أفْرِقة (n., f.) |
| French (language) [3] | الفَرَنْسِيَّة (n., f.) |
| team, company, band, troupe [20] | فَريق ج أفرِقة (n., f.) |
| riddle [22] | فَزّورة ج فَوازير (n., f.) |
| pistachio [21] | فُسْتُق (n., m.) |
| Classical Arabic (*lit.*: "most eloquent") [14] | فُصْحى (superlative) |
| (academic) term, season [5] | فَصْل ج فُصول (n., m.) |
| pure, good, clear, standard, or literary Arabic [22] | فَصيح (adj.) |
| space [22] | فَضاء (n., m.) |
| silver [23] | فِضّة (n., f.) |
| to prefer [14] | فَضَّلَ (يُفَضِّل) تَفْضيل (v.) |
| breakfast [8] | فَطور (n., m.) |
| pie [15] | فَطيرة ج فَطائِر (n., f.) |
| to do [7] | فَعَلَ (يَفعَلُ) فِعْل (v.) |
| only; no more than [5] | فَقَطْ (particle) |
| poor [17] | فَقير ج فُقَراء (n., m.) |
| to think, to reflect, to ponder (not to believe) [20] | فَكَّرَ (يُفَكِّرُ) تَفْكير (v.) |
| idea [14] | فِكْرة ج أفْكار (n., f.) |
| peasant, farmworker [23] | فَلّاح ج ون (n., m.) |
| philosophy [16] | فَلْسَفة ج فَلسَفات (n., f.) |
| patty made from ground beans and spices fried in oil (Syria) [8] | فُلفُل ج فَلافِل (n., m.) |
| green (bell) pepper [20] | فُلَيفُلة (n., f.) |
| cup [8] | فِنْجان ج فَناجين (n., m.) |
| hotel [11] | فُنْدُق ج فَنادِق (n., m.) |
| to understand, to comprehend, to realize [20] | فَهِمَ (يَفْهَمُ) فَهْم (v.) |
| fava beans [8] | فول (n., m.) |
| peanuts [20] | فول (سوداني) (n., m.) |
| physics [5] | فيزياء (n., f.) |
| philosopher [16] | فَيْلَسوف ج فَلاسِفة (n., m.) |

# ق

| | |
|---|---|
| to meet [11] | قابَلَ (يُقابِلُ) مُقابَلة (.v) |
| to drive [23] | قاد (يَقودُ) قِيادة (.v) |
| boat [19] | قارِب ج قَوارِب (.n., m) |
| continent [21] | قارّة ج قارّات (.n., f) |
| rule, principle, basis, foundation, base [20] | قاعِدة ج قَواعِد (.n., f) |
| to say [11] | قالَ (يَقولُ) قَوْل (.v) |
| to do, to perform [16] | قامَ (يَقومُ) قِيام (.v) |
| to gamble [19] | قامَرَ (يُقامِرُ) مُقامَرة، قِمار (.v) |
| law [16] | قانون ج قَوانين (.n., m) |
| Cairo (capital of Egypt) | القاهِرة (.n., f) |
| leader (military) [16] | قائد ج قُوّاد / قادة (.n., m) |
| before [11] | قَبْلَ (.adv) |
| [no meaning; denotes completed action, emphasis, or possibility] [23] | قَد (particle) |
| Jerusalem | القُدْس (.n., f) |
| foot [23] | قَدَم ج أقْدام (.n., f) |
| to serve, to provide [19] | قَدَّمَ (يُقَدِّمُ) تَقديم (.v) |
| old, ancient [10] | قَديم ج قُدَماء (.adj) |
| to read [7] | قَرَأَ (يَقرَأُ) قِراءة (.v) |
| nearby, close [7] | قُرْب (.adv) |
| pumpkin [15] | قَرْع (.n., m) |
| cauliflower [20] | قَرنَبيط (.n., m) |
| close, near [11] | قَريب (.adv) |
| a relative [23] | قَريب ج أقارِب (.n., m) |
| village [16] | قَرية ج قُرى (.n., f) |
| priest [16] | قِسّيس ج قَساوِسة (.n., m) |
| story [23] | قِصّة ج قِصَص (.n., f) |
| short [10] | قَصير ج قِصار (.n., m) |
| to spend time [13] | قَضى (يَقضي) قَضاء (.v) |
| train [14] | قِطار ج قِطارات (.n., m) |
| country (almost exclusively used for Arab countries) [21] | قُطْر ج أقْطار (.n., m) |

| | |
|---|---|
| piece [8] | قِطْعة ج قِطَع (n., f.) |
| cotton [21] | قُطْن (n., m.) |
| heart [23] | قَلْب ج قُلوب (n., m.) |
| to worry [17] | قَلَقَ (يَقْلَق) قَلَق (v.) |
| pencil, pen | قَلَم ج أقلام (n., m.) |
| little [6] | قَليل (adj.) |
| a little [6] | قَليلاً (adv.) |
| wheat [21] | قَمْح (n., m.) |
| moon, satellite [22] | قَمَر ج أقْمار (n., m.) |
| of the moon, lunar [1] | قَمَريّ (adj.) |
| shirt [11] | قَميص ج قُمْصان (n., m.) |
| channel [22] | قَناة ج قَنَوات (n., f.) |
| coffee [8] | قَهْوة (n., f.) |
| arch [14] | قَوْس ج أقْواس (n., m.) |
| powerful, strong [10] | قَويّ ج أقوِياء (adj.) |

# ك

| | |
|---|---|
| like, as [20] | كَـ (prep.) |
| writer, scribe [16] | كاتِب ج كُتّاب / كَتَبة (n., m.) |
| glass [8] | كَأس ج كُؤوس (n., f.) |
| sufficient [20] | كافٍ (الكافي) (active participle) |
| to be (was, were) [11] | كانَ (يَكونُ) كَوْن (v.) |
| December [11] | كانون الأوَّل (n., m.) |
| January [11] | كانون الثاني (n., m.) |
| kebab, minced meat on a skewer with parsley and onion [9] | كَباب (n., m.) |
| big, large; old (in age) [10] | كَبير ج كِبار (n., m.) |
| big [5] | كَبير (adj.) |
| book | كِتاب ج كُتُب (n., m.) |
| writing [13] | كِتابة (n., f.) |
| to write [7] | كَتَبَ (يَكْتُبُ) كِتابة (v.) |
| much, a great deal [13] | كَثير ج كَثيرون / كِثار (n., m.) |
| a great deal [8] | كَثيراً (adverbial) |

| | |
|---|---|
| كَذلِكَ | also, as well [19] |
| كَرَم (n., m.) | hospitality, generosity [23] |
| كُرة ج كُرات (n., f.) | ball, sphere [20] |
| كُرةُ السَلّة | basketball [20] |
| كُرةُ الطاولة | table tennis [20] |
| الكُرةُ الطائرة | volleyball [20] |
| كُرةُ القَدَم | football/soccer [20] |
| كُرةُ الماء | water polo [20] |
| كُرةُ المَضرِب | tennis [20] |
| كُرْسيّ ج كَراسٍ (n., m.) | chair |
| كِرمال | for the sake of (Syrian colloquial) [16] |
| كَريم ج كُرَماء (adj.) | generous [16] |
| كُلّ (n.) | every, all, the whole [12] |
| كِلا (n.) | both [21] |
| كَلام (n., m.) | speech, speaking [23] |
| كَلَّفَ (يُكَلِّفُ) تَكْليف (v.) | to cost [23] |
| كَلَّمَ (يُكَلِّمُ) (v.) | to talk to, to speak with [24] |
| كَلِمَة ج كَلِمات (n., f.) | word [3] |
| كُلِّيَّة ج كُلِّيات (n., f.) | college [2] |
| كَمْ (interrogative particle) | how many/much [3] |
| كَما (particle) | as [17] |
| كَمان | أيضاً (Syrian colloquial) [14] |
| كَهْرَباء (n., f.) | electricity [17] |
| كوسا (n., m.) | zucchini [20] |
| كوفِيّة ج كوفيّات (n., f.) | headdress [10] |
| كيبِل (n., m.) | cable [22] |
| كيلومِتر ج كيلومِترات (n., m.) | kilometer [19] |
| كيمياء (n., f.) | chemistry [5] |

# ل

| | |
|---|---|
| لـ (prep.) | to, for, by [6] |
| لاَ (negative particle) | no |

| | |
|---|---|
| Don't worry about it (said when s.o. thanks you for sth.) [6] | لا شُكْرَ على واجِب |
| necessary [16] | لازِم (active participle) |
| player [23] | لاعِب ج ون (n., m.) |
| because [13] | لأنَّ (particle) |
| kernel, seed [20] | لُبّ ج لُبوب (n., m.) |
| to wear [10] | لَبِسَ (يَلبَسُ) لُبْس (v.) |
| yogurt [13] | لَبَن (n., m.) |
| lightly salted, partially dehydrated yogurt with olive oil [14] | لَبَنة (n., f.) |
| meat [8] | لَحْم ج لُحوم (n., m.) |
| عِنْدَ [19] | لَدى (prep.) |
| for this reason, therefore [14] | لِذلِكَ (demonstrative) |
| delicious, delightful, tasty [20] | لَذيذ (adj., m.) |
| nice [5] | لَطيف (adj.) |
| to play [20] | لَعِبَ (يَلعَبُ) لَعْب (v.) |
| game, play, ride [19] | لُعبة ج لُعبات، ألعاب (n., f.) |
| language [2] | لُغَة ج لُغات (n., f.) |
| of language, linguistic [2] | لُغَويّ (adj.) |
| [expresses completed action with a perfect tense verb] [24] | لَقَد (particle) |
| but [1] | لكِنْ (particle, weak version) |
| but [1] | لكِنَّ (particle, strong version) |
| not (particle used to negate past-tense verbs) [17] | لَمْ (particle) |
| no longer [20] | لَمْ يَعُدْ |
| why [13] | لـماذا (particle) |
| negates future (= will not) [19] | لَنْ + المضارع المنصوب |
| blackboard | لَوح ج ألْواح (n., m.) |
| if you would; please [1] | لَو سَمَحْت |
| color [12] | لَوْن ج ألْوان (n., m.) |
| [Syrian] pound; lira [18] | لَيْرة ج لَيْرات (n., f.) |
| not [1] | لَيْسَ (particle) |
| لِماذا (Syrian colloquial) [14] | لَيْش |
| night [12] | لَيْل (n., m.) |
| (a) night [17] | لَيْلة ج لَيالٍ (n., f.) |

# م

| | |
|---|---|
| م (مِتْر) ج أمْتار (.n., m) | meter [18] |
| ما | what (question particle used in front of nouns) [3] |
| ما (particle) | [particle used to negate past-tense verbs] [10] |
| ما عَدا (particle) | except [17] |
| ماء ج مِياه (.n., m) | water [8] |
| ماء غازيّ ج مِياه غازيّة (.n., f) | soda [20] |
| ماتَ (يموتُ) مَوْت (.v) | to die [22] |
| مادّة ج مَوادّ (.n., f) | school subject, course [4] |
| ماذا | what (used with verbs) [3] |
| ما رأيُك | what's your opinion? [8] |
| ماضٍ (الماضي) (.adj) | previous, last, past [17] |
| ماطِر (.adj., m) | rainy [12] |
| مانِع (active participle) | objection [11] |
| مُباراة ج مُبارَيات (.n., f) | match, game [20] |
| مُبارَك (.n., m) | blessed [15] |
| مُبَكِّر ج مُبَكِّرون (.n., m) | one coming early [13] |
| مَبنى ج مَبانٍ (.n., m) | building, construction [19] |
| مُتَأخِّر ج مُتَأخِّرون (.n., m) | one coming late [13] |
| مَتى (question particle) | when [8] |
| مُتَّحِد (.adj., m) | united [9] |
| مُتحَف ج مَتاحِف (.n., m) | museum [19] |
| مُتَحَمِّس (active participle) | enthusiastic [11] |
| مِترو (.n., m) | metro [18] |
| مُتَزَوِّج ج مُتَزَوِّجون (n., m) | married [1] |
| مُتَفَرِّج ج ون (.n., m) | spectator [20] |
| مُتَقاعِد ج مُتَقاعِدون (.n., m) | retired person [24] |
| مُتَوَسِّط (.adj., m) | intermediate [15] |
| مِثْل ج أمْثال (.n., m) | something similar, like, such as [19] |
| مَجّانيّ (.adj) | free of charge [22] |
| مُجْتَمَع ج مُجْتَمَعات (.n., m) | society, community [23] |

| | |
|---|---|
| magazine [7] | مَجَـلَّة ج مَجَلاّت (n., f.) |
| kitchen sink [18] | مَجْلى ج مَجالٍ (n., m.) |
| accountant [23] | مُحاسِب ج ون (n., m.) |
| accounting [9] | مُحاسَبة (n., f.) |
| lawyer, attorney-at-law, counsel [16] | مُحامٍ ج مُحامون (n., m.) |
| loving [19] | مُحِبّ ج مُحِبّون (n., m.) |
| engine, motor [10] | مُحَرِّك ج مُحَرِّكات (n., f.) |
| Islamic month (*muḥarram*) [11] | مُحَرَّم (n., m.) |
| station [14] | مَحَطّة ج مَحَطّات (n., f.) |
| place; store [1] | مَحَلّ (n., m.) |
| roasted, toasted [20] | مُحَمَّص (n./adj.) |
| ocean [21] | مُحيط ج مُحيطات (n., m.) |
| bakery [18] | مَخْبَز ج مَخابِز (n., m.) |
| laboratory [2] | مُخْتَبَر ج مُخْتَبَرات (n., m.) |
| store, warehouse [24] | مَخْزَن ج مَخازِن (n., m.) |
| [floor] plan, map [18] | مُخَطَّط ج مُخَطَّطات (n., m.) |
| sincere, faithful (sincerely yours) [19] | مُخلِص ج مُخلِصون (n., m.) |
| period, duration [19] | مُدّة ج مُدَد (n., f.) |
| teacher [24] | مُدَرِّس ج مُدَرِّسون (n., m.) |
| school [17] | مَدْرَسة ج مَدارِس (n., f.) |
| stewed [13] | مُدَمَّس (adj.) |
| boss; director [6] | مُدير ج مُدَراء (n., m.) |
| city, town | مَدينة ج مُدُن (n., f.) |
| announcer [22] | مُذيع ج ون (n., m.) |
| to pass, to go by [19] | مَرَّ (يَمُرُّ) مُرور (v.) |
| mirror [18] | مِرْآة ج مَرايا (n., f.) |
| square [21] | مُرَبَّع (adj.) |
| jam, preserve [8] | مُرَبّى ج مُرَبَّيات (n., m.) |
| elevated [18] | مُرْتَفِع (active participle) |
| toilet [18] | مِرْحاض ج مَراحيض (n., m.) |
| center [23] | مَرْكَز ج مَراكِز (n., m.) |
| comfortable [18] | مُريح (adj.) |

| | |
|---|---|
| sick, ill, patient [24] | مَريض ج مَرْضى (n., m) |
| once, one occurrence [13] | مَرّة ج مَرّات (n., f.) |
| crowded [14] | مُزْدَحِم (adj.) |
| farm [23] | مَزْرَعة ج مَزارِع (n., f.) |
| area [21] | مِساحة ج مِساحات (n., f.) |
| help, assistance [6] | مُساعَدة (verbal n.) |
| evening [8] | مَساء (n., m.) |
| swimming pool [2] | مَسْبَح ج مَسابِح (n., m.) |
| hospital [24] | المُسْتَشْفى (n., m.) |
| mosque [19] | مَسجِد ج مَساجِد (n., m.) |
| recorded [23] | مُسَجَّل (adj./n.) |
| recorder [23] | مُسَجِّلة ج مُسَجِّلات (n., f.) |
| theater, stage [19] | مَسرَح ج مَسارِح (n., m.) |
| show, (television) series [13] | مُسَلسَل ج مُسَلسَلات (n., m.) |
| Muslim, one of the Islamic faith [15] | مُسْلِم ج مُسْلِمون (n., m.) |
| boiled [8] | مَسْلوق (passive particle) |
| Christ [15] | المَسيح (n., m.) |
| walk [11] | مَشى (يَمْشي) مَشي (v.) |
| watching [13] | مُشاهَدة (verbal n.) |
| one who is longing, yearning [19] | مُشْتاق ج مُشْتاقون (n., m.) |
| busy [13] | مَشْغول ج مَشْغولون (n., m.) |
| mixed, assorted [16] | مُشَكَّل (passive participle) |
| famous, well-known [14] | مَشْهور ج (ون)، مَشاهير (participle) |
| grill, gridiron [20] | مِشواة ج مَشاوٍ (n., f.) |
| grilled [20] | مَشويّ (adj.) |
| lamp [18] | مِصْباح ج مَصابيح (n., m.) |
| Egypt | مِصْر (n., f.) |
| bank [18] | مَصْرِف ج مَصارِف (n., m.) |
| elevator, lift [19] | مِصعَد ج مَصاعِد (n., m.) |
| factory, plant [23] | مَصْنَع ج مَصانِع (n., m.) |
| made (of/from) [21] | مَصْنوع (مِن) (passive participle) |
| airport [11] | مَطار ج مَطارات (n., m.) |

| | |
|---|---|
| مَطْبَخ ج مَطابِخ (n., m.) | kitchen [8] |
| مَطَر ج أمْطار (n., m.) | rain [12] |
| مُطْرِب ج مُطْرِبون (n., m.) | entertainer [22] |
| مَطْعَم ج مَطاعِم (n., m.) | restaurant [8] |
| مُطِلّ (verbal n.) | overlooking [18] |
| مَعَ (prep.) | with [1] |
| مَعاً (adv.) | together [13] |
| مَعَ أنَّ | though, although [19] |
| مُعايَدة ج مُعايَدات (n., f.) | greeting [17] |
| مُعْتَدِل (adj.) | moderate [12] |
| مَعْجون ج مَعاجين (n., m.) | paste [13] |
| مُعْظَم (n.) | most [12] |
| مَعك حَقّ | you're right [14] |
| مَعْكَرونة (n., f.) | pasta, macaroni [14] |
| مُعَلِّم ج مُعَلِّمون (active participle) | teacher [15] |
| مَعلومة ج مَعلومات (n., f.) | information [15] |
| مَعْنى ج مَعانٍ / المعاني (n., m.) | meaning [3] |
| مَغْرِب (n., m.) | sunset [15] |
| المَغْرِب (n., f.) | Morocco |
| مَغْسَلة ج مَغاسِل (n., f.) | washbasin, bathroom sink [18] |
| مُغَطّىً (بِـ) (passive participle) | covered (with) [21] |
| مُغَنٍّ ج ون (n., m.) | singer [22] |
| مِفْتاح ج مَفاتيح (n., m.) | key |
| مِفْرَش ج مَفارِش (n., m.) | tablecloth [23] |
| مُفَضَّل (n./adj., m.) | preferred, favorite [20] |
| مَفعول (passive participle) | effectiveness, validity [24] |
| مُقابِل (adv.) | opposite, across from [18] |
| مُقابَلة ج ات (n., f.) | interview [22] |
| مُقبِل ج مُقبِلون (n., m.) | coming, next, following [19] |
| مُقَدِّمة ج مُقَدِّمات (n., f.) | introduction [16] |
| مَقْصَف ج مَقاصِف (n., m.) | cafeteria [8] |
| مَقْعَد ج مَقاعِد (n., m.) | seat, bench, armchair [23] |

| | |
|---|---|
| fried [13] | مَقليّ (adj.) |
| place, location [16] | مَكان ج أمْكِنة (n., m.) |
| office [2] | مَكْتَب ج مَكاتِب (n., m.) |
| library, bookstore, bookcase [2] | مَكْتَبة ج مَكْتَبات (n., f.) |
| written [17] | مَكْتوب (n., m.) |
| Mexico [21] | المِكسيك (n., f.) |
| note, observation [24] | مُلاحَظة ج مُلاحظات (n., f.) |
| clothes [18] | مَلبَس ج مَلابِس (n., m.) |
| playground, sports field [2] | مَلْعَب ج مَلاعِب (n., m.) |
| king [16] | مَلِك ج مُلوك (n., m.) |
| queen [23] | مَلِكة ج مَلِكات (n., f.) |
| place of entertainment [14] | مَلْهىً ج مَلاهٍ (n., m.) |
| polluted [23] | مُلَوَّث (adj.) |
| million [19] | مِليون (n., m.) |
| excellent [14] | مُمْتاز ج ون (adj.) |
| enjoyable [23] | مُمْتِع (active participle) |
| actor, representative [22] | مُمَثِّل ج ون (n., m.) |
| kingdom [23] | مَمْلَكة ج مَمالِك (n., f.) |
| who [5] | مَنْ (question particle and relative noun) |
| from, of | مِن (prep.) |
| via; by means of [22] | مِن خِلالِ |
| please [7] | مِن فَضْلِك |
| occasion [15] | مُناسَبة ج مُناسَبات (n., f.) |
| product [21] | مُنتَج ج مُنتَجات (n., m.) |
| scholarship, grant, gift [17] | مِنْحة ج مِنَح (n., f.) |
| since, for [19] | مُنْذُ (prep.) |
| house, residence [23] | مَنزِل ج مَنازِل (n., m.) |
| region [15] | مِنْطَقة ج مَناطِق (n., f.) |
| view, panorama [23] | مَنْظَر ج مَناظِر (n., m.) |
| outlet [21] | مَنْفَذ ج مَنافِذ (n., m.) |
| جَيِّد (Syrian colloquial) [16] | منيح ج امْناح (adj.) |
| engineer [14] | مُهَنْدِس ج مُهَندِسون (n., m.) |

| | |
|---|---|
| occupation, profession [24] | مِهْنة ج مِهَن (n., f.) |
| means of transportation [23] | مُواصَلة ج مُواصَلات (n., f.) |
| agree [8] | مُوافِق (active participle) |
| agreement, approval [6] | مُوافَقَة (verbal n.) |
| found, existing, present [1] | مَوْجود (n., m.) |
| wave [22] | مَوْجة ج ات (n., f.) |
| historian [16] | مُؤَرِّخ ج مُؤَرِّخون (n., m.) |
| banana [20] | مَوْز (n., m.) |
| worker; employee [6] | مُوَظَّف (ج) مُوَظَّفون (n., m.) |
| time, appointment [9] | مَوْعِد ج مَواعيد (n., m.) |
| [cooking] range [18] | مَوْقِد ج مَواقِد (n., m.) |
| [bus] stop, parking lot [18] | مَوْقِف ج مَواقِف (n., m.) |
| birthday, birthplace [15] | مَوْلِد (n., m.) |
| consisting of, comprising [24] | مُؤَلَّف (مِن) (passive participle) |
| hundred [6] | مِئة ج مِئات (n., f.) |
| square, field, arena [19] | مَيدان ج مَيادين (n., m.) |
| birth, birthday [15] | ميلاد ج مَواليد (n., m.) |
| port [19] | ميناء ج مَوانِئ (n., m.) |

## ن

| | |
|---|---|
| waiter [23] | نادِل ج نُدُل (n., m.) |
| window | نافِذة ج نَوافِذ (n., f.) |
| minus [3] | ناقِص (n., m.) |
| to fall asleep; to sleep [9] | نامَ (يَنامُ) نَوْم (v.) |
| plant [23] | نَبات ج نَباتات (n., m.) |
| to spring, to originate, to flow [21] | نَبَعَ (يَنْبُعُ) نَبْع (v.) |
| section, manner, mode, fashion [21] | نَحْو ج أَنْحاء (n., m.) |
| to stay (in a place) [11] | نَزَلَ (يَنْزِلُ) نُزول (v.) |
| relative adjective | نِسْبة (n., f.) |
| person (used in population counts) [19] | نَسَمة ج نَسَمات (n., f.) |
| to forget [13] | نَسِيَ (يَنسى) نِسْيان (v.) |
| textile, tissue, fabric [21] | نَسيج (n., m.) |

| | |
|---|---|
| bulletin, report [22] | نَشْرة ج نَشَرات (n., f.) |
| half [9] | نِصْف ج أَنْصاف (n., m.) |
| to clean [13] | نَظَّفَ (يُنَظِّفُ) تَنظيف (v.) |
| eyeglasses | نَظّارة ج نَظّارات (n., f.) |
| system [22] | نِظام ج أَنْظِمة (n., m.) |
| clean [14] | نَظيف (adj., m.) |
| yes | نَعَم |
| mint, peppermint [23] | نَعناع (n., m.) |
| same [24] | نَفْس ج أَنْفُس (. . .الـ) (n., f.) |
| petroleum, crude oil [21] | نِفْط (n., m.) |
| to be sent into exile, to be expelled [16] | نُفِيَ (يُنْفى) نَفْيٌ (passive v.) |
| to move sth. somewhere; to transport [23] | نَقَلَ (يَنْقُلُ) نَقل (v.) |
| small, spicy mutton sausage [20] | نَقانِق (أو مَقانِق) (n., f. pl.) |
| pure [23] | نَقيّ (adj.) |
| daytime [12] | نَهار (n., m.) |
| end [14] | نِهاية ج نِهايات (n., f.) |
| to get up [13] | نَهَضَ (يَنهَضُ) نُهوض (v.) |
| kind, sort [17] | نَوْع ج أَنْواع (n., m.) |
| sleeping [11] | نَوْم (verbal n.) |
| April [11] | نيسان (n., m.) |

## هـ

| | |
|---|---|
| these [2] | هاتانِ (dual, f., nom.) |
| phone | هاتِف ج هَواتِف (n., m.) |
| these [2] | هاتَيْنِ (dual, f., acc., gen.) |
| Pacific [21] | الهادي (adj.) |
| quiet, serene [23] | هادِئ (adj.) |
| important, significant [19] | هامٌّ ج هامّون (n./adj.) |
| present, gift [23] | هَدِيّة ج هَدايا (n., f.) |
| this | هذا (n., m.) |
| these [2] | هذانِ (dual, m., nom.) |
| these [2] | هذَيْنِ (dual, m., acc., gen.) |

| | |
|---|---|
| this | هذِه (n., f.) |
| pyramid [19] | هَرَم ج أهرام / أهرامات (n., m.) |
| (question particle for yes-no questions) [3] | هَلْ |
| now (Syrian colloquial) [18] | هَلَّق أو هَللأ |
| they | هُم (pron., m., pl.) |
| they | هُما (pron., m., dual) |
| they | هُنَّ (pron., f., pl.) |
| here [9] | هُنا (demonstrative) |
| there, there is/are [1] | هُناكَ (demonstrative) |
| Pacific [21] | الهادي (adj.) |
| to congratulate, to felicitate (on the occasion of) [15] | هَنَّأَ (يُهَنِّئُ) تَهنئة (v.) |
| India [10] | الهِنْد (n., f.) |
| engineering [2] | هَنْدَسَة (n., f.) |
| he | هُوَ (pron.) |
| air [23] | هَواء (n., m.) |
| these (human plural) [2] | هؤُلاءِ (m., pl.) |
| identity [3] | هُوِيّة ج هُوِيّات (n., f.) |
| she | هِيَ (pron.) |

## و

| | |
|---|---|
| and [1] | وَ (conjunction) |
| one [3] | واحِد (n., m.) |
| spacious, large [18] | واسِع (adj.) |
| father, parent [19] | والِد ج والِدون (n., m.) |
| by God, I swear, really (used to add emphasis) [13] | وَاللّهِ |
| to find [17] | وَجَدَ (يَجِدُ) وُجود (v.) |
| there is/are, to exist [18] | وُجِدَ (يوجَدُ) (passive of وَجَد) |
| face [13] | وَجْه ج وُجوه (n., m.) |
| alone, by himself [9] | وَحْدَهُ (adv.) |
| sole, only [5] | وَحيد ج وَحيدون (n., m.) |
| paper | وَرَقَة ج أوْراق (n., f.) |
| ministry, department in an administration [24] | وِزارة ج وِزارات (n., f.) |

| | |
|---|---|
| وَزير ج وُزَراء (n., m.) | minister [16] |
| وِسادة ج وَسائِد (n., f.) | pillow [11] |
| وَسَط ج أوساط (n., m.) | middle, central [21] |
| وُسْطى (adj., f.) | middle [4] |
| وَسيم ج (ون) (adj., m.) | handsome [10] |
| وِشاح ج أوشِحة، وَشائح (n., m) | scarf, sash [23] |
| وَصَلَ (يَصِلُ) وُصول (v.) | to arrive, to reach a destination [11] |
| وَضَعَ (يَضَعُ) وَضْع (v.) | to put [18] |
| وَطَن ج أوطان (n., m.) | homeland |
| وَقْت ج أوْقات (n., m.) | time [20] |
| وَقَعَ (يَقَعُ) وُقوع / وَقْع (v.) | to be located; to fall down [18] |
| وِلاية ج وِلايات (n., f.) | state |
| الوِلاياتُ المُتَّحِدةُ الأمريكيّة (n., f.) | the United States of America [9] |
| وَلَد ج أَوْلاد (n., m.) | boy [5] |
| وُلِدَ (يولَدُ) وُلود (v.) | to be born (passive) [15] |

## ي

| | |
|---|---|
| يا | [vocative particle used to call the attention of the addressee] [3] |
| اليابان (n., f.) | Japan [10] |
| اليابانِيَّة (n., f.) | Japanese (language) [3] |
| يَد ج أَيْدٍ (n., f.) | hand [13] |
| يَسار (n., m.) | left [18] |
| يُمْكِنُكَ (v.) | you (m. sg.) are able [6] |
| يَمين (n., m.) | right [18] |
| يَوْم ج أيّام (n., m.) | day [11] |
| اليَوْم (adv.) | today [11] |
| يَوْمِيّة ج يوميّات (n., f.) | diary, daily journal [11] |

# Index


**A**

absolute object . . . . . . . . . . . . . . 343
accusative 8, 10–13, 34, 52–54, 64, 81–82, 107–110, 123, 127, 137, 146–147, 160, 192, 209, 211, 216, 221, 268, 287–289, 291, 295, 324–325, 343–344, 378, 404, 407, 464, 511
active participle. . . . . 99, 126, 314–316, 346–347, 439, 550
activities (describing) 117, 135, 139, 159, 165–166, 177, 201, 207, 243, 251, 263, 303, 361, 389, 499
added letters (verb forms). 312, 316, 324
addition (*iḍāfa*). . . . . . . . . . . . . .28
adjectives . . . . . .14, 27–28, 36, 64–66, 80, 82–84, 86, 101, 137–138, 148, 157–159, 177, 190–194, 196, 212–214, 273, 290–291, 315, 406, 408, 436–437
adverb . . . . . 9, 101, 128, 135, 137–138, 208, 216–217, 237, 245, 361, 378, 389, 404–405, 413–414, 464, 475, 491–493
adverb of place عِند. . . . . . . . 128, 414
adverbial . . 135, 137–138, 217, 237, 464
affirmative (sentence) . . . . . . . . . 467
agent. . . . . . . 126, 288, 293–295, 314, 318, 346, 374, 488
agreement. . . . . . . . .7, 27, 61, 64–66, 107–109, 177, 190–194, 408, 490, 493
alphabet (table). . . . . . . . . . . . . 545
answer key . . . . . . . . . . . . . . . 564
antecedent. . . . . . . . . . 407–411, 413
Arab culture (notes) . . . 35, 76, 80, 131, 138, 167, 182, 195, 356, 523, 528, 540
Arab states . . . . . . . . . . . . . . . 183
Arabian Gulf . . . . . . . . . . . 183–184
article (definite and indefinite) . 3, 14–15, 17–18, 30–32, 84, 96, 131, 151, 157, 170, 188, 232, 237, 325, 410, 512, 529, 533
arts. . . . . . . . . . . . . . . . . . . . 182
assimilating . . . . . . . . . 3, 14–15, 19
attached pronoun . . . . . . 8–9, 30–31, 117, 120, 123, 128–131, 135, 146, 344, 414–415, 466, 489
attribute . . . . . . . . . 80, 212, 318, 529
augmented verbs . . . . . . . . . 317, 533

**B**

broken plurals . . . . 147–148, 257, 346

**C**

cardinal numbers. . . . 41, 47, 83–84, 95, 107–108, 157, 169, 324–325
case . . . . . . . . . . . . 3, 8, 10–11, 13, 27, 29–32, 52–53, 64–66, 81–84, 99, 107–110, 117, 123, 126–128, 137, 147, 158–159, 177, 188–190, 192–193, 216, 220–221, 257, 268, 287–291, 293–294, 324–325, 333, 343–344, 349, 374, 376, 378, 404–405, 407, 464, 466–467, 488, 493, 511
Christ (Christmas). . . . . 218–219, 298
clause . . . .268, 406–407, 410–411, 434, 512–513
colloquial Arabic . . . xxv, xxvi, 23, 35, 36
colors . . . . . . . . . .314, 321, 423, 436
comment (predicate). . . . . 10, 126, 344
comparative 201, 212–214, 375, 423, 437, 519, 529, 530
completed action قَد . . . . . . . 509–510
compound numbers . . . . . . . 107, 159
computer program. . . . . . . . . . . xix
conditional إنْ. . . . . . . . . . . 512–513
conjunction فَ . . . . . . . . . . 268, 508
conjunction وَ. . . . 6, 159, 169, 171–172
conjunctive *hamza* . . . . . . . . . . . 532
consonant. . . . 15–16, 36, 52, 147, 157, 170, 188–189, 209–210, 292–294, 311, 322, 423, 437, 532, 547
content questions. . . . . .xxii, 41, 43–44

context. . . . . . .xix–xxvii, 4, 42, 51, 64, 69, 77, 86, 98, 105, 119–120, 129, 136, 152, 194, 214, 217, 220, 223, 231, 252, 256, 355, 376, 405, 467, 493, 508
continuous present. . . . . . . 45–46, 95, 103–105, 122, 138, 144, 201, 207, 210, 216–217, 263, 318, 348, 350–351, 361, 372, 389, 404
contrast . .3, 8–10, 13, 212, 263, 268–269
contrastive . . . . . . . . . . . . . . . 269
count noun . . . . . . . . . . . . 157, 171

**D**

*ḍamma*. . . . . . 10, 17, 30, 535–536, 547
declinable . . . . . . . . . . . . . . . . 325
defective. . . 253, 292, 294, 322, 438–439
defective verbs . . . . . . . . . . 292, 439
definite . . . 3, 10, 14–15, 17–18, 30–32, 64, 81–82, 84, 86, 96, 110, 123, 126, 131, 137, 151, 157–159, 169–170, 188, 190, 193–194, 208, 213, 232, 236–237, 290, 325, 373, 406, 410, 439, 488, 492, 512, 529, 533
definite article . . . . . .3, 14–15, 17–18, 30–32, 84, 96, 131, 151, 157, 170, 188, 232, 237, 325, 410, 512, 529, 533
definiteness . . . 30, 32, 84, 158, 177, 190, 193–194, 288
degree . . 95, 98, 101, 137–138, 201, 209, 212–214, 235, 423, 519, 529
demonstrative . . . . . 3, 7, 23, 33–35, 64, 69–70, 263, 270, 271–272, 413–414, 534
deputy agent . . . . . . . . . . . 293–295
diacritical marks . . . . . . . . . . . . 545
dialects . . . . . . . . . . . . xxv, 36, 184
dialogues . .xix, xxii, xxvi, 136, 140, 149, 151
dialogues (DVD) . . . . . . 37, 57, 72, 98
dictionary . . . . . . . . . . .xxiv, 45, 311
diptote. . . . . . .126, 279, 289–291, 511
direct object. . 81–83, 123, 127, 268, 289, 292, 373–374, 489
directions . . 381, 383, 405, 447, 464–465
disjunctive *hamza* . . . . . . . . 532, 534
diving for pearls . . . . . . . . . . . . 184
doer of the action 126, 319, 346, 467, 488
double *ḍamma* . . . . . . . . . 10, 17, 30
double *fatḥa* . 10–11, 17, 30, 52–53, 537
double *kasra* . . . . . . . . 17, 30–31, 82
doubled consonant. . . . . 209, 423, 437
dual . . . . . 7, 12, 34, 45, 61–62, 64–65, 82, 99, 105, 110, 126–127, 137, 144, 190, 192, 201, 208–209, 213–214, 256–257, 288, 315, 333, 343, 345–346, 348, 353, 407–409, 436, 465, 512, 531, 550

**E**

education . . . . . . . . . . . . . 182, 279
emirates . . . . . . . . . . . . . . . . . 183
emphasis . . . . . . . . .64–65, 509–510
endings . . .13–14, 64, 81, 99, 212, 237, 290
enumerating . . . . . . . . . . . . . . 3, 6
exception . .126, 130, 157–159, 253, 333, 344, 447, 466, 468, 532, 534
exercises. . . . .xix–xxiv, xxvi–xxvii, 564
explaining reason . . . . . 333, 344–345
express dislike . . . . . . . . . . . . 137

**F**

family . . . . .xxiii, 75, 78–80, 86–88, 95, 167–168, 177, 180, 182–183, 190, 195, 285, 377, 519, 524, 540
*fatḥa* . . . . 10–11, 17, 30, 52–53, 81, 169, 535–537, 547
feminine. . . . . . . . . .7, 11–12, 27, 29, 33–34, 36, 45, 65–66, 69–70, 84, 99, 103, 105–106, 108–110, 119, 129–130, 138, 144, 147–148, 157–158, 191, 254, 288, 293, 315–316, 345, 348, 373, 407–409, 436, 465, 490, 493, 529–530, 550
feminine superlative . . . . . . . 529–530
final *hamza* . . . . . . . . . . . 535, 537
first name . . . . . . . . . . . 80, 131, 528
fishing . . . . . . . . . . . . . . . . . . 184
five nouns . . . . .220–221, 279, 287, 288
formality . . . . . . . . . . . . . . . . 403
fractions. . . . . . . . . . . . . 159–161
frequency . . 137, 251, 333, 343, 423, 434
fricative . . . . . . . . . . . . . . . . . 549

functional objectives . . . . . . . . . . xxii
functions . . xix, xx–xxi, xxiii, xxv–xxvi, 64, 83, 120, 220, 411, 508–509
future . . . .201, 207, 215–216, 263, 389, 403, 405–406, 531

**G**

gender . . . . . . . . . 7–8, 11–12, 27–28, 34–35, 45, 65–66, 69–70, 82, 84, 86, 99, 104–105, 107–110, 130, 158, 177, 185, 190–192, 207, 255–256, 288, 293, 325, 373, 407–409, 436, 493, 530
genitive . . . . . . . . . . . . . . . 29–31, 34, 64–66, 82, 107–110, 127, 146–147, 158–159, 170–171, 208, 220–221, 236, 287–290, 324–325, 343–344, 376, 378, 405, 407, 488, 511
glossary . . . . . . . . . . . . . . xix, xxiv
glottal stop . . . . . . . . . . 36, 170, 549
grammar . . . . . xx–xxii, xxiv, xxvii, 83
grammar (identification) . . . . 148, 151
grammar (note) . . . . . . . . . 112, 126
grammarians . . . . . . . . . 14, 213, 378
grammars . . . . . . . . . . . .81–82, 318
greetings. . . . . . . . . . . . . . . . . 149
Gregorian calendar. . . . . . . . . . . 219

**H**

habitual action . . . . . . . 139, 423, 434
*hamza* . . 15, 36, 122, 519, 532–538, 547
*hamzatu-l-qaᶜ* . . . . . . . 532, 534, 537
*hamzatu-l-waṣl* . . . . . 15, 532–533, 537
head gear . . . . . . . . . . . . . . . . 184
headdress . . . . . . . . . . . . . 167, 184
hollow verb . . . . . . .215, 253, 292, 294

**I**

*iḍāfa* . . . . . . . .23, 28–32, 56, 529, 533
illustrations . . . . . . . . . . . . . . xxiii
imperative. . . . xxiv, 117, 120–124, 135, 144–145, 243, 252–254, 318, 439, 533, 550–563
imperfect . . . . . . . . 45, 104, 318, 510
inanimate . . . . . 128, 130, 138, 191, 491
indeclinable. . .84, 107, 109, 159, 289, 290
indefinite . . . . . . 3, 10, 17–18, 30–31, 52–53, 64–66, 81–82, 86, 108–110, 123, 126, 137, 151, 160, 171, 193–194, 209, 213, 216, 236–237, 288–289, 291, 373, 410, 413, 439, 493
indefinite antecedent. . . . . . . . . . 410
indicative . .104, 139, 207, 353, 349–351, 406, 439, 513, 534, 550–562
indirect speech . . . . . . . . . . . . .96
infinitive. . . . . . . . . . . . . . . 45, 372
initial *hamza* . . . . . . . . . . . 532–533
inquiring . . . . . . . . . . . . . 117, 119
instrument (noun of) . . . . . . 361, 375
intention . . . . . . . . . . . . . 361, 372
invariable . . . . . . . .108, 161, 325, 465
Islamic calendar . . . . . . . . . . . . 218

**J**

jussive . . . . . . 253, 348–351, 439, 490, 512–513, 550–562

**K**

*kasra*. . . 17, 30–31, 64, 82, 534–536, 547

**L**

language functions . . xix–xxi, xxiii, xxvi
last names . . . . . . . . . . 75, 80–81, 97
learning environment . . . . . . . . xxvii
Learning Objectives . . . . . . . . . . xxii
Levant . . . . . . . . . . . . . . xxv, 35–36
literature. . . . . . . . . . . . . . xxvi, 182
location . . . . 3–4, 43–44, 217, 311, 356, 361, 378, 464–465, 508
lunar calendar . . . . . . . . . . 217, 287

**M**

*madda* . . . . . . . . . . . . . . . . . . 547
map . . . . . . . . . . xxiii, 183, 383, 465
marker. . . . . . . . . . 10–12, 17, 30, 52, 81, 83, 108, 127, 144, 147, 158, 192, 207, 209, 221, 253, 290, 406
masculine . . . . . . . .7, 12, 27, 33–34, 45, 65–66, 69–70, 82, 84, 99, 103, 105, 107–109, 111, 119, 121, 126–127, 137, 144, 146–148, 185–186, 191–192, 196,

208–209, 215, 253–254, 256–257, 288, 211, 315–316, 343, 345, 348, 353, 407–409, 436, 465, 490, 493, 529–530, 550
mass noun . . . . . . . . . . . . . . . 171
matching . . . . . . . . . . . . xxii, xxvii
matching (exercises) . . . 5, 26, 41, 63, 85, 101, 125, 142, 168, 182, 203, 230, 244, 280, 304, 324, 334, 362, 391, 401, 424, 449
medial *hamza*. . . . . . . . . . . . . . 536
Modern Standard Arabic . . . xxiv, xxvii
mood . . . . . . . xxi, xxiv, 348, 439, 488
moon letters . . . . . . . . . . . . .14, 16
morphological patterns . . . . . . . . 311
multiple choice . . . . . . . . . xxii, xxvii
multiple *iḍāfa*. . . . . . . . . . . 135, 151

**N**

names . . . . . . . . . . . . . . . . . . 25, 27, 52, 69, 75–76, 80–81, 97, 117, 125, 131, 167, 177, 184, 187, 217–218, 240, 287, 289, 291, 375, 435
negating a past tense verb . . . . . . . 187
negation . . . . . . .95, 103, 177, 216, 348
negative . . . 9, 46, 50, 103, 137, 235, 253, 466–467
nickname . . . . . . . . . . . . . . . . 528
*nisba*. . . . . . . . . . 23, 27–28, 272, 465
nominal sentence. . .3, 7, 9–11, 126, 209, 211, 216, 221, 237, 271, 295, 344
nominative . . . . . . . 10–11, 27, 34, 64, 99, 107–110, 126–127, 146–147, 159, 161, 192, 209, 211, 216, 221, 268, 287, 288, 293–294, 324–325, 343–344
non-inflecting . . . . . . . . (*see* diptote)
non-rational nouns . . . . . 69, 191, 409
non-restrictive . . . . . . . . . . 409, 413
noun . . . . (comparative nouns) 375, 423, 437; (count nouns) 157, 171; (dual nouns) 61, 64, 82, 126–127, 192, 208–209, 343; (five special nouns) 201, 220, 221, 287; (modified noun) 65, 82, 106–107, 110, 220, 236, 263, 271, 325, 378, 406–407, 493, 511; (not fully inflected nouns) 289; (noun-adjective) 158, 177, 190–193, 408; (noun of instrument) 361, 375; (number-noun agreement) 61, 64; (partitive nouns) 229, 236, 243, 252; (plural nouns) 7, 69, 82, 148, 190, 257, 333, 343; (plurals of nouns) 135, 146; (relative noun) 27, 263, 272, 389, 406–411, 413, 475, 491; (verbal noun) xxiv, 177, 188–190, 311, 314, 373, 489, 519, 531–533, 550
noun phrase. . . . 86, 193–194, 268, 272, 344, 406, 488, 511
number . . . . .6–7, 11–12, 27–29, 34, 41, 45, 47–49, 51, 52, 54, 57, 61, 64–69, 75, 82–84, 86, 95, 104–105, 107–111, 123, 130, 157–159, 161, 166, 169, 171–172, 177, 185, 188, 190–191, 207–208, 236, 254–256, 258, 303, 311, 324–326, 353, 378, 407, 409, 436, 530

**O**

object . . . . . 3, 6–8, 23, 33, 35, 68, 117, 119–120, 128, 177, 191, 491; (object of prepositions) 81, 83, 127, 221, 288–289, 405, 343, 411, 466, 467, 531; (object of verbs) 81, 83, 107, 123, 129, 136, 146, 148, 192, 253, 268, 271, 288–289, 292, 293, 346, 373–374, 411, 466–467, 489, 532
objectives . . . . . xxii–xxiii, xxvii, 3, 23, 41, 61, 75, 95, 117, 135, 157, 177, 201, 229, 243, 263, 279, 303, 333, 361, 389, 423, 447, 475, 499, 519
obligation . . . . . . . . . . . .xxi, 475, 487
oil . . . . . . . . . . . . . . . . . 182, 184
oral. . . xxii–xxiii, xxv, xxvi, 95–96, 169, 181
oral drills . . . . . . . . . . . . . . . .xxvi
ordinal numbers . . . . . 75, 83–84, 157, 161, 169, 303, 324–326, 353
origin . . . . . . . . . . . .44, 80, 99, 315
original letters . . . . . . . . . . 322, 349

**P**

participles . . .xxiv, 99, 311, 315, 333, 346, 348
particles . . . . . . 8, 43–44, 52, 170, 207, 345, 405, 413, 508–509, 530, 533–534
particle أَنَّ . . . . . . . . . . . . . 209, 255
partitive meaning . . . . . . . . . . . 252

partitive nouns . . . . .229, 236, 243, 252
passive. . . . . . xxiv, 279, 292–295, 311, 314, 316, 318, 320, 333, 346–348, 550
passive participle . . . . . . xxiv, 311,314, 316, 333, 346–348, 550
passive voice . . . . . . . . . . . 292, 295
past participle. . . . . . . . . . . . . . 292
past tense . . . 45, 79, 122, 177, 185–187, 210, 215–216, 256, 292, 294–296, 311, 313, 348, 372, 844, 492, 509–510, 512–513, 531, 533
pattern. . . . . 77, 84, 104–105, 137, 185, 188–189, 212–214, 311–313, 315–320, 322, 324, 346, 375, 376, 406, 437–438, 529–531, 550
perfect. . . . . . . . . . . . . . . 318, 509
perfective . . . . . . . . . . . . . . . . 509
permutative. . . . . . . . . . . . 499, 511
person . . . . . . . . . . . . . 12, 45, 80–81, 97–100, 103–105, 120–122, 124, 128, 130, 144–145, 149, 162, 167, 174, 180, 184, 186, 207, 210, 212, 247, 253–256, 268, 293, 310–311, 319, 342, 345, 348, 353, 372, 381, 403, 408–409, 488–490, 533–534, 550
personal pronoun . . . . . . . . . .45, 86
pharyngealized . . . . . . . . . . . . . .15
phrase . . . xxii–xxiii, xxvi–xxvii, 4, 7, 9, 12–13, 16, 28–32, 50–52, 86–87, 100, 110, 120, 128–129, 136–137, 151, 158, 193–194, 217, 237, 252, 255, 268, 270, 272, 287, 325, 340, 344, 355, 356, 374, 405–406, 415, 464, 485, 488, 490, 511, 513, 531, 540
place . . . . . xxv, 8, 10, 12, 29, 43, 45, 80, 87, 99, 122, 128, 136, 148, 158, 184, 207–208, 258, 269, 273, 292, 314, 321, 323, 361, 378, 381, 389, 404, 406, 413, 440, 488, 491, 510, 528
plural . . . . . . . . 7, 11, 12, 27, 34, 52, 61, 64–67, 69–70, 82, 97, 99, 105, 110–111, 126–127, 130, 135, 137–138, 144, 146–148, 171, 185–186, 190–192, 196, 201, 208–209, 213–215, 236, 253–254, 257, 273, 288–291, 315–316, 333, 343, 345–346, 348, 407–409, 436, 488, 512, 529, 531
plural suffix . . . . . . . . . 147, 346, 512
politeness . . . . . . . . . . . . . . . . 120
possession. . . . . . xxiv, 28–29, 44, 117, 128–129, 177, 217
possessive . . . . . 17–18, 29–30, 79, 129, 188, 193, 272, 389, 410, 415, 512
possessive pronoun . . . 17–18, 30, 129, 188, 193, 272, 410
possessive suffix . . . . . . . . . 415, 512
possibility . . . . . . . . . . 475, 489, 510
predicate . . . . . . .7, 9–13, 64, 86, 126, 192, 209, 211, 216, 221, 288, 295, 344
preference. . . . . . . . . . 136, 373, 423
prefix . . . . . . 6, 14–15, 30, 45, 51, 84, 95–96, 104, 121–122, 129, 144, 151, 170–171, 185, 193, 207, 220, 268, 271, 292, 294, 315, 317, 325, 345, 346, 376, 405, 410, 491, 508–509, 529, 533–534
preposition . . . . . . 3–4, 12, 15, 51, 75, 82–83, 107, 112, 127–130, 137, 146, 158–159, 201, 208, 213, 220–221, 243, 252, 255, 257, 263, 270–271, 288–289, 325, 344, 361, 376, 377–378, 381, 389, 405, 409, 411, 413–414, 464, 466–467, 487–488, 491, 529, 531, 534
preposition لِـ . . . . . . . . 112, 128–129, 255, 263, 270–271, 531, 534
prepositional phrase . . . . . . 4, 12, 128, 137, 252, 270, 405, 464
present tense . . . 43, 45–46, 89, 103–105, 121–122, 144, 185, 190, 207, 215–216, 253, 292–294, 313, 345, 348–351, 372, 434, 439, 488, 490, 492, 510, 512–513
profession . . . . . . . . . . . 80, 499, 519
proficiency . . . . . . xx–xxi, xxvi–xxvii
progressive . . . . . . 139, 423, 434–435
pronoun. . .3, 8–9, 11–12, 16, 18, 30–31, 43, 45–46, 69–70, 75, 81, 86–87, 100, 104–105, 117, 120–123, 128–131, 135, 145–146, 169–171, 184, 186, 188, 193, 209, 211, 213, 217, 253, 255, 271–272, 344, 372, 374, 410–412, 414–415, 466, 488–490, 533, 550–563
purpose . . . . . .xx, xxii–xxiii, 312, 376, 403, 537

**Q**

question word . . . . . . . . .43–44, 120

**R**

rational . . . . . 11, 61, 69–70, 130, 191, 408–409, 491

reading passages . . . . . . xix, xxii–xxiv, xxvi–xxvii, 5, 8, 79–80, 87, 102, 141, 151, 164, 167, 179–180, 184–185, 188, 206, 208, 233, 234, 249, 251, 256, 267, 285, 289, 291, 310, 317, 341–342, 353, 375, 413, 434, 486, 488, 507, 513

reason . . . . . . . . . . . . . . . . . . . xxi, 14, 43, 54, 69, 243, 255, 263, 270–271, 273, 333, 343–345, 438, 519, 530

referent . . . . . . . . . . .28–29, 34, 411

relative. . . . . 27, 30, 263, 272, 273, 389, 406–411, 413, 475, 491

relative adjective . . . . . . . . . . . . 273

relative clause. . . . . 406–407, 410–411

relative noun . . . . . . 27, 263, 272, 389, 406–411, 413, 475, 491

request. . . . 54, 117, 120–121, 135–136, 252, 315

restricted class . . . . . . . . . . . . . 533

reverse gender agreement . . . . . 65, 66, 107, 108, 493

root . . . . . . .xx, 45, 84, 158, 185–186, 202, 212, 219, 311–313, 315–317, 319, 321–324, 355, 437–438, 532

**S**

*šadda* . . . . . . . . . . . . . . . . . . 547

salutations. . . . . . . . . . . . . . . . 403

scrambled sentences . . . . . . . . . xxvii

seasons . . . . . . . . . . . . . . . . . 229

seat. . . . . . . 52–53, 101, 121, 534–537

secular Arab countries. . . . . . . . . 183

Semitic months. . . . . . . . . . . . . 217

sentences (nominal) . . . 3, 7, 9–11, 126, 209, 211, 216, 221, 237, 271, 295, 344

separate pronouns . . . . . . . . . . . 550

sequence . . . . xxvi, 146, 201, 208, 258, 370, 434–435, 508–509

singular . . . . . . . . . . . . . .7, 12, 27, 33, 45, 52–54, 64–65, 69–70, 99, 103, 105, 107–110, 121, 126, 130, 137, 144, 146–147, 171, 185, 186, 190–191, 213, 236, 253–257, 311, 315, 345, 348, 353, 407–409, 436, 365, 488–490, 493, 534

sound feminine plurals . . . . . 147, 148

sound masculine plurals. . .82, 126–127, 137, 146, 192, 208–209, 215, 257, 316

sound plural . . . . . . . . . . . . . . .99

sound system . . . . . . . . . . . xxiv, 548

specification . . . . . . . . . . . . . . 127

spelling of *hamza*. . . . . . . . . . . 534

Standard Arabic . . . . . . xxiv, xxvii, 35

stem . . . . . . . . 45, 144, 185–186, 311

stop (glottal) . . . . . . . . . 36, 170, 549

stripped verb . . . . . . . . . . . . . . 317

structural objectives . . . . . . . . . . xxii

subject. . . . . . . . . .xxvi, 7–10, 13, 64, 75–76, 81, 86, 108, 110, 120, 126, 146, 148, 209, 211, 221, 247, 255–256, 268, 271, 288, 293–295, 321, 344, 374, 412, 489, 532

subjunctive . . . .xxi, 333, 344–345, 349, 351, 406, 550–563

substitution. . . . . . . . . . . . 373, 511

suffix. . . . . . 8–9, 11, 17–18, 27, 30–31, 45, 64–65, 82, 95, 99, 101, 104–105, 110, 117, 123, 126, 128, 130, 137, 144, 146–148, 170, 185–186, 188, 193, 207, 209, 212, 253, 272–273, 315, 343–344, 346, 410–411, 415, 466, 489, 512, 531, 535, 537

*sukūn* . . . . . . . . . . . . . . . 535–537

sun letters . . . . . . . . . . . . . . 14–15

superlative . . . 201, 211–214, 437, 519, 529–530

surname. . . . . . . . . . . . . . . . . . .80

**T**

*tanwīn* . . . . . . .17–18, 30–31, 537, 547

temperature scales . . . . . . . . 229, 238

tense . . . . . xx, xxiv (*see also* past tense; present tense)

terms of address . . . . . 52, 95–98, 149, 389, 403, 519, 528

time . . . . . . . . .xx, xxiv, 5, 19, 26, 41,

43, 45, 47, 63, 85, 101, 135, 137–138, 157–161, 165, 169, 172, 174, 184, 202, 205, 207–208, 215–216, 235–237, 247, 252, 254, 314–316, 319, 321, 343–344, 376, 378, 381, 389, 404–405, 423, 434, 475, 490–493, 508, 513, 531
tongue . . . . . . . . . . . . . . . . . . . .xx
topic . . . . . . xxii, 10, 99, 126, 207, 344
transitive . . 117, 123, 292, 317–318, 346
transliteration. . . . . . . . . . . xxiv, 548
triliteral . . . . . . 189, 312, 317, 322, 437

**U**

urban centers . . . . . . . . . . . . 36, 528

**V**

verb . . . . . (imperative verbs) 120–121, 144, 252; (object of verbs) 81, 83, 107, 123, 129, 136, 146, 148, 192, 253, 268, 271, 288–289, 292, 293, 346, 373–374, 411, 466–467, 489, 532; (past-tense verbs) 45, 79, 122, 177, 185–187, 210, 215–216, 256, 292, 294–296, 311, 313, 348, 372, 844, 492, 509–510, 512–513, 531, 533; (present-tense verbs) 43, 45–46, 89, 103–105, 121–122, 144, 185, 190, 207, 215–216, 253, 292–294, 313, 345, 348–351, 372, 434, 439, 488, 490, 492, 510, 512–513; (pronouns suffixed to verbs) 117, 129, 131; (transitive verbs) 117, 123, 346; (verb conjugation) xx, xxiv, 89, 103–104, 190, 256, 550; (verb forms) 45–46, 207, 303, 311–312, 317, 320, 323, 345, 348, 510, 531; (verb position) 255; (verb stem) 45, 185–186; (verbal nouns) xxiv, 177, 188–190, 311–312, 314, 373, 489, 519, 531–533, 550; (verbs with doubled consonants) 209; (weak verbs) 243, 253, 333, 349, 423, 437–440
verbal noun . . . . . . . . . . . .xxiv, 177, 188–190, 311–312, 314, 373, 489, 519, 531–533, 550
vocabulary . . . . . . . . .xxviii, xx, xxii, xxiv, xxvi–xxvii, 20, 38, 51, 58, 73, 79, 92, 114, 124, 133, 149, 153, 174, 198, 224, 240, 259, 276, 285, 299, 329, 355, 357, 385, 418, 442, 470, 492, 496, 515, 541, 615
vocative . . . . . . . . . . . . . 52, 96, 534
volition (verbs of) . . . . . . . . . . . 372
vowel . . . . . . 30, 35–36, 53, 121–123, 126, 128, 144, 147, 161, 170, 189, 192, 215, 220–221, 253–254, 287–288, 290–296, 311–312, 322, 326, 349–350, 438–439, 531, 532, 534–537, 547

**W**

*waṣl* . . . . . . . . 15, 122, 532–533, 537
weak verbs . . . 243, 253, 333, 349, 423, 437–440
weather . . . . . .229, 234–235, 273, 296
weekend. . . . . . . . 207, 218, 234, 237, 251–252, 258, 272, 415, 434, 530
weighting system. . . . . . . . . . . . 535
Western calendar. . . . . . . . . 217–219
women. . . .7, 70, 76, 100, 145, 167, 177, 182–184, 256, 528
word construction . . . . . . . . . . xxvii
writing system . . . . . . . xx, xxii, xxvii

**Y**

Yes/no questions . . . . . . . .43–44, 534

# فِهرِس


إن 512
آنسة 528
أو 43
أوزان الفعل 317
أولائك 34
أي 119–120
أية 119–120
أين 43–44

ب
بدل 511
بضع 493
بضعة 493
بعد 208, 492
بعض 229, 236

ت
تانك 34
تلك 33–34, 70
تمييز 127
تنوين 17–18, 31–34, 527, 547
تينك 34

ج
جر 127
جمع مؤنث سالم 147–148
جمع مذكر سالم 82, 126–127, 137, 146, 192, 208–209, 215, 257, 316
جنوب 464

ح
حالة الجر 127
حالة الرفع 126

ا
أبو 403, 528
أجوف 293
أحرف شمسية 14–15
أحرف قمرية 14, 16
أخ 528
أخت 528
أستاذ 528
أستاذة 528
اسم الآلة 361, 375
اسم التفضيل 529
اسم الفاعل 99, 126, 314, 315, 316, 346, 347, 439, 550
اسم المفعول 314, 316, 333, 346–347, 550
اسم النسبة 27–28, 272
أسماء موصولة 406–407
أسماء موصولة خاصة 407
إضافة 28, 33, 51, 65–66, 86, 110, 120, 127, 135, 151, 171, 193–194, 201, 213–215, 236, 252, 272, 287–289, 333, 343–344, 353, 373, 378, 389, 411, 415, 464–465, 467, 488, 512
افتعل 312, 321, 438, 533
أفعل 316, 319
الـ 14
إلاّ 160–161, 169, 447, 466
التي 389, 407, 411
الذي 389, 406, 491
أم 403, 528
أما 268–269
أمس 408, 413
أنْ 489
أنَّ 201, 208–210, 212, 254

ض
ضمائر الفصل . . . . . . . . . . . . 86

ظ
ظرف . . . . . . . . . . . . . 208, 404
ظرف الزمان . . . . . . . . . 404–405
ظرف المكان . . . . . . . . . 404–405

ع
عدا . . . . . . . . . . 343, 377, 466
عند . . . . . . . . . . 128, 137, 217

غ
غداً . . . . . . . . . . . . . . . 217
غرب . . . . . . . . . . . . . . 464
غير . . . . . . . . . . . . . 466–467

ف
فاعل . . . . 99, 126, 314–316, 346–347, 439, 550
فعل . . . . . . . 45–46, 207, 303, 311–312, 317, 320, 323, 345, 348, 510, 531
الفعل المجرد . . . . . . . . . . . 317
الفعل المزيد . . . . . . . . . . . 317
الفعل المعتل . . . . . . . 353, 437–439
فعلل . . . . . . . . . . . . . . 222
فعلى . . . . . . . . . . . . . . 529
فقد . . . . . . . . . . . . . . . 510

ق
قبل . . . . . . . . . . . . . 208, 492
قد . . . . . . . . . . . . . . 509–510
قمر . . . . . . . . . . . . . . 14–15
قمري . . . . . . . . . . . . . 14–15

ك
كان . . . . . . . . 215–216, 292, 295, 509

حالة النصب . . . . . . . . . . . 127
حرف علة . . . . . 243, 253, 333, 349, 423, 437–440
حروف الجر . . . . . . . . . . . 376

خ
خبر . . . . . . . . . . . . . . 126

د
دكتور . . . . . . . . . . . . . 528

ذ
ذانك . . . . . . . . . . . . . . 34
ذلك . . . . . . . . . . . . 33–34, 70
ذو . . . . . . . . . . . . . 287–289
ذي . . . . . . . . . . . . . 287–289
ذينك . . . . . . . . . . . . . . 34

ر
رفع . . . . . . . . . . . . . . 126

س
ساعة . . . . . . . . . . . 158–161, 169
ست . . . . . . . . . . . . . . 528
سوف . . . . . . . . . . . . 207, 405
سيد . . . . . . . . . . . . . . 528
سيدة . . . . . . . . . . . . . . 528

ش
شرق . . . . . . . . . . . . . . 464
شمال . . . . . . . . . . . . . . 464
شمالي . . . . . . . . . . . . 464–465
شمس . . . . . . . . . . . . . 14–15
شمسي . . . . . . . . . . . . . 14–15

ص
صار . . . . . . . . . . . . . 295, 434

مرة . . . 343
مرفوع . . . 10–11, 27, 34, 64, 99, 107–110, 126–127, 146–147, 159, 161, 192, 209, 211, 216, 221, 268, 287, 288, 293–294, 324–325, 343–344
مصدر . . . 177, 188–190, 311–312, 314, 373, 489, 519, 531–533, 550
مضارع . . . 43, 45–46, 89, 103–105, 121–122, 144, 185, 190, 207, 215–216, 253, 292–294, 313, 345, 348–351, 372, 4343, 439, 488, 490, 492, 510, 512–513
مضارع مجزوم . . . 253–254, 333, 348–351, 353, 375, 439, 390, 512–513, 550, 563
مضارع مرفوع . . . 104, 139, 207, 353, 349–351, 406, 439, 513, 534, 550–562
مضارع منصوب . . . 333, 344–345, 349, 351, 406, 550–563
مضاف . . . 111, 127, 214–215, 343, 353, 512
مضاف إليه . . . 127, 214, 343
معتل . . . 349, 437–439
معرّف . . . 193
معظم . . . 237
مفعول . . . 346–347
مفعول به . . . 127
مفعول مطلق . . . 343
ممنوع من الصرف . . . 126, 279, 289–291, 511
مَن . . . 43–44, 170, 217, 409,
منصوب . . . 127, 160, 192, 209, 211, 216, 221, 255, 2268, 288–290, 295, 333, 343–345, 349–351, 353, 361, 372–375, 377–378, 404, 305–408, 464, 466–467, 488, 511, 530–531, 550–563
ميزان صرفي . . . 311
ميلادي . . . 219

كذلك . . . 414
كسرة . . . 83
كل . . . 237, 343
كلا . . . 465–466
كلتا . . . 465–466
كلتي . . . 466
كلي . . . 466
كم . . . 52–53, 69, 170
كي . . . 530
كيف . . . 44

ل

لـ . . . 530–531
لأنَ . . . 255, 344
لذلك . . . 270, 414
لكن . . . 8–10
لم . . . 348, 490
لماذا . . . 255
لن . . . 405–406, 531
ليس . . . 11–13, 68, 216
ليست . . . 11–13

م

ما . . . 43–44, 52, 69, 172, 187,|344, 348, 377, 409, 491
ما عدا . . . 344, 377
ماذا . . . 43–44, 120
ماضي . . . 185
مبتدأ . . . 126
متى . . . 170, 217
مثال . . . 438
مجرور . . . 29–31, 34, 64–66, 82, 107–110, 127, 146–147, 158–159, 170–171, 208, 220–221, 236, 287–290, 324–325, 343–344, 376, 378, 405, 407, 488, 511
مجزوم . . . 253–254, 333, 348–351, 353, 375, 439, 390, 512–513, 550, 563

ن

نائب فاعل . . . 293–394

ناقص . . . 292, 293, 438

نسبة . . . 23, 27–28, 272, 465

نصب . . . 127, 146–147

نكرة . . . 193

ني . . . 489

ه

هاتان . . . 34

هاتين . . . 34

هؤلاء . . . 34, 70

هجرة . . . 218, 523

هذا . . . 7, 33–35, 70

هذان . . . 34

هذه . . . 7, 33–35, 70

هذين . . . 34

هل . . . 43–44

همزة القطع . . . 532, 534, 537

همزة الوصل . . . 15, 532–533, 537

هنا . . . 7

هناك . . . 7, 14

هو . . . 86–87

هي . . . 86–87

و

وقد . . . 509

## Illustration Credits

All color clip art used throughout the book is copyright © 2009 by Jupiterimages Corporation. The clip art appears on pages 3, 8, 35, 37, 42, 54, 55, 62, 71, 77, 96, 97, 103, 118-120, 135, 138, 140, 159, 162, 163, 177-179, 201, 203, 229, 231, 232, 243, 245, 246, 263, 282, 283, 306, 335-338, 340, 361, 365, 366, 370, 371, 378, 389, 393-398, 424-429, 448, 476, 478, 482, 500-502, and 529.

All black and white illustrations are by Mary Valencia.

The map of the Arab world that appears on page 452 is by William L. Nelson. Details of this map appear on pages 183, 282, 307, 308, 342, and 453. An adapted version of the map appears in the introduction to the book.

Lesson 1 – Page 2, photo by Rabbee alhaj Othman.

Lesson 2 – Page 22, photo of Damascus University building by Raghid Brayez.

Lesson 3 – Page 40, photo by Mahdi Alosh.

Lesson 4 – Page 60, photo of the Umayyad Mosque in Damascus, Syria, by Eric Lafforgue, www.ericlafforgue.com.

Lesson 5 – Page 74, photo by Mahdi Alosh.

Lesson 6 – Page 94, photo by Mahdi Alosh.

Lesson 7 – Page 116, photo of Arabic newspapers by John Wreford, www.johnwreford.com.

Lesson 8 – Pages 134 and 150, photos by Mahdi Alosh.

Lesson 9 – Page 156, photo by Rami Tarawneh.

Lesson 10 – Page 176, photo by Mahdi Alosh.

Lesson 11 – Page 200, photo of Syrian calendar by Mahdi Alosh. Page 204, calendar image by Allen Clark.

Lesson 12 – Page 228, photo by Tim Shea.

Lesson 13 – Page 242, photo of Damascene juice seller by John Wreford, www.johnwreford.com.

Lesson 14 – Page 262, photo by Mahdi Alosh.

Lesson 15 – Page 278, photo of Yousef Al-Azmeh statue in Damascus, Syria, by Mahdi Alosh.

Lesson 16 – Page 303, photo of Saladin statue in Damascus, Syria, by Mahdi Alosh.

Lesson 17 – Page 332, photo by Mahdi Alosh.

Lesson 18 – Page 360, photo of Cairo, Egypt, skyline by Allen Clark.

Lesson 19 – Page 388, photo of Syrian mailbox by Mahdi Alosh.

Lesson 20 – Page 422, photo by John Wreford, www.johnwreford.com.

Lesson 21 – Page 446, photo of Krak des Chevaliers, a former Crusader castle 40 miles east of Tartus, Syria, copyright © 2009 by Jupiterimages Corporation.

Lesson 22 – Page 474, photo of Fairuz by Derbake.

Lesson 23 – Page 498, photo of mask of Tutankhamen's mummy copyright © 2009 by Jupiterimages Corporation.

Lesson 24 – Page 518, photo of Syrian and American passports by Mahdi Alosh.